SolidWorks® 2011 Parts Bible

Matt Lombard

WILEY

Wiley Publishing, Inc.

SolidWorks® 2011 Parts Bible

Published by
Wiley Publishing, Inc.
10475 Crosspoint Boulevard
Indianapolis, IN 46256
www.wiley.com

About the Author

Matt Lombard is an independent engineering consultant specializing in plastic parts and complex shapes. He also writes a blog on SolidWorks, which you can find at www.dezignstuff.com/blog. Matt lives in the picturesque Shenandoah Valley of Virginia, where he enjoys reading the classics and fishing.

Credits

Senior Acquisitions Editor
Stephanie McComb

Project Editor
Jade L. Williams

Technical Editor
Charles Culp

Copy Editor
Marylouise Wiack

Editorial Director
Robyn Siesky

Editorial Manager
Rosemarie Graham

Business Manager
Amy Knies

Senior Marketing Manager
Sandy Smith

Vice President and Executive Group Publisher
Richard Swadley

Vice President and Executive Publisher
Barry Pruett

Senior Project Coordinator
Kristie Rees

Graphics and Production Specialists
Ana Carillo
Andrea Hornberger
Jennifer Mayberry
Jill A. Proll

Quality Control Technicians
Lindsay Amones
Rebecca Denoncour
John Greenough
Melanie Hoffman
Susan Moritz
Dwight Ramsey
Robert Springer

Proofreading
Christine Sabooni

Indexing
Broccoli Information Mgt.

Media Development Project Manager
Laura Moss

Media Development Assistant Project Manager
Jenny Swisher

Media Development Associate Producer
Joshua Frank

Contents

Contents

Contents

Contents

Contents

Contents

Contents

Contents

Contents

Contents

Contents

Contents

Contents

Contents

Acknowledgments

I would like to acknowledge the efforts of the staff at Wiley for their dedication in editing the text of these books. It can be a difficult job making sure that a technical subject is treated properly. I'd also like to thank Charles Culp, the technical editor, for taking the time out of his schedule to make sure the material is accurate. Thanks also to Kim and Zoey, who help with the details in life allowing me to do this kind of work.

Introduction

SolidWorks as a topic of learning is a huge, sprawling expanse. There is a lot to know, and a lot to write about. While I have made every effort to be complete in this book, I'm sure there are some niche topics that have gone untreated. New in 2011, I have taken this book from a single volume of an immense scope to two individual volumes, each still fairly large, one covering parts and part drawings, and the other covering assemblies and assembly drawings. There is some overlap and some gray area between these topics, but I have tried to divide the material in the way that makes the most sense and divides the material evenly. It is certainly recommended for you to get both volumes for your reference.

This book is primarily meant as an encyclopedic desk reference for SolidWorks Standard users who want a more thorough understanding of the software and process than can be found in other available documentation. As such, it is not necessarily intended to be a guide for beginners, although it has elements of that. Nor is it necessarily intended as a classroom guide, but I have seen people use it for that as well.

Possibly the most controversial aspect of the book is that it is not filled with step-by-step tutorials (although there are some). Tutorials have their place, and I believe they are best suited for beginners. You are only a beginner for a short period of time, so this book tries to aim more at intermediate users, and it does so with a more conceptual approach to explaining functionality. I attempt to help you make the decisions about how to apply the tools to your tasks rather than demonstrating simple tasks that you will never need to do again. You will not learn to model a teapot in this book, because in your work, knowing how to model a teapot will probably not help you. You will, however, learn how to make decisions which should enable you to model just about anything you want, including teapots.

To keep the size of the book down, I have tried to avoid topics found only in SolidWorks Professional or Premium, although some discussion of these topics was in places unavoidable.

While the book does point out limitations, bugs and conceptual errors in the software, and from time to time ventures into the realm of opinion, in every case this is meant to give the reader a more thorough understanding of the software and how it is applied in the context of everyday design or engineering practice.

The overall goal of this book is not to fill your head with facts, but to help you think like the software, so that you can use the tool as an intuitive extension of your own process. As your modeling projects get more complex, you will need to have more troubleshooting and workaround skills available to you. Along with best practice recommendations, these are the most compelling reasons to study this book.

Thank you for your interest.

About This Book

You will find enough information here that the book can grow with your SolidWorks needs. I have written tutorials for most of the chapters with newer users in mind, because for them, it is most helpful to see how things are done in SolidWorks step by step. The longer narrative examples give more in-depth information about features and functions, as well as the results of various settings and options.

This book includes many details that come from practical usage and is focused on the needs of professional users, not on student learners. My approach is to teach concepts rather than button pushes.

How This Book Is Organized

This book is divided into six parts.

Part I: Introducing SolidWorks Basics

This part explores basic concepts and terminology used in SolidWorks. You need to read this section if you are new to the software and especially if you are new to 3D modeling or parametric history-based design.

Part II: Building Intelligence into Your Parts

This part takes a deeper look at creating parametric relations to automate changes.

Part III: Creating Part Drawings

This part examines the functionality within the 2D drawing side of the software. Whether you are creating views, making tables, or customizing annotations, these chapters have something for everyone.

Part IV: Using Advanced Techniques

This part examines several types of advanced techniques, such as surface modeling and multi-body modeling. This is information you won't find in other SolidWorks books, explained here by someone who uses the functionality daily.

Part V: Working with Specialized Functionality

Specialized functionality such as sheet metal, , and plastics, requires detailed information. Part V includes these topics because they are key to unlocking all the power available in SolidWorks.

Part VI: Appendixes

The appendixes in this book contain information that was not appropriate in the main body of the text, such as the contents of the DVD and other sources of help.

Icons Used in This Book

This book uses a set of icons to point out certain details in the text. While they are relatively self-explanatory, here is what each of these icons indicates:

Caution

Caution icons warn you of potential problems before you make a mistake. ■

Cross-Reference

Cross-Reference icons point out where you can find additional information about a topic elsewhere in the book. ■

New Feature

The New Feature icon highlights features and functions that are new to SolidWorks 2011. ■

Note

Notes highlight useful information that you should take into consideration, or an important point that requires special attention. ■

On the DVD

This icon points you toward related material on the book's DVD. ■

Tip

Tips provide you with additional advice that makes the software quicker or easier to use. ■

The *SolidWorks 2011 Parts Bible* is unique in its use of these two icons:

Best Practice

Best practice icons point out recommended settings or techniques that are safe in most situations. ■

Performance

Performance icons elaborate on how certain settings, features, or techniques affect rebuild speed or file size. ■

These icons point out and describe techniques and settings that are either recommended or not recommended for specific reasons. Best Practice is usually considered to be very conservative usage, where the stability of the parametrics and performance (a euphemism for *rebuild speed*) are the ultimate goals. These two aspects of SolidWorks models are usually weighed against modeling speed (how long it takes you to create the model).

You should take Best Practice and Performance recommendations seriously, but you should treat them as guidelines rather than as rules. When it comes right down to it, the only hard and fast rule about SolidWorks is that there are no hard and fast rules. In fact, I believe that the only reason to have rules in the first place is so that you know when you can break them. Parametric stability and modeling speed are not always the ultimate goals and are often overridden when work-around techniques are used simply to accomplish a geometric goal.

Because not everyone models with the same goals in mind, a single set of rules can never apply for everyone. You must take the best practice suggestions and apply them to your situation using your own judgment.

My point of view while writing this book has been that of someone who is actually using the software, not of someone trying to sell ideas, nor of someone trying to make the software look good, or even that of an academic trying to make a beautiful argument. I try to approach the software objectively as a tool, recognizing that complex tools are good at some things and not so good at others. Both kinds of information (good and not-so-good) are useful to the reader. Pointing out negatives in this context should not be construed as criticizing the SolidWorks software, but rather as preparing the reader for real-world use of the software. Any tool this complex is going to have imperfections. Hopefully some of my enthusiasm for the software also shows through and is to some extent contagious.

Terminology

An important concept referred to frequently in SolidWorks is *design intent*. As a practical matter, I use the phrase *design for change* to further distinguish design intent from other design goals.

The reader needs to be familiar with some special terminology before continuing. In many cases, I use a SolidWorks vernacular or slang when the official terminology is either not descriptive enough or, as is sometimes the case, has multiple meanings. For example, the word *shortcut* has multiple meanings in the SolidWorks interface. It is used to describe right mouse button menus as well as hotkeys. As a result, I have chosen not to use the word shortcut and instead substitute the words *RMB* and *hotkey*.

I frequently use RMB to refer to right mouse button menus, or other data that you access by clicking the right mouse button on an item. The word *tree* refers to the list of features in the FeatureManager.

Differences are frequently found between the names of features on toolbars and the names in the tool tips, menus or PropertyManager titles. In these cases, the differences are usually minor, and either name may be used.

Most functions in SolidWorks can work with either the object-action or the action-object scenarios. These are also called *pre-select* and *select*, respectively. The Fillet feature shows no difference between using pre-selection and selection, although for some fillet options such as face fillet, pre-select is not enabled. Most features allow pre-selection, and some functions, such as inserting a design table, require pre-selection. Although you cannot identify a single rule that covers all situations, *most* functions accept both.

Frequently in this book, I have suggested enhancement requests that the reader may want to make. This is because SolidWorks development is driven to a large extent by customer requests, and if a large number of users converge on a few issues, then those issues are more likely to be fixed or changed. Again, the enhancement request suggestions are not made to criticize the software, but to make it better. I hope that several of you will join me in submitting enhancement requests.

SolidWorks is an extremely powerful modeling tool, very likely with the best combination of power and accessibility on the MCAD market today. This book is meant to help you take advantage of its power in your work and even hobbyist applications. If I could impart only a single thought to all readers of this book, it would be that with a little curiosity and some imagination, you can begin to access the power of SolidWorks for geometry creation and virtual product prototyping. You should start with the assumption that there is a way to do what you are imagining, and that you should be open to using different techniques.

Whoever you are, I hope that you find insight deeper than simply "what does this button do?" in this book. I hope that you will find an intuition for thinking like the software. Jeff Ray, CEO of the SolidWorks Corporation, has said that the goal is to make the software as "intuitive as a light switch." While most people will agree that they have some work left to achieve that particular goal, I believe that approaching the interface intuitively, rather than attempting to remember it all by rote, is the best method. Good luck to you all.

Contacting the Author

You might want to contact me for some reason. Maybe you found an error in the book, or you have a suggestion about something that you think would improve it. It is always good to hear what real users think about the material, whether you like it or think it could be improved.

The best way to contact me is either through e-mail or through my blog. My e-mail address is matt@dezignstuff.com. You will find my blog at http://dezignstuff.com/blog. On the blog you can leave comments and read other things I have written about the SolidWorks software, CAD, and engineering or computer topics in general. If you want to contact me for commercial help with a modeling project, the previous e-mail address is the best place to start that type of conversation.

Thank you very much for buying and reading this book. I hope the ideas and information within its pages help you accomplish your professional goals.

Part I

Introducing SolidWorks Basics

Introducing SolidWorks

In SolidWorks, you build 3D parts from a series of simple 2D sketches and features such as extrude, revolve, fillets, cuts, and holes, among others. You can then create 2D drawings from the 3D parts and assemblies.

This chapter will familiarize you with some of the tools available to make the transition to SolidWorks, and with some of the basic facts and concepts that you need to know to get the most out of the software.

If you want to start using the software without learning about how or why it works, you can skip directly to Chapter 3 for sketches or Chapter 4 to start making simple parts, assemblies, and drawings. Of course, I recommend you get a bit of background and some foundation first.

Installing SolidWorks for the First Time

Some of you will have SolidWorks installed for you by people in your company or by SolidWorks reseller experts, and some of you will do the installation on your own. Regardless, it is best to make sure that your hardware and software are compatible with the SolidWorks system requirements, available on the SolidWorks Web site at `www.solidworks.com/sw/support/SystemRequirements.html`.

SolidWorks installs natively on both 32- and 64-bit operating systems. It is only supported for Windows XP, Vista, and Windows 7. In all cases, the professional-level OS is recommended. Although, it is possible to install and run SolidWorks under Parallels and Boot Camp on Apple hardware, that configuration is not supported or tested by SolidWorks Corporation or its resellers.

You can find video card requirements at the above link for system requirements. The main concern with a video card for SolidWorks is that it be compatible with OpenGL. Hardware changes too rapidly for me to give specific recommendations here, but generally, nVidia brand boards in the Quadro line are acceptable, as are AMD/ATI brand boards in the FirePro line. You should expect to pay $100 to $500 for a serviceable low- to mid-range video card. Cards that are marketed as game cards, such as the Radeon or GeForce, have known limitations and do not work well with SolidWorks.

In addition to installing the correct hardware, you also need to have a compatible driver version installed. Again, refer to the SolidWorks system requirements Web site.

Whether you are installing SolidWorks or someone else is installing it for you, you should consider purchasing a copy of the *SolidWorks Administration Bible* (Wiley, 2010), which contains all the information you need on installing, configuring, and troubleshooting SolidWorks.

Alternatively, you might not want to get that involved at first. You can install the software with all defaults just to get started, using it as a practice installation, especially if you intend to learn as much as you can about it, and then come back and do a more thorough job of implementing it later. If this is the case, just put the DVD in the drive and accept all the defaults. In the Summary page, shown in Figure 1.1, you can choose to change the disk installation location and choose which products are installed.

FIGURE 1.1

Changing installation settings on the Summary install page

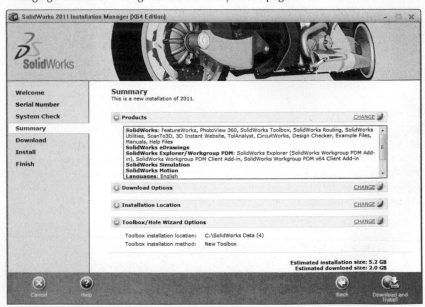

You should count on the installation requiring about 6GB of space on your hard drive, depending on the options you select to install. The locations of files on your computer will vary by SolidWorks version, by your operating system, and by your own installation choices, but the bulk of the files are placed into two separate folders: the Program Files folder (C:\Program Files\SolidWorks Corp\ SolidWorks) and the Toolbox Data folder (C:\SolidWorks Data).

SolidWorks 2011 also creates a folder in the My Documents folder called GaBi which appears to only have empty folders, but you should not remove it. Also in My Documents are two folders called SolidWorks Downloads and SolidWorks Visual Studio Tools for Applications. Both of these should also remain where they are. The SolidWorks Downloads folder is a good place to look for items that are downloaded automatically from the Background Downloader or the SWIM.

When installing any software, it is best practice to exit out of all other software first, turn off antivirus software, make sure you have enough hard drive space and otherwise meet the system requirements outlined on the SolidWorks System Requirements Web page, and reboot when the installation is complete.

You can also install without a DVD, using downloaded data instead. To do this, you need a subscription account for the Customer Portal area of the SolidWorks Web site at `www.solidworks.com/sw/support/Subscription Services.html`.

Trial installations, network licenses, student versions, administrative images, and other special cases may require that you contact your reseller for technical support.

Starting SolidWorks for the First Time

SolidWorks has many tools for beginning users that are available when the software is installed. A default installation presents you with several options when the software is started the first time. Following is a description of these options, and how you can most benefit from them.

If you plan to go to formal SolidWorks reseller-based training classes, it is a very good idea to go through some of the tutorials mentioned in this section first; this way you are prepared to ask educated questions and have a leg up on the rest of the class. You will get more out of the training with the instructor if you have seen the material once before.

Examining the SolidWorks license agreement

It is useful to be familiar with what this document says, but the agreement does not have any bearing on learning how to use the software other than the fact that it allows for a Home Use License. Many users find this part of the license agreement helpful. The primary user of the license at work is also allowed to use the license at home or on a portable computer. This is often a good option for learning techniques, doing additional practice, or completing the design of that deck or soapbox derby car. If your employer uses floating licenses, the rules are somewhat different. Contact your reseller for details.

Viewing the Welcome to SolidWorks screen

The Welcome to SolidWorks screen, shown in Figure 1.2, is the next thing to greet you. This helps you establish what type of tools you would like to see in the interface and gives you some help options. You may not get the chance to see this dialog box if someone else, such as an IT person, has installed and done an initial test on your software for you.

If you make a choice that you would like to change later, the options presented in this dialog box are also available elsewhere. Although you will not see this dialog box again, the interface is highly customizable and options exist for most things you might want to change. Chapter 2 covers interface customization in more detail.

FIGURE 1.2

The Welcome to SolidWorks screen

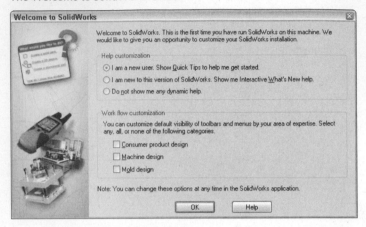

Using Quick Tips

The Quick Tips setting enables balloons with tips to help you get started with several tasks. For example, the first Quick Tip you see may be the one shown in Figure 1.3. When you begin to create your first document in SolidWorks, a Quick Tip helps guide you on your way.

FIGURE 1.3

The SolidWorks Document Quick Tip

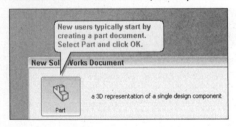

As you continue working, Quick Tips displays a box, shown in Figure 1.4, at the lower-right corner of the Graphics Window that offers context-sensitive help messages. As you work with the software, these messages change to remain relevant to what you are doing.

You can turn Quick Tips on or off by clicking the small square on the Status Bar in the lower-right corner, as shown in Figure 1.5. You can turn the Status Bar on or off in the View menu; however, the Status Bar serves many useful purposes for all users, so I recommend you leave it active. You can also turn Quick Tips off in the Help menu by deselecting Quick Tips. The on/off setting is document-type sensitive, so if you deselected Quick Tips off in part mode, you will need to do it again for assemblies and drawings, as well. Quick Tips are a great way to get going or to get a little refresher if it has been a while since you last saw the software.

FIGURE 1.4

The main Quick Tip window

FIGURE 1.5

Turning Quick Tips on or off

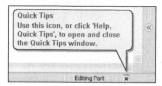

Creating a new document

 To start a new SolidWorks document, click the New icon in the title bar of the SolidWorks application. With standard functions such as creating a new document, SolidWorks works just like a Microsoft Office application, and the icons even look the same.

The first time you create a document, SolidWorks prompts you to select units for your default templates, as shown in Figure 1.6. This is an important step, although you can make changes later if needed. SolidWorks stores most of the document-specific settings in document templates, which you can set up with different settings for each type of document — parts, assemblies, and drawings. More information on part and assembly templates can be found later in this chapter. Drawing Templates are described in detail in Chapter 14.

FIGURE 1.6

The default template units selection

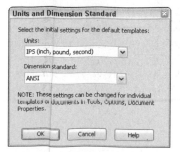

One of the most common questions new users ask is how they can change the default so that new documents come up with a certain type of units every time. Units in new documents are set within the templates. To create a part with inch units, use a template with inch units. You can have as many templates as you want, and can have a different template for each type of units you might use.

ISO (International Organization for Standardization) and ANSI (American National Standards Institute) standards use different methods of projecting views, and these standards are controlled by templates. ISO is typically a European standard and uses First Angle Projection, while ANSI is an American standard and uses Third Angle Projection. The standard projection used throughout this book is Third Angle.

The difference between Third and First angle projections can cause parts to be manufactured incorrectly if those reading the prints (or making the prints) do not catch the difference or see that there is some discrepancy. Figure 1.7 demonstrates the difference between the two projection types. Make sure to get the option correct. If someone else, such as a computer specialist who is not familiar with mechanical drafting standards, initially sets up SolidWorks on your computer, you will want to verify that the default templates use the correct standards, units, and projection method.

FIGURE 1.7

Differences between First (left) and Third (right) angle projections

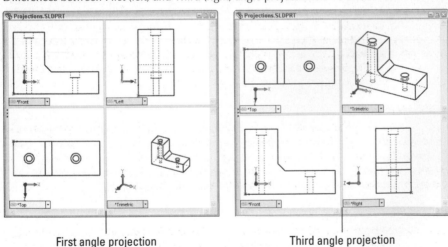

First angle projection   Third angle projection

Another setting affecting projections that you will want to check can be accessed by choosing Tools ⇨ Options ⇨ Display/Selection ⇨ Projection type for four-view viewport. This does not follow the dimensioning standard selected for the default templates or the country in which the software is installed.

Exploring SolidWorks documentation

Several types of documentation are available to help SolidWorks learners along their path. A great place to start is the SolidWorks Resources tab in the Task Pane (on the right side of the screen). This is the first tab in the list and has the Home icon. The Getting Started option in the SolidWorks Resources tab is shown in Figure 1.8.

FIGURE 1.8

The Getting Started option on the SolidWorks Resources tab of the Task Manager

The terminology SolidWorks has used over the past several releases has changed and may seem confusing to some of you. In 2007, SolidWorks changed the name Online User's Guide to SolidWorks Help. This is a help file on the local computer; it is not online in that it is not on the Internet. In 2010, the SolidWorks Web Help option was added to the Help menu. This option is online in that it is on the Internet.

Accessing tutorials

You can access several tutorials by selecting the SolidWorks Tutorials option from the Help menu. There you will find a list of tutorials on subjects from sheet metal to macros in parts, assemblies, and drawings. These tutorials are certainly worth your time and will build your skills and knowledge of basic functionality. This *SolidWorks Bible* distinguishes itself from the tutorials by going into far more detail and depth about each function, adding information such as best practices, performance considerations, and cautionary data, acting as a thorough desk reference. The purpose of this book is not to duplicate all the resources for beginners, but to take the information into far more depth and detail and answer the "why" questions instead of just the "how" questions.

Keeping up with what's new

With every release, SolidWorks publishes a What's New document to help you keep up to speed with the changes. This is typically a PDF file with accompanying example files. If you have missed a version or two, reading through the What's New files can help get you back on track. (You can find every What's New document on Ricky Jordan's blog, at `http://rickyjordan.com`.) Again, don't expect many details or interface screen shots; it introduces you to the basic changes.

Moving from 2D to 3D

The Help menu contains a selection called Moving from 2D to 3D. It is intended to help transitioning users acclimate to their new surroundings. Terminology is a big part of the equation when making this switch and figures prominently in the Moving from 2D to 3D help file.

Likely, the most helpful sections in Moving from 2D to 3D are Approach to Modeling and Imported AutoCAD Data. The information in these categories is useful whether you are coming to SolidWorks from AutoCAD or from another CAD package.

Exploring SolidWorks Help

SolidWorks Help (formerly The Online User's Guide) is the new Help file. There are two formats: the traditional Help format and a Web-based help file. You can use Search capabilities to find what you are looking for. The SolidWorks Help has tutorials and a separate API (application programming interface) help file. Frankly, it lacks detail and often skips over important facts such as what you might use a certain function for, what the interface looks like, or where you might find the command in the first place. This *SolidWorks Bible* fills in the gaps in information about the standard version of the software.

Checking out the Tip of the Day

The SolidWorks Tip of the Day is displayed at the bottom of the SolidWorks Resources tab in the Task Pane. Cycling through a few of the tips or using them to quiz coworkers can be a useful skills-building exercise.

Switching from hardcopy documentation

Unfortunately, hardcopy documentation has dwindled from all software companies. Software suppliers often claim that keeping up with the changes in print is too much work and inefficient. This is the same reason that SolidWorks gives for changing from help files that are on your local computer to help files that are only available across the Internet. Still many users prefer to have a physical book in their hands, one they can spread out on the desk next to them; earmark, highlight, and mark with Post-its; and take notes in, as evidenced by you holding this book at this moment. Electronic documentation certainly has its advantages, but hardcopy also has its place.

Identifying SolidWorks Documents

SolidWorks has three main data type files: parts, assemblies, and drawings; however, there are additional supporting types that you may want to be familiar with if you are concerned with customization and creating implementation standards. Table 1.1 outlines the document types.

TABLE 1.1

Document Types

Design Documents	Description
.sldasm	SolidWorks assembly file type
.slddrw	SolidWorks drawing file type
.sldprt	SolidWorks part file type

Templates and Formats	Description
.asmdot	Assembly template
.asmprp	Assembly custom properties tab template
.drwdot	Drawing template
.drwprp	Drawing custom properties tab template
journal.doc	Design journal template
.prtdot	Part template
.prtprp	Part custom properties tab template

Templates and Formats	Description
.sldbombt	BOM template (table-based)
.sldtbt	General table template
.slddrt	Drawing sheet format
.sldholtbt	Hole table template
.sldrevtbt	Revision table template
.sldwldtbt	Weldment cutlist template
.xls	BOM template (Excel-based)

Library Files	Description
.sldblk	Blocks
.sldlfp	Library part file

Styles	Description
.sldgtolfvt	Geometric tolerance style
.sldsffvt	Surface finish style
.sldweldfvt	Weld style

Symbol Files	Description
gtol.sym	A symbol file that enables you to create custom symbols
swlines.lin	A line style definition file that enables you to create new line styles

Others	Description
.btl	Sheet metal bend table
calloutformat.txt	Hole callout format file
.sldclr	Color palette file
.sldreg	SolidWorks settings file
.sldmat	Material database
.sldstd	Drafting standard
.swb, swp	Macros, macro features
.txt	Custom property file, sheet metal bend line note file
.xls	Sheet metal gauge table

Saving your setup

If you have taken time to set up a computer and then need to reinstall SolidWorks, move to another computer, or duplicate the setup for another user, you need to copy out the files you have used or customized. By default, all these files are located in different folders within the SolidWorks installation directory. Chapter 2 deals with interface settings and creating a registry settings file to copy to other computers or use as a backup.

Best Practice

It is especially important to have copies of these files in a location other than the default installation folder when you are doing complex implementations that include templates of various types of tables or customized symbol files. Uninstalling SolidWorks or installing a new version will wipe out all your hard work. Choose Tools ⇨ Options ⇨ File Location to save these files in separate library folders on the local hard drive or on a network location. ■

Using templates

I have included some of my part and assembly templates on this book's DVD for you. Copy these files to the folder specified at Tools ⇨ Options ⇨ File Locations ⇨ Document Templates.

When you begin to create a new document, and the New SolidWorks Document dialog box gives you the option to select one of several files to start from, those files are templates. Think of templates as "start parts" that contain all the document-specific settings for a part (Tools ⇨ Options ⇨ Document Properties). The same concept applies to assemblies and drawings. Templates generally do not have any geometry in them (although it is possible).

Tip

The Novice interface for the New SolidWorks Document dialog box (File ⇨ New SolidWorks Document) only enables you to select default templates. The Advanced interface enables you to select any available template. ■

As shown in Figure 1.9, several tabs can be displayed on the advanced interface. Each of these tabs is created by creating a folder in the template directory specified in the Options dialog box (Tool ⇨ Options). To remove any confusion, I want to note that in Figure 1.9, the Advanced interface shows the button labeled Novice, and the Novice interface shows the button labeled Advanced.

Having multiple document templates available

Having multiple templates available gives you many options when starting a new document. This offers an advantage in many situations, including the following:

- Standardization for a large number of users
- Working in various units
- Preset materials
- Preset custom properties
- Parts with special requirements, such as sheet metal or weldments
- Parts and assemblies with standardized background colors
- Drawings of various sizes with formats (borders) already applied
- Drawings with special notes already on the sheet

Cross-Reference

Drawing templates and formats are complex enough that I cover them in a separate chapter. Chapter 14 discusses the differences between templates and formats and how to use them to your advantage. This chapter addresses part and assembly templates. ■

FIGURE 1.9

The Novice and Advanced interfaces for the New SolidWorks Document dialog box

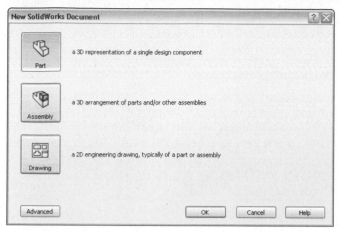

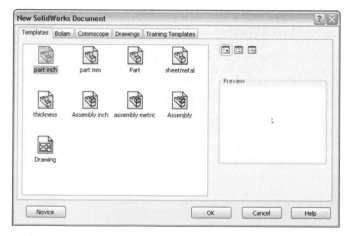

Depending on your needs, it might be reasonable to have templates for metric and inch part and assembly, templates for steel and aluminum, and templates for sheet metal parts and for weldments, if you design these types of parts. If your firm has different customers with different requirements, you might consider using separate templates for each customer. Over time, you will discover the types of templates you need, because you will find yourself making the same changes repeatedly.

You should also note that in SolidWorks 2011 templates can also control document scenes. A system option controls whether the document scene or a system background color option is the default. The default setting for this gives the document scene precedence over the system background color settings. See Chapter 5 for more details on scenes and background colors.

To create a template, open a document of the appropriate type (part or assembly), and make the settings you want the template to have; for example, units are one of the most common reasons to make a separate template, though any Document Property setting is fair game for a template, from the dimensioning standard used to the image quality settings. You can find these settings through the menus at Tools ⇨ Options ⇨ Document Properties.

Some document-specific settings do not appear in the Document Properties dialog box. Still, these settings are saved with the template. Settings that fall into this category are the View menu entity type visibility option and the Tools ⇨ Sketch Settings menu options.

Custom Properties are another piece of the template puzzle. If you use or plan to use BOMs (Bills of Materials), PDM (Product Data Management), or linked notes on drawings, you need to take advantage of the automation options available with custom properties. Setting up custom properties is covered in detail in Chapter 14.

In addition, the names of the standard planes are template specific. For example, the standard planes may be named Front, Top, and Side; or XY, XZ, and ZY; or Plane1, Plane2, and Plane3; or North, Plan, and East; or Elevation, Plan, and Side for different uses.

Locating templates

You can set the location of the templates folder at Tools ⇨ Options ⇨ File Locations ⇨ Document Templates. The folder location may be a local folder or a shared network folder. Multiple folders may be specified in the list box, each corresponding to a tab in the New Document's Advanced interface.

After all the Document Properties, custom properties, and other settings are set to your liking and you are ready to save the file as a template, choose File ⇨ Save As and select Part Templates in Files of Type. SolidWorks prompts you to save the template in the first folder listed in the File Locations list. You can create assembly templates the same way, except you change the settings for an assembly document.

You can also create additional tabs on the New SolidWorks Document dialog box by making subfolders in the main folder in the File Locations area. For example, if your File Locations list for Document Templates looks like Figure 1.10, your New SolidWorks Document dialog box will look like Figure 1.11.

FIGURE 1.10

The Tools ⇨ Options ⇨ File Locations list

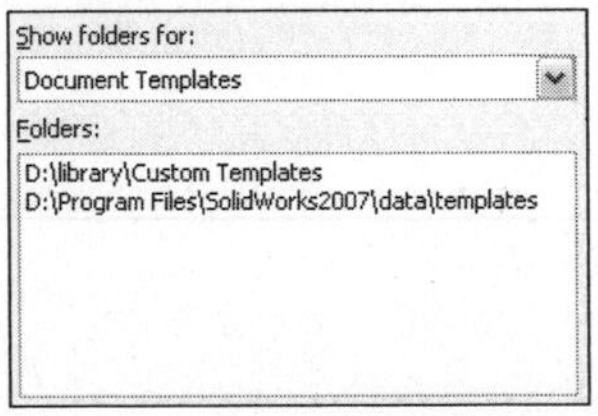

Adding subfolders to either of the locations listed in File Locations results in additional tabs in the New SolidWorks Document dialog box, as shown in Figures 1.12 and 1.13.

FIGURE 1.11

The New SolidWorks Document dialog box

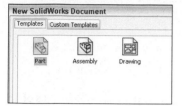

FIGURE 1.12

Additional subfolders added to a File Locations path

FIGURE 1.13

The tabs associated with the subfolders in New SolidWorks Document dialog box

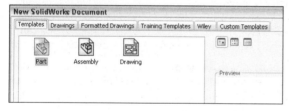

Using default templates

Default templates are established at Tools ⇨ Options ⇨ Default Templates. The default templates must be in one of the paths specified in File Locations. Figure 1.14 shows the Default Templates settings.

FIGURE 1.14

The Tools ⇨ Options ⇨ Default Templates settings

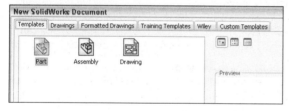

There are two Default Template options: Always use these default document templates and Prompt user to select document template. The Default Template options apply to situations when a template is required by an automatic feature in the software such as an imported part or a mirrored part. In this situation, depending on the option selected, the system automatically uses the default template or the user is prompted to select a template.

Performance

Allowing the software to apply the default template automatically can have a great impact on speed. This is especially true in the case of imported assemblies, which would require you to select templates manually for each imported part in the assembly if the Prompt user to select document template option is selected. ■

Sharing templates

If you are administering an installation of a large number of users, or even if there are just a couple of users working on similar designs, shared templates are necessary. If every user does what she thinks best, you may get an interesting combination of conflicting ideas, and the consistency of the company's documentation may suffer. Standardized templates cannot make users model, assemble, and detail in exactly the same way, but they do start off users on the same foot.

To share templates among several users, create a folder for templates on a commonly accessible network location, preferably with read-only access for users and read-write permissions for administrators. Then point each user's File Locations and Default templates to that location. Access problems due to multiple users accessing the same files do not arise in this situation because users copy templates to create new documents and do not use them directly.

Caution

One of the downfalls of this arrangement is that if the network goes down, users no longer have access to their templates. This can be averted by also putting copies of the templates on the local computers; however, it has the tendency to undermine the goal of consistent documentation. Users may tend to use and customize the local templates rather than use the standardized network copies.

CAD administration and organizing any group of people on some level always comes down to trusting employees to do the right thing. There is no way to completely secure any system against all people trying to work around the system, so you must rely on hiring people you can train and trust. ■

Understanding Feature-Based Modeling

You need to be familiar with some terminology before diving into building models with SolidWorks. Notice that I talk about "modeling" rather than "drawing," or even "design." This is because SolidWorks is virtual prototyping software. Whether you are building an assembly line for automotive parts or designing decorative perfume bottles, SolidWorks can help you visualize your geometrical production data in the most realistic way possible without actually having it in your hand. This is more akin to making a physical model in the shop than drawing on paper.

"Feature-based" modeling means that you build the model by creating 2D sketches and applying processes (features) to create the 3D shape. For example, you can create a simple box by using the Extrude process, and you can create a sphere using the Revolve process. However, you can make a cylinder using either process, by revolving a rectangle or extruding a circle. You start by visualizing the 3D shape, and then apply a 3D process to a 2D sketch to create that shape. This concept on its own is half of what you need to know to create models with SolidWorks.

Figure 1.15 shows images of simple feature types along with the 2D sketches from which they were created.

FIGURE 1.15

Simple extruded and revolved features

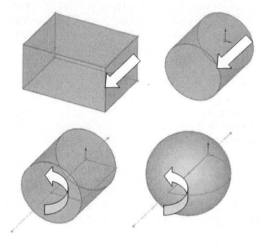

Many different feature types in SolidWorks enable you to create everything from the simplest geometry shown in Figure 1.15 to more complex artistic or organic shapes. In general, when I talk about modeling in this book, I am talking about *solid* modeling, although SolidWorks also has a complete complement of surfacing tools. I discuss the distinction between solid and surface modeling in Chapter 20.

Cross-Reference

To learn more about surfacing in SolidWorks, refer to the SolidWorks Surfacing and Complex Shape Modeling Bible (Wiley, 2008) for a complete surfacing reference. ■

Table 1.2 lists some of the most common features that you find in SolidWorks and classifies them according to whether they always require a sketch, a sketch is optional, or they never require a sketch.

TABLE 1.2

Feature Types

Sketch Required	Sketch Optional	No Sketch (Applied Features)
Extrude	Loft	Fillet
Revolve	Sweep	Chamfer
Rib	Dome	Draft
Hole Wizard	Boundary	Shell
Wrap	Deform	Flex

In addition to these features, other types of features create reference geometry, such as curves, planes, axes, surface features (Chapter 20); specialty features for techniques like sheet metal (Chapter 21); plastics/mold tools (Chapter 24).

Understanding History-Based Modeling

In addition to being feature-based, SolidWorks is also history based. To show the process history, there is a panel to the left side of the SolidWorks window called the *FeatureManager*. The FeatureManager keeps a list of the features in the order in which you have added them. It also enables you to reorder items in the tree (in effect, to change history). Because of this, the order in which you perform operations is important. For example, consider Figure 1.16. This model was created by the following process, left to right starting with the top row:

1. **Create a sketch.**
2. **Extrude the sketch.**
3. **Create a second sketch.**
4. **Extrude the second sketch.**
5. **Create a third sketch.**
6. **Extrude Cut the third sketch.**
7. **Apply fillets.**
8. **Shell the model.**

FIGURE 1.16

Features used to create a simple part

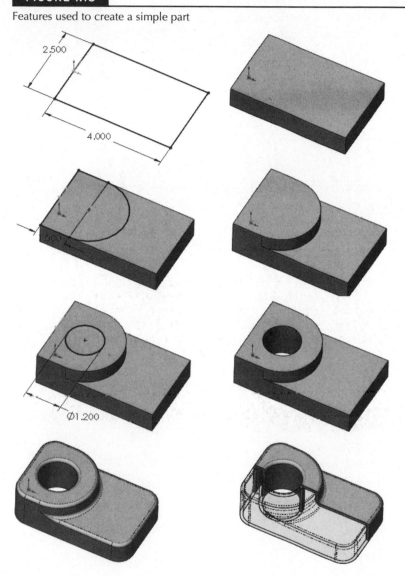

If the order of operations used in the previous part were slightly reordered (by putting the shell and fillet features before Step 6), the resulting part would also look slightly different, as shown in Figure 1.17.

FIGURE 1.17

Using a different order of features for the same part

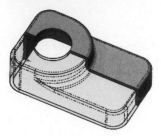

Figure 1.18 shows a comparison of the FeatureManager design trees for the two different feature orders. You can reorder features by dragging them up or down the tree. Relationships between features can prevent reordering; for example, the fillets are dependent on the second extruded feature and cannot be reordered before it. This is referred to as a *Parent/Child relationship*.

Cross-Reference

Reordering and Parent/Child relationships are discussed in more detail in Chapter 12. ■

FIGURE 1.18

Compare the FeatureManager design trees for the parts shown in Figure 1.16 and Figure 1.17.

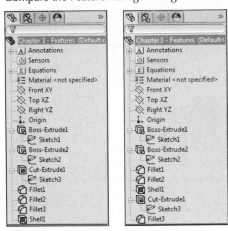

On the DVD

The part used for this example is available in the material on the DVD, named Chapter 1 — Features.SLDPRT. ■

The order of operations, or *history*, is important to the final state of the part. For example, if you change the order so that the shell comes before the extruded cut, the geometry of the model changes, removing the sleeve inside instead of the hole on top. You can try this for yourself by opening the part indicated previously, dragging the Shell1 feature in the FeatureManager, and dropping it just above the Cut-Extrude1 feature.

Note
You can only drag one item at a time in the FeatureManager. Therefore, you may drag the shell, and then drag each of two fillets, or you could just drag the cut feature down the tree. Alternatively, you can put the shell and fillets in a folder and drag the folder to a new location. Reordering is limited by parent-child relationships between dependent features. ■

Cross-Reference
You can read more about reordering folders in Chapter 12. ■

In some cases, reordering the features in the FeatureManager may result in geometry that might not make any sense; for example, if the fillets are applied after the shell, they might break through to the inside of the part. In these cases, SolidWorks gives an error that helps you to fix the problem.

In 2D CAD programs where you are just drawing lines, the order in which you draw the lines does not matter. This is one of the fundamental differences between history-based modeling and drawing.

Features are really just like steps in building a part; the steps can either add material or remove it. However, when you make a part on a mill or lathe, you are only removing material. Some people choose to model following manufacturing methods, so they start from a piece of stock and apply features that remove material. This approach works best for machining, but doesn't work well for molding, casting, sheet metal, or progressive dies. The FeatureManager is like an instruction sheet to build the part. When you reorder and revise history, you change the order of operations and thus the final result.

Sketching with Parametrics

Sketching is the foundation that underlies the most common feature types. You will find that sketching in parametric software is vastly different from drawing lines in 2D CAD.

Dictionary.com defines the word *parameter* as "one of a set of measurable factors . . . that define a system and determine its behavior and [that] are varied in an experiment." SolidWorks sketches are parametric. What this means is that you can create sketches that change according to certain rules, and maintain relationships through those changes. This is the basis of parametric design. It extends beyond sketching to all the types of geometry you can create in SolidWorks. Creating sketches and features with intelligence is the basis of the concept of Design Intent, which I cover in more detail later in this chapter.

In addition to 2D sketching, SolidWorks also makes 3D sketching possible. Of the two methods, 2D sketches are by far more widely used. You create 2D sketches on a selected plane, planar solid, or surface face and then use them to establish shapes for features such as Extrude, Revolve, and others. Relations in 2D sketches are often created between sketch entities and other model edges that may or may not be in the sketch plane. In situations where other entities are not in the sketch plane, the out-of-plane entity is projected into the sketch plane in a direction that is normal to the sketch plane. This does not happen for 3D sketches.

You can use 3D sketches for the Hole Wizard, routing, weldments, and complex shape creation, among other applications.

Cross-Reference

For more information on 3D sketching, please refer to Chapter 6. ■

For a simple example of working with sketch relations in a 2D sketch, consider the sketch shown in Figure 1.19. The only relationships between the four lines are that they form a closed loop that is touching end to end, and one of the corners is coincident to the part origin. The small square icon near the origin shows the symbol for a *coincident* sketch relation. These sketch relations are persistent through changes and enable you to dynamically move sketch elements with the cursor on the screen. The setting to enable or disable displaying the sketch relation symbols is found at View ⇨ Sketch Relations.

FIGURE 1.19

A sketch of four lines

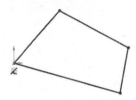

If you drag any of the unconstrained corners (except for the corner that is coincident to the origin), the two neighboring lines will follow the dragged endpoint, as shown in Figure 1.20. Notice the ghosted image left by the original position of the sketch. This is helpful when experimenting with changes to the sketch because you can see both the new and the old states of the sketch. The setting to enable or disable this ghosted position is found at Tools ⇨ Options ⇨ Sketch ⇨ Ghost Image on Drag.

FIGURE 1.20

Dragging an endpoint

If you add a parallel relation between opposing lines, they now act differently, as shown in Figure 1.21. You add a parallel relation by selecting the two lines to make parallel and selecting Parallel from the PropertyManager panel. You can also select the Parallel relation from the context bar that pops up in the graphics window when you have both lines selected.

Cross-Reference

You can read more about the PropertyManager in Chapter 2. ∎

Dragging an endpoint where lines have relations

Next, add a second parallel and a horizontal relation, as shown in Figure 1.22. If you are following along by re-creating the sketch on your computer, you will notice that one line has turned from blue to black.

Horizontal and parallel relations are added.

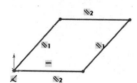

The line colors represent sketch states. It may be impossible to see this in the black and white printing of this book, but if you are following along on your own computer, you can now see one black line and three blue lines. Sketch states include Underdefined, Overdefined, Fully Defined, Unsolvable, Zero Length, and Dangling, and are described as follows:

- **Blue: Underdefined.** The sketch entity is not completely defined. You can drag a portion of it to change size, position, or orientation.

- **Black: Fully Defined.** The sketch entity is fully defined by a combination of sketch relations and dimensions. A sketch cannot be fully defined without being connected in some way to something external to the sketch, such as the part origin or an edge. (The exception to this rule is the use of the Fix constraint, which, although effective, is not a recommended practice.)

- **Red: Overdefined — Not Solved.** When a sketch entity has two or more relations and one of them cannot be satisfied, the unsatisfied will be red. For example, if a line has both Horizontal and Vertical relations, and the line is actually vertical, the Vertical relation will be yellow (because it is conflicting but satisfied), and the Horizontal will be red (because it is conflicting and not satisfied).

- **Yellow: Overdefined — Conflicts.** Solving the sketch relations would result in a zero-length entity; for example, this can occur where an arc is tangent to a line, and the center-point of the arc is also coincident to the line.

- **Brown: Dangling.** The relation has lost track of the entity to which it was connected.
- **Pink.** The pink sketch status is no longer used.

There can be entities with different states within a single sketch. In addition, endpoints of lines can have a different state than the rest of the sketched entity. For example, a line that is sketched horizontally from the origin has a *coincident* at one endpoint to the origin, and the line itself is *horizontal*. As a result, the line and first endpoint are black, but the other endpoint is underdefined because the length of the line is not defined. Sketch states are indicated in the lower-right corner of the graphics window and in the status bar. You can see that dragging one corner allows only the lines to move in certain ways, as shown in Figure 1.23.

FIGURE 1.23

Sketch motion is becoming more constrained.

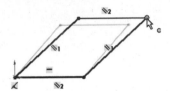

In addition to sketch relations, dimensions applied using the Smart Dimension tool are also part of the parametric scheme. If you apply an angle dimension (by clicking the two angled lines with the Smart Dimension tool) about the origin and try dragging again, as shown in Figure 1.24, you see that the only aspect that is not locked down is the length of the sides. Notice also that when the angle dimension is added, another line turns black.

FIGURE 1.24

Open degrees of freedom can be dragged.

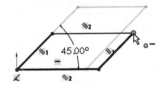

Finally, adding length dimensions for the unequal sides completes the definition of the sketch, as shown in Figure 1.25. At this point, all lines have turned black. This state is called "fully defined." Between the dimensions and sketch relations, there is enough information to re-create this sketch exactly.

Best Practice

It is considered best practice to fully define all sketches. However, there are times when this is not practical. When you create freeform shapes, generally by using splines, these shapes cannot easily be fully defined, and even if they are fully defined, the extra dimensions are usually meaningless, because it is impractical to dimension splines on manufacturing drawings. ■

The fully defined sketch cannot be dragged, and there are no degrees of freedom.

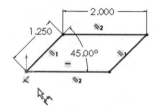

Parametric relations within a sketch control how the sketch reacts to changes from dimensions or relations within the sketch or by some other factor from outside the sketch. Other factors can also drive the sketch, such as equations, other model geometry that is external to the sketch, and even geometry from another part in an assembly, as you shall see later.

Understanding Design Intent

Design Intent is a phrase that you will hear often among SolidWorks users. I like to think of it as "design for change." Design Intent means that when you put the parametric sketch relations together with the feature intelligence, you can build models that react to change in predictable ways. This gives you a great deal of control over changes.

An example of Design Intent could be a statement that describes general aspects that help define the design of a part, such as "This part is symmetrical, with holes that line up with Part A and thick enough to be flush with Part B." From this description, and the surrounding parts, it is possible to re-create the part in such a way that if Part A or Part B changes, the part being described updates to match.

Some types of changes can cause features to fail or sketch relations to conflict. In most situations, SolidWorks has ample tools for troubleshooting and editing that you can use to repair or change the model. In these situations, it is often the Design Intent itself that is changing.

Best Practice

When editing or repairing relations, it is considered best practice to edit rather than delete. Deleting often causes additional problems farther down the tree. Many users find it tempting to delete anything that has an error on it. ■

Editing Design Intent

One of the most prominent aspects of design in general is change. I have often heard it said that you may design something once, but you will change it a dozen times. This concept carries over into solid modeling work. Design Intent is sometimes thought of as a static concept that controls changing geometry. However, this is not always the way things are. Design Intent itself often changes, thus requiring the way in which the model reacts to geometric changes to also change. Fortunately, SolidWorks has many tools to help you deal with situations like this.

Choosing sketch relations

Seeing the sketch relation symbols is the best tool for visualizing Design Intent. You can show or hide icons that represent the relations by choosing View ⇨ Sketch Relations. When shown, these relations appear as an icon in a small colored box in the graphics area next to the sketch entity. Clicking the icon highlights the sketch elements involved in that relation. Refer to Figures 1.19 through 1.25 for examples of these relations.

Tip

The View Sketch Relations option is an excellent candidate for use with a hotkey, thus enabling you to easily toggle it on and off. ■

Cross-Reference

For more information on creating and managing hotkeys, see Chapter 2. ■

You can use the sketch relation icons on the screen to delete relations by selecting the icon in the graphics area and pressing Delete on the keyboard. You can also use them to quickly determine the status of sketch relations by referring to the colors defined earlier.

Selecting display/delete relations

 The Display/Delete Relations tool enables you to list, sort, delete, and repair sketch relations. You can find the Display/Delete Relations tool on the Sketch toolbar. The sketch status colors defined earlier also apply here, with the relations appearing in the appropriate color. (Relations are not shown in blue or black, only the colors that show errors, such as red, yellow, and brown.) This tool also enables you to group relations by several categories:

- All in This Sketch
- Dangling
- Overdefining/Not Solved
- External
- Defined in Context
- Locked
- Broken
- Selected Entities

In the lower Entities panel of the Display/Delete Relations PropertyManager, shown in Figure 1.26, you can also replace one entity with another, or repair dangling relations.

FIGURE 1.26

The Display/Delete Relations PropertyManager enables you to repair broken relations.

Cross-Reference

You can read more about repairing dangling entities in Chapter 12. ∎

Using suppressed sketch relations

Suppressing a sketch relation means that the relation is turned off and not used to compute the position of sketch entities. Suppressed relations are generally used in conjunction with configurations.

Cross-Reference

Configurations are discussed in detail in Chapter 11. ∎

Working with Associativity

In SolidWorks, associativity refers to links between documents, such as a part that has an associative link to a drawing. If the part changes, the drawing updates as well. Bidirectional associativity means that the part can be changed from the part or the drawing document window. One of the implications of this is that you do not edit a SolidWorks drawing by simply moving lines on the drawing; you must change the model, which causes all drawing views of the part or assembly to update correctly.

Other associative links include using *inserted* parts (also called *base* or *derived* parts), where one part is inserted as the first feature in another part. This might be the case when you build a casting. If the part is designed in its "as cast" state, it is then inserted into another part where machining operations are performed by cut features and the part is transformed into its "as machined" state. This technique is also used for plastic parts where a single shape spans multiple plastic pieces. A "master part" is created and split into multiple parts. An example would be a mouse cover and buttons.

One of the most important aspects of associativity is file management. Associated files stay connected by filenames. If a document name is changed, and one of the associated files is not updated appropriately, the association between the files can become broken. For this reason, you should use SolidWorks Explorer to change names of associated files. Other techniques will work, but there are some techniques you should avoid.

Best Practice

It is considered poor practice to change filenames, locations, or the name of a folder in the path of documents that are referenced by other documents with Windows Explorer. Links between parts, assemblies, and drawings can be broken in this way. Using SolidWorks Explorer or a PDM application is the preferred method for changing filenames. ∎

On the DVD

Refer to the DVD to find video tutorials for Finding Help, Parametric Sketching, and Working with Templates.

Tutorial: Creating a Part Template

This simple tutorial steps you through making a few standard part templates for use with inch and millimeter parts, as well as making some templates for a couple of materials.

1. Choose Tools ⇨ Options ⇨ System Options ⇨ File Locations and then select Document Templates from the Show folder for list.

2. Click the Add button to add a new path to a location outside of the SolidWorks installation directory where you have copied the templates from the DVD with this book; for example, D:\Library\Templates.

3. Click OK to dismiss the dialog box and accept the settings.

4. Choose File ⇨ New from the menu.

5. Select any part template.

6. Choose Tools ⇨ Options ⇨ Document Properties ⇨ Drafting Standard.

7. Make sure the ANSI standard is selected.

8. Click the Units page.

9. **Change the unit system to IPS, inches with three decimal places, using millimeters as the dual units with two decimal places. Set angular units to Degrees with one decimal place.**

10. **Change to the Grid/Snap page.**

11. **Turn off Display grid.**

12. **Change to the Image Quality page.**

13. **Move two-thirds of the way to the right, so it is closer to High.** Make sure the Save tessellation with part document option is selected.

14. **Click OK to save the settings and exit the Tools ⇨ Options dialog box.**

15. **Click the right mouse button (RMB) on the Materials entry in the FeatureManager, and select 1060 Alloy from the list.** If it is not there, click Edit Material and find it from the larger list.

16. **Choose File ⇨ Properties, and click the Custom tab.**

17. **Add a property called Material of type Text.** In the Value/Text Expression column, click the down arrow and select Material from the list. Notice that the Evaluated Value shows 1060 Alloy.

18. **Add another property called description and give it a default value of Description.** At this point, the window should look like Figure 1.27.

FIGURE 1.27

Setting up Custom Properties

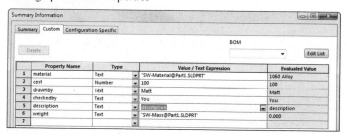

19. **Click OK to close the Summary Information window.**

20. **Change the names of the standard planes by clicking them twice slowly or clicking once and pressing F2.** Rename them **Front**, **Top**, and **Side**, respectively.

21. **Ctrl+select the three planes from the FeatureManager, click the RMB, and select Show** (the eyeglasses icon).

22. **From the View menu, make sure that Planes is selected.**

23. **Click the RMB on the Front plane and select Sketch.**

24. **Select the Line tool and click and drag anywhere to draw a line.**

25. **Select the Smart Dimension tool and click the line, then click in the space in the Graphics Window to place the dimension. If you are prompted for a dimension value, press 1 and click the check mark, as shown in Figure 1.28.**

FIGURE 1.28

Drawing a line and applying a dimension

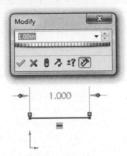

26. **Press Esc to exit the Dimension tool and click the RMB on the displayed dimension and select Link Value.**

27. **Type** thickness **in the Name box, and click OK.**

28. **Press Ctrl+B (rebuild) to exit the sketch, select the sketch from the FeatureManager, and press Delete on the keyboard.**

Note

You do the exercise of creating the sketch and deleting it only to get the link value "thickness" entered into the template. Once you've done it, every part made from this template that uses an Extrude feature will have an option box for Link to Thickness, which enables you to establish a thickness variable automatically for each part you create. This is typically a sheet metal part feature, but you can use it in all types of parts. ∎

29. **Choose File ⇨ Save As and then select Part Template from the drop-down list.** Ensure it is going into your template folder by giving it an appropriate name reflecting the inch units and 1060 material, and then click Save.

30. **Edit the material applied to change it from 1060 Alloy to Plain Carbon Steel, and save it as another template with a different name.**

31. **Change the primary units to millimeters with two places, and save as a third template file.**

32. **Exit the file.**

Tutorial: Using Parametrics in Sketches

What separates parametric CAD tools from simple 2D drawing programs is the intelligence that you can build in to a parametric sketch. In this tutorial, you learn some of the power that parametrics can provide in both structured (using actual dimensions) and unstructured (just dragging the geometry with the mouse) changes.

1. **Open a new SolidWorks document by clicking the New toolbar button or by choosing File ⇨ New.**

2. **From the list of templates, select a new part template, either inch or millimeter.**

3. **Press the Spacebar on the keyboard to open the View Orientation dialog box, and double-click the Front view.**

4. **Right-click the Front plane in the FeatureManager, or whatever the first plane listed is, and select Sketch.**

5. **Click the View menu, and make sure the Sketch Relations item is depressed.** This shows small icons on the screen to indicate when parametric relations are created between sketch entities.

6. **Click the Circle from the Sketch toolbar (choose Tools ⇨ Sketch Entities ⇨ Circle).**

7. **Sketch a circle centered on the Origin.** With the Circle tool activated, click the cursor at the Origin in the graphics area. The Origin is the asterisk at the intersection of the long vertical red arrow and the short horizontal red arrow. After clicking the first point, which represents the center of the circle, move the cursor away from the Origin, and click again, which will establish the radius of the circle. (You can also click and drag between the circle center and the radius if you prefer.) Figure 1.29 shows the result.

FIGURE 1.29

Sketching a circle

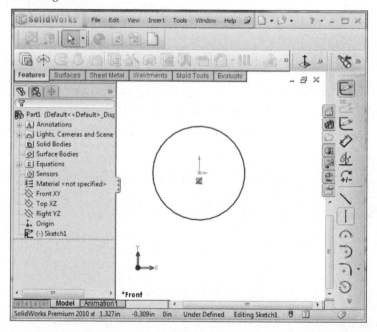

8. **Deactivate the circle by clicking its toolbar icon or pressing the Esc key on the keyboard.** Now click and hold the cursor on the circle, then drag it to change the size of the circle. The center of the circle is locked to the Origin as the Coincident icon near the Origin appears. The radius is undefined, so it can be dragged by the cursor. If the centerpoint were not defined, the location of the center of the circle could also be dragged.

9. **Activate the 3 pt Corner Rectangle.** To find it through a menu, choose Tools ➪ Sketch Entities ➪ 3pt Corner Rectangle.

10. **Click the first point inside the circle, click the second point outside the circle, and click the third point such that one end of the rectangle is completely inside the circle.** Use Figure 1.30 as a reference. Avoid making any two points vertical or horizontal from one another. You will learn in Chapter 3 about how to control automatic relations in more detail.

FIGURE 1.30

Sketching a three-point rectangle

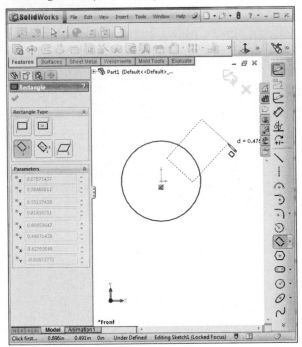

11. **Activate the Centerline tool by choosing Tools ➪ Sketch Entities ➪ Centerline.** Click and hold the left mouse button first at the Origin; then at the midpoint of the far end of the rectangle release the mouse button, as shown in Figure 1.31. When the cursor gets close to the midpoint of the end of the rectangle, it snaps into place. Press Esc to turn off the Centerline tool.

12. **Select the centerline and Ctrl+select the line with which it shares the midpoint relation.** After making the second selection, do not move the cursor, and you will see a set of options in a popup context toolbar. Click the Make Perpendicular icon, as shown in Figure 1.32, and the rectangle becomes symmetric about the centerline.

FIGURE 1.31

Creating a midpoint relation between a centerline and a line

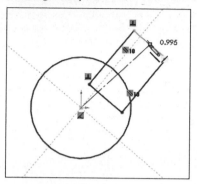

FIGURE 1.32

Making the rectangle symmetric about the centerline

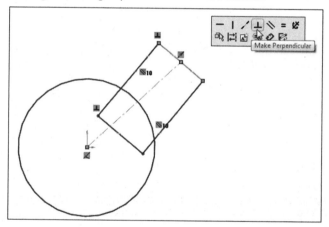

13. **Drag one of the corners of the rectangle from inside the circle and drop it on the circumference of the circle itself.** The point here is that you want the corner of the circle to be right on the circle always. A coincident relation is created by the drag-and-drop action. Now when you move either the circle or the rectangle, the other may change in size. Try dragging the circle itself, a corner point of the rectangle, or a line of the rectangle. Try dragging the centerline and the free endpoint of the centerline. Notice that the result of moving each different sketch entity is different from any of the others.

 14. **Click the Smart Dimension tool in the Sketch toolbar or choose Tools ⇨ Dimensions ⇨ Smart.** Click the outside end line of the rectangle, and move the cursor away from the line. You can align the dimension one of three ways: measuring the horizontal dimension of the

33

line, the vertical dimension, or the dimension aligned with the angle of the line. When the dimension is aligned with the angle, as shown in Figure 1.33, click the RMB. This locks in that orientation and enables you to select a location for the dimension without affecting its orientation. Click to place the dimension. If the dimension does not automatically give you the opportunity to change the dimension, double-click the dimension and change it to 0.5 inch or 12 mm. If this is larger than the diameter of the circle, notice that the circle changes to accommodate the new width.

FIGURE 1.33

Placing a dimension on an angled line

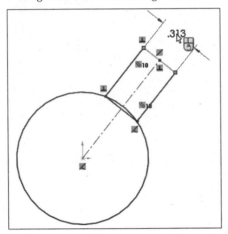

15. **Drag the endpoint of the centerline around the center of the circle to see how the sketch reacts.** Notice that the dimension added to the rectangle keeps it a constant width and makes it react more predictably.

16. **Put a dimension on the circle. Click the circumference of the circle with the Smart Dimension tool, and then place the dimension anywhere on the screen without clicking any other geometry.** Notice that diameter values of less than the dimension created in Step 14 cause errors. This makes geometrical sense. Change the diameter value to 1 inch or 25 mm.

17. **Drag the endpoint of the centerline again.** Notice that as you define more sizes and relationships between sketch entities, the motion of the sketch as you drag becomes more constrained and predictable.

18. **Activate the Smart Dimension tool again.** Click the Top plane from the FeatureManager and then click the centerline. This creates an angle dimension. Position the angle dimension and change its value to 60 degrees, as shown in Figure 1.34.

19. **Double-click any dimension and use either the up and down arrows to the right of it or the scroll wheel below it to change the value, as shown in Figure 1.35.** Notice that not all values of all dimensions produce valid results. Also, notice that the entire sketch is black except for the outer end of the rectangle, which is now blue. This is the only thing you can now drag.

FIGURE 1.34

Creating an angle dimension

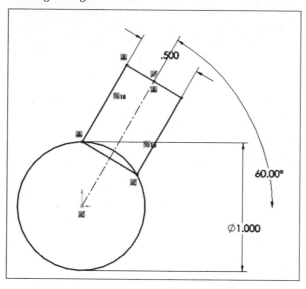

FIGURE 1.35

Using arrows or scroll wheel to change dimension values

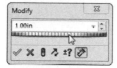

Summary

While product development is about design, it is even more about change. You design something once, but you may modify it endlessly (or it may seem that way sometimes). Similarly, SolidWorks is about design, but it really enables change. Think of SolidWorks as virtual prototyping software that enables you to change your prototype rather than having to make a new one. Virtual prototypes will never completely replace physical models, but they may reduce your dependence on them to some extent.

SolidWorks is also about reusing data. Associativity enables you to model a part once and use it for Finite Element Analysis (FEA), creating 2D drawings, building assemblies, creating photorealistic renderings, and so on. When you make changes to the model, your drawing is automatically updated, and you don't have to reapply FEA materials and conditions or redo the rendering setup. Associativity saves you time by reusing your data. Associativity and change driven by feature-based and history-based modeling can take some getting used to if you have had limited exposure to it, but with some practice it becomes intuitive, and you will see the many benefits for enabling change. Parametric sketching and feature creation help you to maintain Design Intent as well as adjust it as necessary.

Navigating the SolidWorks Interface

The SolidWorks interface offers a wide range of tools. You will find more than one way to do almost everything. There is no one best way to use the interface; and each method has strengths and weaknesses depending on the task, and depending on the individual.

In this chapter, I will start by displaying the entire default interface, but in the rest of the book I will only show a reduced interface, mainly to save space and keep the focus on the graphics window.

Once you have mastered the various interface elements and customized your SolidWorks installation, working with the software becomes much more efficient and satisfying. You may find your mastery of the interface comes with practice and experience. Many existing users may discover features in this book that they were not aware of, even though they have been trained and have used the software for years.

I explain each interface element identified in Figure 2.1 in detail within this chapter.

You might want to put a bookmarker in this page and refer back to Figure 2.1 often, as much of the interface discussion refers to elements illustrated in this figure.

IN THIS CHAPTER

Discovering elements of the SolidWorks interface

Customizing the interface to work for you

Exploring the interface

FIGURE 2.1

Elements of the SolidWorks interface

FeatureManager, ConfigurationManager, DimXpertManager, DisplayManager tabs

CommandManager tabs

CommandManager

PropertyManager (detached)

Application Window controls

SolidWorks Search

Document Window controls

Confirmation Corner

Display pane expander

Title Bar menu

Title Bar toolbar

Title bar

"S" toolbar

Sketch cursor

Task pane

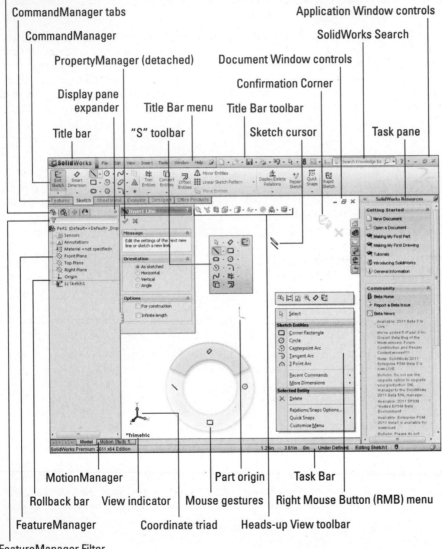

MotionManager

Part origin

Task Bar

Rollback bar   View indicator   Mouse gestures   Right Mouse Button (RMB) menu

FeatureManager   Coordinate triad   Heads-up View toolbar

FeatureManager Filter

Identifying Elements of the SolidWorks Interface

The major elements of the SolidWorks interface are the graphics window, where all the action takes place, the FeatureManager, which is the list of all the features in the part, the PropertyManager, where most of the data input happens, and the CommandManager and toolbars, where you access most of the commands in the software.

Figure 2.1 shows the default interface with a couple of exceptions. First, I have pinned the Title Bar menu in place. Second, I have detached the PropertyManager. Throughout the rest of this book, I will use a simplified CommandManager display (without the text on the buttons), and I may use the Sketch toolbar independent from the CommandManager to minimize CommandManager tab switching. I may also deactivate the Heads-up View toolbar to keep the display area clean, and use the whole Right Mouse Button (RMB) menu rather than the default Context Menus at the top of the truncated RMB menu.

Using the CommandManager and toolbars

In some respects, the CommandManager resembles the Microsoft (MS) Ribbon interface found in Office 2007 applications. SolidWorks did not do a strict implementation of the MS Ribbon, because it wanted to add more customizability. A far more complete array of interface configuration possibilities awaits you with SolidWorks 2011. In this section of the chapter, I show you how to make the CommandManager work for you and how to use regular or flyout toolbars to replace it effectively.

Exploring the CommandManager

The CommandManager is an area of the interface that you can use to flip between sets of related commands. It does not necessarily save space, and I don't believe it helps you to work faster. However, it does make your workspace a bit more organized. The main purpose of the CommandManager is to give you easy access to all commands without fumbling with the menus, and even access to customized groups of icons that are not available on a single default toolbar, without cluttering the entire screen with toolbars.

The CommandManager accomplishes this by providing small tabs under the left end of the toolbar area to enable you to switch the collection of tools that appears. Figure 2.2 shows the CommandManager in customize mode, showing all the tabs available in a default setup. To get the CommandManager into customize mode, right-click one of the CommandManager tabs and select Customize CommandManager. Alternatively, you can choose Tools ➪ Customize.

Note

To access the pull-down menus in a default setup, place the cursor over the SolidWorks logo or the small flyout triangle to the right of it in the upper-left corner of the SolidWorks window. Figure 2.2 shows the flyout for pull-down menus pinned in place. To keep the menu in that position, click the pushpin on the right end of the flyout menu bar. ■

FIGURE 2.2

Customizing the CommandManager

Customizing the CommandManager

Notice the last tab along the bottom of the CommandManager on the right. If you want to add another tab, you can right-click this tab and select the tab you want to add. You can also select to add a blank tab and populate it with individual buttons. Figure 2.3 shows a detail of the Add Tab menu options after you right-click the tab.

FIGURE 2.3

Adding tabs to the CommandManager

You can also left-click the special tab on the right and skip the Add Tab menu. To add individual buttons, first find the button you want to add in the Customize dialog box by choosing Tools ➪ Customize. Click the Commands tab in the Customize dialog box, and then switch the CommandManager to the tab you want to add the button to, and drag the button from the Customize dialog box to the CommandManager. You can remove buttons from the CommandManager by dragging them into the blank graphics window area.

Docking the CommandManager

In SolidWorks, you can undock the CommandManager and leave it undocked, pull it to a second monitor, or dock it vertically to the left or right. To undock it, click and drag on any non-toolbar button area of the CommandManager, such as around the border. To re-dock an undocked CommandManager or to change its docking location, drag it onto one of the docking stations around the screen. Figure 2.4 shows the CommandManager undocked.

Using Auto Collapse

The small box with the arrows in it in the upper right-hand corner of the undocked CommandManager and the undocked PropertyManager is the Auto Collapse option. There seem to be some inconsistencies in the way this option works with certain undocked PropertyManagers. You may have to resize undocked PropertyManagers manually for various features. When the option is active, the PropertyManager is supposed to expand and collapse automatically and should not require scroll arrows unless the PropertyManager is larger than your monitor's height. In the condition it is shown in Figure 2.4, the undocked CommandManager will not collapse, but if you click Auto Collapse, the arrows go away, and the entire CommandManager acts like a big flyout toolbar. This can be very handy because it saves a lot of space on the screen, but at the same time it requires additional mouse movement to open it up. This is the common trade-off in this interface — you can trade screen space for additional mouse movement or clicks.

FIGURE 2.4

The undocked CommandManager without text labels

Mixing the CommandManager with toolbars

To put a toolbar inline with the CommandManager, drag the toolbar close to the right-hand end of the CommandManager. A space on that row or column will open up. The amount of space that opens up depends on the CommandManager tab with the longest set of icons, even if that tab is not showing. To increase the amount of space available for a toolbar on the same row as a CommandManager, enter Customize CommandManager mode by right-clicking a tab and selecting Customize CommandManager. Then cycle through the available tabs, looking to see which one has the most icons. Remove icons from the tab with the most. This makes more room for toolbars to the right of the CommandManager.

Basing tabs on document types

SolidWorks remembers which tabs to show on a per document type basis. This means that when you are working on a part document, you will have one set of tabs. When you switch to an assembly document, you will see a different set of tabs. The same goes for drawings. Notice that in Figure 2.3, in the right mouse button (RMB) menu, the options Copy Tab to Assemblies and Copy Tab to Drawings appear. These options make it easier to set up customizations that apply for all document types.

Changing the appearance of the CommandManager

When users see the CommandManager for the first time, they often ask how to hide the text. You can turn off the text in one of two ways. The easiest way is to right-click in the CommandManager and deselect the Use Large Buttons with Text option, as shown in Figure 2.5.

I will use the interface with the hidden text for the rest of the book, primarily to save space on the printed page. You can't be a beginner forever, and so it is time to learn those feature icons. Remember that if you need help with the name of an icon, you can hover the cursor over the icon and a tool tip will tell you what it is.

Another way to remove text from the CommandManager is to remove it only from selected icons. To do this, first enter the customize mode by choosing Tools ➪ Customize or right-click a CommandManager tab and select Customize CommandManager, and then right-click a button in the CommandManager and change the Show Text setting, as shown in Figure 2.6. The Show Text option is only available when Use large buttons with text is enabled.

Adding or removing text from the CommandManager buttons

Changing the text setting for individual buttons in the CommandManager

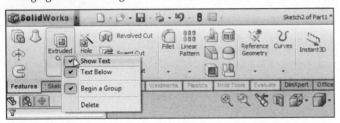

Notice also that the text by default goes to the right side of the icon, but using the RMB menu, you can put the text beneath the icon. With these options and some patience to go through the entire interface, you can almost totally customize the appearance and function of your CommandManager.

The most streamlined and space-efficient way to set up the CommandManager is to remove the text. This arrangement is shown in Figure 2.5, in the lower image. Notice that the CommandManager without text takes up the same amount of height as a normal toolbar, with the added room for the tabs at the bottom. The text can be useful for new users or features that you do not commonly use. Also, notice that with the text turned off, you have room for more toolbar space at the right-hand side of the CommandManager.

The final setting for the CommandManager appearance is the size of the icons. You have control over the size of the icon images in the CommandManager. You can find this setting in the Customize dialog box (Tools ⇨ Customize), and it is shown in the upper-right side of Figure 2.7. The difference between large and small icons is shown in the lower part of the figure.

This setting applies to all the toolbar icons except the Menu Bar, RMB menu, and Context Bar icons. The setting does apply to the S shortcut toolbar and the Heads-up View toolbar, which I discuss later in this section. Large icons can be useful on displays with very high resolution, in particular on laptops where the screen itself may be small but the resolution is very high. All the screen shots in this book are taken with the Large Icons option turned on for improved visibility. There is often a small difference between the appearance of the large and small icons, aside from size.

Recognizing the limitations of the CommandManager

If you undock the CommandManager, you cannot reorient the tabs horizontally. They remain vertical. In addition, you cannot place multiple rows of toolbars on the same row as a CommandManager using large buttons with text. You cannot dock the CommandManager to the bottom of the SolidWorks window. Another minor limitation is that although SolidWorks enables you to place toolbars at the right end of the CommandManager as well as above it, it does not allow you to place them to the left of the CommandManager or below it.

FIGURE 2.7

Setting large icons

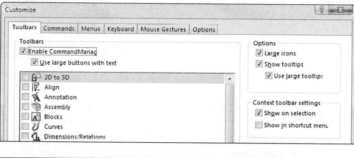

Using toolbars

The point of the CommandManager is to enable you to have many toolbars available to you in a single click, with the main goals being organization and saving space. SolidWorks is a complex program, with a sprawling interface. The CommandManager does a good job of making most of it available to you quickly without taking up a lot of space. Unfortunately, when you save one thing, you usually wind up giving up something else. Interface setup is frequently about compromise or balancing conflicting concerns. In the case of the CommandManager, the compromise is between screen space, mouse travel, and clicks. You may find yourself clicking frequently back and forth between the Sketch and Features tabs. For this reason, in my interface setup, I put the Sketch toolbar vertically on the right side of the graphics window and remove it from the CommandManager. This enables me to see the Sketch and Features toolbars at the same time and greatly reduces the number of times I have to click back and forth between the CommandManager tabs.

The SolidWorks interface performs best with some customization. No two people set it up exactly the same, but everyone needs some adjustment because they might be working on specialized functionality such as molds or surfacing, or they might work with limited functionality, such as predominantly revolved features. Of course, customization can also accommodate personal preferences, for example, if one user prefers to use hotkeys and another uses menus or even the S key.

You can enable and disable toolbars in several ways. To enable a toolbar, right-click in a toolbar area and you will be presented with a list of toolbars in SolidWorks. Another way to do this is to use the Customize dialog box by choosing Tools ⇨ Customize, or the Customize option near the bottom of the RMB toolbar list. Yet another way is to choose View ⇨ Toolbars.

Exploring the Heads-up View toolbar

The Heads-up View toolbar appears along the middle of the top edge of the graphics window. Figure 2.8 shows the default arrangement of the Heads-up View toolbar, and it is shown in relation to the rest of the interface in Figure 2.1.

FIGURE 2.8

The Heads-up View toolbar

You can customize the Heads-up View toolbar by using the Toolbars dialog box (Tools ⇨ Customize ⇨ Toolbars). Customization includes turning the Heads-up View toolbar on or off and adding or removing buttons. These customization options were introduced in SolidWorks 2010. Previously, you could not turn it off, and it had a special way of adding and removing toolbar buttons. If you have multiple document windows or multiple view ports showing, the Heads-up View toolbar only shows in the active window or view port. This toolbar often overlaps with other interface elements when several windows are tiled or if the active window is not maximized, such as the PropertyManager if it is pulled out of the FeatureManager.

Cross-Reference

Chapter 3 covers the Confirmation Corner in more detail. ■

Exploring the Menu Bar toolbar and menu

The Menu Bar toolbar is found just to the right of the SolidWorks logo on the title bar in the top-left corner of the SolidWorks window. By default, it contains most of the elements of the Standard toolbar, and it is available even when no documents are open. It uses mostly flyout toolbar icons, so again it follows the trend of saving space at the expense of an extra click. This toolbar can be customized in the same way as normal toolbars in the Customize dialog box in the Commands tab. This toolbar cannot be turned off, but you can remove all the icons from it.

Note

You could run the SolidWorks interface from just the CommandManager without any additional toolbars; you could do the same with just the Menu Bar toolbar, customizing it with all flyout toolbars. The main advantages of the Title Bar toolbar are that it is visible when no documents are open, and that it makes use of otherwise wasted space in the title bar. You might set up the interface for a 12-inch normal aspect display laptop very differently from that of a desktop unit with a 24-inch-wide screen. ■

There is also a Menu Bar Menu, which is hidden by default. The SolidWorks logo in the upper left of the SolidWorks window or the small triangle next to the logo serve as a flyout to expand the main SolidWorks menus. You can pin the menus in place using the pushpin shown at the right end of the menus in Figure 2.9. When the menu is pinned, the toolbar moves to the right to accommodate it.

Note

The 3Dcontrol menu entry is not part of base SolidWorks; it is part of the 3Dconnexion (spaceball) driver. ■

Notice that on low resolution or non-maximized SolidWorks windows, you can run into some space problems if the Menu Bar Menu is pinned open. Figure 2.9 shows the SolidWorks 2011 interface with all default settings displayed at 1024 × 768 resolution, which is a common resolution when using digital LCD projectors or small notebook computers. You need to examine the changes in the SolidWorks interface with display size in mind. You might consider having different sets of settings for using a laptop at a docking station with a large monitor, using the laptop with a small monitor, or using the computer with a low-resolution digital projector.

FIGURE 2.9

The Menu Bar toolbar and menu

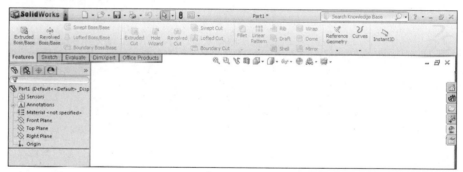

Looking at the Flyout toolbar buttons

SolidWorks saves space by putting several related icons on the flyout toolbars. For example, the Rectangle tool has several different ways to make a rectangle, with a button for each, and they are all on the rectangle flyout.

You can see all the available flyouts in the Customize menu (Tools ➪ Customize), under the Commands tab, in the first listing in the window, Flyouts.

The purpose for flyouts is primarily to save toolbar space when several tools are closely related. SolidWorks has set up flyouts in two configurations: flyouts that always maintain the same image for the front button (such as the Smart Dimension flyout) and flyouts that use the last used button (such as the Rectangle flyout).

Toolbar flyouts are listed in Tools ➪ Customize ➪ Commands and are listed from 2D to 3D through the Weldments toolbar. After Weldments in the list, the flyouts are Similar Function flyouts. You can change the order of the items in the flyouts by changing the order of the items in the toolbars. Just display the original toolbar and choose Tools ⇨ Customize to reorder it to your liking. These toolbars will always have the same icon on the top. For example, if you use the Reference Geometry flyout to access the Axis command, the image for the Plane icon will remain on top. The image on top is considered the most commonly used function of that group of tools, and so remains on top.

Add-in flyouts, such as the FeatureWorks flyout, are controlled by that specific add-in and again keep the same icon always on top.

The flyouts used for tools of similar function are split between using the most recently used tool icon on top and keeping a consistent icon on top. The only tools that appear to follow the latest icon method are the Sketch Entities tools. Sketch tools and other flyouts use a hard-coded top image.

Exploring the Context toolbars

Context toolbars are toolbars that appear in the graphics window when you right-click or left-click something. When you right-click, a context toolbar appears at the top of the RMB menu and shows the functions that SolidWorks deems the most commonly used functions. This is a static list and does not change as you use the buttons. These functions are removed from the RMB menu and replaced with the Toolbar icon in a toolbar above the abbreviated RMB menu, as Figure 2.10 shows.

FIGURE 2.10

The right-click menu and context toolbar

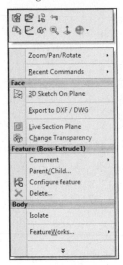

An identical toolbar appears when you click (left-click) an item on screen. When this toolbar appears with a left-click, the rest of the RMB menu does not appear. Tool tips are available if you do not recognize the icons on the toolbar. For reference, the icons in the context toolbar atop the RMB menu (the icons without text) shown in Figure 2.10 are in order from the upper-left: Edit Feature, Edit Sketch, Suppress, Rollback, Select Other, Sketch, Hide Body, Zoom To Selection, Normal To, and Appearance Callout. Notice that these selections do not reappear in the main RMB menu.

These context toolbars are not editable, but you can turn them off and put the RMB menu back to its complete configuration. To turn off the context toolbars, click the context toolbar and choose Tools ⇨ Customize. Use the options on the right side of the main Toolbars tab, as shown in Figure 2.11.

FIGURE 2.11

Context toolbar settings

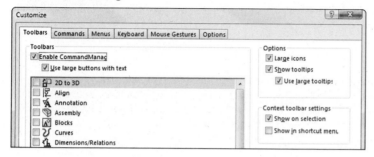

I find that the RMB context toolbars are distracting because they force you to read a two-dimensional list of icons and a one-dimensional list of text. To me, this is just too confusing. I turn these off so that the RMB menus look like they always did. However, I do find left-click context toolbars useful for things like Hide Sketch, Edit Feature, Edit Sketch, Appearance Callout, sketch relations, and so on. When I use the RMB menus, I'm looking for a more general function. When using the left-click context bars, I'm looking for something specific that I know is there. In Figure 2.11, the Show on selection check box option simply refers to the left-click toolbar, and Show in shortcut menu check box option refers to the RMB menu.

The purpose of the context toolbars is to save space by condensing some commands into a toolbar without text instead of a menu with icons and text. The left- and right-click toolbars are the same, but they work differently. The left-click context toolbar fades as you move the cursor away from it and becomes darker as you move the cursor toward it. Once it fades past a certain point, you cannot get it back, except if you have Ctrl+selected multiple entities. The context toolbar does not appear until you release the Ctrl key. To get a context menu to show up again after it has faded, you can just move the cursor back to approximately where the toolbar would have been and press Ctrl again. This works only for multiple selection menus where Ctrl was used to multi-select. The functionality is probably a bug, or unintentional in any case, or else it would also work somehow for single selections.

Exploring the Shortcut "S" toolbar

The Shortcut toolbar is also known as the "S" toolbar because by default you access it by pressing the S key. You can customize this toolbar for each document type and another for sketches, so it can have different content for sketches, parts, assemblies, and drawings. To customize the "S" toolbar, right-click it when it is active and click Customize from the RMB menu, as shown in Figure 2.12.

Many people claim to have customized the "S" toolbar to such an extent that they have been able to remove the CommandManager and all other toolbars from their interface. This is possibly true if you use a limited number of sketch entities, sketch relations, and feature types, or make extensive use of flyouts on the "S" toolbar. However, if you work with a wide range of tools (say, surfacing, sheet metal, and plastic parts), you may need some additional toolbar space. It is completely believable to have access to most of the software's function with the "S" toolbar and either the Menu Bar toolbar or the CommandManager. CommandManager by far gives you the most flexibility, but it also requires the most space.

FIGURE 2.12

Right-click on the Shortcut "S" toolbar to customize it.

The "S" key shortcut may conflict with another keyboard customization you have done, depending on how your software was installed. To change the "S" toolbar key to another character or to reassign it, follow the directions for creating and maintaining hotkeys later in this chapter in the section on customization. It is referenced as the Shortcut Bar in the Keyboard list (Tools ➪ Customize ➪ Keyboard).

Using Tool tips

Tool tips come in two varieties: large and small. Large tool tips show the name of the tool and available shortcut keys, along with a brief description of what it does. Small tool tips show only the tool's name and shortcut keys. To change the tool tip display from large to small, or to deselect the tool tip display altogether, choose Tools ➪ Customize. The options for using large tool tips and showing tool tips appear in the upper-right corner, as shown in Figure 2.11. In addition to the tool tip balloons, tips also appear in the status bar at the bottom of the screen when the cursor is over an icon. Figure 2.13 shows a comparison between large and small tool tips.

FIGURE 2.13

SolidWorks uses large tool tips by default.

Note

The Customize option (Tools ➪ Customize) is inactive unless a SolidWorks document is open. To access the Customize dialog box, first open a SolidWorks part, assembly, or drawing and then choose Tools ➪ Customize from the menu. Customize is different from the Customize Menu option found in all SolidWorks menus. The Customize Menu option is discussed later in this chapter. ■

Managing toolbars

After all that, if you still feel you need to work with standard toolbars, it is easy to move, select and deselect, and add icons to toolbars. It is important to remember that different document types retain different toolbar settings; for example, the toolbars that you see with a part open are different from the toolbars that you see for drawings.

When you are working on parts, it is important to have both the Sketch and the Features toolbars active. When you are working on a drawing, you will never use the Features toolbar, but you will frequently use the Sketch toolbar. Likewise, for assemblies, you may want to display some additional toolbars and eliminate others. For this reason, when you change from a part document to a drawing document, you may see your display adjust because the changing toolbars increase or decrease the amount of space that is required.

Best Practice

It is best practice to set up the toolbars for each document type so that they take up similar amounts of space — for example, two rows on top and one column to the right. This way, changing between document types is not so jarring, and the graphics area does not need to resize for each change. ■

Moving toolbars

To move a toolbar, you can click with the cursor at the dotted bar on the left end of the toolbar, as shown in Figure 2.14. The cursor changes to a four-way arrow and you can then drag the toolbar where you want it. Toolbars dock either vertically or horizontally. You can resize undocked toolbars so that they have rows and columns. This arrangement is typically used with the Selection Filter toolbar, which is often left undocked and compressed into a block that is three or four columns wide.

If the SolidWorks window is not wide enough for the toolbar to fit entirely in the screen, double arrows like those shown in Figure 2.15 appear at the end of the truncated toolbar. When you click the double arrows, a flyout toolbar appears with the missing icons, as shown in Figure 2.16.

FIGURE 2.14

Dotted bars enable you to move toolbars.

FIGURE 2.15

A truncated toolbar showing double arrows

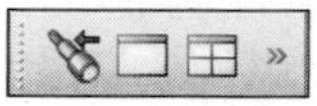

FIGURE 2.16

You can display all of a truncated toolbar by clicking the double arrows.

Using flyout toolbars

You can use any toolbar as a flyout toolbar. Figure 2.17 shows the list of all flyout toolbars, which is the same as the list of *all* toolbars. Flyout toolbars are a nice space-saving feature for tools that you use infrequently, but frequently enough to want to avoid going through the menus. To use a toolbar as a flyout, select it from the Flyout toolbars list and drag it onto an existing toolbar. It displays with an arrow to the right. Clicking the arrow causes all the tools to scroll out temporarily until you click a toolbar icon or anything else.

To add icons to a flyout toolbar, temporarily show the regular toolbar that corresponds to the flyout toolbar and add icons to the regular toolbar. When you are done adding or removing icons, turn off the regular toolbar; the changes are applied to the flyout.

FIGURE 2.17

The Flyout toolbars are on the Commands tab in the Customize dialog box.

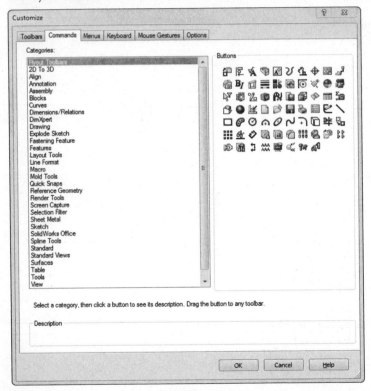

Tip

If you want to create a separate toolbar, you can commandeer an existing one for your own purposes. For example, because I do not use the Tools toolbar, I have removed all the regular icons from it and replaced them with relevant flyout toolbars, which I do use extensively. This enables me to consolidate space and not have unused icons on my toolbars. Alternatively, creating a custom CommandManager tab and putting on it what you like is much easier. ■

Working in Full Screen mode

Full Screen mode enables you to toggle quickly to the display so that only the graphics window and the Task pane appear; the FeatureManager, menus, toolbars, and status bar are all hidden. Alternatively, you can hide just the FeatureManager or the toolbars.

In Full Screen mode, you can still access the menus by clicking the cursor along the top border of the window, as shown in Figure 2.18.

- To toggle to Full Screen mode, press the F11 key.
- To toggle the toolbar display, press the F10 key (see Figure 2.18).
- To toggle the FeatureManager display, press the F9 key.

Customizing your workflow

When you first install and run the SolidWorks software, the SolidWorks Welcome screen shown in Figure 2.19 offers you the option to customize the interface using one of three preset option packages. Special menu and toolbar settings are made for Consumer product design, Machine design, or Mold design. After the software is initially installed, you only see this screen once, but you can change all the options in other places, including the Options tab in the Customize dialog box.

FIGURE 2.18

The SolidWorks window with all toolbars hidden using the F10 key

FIGURE 2.19

The Welcome to SolidWorks screen

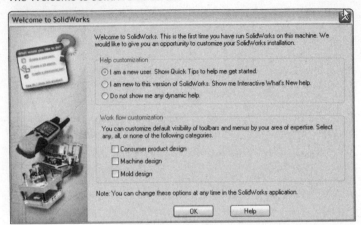

The three-workflow customizations affect the interface as follows:

- Consumer product design adds the Surfaces toolbar to the CommandManager.
- Machine design adds Sheet Metal and Weldments toolbars to the CommandManager.
- Mold design adds Surfaces and Mold Tools toolbars to the CommandManager.

Similar changes are made to the menus to hide or show menu selections as appropriate. You can find more information about hiding and showing menu items later in this chapter.

If you want to select a different option after the initial setup, choose Tools ➪ Customize and click the Options tab, where you can specify a different choice. Figure 2.20 shows the Options tab of the Customize dialog box.

FIGURE 2.20

The Options tab of the Customize dialog box, where you can select a different workflow customization

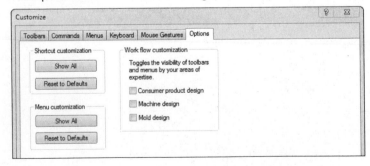

Controlling menus

Everyone has his own style of working. For example, some people like to use menus and others do not. Some like to use hotkeys and others like the mouse. Modify Section View is an example of a tool that you cannot access via toolbars. It can only be accessed via the menus.

The most frequently used menu items are in the View, Insert, and Tools menus. All the menus shown in this section have all the possible options selected. As a result, the View menu in Figure 2.21 may contain options that are not available on your computer. Customizing menus is covered later in this chapter. Figure 2.21 also shows the Insert and Tools menus, along with an image of a menu with the Customize Menu mode activated.

FIGURE 2.21

Popular menus

View menu

Insert menu

Tools menu

Customizing the Tools menu

You use the View menu primarily for turning on or off the visibility of entity types such as planes, sketches, or temporary axes. You can also do this by using hotkeys or by putting extra items on the View toolbar.

The Insert menu is used mostly for creating feature types for which you do not have a toolbar icon on the screen. For example, although the Move Face tool is on the Mold Tools toolbar, it has many uses aside from mold design. You can find the Move Face tool by choosing Insert ➪ Face.

The Tools menu is used primarily for sketch entities or tools for which you have no icon on the screen. Several other commonly used tools, such as Measure, Equations, Customize, and Options, are also available in this menu.

You can customize menus by adding or omitting items. By using the Customize Menu option at the bottom of any menu — including shortcut (RMB) menus — you can remove items from any menu by clearing the check boxes next to tools that you do not use. To bring back the removed items, you can either go back to the Customize Menu or choose Tools ➪ Customize ➪ Options and click the Reset to Defaults buttons for menu and shortcut customization.

Note

Be careful not to confuse this Customize Menu selection with the Customize menu selection on the Tools menu. Figure 2.21 shows the Tools menu being customized. In addition, I do not recommend removing items from the menus. It doesn't take much for someone to need one of those items and no one remembers that it was supposed to be there or how to get it back. ∎

Interpreting SolidWorks Use of the Word "Shortcut"

Between the SolidWorks and Microsoft interfaces, the word *shortcut* is used in several overlapping and confusing ways. Users replace most of the SolidWorks occurrences with words they use every day. The following list describes where SolidWorks and Microsoft users might encounter the word *shortcut* as a formal name for interface functionality, and how they might understand it.

- **The Windows Shortcut** link to another file or folder. Most users still refer to this link as a *shortcut* or *desktop shortcut*.

- **Shortcuts** (as identified in the SolidWorks Help under Shortcut ➪ Keys) are either accelerator keys or keyboard shortcuts. Users refer to accelerator keys as *Alt-keys*, and to keyboard shortcuts as *hotkeys*.

- **Shortcut menus** are commonly called the right mouse button (RMB) menus, and have detached toolbars called context bars for both right- and left-click options. These are commonly known as the *RMB bar* and the *LMB bar*.

- **Shortcut tabs** (found as the "shortcut" entry in the SolidWorks Help) presumably refer to DriveWorksXpress functionality, although there is no direct mention of that in the Help entry. DriveWorksXpress is described in more detail in the *SolidWorks 2011 Assemblies Bible* (Wiley, 2011).

- **Shortcut bars** are commonly known as the *S key toolbar*.

If you use the alternate terminology offered here, it will be clear to all users what you are talking about.

The Options dialog box (Tools ⇨ Customize ⇨ Options), shown in Figure 2.20, contains the Shortcut (RMB) menu and Menu customization options. These options enable you to show all the menu items for both types of menus in a single stroke. By default, some items are hidden in various menus. Keyboard customization is discussed later in this chapter. Keyboard shortcuts are generally referred to as *hotkeys*.

Changing cursors

SolidWorks cursors are context sensitive and change their appearance and function depending on the situation. Sketching cursors display a pencil and the type of sketch entity that you are presently sketching. Sketch cursors also display some dimensional information about the entity that you are sketching, such as its length or radius. Sketch cursor feedback is necessary for fast and accurate sketching.

Cross-Reference

To learn more about sketch cursor feedback, see Chapter 3. ∎

The Select cursor changes depending on the item over which you have positioned it. Cursor symbols also help remind you when selection filters are active. The cursor is frequently available as an OK button. For example, after selecting edges for a Fillet feature, the RMB functions as an OK button. Figure 2.22 shows various cursors and their significance.

FIGURE 2.22

Various SolidWorks cursors

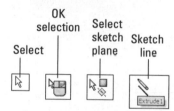

Working with models in the FeatureManager and PropertyManager windows

The FeatureManager window is the panel to the left of the screen, which shows an ordered list of features describing how the part was built. SolidWorks users spend a fair amount of time using the FeatureManager to edit or inspect models. Figure 2.23 shows the FeatureManager for a simple model.

Using the FeatureManager

 There is a splitter bar at the top of the FeatureManager that enables you to split the FeatureManager window into two windows, enabling you to display the FeatureManager and another window, such as the PropertyManager. Small arrows in the middle of the right separator can collapse the FeatureManager to increase screen space. The F9 key also collapses or opens the FeatureManager (refer to Figure 2.23).

FIGURE 2.23

The FeatureManager for a simple model

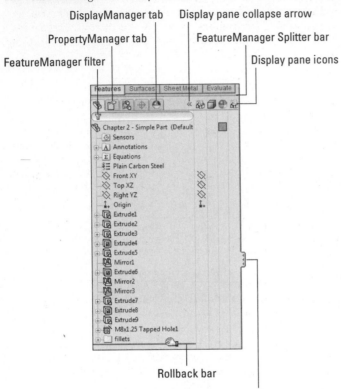

DisplayManager tab

Display pane collapse arrow

PropertyManager tab

FeatureManager Splitter bar

FeatureManager filter

Display pane icons

Rollback bar

FeatureManager collapse tab

Looking at the Display pane

 You can open the Display pane flyout from the FeatureManager by using the double arrows at the top-right corner of the FeatureManager. The Display pane helps you to visualize where appearances, display styles, or hidden bodies have been applied in a part document and additional functions in an assembly document. The display pane is helpful when you're looking for colors that are applied to the model at some level other than the part level.

Cross-Reference

Appearances are covered in more detail in Chapter 5. ■

Looking at the Rollback bar

 The Rollback bar at the bottom of the FeatureManager enables you to see the part in various states of history. Features can be added while the rollback bar is at any location. The model can also be saved while rolled back.

Looking at the FeatureManager filter

 One of the most useful elements of the FeatureManager is the FeatureManager filter. The filter resides at the top of the FeatureManager. If you type text in the filter, SolidWorks searches feature names, descriptions, comments, tags, and dimension names for text matching the string, and only shows matching features in the window. This also works in assemblies, where you can filter for part names or document properties. The filter is very useful for quickly finding parts, features, mates, or anything else that shows up in the part or assembly FeatureManager.

Using the PropertyManager

 The PropertyManager is where you go to set most of the feature parameters and where you edit the properties of selected items such as sketch elements. You can manually switch to the PropertyManager using the tabs on the top of the Display panel or allow it to pop up automatically when your input is needed. The leftmost tab in the row of icons is the FeatureManager tab, the second from the left is the PropertyManager tab, the second from the right is the ConfigurationManager tab, and the rightmost tab is the DimXpertManager. Other icons may also appear in this area for drawings or if you have add-ins such as PhotoWorks or SolidWorks Simulation (formerly COSMOS) turned on. The ConfigurationManager tab appears with more detail in Chapter 11

One of the benefits of putting all of the data entry into the PropertyManager is that it saves a lot of space on the screen. On the other hand, you will often need to make a selection from the FeatureManager at the same time that the PropertyManager pops up and takes its place. You can disable this automatic popup behavior by choosing Tools ➪ Options ➪ System Options ➪ General and selecting the Auto-show PropertyManager setting.

My favorite option for dealing with the PropertyManager is to detach it from the FeatureManager so that you can see the two side by side instead of one or the other. To detach the PropertyManager, drag its icon from the tabs out into the graphics area and release. Once the PropertyManager is detached, you can move it to a second monitor, float it within the SolidWorks window, or dock or reattach it. To put it back in its place under the FeatureManager, just drag it back on top of the FeatureManager using one of the docking station symbols on the screen, allow it to snap into place, and release it.

Caution

The detached PropertyManager does not automatically expand to match the size of the data included in it. You will often have to widen or lengthen the size of the detached PropertyManager window to see everything in it. This is a bug that has been around since this functionality was introduced. ■

If you do not like the detachable PropertyManager, you can use the splitter bars either to put the FeatureManager on top and the PropertyManager beneath or use the flyout FeatureManager. When creating or editing a feature, you can access the flyout FeatureManager by double-clicking the name of the feature at the top of the PropertyManager. The flyout FeatureManager is displayed just to the right of the regular FeatureManager, in the main graphics window, and is transparent to enable you to see the model through it. The various ways of combining the FeatureManager and PropertyManager are shown in Figure 2.24.

The detached PropertyManager, the split FeatureManager, and the flyout FeatureManager

Detached PropertyManager

Flyout FeatureManager

Split
FeatureManager

Introducing the DisplayManager

The terminology around the various interface devices that are used to show, edit, and place colors (appearances) on part and assembly models becomes more complex with every release. SolidWorks 2011 introduces the DisplayManager. This interface element is separate from the Display pane and the Appearances panel of the Task pane. The DisplayManager helps you understand the various display-related items that might be applied to your model. Figure 2.25 shows the DisplayManager with the Appearances active. Chapter 5 discusses the DisplayManager in more depth.

The DisplayManager helps you sort through everything that affects how the model looks.

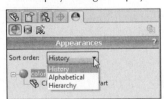

Getting around the Task pane

By default, the Task pane sits to the right of the SolidWorks screen, although you can undock it entirely. If you want to keep it open, click the pushpin in the upper-right corner of the pane. The Task pane is shown in Figure 2.26.

FIGURE 2.26

The Task pane

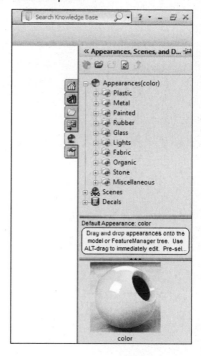

The Task pane is the home for several panels:

- **SolidWorks Resources.** These are useful links for templates, tutorials, tech support, news, GlobalSpec search, Tip-of-the-Day, and other resources.
- **Design Library.** This includes locally stored libraries, Toolbox, and 3D Content Central. This tab also contains "SolidWorks Content," which consists of additional library resources that can be downloaded directly from the Task Pane.
- **File Explorer.** This is a Windows Explorer interface that you can use to browse for files.
- **SolidWorks Search.** This panel allows you to perform searches that include the SolidWorks Knowledge Base and the SolidWorks Community Forum, as well as filename and custom properties for SolidWorks files on your computer or network.
- **View Palette.** This palette enables you to visually select views and drag them onto a drawing sheet.

- **Appearances, Scenes, and Decals.** This panel enables you to select appearances and scenes for your SolidWorks documents. SolidWorks has also moved decals into the SolidWorks Standard level of the software instead of being part of the rendering software.

- **Custom Properties.** The custom property tab in Task pane enables you to create a custom interface that goes inside this Task Pane tab that will help you enter custom property data quickly, easily, and accurately.

- **Recovered Documents.** After a crash, auto-recovered documents are listed in this special purpose Task Pane tab.

Getting familiar with the Status bar

The status bar is a nonintrusive way in which SolidWorks communicates information back to the user. It is located at the bottom of the screen, and you can enable it from the View menu. Figure 2.27 shows the status bar in action.

FIGURE 2.27

The status bar showing a tool tip for the Sketch Circle tool

Sketches a circle. Select the center of the circle, then drag to set its radius.   -1.995in   0.364in   0in   Under Defined   Editing Sketch2

The status bar can display the following information, indicators, and icons:

- Progress as parts, assemblies, or drawings load
- Tool tips for commands
- Measurements
- The sketch status for an active sketch
- In-context editing
- Suspend automatic rebuilds
- Icons that enable you to turn Quick Tips off or on
- The sheet scale for drawings
- The cursor position for drawings and sketches
- Whether you are editing the sheet, sheet format, or view of a drawing

Assigning tags

Tags work like document properties, except that they do not need a property name; they just use a value. A tag could be considered simply a keyword that you can associate with a part in an assembly or even a feature in a part. Tags can be searched by SolidWorks Explorer or by the FeatureManager Filter. You can assign tags by clicking the yellow tag icon on the status bar in the lower-right corner of the SolidWorks window. Figure 2.28 shows a tag being added to a feature.

Making use of Quick Tips

Quick Tips appear in the popup window in the lower-right corner of the graphics window. They can change as you work so that they are sensitive to the context in which you are working. They are a great way for new users or infrequent users to learn or be reminded of the next steps available to them. You can activate and deactivate Quick Tips by clicking the question mark icon in the lower-right corner of the SolidWorks window on the status bar. Figure 2.29 shows the Quick Tips window in action.

FIGURE 2.28

Adding a tag to a feature

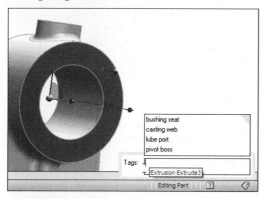

FIGURE 2.29

Quick Tips in action

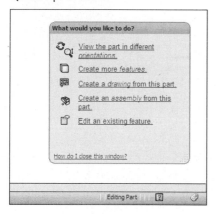

Using SolidWorks Search

You can find SolidWorks Search in the upper-right corner of the SolidWorks application window, on the title bar, as shown in Figure 2.30.

FIGURE 2.30

Accessing SolidWorks Search

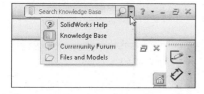

SolidWorks Search enables you to search the SolidWorks Help, Knowledge Base, or community forums for information (some of these require an Internet connection and login), as well as look for SolidWorks models on your local or network drives.

Searching for files

The file searches include 3D ContentCentral, SolidWorks Explorer, and SolidWorks Workgroup PDM if it is installed. Figure 2.31 shows the interface for searching for files.

FIGURE 2.31

Using SolidWorks Search to search for files

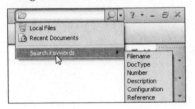

To configure where SolidWorks is going to search for files, you can use the options at Tools ➪ Options ➪ File Locations ➪ Search Paths. Remember that SolidWorks follows search rules that force it to look in directories that may not be obvious to you, including recent folders where you have saved documents and other directories. You can also select custom properties to search from the drop-down list.

Figure 2.32 shows the result list displayed in the Search tab of the Task pane. This allows you to quickly view the search results along with the filenames to pick out the files you are looking for.

FIGURE 2.32

Browsing search results

Searching for help

SolidWorks Search appears to only work with the Web Help feature. As a result, if you do not have an Internet connection, you cannot access the Help feature through Search, and the KB and forums are also Web based. If you have no Internet connection, just look through the local Help feature manually.

Figure 2.33 shows the results of searching the Knowledge Base for the phrase "installation recommendations." There are plenty of relevant entries to browse. A similar results window appears if you choose to search the forums.

Searching the Knowledge Base for installation tips

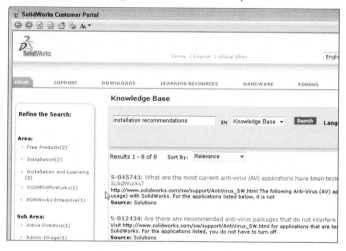

There is not a way to search all three sources of technical information at the same time. Thus, to search all three locations, you have to search each one individually.

Using the 2D Command Line Emulator

This is a tool specifically for people who are coming to SolidWorks from AutoCAD. As the name suggests, it adds a command line to the bottom of the SolidWorks window that works like the AutoCAD command line in most respects. The available commands are somewhat limited compared to those that are available in AutoCAD. This tool only functions in the 2D sketch mode, on a drawing sheet, or in a drawing view; it does not work in a 3D sketch. The 2D Command Line Emulator is shown in Figure 2.34.

Available sketch tools in the 2D Command Line Emulator include Align, Arc, Array, 'Cal, Chamfer, Chprop, Circle, 'Color, Copy, DDcolor, Dim, Dist, Ellipse, Erase, Exit, Extrude, Fillet, 'Grid, Line, List, Massprop, Mirror, Move, Offset, 'Ortho, 'Osnap, 'Pan, Plot, Point, Polygon, Qsave, Rectangle, 'Redraw, 'Redrawall, Revolve, Rotate, Save, Saveas, 'Snap, Spline, Trim, U (undo), 'Units, 'View, and 'Zoom. You can use commands preceded by an apostrophe (') as transparent commands without exiting an active command. Notice that even the cursor changes to crosshairs.

FIGURE 2.34

The 2D Command Line Emulator in action

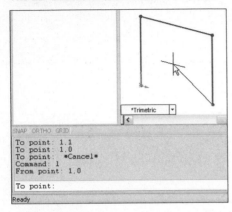

Best Practice

The best way to learn a new software package is to embrace the new way, not to cling to the old way. Although AutoCAD users may find the 2D Command Line Emulator more comfortable to work with, you will not achieve the same results as you will with the SolidWorks default-sketching mode. For example, the resulting sketch entities created using the 2D Command Line Emulator are not constrained in any way, and the endpoints do not even merge. You can deselect the 2D Command Line Emulator by going to Tools ⇨ Add-ins. ■

Note

The 2D Command Line Emulator is not available on 64-bit versions of SolidWorks. ■

Making the Interface Work for You

As engineers and designers, we all like to tinker with things to optimize efficiency and to apply our personal stamp. When the SolidWorks software is installed, the interface is functional, but not optimal. Earlier in this chapter, I discussed managing and customizing toolbars and menus. In the remainder of this chapter, I will focus more on customizing the interface and suggest some strategies that you might use to help customize your work environment.

Customizing colors

You need to be aware of a few things before you change the standard colors in the SolidWorks interface. The first is that SolidWorks does not automatically alter text color to contrast with your background. As a result, if you set the background to black, and the text is black, you won't be able to see the text. This may seem obvious to some people, but AutoCAD automatically changes text color to contrast with the viewport background, and so AutoCAD users may take this functionality for granted.

Exploring default selection colors

All the interface colors are controlled in the Systems Options Colors dialog box. You can access the dialog box by choosing Tools ➪ Options ➪ Colors. The selection color in particular is set at Selected Item 1, as shown in Figure 2.35.

FIGURE 2.35

Changing interface colors

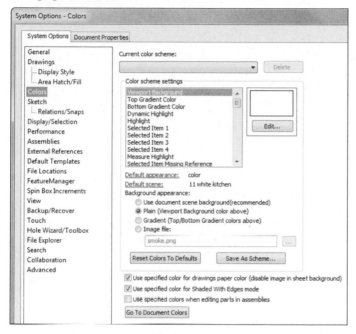

Notice that you can set a color scheme. I recommend that if you want to change the colors used in the interface, you save the settings as a color scheme so that the scheme can be re-created easily later or copied to another computer. Color schemes are stored in the Windows registry, not as separate files. To transfer color settings to another computer, you will need to either use the Copy Settings Wizard or manually copy data from the Windows registry.

Before making changes, you might consider saving your initial settings as a separate scheme so you can get back to them if you need to.

Caution

Making changes to the Windows registry can adversely affect software installation and hardware performance. You should not attempt changes to the registry unless you know exactly what you are doing. ■

Selecting background options wisely

You should avoid some colors for the background, or you should make some changes if you choose these colors. Black is used with fully defined sketches, dimensions, FeatureManager text, and annotations. Blue can mask the underdefined sketch color. Bright green (or blue, depending on the version you are using) can cause problems with seeing selected items. Bright red, aside from being a terrible color to stare at all day, also does not contrast well with some of the red highlights and error colors.

You might think that no matter which color background you select, aside from the default, the items or features are difficult to see. For this reason, many users choose a gradient background, which enables them to pick colors where items are always visible on one-half of the screen or the other. Staring at a white screen all day can be uncomfortable for your eyes, so pick colors that enable you to see everything with "reasonable" contrast, yet are not glaringly bright. Very high contrast is hard on the eyes, and low contrast may make it difficult to distinguish items on the screen.

You have to consider what the purpose of the background is. Some people doing presentations may want the background to be attractive while otherwise staying out of the way. Others may only need the background to contrast with whatever is in front of it in a way that does not strain anyone's eyes. For writing a book, the background generally needs to be white to match the page. No one scheme will suit all needs.

In addition to colors and gradients, you can use an image as the graphics window background. This gives you a wider range of customization capabilities, and several sample images are already available in the default settings. Also, be aware that document scene backgrounds are document specific and override system options.

RealView also adds some capabilities with *scenes*. Scenes can be applied from the Appearances, Scenes, and Decals tab on the Task pane. Most of the display settings work in conjunction with RealView, which is an advanced display mode. Depending on your graphics card, your computer may or may not be capable of using RealView. SolidWorks offers three different types of scenes: Basic, Studio, and Presentation. Of these, I find the Studio scenes to be the best when I need a reflective floor with shadows; otherwise, I stick with the Basic scenes. I find it distracting to use either reflections or shadows in models while working. However, a nice, shiny RealView appearance to the part is often useful, especially for visualizing curvature on curvy parts. I describe RealView, along with scenes, in more detail in Chapter 5.

Customizing strategies

You can easily customize many aspects of the SolidWorks interface, including:

- Toolbars
- Menus
- Background colors or images
- PropertyManager skins
- Task pane location
- Hotkeys
- Macros
- Custom application programming

Whether or not you should customize each of the previous items depends partially on how much time and energy you have to spend, how much you work with others, whether you share your workstation with other users, and how much money you are ready to dedicate in the case of custom programming.

Considering hotkey approaches

Some of us old-timers prefer to use the keyboard instead of the mouse. If your hand-eye coordination is as bad as mine is, you may also choose this approach. I can type without looking at the keyboard, but when I use the mouse, it takes me a few seconds to aim at an icon and hit it accurately. This means that I customize SolidWorks to use as many hotkeys as possible, and remove icons from the interface if I have them on hotkeys. Unfortunately, my memory is as bad as my eyesight, and so remembering 75 hotkey commands is a bit of a problem. I admit to having a printed list of hotkeys taped to the side of my monitor. While I know that needing to read the list to find a particular hotkey defeats most of the purpose of using them in the first place, I just accept it as a learning aid. This is a self-solving problem, because the hotkeys that I use the most are the ones that I learn most quickly.

I generally do not advocate trying to standardize a hotkey scheme across multiple users, unless the users all agree to it. The underlying reason for writing this section is that everyone remembers things differently in the first place.

Any command that I use more than a few times an hour is worth assigning to a hotkey. I like to use alliteration when assigning keys to help with my faulty memory. The most frequently used commands are assigned single-letter hotkeys, and the less frequently used commands are assigned combinations. Thus, Tools Options is linked to O, Measure to M, Select Vertex to Shift+V, and Curve Projected to Ctrl+J (Ctrl+P is the Windows standard for the Print command). Other people like to group keys into easy-to-reach combinations; this is why the Q, W, A, S, Z, and X keys are often assigned first for right-handed mouse users.

Organizing hotkeys

Hotkeys are assigned and organized in the Keyboard dialog box (Tools ⇨ Customize ⇨ Keyboard), as shown in Figure 2.36. This interface enables you to see all the hotkeys (called *shortcuts* in the list) easily. If you try to enter an existing hotkey, SolidWorks issues a prompt, telling you that the key is assigned to another command and its name. The prompt asks you whether you want to clear the other instance of the hotkey and make the new one active. You can also print out or copy to the Clipboard a list of only commands that use hotkeys.

Because the list of commands is so long, a Search function is available, and a drop-down arrow makes only the commands from a selected menu visible. The list of commands is organized by menu name, and the menus are listed as they occur in the interface. Fortunately, on the Keyboard tab, SolidWorks enables you to sort, using the column headers to list the menus, commands, or hotkeys in alphabetical order, simply by clicking the column header. This is a highly usable interface, one of my favorite interface changes in the last several releases.

Hotkeys for menu items are listed on the right side of the regular drop-down menus. These serve more as a learning aid than interface elements. Figure 2.37 shows a drop-down menu with hotkey combinations on it.

FIGURE 2.36

The Keyboard dialog box (Tools ➪ Customize ➪ Keyboard) and the mouse gesture donut

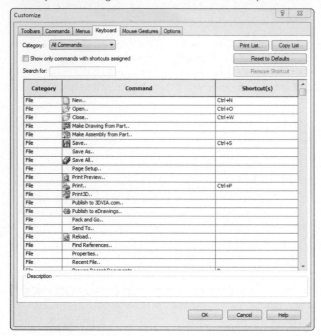

FIGURE 2.37

Drop-down menus contain reminders of the hotkey combinations.

Using mouse gestures

You can customize and use a mouse gesture interface, shown in the second image of Figure 2.37. To make the interface appear, just drag the RMB slightly, about 14 inch. Once you get used to the interface, a drag of about 34 inch in a single motion will activate the commands.

Note

I have found that this interface works best when you have memorized the commands available at various positions around the donut. You can set it to use four or eight divisions. Accuracy is more difficult with the larger number of divisions. ■

You can establish the donut in four or eight segments; it comes set to four by default. You can also do the customization in the Customize dialog box (Tools ⇨ Customize) using the Mouse Gestures tab. The advantage of this interface is that it is very easy to invoke. I like the way you can use the default setup to control views. The mouse moving in a particular direction is easily associated with a view direction, so it should be easy to remember.

Mouse gestures will probably not replace hotkeys or the "S" toolbar, but they do add effective quick access for a few functions.

Using the keyboard

Moving between the mouse and the keyboard can be bothersome and time-consuming. In addition to the hotkey approach, you can use another keyboard method to save time. Many users become adept at using the Alt-key combinations to invoke menu items. Most menu items in Windows applications contain a single underlined letter.

To access a top-level menu, you can hold down the Alt key and press the underlined letter for that menu, and then just press an underlined letter in the menu to access specific commands. This technique enables you to navigate most of the interface without using the mouse. For example, to exit SolidWorks, instead of using the mouse to click the red X in the upper-right corner, you could press Alt+F, X. In Figure 2.38, you can see that the F in File is underlined, as is the X in Exit.

FIGURE 2.38

Alt-Keys in the File menu

You may potentially run into conflicts when using Alt-keys. A combination of Alt + another keyboard key is a valid use of a hotkey combination. If you use any Alt hotkey combinations, it is likely that you have seen a conflict like this. In cases of conflict, the hotkey combination seems to gain priority over the Alt-key accelerator.

Minimizing icons

In order to maximize valuable space on the monitor, many SolidWorks users strive to minimize the number of toolbar icons on the screen, or confine them to two rows of toolbars. You can do this by using the CommandManager, flyout toolbars, the "S" toolbar, right-click toolbars, and hotkeys, and removing unused icons, as well as the other techniques discussed here.

Having an uncluttered workspace is definitely a plus, but having easy access to commands is the real purpose of an interface in the first place. You need to strike a balance between too much and not enough. The more kinds of work you do in SolidWorks, the more tools you will need to have available. If you only create relatively simple machined parts and drawings, you will need fewer tools available than someone who creates complex plastic part assemblies with rendering and animation.

Contemplating device approaches

If you have never used a Spaceball or equivalent view-manipulation device, you should consider it. They are wonderful devices and do far more than just spin the view. Most of the devices also have several programmable buttons that you can link to menu items. They can move drawing views, parts within assemblies, and even manipulate selected objects in other Office applications and Web browsers.

Using touch and multi-touch support

I have written portions of this book on a tablet PC. A tablet might not be ideal for long periods of SolidWorks usage. However, I use it regularly for presentations and even modeling when I really want to get the feel of drawing a line by hand. The stylus is not quite as intuitive as a pencil, but it is less of an impediment to the tactile feel of actual drawings than a clunky mouse. Tablets are a great option when used in combination with the new touch functions in SolidWorks, such as mouse gestures.

The mouse gestures functionality is considered a tool well suited to a tablet interface, where flicking the stylus is easier than mouse clicking. This is a single-touch technique, since the stylus typically adds only a single point of contact with the screen.

Multi-touch devices are still rare in the CAD-enabled office, but they are becoming more widely available. In preparation for this future functionality that seems ideally suited to visual applications such as CAD and 3D, SolidWorks has added functionality to take advantage of these tools. Multi-touch Action Mappings, as the SolidWorks Help refers to them, are intuitive two-finger motions that enable you to control the view for actions like:

- Zoom in or out
- Rotate
- Pan
- Roll
- Zoom to fit
- Right-click

SolidWorks gave these special actions a new page in the Options dialog, shown in Figure 2.39.

FIGURE 2.39

SolidWorks special settings for multi-touch controls

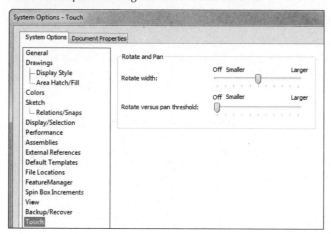

While SolidWorks does not yet support devices such as smart phones, Samsung Galaxy Tab, Motorola Xoom, or the iPad, you can find touch and multi-touch support from Windows-based convertible PC tablets offered by HP and Lenovo. You can also use devices like the Wacom Cintiq digitizers and touch and multi-touch monitors from most of the major monitor manufacturers in sizes conducive to CAD.

Support for phone-based tablets with alternative OSes such as Google Android or iOS including others will come when SolidWorks delivers what is now known as SolidWorks V6, which will be OS independent, and accessed via a Web browser. SolidWorks management estimates this is less than five years away.

Accessing macros

Macros are short snippets of programming code that have a particular function. Most macros are small and intended for simple tasks that are repeated many times, such as changing selected dimensions to four decimal places or zooming the screen so that it is sized 1:1 (actual size). Macros may be recorded, written from scratch, or a combination where you record a particular action for use as a starting point and then embellish it manually from there. Recorded macros may not always record the parts of the action that you want to make into a macro, but you can edit them manually to include anything that you can program with the SolidWorks API (application programming interface), which is included with the base SolidWorks package at no extra cost.

To access macros by using hotkeys, follow these steps:

1. **Make a folder in your SolidWorks installation directory called "macros."**
2. **Copy macros into this folder.**
3. **Start (or restart) SolidWorks.**
4. **Choose Tools ➪ Customize ➪ Keyboard.**
5. **Scroll to the bottom of the list under the Macros category and then assign hotkeys as you would for standard SolidWorks commands.**

Whether you are skilled at writing or recording macros, or you are just using macros collected from other people, they can be huge time-savers and offer functionality that you would not otherwise be able to access.

Saving custom interface settings

Once you have set up your menus and toolbars, worked out all of custom colors, figured out your hot-key usage, and connected your macros, you don't want to lose these settings when you reinstall the software or move to a different computer. Another user may want to share your settings, or you may want to transfer them to your home computer (for modeling the new deck or the doghouse, of course). Fortunately, these settings are very portable.

You can use the Copy Settings Wizard to save these settings out to a file. Access the wizard by choosing Start ⇨ Programs ⇨ SolidWorks 2010 ⇨ SolidWorks Tools ⇨ Copy Settings Wizard. This creates a file with an *.sldreg file extension. You can restore settings by double-clicking this file on a computer that has SolidWorks installed on it.

Note
You may need to have administrator access to your computer to apply a SolidWorks registry file. ■

The SolidWorks settings are actually Windows registry settings. The file that is saved by the wizard is just a registry file that has a different extension to prevent it from being applied too easily. Saved-out Windows registry files have a *.reg file extension, and you can integrate them into the registry by simply double-clicking them. If you are not familiar with the Windows registry, you should not make direct changes, because even small changes can cause serious problems with your operating system, installed software, or even hardware. The settings that are saved out by the Copy Settings Wizard are safe to transfer between computers. In order for the Copy Settings Wizard to work, you need to have Administrator-level access to your computer. The Copy Settings Wizard is shown in Figure 2.40.

FIGURE 2.40

The Copy Settings Wizard

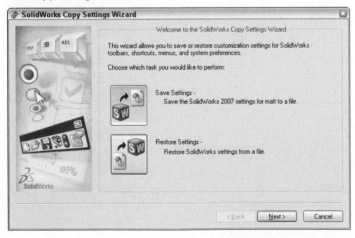

Working with multiple document windows

You may sometimes have the luxury of working on a single part at a time, but more often you will find yourself with several documents open at once. This is a common situation for most users. Fortunately, SolidWorks has several methods for dealing with "information overload" to help you sort through it all.

Managing windows

Like most Windows applications, SolidWorks can arrange the open document windows in one of several ways that are available through the Window menu (see Figure 2.41):

- **Cascade.** Most useful for accessing documents that are to be edited one by one.

- **Tile Horizontally.** Most useful for comparing wide and short parts side by side.

- **Tile Vertically.** Most useful for tall, narrow parts, or documents where you want to compare items in the FeatureManager.

- **Arrange Icons.** When windows are minimized to icons, this menu selection arranges the icons neatly, starting in the lower-left corner of the window.

FIGURE 2.41

The Window menu

The images in Figure 2.42 are meant to show the arrangement of the windows, not the content of the windows. Also, remember that you can use the F9 key to close the FeatureManager, the F10 key to remove the toolbars to create extra interface space when arranging several windows in the graphics window, and the F11 key to remove portions of the interface and enable you to work full screen.

FIGURE 2.42

Window Arrangements: cascade and tiled

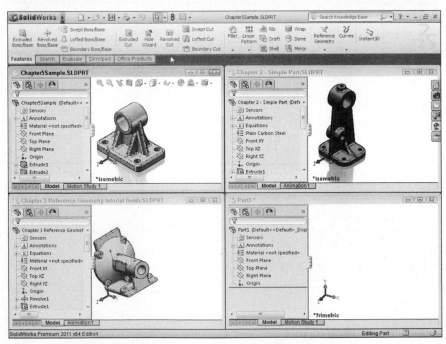

Changing windows

You can use several techniques to change from one SolidWorks window to another. By clicking on the Window menu, you can view a list of open document windows (refer to Figure 2.41). You can then select the desired window directly from this menu, as shown in Figure 2.43. Press Ctrl+Tab to open the Open Documents dialog box (see Figure 2.43). This enables you to select the document visually that you want to open.

FIGURE 2.43

The Open Documents dialog box

Additionally, by default the R hotkey opens the Recent Documents dialog box, similar to the Recent Documents list in the File menu. This can also be accessed via the File menu if necessary. The Recent Documents dialog box is shown in Figure 2.44.

FIGURE 2.44

The Recent Documents dialog box

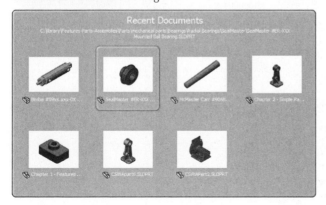

Getting to Know the Interface

By this point, you have learned quite a bit about all the tools involved in using the SolidWorks interface. In this tutorial, you get some hands-on practice at manipulating the interface. This tutorial is intended to reinforce the following skills:

- Adding and removing toolbars
- Adding and removing toolbar buttons
- Adding and removing items from drop-down and RMB menus
- Setting up the CommandManager
- Setting up hotkeys
- Linking a hotkey to a macro
- Changing interface colors

Also, don't forget to check out the video tutorials on the DVD for this chapter. The videos cover CommandManager, FeatureManager, and PropertyManager, along with the Graphics Window and Shortcuts.

Copying the existing settings

Regardless of what your initial settings are, you do not want to lose them. Before you start to make changes to your system, you should save out the existing settings to a file from which they can be recovered. You can do this using the Copy Settings Wizard, as shown in Figure 2.40.

To use the Copy Settings Wizard, follow these steps:

1. **Close SolidWorks.**
2. **Choose Start ⇨ Programs ⇨ SolidWorks 2011 ⇨ SolidWorks 2011Tools ⇨ Copy Settings Wizard.**
3. **Select Save Settings, and click Next.**
4. **Enter a location and a name for the file.**
5. **Select the items that you would like to save.** For the purposes of this tutorial, make sure that the following options are selected: Keyboard Shortcuts, Menu Customization, Toolbar Layout, and All Toolbars.
6. **Click Finish.** Browse to the location where you saved the file and make sure that it is there.

Applying default settings to interface items

You can set the interface back to the default settings using one of two methods. The first method, editing the Windows registry, may not be available to all users. It requires Administrator access to your computer and a good familiarity with Windows.

Caution

Editing the Windows registry can be dangerous if you make a mistake. Do not attempt this method if you have any doubts about what you are doing. ■

To set SolidWorks back to its default settings by editing the Windows registry, follow these steps:

1. **Close SolidWorks.**
2. **Choose Start ⇨ Run.**
3. **Type** regedit, **and click OK.**
4. **Browse to** HKEY_CURRENT_USER\Software\SolidWorks\SolidWorks 2010 **or the appropriate folder for the version that you are using.**
5. **To return all settings in SolidWorks to default, rename the entire SolidWorks 2010 folder to include "(old)" at the end of the filename.**
6. **Close the Registry Editor.**
7. **The folder is re-created when SolidWorks starts up again, and is populated with default values.** If you need to get the previous folder back, you can delete the new one and rename the old one to remove the "(old)" from the name.

The second method, which is less risky but less complete, is to go to the main settings locations and use the tools provided to return settings to their defaults. Restart SolidWorks and create a new blank document (you cannot display the Customize dialog box without a document open). To access the resets for the interface, do the following:

1. **Choose Tools ⇨ Options ⇨ General ⇨ Reset, and go to the bottom-left area of the dialog box.**
2. **Choose Tools ⇨ Customize ⇨ Toolbars ⇨ Reset, and go to the bottom-left area of the dialog box.**
3. **Choose Tools ⇨ Customize ⇨ Menus ⇨ Reset All, and go to the right side of the dialog box.**
4. **Choose Tools ⇨ Customize ⇨ Keyboard ⇨ Reset to Defaults, and go to the upper-right area of the dialog box.**
5. **Choose Tools ⇨ Customize ⇨ Options; there are two Reset to Defaults buttons along the left side of the dialog box.**

Customizing the CommandManager

Now that you have restored the default settings, you can begin customizing the interface with the CommandManager. To do this, open a part document or create a new one, then click the RMB anywhere on the CommandManager, and deselect the Use Large Buttons with Text option, as shown in Figure 2.45. When you have done this, the check mark should no longer appear in front of the option.

FIGURE 2.45

Deselect the Use Large Buttons with Text option.

Next, add some toolbars to CommandManager, as follows:

1. **RMB-click the CommandManager tabs and select Customize CommandManager.**

2. **Click (left-click) the New Tab icon at the right end of the CommandManager tabs and select Surfaces, Sheet Metal, and Annotations. Deselect the Sketch tab by right-clicking it and selecting Hide Tab.** The new tab icon is shown in Figure 2.46.

FIGURE 2.46

Adding tabs to the CommandManager

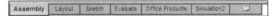

3. **In the Customize dialog box, select the Large Icons option.**

4. **Turn the Sketch toolbar on, but not inside the CommandManager; use the Toolbars tab of the Customize dialog box.** Dock the Sketch toolbar to the right side of the window.

5. **Select the Standard Views toolbar and drag it to the right end of the CommandManager.** Now drag a couple of buttons off it, such as the bottom, or left, or back views.

6. **On the Commands tab of the Customize dialog box, select the Flyout toolbars entry, and drag any Flyout toolbars from the Customize dialog box to the Menu Bar toolbar.** Figure 2.47 shows this step in action.

FIGURE 2.47

Adding flyouts to the Menu Bar toolbar

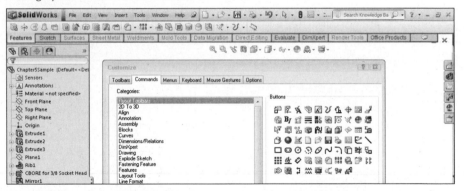

7. **With the Commands tab of the Customize dialog box still active, click on the View Category.**

8. **Add or remove tools until this toolbar has the tools you want to use on it. If you want to deselect the Heads-UP View toolbar, activate the Toolbars tab in Customize, and deselect the View (Heads-Up) option.**

9. **Run your cursor over the main menu flyout and use the pushpin to pin the menu open**.

10. **Choose Tools ⇨ Customize ⇨ Options and select both Show All buttons for Shortcut customization and Menu customizations.** This removes the double arrows at the bottoms of RMB menus. This setting is shown in Figure 2.48.

FIGURE 2.48

Removing truncated menus

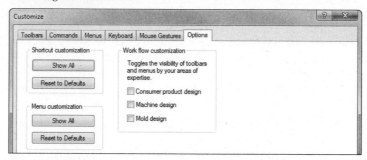

11. While still in the Customize dialog box, change to the Toolbars tab and deselect the Context Toolbar Settings ⇨ Show In Shortcut Menu option to disable the right-click context toolbar to put the RMB menus back to their pre-2008 state (all entries in menu use text).

12. Click and drag the PropertyManager tab (second tab from the left) from the FeatureManager, and dock it just to the right of the FeatureManager under the CommandManager tabs. The display should now look like Figure 2.49.

FIGURE 2.49

The customized SolidWorks interface

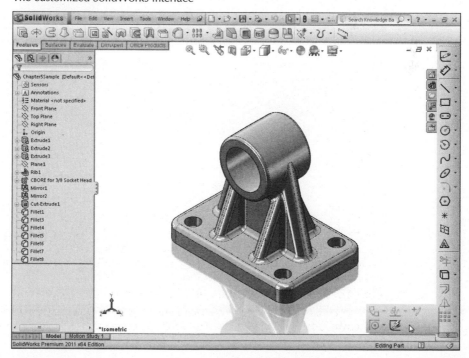

The small flyout in the lower-right corner of Figure 2.49 is the remainder of the Sketch toolbar that does not fit on the screen. This screen shot was taken on a monitor with large icons at 1024 × 768 resolution. At such a low resolution, long toolbars do not fit on the screen, and the remaining icons are activated by the two small arrows at the end of the toolbar.

Customizing menus

If you always do the same types of work, or more importantly, *never* do certain types of work, you might consider customizing some menus to remove items that you never use. Customization applies to both the main drop-down menus and the context-sensitive RMB menus. To customize a menu, follow these steps:

1. **Choose Insert ⇨ Customize Menu with a part document open.** Note that Customize Menu is different from Customize.

2. **Deselect the menu items Sketch from Drawing, DXF/DWG, Object, and Hyperlink (see Figure 2.50).** Click anywhere outside the list to close it.

3. **Click on the Insert menu to ensure that the deselected items have been removed.**

FIGURE 2.50

Customizing the Insert menu

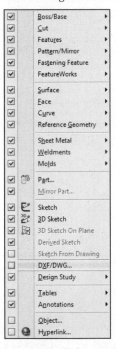

4. **RMB-click the Right plane in the FeatureManager.**

5. **Select Customize Menu.**

6. **Deselect Section View.** Click anywhere outside the list to close it.

7. **RMB-click the Right plane to verify that Section View has been removed.**

Changing interface colors

This tutorial does not depend on RealView capabilities, but later work will. To find out whether your computer is RealView capable, check your video card and driver version against the list on the SolidWorks Web site for system requirements. On the main page of the site, follow the link Support ⇨ System Requirements ⇨ Graphics Card Drivers.

Before starting this tutorial, make sure the RealView icon is disabled. You can deselect RealView by choosing View ⇨ Display ⇨ RealView Graphics or by using the gold ball toolbar icon on the Heads Up View toolbar.

Cross-Reference

For more information on RealView graphics, see Chapter 5. ∎

Edit the colors used in the interface:

1. **Choose Tools ⇨ System Options ⇨ Colors.** Make sure the "Plain (Viewport Background color above)" option is selected.

2. **Change the Viewport Background color, first in the Color Scheme Settings list, to a light gray color, then click OK and make sure the setting was applied.**

3. **Return to the Colors dialog box by choosing Tools ⇨ System Options ⇨ Colors, click the Save As Scheme button, and save the color scheme as Plain Gray.**

4. **Now select the Gradient option, and select the top and bottom gradient colors (second and third in the top list).** Click OK and see how you like the gradient display. Adjust the colors until you are happy with them.

5. **Return to the Colors dialog box by choosing Tools ⇨ System Options ⇨ Colors, click the Save As Scheme button, and save the color scheme as Gradient.** Figure 2.51 shows the Colors dialog box.

6. **Use the Current color scheme drop-down list at the top to change the color schemes between the newly saved schemes.**

Adding hotkeys

For many users, hotkeys are an integral part of the everyday experience of using SolidWorks. You can easily assign hotkeys and manage the assignments by following these steps:

1. **Choose Tools ⇨ Customize ⇨ Keyboard.**

2. **In the Search For text box, type** Options.

3. **Click in the Shortcut column, and type** O.

4. **Click again in the Search For text box, and type** Customize.

5. **Click in the text box next to the Tools ⇨ Customize entry and press Ctrl+C.** Click No to the question of whether you want to reassign the hotkey. Press Ctrl+T instead.

6. **Click OK to exit the Customize dialog box.**

7. **Press the O key to open the Options tab. Click OK to exit.**

8. **Press Ctrl+T to open the Customize dialog box. Click OK to exit.**

9. **Press Alt+F, and then click the Close button to exit SolidWorks.**

FIGURE 2.51

The Colors settings

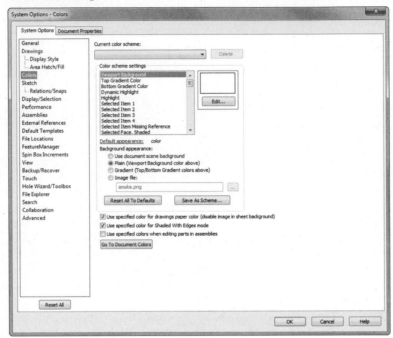

Combining macros with hotkeys

The following steps show you how to link a macro to a hotkey:

On the DVD

You can use the macro called **rectangle.swp**, located on the DVD. ■

1. **Find your SolidWorks installation directory.** By default, this directory is `C:\Program Files\SolidWorks Corp\SolidWorks`.

2. **Create a folder called Macros in the SolidWorks directory and put the rectangle.swp macro in it.**

3. **Open SolidWorks.**

4. **Create a new blank part document.**

5. **Press Ctrl+T to access the Customize dialog box.**

6. **Click the Keyboard tab.**

7. **In the Search For text box, type** rectangle.

8. **Click in the Shortcut column next to the listing with the Category of Macros, and press R.**

9. **Click OK to exit the Customize dialog box.**

10. **Press R.** The rectangle macro runs and draws a sketch rectangle on the Front plane, centered on the origin.

11. **Press Ctrl+S to access the Windows standard hotkey for the Save command.** Name the part **rectangle.sldprt** and save it to a workspace directory.

12. **Press Alt+F and then click Close to exit SolidWorks.**

The use of Alt-keys and hotkeys is somewhat exaggerated in this tutorial, but it is intended to get you used to working with them.

Summary

The SolidWorks interface has many elements because SolidWorks has so much functionality. You can access most elements multiple ways, which can be liberating because it offers options, but it also can add to the confusion because there is so much to know. You do not need to know every way to do everything; you only need to know the best way for you. After using this chapter to find the various ways of using the interface, you can develop the way that is most comfortable for you and stick with it.

Be aware that every couple of releases, SolidWorks changes the interface, and often, they use the most radical options available as the new defaults. Keep a copy of your settings file with you, so you can restore settings or take your settings to another computer quickly if you need to re-set up.

Working with Sketches

The workflow for most SolidWorks features goes like this:

1. Create a sketch
2. Use the sketch to create a feature
3. Repeat

So the first step to leaning how to create models in SolidWorks is to learn how to sketch. If you are coming from another parametric 3D modeler, many of your skills will be transferable to SolidWorks. If you are coming from a 2D application, sketching is just like drawing except that you do it in smaller chunks and on planes in 3D space. If you have never used CAD before, think of the sketch-feature relationship as creating a simplified 2D drawing that represents a portion of the part that you can make with some sort of process such as extruding the shape in the 2D drawing, or revolving it.

So far, in this book, you have looked mainly at concepts, settings, and setup, which is necessary but mundane business. In this chapter, you begin to learn how to control parametric relationships in sketches. Then in later chapters, you begin to build models, simple at first, but gaining in complexity and always demonstrating new techniques and features that build your modeling vocabulary. Beyond this, you use the parts to create drawings.

This chapter deals entirely with sketches in parts. However, you will be able to apply many of the topics I cover here to assemblies. Some related topics, such as layout sketches, have functionality that is exclusive to assemblies, and these topics are covered in the assemblies' book, *SolidWorks 2011 Assemblies Bible* (Wiley, 2011).

When you open a sketch, several tools become available, specifically all the sketch entities and tools. Conversely, you cannot do several things *until* you open a sketch. For example, you cannot apply a Fillet feature while a sketch

IN THIS CHAPTER

Beginning a sketch

Distinguishing sketch entities

Creating relationships in sketches

Examining sketch settings

Using sketch blocks in parts, assemblies, and drawings

Using reference geometry

Learning to use sketch relations tutorial

Using blocks and belts tutorial

Referencing geometry tutorial

is open. Open sketches and selection filters are two very common sources of frustration for new users. Several indicators exist to let you know when you are in Sketch mode:

- The title bar of the SolidWorks window displays the text Sketch X of Part Y.
- The lower-right corner of the status bar displays the text Editing Sketch X.
- The Confirmation Corner displays a sketch icon in the upper-right corner of the graphics window.
- The Sketch toolbar button displays the text Exit Sketch.
- The red sketch Origin displays.
- If you are using the grid, it displays only in Sketch mode.

While most users find the sketch grid annoying or distracting, when teaching, I've always used the grid to remind students when they are in Sketch mode. If you forget or would like a visual cue, the sketch grid is a useful option.

Opening a Sketch

Sketches must be either open or closed, and you can only have one sketch open at a time. SolidWorks uses many indicators to show the state of a sketch, including the Confirmation Corner and the Task Bar.

Several methods exist to open new sketches in SolidWorks:

- Click a sketch entity toolbar button from the Sketch toolbar; SolidWorks prompts you to select a sketch plane. When you select the plane, the sketch opens.
- Preselect a plane or planar face and then click either a sketch entity button or the Sketch button.
- Use the left mouse button to click context toolbar — click a face or plane and select the Sketch icon.
- Use the right mouse button (RMB) to click a plane or planar face and select Insert Sketch. Planes can be selected from either the graphics window or the FeatureManager.

You can open existing sketches several ways:

- Right-click a sketch in the FeatureManager or graphics window, and select Edit Sketch.
- Select a sketch from the FeatureManager or graphics window, and click the Sketch button on the Sketch toolbar.
- Left-click a sketch or feature and click the Edit Sketch icon from the context toolbar.
- Double-click a sketch with the Instant 3D tool active.

Identifying Sketch Entities

The first step in creating most SolidWorks parts is a sketch. This will usually be a 2D sketch, although you can also use 3D sketches. A 2D sketch is simply a collection of 2D lines, arcs, and other elements that lie together on a plane; it usually also contains relations and/or dimensions between the entities so that the sketch can automatically adjust to changes because each sketch entity understands its function.

SolidWorks sketch entities include many types, some of which you will use all the time, and some of which you may not use, even if you spend years working with the software. Next, I identify each entity type. This enables you to see it at least once and know that it is available if you need it at some point.

Using the Sketch toolbar

In this section, I identify the default buttons on the Sketch toolbar, followed by the rest of the entities that you can access by choosing Tools ➪ Customize ➪ Commands ➪ Sketch.

 The Sketch tool opens and closes sketches. You may notice that the name of the button changes depending on if the sketch is open or closed. If you preselect a plane or planar face and then click the Sketch button, SolidWorks opens a new sketch on the plane or face. If you preselect a sketch before clicking the Sketch button, SolidWorks opens this sketch. If you preselect an edge or curve feature before clicking the Sketch button, SolidWorks automatically makes a plane perpendicular to the nearest end of the curve from the location you picked. If you do not use preselection, and only click the Sketch tool with nothing selected, SolidWorks prompts you to select a plane or planar face on which you want to put a new sketch, or an existing sketch to edit.

 The 3D Sketch tool opens and closes 3D sketches with no preselection required. 3D sketch is covered in more detail in Chapter 31.

 The Smart Dimension tool can create all types of dimensions used in SolidWorks, such as horizontal, vertical, aligned, radial, diameter, angle, and arc length. You can create dimensions several ways, as shown in Figure 3.1:

- By selecting a line and placing the dimension
- By selecting the endpoints of the line and placing the dimension
- By selecting a line and a point and placing the dimension
- By selecting a pair of parallel lines and placing the dimension

FIGURE 3.1

Selection options for linear Smart Dimension

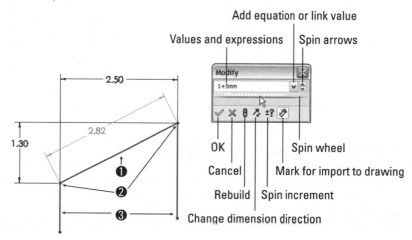

Selecting the line is the easiest and fastest method. Selecting parallel lines on the ends is not recommended because if you delete either of the selected lines, the dimension is also deleted; however, sometimes this method is necessary.

You can use the first and second techniques for the angled line shown in Figure 3.1 to create any of the three dimensions shown. To accomplish this task, drag the cursor while placing the dimension until the witness lines snap to the orientation you want.

Tip

To lock the orientation of a dimension while moving the cursor to place the actual dimension value, click the RMB. To unlock it, click the RMB again. The RMB cursor appears as a lock when the functionality is unavailable and an unlock icon when it is. ■

The third technique locks you into the horizontal orientation because of the orientation of the selected lines.

Note

In some situations, you may run into lines that appear to be parallel but are not exactly so. This will result in an angle dimension instead of a linear dimension. Here, you can select one of the lines and one endpoint. SolidWorks requires parallelism be precise, and situations where lines aren't exactly parallel happen if the angular measurement is off in the second or third decimal place, measuring in degrees. Imported 2D drawings and reverse-engineered 3D models can be particularly susceptible to this type of error. ■

Caution

When you select lines to establish a dimension instead of endpoints, both of the lines gain an implied parallel relation that prevents them from moving as you might predict. In the example shown in Figure 3.1, neither of the end lines can be angled unless you remove the dimension.

Another issue with adding dimensions to lines is that if you delete either line, the dimension is also deleted. This is not true for the first and second techniques, where as long as the endpoints remain, the dimension remains. ■

You can change Smart Dimension values several ways. The most direct way is to simply key in a value such as 4.052. The software assumes document units unless you key in something specific. You could also key in an expression, even with mixed units, such as 8.5 mm/2+.125 or 25.4+.625 in. You can also key in negative dimensions, which function the same as the Change Sense button in the Modify box.

Another way to put a value into the Modify box is to click the down arrow to the right of the value field, and select either to use an equation to calculate a value or a Link Value. A Link Value is like a variable name to which you can assign a value. You can link multiple dimension values to that Link Value. In sheet metal parts, the default Link Value of Thickness is used; if you change the thickness in one feature, it changes for all the sheet metal features.

To the right of the drop-down arrow is a pair of up and down spin arrows that enable you to change the value in the Modify box by a set increment amount. You set the increment in Tools ➪ Options ➪ System Options ➪ Spin Box Increments. You can also store multiple increment values within the Increment Value icon on the Modify box.

The final way to change the value in the Modify box is by using the wheel underneath the value field. The wheel uses the default increment value. Pressing Ctrl while using the wheel multiplies the increment by ten, and pressing Alt while using the wheel divides the increment by ten.

Here is a look at the Dimension Properties interface.

- **Radial.** You create the dimension by selecting an arc and placing the dimension. If you want a radial dimension of a complete circle, you must right-click the dimension after you create it, select Display Options, and select the Display as Radius/Display as Diameter toggle, as shown in Figure 3.2. Alternatively, you could use the Radius or Diameter leader display options on the Leaders tab of the Dimension PropertyManager.

FIGURE 3.2

The Dimension Properties interface

- **Diameter.** You can create the dimension by selecting a complete circle and placing the dimension. If you want a diameter dimension for an arc, use the RMB menu or Dimension Properties dialog box and select the Diameter Dimension option.

Note

Along with the Radial and Diameter dimensions, you may also want to dimension between arcs or circles, from tangent or nearest points. To do this, press the Shift key and select the Smart Dimension tool to select the arcs near the tangent points. Alternatively, to change a dimension from a center-to-center dimension to a max-to-max dimension, you can drag dimension attachment points to tangent points or use the dimension properties. ■

- **Angle.** You can create the angle dimension one of two ways. If the angle to be driven is between two straight lines, simply select the two straight lines and place the dimension. If you are creating an included angle dimension for an arc where there are not necessarily any straight lines drawn, then with the Smart Dimension tool active, first select the vertex of the angle, and then the two outlying points, as shown in Figure 3.3.

FIGURE 3.3

Creating an included angle dimension

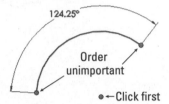

124.25°

Order
unimportant

●←Click first

- **Arc Length.** You can create the dimension by selecting an arc and its endpoints with the Smart Dimension tool.

 The Line tool creates straight lines using one of two methods:

- **Click+Click.** Used for drawing multiple connected end-to-end lines. Click and release the left-mouse button to start the line; each click and release ends the previous line and starts a new one. Double-click, press Esc, or deselect the Line tool to end.

- **Click and Drag.** Used to draw individual or unconnected lines. Click, drag, and drop. The first click initiates the line, and the drop ends it.

Note

The click+click and click and drag methods have been treated equivalently by SolidWorks until recent releases. Some new functions like Enable on-screen numeric input seem to function better with click+click than click and drag. ∎

Alternate methods for drawing lines include horizontal, vertical, angle, and infinite lines. The interface for these options appears in the PropertyManager, as shown in Figure 3.4.

- **Horizontal, Vertical.** These settings require you to select a starting point and an ending vertical or horizontal position. There does not seem to be any compelling reason to use this instead of the regular line command.

- **Angle.** This setting enables you to specify an angle and drag a line at this angle. Again, I can find no compelling reason to use this tool.

- **Infinite length.** SolidWorks parts have a working space limited to 1000 meters on a side, centered on the Origin. Infinite lines extend well beyond this, although you cannot draw or dimension a regular line outside of this box. I have not come across a compelling use for this feature.

FIGURE 3.4

The Insert Line PropertyManager interface

Note

The Add Dimensions option exists in several sketch entity PropertyManagers and adds Smart Dimensions to newly sketched entities. The option only appears in the sketch entity PropertyManager if the setting at Tools⇨Options⇨ Sketch⇨Enable on-screen numeric input on entity creation is selected.

The on-screen numeric input is not the same as the Input Dimension Value function, and, in fact, it overrides that option. You cannot input dimension values when using the Add Dimensions in conjunction with click and drag sketching. It appears to be intended for click+click sketching only, so that you can enter values between clicks. ■

 The Corner Rectangle tool creates a rectangle by clicking one corner and dragging to the diagonal corner. This action creates four lines with Horizontal and Vertical sketch relations, as appropriate. The Corner Rectangle is also available as a flyout icon with a Corner Rectangle, Center Rectangle, 3 Point Corner Rectangle (rectangle at an angle), and 3 Point Center Rectangle, as well as a Parallelogram. Figure 3.5 shows the flyout and flyout icons, and the PropertyManager for the Rectangle, which also enables you to switch types of rectangle easily.

FIGURE 3.5

The Rectangle flyout with associated icons

Notice the Add dimensions check box in the PropertyManager. Selecting this box while creating a rectangle causes the software to add dimensions aligned with the sides of the rectangle. This option is also available for lines, arcs, and circles.

Note that if you use this option in conjunction with the Enable on-screen numeric input on entity creation setting, found at Tools ⇨ Options ⇨ Sketch, it makes creating sketch entities to the correct size immediately much easier.

 The Circle tool creates a circle using one of two methods, which are available from either the flyout icon or the Circle PropertyManager:

- **Center Creation.** Click the center of the circle and drag the radius. The Circle PropertyManager calls this function *center creation*.

- **Perimeter Creation.** To create a circle using this technique, you must select the Perimeter Creation option from the Circle PropertyManager window after clicking the Circle tool. There is also a separate Perimeter Creation toolbar button and a menu selection for Tools ⇨ Sketch Entities ⇨ Perimeter Circle. This only creates tangent relations with other entities in the current sketch; if you are building a circle from model edges or entities in other sketches, you need to apply the relations manually. SolidWorks calls these functions *perimeter creation*.

  - **Tangent to Two Entities.** Start the circle with the cursor near one line in the sketch. A Tangent symbol appears by the cursor with a yellow background. Click and drag the diameter to the second tangent entity, where a similar cursor symbol should appear. Release the mouse button and right-click the green check mark icon. This process is shown in Figure 3.6.

FIGURE 3.6

Creating a perimeter creation circle

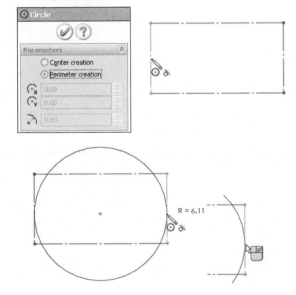

- **Tangent to Three Entities.** Use the same process for Tangent to two entities, but omit the right-click of the green check mark icon. After dropping on the second tangent, drag again to the third tangent entity.

The Centerpoint Arc tool creates an arc by clicking the center, dragging the radius, and then clicking and dragging the included angle of the arc. The first two steps are exactly like the Center-Radius circle.

The Tangent Arc tool creates an arc tangent to an existing sketch entity. Depending on how you move the cursor away from the end of the existing sketch entity, the arc can be tangent, reverse tangent, or perpendicular, as shown in Figure 3.7.

FIGURE 3.7

Using the Tangent Arc feature

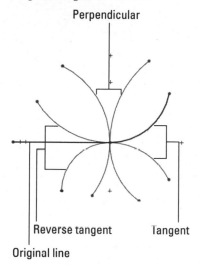

Another way to create a tangent arc (called auto-transitioning) is to start drawing a line from the end of another sketch entity, and while holding the left mouse button, press the A key; or return the cursor to the starting point and drag it out again. This second method can be difficult to master, but it saves time compared to any of the techniques for switching sketch tools.

The 3 Point Arc tool creates an arc by first establishing endpoints, and then establishing the included arc, as shown in Figure 3.8. Again, this tool also works using the click+click or click and drag methods.

FIGURE 3.8

Creating a three-point arc

 The Sketch Fillet tool creates a sketch fillet in one of two ways. Either you can select the endpoint where the sketch entities intersect or you can select the entities themselves, selecting the portion of the entity that you want to keep. Figure 3.9 illustrates both techniques.

FIGURE 3.9

Creating a sketch fillet

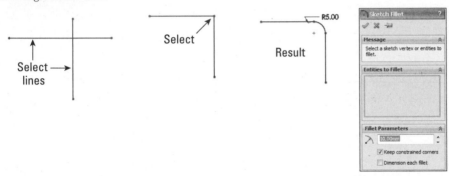

The Sketch Chamfer tool is on the same flyout as the Sketch Fillet by default. Sketch Chamfer does not have a list selection box the way that fillet does, and does not use a preview like the fillet.

Sketch Fillets

While the Sketch Fillet tool is easy to use and may align with your way of working in a 2D program, it is not considered best practice to use sketch fillets extensively. Some reasons for this include:

- Large changes in the size or shape of the rest of the sketch can make the feature built from the sketch to fail.

- SolidWorks (and other parametric programs as well) often has difficulty solving tangent arcs in some situations. You may see fillets flip tangency or go around 270° instead of just 90°. Using many fillets in a sketch can often cause trouble.

- If you want to remove the fillets temporarily, there is no good way to do this if you have used sketch fillets.

- Sometimes feature order requires that other features, such as draft, come before the fillet, which is difficult to do if they are part of the sketch.

- Sometimes a 2D fillet simply cannot create the required 3D geometry.

Fillet features are the preferred method for creating rounds and fillets. The same can be said for chamfers. Still, sometimes you need to use tangent arcs in sketches. You will have to decide which way works best for you.

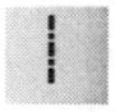

The Centerline tool follows the same methods as regular lines and is called a *construction line* in some cases. Other construction entities, such as construction circles, are not available directly, but you can create them by selecting the For Construction option in the PropertyManager for any entity.

The Spline tool draws a freeform curve. Splines may form either a single closed loop or an open loop. In either case, the spline is not allowed to cross itself. You can draw a spline by clicking each location where you want to add a control point. Figure 3.10 identifies the elements of a spline. The detail image shows the structure of a spline handle.

FIGURE 3.10

The structure of a spline and spline handles

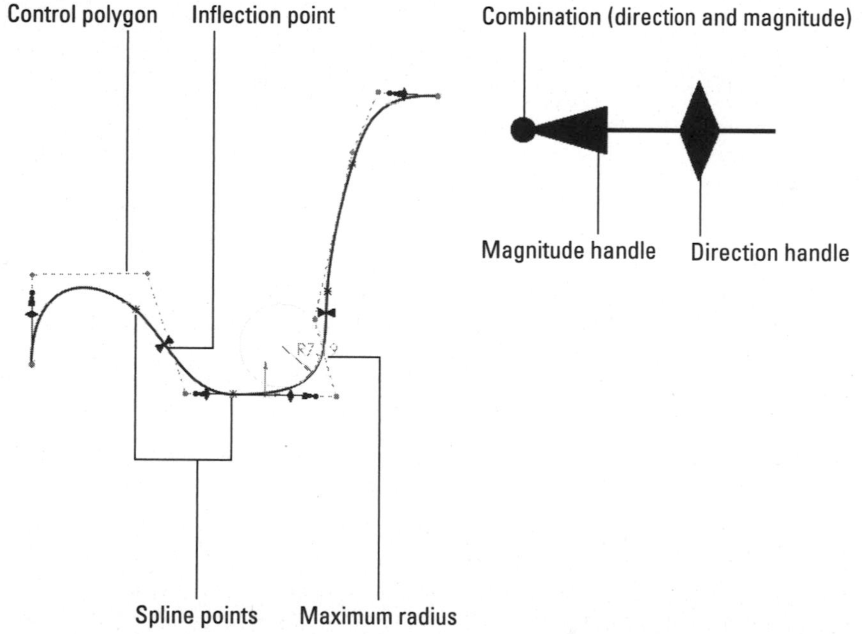

Splines are used mainly for freeform complex shapes in 2D and 3D sketches, although you can also use them for anything in which you would use other sketch elements. If you need more information on splines and complex shape modeling, refer to the *SolidWorks Surfacing and Complex Shape Modeling Bible* (Wiley, 2008).

The Point tool creates a sketch point. Aside from limited cases of lofting to a point or using a point as a constraint sketch in a Fill feature, sketch points are usually used for reference or for the location of the centerpoint of Hole Wizard features.

You can also use the sketch point as a virtual sharp. If two sketch entities do not actually intersect because of a fillet or chamfer, selecting the two entities and clicking the Point tool creates a point at the location where they would intersect if they were extended. This is useful for dimensioning to the sharp. Virtual sharp display is controlled by a Document Property setting.

 The 3D Sketch Plane tool creates a plane in a 3D Sketch. I discuss 3D Sketches in more detail in Chapter 6. By sketching on planes within a 3D sketch, you get most of the benefits and usage of 2D sketches, and you do not have to deal with history between sketches. Before committing too much work to this course, you should look into some of the shortcomings of 3D Planes. The planes are treated just like any other entity in the 3D sketch, which means you can assign sketch relations to them, but it also means that they can move around within the sketch like sketch entities.

 The Add Relation tool displays a PropertyManager window that enables you to apply sketch relations. This interface appears to be obsolete because it is easier to simply select sketch items and apply relations via the context toolbar or in the PropertyManager window that appears automatically when you select them; however, there are some subtle workflow-related reasons for using this tool.

Two advantages exist to using the Add Relations dialog box over simply selecting sketch entities and adding relations. When the Add Relation PropertyManager is active, you do not need to use the Ctrl key to select multiple entities. You also do not need to clear a selection before making a new selection for the next relation. These two reasons sound minor, but if you have a large number of sketch relations to apply, the workflow goes much more smoothly using this tool than the default method.

 The Display/Delete Relations tool enables you to look through the relations in a sketch and sort them according to several categories. From this window, you can delete or suppress relations and replace entities in relations.

 The Quick Snaps flyout tool enables you to quickly filter types of entities that sketch elements will snap to when you move or create them. To access the tools, click the drop-down arrow to the right of the toolbar button.

 The Mirror Entities tool mirrors selected sketch entities about a single selected centerline and applies a Symmetric sketch relation. In addition, a Dynamic Mirror function is described later in this chapter.

Note

PropertyManagers for sketch tools such as Mirror, Convert Entities, Sketch Fillet, and Intersection Curve now include a selection box for the entities to be used in the operation. The Offset PropertyManager is one that is conspicuously missing this functionality.

The workflow for the sketch tools with the selection boxes generally feels interrupted, in comparison to the workflow in SolidWorks versions before the selection boxes existed. To overcome this problem, you can deselect the push pin, and on the next execution of the tool, preselect the entities that would go into the selection box and then click the toolbar icon. ∎

 The Convert Entities tool converts edges, curves, and sketch elements from other sketches into entities in the current sketch. When edges are not parallel to the sketch plane, the Convert Entities feature projects them into the sketch plane. Some elements may be impossible to convert, such as a helix, which would produce a projection that overlaps itself. Sketch entities created using Convert Entities get an On-Edge sketch relation.

The Offset Entities tool works like the Convert Entities feature, except that it offsets the sketch to one side or the other of the projection of the original edge, sketch, or curve. Figure 3.11 shows the interface for this command.

FIGURE 3.11

The Offset Entities interface

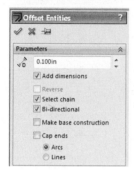

The options available in the Offset Entities interface are as follows:

- **Add dimensions.** Constrains offset sketch entities. Instead of the On-Edge relations, Offset Entities creates an Offset sketch relation that cannot be re-created manually.
- **Reverse.** Changes the direction of the offset.
- **Select chain.** Selects continuous end-to-end sketch entities.
- **Bi-directional.** Offsets to both sides simultaneously.
- **Make base construction.** If you are offsetting sketch entities within the active sketch, this option converts the original sketch entities to construction sketch geometry.
- **Cap ends.** Is available only when you have selected the Bidirectional option. Capping the ends with arcs is an easy way to create a slot from a sketch of the centerline. This function works with all sketch entities; it is not limited to straight slots. Figure 3.12 shows examples of the Cap ends option.

Caution

The Offset Entities command may fail if the offset distance is greater than the smallest radius of curvature, and you are attempting to offset to the inside of the arc. ∎

In addition to the bidirectional offset with capped ends, SolidWorks also has slot sketch entities for straight and curved slots, which are covered later in this chapter. Composite slots (made of a combination of straight and curved sections) still require the offset method.

The results of using offset entities cap ends

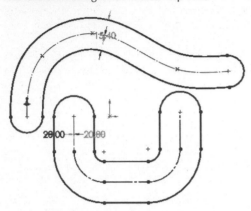

 The Trim tool is actually several functions rolled into one, and it is an extremely powerful tool for editing sketches. Trim Entities allows several methods for trimming, as well as extending and deleting sketch entities. Figure 3.13 shows the PropertyManager interface for this function.

The Trim interface

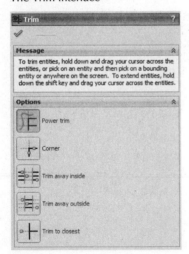

- **Power trim.** Trims by dragging a cursor trail over multiple entities. The entities that you drag the cursor over are trimmed back to the next intersecting sketch entity. Each time you trim an entity, a red box remains until you trim the next entity. If you backtrack with the cursor and touch the red box, this trim is undone. This option is best used when you need to trim a large number of entities that are easy to hit with a moving cursor. Figure 3.14 shows the Power Trim feature in action.

  You can also use power trim to extend sketch entities along their paths by dragging the endpoints. Regular dragging can also change the position or orientation of the rest of the entity, but by using the Power trim feature you affect only the length.

FIGURE 3.14

The Power trim feature in action

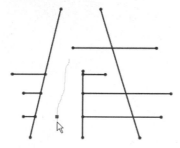

- **Corner.** Trims or extends two selected entities to their next intersection. When you use the Corner option to trim, the selected portion of the sketch entities is kept, and anything on the other side of the corner is discarded. Figure 3.15 shows two ways that the Corner option can work.

FIGURE 3.15

Using the Corner option

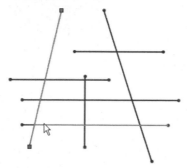 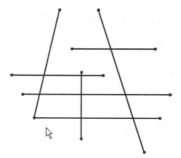

- **Trim away inside.** Trims away selected entities inside a selected boundary. The boundary may consist of a pair of sketch entities or a model face (edges of the face are used as the boundary). Only entities that cross both selected boundaries (or cross the closed loop of the face boundary twice) can be trimmed. This option does not trim a closed loop such as a circle, ellipse, or closed spline.

- **Trim away outside.** Functions exactly like the Trim away inside option, except that sketch entities outside of the boundary are discarded. The Trim away inside and Trim away outside options are illustrated in Figure 3.16.

FIGURE 3.16

Using the Trim away inside and Trim away outside options

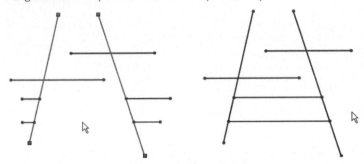

- **Trim to closest.** This is the default setting. Clicking a sketch entity will:
  - Trim it back to the next entity if there is only one crossing entity
  - Trim between two crossing entities if there is more than one
  - Delete the entity if there are no crossing entities

  In all cases, the selected section of the entity is removed. The Trim to closest option can also extend when you drag one entity to another; if an intersection is possible, the first entity is extended to the second entity. Figure 3.17 illustrates how the Trim to closest option functions.

FIGURE 3.17

Using Trim to closest to extend

The Construction Geometry tool toggles between regular sketch entities and construction entities. Construction sketch entities are not used to create solid or surface faces directly; they are only used for reference — for example, revolve centerlines, extrude and pattern directions, and so forth. Be careful with the icon for this function, because it looks almost identical to the No Solve Move icon, especially as printed here in gray scale.

Note

The icons for Hide/Show Edges, No Solve Move, and Construction Geometry look substantially similar, and in this black and white book they may be indistinguishable. ■

 The Stretch sketch tool is intended for use in sketches where there are enough dimensions to make a particular change difficult by changing dimensions only. It is similar in purpose and use to the AutoCAD Stretch function because it was loosely modeled after the AutoCAD functionality. Stretch enables you to specify a change that will change several dimensions simultaneously. Figure 3.18 shows the initial, intermediate, and final states of the sketch being stretched.

FIGURE 3.18

Using the Stretch sketch tool

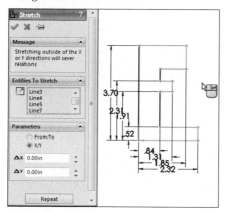 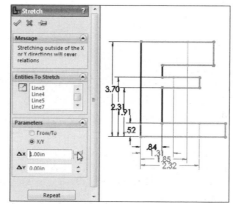

Tip

The main ideas to remember with the Stretch tool are that it is used to stretch dimensioned lines, and that you need to select the lines that will lengthen or shorten as well as the lines that will move. Because of this, selecting entities for Stretch is best done with the right-to-left window selection, which also selects any items that the selection box crosses. (Left-to-right window selection only selects items that are completely within the selection box.) ■

Caution

Figure 3.18 shows the X/Y option being used, but if you use the From/To option, be aware that it may unexpectedly delete some sketch relations. ■

The Move, Rotate, Copy, and Scale sketch tools operate on selections within a sketch. You can use these tools with pre- or post-selection methods. These tools delete existing sketch relations when necessary to accomplish the task. For example, if you want to move a rectangle connected to the origin, the Move tool will delete the Coincident relation between the sketch endpoint and the origin. If you want to rotate a rectangle, the Rotate tool will delete all the horizontal and vertical relations on the entities being rotated. This operation may result in a completely underdefined sketch. SolidWorks does not warn you that sketch relations are being deleted.

If you use the Scale tool on a fully defined sketch, SolidWorks will scale the position of the selected entities, deleting sketch relations if necessary to do so, but no dimensions will be scaled or deleted.

Caution

Be careful when using these sketch tools. They can delete sketch relations without warning. ■

These sketch tools were originally put in the software to avoid some of the complexities and limitations of the Modify Sketch tool, which can also move, copy, rotate, and scale sketches. Figure 3.19 shows the simple interface for the Move Entities command. Select the entities to move in the upper box and the method to move them below.

FIGURE 3.19

The Move Entities interface

Select is usually used to turn off the previous command and return the cursor to its default state.

Grid/Snap is used to open the Grid/Snap section of Tools ➪ Options ➪ Document Properties.

Parallelogram is used to draw a parallelogram (adjacent sides are not perpendicular, and opposite sides are parallel). Click one corner of the parallelogram, then click the second and third corners. Works like the 3 Point Rectangle except that adjacent sides are not perpendicular.

Polygon creates a regular *n*-sided polygon in the same way as a circle. Click the center and drag the radius. You need to set the number of sides in the PropertyManager before clicking in the graphics window.

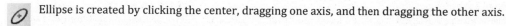 Ellipse is created by clicking the center, dragging one axis, and then dragging the other axis.

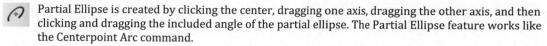 Partial Ellipse is created by clicking the center, dragging one axis, dragging the other axis, and then clicking and dragging the included angle of the partial ellipse. The Partial Ellipse feature works like the Centerpoint Arc command.

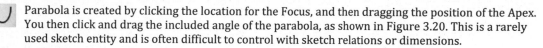 Parabola is created by clicking the location for the Focus, and then dragging the position of the Apex. You then click and drag the included angle of the parabola, as shown in Figure 3.20. This is a rarely used sketch entity and is often difficult to control with sketch relations or dimensions.

FIGURE 3.20

Drawing a parabola

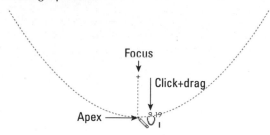

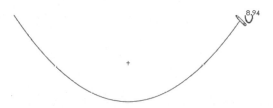

 Spline on Surface is used in 3D sketches to draw a freeform spline on any 3D surface. The Spline on Surface feature can cross face boundaries as long as the faces are at least tangent (ideally curvature continuous) across the edge. Spline on Surface can be used to trim surfaces or create split lines.

 Sketch Text creates editable text in sketches using TrueType fonts installed in your Fonts folder. Some fonts produce sketches that are unusable for solid features, due to violating sketch rules with overlapping or zero thickness. You need to be careful which fonts you select, but I have had success with a wide variety of fonts I have found on the Internet. Sketch Text may be dissolved into lines and arcs so that you can edit them manually. Dissolve is available on the RMB menu. Figure 3.21 points out the key elements of the Sketch Text interface.

FIGURE 3.21

The Sketch Text interface

 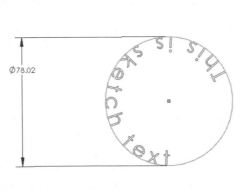

Note

Note that the Link To Property icon enables you to link sketch text to a custom property, or a configuration specific custom property. Using configurations and properties to drive sketch text can be a valuable function. ∎

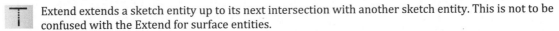 Intersection Curve, in 2D sketches, creates sketch entities where the sketch plane intersects selected faces. In 3D sketches, the Intersection Curve sketch tool creates sketch entities where any types of selected faces intersect. This can be an extremely useful tool in many situations.

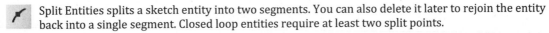 Face Curves applies the underlying U-V isoparameter mesh to a selected face. It is most commonly used as an evaluation tool for complex surfaces, but you can also use it to create curves to rebuild faces. Accepting the results by clicking OK creates a separate 3D sketch for each spline. Figure 3.22 shows the original surface and the results of using face curves on a complex lofted surface.

Extend extends a sketch entity up to its next intersection with another sketch entity. This is not to be confused with the Extend for surface entities.

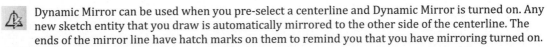 Split Entities splits a sketch entity into two segments. You can also delete it later to rejoin the entity back into a single segment. Closed loop entities require at least two split points.

 Dynamic Mirror can be used when you pre-select a centerline and Dynamic Mirror is turned on. Any new sketch entity that you draw is automatically mirrored to the other side of the centerline. The ends of the mirror line have hatch marks on them to remind you that you have mirroring turned on.

 Linear Pattern creates a one- or two-directional pattern of sketch entities. You can define spacing and angles. Figure 3.23 shows the interface and the results of this function.

FIGURE 3.22

Using face curves on a complex surface

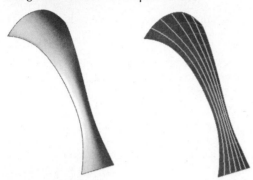

FIGURE 3.23

The Linear Pattern interface

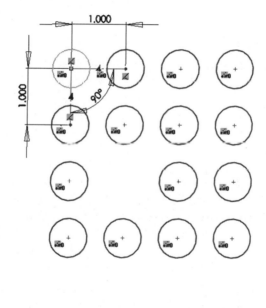

 Circular Sketch Pattern creates a circular pattern of sketch entities.

Best Practice

You should use sketch patterns as little as possible. For many of the same reasons that fillet features are preferred over sketch fillets, pattern features are preferred over sketch patterns. Sketch patterns are not as editable or as flexible as feature patterns. They solve slowly, especially when you pattern many entities. Best practice is to avoid sketch patterns unless there is no alternative. ■

 Make Path is intended to help create machine-design motion in sketches, in particular, cam type motion. Although it is helpful, you do not need to make a block of the cam first. You can then right-click the block and select Make Path. A tangent relation to a path enables a follower to roll around the entire perimeter.

 Modify Sketch is one of my favorite sketch tools, but it has been falling out of favor in more recent versions of SolidWorks because of the improvements to tools such as Move Sketch. It is also one of few remaining dialog box interfaces in the software. The Modify Sketch tool is flexible and powerful, and enables you to move, rotate, and scale the sketch, as well as mirror about a horizontal or vertical axis or about both axes simultaneously. Figure 3.24 shows the interface, which consists of a dialog box, a special Origin-like symbol, and a context-sensitive cursor.

FIGURE 3.24

The Modify Sketch interface

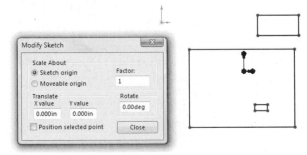

Both the left and right mouse buttons have special functions, which change when the cursor is moved over the three knots on the special Modify Sketch Origin. The RMB enables you to mirror or rotate the sketch, and the left mouse button (LMB) enables you to move the Origin or move the sketch.

This function has some limitations when you use it with sketches that have external relations. Certain functions may be disabled or a warning message may appear, saying that you need to remove external relations to get a particular function to work correctly.

 No Solve Move enables the moving of sketch entities without solving any relations in the sketch. If you select this option and you move an entity with relations that would otherwise not allow it to move (such as a collinear relation), you are prompted with a choice to delete the existing relation and continue or copy the entity without the relation. As mentioned earlier, be careful with the icon for this function because it looks almost identical to the Construction Geometry icon, especially as printed here in gray scale.

 Sketch Picture is a picture that is placed in the sketch, lies on the sketch plane, and is listed in the FeatureManager indented under the sketch. The Sketch Picture may be suppressed independently from the rest of the sketch, and when the sketch is hidden the picture is not visible. You can easily move, resize, and rotate Sketch Pictures, as well as apply a transparent background color to them.

Sketch Pictures are usually used for tracing over or as a planar decal without the need for PhotoWorks. Figure 3.25 shows the controls for manipulating the Sketch Picture feature.

The Sketch Picture interface

 Equation Driven Curve is a sketch spline driven by either an explicit or parametric equation, as shown in Figure 3.26. An explicit equation is in the form $y = f(x)$, while a parametric equation uses multiple equations driven by a common parameter value of the form, such as

$$x = cos(t)$$
$$y = sin(t)$$
$$0 > t > pi$$

where t is a number in radians.

The result is a proportional spline in a sketch, not a curve feature as the name suggests. The capability exists to drag the spline itself, or its endpoints, in 2D or 3D and SolidWorks calculates the new transformation. To reposition a sketch, use sketch relations and dimensions.

If you start an Equation Driven Curve in a 2D sketch, you get the form for a 2D curve equation. If you start in a 3D sketch, you get the form for a 3D curve. Once these splines are created, you cannot remove the relation to the equation and manually edit the spline; they are tied to the equation until you delete the entire spline.

One way to get around this limitation would be to create an equation-driven curve in one sketch, and then open another sketch and use convert entities to copy the spline, delete the On Edge relation, and use Simplify Spline to add control points to it. This is a technique commonly used with other types of curves; it does not enable you to update the overall size or shape of the spline through the equation, but you can manually adjust sections of a curve originally created from equations. Examples of where this might be useful would be a lead in or lead out on a cut thread, a special attachment loop in the middle of a spring, or a flare around the edge of a lens or reflector dish for mounting.

FIGURE 3.26

The Equation Driven Curve PropertyManager

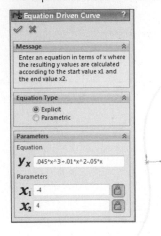
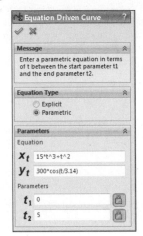

 Straight Slot and Curved Slot draw slots of a given width and length with full rounds on the ends. All the slot sketch entities can be seen in the PropertyManager shown in Figure 3.27. If you need to draw a composite slot or a slot with multiple entities, you will need to use the bi-directional sketch offset with capped ends mentioned earlier.

FIGURE 3.27

The PropertyManager for the slot sketch entities

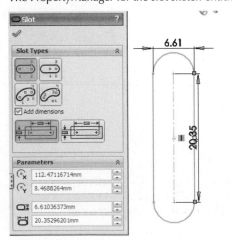

Using the Dimensions/Relations toolbar

The Dimensions/Relations toolbar has a few tools that you have already seen, but as the name suggests, it also contains tools that will either help you to create or investigate dimensions and sketch relations. Figure 3.28 shows the default toolbar, but in the following pages, you look at all the available tools you can see at Tools ⇨ Customize ⇨ Commands ⇨ Dimensions/Relations.

The Dimensions/Relations toolbar

- • **Smart Dimension.** Lets you dimension the sketch entity and combines several dimensioning methods into a single tool, such as horizontal, vertical, aligned, radial, diameter, and so on.

- • **Horizontal Dimension.** Applies a dimension to a sketch entity that drives the horizontal distance between the endpoints.

- • **Vertical Dimension.** Works like a horizontal dimension but vertically.

- • **Baseline Dimensions.** Creates dimensions only in *drawing* documents. Baseline Dimensions are different from most of the dimension tools that you find on the Dimensions/Relations toolbar in that they can create driven dimensions on view geometry or driving dimensions on sketch geometry in a drawing, but cannot be used on sketch geometry in parts. Baseline Dimensions start from a single reference; then as you select additional references, additional dimensions are stacked (see Figure 3.29).

FIGURE 3.29

Baseline Dimensions on a drawing

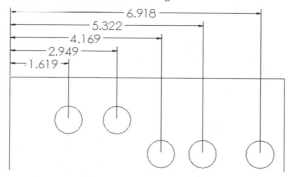

- • **Ordinate Dimensions.** Drives dimensions where a set of ordinate dimensions originate from a common zero point. To use these dimensions, simply click a zero location, place the zero dimension, and then click additional points. The dimensions are placed and are automatically aligned to the rest of the dimensions.

Note
If a line is not selected as the zero reference entity, the Ordinate Dimension feature defaults to a Horizontal Ordinate. ◼

You can remove Ordinate Dimensions from the common alignment by right-clicking the dimension and selecting Break Alignment. Ordinate Dimensions will jog automatically if SolidWorks senses that the dimensions are getting too close to one another. You can also jog them manually. After you create the Ordinate Dimension set, you can add to it by accessing the Add to Ordinate command through the RMB menu. All the options for Ordinate Dimensions are shown in Figure 3.30.

Not all the listed options are available in the model sketch environment; some are available only in drawings.

 Horizontal and Vertical Ordinate Dimensions have the same function as the regular Ordinate Dimensions, except that they only drive horizontal and vertical dimensions, respectively.

 Chamfer Dimension is another type of dimension that is only driven and only applied in drawing documents. It works by first selecting the chamfered edge and then selecting the angle reference edge. It produces dimensions like the one shown in Figure 3.31.

FIGURE 3.30

Options for Ordinate Dimensions

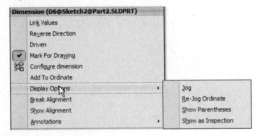

FIGURE 3.31

Applying a chamfer dimension

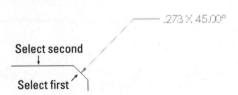

Automatic Relations toggles to enable or disable the automatic creation of sketch relations while sketching. This toggle is also available through Tools ➪ Sketch Settings ➪ Automatic Relations. Automatic relations help you to create intelligent sketches with less manual intervention. Although using them takes a little practice, it is well worth the effort.

Caution

As with any automatic function, there are times when automatic relations will do things that you do not expect or want. While you are sketching, it is recommended that you watch the cursor and the relations that it automatically applies. ■

While sketching, symbols appear on the cursor to show that a relation will automatically be created. These symbols have a yellow background and will apply horizontal, vertical, coincident, tangent, parallel, and perpendicular relations. Figure 3.32 shows two situations where automatic relations are applied — a horizontal and a tangent relation.

FIGURE 3.32

Some automatic relations that appear on the cursor

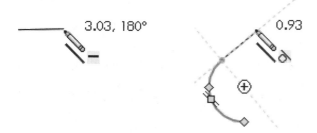

Inferencing in Sketch

Although SolidWorks users (even experienced ones) often confuse Inferencing and Automatic Relations, these functions are not the same. *Inferencing* refers to the blue dotted lines that display in Sketch mode when the cursor aligns with endpoints, centerpoints, or the Origin. Inferencing does not create sketch relations, with one exception. If both ends of a line pick up the same inference to the same point, SolidWorks will add that inference as an automatic relation.

When the cursor displays a small sketch relation symbol with a yellow background, this means that an automatic relation is going to be applied. If the relation symbol has a white background, the relation is inferenced but not applied as an actual sketch relation. The symbols with the blue (the color may also be green in SolidWorks 2008 or later) background are relations that have been applied to existing sketch entities. The symbols look the same, regardless of background color. Be aware that differences in versions and differences in color schemes can cause these colors to be different on your system.

Table 3.1 shows the symbols for the various inferences, automatic relation cursors, and applied sketch relations. The difference between the three types is simply the background colors: white, yellow, and blue, respectively.

TABLE 3.1

Symbols

	Along X		Along Y		Along Z
	At Intersection of Two Faces		Coincident		Collinear
	Concentric		Coradial		Equal
	Equal Curvature		Fix		Horizontal
	Intersection		Midpoint		Offset
	On Edge		On Surface		Parallel
	Perpendicular		Pierce		Symmetric
	Tangent		Vertical		Display/Delete Relations
	Fully Define Sketch				

The Fully Define Sketch interface uses sketch relations and dimensions to fully define the active sketch. It enables you to select which types of sketch relations and dimensions will be used to do this. Figure 3.33 shows the Fully Define Sketch interface. Be careful of this icon because it looks almost identical to the Sketch icon.

If you are familiar with older versions, the Fully Define Sketch function was formerly called Auto Dimension and has absorbed the functionality of Scan Equal and Add Relations. This function is very useful when used with imported sketch data. If you do not like the automatic dimensioning scheme, you can at least take advantage of the automatic sketch relations.

Best Practice

The Fully Define Sketch function does not necessarily use the best dimensioning practice for manufacturing drawings or for Design Intent. This tool is best used in situations when baseline and ordinate dimensions are appropriate. ■

FIGURE 3.33

The Fully Define Sketch interface

Exploring Sketch Settings

In addition to sketch tools, another important aspect of controlling sketches is sketch settings. Sketch settings are found in two different locations. The first location is at Tools ⇨ Options ⇨ Sketch. In this chapter, I cover the settings found at the second location, Tools ⇨ Sketch Settings. These settings mainly affect sketch relations.

- **Automatic Solve** is turned on by default. As you make changes to a sketch by adding relations or changing dimensions, SolidWorks automatically and immediately updates the sketch to reflect the changes. When the Automatic Solve setting is turned off, these changes are deferred until you exit the sketch or turn the Automatic Solve setting back on. The setting can be useful to prevent intermediate solutions (for example, when half of the changes are made) that may cause problems with the sketch, and when you are confident that the outcome will be correct. It is a rarely used option, and you could probably exist just fine without even knowing this option was there at all.

  If you import a large drawing from the DXF or DWG format, these drawings import as sketch entities into either a SolidWorks sketch or a drawing. SolidWorks may automatically turn off the Automatic Solve setting for performance (speed) reasons on files of this type.

- **Enable Snapping** is turned on by default. It enables the cursor to snap to the endpoints of existing sketch entities to help you make cleaner sketches. When you turn this setting off, Automatic Relations is also disabled (although the icon for the setting remains depressed, Automatic Relations are not created). Holding down the Ctrl key while sketching disables snapping. Holding down the Ctrl key while dragging sketch entities functions like copying sketch geometry. The No Solve Move is discussed in the Sketch toolbar section.

- **Detach Segment on Drag** is turned off by default. When you turn this setting on, the Detach Segment on Drag feature enables you to pull a single sketch element away from a chain of elements. For example, if you had a rectangle and you wanted to detach one of the lines from the rest of the rectangle without using this setting, you would have to draw extra geometry and then trim and delete lines in order to release the endpoints.

Best Practice

It is recommended that you leave Detach Segment on Drag off. Turn it on only when you need it, and then immediately turn it off again. This setting can be hazardous for everyday use, because it enables you to simply drag sketch elements that may be otherwise fully defined. ∎

- **Override Dims on Drag** is off by default. When you turn this setting on, it enables you to drag fully defined sketch geometry, and the dimensions will update to match the dragged size. This is another setting that you should use sparingly. It can be useful for doing concept work, but you should leave it off when working with production data for obvious reasons.

Note

Combining Override Dims on Drag with Instant3D can be very handy for concept work, enabling you to drag sketches, model faces, and edges easily. ∎

Using Sketch Blocks

Sketch blocks are collections of sketch entities that can be treated as a single entity and can be reused within a single document or shared between documents. You can use sketch blocks in parts, assemblies, and drawings. To create a sketch block, select a group of sketch entities and click the Make Block button on the Blocks toolbar, or select Tools ➪ Blocks ➪ Make. Pre-selection is not necessary; you can also select the entities after you invoke the command.

Blocks may be internal to a particular document, or they may be saved as an external file. The externally saved block may be linked to each document where it is used, so that if the block is changed, it updates in the documents where it is used.

You can use blocks in conjunction with the Make Path function mentioned earlier in this chapter to create functional layouts for mechanisms. You can also use blocks in an assembly to build parts in-context. Refer to the *SolidWork 2011 Assemblies Bible* (Wiley, 2011) for a more in-depth examination of the assemblies aspects of blocks in SolidWorks.

The following is a description of the various tools that are available on the Blocks toolbar:

- **Make Block.** Creates a sketch block from selected sketch entities. You can position a manipulator to denote the insertion point for the block. Blocks may attach at any entity endpoint, but the insertion point follows the cursor.

- **Edit Block.** Enables you to edit an existing block as if it were a regular sketch.

- **Insert Block.** Enables you to select from a list of open blocks or browse to a location where blocks are stored. You can edit the insertion point by using the Edit Block function.

- **Add/Remove.** Enables you to add or remove sketch entities from the block without deleting them from the sketch while editing a block.

- **Rebuild Block.** Allows changes to a block to be reflected in any external relations without exiting the block. For example, if you have a block in a sketch and a sketch line is coincident to one of the endpoints in the block, you may edit the block such that the referenced endpoint moves. As a result, the line in the sketch will not move until you exit the block or use the Rebuild Block function.

• **Save Block/Save Sketch As Block.** Saves a selected block to an external file (with the *.sldblk extension) or saves the selected sketch as a block.

 • **Explode Block.** Removes all the sketch entities from a block and brings them into the current sketch.

• **Belt/Chain.** Enables you to make a belt or chain around a set of pulleys. Each pulley must be a block. After activating the command (by right-clicking on a sketch or block), you can select each pulley and use the arrow on the pulley to switch the side of the pulley to which the belt goes. You can also compensate for the thickness of the belt (this is important when both sides of the belt are in contact with pulleys) and drive the pulley arrangement using the length of the belt. Figure 3.34 shows the Belt/Chain dialog box.

FIGURE 3.34

The Belt/Chain dialog box

Working with Reference Geometry

Reference geometry in SolidWorks is used to help establish locations for geometry that you can't physically touch, such as planes, axes, coordinate systems, and points. You often use reference geometry to establish a characteristic of the finished solid model before the model is created or to include an item that you may want to mate another part to in an assembly later. Mate References are also classified as Reference Geometry.

The importance of working with reference geometry becomes obvious in situations where you need to create geometry that doesn't line up with the standard planes. You might use planes to represent faces and axes to represent the centers of holes. Axes are often used to establish a direction, such as in plastic parts where, because of draft, you never truly have any vertical edges; an axis is frequently used to establish the direction of pull for the mold.

Coordinate systems come in handy, especially when translating a part from one system to another for the purpose of machining or some type of analysis. SolidWorks users usually model in such a way that the modeling work is made simpler by the choice of how the part origin is positioned relative to features of the part, but rapid prototyping, machining, mold building, and sheet metal manufacturing applications may have different requirements. As a part modeler, you cannot account for the needs of all downstream applications with your initial choice of origin placement, but you can always create a reference coordinate system for those downstream applications to use.

Creating planes

 Planes are the most commonly used type of reference geometry because they are used for sketching, cutting, as extrude end conditions, and more. The Plane feature PropertyManager and its functionality have changed significantly in recent versions. With the new interface, shown in Figure 3.35, you start by selecting model items (faces, edges, points, vertices, or other sketch or reference geometry) that you want to use to create the plane. The new plane uses constraints like sketch relations from the selected references. For example, in Figure 3.35, the new plane is tangent to the selected First Reference cylindrical face and at an angle to the selected Second Reference of a plane.

Creating a new plane from a set of selections and constraints

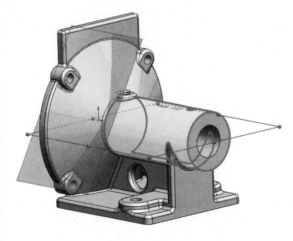

The good news about this method is that there are far more options for creating planes than in the previous method, but the bad news is that the options are not all spelled out anywhere. You have to make a selection before it shows you the available constraints. The older interface presented the available options right up front, but there were fewer to choose from. Hopefully this interface matures in the future. Meanwhile, you may need to experiment to see what works best for the type of modeling you do.

Note

For longtime users, when you start using the new Plane functionality, it may be best to try to ignore the new interface and simply make the same types of selections that you made in the past. The new Plane functionality will work perfectly that way. If you are a new user, just think of how you would like to specify the new plane, given the available geometry, and give it a try. The available options are not documented, so working with this interface requires some blind trust on the part of the user. The tool is quite powerful, but you will need to spend time experimenting with it. Even then, you will be unsure whether you are missing important options. ∎

Working with axes

You can use axes to create pivot points in a part where you do not have any hole-type geometry for mating with other parts, or as a direction of pull for plastic parts or molds. Axes are frequently used to establish direction. Figure 3.36 shows that the first three features in a plastic part are axes established from the standard planes.

FIGURE 3.36

Using axes to establish direction

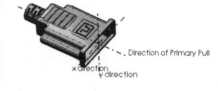

Consider using axes set up in this way as standard features in your template files. They can be effective in assemblies for moving parts in orthogonal directions and in parts for pattern or draft directions.

Note

The interface for the Axis feature has not been changed to match the Plane interface. Notice that the methods for creating an axis are spelled out clearly in the interface. I expect to eventually see a change to Axis to make it match the Plane interface. ∎

Using Coordinate Systems

Coordinate Systems in SolidWorks are primarily used for import and export, but can also be used for mating, mass properties, and other purposes. Coordinate Systems are usually located by a point to determine location or a set of edges to determine direction. Figure 3.37 shows the PropertyManager for assigning a coordinate system, along with the Export Options dialog box, which you can access from the Save As dialog box when the Files of Type drop-down is set to an export format.

FIGURE 3.37

Use Coordinate Systems to export parts and assemblies with a new origin location.

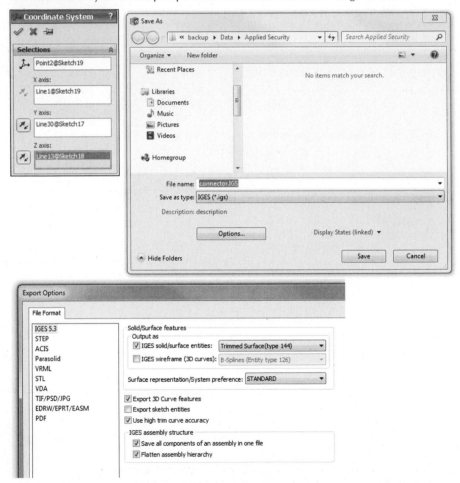

To use the coordinate system when saving as a translated file type such as IGES or Parasolid, click the Options button, as shown in Figure 3.37; at the bottom of the Export Options dialog box, a selection box for Output coordinate system appears.

To use the coordinate system with mass properties, choose Tools ⇨ Mass Properties from the menu, and then select the Output coordinate system, as shown in Figure 3.38.

FIGURE 3.38

Assigning the coordinate system with a well-hidden setting

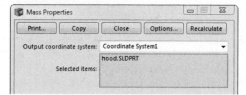

Using points as reference geometry

 The Point reference geometry feature is infrequently used; however, in some situations there is nothing else that does the job quite as well. This is not the same as a sketch point and does not require a sketch to be open; it is just a reference point that you can place in space. Figure 3.39 shows the PropertyManager for the Point reference geometry feature.

FIGURE 3.39

The Point reference geometry feature has several modes of point creation you won't find elsewhere.

My favorite Point placement method is the Along Curve Distance option (the bottom one in Figure 3.39). It enables you to create several regularly spaced points along a curve.

Tutorial: Learning to Use Sketch Relations

Although, it is useful to read through the definitions and functions of all the sketch entities, tools, and relations, using your mouse to create is what this is all about. This tutorial makes sure that you get to know all the major functions in SolidWorks sketches. Almost every part that you build will start with a sketch, so this is a skill worth mastering. Follow these steps to learn about sketch relations:

On the DVD

The `BibleInchTemplate.prtdot` template used in this tutorial is in the Chapter 3 folder on the DVD. ■

1. **Open a new part using a template that you set up in the Template tutorial from Chapter 1.** If you do not have this template, there is one provided for you on the DVD named `BibleInchTemplate.prtdot`. Copy it to your templates folder and use it to create a new part. You may also use a SolidWorks default template.

2. **Select the Front plane in the FeatureManager, and click the Sketch button on the Sketch toolbar.** Click the Line tool from the Sketch toolbar.

3. **Move the cursor near the Origin; the yellow Coincident symbol appears.**

4. **Draw a line horizontal from the Origin.** Remember that there are two ways to sketch the line: Click+click or click and drag. Make sure that the line snaps to the horizontal and that there is a yellow Horizontal relation symbol. The PropertyManager for the line should show that the line has a Horizontal relation. Also notice that the line is black, but the free endpoint is blue (after you hit Esc twice to clear the tool, then clear the selection). This means that the line is fully defined except for its length. You can test this by dragging the blue endpoint.

5. **Click the Smart Dimension tool on the Sketch toolbar, use it to click the line that you just drew, and place the dimension.** If you are prompted for a dimension, type **1.000**. If not, then double-click the dimension; the Modify dialog box appears, enabling you to change the dimension. The setting to prompt for a dimension is found at Tools ➪ Options ➪ General, Input Dimension Value.

6. **Draw two more lines to create a right triangle to look like Figure 3.40.** If the sketch relations symbols do not show in the display, turn them on by clicking View ➪ Sketch Relations. You may want to set up a hotkey for this, because having sketch relations is useful, but often gets in the way. Note that the sketch relation symbols may also be green, depending on how your software is installed.

FIGURE 3.40

Draw a right triangle.

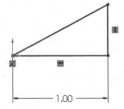

---

7. **Drag the blue endpoint of the triangle.** Dragging endpoints is the most direct way to change the geometry. Dragging the line directly may also work, but this sometimes produces odd results. The sketch leaves a ghost when dragging so that you can see where you started. Note that the setting for leaving a ghost when dragging a sketch is found at Tools ➪ Options ➪ Sketch, Ghost Image On Drag.

8. **Click the Smart Dimension tool, and then click the horizontal line and the angled line.** This produces an angle dimension. Place the angle dimension and give it a value of 30°.

9. **Click the Sketch Fillet tool, set the radius value to 0.10 inches, and click each of the three endpoints.** Where the 1.000-inch dimension connects to the sketch, SolidWorks has created *virtual sharps*. Figure 3.41 shows the sketch at this point. You may now want to turn off the Sketch Relations display because the screen is getting pretty busy. You can find this setting at View ➪ Sketch Relations.

FIGURE 3.41

The resulting sketch after you perform Step 9

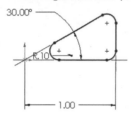

10. **Draw a line starting from the midpoint of the angled line.** The midpoint should highlight when you move the cursor close to it. Draw the line perpendicular to the angled line. A dotted yellow line appears, showing where the perpendicular lies. When you follow this line, the yellow perpendicular symbol appears on the cursor. Make this line approximately .25 inches long. Feedback on the cursor also shows the length of the line as you draw it.

11. **Draw two more lines ending at the endpoint of the sketch fillet, as shown in Figure 3.42.** Use the Inferencing lines to line up the second angled line with the end of the arc.

12. **Click the Trim tool from the Sketch toolbar.** Make sure that the Trim option is set to Closest. Click the angled line of the triangle between the two lines sketched in Step 11. This trims out that section and makes the sketch a single closed loop. A warning may appear because you have a Midpoint relation to the line being trimmed; you no longer want this relation, but you want the lines to intersect at their endpoints. Select Yes at the prompt.

13. **Click the Smart Dimension tool.** Use it to create aligned dimensions on the short line (.25 inches) and one of the long lines (.125 inches). You may now want to reorganize some of the dimensions if the display is becoming crowded.

14. **At this point, two of the lines should be blue, but it may not be clear why they are not defined.** Select one of the blue lines and drag it. Notice that what changes is the arc nearest the Origin. This changes in a way that is not useful for this part. To lock this line where it needs to be, select the blue line nearest the Origin and the centerpoint of the arc nearest the Origin, and give them a Coincident relation in the PropertyManager. The result is a fully defined sketch, as shown in Figure 3.43.

FIGURE 3.42

The resulting sketch after you perform Step 11

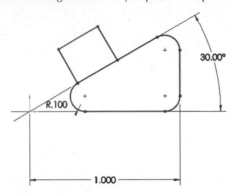

FIGURE 3.43

The resulting sketch after you perform Step 14

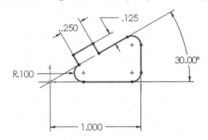

15. **Save the part with the name** Sketch Relations Tutorial.sldprt. **Close the part.**

Tutorial: Using Blocks and Belts

Sometimes I am amazed at the things that can be done in SolidWorks, even with fairly simple tools. This is one of those times. If you design machines, this tutorial will have some extra meaning for you. If you do not design machines, Blocks and Belts are still valuable tools to have in your toolbox ready to use in various situations. Follow these steps to learn about using Blocks and Belts.

1. **Open a new part with inches as the units.**

2. **Draw a sketch on the Front plane as shown in Figure 3.44, with four lines connected to the Origin.** Exit the sketch and rename it Layout Sketch, either by clicking twice on the name of the feature in the FeatureManager or by selecting it and pressing F2.

3. **Open a second sketch on the Front plane, and draw a circle centered on the Origin with a 6-inch diameter.**

4. **Inside the circle, draw a Centerpoint rectangle centered on the Origin.**

FIGURE 3.44

The layout sketch

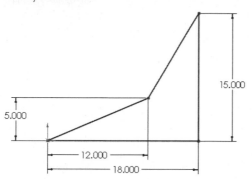

5. **Select two adjacent sides of the rectangle and make an Equal sketch relation between them.** (This makes the rectangle into a square.)

6. **Click the Smart Dimension tool, and apply a 1.000-inch dimension to one side of the square.** Turn off the Smart Dimension tool by clicking it again on the toolbar or pressing Esc.

7. **If the Blocks toolbar is not active, activate it and then select Make Block.** You can also access this command through Tools ⇨ Block ⇨ Make.

8. **Window select the circle and the square by clicking and dragging a box that includes all the items in the sketch.** The PropertyManager to the left displays a circle and six lines that are to be made into a block.

9. **Expand the Insertion Point panel in the PropertyManager.** This causes a blue manipulator Origin to appear in the graphics window. Click this Origin and drag it onto the center of the circle. Then click the green check mark icon to exit the Make Block dialog box. This is shown in Figure 3.45.

FIGURE 3.45

Creating a block

 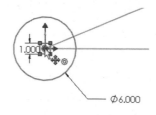

10. **The items in the block now turn gray.** Click anywhere on the block and drag it out of the way. Then drag the center of the circle and drop it on the part Origin.

11. **Click the Insert Block tool on the Blocks toolbar.** Place the block on the opposite sharp corner of the layout sketch.

12. **Create another block that is identical to the first one, except that it has a diameter of 3 inches instead of 6 inches.** You can do this by selecting the first block, clicking Edit Block from the toolbar, and copying (Window select and Ctrl+C). Then exit the Edit Block and paste (Ctrl+V) in the regular sketch. Make sure to also change the insertion point for this second block to the center of the circle.

13. **Insert a second instance of this second block, and make sure that both of them have the center of the circle at the two remaining intersection points of the four-sided shape of the layout sketch.** At this point, your sketch should look like Figure 3.46.

FIGURE 3.46

Block placement

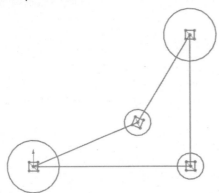

14. **Click the Belt/Chain tool on the Blocks toolbar.** Select the blocks in counterclockwise order, starting at the Origin. On the last pulley, you will have to click the arrow to get the belt to go the correct way around the pulley. Use Figure 3.47 as a guide.

15. **Make sure that the Engage Belt option is selected.** This enables you to make the pulleys move in the same way that they would in a real belt-driven mechanism.

16. **Click the Use Belt Thickness option and assign .25 inches for the thickness.** The belt should be offset from the pulleys.

17. **Click the green check mark icon.**

18. **Click and drag one of the corners of the square in a pulley.** All the pulleys should turn as if this were a real mechanism. The ratios are also observed because the small pulleys rotate faster than the large ones.

19. **Save this part as** `Blocks and Belts Tutorial.sldprt`. Exit the part.

FIGURE 3.47

Creating the belt around the pulleys

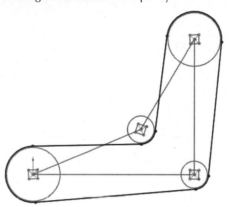

Tutorial: Creating Reference Geometry

This tutorial steps you through creating reference geometry on an existing part in preparation for locating 3D features.

On the DVD

The `Chapter 3 Reference Geometry.SLDPRT` file (or drawing) used in this tutorial is in the Chapter 3 folder on the DVD. ∎

1. **Open the file from the DVD in the Chapter 3 folder called** `Chapter 3 Reference Geometry - start.sldprt`.

2. **In the FeatureManager filter, type** plane1. Double-click Plane1 in the FeatureManager, then double-click the 3.25-inch dimension on the screen and change it to 3.35 inches. Click the rebuild symbol (traffic light) and watch the update. This plane locates the mounting base of the part.

   When you are done, click the X at the right end of the FeatureManager filter to clear the result. Pressing Esc does the same thing.

3. **Click the Axis toolbar button from the Reference Geometry flyout menu (on the Features tab of the CommandManager in a default install).**

4. **Select the inside face of a hole on the part, as shown in Figure 3.48.** This creates an axis on the centerline of the hole. You should note that a temporary axis already exists for all cylindrical faces, but making a true axis feature helps this one stand out as different from the other holes on the part.

FIGURE 3.48

Making one hole stand out by creating an axis feature

The selection of the Cylindrical/Conical Face option should be automatically activated by your selection of the cylindrical face of the hole. Accept the result with the green check mark when the selections and settings are complete.

 5. **Click the Plane toolbar button from the Reference Geometry flyout on the Features tab of the CommandManager.**

6. **Select the large cylindrical face of the part as the First Reference and the axis you just created as the Second Reference.** Make sure the First Reference uses the Tangent constraint and the Second Reference uses the Coincident constraint. This makes a plane tangent to the main cylinder in the part that goes through the patterned hole, as shown in Figure 3.49.

FIGURE 3.49

Creating a plane from tangent and coincident constraints

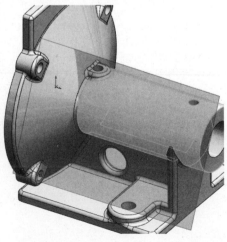

Click the green check mark to accept the result.

7. **Open a new sketch on the new plane.**

8. **Click the View menu and activate the Temporary Axes option.** You should now see blue axes (without names) appear along the centerlines of every conical or cylindrical face on the model (except for faces created by fillet or chamfer features).

Note

If the view is already normal to the selected plane, and you double-click Normal To, the view switches to 180 degrees opposite. For this exercise, it doesn't matter which way you view the part, but from the top is better than from the bottom because the view is clearer. ■

9. **Select the sketch plane either from the graphics window or the FeatureManager. Press the Spacebar on the keyboard and double-click Normal To.** There are other ways to access this command, but this is the method that will work regardless of your interface setup. You can use whatever method you prefer.

10. **Use the Centerpoint Rectangle to create a rectangle centered around the temporary axis of the large cylindrical face.** Make sure that the centerpoint, which is the first click you make, picks up a coincident automatic relation with the temporary axis. Make sure the second click to place the corner of the rectangle does not pick up any automatic relations.

You can tell if any relations have been applied if you go to the View menu and activate Sketch Relations. Make sure the centerpoint has a coincident relation and that none of the corners has any relations.

Note

The temporary axis is not on the same plane as the sketch plane, so if the view is not normal to the sketch plane, picking up an automatic relation between the centerpoint of the rectangle and the temporary axis will be difficult. ■

11. **Use the Smart Dimension tool to apply dimensions, as shown in Figure 3.50.** Note that the 3.450-inch dimension goes to the part origin on the left. You can select this from either the graphics window or the FeatureManager.

Best Practice

It is best practice to dimension or create sketch relations to items that have the fewest other relations. You should try to use the part origin and standard planes when possible. Dimensioning to reference geometry is better than dimensioning to model edges, although this is not always possible. Experienced users will immediately recognize the need for removing layers of references to prevent restrictive parent-child relations and broken or dangling relations. For beginning users, after you have some experience with making changes to models where relations have been applied carelessly, being more selective with sketch and dimension references will look more attractive to you. ■

FIGURE 3.50

Dimensioning the new sketch

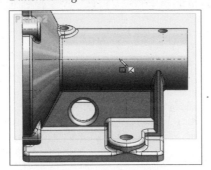
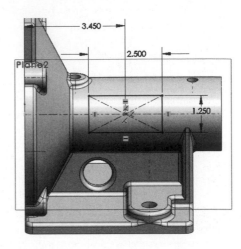

 12. Click the Extrude toolbar button on the Features tab of the CommandManager. Rotate the model (by dragging with the mouse wheel depressed) slightly so you can see the side of the extrusion preview, as shown in Figure 3.51.

FIGURE 3.51

Creating the extrusion from the new sketch

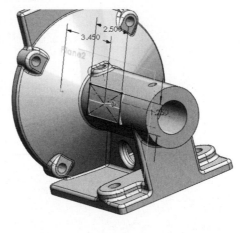

You may have to adjust the direction of the extrude using the icon with the arrows just below the Direction1 heading in the Boss-Extrude PropertyManager.

13. Use the Up To Next end condition, which makes the sketch go up to the next solid that it encounters.

14. Use the View menu to turn off the display of Axes, Temporary Axes and Planes.

Summary

Sketching in SolidWorks is something that you will do almost every time you open the software. A lot of automated functions are available that can enable you to do much of the work for you. You also have a lot of control to make changes manually. Remember that the best way to create most sketches is to use automatic relations when you can, sketch the approximate shape that you want to make, and then either drag it to pick up automatic relations, add dimensions, or add relations manually. Remember that you can use the left-click context toolbar to speed up adding relations manually.

The options for creating intelligent relationships that establish your Design Intent, as well as SolidWorks's capabilities in laying out mechanisms, is only limited by your imagination. The more familiar you become with the tools in your toolbox, the more of a craftsman you can become with this software.

Reference geometry is an essential part of creating and controlling relationships in any parametric model. Reference geometry is usually more stable than solid geometry, so sketch relations and dimensions should use reference geometry as references when possible.

Creating Simple Parts and Drawings

G ood modeling practice is based on robust design intent. This just means that you should try to build parts that can adapt easily to changes. This section of the book begins with questions that you need to ask to make good models.

Beginning to create simple parts will help you understand techniques used in more complex modeling projects. Learning on simple tools and then expanding your skills helps you to understand best practice issues, which makes you a better contributor to a team environment.

Discovering Design Intent

By asking questions about the part's function before you start modeling or designing, you can create a model that will be easier to edit, easier to properly place into an assembly, easier to detail in drawings, and easier for other SolidWorks users to understand when someone else has to work on your models. Whether you are doing the modeling for someone else or doing the design and modeling for yourself may make a difference in how you approach the modeling task.

The purpose of these questions is to help you establish design intent. The term *design intent* is a statement of how the part functions and how the model reacts to modeling changes.

It may help if you try to put the design intent into words to help you focus on what is important in the design. An example of a statement of design intent is "This part is symmetric about two planes, is used to support a 1.00" diameter shaft with a constant downward load of 150 pounds using a bronze bushing, and is bolted to a plate below it." This does not give you enough information to design the part, but it does give you information about two surfaces that are important (a hole for the bushing and the bottom that touches the mounting plate), as well as some general size and load requirements. The following questions can help you develop the design intent for your own projects.

Using symmetry

Symmetry is an important aspect of design intent. Taking advantage of symmetry can significantly reduce the time needed to model the part. Symmetry can exist on several levels:

- Sketch symmetry
- Individual feature symmetry
- Whole-part symmetry
- Axial symmetry (a revolved part)
- "Almost" symmetry (the whole part is symmetrical, except for a few features)
- Left and right symmetrical versions of the part
- Assembly symmetry

Determining primary or functional features

This is probably the most important question. Primary or functional features include how the part mounts or connects to other parts, motion that it needs to accommodate, and additional structure to support loads.

Often it is a good idea to create a special sketch as the first feature in the part that lays out the functional features. This could be as simple as a straight line to denote the bottom and a circle to represent the position and size of a mating part, or as complex as full outlines of parts and features from all three standard planes. This technique is called a *layout sketch*, and it is an important technique in both simple and complex parts. You can use layout sketches for anything from simply drawing a size-reference bounding box to creating the one point of reference for all sketched features in the part. You can use multiple layout sketches if a single sketch on one plane is not sufficient.

Predicting change

When the marketing department gets out of their meeting at 4:45 pm, what changes do you need to be prepared for so that you can still be out the door by 5:00 pm? No one expects you to be able to tell the future, but you do need to model in such a way that your model easily adapts to future changes. As you gain experience with the software and engineering design processes, keep this idea in mind; you will develop some instincts for the type of modeling that you do.

Determining the manufacturing method

Modeling for the casting process is very different from modeling for the machining process. When possible, the process should be evident in your modeling. There are times when you will not know which process will be used to create the part when you start to create a model. If you are simply making an initial concept model, you may not need to be concerned about the process. In these cases, it may or may not be possible to reuse your initial model data if you need to make a detailed cast part from your non-process-specific model. Decisions like this are usually based on available time, how many changes need to be made, and a determination of the risk of making the changes versus not making the changes, as well as which decision will cost you the most time in the long run.

Sometimes it makes sense to allow someone else to add the manufacturing details. A decision like this depends on your role in the organization and your experience with the process compared with that of other people downstream in the manufacturing process. For example, if you are not familiar with the Nitrogen Gas Assist process for molding polypropylene, and you are modeling a part to be made in that process, you might consider soliciting the help of a tooling engineer or passing the work on to someone else to add engineering detail.

Best Practice

As engineers, we are typically perfectionists. However, there always needs to be a balance between perfection and economy. Achieving both simultaneously is truly a rare event. Still, you should be aware that problems left by the designer for other downstream applications to solve (such as machining, mold making, and assembly) also have an impact on the time and cost of the project. ■

Identifying secondary operations

When working with any manufacturing process, some secondary processes are generally required. For example, if you have a cast part, you may need to machine the rough surface to create a flat face in some areas. You may also need to ream or tap holes. In plastic parts, you may need to press in threaded inserts.

SolidWorks includes special tools you can use to document secondary operations:

- **Configurations.** This SolidWorks technique enables you to create different versions of a part. For example, one configuration may have the features for the secondary operations suppressed (turned off) and showing just the part as cast, while the other configuration shows the part as machined.

Cross-Reference

Chapter 11 discusses configurations and feature suppression in depth. ■

- **Insert Part.** This SolidWorks technique enables you to use one SolidWorks part as the starting point for a second part. For example, the as-cast part has all the features to make the part, but it is inserted as the first feature in the as-machined part, which adds the cuts required by the machining process.

Creating multiple versions

Sometimes size-based versions of parts have to be created or versions based on additional features. If these are simple, they can also be handled with configurations, but you need to plan this flexibility in advance.

Creating a Simple Part

You need to practice some of the skills you will learn on simple parts. Chapter 2 introduced the tools and features you will use, and this chapter teaches you how to string the simple features together intelligently. In this section, I'll show you how to build the simple part shown in Figure 4.1. While the shape is simple, the techniques used and discussed here are applicable to a wide variety of real-world parts. The discussion on how to model the part contains information on some of the topics you need to understand in order to do the work.

FIGURE 4.1

A simple machined part

Deciding where to start

Deciding where to start can be more difficult than it sounds, especially for new users. For this reason, I will go through some sample parts and discuss possible starting points. Figure 4.2 shows the first part. For reference, all of these parts are found on the DVD included with this book.

FIGURE 4.2

Deciding where to start

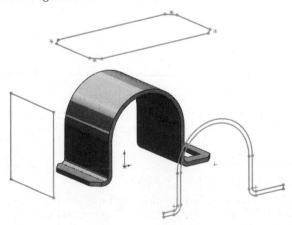

When you are trying to decide how to model geometry in SolidWorks, you should be thinking of a 2D shape and a process. You typically create prismatic shapes by using an Extrude feature and round shapes by using a Revolve feature. Features can also add material (boss) or remove material (cut). Obviously, your first feature has to add material.

If you look at the 3D geometry and see it as a series of 2D drawing views arranged in 3D space (as shown in Figure 4.2), you are on your way to deciding where to start.

The part in Figure 4.2 has flat and round faces, but if you examine it, you can create the overall shape using a single extrude. The best option in this case would be to start with a sketch like the one in the lower-right corner, and extrude it. This is a good beginning. Although you can make the same part starting from any of the three sketches, the one in the lower-right corner gets you closest to the final shape.

Also realize that you don't need to make all of the geometry in a single feature. It is often best to use multiple features for elements such as holes, fillets, chamfers, and other groups of geometry that can be separated out from the main shape.

You might look at the part and see many ways to create it, but the most straightforward way is to use a main extrude, a rectangular cutout, and four chamfers, as shown in Figure 4.3.

FIGURE 4.3

Breaking down the features in this part

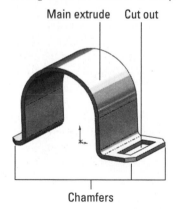

Main extrude   Cut out

Chamfers

Also notice where the part is placed in relation to the Origin. Different people might do this differently, and the same person might even do it differently depending on the function of the part. In this case, the Origin is aligned with the center of the round shape and at the bottom of the flat face. The placement of the Origin suggests that this part sits on the flat face of another part and may hold a cylindrical face of another part.

If you open the part from the DVD, you will notice that the Origin is also placed in the middle of the extrusion depth. This suggests that the part is symmetrical from front to back.

If you are new to 3D modeling, this might be a lot to take in all at once, but you should try to keep the ideas presented here in mind as you work through your first several parts, or when you examine SolidWorks parts made by more-experienced users.

Figure 4.4 shows another part with other features. Again, you can choose from several ways to make this part.

FIGURE 4.4

Identify the best starting point for this part.

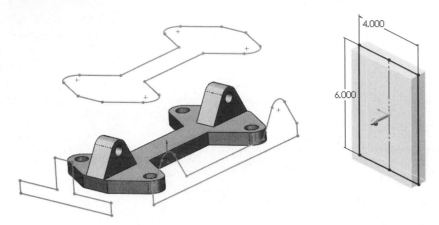

In this case, the best option is to use the one on top. This is because the other two profiles would add geometry that you would have to remove later. Notice that the holes in the part are not represented in any of the profiles. This is because holes are often added as separate features later.

Returning to the part in Figure 4.1, it should be clear enough that this part would be best started from a rectangle, although the rectangle could come from any of the three directions. I personally try to use the biggest sketch that will create a solid that requires the fewest number of cuts. The first feature that you create should also be positioned relative to the Origin. Whether there is a corner of a rectangle that is coincident to the Origin, the rectangle is centered on the Origin, or dimensions are used to stand the rectangle off from the Origin at some distance, you need to lock the first feature to the Origin with every part you build.

When working with a simple part, the entire part can sometimes be described as rectangular or cylindrical. In cases like these, it is easy to know where to start: you simply draw a rectangle or a circle, respectively. On complex parts, it may not be obvious where to start, and the overall part cannot be said to have any simple shape. In cases like these, it may be best to select *the* (or *a*) prominent feature, mounting location, functional shape, or focus of the mechanism. For example, if you were to design an automobile, what would you designate as the 0,0,0 Origin? The ground might be a reasonable location as would the plane of the centers of the wheels. As long as everyone working on the project agrees, many different reference points could work. With that in mind, it seems logical to start the rectangular part by sketching a rectangle. Select the Top plane and sketch a centerpoint rectangle centered on the part Origin.

Building in symmetry

Your next decision is about part symmetry. This part is not completely symmetrical: modeling a quarter of it and mirroring the entire model twice is not going to be the most effective technique. Instead, you should build the complete part around the Origin and mirror individual features as appropriate. To start this type of symmetry, you need to sketch a rectangle centered on the Origin.

Figure 4.5 shows a centerpoint rectangle that has been sketched with the centerpoint at the part Origin. This creates symmetry in both directions. You can use additional construction geometry and sketch relations to make the rectangle only symmetrical side to side.

FIGURE 4.5

Using a centerpoint rectangle to build symmetry about the Origin

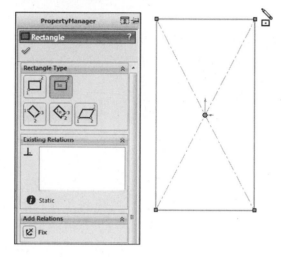

Tip

To make a rectangle work like a square, use an Equal sketch relation on two adjacent sides. This only requires a single dimension to drive the size of the square. ∎

 Beginning with the rectangle you sketched in the previous section, apply one horizontal dimension by clicking the Smart Dimension tool on a single horizontal line, placing the horizontal dimension (4.00 inches), by clicking a vertical line, placing the vertical dimension (6.00 inches). The sketch is fully defined at this point because both the size and position of the rectangle have been established.

Best Practice

If you are dimensioning a horizontal line, the best way to do it is to simply select the line and place the dimension. Selecting the line endpoints can also work, but selecting the vertical lines on either side of the horizontal lines is not as robust. The problem is that if you use this third method, deleting either of the vertical lines causes the dimension to be deleted. In the first two dimensioning methods, dimensions are not deleted unless you remove one of the endpoints, which requires deleting two lines: the horizontal line and one of the vertical lines. ∎

Making it solid

 Next, click Extrude in the Features toolbar or choose Insert ➪ Boss/Base ➪ Extruded. In the Direction 1 panel, select Mid Plane as the end condition. SolidWorks takes the distance that you entered and extrudes it symmetrically about the sketch plane. Enter **1.00 inch** as the distance.

Extrude Feature Options

The Extrude feature is one of the staples of SolidWorks modeling. Depending on the type of modeling that you do, the Extrude feature may be one of your main tools.

The Extrude interface

Extruding from a selection

The From panel establishes where the Extrude feature starts. By default, SolidWorks extrudes from the sketch plane. Other available options include:

- **Surface/Face/Plane.** The extrude begins from a surface body, a face of a solid, or a reference plane.
- **Vertex.** The distance from the sketch plane to the selected vertex is treated as an offset distance.
- **Offset.** You can enter an explicit offset distance, and you can change the direction of the offset.

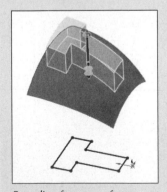

Extruding from a surface

Cross-Reference

Surface features are discussed in detail in Chapter 20. ∎

Understanding Direction 1 and Direction 2

Direction 1 and Direction 2 are always opposite one another. Direction 2 becomes inactive if you select Mid Plane for the end condition of Direction 1. The arrows that display in the graphics window show a single arrow for Direction 1 and a double arrow for Direction 2. For the Blind end condition, which is described next, dragging the arrows determines the distance of the extrude.

 Each of the end conditions is affected by the Reverse Direction toggle. This toggle simply changes the default direction by 180 degrees. You need to be careful when using this feature, particularly when using the Up to end conditions, because if the entity that you are extruding up to is not in the selected direction, an error results.

Following is a brief description of each of the available end conditions for the Extrude feature:

- **Blind.** Blind in this case means an explicit distance. The term is usually used in conjunction with holes of a specific depth, although here it is associated with a boss rather than a hole.

- **Up to Vertex.** In effect, Up to Vertex works just like the Blind end condition, except that the distance is parametrically controlled by a model vertex or sketch point.

- **Up to Surface.** Up to Surface could probably be better named *Up to Face*, because the end does not necessarily have to be an actual surface feature. This end condition may display a warning if the projection of the sketch onto the selected face extends beyond the boundary of the face. In that case, it is advisable to knit several faces together into a surface body and to use the Up to Body end condition.

- **Offset from Surface.** By default, Offset from Surface extrudes until it reaches a specified distance from a selected surface. There are two methods for determining the type of offset and one to determine direction.

  - The default offset method behaves as if the selected surface were offset radially, so that a surface with a 4-inch radius and a 1-inch offset would give a curvature on the end of the extrude of a 3-inch radius.

  - The second method, called Translate Surface, behaves as if the surface were *moved* by the offset distance.

  - Reverse Offset refers to when the offset stops short of the selected face or when it goes past it.

- **Up to Body.** The Up to Body end condition is very useful in many situations, especially when receiving the error message, "The end face cannot terminate the extrusion," from the Up to Surface end condition.

- **Mid Plane.** The Mid Plane end condition eliminates the Direction 2 options and divides the extrude distance equally in both directions; for example, if you specify a 1.00-inch Mid Plane, SolidWorks extrudes .50 inches in one direction and .50 inches in the other direction.

- **Through All.** The Through All end condition is available only when there is already solid geometry existing in the part. When used for an extruded boss (which adds material), it extrudes to the distance of the farthest point of the solid model in a direction perpendicular to the sketch plane. When used for a cut, it simply cuts through everything.

continued

continued

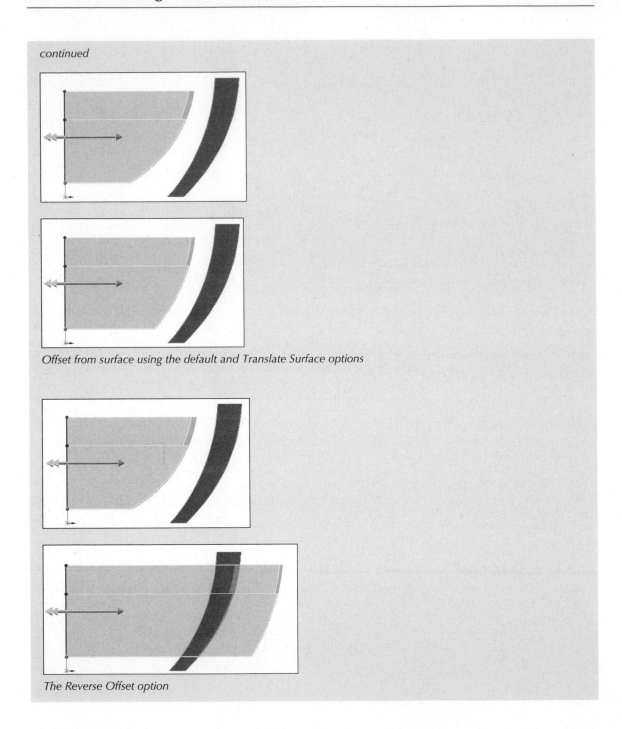

Offset from surface using the default and Translate Surface options

The Reverse Offset option

- **Up to Next.** Up to Next extrudes the feature until it runs into a solid face that completely intercepts the entire sketch profile. If a portion of the sketch hangs over the edge of the face, the extrude feature will keep going until it runs into a condition that matches that description, which may be the outer face of the part in the direction of the extrusion.

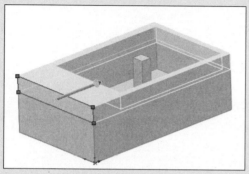

The Up to Next end condition used with a Cut extrude

By default, the Direction of Extrusion is normal to the sketch plane, but you can also select a linear entity such as an edge or axis as the direction. All the end-condition options are still available when you manually define the Direction of Extrusion as something other than the default.

You can also assign a draft option to an extrusion as it is created, and you can control the draft separately for Direction 1 and Direction 2.

Best Practice

When dealing with molded or cast parts, certain types of features, such as draft, fillets, and shells, are often the targets of users trying to assign best practices. This is partially because using draft, fillets, and shells is very much like playing Rock, Paper, Scissors; the only way to win this game is by luck. Arranging the features in the correct order so that the model is efficient and achieves the desired results is challenging. It is usually best to apply draft as a separate feature rather than using it in the definition of the Extrude feature. It is also best to apply draft after most of the modeling is done, but before you apply the cosmetic fillets and before you use the shell feature. ∎

Using the Thin Feature Panel

The Thin Feature panel is activated by default when you try to extrude an open loop sketch (a sketch that does not fully enclose an area). The end-condition options remain the same. What changes is the feature applies a thickness to the sketch elements in the manner of a sheet metal part, thin-walled plastic part, or a rib. The Thin Feature panel of the Extrude PropertyManager, along with a representative thin feature extrusion.

continued

continued

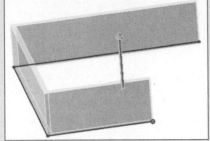

The Thin Feature panel and a thin feature extrusion

The Cap Ends option is available only when you specify a Thin Feature to be created from a closed loop sketch. This creates a hollow, solid body in a single step. You can also use Thin Features with cuts, and they are very useful for creating slots or grooves.

Using contour selection

Contour selection enables you to select areas completely bounded by sketch entities for use with features such as Extrude. For example, you could use a sketch like the number sign (#). You can use contour selection to select the box in the center, which is completely bound by sketch elements. The image below shows an extrude feature making use of contour selection in a sketch.

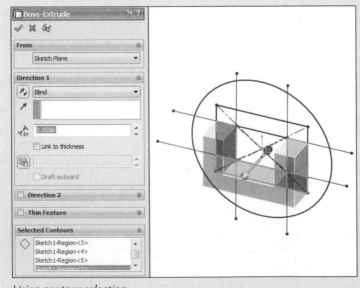

Using contour selection

The part used in the above image is on the DVD, and is called Chapter 4 — Contour Selection.sldprt.

SolidWorks works best when the sketches are neat and clean, when nothing overlaps, and when no extra entities exist. However, when you need to use a sketch that does not meet these criteria, you can use this alternative method.

Best Practice
I believe this feature was introduced into SolidWorks only to keep up with other CAD packages, not because it is a great feature. I do not recommend using contour selection on production models. It is useful for creating quick models, but the selection is too unstable for data that you may want to rely on in the future. The main problem is that if the sketch changes, the selected area may also change, or SolidWorks may lose track of it entirely. ■

Using Instant 3D

Instant 3D enables you to pull handles to create extrusions and to drag model faces to change the size and location of features. Several feature types enable you to use arrows to adjust elements visually of parametric features and sketches. The function largely replaces and expands on the older functionality called Move/Size Features. Figure 4.6 shows the arrows added by Instant 3D, which are the handles that you pull on to create a solid from a sketch or edit an existing feature. Notice also that you can make cut features with Instant 3D. In fact, you can change a boss feature into a cut. I'm sure this is a neat sales demo trick, but I'm not aware of any practical application of changing a boss into a cut.

One of the attractive things about Instant 3D is that it allows you to make changes to parts quickly without any consideration for how the part was made. For example, the cylindrical part was made from a series of extrudes, with a hole cut through it with draft on the cut feature. The flat faces can be moved, and the cylindrical faces offset. Behind the scenes, SolidWorks figures out which sketches or feature parameters of which features have to be edited. This saves you time searching the FeatureManager to figure out which features or sketches control a given face. As you work through more complex parts, you will see how handy this can be at times. You can activate or deactivate Instant 3D using the icon on the Features toolbar.

Note
When combined with the sketch setting Override Dims on Drag, Instant 3D can be a powerful concepting tool, even on fully dimensioned sketches. ■

Instant 3D also offers a tool called Live Section. Live Section enables you to section a part with a plane, and you can drag the edges of the section regardless to which features the edges belong. To activate Live Section, right-click a plane that intersects the part and select Live Section Plane. Live Section is shown on the cylindrical part in Figure 4.6.

Instant 3D can also be an effective tool when used in conjunction with the direct editing type of tools such as Move Face. In fact, Instant 3D mimics some of the direct edit type of functionality found in applications such as Sketchup and Spaceclaim.

Chapter 23 discusses the direct edit theme in more detail, and revisits the Instant 3D manipulators in that light.

FIGURE 4.6

Using Instant 3D and Live Section

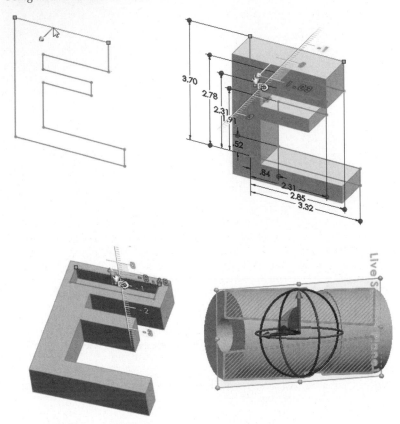

Making the first extrude feature

Going back to the sketch in Figure 4.5, I will show you how to continue building the part using the newly learned tools. By centering the sketch on the Origin and extruding by using a Mid Plane end condition, the initial block is built symmetrically about all three standard planes, with the part Origin at the center. In many parts, this is a desirable situation. It enables you to create mirrored features using the standard planes, and helps you to assemble parts together in an assembly later, when parts must be centered and do not have a hard face-to-face connection with other parts. Figure 4.7 shows the initial feature with the standard planes.

Note

When you create a feature from a sketch, SolidWorks hides and absorbs (consumes) the sketch under the feature in the FeatureManager, so you need to click the plus sign next to the feature to see the sketch in the tree. You can right-click the sketch in the FeatureManager to show it in the graphics window. ■

FIGURE 4.7

An initial extruded feature centered on the standard planes

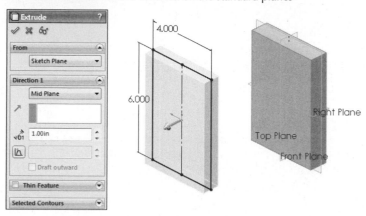

The next modeling step is to create a groove on the back of the part. How is this feature going to be made? You can use several techniques to create this geometry. List as many techniques as you can think of, whether or not you know how to use them. Later, I will go through several techniques that work.

Tip

One of the secrets to success with SolidWorks, or indeed any tool-based process, is to know several ways to accomplish any given task. By working through this process, you gain problem-solving skills as well as the ability to improvise when the textbook method fails. ■

Figure 4.8 shows multiple methods for creating the groove. From the left to the right, the methods are a thin feature cut, a swept cut, and a nested loop sketch.

FIGURE 4.8

Methods for creating the groove

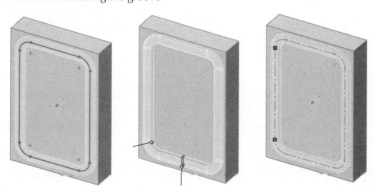

With a thin feature cut, you sketch the centerline of the groove, and in the Cut-Extrude feature, select the Thin Feature option and assign a width and depth. The option on the right is what is called a "nested loop," because it has a loop around the outside of the slot and another around the inside. Only the material between the loops is cut away. The method in the center is a sweep where the cross section of the slot is swept around a path to make the cut.

Another potential option could include a large pocket being cut out, with a boss adding material back in the middle. Each option is appropriate for a specific situation. The thin feature cut is probably the fastest to create, but also the least commonly used technique for a feature of this type. Most users tend to use the nested loop option (one loop inside another).

Controlling relative size or direct dimensions

You can control the size of the groove as an offset from the edges of the existing part or you can drive the dimensions independently. Again, this depends on the type of changes you anticipate. If the groove will always depend on the outer size of the part, the decision is easy — go with the offset from the outside edges. If the groove changes independently from the part, you need to re-create dimensions and relations within the sketch to reflect different design intent.

Creating the offset

You need to consider one more thing before you create the sketch. What should you use to create the offset — the actual block edges or the original sketch? The answer to this is a Best Practice issue.

Best Practice

When creating relations that need to adapt to the biggest range of changes to the model, it is best to go as far back in the model history as you can to pick up those relations. In most cases, this means creating relations to sketches or reference geometry rather than to edges of the model. Model edges can be fickle, especially with the use of fillets, chamfers, and drafts. The technique of relating features to driving layout sketches helps you create models that do not fail through the widest range of changes. ∎

To create the offset for your part, follow these steps:

1. **Open a sketch on the face of the part.** To create the offset, expand the Extrude feature by clicking the plus icon next to it in the FeatureManager so that you can see the sketch. Regardless of how it displays here, this sketch appears before the extrude in the part history. Right-click the sketch and select Show.

Tip

You can view individual sketches and reference geometry entities such as planes from the RMB menu. The global settings for the visibility of these items are found in the View menu. You can access these items faster by using the View toolbar, or by linking the commands to hotkeys. ∎

2. **Right-click the sketch in the graphics window and click Select Chain.** This selects any non-construction, end-to-end sketch entities. Click Offset Entities on the Sketch toolbar. Offset to the inside by .400 inches. Apply .500-inch sketch fillets to each of the corners.

3. **Click Extruded Cut on the Feature toolbar.** By default, the extruded cut will cut away everything inside the closed profile of the sketch. Look down the FeatureManager window and select the check box on the top bar of the Thin Feature panel. Make the cut Blind, .100 inch. The Thin Feature type should be set to Mid Plane with a width of .400 inches. The PropertyManager and graphics window should look like Figure 4.9.

FIGURE 4.9

Creating the groove with a thin feature cut

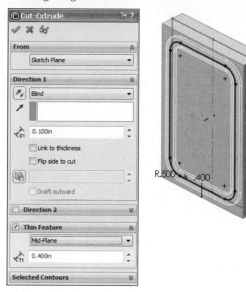

Using sketch techniques

Although you could create the next two features more easily and efficiently using a cut, I will show you how to create them as two extrudes. The intent here is to show some useful sketch techniques rather than optimum efficiency. Begin with the part from the previous section and follow these steps:

1. **Open a new sketch on the large face opposite from the groove.** Draw a corner rectangle picking up the automatic coincident relation to one corner and then dragging across the part and picking up another coincident to the edge on the opposite side. Figure 4.10 shows the rectangle before and after this edit.

Tip

If you want to continue using the recommended best practice mentioned earlier of making relations to sketches rather than model edges, here are a few tips. In some situations (such as the current one), the sketch plane is off-set from the sketch that you want to make relations to, and the best bet is to use the Normal To view. The next obstacle is making sure that automatic relations pick up the sketch rather than the edge, and so you can use the Selection Filter to select sketch entities only. ■

2. **Delete the Horizontal relation on the line that is not lined up with an edge.** This enables you to drag it to an angle or apply the dimensions shown in Figure 4.10.

3. **Extrude sketch to a depth of 0.25 inch.**

    You can delete the Horizontal relation by selecting the icon on the screen and pressing Delete on the keyboard. As a reminder, you can show and hide the sketch relation icons from the View menu. You can check to ensure that the relations were created to the sketch rather than the model edges by clicking the Display/Delete Relations button on the Sketch toolbar, clicking the relation icon to check, and expanding the Entities panel in the PropertyManager. The Entities box shows where the relation is attached to, as shown in Figure 4.11. In this case, it is a point in Sketch1. Without custom programming, there is no way to identify items in a sketch by name, but you already know which point it is; you just needed to know whether it was in the sketch or on the model. The second sketch trick involves the use of a setting.

FIGURE 4.10

Edits to a rectangle

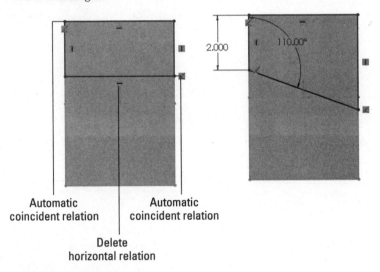

Automatic coincident relation   Automatic coincident relation

Delete horizontal relation

FIGURE 4.11

The Display/Delete Relations dialog box

4. **Choose Tools ⇨ Options ⇨ Sketch and ensure that Prompt to Close Sketch is turned on; then click OK to close the dialog box.**

5. **Open another new sketch on the same face that was used by the last extrusion.** Draw an angled line across the left and bottom sides of the box with the dimensions shown in Figure 4.12. In this case, for this technique to work, the endpoints of the line have to be coincident with the model edges rather than the sketch entities.

   This line by itself constitutes an open sketch profile, meaning that it does not enclose an area and has unshared endpoints. Ordinarily, this results in a Thin Feature, as described earlier, but when the endpoints are coincident with model edges that form a closed loop and the setting mentioned previously is turned on, SolidWorks automatically gives you the option of using the model edges to close the sketch. This saves several steps compared to selecting, converting, and trimming manually.

FIGURE 4.12

Using the prompt to close a sketch setting

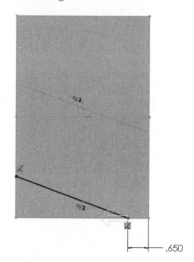

6. **Click the Extrude tool on the Features toolbar.** Answer yes to the prompt, and double-click the face of the previous extrusion. SolidWorks automatically uses the face that you double-clicked for an Up to Surface end condition. This is a simple way of linking the depths of the two extrusions automatically. Again, this entire operation could have been handled more quickly and efficiently with a cut, but these steps demonstrate an alternative method, which in some situations may be useful.

Using the Hole Wizard

The next features that you will apply are a pair of counterbored holes. SolidWorks has a special tool that you can use to create common hole types, called the Hole Wizard. The Hole Wizard helps you to create standard hole types using standard or custom sizes. You can place holes on any face of a 3D model or constrain them to a single 2D plane or face. A single feature created by the Hole Wizard may create a single or multiple holes, and a feature that is not constrained to a single plane can create individual holes originating from multiple faces, non-parallel, and even non-planar faces (holes may go in different directions). All holes in a single feature that you create by using the Hole Wizard must be the same type and size. If you want multiple sizes or types, you must create multiple Hole Wizard features.

To apply counterbored holes to your part, follow these steps:

1. **Select the face that the groove feature was created on, and click the Hole Wizard tool on the Features toolbar.** Then set the hole to Counterbored, set the type to Socket Head Cap Screw, the size to one-quarter, and the end condition to Through All, as shown in Figure 4.13.

FIGURE 4.13

The Hole Wizard Hole Specification interface

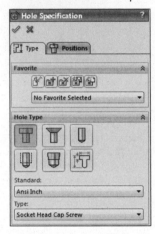

2. **Next, click to select the Positions tab at the top of the PropertyManager.** This is where you place the centerpoints of the holes using sketch points. It is often useful to create construction geometry to help line up and place the sketch points. Make sure the plane or face that the holes originate from is selected in the Positions tab.

3. **Draw two construction lines, horizontally across the part, with Coincident relations to each side.** Select both lines and give them an Equal relation. The point of this step is to evenly space holes across the part without dimensions or equations.

Tip

Although several methods exist to make multiple selections, a box or window selection technique may be useful in this situation. If the box is dragged from left to right, only the items completely within the box are selected. If the box is dragged from right to left, any item that is at least partially in the box is selected. ■

Tip

SolidWorks displays an error if you try to place a sketch point where there is an existing sketch entity endpoint. If you build construction geometry in a sketch and want to place a sketch point at the end of a sketch entity, you have to create the sketch point to the side where it does not pick up other incompatible automatic sketch relations, and then drag it onto the endpoint. ■

4. **Place sketch points at the midpoint of each of the construction lines.** If there is another sketch point other than the two that you want to make into actual holes, delete the extra points. Dimension one of the lines down from the top of the part, as shown in Figure 4.14. All the sketch relation icons display for reference. Click OK to accept the feature once you are happy with all the settings, locations, relations, and dimensions.

FIGURE 4.14

Placing the centerpoints of holes

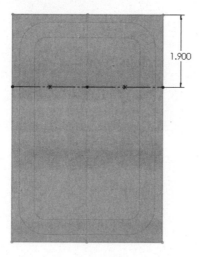

Cutting a slot

The Hole Wizard does not specifically enable you to cut slots. However, SolidWorks has Slot sketch entities, or you can use one of the following methods to cut a slot:

- **Use one of the Slot sketch tools.** SolidWorks has straight and arc slot options on the sketch toolbar.

- **Explicitly drawing the slot.** Draw a line, press A to switch to the Tangent Arc tool, draw the tangent arc, and press A to switch back to the Line tool, and so on. Although you can press the A key to toggle between the line and arc functions, you can also toggle between a line and a tangent arc by returning the cursor to the line/arc first point.

- **Rectangle and arcs.** Draw a rectangle, place a tangent arc on both ends, and then turn the ends of the rectangle into construction entities.

- **Thin feature cut.** As you did earlier with the groove, you can also create a Thin Feature slot, although you need to follow additional steps to create rounded ends on it.

- **Offset in Sketch.** By drawing a line, and using the Offset with Bi-directional, Make Base Construction, and Cap Ends settings, it is easy to create a slot from any shape by drawing only the centerline of the slot.

- **Library feature.** A library feature can be stored and can contain either simple sketches or more complex sets of combined features. The library feature is a good option for the counterbored slot used in this example.

Hole Wizard: Using 2D versus 3D Sketches

Hole Wizard holes use either a 2D or a 3D sketch for the placement of the hole centers. You can define the centers by simply placing and dimensioning sketch points. Starting with SolidWorks 2010, the 2D sketch type is used by default, with the 3D sketch type only being used when you specify it in the Positions tab of the Hole Wizard tool.

The following image shows a part with various types of holes created by the Hole Wizard, including counterbored, countersunk, drilled, tapped, and pipe-tapped holes. The part is shown in section view for clarity; however, the drilled hole is not shown in the figure.

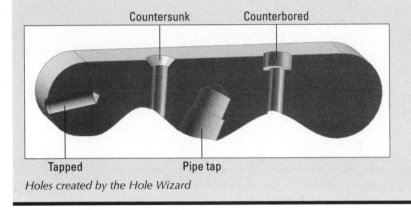

Holes created by the Hole Wizard

To cut slots in your part, follow these steps:

1. **In this case, use the Centerpoint Straight Slot option.** Slots are easiest to create with the Click-click method rather than Click+drag. Click near where you want the center of the slot. Click again for the center of one end; then click a third time for the width/end radius. The Slot PropertyManager is shown in Figure 4.15.

   Create a horizontal sketch relation between the origin and the centerpoint of the slot. Add dimensions as shown in Figure 4.15.

Note

Using the Add dimensions option in the Slot PropertyManager can help you size the slot more quickly. This does not require the Enable on screen numeric input option to be turned on. ■

2. **From this sketch, create an extruded cut that extrudes up to the surface of the counterbore in the holes.** The through hole for the counterbored slot is also a slot, and so you can use the same technique.

3. **Open a sketch on the bottom of the previous slot, and draw a straight slot.** Make the new slot 0.05 inch smaller than the first slot. You can create a cut using the Through All end condition.

FIGURE 4.15

Creating a slot

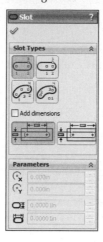

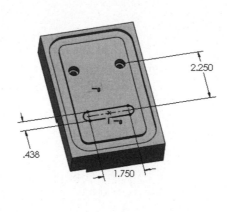

Tip

Picking up relations automatically may seem difficult at first, but with some practice, it becomes second nature. When trying to find the center of an arc, the centerpoint is usually displayed and is easy to select. However, when making a relation to an edge, the centerpoint does not display by default. To display it, hold the cursor over the arc edge for a few seconds; a marker that resembles a plus sign inside a circle will show you where the center is, thus enabling you to select it with a sketch tool and pick up the automatic relations. ■

In Figure 4.16, the first centerpoint has already been referenced, and the cursor is trying to find the centerpoint of the other end of the slot.

FIGURE 4.16

Applying automatic relations to a circular edge

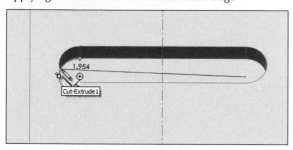

Creating fillets and chamfers

As mentioned earlier, it is considered a best practice to avoid using sketch fillets when possible, using feature fillets instead. Another best practice guideline is to put fillets at the bottom of the design tree,

153

or at least after all the functional features. You should not dimension sketches to model edges created by fillets unless there are no better methods available. Several chapters could be written just about fillet types, techniques, and strategies in SolidWorks. Chapter 7 deals with more complex fillet types.

Best Practice

Do not dimension sketches to model edges that are created by fillets. While the previous best practice about relations to sketch entities instead of model edges was a mild warning, you must heed this one more carefully. ■

To add fillets and chamfers to your part, follow these steps:

1. **Initiate a Fillet feature, and select the four short edges on the part.** Set the radius value to .600 inches. Click OK to accept the Fillet feature.

Tip

When selecting edges around a four-sided part, the first three edges are usually visible and the fourth edge is not. You can select invisible edges by expanding the Fillet Options panel of the Fillet PropertyManager, and selecting the Select through faces option. When you have a complex part with many hidden edges, this setting can be bothersome, but in simple cases like this, it is useful. Figure 4.17 shows this option in action. ■

FIGURE 4.17

Selecting an edge through model faces

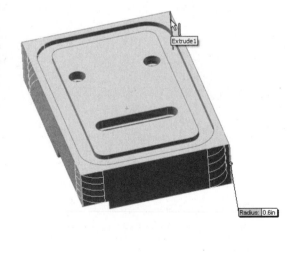

2. **Apply chamfers to the edges of the angled slot through the part, as indicated in Figure 4.18.** Make the chamfers .050 inches by 45 degrees.

   Chamfers observe many of the same best practices as fillets.

Tip

Feature order is important with features like chamfers and fillets because of how they both tend to propagate around tangent edges. Although you can turn this setting off for both types of feature, it is best to get the correct geometry by applying the features in order. ■

Cross-Reference

The Fillet Xpert, which helps you to manage large numbers of overlapping fillets by automatically sorting through feature order issues, is discussed in detail in Chapter 20. ■

3. **Select the four edges that are indicated for fillets in Figure 4.18.** Apply .050-inch-radius fillets.

4. **Apply a last set of .050-inch chamfers to the backside of the counterbores and slot.**

FIGURE 4.18

Edges for fillet and chamfer features

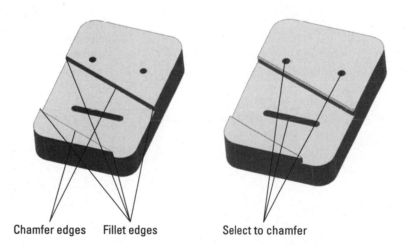

Chamfer edges   Fillet edges   Select to chamfer

The finished part is simple, but you have learned many useful techniques along the way.

On the DVD

You will find two video tutorials on the DVD for this chapter. One of them deals with the concept of feature-based modeling, and the other is a demonstration of creating a simple part and drawing. ■

Tutorial: Making a Simple Drawing

In SolidWorks, drawing views are created from the 3D model. Even the most complex section views are almost free, because they are simply projected from the 3D model. When you make changes to the 3D model, all 2D views update automatically. You can handle dimensions in a couple of ways, either using the dimensions that you used to create the model or placing new dimensions on the drawing (best practice for modeling is not necessarily the same as best practice for manufacturing drawings). To make a simple drawing of a SolidWorks native part, follow these steps:

1. **Click the New button from the Standard toolbar or choose File ⇨ New.** From the New SolidWorks Document window, select the Drawing template. The template contains all the document-specific settings.

2. **After selecting the drawing template, the Sheet Format/Size dialog box appears, as shown in Figure 4.19.** Select the D-Landscape sheet size, as well as the format that automatically associates with that sheet size, and click OK. If the Model View PropertyManager appears, click the red X icon to exit.

FIGURE 4.19

The Sheet Format/Size dialog box

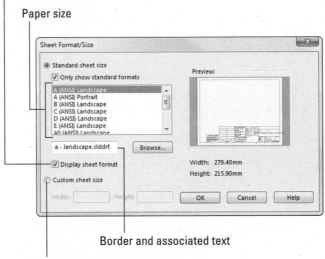

Deselect for a blank drawing sheet

Paper size

Border and associated text

Select for a custom size paper

3. **Before creating any views on the drawing, set up some fields in the format to be filled out automatically when you bring the part into the drawing.** Right-click anywhere on the drawing sheet (on the paper) and select Edit Sheet Format.

4. **Zoom in to the lower-right corner of the drawing.** Notice that there are several variables with the format $PRPSHEET:{Description}. These annotations are linked to custom properties. Some of them have properties with values (such as the Scale note), and some of the properties do not have values (such as the Description).

5. **Add an annotation in the Drawn row, in the Date column.** You can add annotations by choosing Insert ⇨ Annotations ⇨ Note, or by activating the Annotations toolbar in the CommandManager and clicking the Note button. Type today's date as the text of the note.

Caution

If you are using a SolidWorks default template and a circle appears around your note, and then use the Text Format PropertyManager that appears when you are creating a note, expand the Border panel, and change the Circle option to None. ■

6. **Add another note, this time to the Name column.** Do not type anything in the note, but click the Link to Properties button in the Note PropertyManager to create a link to a custom property. In the Link to Property dialog box, click the Model in View Specified option in Sheet Properties. Type **user** in the drop-down text box below the option. This now accesses a custom property in a part or assembly that is put onto this drawing and called "user," and will put the value where the note is placed.

7. **To return to Edit Sheet mode (out of Edit Format mode), select Edit Sheet from the RMB menu.** A little text reminder message appears in the lower-right corner on the status bar to indicate whether you are editing the Sheet or the Format.

8. **From the Drawings toolbar, click the Standard 3 View button, or through the menus, choose Insert ⇨ Drawing View ⇨ Standard 3 View.** If the Chapter4SimpleMachinedPart document does not appear in the list box in the PropertyManager, then use the Browse button to select it. When you click the OK button, the three drawing views are created.

9. **Drawing views can be sized individually or for each sheet.** The Sheet Properties dialog box in Figure 4.20 shows the sheet scale. If this is changed, all the views on the sheet that use the sheet scale are updated. If you select a view and activate the Drawing View PropertyManager, you can use the Scale panel to toggle from Use Sheet Scale to Use Custom Scale.

FIGURE 4.20

First angle versus third angle projections

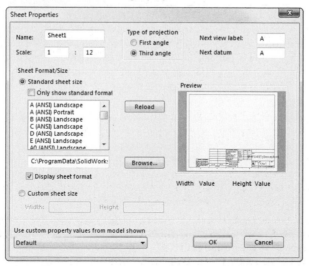

Caution

In the United States, drawings are traditionally made and understood using the Third Angle Projection, which is the ANSI (American National Standards Institute) standard. In Europe, drawings typically use First Angle Projection, which is the ISO (International Organization for Standardization) standard. If you are not careful about making and reading your drawings, you could make a serious mistake. There are times when in the United States, the SolidWorks software will install with ISO standard templates, which will project views using First Angle Projection. When you're using a template that you are unfamiliar with, it is a good idea to check the projection method. To do this, right-click the drawing sheet and select Sheet Properties. The Type of projection setting appears in the top middle of the dialog box, as shown in Figure 4.20. This dialog box looks similar to the Sheet Format/Size dialog box, but it has some additional options, including the projection type. ■

10. **To create an Isometric view, activate the Drawings toolbar in the CommandManager, and click the Projected View button.** Then select one of the existing views, and move the cursor at a 45-degree angle. If you cannot place the view where you would like it to go, press the Ctrl key to break the alignment and place the view where you want it.

11. **You can change the appearance of the drawing view in several ways.**

    - **View ➪ Display ➪ Tangent Edges with Font** uses phantom line type for any edge between tangent faces.

    - **View ➪ Display ➪ Tangent Edges Removed** completely removes any tangent edges. This is not recommended, especially for parts with many filleted edges, because it generally displays just the outline of the part.

    - **Shaded** or **Wireframe** modes can be used on drawings, accessed from the View toolbar.

    - **Perspective** views must be saved in the model as a named view and placed in the drawing using the view name.

    - **RealView** drawing views are not available on a drawing except by capturing a screen shot from the model and placing this screen shot in a drawing. The same applies to PhotoWorks renderings.

12. **Look at the custom properties that you created in the title block.** The date is there because you entered a specific value for it, but the Name field is not filled in. This is because there is no User property in the part. Right-click the part in one of the views and select Open Part. In the part window, choose File ➪ Properties, and in the Property Name column, type the property name **user**, with a value of your initials, or however your company identifies people on drawings. The Properties dialog box, also called Summary Information, is shown in part in Figure 4.21.

FIGURE 4.21

The Custom Properties entry table

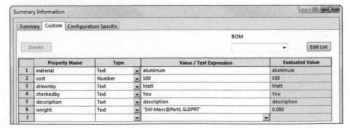

Cross-Reference

When used in models and formats, Custom Properties are an extremely powerful combination, especially when you want to fill in data automatically in the format, in a BOM (Bill of Materials), or a PDM (Product Data Management) product. These topics are discussed in more detail in Chapter 14. ■

13. **When you flip back to the drawing (using Ctrl+Tab), the Name column now contains the value of your initials.**

14. **Click the Section View button on the Drawings toolbar.** This activates the Line command so that you can draw a section line in a view. When sketching, a line can go either on the Sheet or in a view. This is similar to the distinction between the Sheet and the Format. To make a section view, the section line sketch must be in the view. You will know that you are sketching in a view when a pink border appears around the view. You may also use Lock View Focus from the RMB menu to lock view focus manually.

15. **Bring the cursor down to the circular edge of the slot to activate the centerpoint of the arc.** Once the centerpoint is active, you can use the dotted inference lines to ensure that you are lined up with the center. Another option is to create manually sketch relations. Turning on temporary axes displays center marks in the centers of arcs and circles. Figure 4.22 shows the technique with the inference lines being used. Draw the section line through the slot and then place the section view.

FIGURE 4.22

Creating a section view

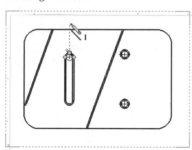

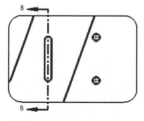 

SECTION B-B

16. **As mentioned earlier, you can use two fundamentally different methods for dimensioning drawings:**

- **Model Items** imports the dimensions used to build the SolidWorks model and uses them on the drawing. These dimensions are *bidirectionally associative*, meaning that changing them on the drawing updates the model, and changing them on the model updates them in the drawing. On the surface of things, this sounds too good to be true, and it is. The potential problems are that you might not model things the way you would dimension them for the shop. You have to answer several questions for yourself, such as do the leader lines go to the right locations or can they be moved, and the dimensions usually come in in such a way that they require quite a bit of moving them around.

- **Reference (driven) Dimensions** can be applied to the drawing view directly. These are only associative in one direction, meaning that they measure what is there, but they do not drive the size or position of the geometry. All changes must be made from the model. Again, on the face of things, this appears to be redundant and a waste of time, but in my personal estimation, by the time you finish rearranging dimensions, checking to ensure that you have everything you need and hiding the extraneous dimensions, you are usually far better off using reference dimensions.

Best Practice

Users have strong opinions on both sides of this issue. The best thing for you to do is to use both methods and decide for yourself. ■

17. **If you choose to use the Model Items approach, you can do this by choosing Insert ⇨ Model Items.** Then specify whether the dimensions should come from the entire model or just a selected feature. You also need to ask whether the dimensions should come into all views or just the selected one, and whether you want just a certain type of dimension, annotation, or reference geometry.

18. **Once the dimensions are brought in, you need to move some of them from one view to another, which you can do by Shift+dragging the dimension from the old location to the new location.** Ctrl+dragging predictably copies the dimension. You can move views by dragging an edge in the view.

Sheet versus Sheet Format

With new and even experienced users, there is some confusion around the Sheet versus Sheet Format issue. Part of the confusion is due to SolidWorks terminology. SolidWorks names the two items Sheet and Sheet Format. In this book, I simply use the terms *Sheet* and *Format* to avoid linking the two items with a common first name. It would be better yet if *Format* were changed to *Border* or *Title Block* so that the name more closely matched the function.

In a SolidWorks drawing, you are editing either the sheet or the format. When editing the sheet, you can perform actions such as view, move, and create views, but you cannot select, move, or edit the lines and text of the drawing border. When editing the format, you can edit the lines and text that make up the drawing border, but the drawing views disappear.

Often, users save a template that already contains a format, and save themselves some time every time they create a new drawing.

While you cannot change templates after you create a document, you can swap and update formats and change sheet sizes.

Summary

This chapter helps to lay the foundation for the more detailed information that will follow. The chapters in Part I include recommendations and answers to questions that help you to develop an intuition for how SolidWorks software operates, which is the most crucial kind of knowledge when troubleshooting a modeling or editing problem.

This chapter has glossed over many of the important details in order to give you a quick overview of the basic functionality in SolidWorks for the three main data types: Parts, Assemblies, and Drawings. Later chapters expand on this information significantly.

Using Visualization Techniques

Visualizing geometry is part of the overall mission of SolidWorks software. Visualizing 3D CAD data is more than seeing shaded solids or shiny surfaces; it includes being able to see the interior and exterior at the same time and using sections, transparency, wireframe, and other tools or techniques. SolidWorks takes it so much further than just being able to see things in 3D; you can look at some parts of an assembly in wireframe while others are transparent and others are opaque. You can see a part with a reflective appearance. You can create section views in parts and assemblies to visualize internal details.

My aim with this chapter is to show you important capabilities that will expand how you can use SolidWorks, and maybe even change the way you use the tools or look at modeling tasks. At the same time, these techniques may provide some of the awe and wonder we sometimes experience while using incredible 3D tools to do actual work. If I sound a little enthusiastic about this topic, it is because visualization is the part of this software that really brings your imagination to life. It can be the source of real inspiration and allows you to communicate geometrical ideas with other people that might not be possible any other way.

Manipulating the View

One of the most important skills in SolidWorks is manipulating the view. This is something you'll do more frequently than any other function in SolidWorks; so learning to do it efficiently and effectively is very important, whether you look at it as rotating the model or rotating the point of view around the model. The easiest way to rotate the part is to hold down the middle mouse button (MMB) or the scroll wheel and move the mouse. If your mouse does not have a middle button or a scroll wheel that you can use as a MMB, then you can use the Rotate View icon on the View toolbar, or the icon on the Heads-up View toolbar. The Heads-up View toolbar is shown in its default state in Figure 5.1.

FIGURE 5.1

Use the Heads-up View toolbar to easily access most visualization tools.

The Heads-up View toolbar can be customized and disabled using the same method that you use for all other toolbars, through the Tools ⇨ Customize dialog.

Tip

Some mouse drivers change the middle-button or scroll-wheel settings to do other things. Often, you can disable the special settings for a particular application if you want SolidWorks to work correctly and still use the other functionality. For example, the most common problem with mouse drivers is that when the model gets close to the sides of the graphics window and the scroll bars engage, the middle mouse button suddenly changes its function. If this happens to you, you should change the function of the MMB to Middle Mouse Button from its present setting. ∎

Using arrow keys

You can use the arrow keys on the keyboard to manipulate the view in predictable and controllable ways. You can use the Shift, Ctrl, and Alt keys to add to the behavior.

The arrow keys enable you to rotate to the following views:

- **Arrow.** Rotate 15 degrees. To customize this setting, choose Tools ⇨ Options ⇨ View.
- **Shift+arrow.** Rotate 90 degrees.
- **Alt+arrow.** Rotate in a plane flat to the screen.
- **Ctrl+arrow.** Pan.

Using the middle mouse button

Most, if not all, mice sold today have middle mouse buttons (MMBs), usually in the form of a clickable scroll wheel.

The MMB or scroll wheel has several uses in view manipulation:

- **MMB alone.** Rotate.
- **Click or hover on edge, face, or vertex with MMB, and then drag MMB.** Rotate around selected entity.
- **Ctrl+MMB.** Pan.
- **Shift+MMB.** Zoom.
- **Double-click MMB.** Zoom to fit.

- **Scroll with wheel.** Zoom in or out. To reverse direction of the zoom setting, choose Tools ➪ Options ➪ View.
- **Alt+MMB.** Rotate in a plane flat to the screen.

Using mouse gestures

Mouse gestures are an interface method that you can customize to do anything a SolidWorks toolbar button can do, but by default, it controls view orientation. Figure 5.2 shows the default configuration of the mouse gesture donut.

FIGURE 5.2

Click+drag the right mouse button (RMB) to access the commands on the donut.

It may take a little time for you to get used the interface. It works best when you understand what the commands are before you use them, so that you can invoke the Top View command in a single motion. It does not work well if you have to initiate the interface with a very short RMB drag, then drag again to select the command. For this reason, it might be better to limit the donut to four commands rather than eight, and set it up intuitively such that the top view is an RMB stroke up, a right view is an RMB stroke to the right, and so on.

You can customize the mouse gesture donut in the Tools ➪ Customize ➪ Mouse Gestures. This works much like the Keyboard (hotkey) customization, where you can turn gestures on or off, set the mouse gesture donut to four or eight sections, and any gesture direction to any available command.

Using the View toolbar

The View toolbar, shown in its entirety in Figure 5.3, contains the tools that you need to manipulate the view in SolidWorks. Not all of the available tools are on the toolbar by default, but I have added them here for this image. To customize your own View toolbar, you must use choose Tools ➪ Customize from the menu and select the Commands tab. Then click the View toolbar, and either drag items from the Customize dialog box to the View toolbar to add them or from the View toolbar into the empty graphics area to remove them. You can use all of these tools with part and assembly models but only a few of them with drawings.

The toolbar that holds tools for direct access to standard named views such as Front, Top, and Normal To is called the Standard Views toolbar and is described later in this chapter.

FIGURE 5.3

The View toolbar

Adding scrollbars and splitters

An option exists to add scrollbars and view pane splitters to the graphics window. To use it, choose Tools ⇨ Options ⇨ Display/Selection, Display Scrollbars in graphics view. This selection will be grayed out if any SolidWorks documents are open (so you must close all SolidWorks documents to change it). When you zoom in such that the part/assembly/drawing is partially off the screen, the scrollbars will activate on the right side and bottom of the SolidWorks window, enabling you to scroll up and down as well as left and right to pan the view. Scrollbars and splitters are turned off by default. You cannot turn off one or the other; scrollbars and splitters come as a package deal.

Figure 5.4 shows a detail of the bottom-right corner of the SolidWorks graphics window, where you find the scrollbars and splitters. Notice the cursor in the lower right over one of the splitters. The splitters can be easy to miss if you do not know what they look like.

FIGURE 5.4

Scrollbars and splitters controls can be turned on or off.

The splitters enable you to split the main graphics window into multiple view ports. The options are two ports horizontally, two ports vertically, or four view ports. The splitter bars are located at the intersection of the scrollbars in the lower-right corner of the graphics window. Of course, you can also use the icons on the Standard Views toolbar for splitting the view into two vertical ports, two horizontal ports, or four ports, the Heads-up View toolbar, or the View Orientation flyout.

Once a viewport has been split, you can remove the split with the toolbar icons, either by dragging the border back to the edge of the display window or by double-clicking the split border. If the view has been split into four, you can set it back to a single viewport by double-clicking the intersection of the horizontal and vertical port borders.

Using the Magnifying Glass

You can invoke the Magnifying Glass by pressing G, and dismiss it when you select something or when you press Esc. To change the hotkey it is associated with, choose Tools ➪ Customize ➪ Keyboard. Magnifying Glass is listed in the Other category. The Magnifying Glass is intended to magnify a small area of the view to enable you to make a more precise selection.

The magnified area follows your cursor as it moves, and you can zoom in and out by scrolling the MMB. Ctrl-dragging the MMB keeps the Magnifying Glass centered on the cursor. Pressing Alt creates a section view parallel to the view, and scrolling the wheel with Alt pressed moves the section plane farther away or closer. Figure 5.5 shows the Magnifying Glass in operation, cutting a section view through a part.

FIGURE 5.5

Using the Magnifying Glass with the section view

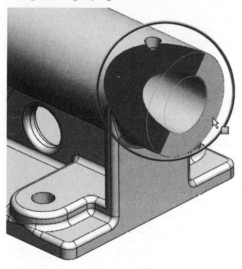

Note

The intended purpose of the Magnifying Glass is to select small items. You may use it to inspect things, but remember it will disappear as soon as you select something. ■

Clicking the Triad axes

The Triad is the multicolored coordinate axis in the lower-left corner of the SolidWorks graphics window. You generally use it passively to see how the view is oriented and to get X, Y, Z reference directions for features that need it.

To use the Triad to control the view orientation, try the following:

- **Click an axis.** The view will rotate to point this axis out of the screen.
- **Click an axis a second time.** This axis will point into the screen.

- **Shift-click an axis.** This view will spin 90 degrees about that axis (using the right-hand rule).
- **Alt-click an axis.** This view will spin 15 degrees (or the default view rotation angle) around the axis.

When you are in a named view, a little box in the lower-left corner shows the name of the view. This includes standard named views and custom named views. Anything that shows up in the View Orientation box (accessed by spacebar) displays a name in the corner. Figure 5.6 shows the Triad and the named view box in the lower-left corner.

FIGURE 5.6

The Triad and named view box

*Right

By Shift-clicking an axis of the triad, the view is rotated 90 degrees from the original orientation. Alt-clicking rotates the view around the clicked axis by the view rotation increment set in Tools ⇨ Options ⇨ View, which is 15 degrees by default. Pressing Ctrl in conjunction with any of these causes the view to rotate in the opposite direction. Therefore, if pressing Shift-click makes the view rotate against the right-hand rule about the clicked axis, pressing Ctrl+Shift-click makes the view rotate with the right-hand rule.

Using the View Tools

SolidWorks has many additional tools for managing the view, and you can easily access them through the Heads Up View toolbar, hotkeys, or the normal toolbars and menus.

The tools in this section will help you to control how you view parts and assemblies. The following tools are mainly found in the View, View ⇨ Display, and View ⇨ Modify menu areas.

- **Zoom to Fit.** Resizes the graphics window to include everything that is shown in the model. You can also access this command by pressing the F key, or double MMB-clicking.

- **Zoom to Area.** When you drag the diagonal of a rectangle in the display area, the display resizes to fit it. The border size around the fit area is fixed and cannot be adjusted. This only zooms in, not out.

- **Zoom In/Out.** Drag the mouse up or down to zoom in or out, respectively. You can also access this command by holding down the Shift key and dragging up or down with the MMB. The hotkey Z and Shift+Z work for Zoom Out and Zoom In, respectively. The percentage of the zoom is a fixed amount and cannot be adjusted. You can also use the scroll wheel to zoom in and out, and if you are accustomed to using a different CAD product where the scroll works the opposite way, a setting exists at Tools ⇨ Options ⇨ View that allows you to reverse the function of the scroll wheel.

- **Zoom to Selection.** Resizes the screen to fit the selection. You can also access this command by right-clicking on a feature in the FeatureManager. For example, if you select a sketch from the FeatureManager and right-click and select Zoom to Selection, the view positions the sketch in the middle of the screen and resizes the sketch to match the display. The view does not rotate with Zoom to Selection.

Tip

A reciprocal function enables you to find an item in the tree from graphics window geometry. If you right-click a face of the model, then you can select Go to Feature in Tree, which highlights the parent feature. ∎

- **Zoom about Screen Center.** Enables you to zoom straight in and straight out. This tool is off by default. The default behavior is that zooming works around the cursor. If the cursor is off to one side, zooming in and out can cause the view to "walk" away from that side. This command is only found in the menus at View ⇨ Modify and does not have an icon.

- **Draft, Undercut, and Parting Line Analysis.** Evaluates the manufacturability of plastic and cast parts. These three types of geometric analysis are discussed in more detail in the discussion on model evaluation in Chapter 12.

- **Rotate View.** Enables you to orbit around the part or assembly using the left mouse button (LMB). You can also access this command by using the MMB without the Toolbar icon.

- **Roll View.** Spins the view on the plane of the screen.

- **Pan.** Scrolls the view flat to the screen by dragging the mouse. You can also access this command by holding down the Ctrl key and dragging the MMB without using the Toolbar icon, or with Ctrl+arrow.

- **3D Drawing View.** Enables you to rotate the model within a drawing view to make selections that would otherwise be difficult or impossible. This is of no use in part and assembly models.

- **Standard Views flyout toolbar.** The Standard Views toolbar is discussed later in this chapter. The flyout enables you to access all the Standard Views tools. This button is also called the View Orientation flyout, depending on where you see it.

- **Wireframe.** Displays the model edges without the shaded faces. No edges are hidden.

- **Hidden Lines Visible (HLV).** Displays the model edges without the shaded faces. Edges that would be hidden are displayed in a font.

- **Hidden Lines Removed (HLR).** Displays the model edges without the shaded faces. Edges that are hidden by the part are removed from the display.

- **Shaded with Edges.** The model is displayed with shading, and edges are shown using HLR. Edges can either be all a single color that you set in Tools ⇨ Options ⇨ Colors (typically black), or they can match the shaded color of the part. Tools ⇨ Options ⇨ Document Properties ⇨ Colors is where you find the document specific setting to use the same color for shaded and wireframe display, which becomes very useful in an assembly when all the parts shown in wireframe are the same color as they are when they are shaded, instead of all being black.

- **Shaded.** The model is displayed with shading, and edges are not shown.

- **Shadows in Shaded Mode.** When the model is displayed shaded, a shadow displays "under" the part. Regardless of how you rotate the model, when Shadows are initially turned on, the shadow always starts out parallel to the standard plane that is closest to the bottom of the monitor. As you rotate the model, the shadow moves with it. If Shadows are turned off and then on again, they again display parallel to the standard plane that is closest to the bottom of the monitor.

• **Section View.** Sections the display of the model. Figure 5.7 shows the Section View command at work. You can use up to three section planes at once. Solid and surface models as well as assemblies can be sectioned. You can use the spin boxes, enter numbers manually, or drag the arrows that are attached to the section planes to move the section through the model. Section planes can also be rotated by dragging the border of the plane.

The Section View tool

Clicking the check mark icon in the Section View PropertyManager enables you to continue working with the sectioned model, although you may not be able to reference edges or faces that are created by the section view. It is only a displayed section; the actual geometry is not cut.

Section Views can be saved either to the View Orientation box or to the Annotation View folder, which enables section views to be reused on the drawing. Annotation Views are described in more detail in Chapter 16.

Once you are working in a section view, if you want to alter it, you can access Modify Section view through the menus at View ➪ Modify ➪ Section View. You should notice that no toolbar icon exists for modifying a section view. You have to access this command through the menus, or by turning off then turning back on the Section View tool. You might also notice that a Modify Section View is available in the hotkey assignment area, Tools ➪ Customize ➪ Keyboard.

 • **RealView.** Creates a more realistic reflective or textured display for advanced material selections. This feature does not work with all graphics hardware, so check the SolidWorks system requirements Web site to see if it supports your hardware. An entire section of this chapter is devoted to the various tools available with RealView graphics.

- **Edit Appearance.** Edit Appearance enables you to apply colors, textures, and materials to faces, bodies, features, parts, and components. Appearance and display issues comprise a large portion of the SolidWorks interface.

Zebra Stripes

Another geometrical analysis tool that helps you visualize the quality of transitions between faces across edges. Zebra Stripes simulates putting a perfectly reflective part in a room that is either cubic or spherical and where the walls are painted with black-and-white stripes. In high-end shape design, surface quality is measured qualitatively using light reflections from the surface. Reflecting stripes makes it easier to visualize when an edge is not smooth.

The three cases that Zebra Stripes can help you identify are as follows (see Figure 5.8):

- **Contact.** Surfaces intersect at an edge but are not tangent across the edge. This condition exists when stripes do not line up on either side of the edge.

- **Tangency.** Surfaces are tangent across an edge but have different radius of curvature on either side of the edge (non-curvature continuous). This condition exists when stripes line up across an edge, but the stripe is not tangent across the edge.

- **Curvature continuity.** Surfaces on either side of an edge are tangent and match in radius of curvature. Zebra Stripes are smooth and tangent across the edge.

FIGURE 5.8

Zebra Stripes

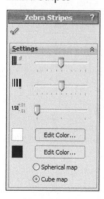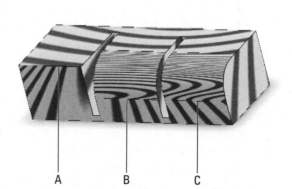

In Figure 5.8, the Zebra Stripes in example A do not match across the edge labeled A at all. This is clearly the non-tangent, contact-only case. Example B shows that the stripes match in position going across the indicated edge, but they change direction immediately. This is the tangent case. Example C shows the stripes flowing smoothly across the edge. This is the curvature continuous case.

You can use the remaining icons in the View toolbar to toggle the display of various types of entities from reference geometry to sketches.

Tip

Consider using hotkeys to toggle the display of your favorite items to hide and show. I use T for Temporary Axes, P for Planes, R for Origins, and so on. ■

View Orientation

 You can activate the View Orientation box by pressing the spacebar. View Orientation, shown in Figure 5.9, keeps all named views, saved section views, and standard views. Tools in the box also enable you to update standard views to the current view or to reset standard views to their defaults. Be aware that a toolbar button on the View toolbar is also called View Orientation.

FIGURE 5.9

The View Orientation dialog box

The Standard Views flyout is called either Standard Views or View Orientation, depending on where you see it. The View Orientation dialog box contains the following controls:

 • **Push Pin.** Keeps the dialog box active.

 • **New View.** Creates a new custom-named view.

 • **Update Standard Views.** Sets the current view to be the new Front view; all other views update relative to this change. This also updates any associated drawing views, but does not move any geometry or change plane orientation.

 • **Reset Standard Views.** Resets the standard views so that the Front view looks normal to the Front plane (Plane1, XY plane).

 • **Previous View** (undo view change). You can access this tool by pressing the default hotkey Shift+Ctrl+Z.

The Standard Views toolbar

I have already mentioned the Standard Views flyout on the View toolbar, but here I describe the tools it contains in detail. Figure 5.10 shows the Standard Views toolbar in its default configuration.

By default, the Standard Views toolbar contains the View Orientation button, a tool from the View toolbar. The View Orientation button is discussed in detail earlier in this section.

The Standard Views toolbar

 Normal To has three modes of operation:

- **First Mode.** Click a plane, planar face, or 2D sketch. When you click Normal To, the view reorients normal to the selected plane, face, or sketch and zooms to fit the model in the view. This method is shown in Figure 5.11.

The result of using Normal To on the end rib angled face

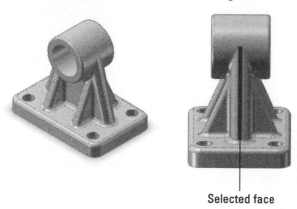

Selected face

- **Second Mode.** Click Normal To a second time. The view rotates 180° to display the opposite direction.
- **Third Mode.** After making the first selection, Ctrl+select another planar entity. The view is normal to the first selection, and the second selection is rotated to the top. This method is shown in Figure 5.12.

FIGURE 5.12

Using Normal To with Second Selection to define the top

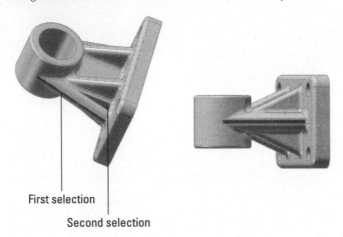

First selection

Second selection

Annotation views

Annotation views enable you to group annotations that were made in the 3D model into views that will be used on the drawing. They are collected under the Annotations folder in the FeatureManager for parts and assemblies. Annotation views can be created either automatically, when 3D annotations are added, or manually. An Unassigned Items annotation view acts as a catchall for annotations that are not assigned to any particular views. In the 3D model, you can use the views to reorient the model and display annotations. As mentioned earlier, annotation views can also capture a model section view to be shown in a drawing view. The Annotation views are shown for the Chapter5SampleCasting part in Figure 5.13.

FIGURE 5.13

Annotations views for Chapter5SampleCasting.sldprt

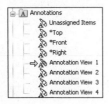

Using the DisplayManager

The DisplayManager is new in SolidWorks 2011. It organizes all of the display and visual information into a form that makes it easier to understand and control. The DisplayManager has buttons that you click to separately list Appearances, Decals, and Scenes, Lights, and Cameras. You can find the DisplayManager as a tab in the FeatureManager window area. Figure 5.14 shows the Appearances data for a part with a material and color applied to two faces and a feature.

FIGURE 5.14

Using the DisplayManager to manage appearances

Appearances in SolidWorks are a combination of color and texture, along with a property that looks like material but is not. Just think of appearance as being color and texture, and the topic is easier to understand.

In order to have appearances display and sort in the DisplayManager, you have to first apply appearances. Most of the appearances are meant to look like idealized materials in real life. Polished, cast, knurled, machined, sand blasted, and other surface finish types are available to add realism to your models. However, you might simply want each part to be a different color to help identify the different parts, using an abstract scheme in place of a realistic one.

Applying appearances

You can apply appearances to faces, bodies, features, parts, assembly components, or even the top-level assembly. Even if you don't apply an appearance, every part and assembly template starts with a default appearance, which is white, glossy plastic. If you use old SolidWorks templates, this default appearance may not apply to you.

You can apply appearances in several ways:

- **Double-click**: Double-clicking an appearance in the Appearances panel of the Task Pane applies the appearance to the document (part or assembly).

- **Drag-and-drop**: Dragging an appearance from the Appearances panel of the Task Pane enables you to drop it on geometry in the graphics window. When you do this, a toolbar pops up and presents you with several options. Figure 5.15 shows this toolbar with the options for Face, Feature, Body, and Part.

FIGURE 5.15

Determining a target for the appearance

- **Context toolbar**: You can also invoke the Appearance function from the context bars (left- or right-click). You can do this with pre-selection or no selection. This method also gives you options for the target to which to apply the appearance, the face, feature, body, or part. Figure 5.16 shows this method.

175

FIGURE 5.16

Using context toolbars to apply an appearance

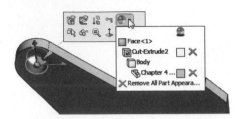

Differentiating appearances and materials

It is easy to confuse appearances and materials. The biggest reason for this is that in many cases, appearances have the same names as materials, and the texture associated with the appearance typically also has the name of a material. SolidWorks has appearances with names such as high gloss plastic, wrought iron, and chromium plate.

It may become even more confusing because materials (which you can assign from the FeatureManager on the left) have appearances (which you assign from the Task Pane on the right) assigned to them. For example, you could assign an appearance called polished aluminum to a material called AISI 304.

You cannot use appearances to assign mass properties (such as density or stiffness) to a part, but you can use materials to assign an appearance as well as mass properties to a part. Figure 5.17 shows the RMB menu for editing material, which you invoke from the Material folder in the FeatureManager.

FIGURE 5.17

Editing a material

Materials assign properties to your parts for drawing hatch and mass properties, as well as simulation. Notice in Figure 5.18 that the second tab allows you to assign an appearance to the material. You can use this interface to create your own custom materials.

FIGURE 5.18

Editing or creating custom materials

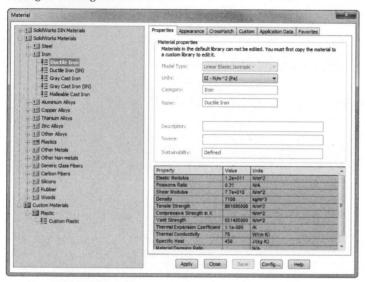

Understanding appearances

Appearances are made up of a combination of color, illumination properties, a surface finish image, and image mapping settings. You can control all these options in the Advanced interface of the Appearances PropertyManager, as shown in Figure 5.19. To access this interface, click the Appearance icon in the Heads Up View toolbar, and click the Advanced button at the top of the PropertyManager.

FIGURE 5.19

Controlling the components of appearance

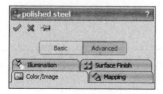

You can adjust the default appearances that install with SolidWorks when you apply them to your models. For example, you can apply a shiny, reflective appearance such as Stainless Steel, but then adjust its color to blue or red. You could apply a cast iron appearance and then increase the roughness. You might apply a brushed aluminum appearance, and change the direction of the brush lines.

You could apply a reflective glass appearance, then reduce the reflectivity and increase the transparency. You might apply a knurled steel appearance to a cylindrical part, and adjust the mapping so that the knurled image does not smear improperly across a face. Figure 5.20 shows the contents of the Color/Image, Mapping, Illumination, and Surface Finish tabs of the Appearances PropertyManager, where you can adjust all of these settings and more.

FIGURE 5.20

Adjusting the display properties in the Appearances PropertyManager

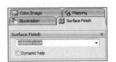

Understanding overrides

Keeping track of colors and appearances in SolidWorks can be difficult. The scheme and terminology seem to change with every release, and SolidWorks 2011 is no exception in this regard. For example, many users have difficulty understanding when one color overrides another color, and how to remove layers of applied colors or appearances. The functionality called Overrides existed in previous versions, but is now more prominent in 2011.

Here is the hierarchy that SolidWorks uses when applying colors (appearances):

- Default
- Part
- Body

- Feature
- Face
- Component
- Assembly

You should read this list with the words "...is overridden by..." between the items. So the default appearance is overridden by anything else, and an appearance that you apply to the assembly overrides everything else. You can also think of this list as being sorted from the weakest to the strongest.

In Figure 5.14, the DisplayManager shows the colors and appearances listed by history, which refers to the order in which they were added to the model. Figure 5.21 shows the appearances sorted by hierarchy, using the order established by Overrides. The Sort Order drop-down list allows you to select from History, Hierarchy, and Alphabetical sorting.

FIGURE 5.21

Sorting appearances and colors by hierarchy

There is no simple way of describing the entire appearances method. It is unnecessarily complex and does not always work as described. You may find times where a face clearly has an altered appearance, but SolidWorks says it does not and moreover won't allow you to remove or change the appearance.

Using appearances with Display States

Display States are covered in more detail later in this chapter. You will also need to understand configurations (see Chapter 11) to completely grasp the use of appearances with Display States. You can assign appearances to apply to all Display States or just to the current Display State. Display States in turn can be linked or unlinked to configurations, and some display properties such as color can be controlled by configurations. The control of appearances and colors for Display States and configurations is convoluted at best. This is a warning that mixing changes to these four items can result in colors that you can either not remove or not apply. It is difficult to say how much of this is due to bugs and how much is due to convoluted logic and too many sources of control. You can control the setting for which Display States an appearance change will apply to. You do this in the Display States panel at the very bottom of the Appearances PropertyManager, as shown in Figure 5.22 on the left.

You can find the Display States interface at the bottom of the ConfigurationManager, as shown in Figure 5.22 on the right.

FIGURE 5.22

Controlling appearances with Display States

Removing appearances

Once you have applied appearances to a part, you may want to remove them later. You can think of multiple appearances applied to various overrides within the part as an old chair with many layers of paint. In this case, you can remove those layers of paint one by one until you get down to the base material, which in this case would be the default material.

Look at Figure 5.23. Notice that there is a red X to the right of each entity — face, feature, body, and part — and another one at the bottom. Each red X enables you to remove a layer of paint from this part. This example is hopefully more extreme than what you will normally deal with, where separate colors have been applied to each entity: white to the face, blue to the feature, pink to the body, and gray to the part. You can remove any color applied at any level just by clicking the red X. Clicking the bottom red X removes all of the overrides (all of the face, feature, body, part, and other colors that have been applied) and assigns the default appearance for that part.

FIGURE 5.23

Removing layers of appearances from a part

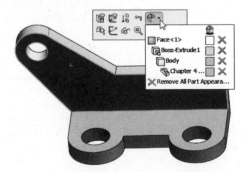

You can assign the default appearance in a part or assembly template, or reassign it in an existing part. To do this, open the Appearances, Scenes, and Decals tab in the Task Pane, find an appearance that you like, and right-click it. Figure 5.24 shows the menu that appears.

FIGURE 5.24

Assigning a default appearance

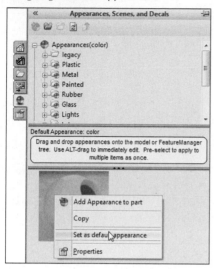

To save this appearance to a part template, assign the default appearance in an empty part document with settings that you want to use, set the default appearance, and save the empty part as a part template.

Using decals

Starting in SolidWorks 2011, decals have been moved into SolidWorks Standard (base level SolidWorks) and no longer require rendering software. All decals used in a model are listed in the Decal area of the DisplayManager.

To apply a decal, you can use the Appearances, Scenes, and Decals tab of the Task Pane to access the stock or sample images, or you can right-click in the open area of the Decals DisplayManager and select Add Decal. This brings up the Decals PropertyManager, shown in Figure 5.25.

You can use *.bmp, *.jpg, *.tif, and *.png images as decals in SolidWorks. The images can be mapped onto flat, cylindrical, or spherical surfaces. You can uses masks or images with an alpha channel to create transparent parts of the decal. You can also select a color of the image to set to transparent. Only *.tif and *.png images can use alpha channel transparency.

You can size, position, and rotate the decal on the screen with handles, as shown in Figure 5.26. You can use any of the corner nodes on the image to resize the decal. Dragging anywhere inside the image border moves the decal, and dragging the yellow ball in the center of the image rotates it.

Working with the Decals PropertyManager

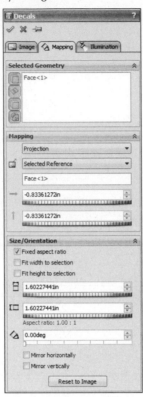

Sizing and positioning the decal

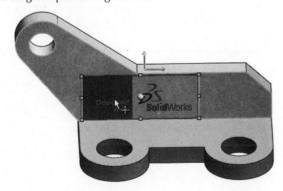

Using scenes, lights, and cameras

Scenes, lights, and cameras are important for visualization and rendering. Rendering is not covered in this book because PhotoView 360 (the replacement for the now-defunct PhotoWorks 2) is not part of the SolidWorks Standard package. The Scene, Lights, and Cameras DisplayManager is shown in Figure 5.27.

Using the Scene, Lights, and Cameras DisplayManager

Controlling scenes

In SolidWorks, a scene is composed of three things: a background, which may be an image, a gradient, or a color; a floor, on which shadows and reflections are cast; and an environment, which is a wrap-around 3D image (*.hdr or *.hdri — high dynamic range images) that provides light to the model in a rendering and will reflect on the model if the model is a highly reflective material. If the environment is hidden, you only see the background. You can also hide the floor so there are no shadows or reflections and the model appears to hang in space.

Be aware that the small, square image shown for each scene in the Task Pane is a rendering of the scene and does not reflect how the scene will look in the graphics window. For most of this book, I have used the Plain White scene, but my screenshots do not look at all like the preview image.

Floors and environments may only appear when you do a rendering. If you want to remove shadows from the modeling window while you work, use the View Settings icon in the Heads Up View toolbar to do this. This is shown in Figure 5.28.

Turning off shadows in the modeling window

When you are using Shadows in shaded mode you can take advantage of a special scene called Ambient Occlusion. With this combination, the SolidWorks model can throw shadows on itself, and holes in the model will appear in shadow. It gives some of the effect of a rendering, but it is just the RealView display.

Ambient Occlusion has some limitations, such as it does not show shadows on the part while rotating, only when you stop rotating the view. It also only works when in shaded mode (with or without edges), and when the Shadows in shaded mode option is turned on in the View ➪ Display menu.

Figure 5.29 shows a part using Ambient Occlusion, along with the studio scenes folder showing that scene.

FIGURE 5.29

Ambient Occlusion scene gives more realistic shadows without rendering

If you want to turn off reflections on the floor while modeling, you can apply a Basic scene or turn off the reflective floor in the Scene PropertyManager, as shown in Figure 5.30. From here you can also perform other common tasks such as aligning the floor with a different plane, offsetting the floor, and adjusting the brightness of the scene.

FIGURE 5.30

The Scene PropertyManager allows you to turn off the reflective floor while modeling.

To apply a scene to a document, you can use the Appearances, Scenes, and Decals tab of the Task Pane, expand the Scenes heading, choose from Basic, Studio, or Presentation scenes, and double-click or drag the scene into the graphics area. The differences between Basic, Studio, and Presentation scenes are as follows:

- **Basic** scenes use only a background color.
- **Studio** scenes use a gradient background.
- **Presentation** scenes use an HDRI image, so that the image rotates with the part as you rotate the view.

In a recent version, SolidWorks made scenes a document property, so they are now controlled by each individual document, and made that the default option. You can override the default with a system option, Tools ⇨ Options ⇨ Colors, and change the Background Appearance setting to anything except the first option: Plain, Gradient, or Image.

Turning on the lights

Lights for the model display in the graphics window are slightly different from the lights for rendering. A certain amount of overlap between OpenGL graphics (normal display) and PhotoView 360 exists. The main difference is that the environment (spherical HDRI image) does not affect the lighting in the model. It does reflect on the model, but does not illuminate it. The lighting in a rendering is predominantly from the environment. You can observe this by editing the scene, going to the Advanced tab, and using the Environment Rotation slider to see what happens. The bright and dark faces do not change, but the reflections do change.

You can add separate lights by right-clicking on the Lights folder in the DisplayManager and selecting one of the new light options shown in Figure 5.31.

FIGURE 5.31

Adding lights to the scene

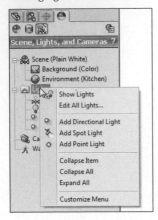

The light appears as an icon in 3D space, which you can drag around. You can also use the PropertyManager for editing the light to key in a specific XYZ location for the light source or direction.

Tip

To use a combination of rotating the view and moving the light icon in 3D space, you can use the Lock To Model option so that the light moves with the model when you rotate the model. ■

The symbols shown in Figure 5.30 to the left of the Directional 17 and Directional 18 lights show that the light is On in SolidWorks, and Off in PhotoView.

The easiest and most effective thing to do when you have a part that just displays dark for some reason is to add a single Point light to a model.

The Ambient setting raises the overall brightness of the part, the Brightness setting refers to just the light, and the Specularity slider controls how lights shine or create "hot spots" on curved faces of models. You can even edit the color of a light to give a part a two-tone effect. If you have a blue part and apply a red light that sits to one side of the model, you can get very interesting color effects where the red light reflects off of the surfaces of the part. Lighting effects are most dramatic on curved parts. Parts that are made mostly of flat faces do not reflect light as smoothly as curved faces. This is why even adding small fillets to a rectangular model can help make the part look nicer (more realistic) for presentation purposes. Figure 5.32 shows a comparison of a model with filleted edges compared to a model with perfectly sharp edges.

Working with cameras

You create cameras through the RMB menu on the Scene, Lights, and Cameras DisplayManager, as shown in Figure 5.33. When you add a camera, an interface displays in the PropertyManager, as shown in Figure 5.34.

FIGURE 5.32

Demonstrating the difference between the appearance of a part with fillets and a part with sharp corners

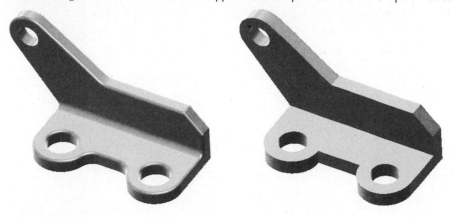

FIGURE 5.33

Adding a new camera with the Camera PropertyManager

In this interface, you can position the Camera object by dragging the triad. To resize the Field of View box, use the controls in the Field of View panel in the PropertyManager. In the graphics window, you can use the left panel to target and position the camera, while the right panel shows the view through the camera.

FIGURE 5.34

Positioning a camera with split windows

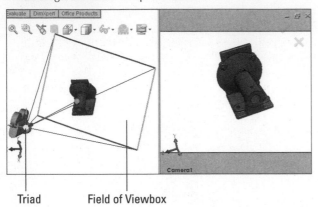

Triad   Field of Viewbox

You get the most lifelike perspective from a lens setting of about 50 mm. Shorter distances produce wide angle or fish eye lens effects. Larger settings make it look like a telephoto lens. It should be noted that perspective within SolidWorks works much differently. Within SolidWorks, the setting is based on how many object lengths you are away from the object. So if a person is approximately 6 feet tall, and you are rendering that person, you would set your perspective as a factor of six. Three object lengths would be 18 feet.

The Depth of Field panel of the Camera PropertyManager is not shown, because it requires that PhotoView be added in. Depth of field can make objects outside of the focus area slightly out of focus, which can greatly add to the realism of renders.

You can use three methods to switch the graphics window to the Camera view:

- Through the View Orientation dialog box (which you access through the spacebar)
- Through the View Orientation popup menu (in the lower-left area of the graphics window)
- Through the RMB menu on the camera in the Lights, Cameras, and Scene folder in the FeatureManager

When you switch the view to the Camera view, the regular Rotate View command does not function. Rotating the view means moving the camera. You can move the camera by editing the Camera properties, reposition the camera by dragging the triad, or rotate the view while looking through the camera using the Turn Camera tool.

- **Camera View.** Views the model through a camera. You can use cameras for:
  - Viewing the model from a particular point of view.
  - Creating renderings with perspective and depth-of-field (focus) blur; this feature is only available when PhotoView 360 is added in.
  - Animating the position and target of the point of view in an animation. This feature is only available when a Motion Study is active.

- **Turn Camera.** Enables you to rotate the camera view when looking through the camera without editing the Camera properties. You must be looking through the camera and it must be unlocked for this to work. Dragging with the MMB does the same thing if the camera is unlocked.

- **Draft Quality HLR/HLV.** Toggles between low-quality (draft) and high-quality edge Hidden Lines Removed (HLR) or Hidden Lines Visible (HLV) display. This affects display speed for complex parts or large assemblies. When in draft-quality mode, edge display may be inaccurate.

- **Perspective.** Displays the model in perspective view without using a camera. If you want to create a perspective view on a drawing, you must create a custom view in the View Orientation dialog box with Perspective selected. You can adjust perspective through View ➪ Modify ➪ Perspective by adjusting the relative distance from the model to the point of view. Relative distance is measured by the size of the bounding box of the model; therefore, if the model fits into a box roughly 12 inches on a side and the perspective is set to 1.1, the point of view is roughly 13 inches from the model. For more accurate perspective, you can use a camera.

Caution

Perspective view and sketching do not work well together. Sketches and dimensions look distorted and incorrect with perspective turned on. I recommend disabling perspective view when sketching. ■

- **Curvature.** A geometrical analysis tool that applies a color gradient to the part based on the local curvature. You can also apply curvature display to individual surfaces through the RMB menu. With some hardware, curvature display can take more time to generate for complex models.

Performance

Settings in Tools ➪ Options ➪ Performance can greatly affect rebuild speed if curvature display data is regenerated for each part rebuild. You should leave this at the default setting, which is Only on Demand. ■

Using RealView

RealView is the display technology behind the fancy appearances of SolidWorks models. The reflections and lighting depend on RealView. If you turn off RealView or if you don't have hardware that supports it, you can't get the great displays. RealView does not affect rendering, just the live display. Check the system requirements listed on the SolidWorks Web site for information about whether your video card supports RealView.

In some situations, you can use RealView instead of rendering. In these cases, RealView acts as a real-time renderer. The main advantages that rendering software such as PhotoView 360 holds over RealView are improved anti-aliasing control, improved shadow control, indirect illumination, global illumination, caustics, and effects such as depth of field from a camera.

You can even use RealView as a diagnostic tool for smooth transitions between surfaces because RealView appearances apply a reflective surface to a part and then apply a reflective background. This is essentially what the Zebra Stripes functionality is doing, but Zebra Stripes applies a specific reflective background to make examining curvature continuity across edges more straightforward.

You can turn RealView on or off by using the golden sphere icon that displays by default on the Heads Up View toolbar. If this icon is grayed out, then your system is not equipped with an appropriate RealView-capable graphics card. Generally, you need an nVidia Quadro series or higher to get RealView capabilities, and an appropriate graphics driver must be installed with the hardware. (NVS series cards are not 3D cards and will not enable RealView.) Some ATI FireGL cards and all FirePro cards will also work.

Exploring the Display Pane

The Display Pane flies out from the right side of the FeatureManager and displays a quick list of which entities have appearances, transparency, or other visual properties assigned. It also shows hidden parts or bodies for assemblies and multibody parts. The Display Pane is shown in Figure 5.35.

FIGURE 5.35

The Display Pane allows you to control display elements of your SolidWorks model.

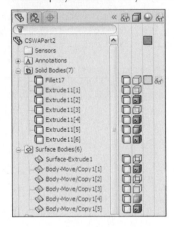

This tool to some extent duplicates the DisplayManager, but it also provides a quick summary of most of the display information, including wireframe/shaded display mode, transparency, hide/show state, and color. It works in both parts and assemblies, and is a highly valuable tool. Between the DisplayManager and the Display Pane, you can easily manage one of the most confusing areas of the SolidWorks software: Appearances.

Applying Color Automatically to Features

You can use the settings found at Tools ⇨ Options ⇨ Document Properties ⇨ Model Display to automatically color certain types of features with specific colors. For example, you can color all Shell features red as you create them.

This function has worked intermittently for many years. For example, you can assign Boss features to always be red, and that works. You can assign surface features to always be yellow, and it works for Extrude, Revolve, Planar, Offset, Loft, and Sweep surfaces, but not for Boundary, Fill, or Ruled.

Using Edge Display Settings

Earlier in this chapter, I discussed the Shaded with Edges display style. Some people think that this makes the parts look "cartoony." I agree, especially when the default black edges are used, but the display improves when the edge color matches the shaded part color. In any case, sometimes this method is necessary to see the breaks between faces, especially fillets. Cartoony or not, it is also useful.

Taking this one step further, you can also make use of the tangent edge settings. These settings are found in the View ⇨ Display menu. The settings are

- **Tangent Edges Visible.** Displays tangent edges as solid lines, just like all other edges.
- **Tangent Edges as Phantom.** Displays tangent edges in a phantom line font.
- **Tangent Edges Removed.** Displays only non-tangent edges.

The tangent edges removed setting leaves parts looking like a silhouette. I prefer the phantom setting because I can easily distinguish between edges that will actually look like edges on the actual part and edges that only serve to break up faces on the model. The tangent edges visible setting conveys no additional information and is the default setting. Figure 5.36 shows a sample part with all three settings.

FIGURE 5.36

Samples of the tangent edge settings

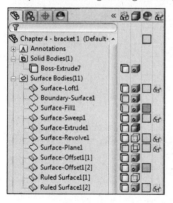

Tutorial: Applying Visualization Techniques

Visualization is a key factor when working with SolidWorks software. Whether it is for a presentation of your design to customers or management or simply checking the design, it is important to be able to see the model in various ways. This tutorial guides you through using several tools and techniques.

1. **If the part named** `Chapter5Sample.sldprt` **is not already open, open it from the DVD.** If it is open and changes have been made to it, choose File ⇨ Reload ⇨ OK.
2. **Practice using some of the controls for rotating and zooming the part.** In addition to the View toolbar buttons, you should also use Z and Shift+Z (Zoom Out and In, respectively), the arrow keys, and the Ctrl+, Shift+, and Alt+arrow combinations.

3. **Use the MMB to select a straight edge on the part, and then drag it with the MMB.** This rotates the part about the selected entity. Also, apply this technique when selecting a vertex and a flat face.

4. **Select the name of the part at the top of the FeatureManager.**

5. **Click the Appearance button from the Heads-up View toolbar at the top of the graphics window.**

6. **Click the color you want in the Favorite panel.** The model should change color. If you click and drag the cursor over the colors, the model changes color as you drag over each new color. You can also drag appearances from the Task Pane. Figure 5.37 shows interfaces for both methods.

FIGURE 5.37

Use the Appearances PropertyManager to change color and material.

7. **If the Color panel is not expanded, click the double arrows to the right to expand it.** Select the colors you want from the continuous color map. Again, click and drag the cursor to watch the part change color continuously.

8. **Create a swatch.** In the Favorite panel, select the Create New Swatch button and call the new swatch color file `BibleColors`.

9. **Select a color from the Color Properties continuous map; the Add Selected Color button becomes active.** Clicking the button adds the color to the swatch palette. You can add several colors to the palette to use as favorites later on.

Tip

You will be able to access these colors again later by selecting `BibleColors` from the drop-down list in the Favorite panel. You can transfer the colors to other computers or SolidWorks installations by copying the file `BibleColors.slddclr` from the `<SolidWorks installation directory>\lang\english` folder (or the equivalent file for your installed language). ■

10. **In the Appearance panel, move the Transparency slider to the right, and watch the part become transparent.**

11. **To prevent the Appearance window from closing after every change, click the pushpin at the top of the window.**

12. **Click the green check mark icon to accept the changes; note that with the pushpin icon selected, the window remains available.**

13. **Expand the flyout FeatureManager in the upper-left corner of the graphics window, as shown in Figure 5.38, so that all the features in the part are visible.**

FIGURE 5.38

The flyout FeatureManager

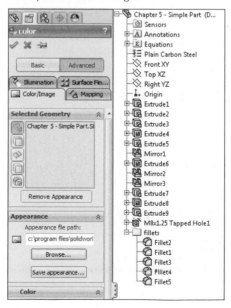

14. **Select the features Extrude1, Fillet7, and Fillet6 from the FeatureManager so that they are displayed in the Selection list of the Appearances window.** Select a color from the BibleColors swatch palette that you have just created.

15. **Click the check mark icon to accept the changes and clear the Selection list.**

16. **Select the inside face of the large cylindrical hole through the part and assign a separate color to the face.**

17. **Click the check mark icon to accept the changes, and click the red X icon to exit the command.**

18. **Expand the Display pane (upper-right area of the FeatureManager).** You should see color and transparency symbols for the overall part, and color symbols for three features. There is no indication of the face color that is applied.

19. **Remove the colors.** Open the Appearances window again, re-select the three features (Extrude1, Fillet7, and Fillet6), and click the Remove Color button below the Selection list. Do the same with the colored face. Return the part transparency to fully opaque.

20. **Click the check mark icon to accept the changes.**

21. **Change the edge display to Shaded (without edges).** Then change to a Wireframe mode. Finally, change back to Shaded with Edges.

22. **Choose View ⇨ Display ⇨ Tangent Edges as Phantom.** Figure 5.39 shows the difference between Tangent Edges Visible, as Phantom, and Removed settings.

Tip

Using the Tangent Edges as Phantom setting is a quick and easy way to look at a model to determine whether face transitions are tangent. It does not help to distinguish between tangency and curvature continuity; you need to use Zebra Stripes for that. ∎

23. **Switch back to Shaded display.**

24. **If you do not have a RealView-capable computer, then skip this step.** Ensure that the RealView button in the View toolbar is depressed. Click the Appearances/Scenes tab on the Task Pane to the right of the graphics window. Expand Appearances ⇨ Metal ⇨ Steel; then in the lower pane, scroll down to the Cast Carbon Steel appearance.

25. **Turn the part over, select the bottom face, and drag and drop the appearance from the Task Pane. Apply the appearance just to the bottom face using the popup toolbar that appears.** The rest of the part should retain the semi-reflective surface, as shown in Figure 5.40. Click the check mark icon to accept the change.

FIGURE 5.39

Tangent Edge display settings for a shaded model

FIGURE 5.40

Applying an appearance to a face

26. **Click the Section View button on the View toolbar.** Drag the arrows in the middle of the section plane back and forth with the cursor to move the section dynamically through the part, as shown in Figure 5.41.

FIGURE 5.41

A section view

27. **Select the check box next to the Section 2 panel name and create a second section that is perpendicular to the first.**

28. **Click the green check mark icon to accept the section.** Notice that while in the Section View PropertyManager, the RealView material does not display, but once you close the dialog box, RealView returns.

Summary

Visualization is a key function of the SolidWorks software. It can either be an end to itself if you are showing a design to a vendor or client or it can be a means to an end if you are using visualization techniques to analyze or evaluate the model. In both cases, SolidWorks presents you with an astounding list of tools to accomplish the task. The tools range from the analytical to the cosmetic, and some of the tools have multiple uses.

Part II

Building Intelligence into Your Parts

Getting More from Your Sketches

P revious chapters have described the basic tools for sketching. This chapter takes you to the next level, teaching you about more advanced sketch tools, how to edit and manipulate sketches, and how to work with sketch text, sketch pictures, and sketch colors. At the end of this chapter, with a little practice to reinforce the tools and techniques, you should feel like you have mastered the topic of SolidWorks sketching and can handle almost any problem that is thrown at you.

Editing Sketch Relations

Delete is not an editing option. In time, you will find that this is good advice, even if you don't agree with it now. There are times to delete instead of editing, but you should delete only when it is necessary. In my own work, I sometimes go to extreme lengths to avoid deleting sketch entities, often just to stay in practice, but also because deleting sketch entities, or even features in a part, increases the likelihood that sketch or mate relationships will be broken.

The main reason to avoid using Delete is that when you are editing a sketch that has other features that are dependent on it, the dependent features may lose their references, or *go dangling*. Because of this, even when you can use the Delete command instead of making edits, it is still a good practice to edit instead. Deleting relations is not as critical as deleting sketch entities, unless the relations are referenced by equations or design tables.

Best Practice

Before deleting sketch entities, try to understand what types of relationships the change will affect downstream. Be sure to consider other sketch relationships within the current part, mates, and in-context relations and even mates in the assembly, and things of this nature. In fact, it is best to have all of this in mind when you are creating relationships to begin with. Try to make relations to the most stable entities available, which usually means having sketches and reference geometry entities as high up in the tree as possible. ∎

Using Display/Delete Relations

 Display/Delete Relations is your primary tool when dealing with sketch relations. It is particularly useful for sorting relations by the various categories shown in Figure 6.1. The capability to show sketch relations in the graphics window is nice; sorting them in a list according to their state makes this feature even more useful. To show the sketch relation symbols on the screen beside the sketch entities, use the menu selection View ➪ Sketch Relations.

FIGURE 6.1

The Display/Delete Relations PropertyManager

Sketch relations in the Display/Delete Relations dialog box can be divided into the following categories:

- **All in this sketch.** Shows all the relations in the active sketch.

- **Dangling.** Shows only the dangling relations. Dangling relations appear in a brownish-green or olive color, and represent relations that have lost one of the entities that drives the relation. You can repair dangling relations by selecting the entity with the dangling relation, and then dragging the red dot onto the entity to which it should have the relation.

- **Overdefining/Not Solved.** Overdefined relations are any set of conflicting or redundant instructions that are given to a sketch entity, and appear in red. If a line has conflicting relations, but it can still meet the requirements, it turns red. If a line has conflicting relations, and it cannot meet the requirements, it turns pink. If solving the line would result in a zero length line or some other impossible situation, it turns yellow.

  The Not Solved condition causes sketch entities to turn pink and often accompanies other entities that are overdefined. Not Solved typically refers to a dimension or relation that cannot be applied because of the conflict. The lower-right corner of the screen and the status bar show flags warning that the sketch is overdefined, as shown in Figure 6.2.

  When an overdefined situation exists, all the relations and dimensions in a sketch often become overdefined. This can look like a daunting task to repair, especially when the entire problem is caused by a single relation. Do not automatically delete everything. Instead, try deleting or suppressing the last dimension or relation that was added, or a single relation that looks suspect. You can suppress a dimension by setting it to Driven in the right mouse button (RMB) menu, and you can suppress relations in the Display/Delete Relations PropertyManager.

FIGURE 6.2

An overdefined sketch

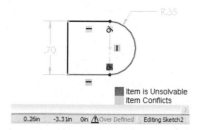

- **External.** External relations connect with an entity outside the active sketch. This includes the part Origin, or any model edges. The term *external relations* can also signify any relations outside of the part.

- **Defined in Context.** Any relation between features in one part in an assembly and another part is considered an in-context relation.

- **Locked (Broken).** External relations (outside the part) may be locked or broken to increase speed and to lock out parametric changes. There is no advantage of breaking relations rather than locking them. Both are ignored, but locked relations can be unlocked; broken relations can only be deleted.

- **Selected Entities.** Sketch relations are shown only for the selected sketch entities.

Cross-Reference

In-context design, also called top-down, as well as locked and broken relations are covered in detail in the SolidWorks 2011 Assemblies Bible (Wiley, 2011). ■

Caution

Some of the relations listed in the Display/Delete Relations dialog box may be colored to signify the state of the relation. Unfortunately, colored relations are typically placed at the top of the list to attract attention, but when you select them, they are always gray, and so the advantage of color-coding is always defeated for the first relation in the list. The only way around this is to select a relation other than the first one in the list. If there is only one relation in the list, you cannot see the state color. ■

A setting in Tool ⇨ Options controls the display of errors. You can choose Tools ⇨ Options ⇨ Feature-Manager to find an option called Display Warnings, where you can choose Always, Never, and All but Top Level. When a sketch contains sketch relations with errors, they display as warning signs on the sketch and will propagate to the top level of a part or assembly if you have selected the Always option.

Using SketchXpert

The SketchXpert, shown in Figure 6.3, can help you to diagnose and repair complex sketch relation problems. The Diagnose button at the top creates several possible solutions that you can toggle through using the forward and backward arrow buttons in the Results panel. The Manual Repair button displays all the relations with errors in a window where you can delete them manually.

By selecting the option at the very bottom of the dialog box (*Always open this dialog when sketch error occurs*), you can make the SketchXpert appear whenever a sketch error occurs. To display the SketchXpert manually instead of automatically, you can access it by right-clicking in a sketch.

FIGURE 6.3

The SketchXpert dialog box

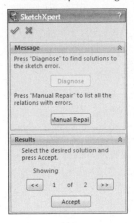

Working with Sketch Entities

SolidWorks offers several different tools to help you move sketch entities around in a sketch. In SolidWorks, it is usually recommended to keep the sketch as simple as you can, and to create patterns using feature patterns rather than sketch patterns. The following section discusses the main tools for moving and copying sketch entities.

Moving entities

 Move entities enables you to move selected sketch entities by either selecting From and To points, or by typing in XY coordinates for the move. When the Keep relations option is unselected, the Move tool automatically detaches sketch segments whose endpoints are merged, as shown in Figure 6.4. If Keep relations is selected, SolidWorks moves the entities and tries to maintain the sketch relations and merged points. All the tools have a pushpin icon in the interface. You can use the tool multiple times in succession when the pushpin icon is pushed in; tools with the pushpin are deactivated after one use if the pushpin icon is not pushed in.

FIGURE 6.4

FIGURE 6.4

Using the Move tool

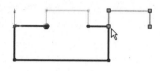

Rotating entities

 Rotate entities rotates selected entities in a sketch in the same way that Move entities works. You can drag the angle or type it in manually. The green check mark icon is on the RMB, as shown in the cursor display in Figure 6.5.

The Keep Relations option does not actually keep any relations — it deletes the Horizontal and Vertical relations in the sketch, as shown in Figure 6.5 — but it does keep the merged endpoints, as shown in the rightmost image of Figure 6.5. This can be useful, especially considering how many sketch relations it would take to make a sketch move like this naturally.

FIGURE 6.5

Using the Rotate tool

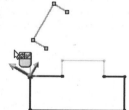
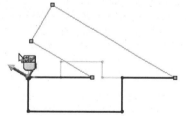

Copying entities

 The Copy entities tool works exactly like the Move entities tool, except that it copies instead of moving. The Copy entities tool enables you to copy selected sketch entities by either selecting From and To points or by typing in XY coordinates to place the copy. SolidWorks copies the entities and tries to maintain the sketch relations and merged points.

Scaling entities

 Scale entities is one of those functions probably best left alone. This is because the results are erratic and unpredictable, particularly if there are dimensions on the sketch. This tool works on a selection of entities, particularly on an isolated selection that is not connected to other entities in the sketch. The PropertyManager for the Scale Entities tool is shown in Figure 6.6.

FIGURE 6.6

The Scale PropertyManager

Modifying sketch

 The Modify Sketch tool has been available in SolidWorks for a long time, but it has been superseded by some of the newer tools mentioned previously. However, it still has some unique functionality that is not covered by any other sketch tool. Modify sketch works on the entire sketch rather than on selections from the sketch, and it works best if there are no external relations between sketch entities and anything outside the sketch. It can also work on a sketch without the sketch being active. While most feature and tool interfaces have been moved to the PropertyManager, Modify sketch still uses a dialog box, as shown in Figure 6.7, that floats in the graphics window.

FIGURE 6.7

The Modify Sketch dialog box

The Modify Sketch dialog box enables you to perform the following functions:

- **Scale About.** The Scaling function in the Modify Sketch tool enables you to scale about either the part Origin or the Moveable Origin. The Moveable Origin is the black origin symbol with knobs on the ends of the axes and at the intersection. The Moveable Origin can be moved and even snapped to entities that are internal or external to the sketch.

- **Translate.** The Translate function of the Modify Sketch tool enables you to click and drag to move the entire sketch, or to select a point and move it to a specific set of coordinates that you type in. If the sketch is dragged onto an external entity and picks up an automatic relation, then a message may appear saying that you can now use Modify sketch only for rotating the sketch because there is an external relation.

- **Rotate.** The Rotate function of the Modify Sketch tool enables you to position the Moveable Origin to act as the center of rotation, and to either type in a rotation angle or drag with the right-mouse button to rotate, as indicated by the cursor.

When you place the cursor over the knobs on the Moveable Origin, the cursor symbols change to indicate the functionality of the RMB. These cursors are shown in action in Figure 6.8. The cursors enable mirroring about X, Y, or both simultaneously.

FIGURE 6.8

The Modify Sketch tool cursors

Note

The one thing about Modify Sketch that many people find unsettling is that the red sketch origin moves and rotates along with the rest of the sketch. Once you make peace with the fact that you can't use the red sketch origin for much anyway, this becomes unimportant. ∎

Copying and pasting sketch entities

Probably the simplest way to copy sketch entities in a sketch is to select the entities and use Ctrl+C and Ctrl+V or one of the many other methods available for this purpose (such as the RMB button menu, the Edit menu, and Ctrl+dragging).

In addition to copying selected entities within an active sketch, you can also select a sketch from the FeatureManager and then copy and paste it to a selected plane or planar face (if you are not in a sketch to begin with). This creates a new sketch feature in the FeatureManager that is not related to the original, although it does maintain internal dimensions and relations. (External relations are not copied with the sketch.) This is particularly useful when setting up certain types of lofts that use several profiles that can be created from a single copied profile. Copying and pasting is a fast and effective method of putting sketches on planes.

Copying a sketch is similar to the derived sketch (addressed later in this chapter), except that with a copied sketch there is no link, and with the derived sketch the new and old sketches remain identical through changes to the original sketch.

Dragging entities

If a selected set of sketch entities has no external relations, then you can select it as a group and move it without distorting or resizing the sketch. For best results with this technique, avoid dragging endpoints — drag an actual line.

Creating a derived sketch

A derived sketch is a parametrically linked copy. The original parent and derived sketches do not need to have any geometrical relation to one another, but when the parent sketch is changed, the dependent derived copy is updated to stay in sync.

To create a derived sketch, you can select a plane or planar face, Ctrl+select the sketch of which you want to make the parametric copy, and then choose Insert ⇨ Derived Sketch.

When you create a derived sketch, you cannot change its shape or size; it works like a block of a fixed shape driven by the parent. However, you can change the position and orientation of the derived sketch. Figure 6.9 shows a derived sketch and its parent. Modify Sketch is a great tool to use for manipulating derived sketches that are not related to things outside the sketch, especially for mirroring or rotating.

FIGURE 6.9

A derived sketch and its parent

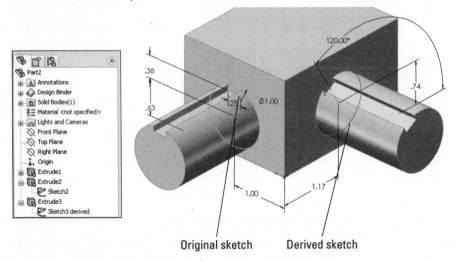

Original sketch   Derived sketch

Using Sketch Pictures

Sketch pictures are images that are placed in a sketch on a sketch plane. You can size and rotate the images, give them a transparent background, trace over them, and suppress them. They display as a child of the sketch in the FeatureManager. Image types that you can use as sketch pictures are BMP, GIF, JPEG, TIFF, PNG, PSD, and WMF.

To bring a picture into a sketch, the sketch must first be active. Click Sketch Picture on the Sketch toolbar (it is not there by default, and so you may need to drag it onto the Sketch toolbar from the Tools ⇨ Customize ⇨ Commands dialog box). You can also access this command by choosing Tools ⇨ Sketch Tools ⇨ Sketch Picture from the menu. You cannot use sketch pictures in assembly sketches, but you can use them in a part sketch in an assembly.

To change the size of a sketch picture, you can double-click it and drag one of the handles around the outside of the image. When the picture comes into the sketch, it is usually too big, having been sized at a ratio of 1 pixel to 1 mm. To size a picture accurately, you should include a ruler or an object of a known size in the image. If you cannot do this, the next best thing is to guess the size. Draw a line in your sketch and dimension it to approximately the size of something that is recognizable in the image, and then move the image by clicking and dragging it to lay the dimensioned sketch entity as close over the object in the image as possible.

You can rotate and mirror images, as well, using the Sketch Picture PropertyManager. Images are opaque, and you cannot see the model through them, but at the same time, you also cannot see the images through the model. They are like flat pieces of paper that are pasted to the model or hanging in space.

You can add transparency to images, either by selecting a color or by using the built-in transparency in the image file (alpha channels are only available in certain types of image files). When you select a color to be transparent, you will also need to increase both the Matching Tolerance and the Transparency value sliders, which are by default set to their minimum values.

Caution

If a sketch picture has had user-defined transparency applied to it, and you double-click the picture, SolidWorks automatically bumps you into the eyedropper mode, which selects a color to be transparent. A single extra click in this mode can make a mess of your Sketch Picture transparency settings by changing the selected transparency color. ■

Sketch pictures cannot be shown on a drawing associatively. The only way to do this is to capture an image of the sketch picture that is being shown in the model, and put this image in the drawing. PhotoView 360 does not use sketch pictures, either, and Decals are a separate item altogether.

Tip

Although the most common use for the sketch picture is as a tracing guide, you can use it for a wide variety of other purposes. For example, any sort of logo, decal, or display that is on a flat surface can be shown as a sketch picture. ■

Best Practice

Best practice for using sketch pictures is to put them into a separate sketch near or at the top of the FeatureManager. Even though you can have sketch entities in a Sketch Picture sketch, I recommend keeping them in separate sketches. This is because when you use the sketch entities for an extrude or a loft guide curve, this sketch will be consumed under that feature, meaning the image becomes buried somewhere in your model rather than being easily accessible at the top of the FeatureManager. ■

Using three views

When building a model from images, it is often helpful to have three or more images from orthogonal views, similar to re-creating a part from a 2D drawing. If you have a left and a right view, it may be a good idea to put them on planes that are slightly separated so that the images are not exactly on top of one another, which makes them both hard to see. Putting them on slightly offset planes means that one will be clearly visible from one direction and the other visible from the other direction.

Each sketch picture must be in a separate sketch. Figure 6.10 demonstrates the use of multiple sketch pictures to trace the outline of a vehicle, with the partially complete model shown with the images.

Using multiple sketch pictures

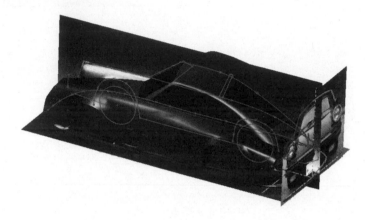

Additionally, you can put multiple sketch pictures inside a single sketch if you want to do that. Both images show up in the FeatureManager, and both can be displayed at the same time, although you may have difficulty if you want to put them on top of one another.

Compensating for perspective

When taking digital photographs to be used as sketch pictures in SolidWorks, you have to consider how perspective affects the image. Perspective can make it difficult to size items in the foreground or background. You should be aware of this, as well as that objects at different distances from the camera will appear at distorted sizes. If you are taking the pictures that will be used as sketch pictures, you can minimize the effects of perspective by standing farther away from the object and using zoom on the camera if possible.

Estimating sharp edges

When you are drawing a sketch of an object, you are usually drawing theoretically sharp corners of the model. Real parts usually have rounded corners, so you may have to use your imagination to project where the 3D surfaces would intersect at an edge minus the fillets.

When you are reverse-modeling a part from images, you are not using an exact science. It is better than not being able to put pictures into the sketch, but there is nothing about it that can be considered precise.

Using Auto Trace

Auto Trace is an add-in that you can select by choosing the Tools ⇨ Add-ins menu. Auto Trace is intended to trace between areas of contrast in sketch pictures, creating sketch entities. To use Auto Trace, make sure the add-in is activated. Activating the Auto Trace add-in activates a set of arrows at the top of the Sketch Picture PropertyManager. There is nothing to identify the functionality with the Auto Trace name. Figure 6.11 shows the Sketch Picture and Auto Trace PropertyManagers. The sliders for the Auto Trace functionality do not point out which end is high and which is low.

FIGURE 6.11

The Sketch Picture and Auto Trace PropertyManagers

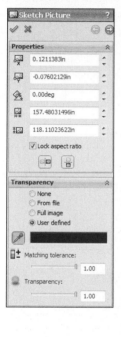

Auto Trace works best with solid blocks of black and white in the Sketch Pictures. To achieve this, you may need to use image processing software and reduce your picture to a two-color (black and white) bitmap, TIF, or PNG image. Even if this pre-processing gives perfect results, don't expect much from Auto Trace.

I can't imagine a situation in which I would use this myself or recommend anyone else use it. In all cases, including idealized demonstration images or those in which traced images would be of the most benefit to the user, such as logos with complex curvature, I believe it would be faster and more accurate to do the tracing manually, even it means using splines.

Using Sketch Text

Sketch text uses TrueType fonts to create text inside a SolidWorks sketch. This means that any TrueType font that you have can be converted to text in solid geometry; this includes Wingdings and symbol fonts. Keep in mind that some characters in certain fonts do not convert cleanly into SolidWorks sketches. Sketch text still has to follow the rules for sketching and creating features such as closed contours, as well as not mixing open and closed contours.

You can make sketch text follow a sketch curve; to space it evenly along the curve, you can control character width and spacing, as well as overall size, by specifying points or actual dimensions. Sketch text can also be justified right, left, centered, and evenly, as well as reversed, rotated, and flipped upside down. Figure 6.12 shows the Sketch Text PropertyManager and some examples of sketch text options.

FIGURE 6.12

Examples of sketch text

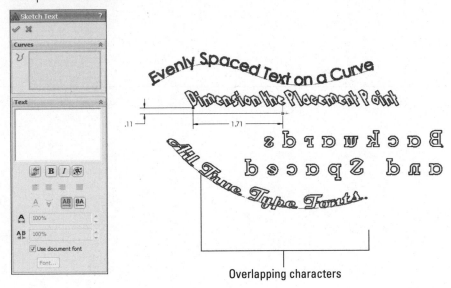

Overlapping characters

The icons in the Sketch Text PropertyManager are self-explanatory, other than the Rotated Text option, which rotates individual letters (as shown in the *Dimension the Placement Point* text in Figure 6.12), and not the whole string of text.

You can use the Sketch Text tool multiple times in a single sketch to make pieces of text with different properties. Each string of text has a placement point located at the lower left of the text. This point can be given sketch relations or dimensions to locate the text.

If the text overlaps in places, as shown in Figure 6.12, you can correct this in a couple of ways. First, you can extrude it with the Merge option unselected so that each letter is created as a separate solid body. You can also explode sketch text so that it becomes simply lines and arcs in a sketch, which you can edit the same as any other sketch. You can also adjust the Width Factor and Spacing settings.

Starting in the 2010 version of SolidWorks, you can link the text to a custom property. This means that sketch text can be changed with configurations. Configurations are covered in a later chapter. The text used to extrude a feature can come from Custom Properties, which can be driven by a design table or directly through the Sketch Text PropertyManager.

Performance

Sketch Text can dramatically slow down the performance of your SolidWorks part. If you write an entire paragraph of text in a sketch and use that text to extrude a solid feature, you are likely to notice that the part runs much more slowly. One way to avoid this is to suppress the feature and only turn it on when needed. ■

Using Colors and Line Styles with Sketches

Custom colors and line styles are usually associated with drawings, not sketches; in fact, they are most valuable when used for drawings. In sketches, this functionality is little known or used, but is still of value in certain situations.

Working in Color Display mode

 In drawings, you can use the Color Display Mode button to switch sketch entities on the drawing between displaying the assigned line or layer color and displaying the sketch status color. It has exactly the same effect in part and assembly sketches.

When you select the button, the sketch state colors are used. When the button is not selected, any custom colors that you have applied to the sketch entities appear. If the button is not selected and you have not applied colors to the entities, then the default sketch state colors are used.

You can use sketch colors for emphasis, to make selected sketch entities stand out, or to make sketches with various functions immediately distinguishable. Color Display mode only has an effect on an active sketch. Once a sketch is closed, it returns to the gray default color for inactive sketch entities.

Assigning line color

 Line color enables you to assign color to entities in an active sketch. The Color Display Mode tool determines whether the assigned color or the default sketch status colors are used.

Using the Edit Sketch Or Curve Color tool

 You can use the Edit Sketch Or Curve Color tool to assign color to an inactive sketch or to a sketch block. The color that you assign to sketches in this way displays only when the sketch is inactive, instead of the default gray color. The sketches also follow the toggle state of the Color Display Mode button. For example, if the Color Display Mode button is selected, then inactive sketches display as gray. When the Color Display Mode button is unselected, then inactive sketches display in any color that you have assigned by using the Edit Color tool.

When you use this tool to color a sketch block, the block displays the color inside the active sketch. You cannot use the Line Color tool mentioned earlier to assign color to a block.

Assigning line thickness and line style

The Line Thickness and Line Style tools function independently from the Color Display Mode button, but they are still used only when the sketch is active. As soon as a sketch that contains entities with edited thickness and style is closed, the display goes back to the normal line weight and font.

To assign a thickness or a style, you can select the sketch entities to be changed, click the button, and then select the thickness or style. Although a single sketch entity may have only a single thickness or style, you can use multiple thicknesses or styles within a single sketch. Figure 6.13 shows a sketch with the thickness and style edited.

Cross-Reference

Line thickness and line styles are covered in more detail in the discussion of drawings in Chapter 18. ■

FIGURE 6.13

A sketch with edited line thickness and line style

Using Other Sketch Tools

SolidWorks has a lot of functionality that overlaps between multiple topics. The following tools could appear in other sections of the book, but I include them here because they will help you work with and control 2D sketches in SolidWorks. Almost everybody who opens the SolidWorks software at one time or another has to use a sketch, so these tools could be applied by a wide swath of users.

Working with RapidSketch

As the name suggests, RapidSketch is meant to help you rapidly create a number of sketches on different planes or flat faces. As you move a sketch cursor over flat faces of a model, the faces highlight to indicate that you can start a new sketch there.

The workflow with this tool is that you start in one sketch, with an active sketch tool, move the cursor over another plane or face without exiting the first sketch, and start sketching the entity on the new plane.

The only real downside of using RapidSketch is that if you sketch on a particular plane or face where other planes or faces might be visible in the background, SolidWorks might interpret certain selections as trying to change sketch planes. To get back to a previous sketch, deactivate the current sketch tool (for example, by pressing Esc) and double-click the previous sketch you want to return to. To move to a later sketch, use the normal sketch exiting techniques.

RapidSketch is a rarely used function in SolidWorks. It has been available for several releases now, but it has not caught on with users. I have yet to see a compelling case for its use.

Adding Sensors

You can add Sensors in the SolidWorks FeatureManager for parts and assemblies by right-clicking the Sensors folder and selecting Add Sensor. You can find the Sensors folder at the top of the FeatureManager. If you cannot find the Sensors folder, choose Tools ⇨ Options ⇨ FeatureManager and make sure the Sensor folder is set to Show.

You are not limited to using sensors only when working with sketches; you can use them outside of sketches in parts and assemblies to warn you when various types of parameters meet various types of criteria.

Figure 6.14 shows the Sensor PropertyManager. You can create sensors for measurements, simulation data, or mass properties. The reason I have included Sensors in this chapter is the measurement options, which enable you to select a dimension and set a range of values or criteria for which you want to be notified. The dimension can be a driving (black) sketch dimension, a driven (gray) dimension on a sketch, or even a driven dimension placed directly on solid geometry.

FIGURE 6.14

The Sensor PropertyManager

Figure 6.14 shows what happens when a sensor finds a condition that you asked it to notify you about.

In addition to turning Sensor alarms on or off, you can also suppress Sensors when they are no longer needed or to improve performance.

Sensors are a great way to keep an eye on particular values, such as wall thickness or clearance between parts. You can use a Sensor to monitor any value you want to monitor but don't drive directly.

Using metadata for sketches

Metadata in SolidWorks is non-geometrical text information. Metadata is particularly helpful as keywords in searches as well as in Product Data Management (PDM) applications. If you don't use metadata within your CAD documents, it can be easy to forget that it is there at all.

You can use the following items as metadata in SolidWorks files:

- Sketch and feature names
- Sketch and feature comments (access comments via the RMB menu)
- Custom Properties
- Design Binder documents
- Tags for features (located on Status Bar in the lower-right corner)

Metadata searches can be particularly useful in large assemblies or parts with long lists of features that you need to find or search through. You can conduct searches for metadata through the FeatureManager Filter at the top of the FeatureManager. The Advanced Search function in assemblies can also search metadata sources. SolidWorks Explorer is a good first-level data management solution that can search, display, and edit metadata and previews. Windows Explorer can also search properties and tags.

Creating construction geometry

In SolidWorks, the only construction geometry that can be created directly is the construction line. All other sketch entities can be converted to construction geometry by selecting the Construction Geometry option within the sketch entity's PropertyManager or by using the Construction Geometry toggle toolbar button.

SolidWorks terminology is inconsistent, because it sometimes refers to construction lines as centerlines. The two are really the same thing. Centerlines are used for revolved sketches and mirroring, but there is no difference between a centerline and a construction line in SolidWorks.

Construction geometry is useful for many different types of situations. I use it frequently for reference sketch data. You can make sketch relations to construction geometry and can use it for layout sketches or many other purposes limited mainly by your needs and imagination.

Sketching in 3D

 The 3D sketch is an important tool for creating weldments (and many other features) in SolidWorks. Structural frames are a large part of the work that is typically done using weldment functionality in

SolidWorks, and frames are most often represented as 3D wireframes. You can do this with a combination of 2D sketches on different planes, with a single 3D sketch, or with a combination of 2D and 3D sketches. If you have confidence in your ability to use 3D sketches, then that is the best way to go. Three-dimensional sketches can be challenging, but they are certainly manageable if you know what to expect from them.

Earlier chapters discuss the tools that are available for 3D sketches; this chapter covers techniques for 3D sketching.

Navigating in space

When drawing a line in a 3D sketch, the cursor and Origin initially look like those shown in Figure 6.15. The large red Origin is called the *space handle*, with the red legs indicating the active sketching plane. Any sketch entities that you draw lie on this plane. The cursor also indicates the plane to which the active sketching plane is parallel. The XY graphic shown in Figure 6.15 does not mean that the sketch is going to be *on* the XY plane, just parallel to it.

FIGURE 6.15

The space handle and the 3D sketch cursor

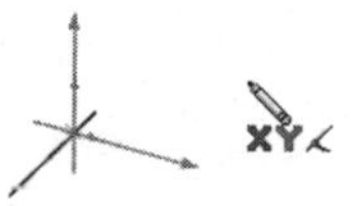

Pressing the Tab key causes the active sketching plane to toggle between XY, YZ, and ZX. The active sketching plane indication does not create any sketch relations; it just lets you know the orientation of the sketch entities that are being placed. If you want to create a skew line that is not parallel to any standard plane, you can do this by sketching to available endpoints, vertices, Origins, and so on. If there are not any entities to snap to, then you need to accept the planar placement, turn off the sketch tool, rotate the view, and move one end of the sketch entity.

An excellent tool to help you visualize what is happening in a 3D sketch is the Four Viewport view. This divides the screen into four quadrants, displaying the Front, Top, and Right views in addition to the trimetric or isometric view. You can sketch in any of the viewports, and the sketch updates live in all of the viewports simultaneously. This arrangement is shown in Figure 6.16. You can easily access the divided viewport screen by using buttons on the Standard Views toolbar. You can also manually split the screen by using the splitter bars at the lower-left and upper-right ends of the scroll bar areas around the graphics window. These window elements are also described in Chapter 2.

When unconstrained entities in a 3D sketch are moved, they move in the plane of the screen. This can lead to unexpected results when viewing something at an angle, moving it, and then rotating the view, which shows that it has shot off into deep interplanetary space. This is another reason for using the Four Viewport view, which enables you to see what is going on from all points of view at once.

FIGURE 6.16

The Four Viewport view

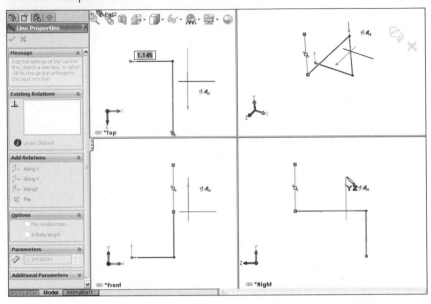

Exploring sketch relations in 3D sketches

Sketch relations in 3D sketches are not exactly the same as in 2D sketches. Improvements have been made in the past several versions, but 3D sketches still lack some important bits of functionality. Pierce is not applicable in a 3D sketch, and is replaced by Coincident, because in 3D sketches there is no difference between Pierce and Coincident. Relations are not projected into a plane in a 3D sketch the way they are in 2D.

On the other hand, several other relations are available in 3D sketches that are not found in 2D sketches, such as AlongX, AlongY, AlongZ, and OnSurface.

As mentioned earlier, relations in 3D sketches are not projected like they are in 2D sketches. For example, an entity in a 2D sketch can be made coincident to an entity that is out of plane. This is because to make the relation, the out-of-plane entity is projected into the sketch plane, and the relation is made to the projection. In a 3D sketch, Coincident means Coincident, with no projection.

As a general caution, keep in mind that solving sketches in 3D is more difficult than it is in 2D. You will see more situations where sketch relations fail, or flip in the wrong direction. Angle dimensions in particular are notorious in 3D sketches for flipping direction if they change and go across the 180-degree mark. When possible, it is advisable to work with fully defined sketches, and also to be careful (and conservative) with sketch relations.

For example, the sketch shown in Figure 6.17 cannot be fully defined without also overdefining the sketch. The main difficulty is that the combination of the tangent arc and the symmetric legs of the end brace cannot be located rotationally, even using the questionable reliability of 3D planes that are discussed next.

FIGURE 6.17

Three-dimensional sketches may be difficult to fully define.

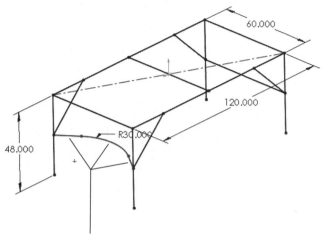

This set of sketch entities cannot be located rotationally within the 3D sketch

Using planes in space

 It is possible to create planes directly in 3D sketches. These planes work like regular planes starting in SolidWorks 2010, where they are defined by constraints and selections rather than selecting a type of method to define a plane. Sketches can be created on these planes, and move with the planes. Having planes in the sketch also enables planar sketch entities such as arcs and circles in 3D sketches.

Unfortunately, there is a lot to watch out for with 3D planes, as they are called. The first thing to watch out for is that they do not follow their original definition like normal Reference Geometry type planes. Figure 6.18 shows the PropertyManager interface for creating 3D planes; however, keep in mind that the plane does not maintain the original relation to these initial references. The parent-and-child relations that SolidWorks users are used to are suspended for this one function, or work in the reverse from what you normally expect.

3D planes cannot be fully defined unless there is some sketch geometry on the plane that is in turn related to something else. Limited types of sketch relations can be applied directly to the plane itself, Horizontal and Vertical relations cannot be applied directly to the plane to orient it. Horizontal and Vertical relations of entities on the plane are relative only to the plane and not to the rest of the part, and so making a line horizontal on the plane does not mean anything when the plane rotates (which it is free to do until it is somehow constrained to prevent this).

Beyond this, when a plane violates a sketch relation, the relation is not reported, which severely limits the amount of confidence that you can place in planes that are created in this way. The biggest danger is in the plane rotating, because that is the direction in which it is most difficult to fully lock down. The best recommendation I can make here is reference sketch lines given some relations to something stable, preferably outside of the 3D sketch.

FIGURE 6.18

The 3D planes PropertyManager

If you choose to use these planes, to activate the plane for sketching, you can double-click the plane with the cursor. The plane is activated when it displays a grid. You can double-click an empty space to return to regular 3D Sketch mode. The main thing that you give up with abandoning 3D sketch planes is the ability to use the dynamic drag options when all loft or boundary sketches are made in a single 3D sketch, which I have never used except to demonstrate the idea once.

Using planar path segments

Some path segments that are allowed in 3D sketches can only be used if they are sketched on a plane. These entities include circles and arcs, and can include splines, although splines are not required to be on a plane. It has already been mentioned that to sketch on a 3D Plane (a plane created within the 3D sketch), you can simply double-click the plane.

To sketch on a standard plane or reference geometry plane, you can Ctrl+click the border of the plane with the sketch entity icon active, or double-click the plane. The space handle moves, indicating that newly created sketch entities will lie in the selected plane.

Defining dimensions

 Dimensions in 2D sketches can represent the distance between two points, or they can represent the horizontal or vertical distance between objects. In 3D sketches, dimensions between points are *always* the straight-line distance. If you want to get a dimension that is horizontal or vertical, you should create the dimension between a plane and a point (the dimension is always measured normal to the plane) or between a line and a point (the dimension is always measured perpendicular to the line). For this reason, reference sketch geometry is often used freely in 3D sketches, in part to support dimensioning.

Using 3D sketch summary

Three-deminisional sketches are extremely powerful for many different applications. The problem is that they are also limited in some of their capabilities, and they do not work exactly like 2D sketches. You will benefit from knowing how to use 3D sketches at some point, even if it isn't every day.

Tutorial: Editing and Copying

This tutorial guides you through some common sketch relation editing scenarios and using some of the Copy, Move, and Derive tools. Follow these steps to learn about editing and copying sketches:

1. **Open the part named** `Chapter6 Tutorial1.sldprt` **from the DVD.** This part has several error flags on sketches. In cases where there are many errors, it is best to roll the part back and go through the errors one by one.

2. **Drag the rollback bar from just after the last fillet feature to just after Extrude3.** If Extrude3 is expanded so that you can see Sketch3 under it, drop the rollback bar to after Sketch3. If a warning message appears, telling you that Sketch3 will be temporarily unabsorbed, select Cancel and try the rollback again. Figure 6.19 shows before and after views for the rollback.

FIGURE 6.19

FIGURE 6.19

Rolling the part back to Extrude3

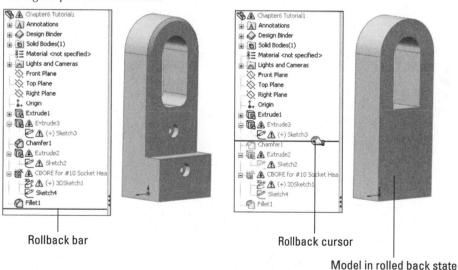

Rollback bar

Rollback cursor

Model in rolled back state

3. **Edit Sketch3 and deselect the Sketch Relations display (View ➪ Sketch Relations).** Relations with errors will still be displayed. Click Display/Delete Relations on the toolbar (the Eyeglasses tool), and set it to All in This Sketch. Notice that all the relations conflict, but only one is unsolvable: the Equal Radius relation. This appears to be a mistake because the two arcs cannot be equal.

4. **Delete the Equal Radius relation.** Select the relation in red and click the Delete button in the PropertyManager. (You can also press the Delete key on the keyboard.) The sketch is still not fixed.

5. **Click the green check mark icon to close the Display/Delete Relations PropertyManager.**

6. **Right-click the graphics window and select SketchXpert; then click Diagnose.**

7. **Using the double arrows in the Results panel, toggle through the available solutions.** All the solutions except one remove sketch relations. Accept the one solution that removes the dimension. This is shown in Figure 6.20. The sketch no longer shows errors in the graphics window, but it still does in the FeatureManager.

FIGURE 6.20

Using the SketchXpert to resolve an overdefined sketch

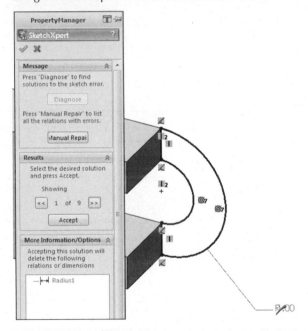

8. **Close the sketch.** Notice that the error flag does not disappear until the sketch has been repaired and closed.

9. **Use the rollback bar to roll forward to after Extrude2 and Sketch2.** Figure 6.21 shows the tool tip message that appears if you place the cursor over the feature with the error. With time, you will begin to recognize the error messages by a single keyword or even by the shape of the message text. This message tells you that there is a *dangling* relation — a relation that has lost one of the entities.

FIGURE 6.21

A tool tip gives a description of the error.

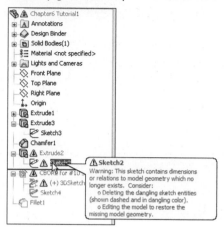

10. **Edit the sketch (see Figure 6.22).** If you show the Sketch Relation icons again, the errors will be easier to identify. When you use Display/Delete Relations (Tools ⇨ Relations ⇨ Display/Delete Relations), the first two Coincident relations appear to be dangling. Clicking the relation in the Relations panel of the Display/Delete Relations PropertyManager shows that one point was coincident to a line and the other point was coincident to a point.

11. **Click the name of the dangling entity in the Entities panel of the PropertyManager; then click the vertex indicated in Figure 6.18 in the Replace box at the bottom.** When you have fixed the errors, exit the sketch and confirm that the flag is no longer on Sketch2.

    An easier way to repair the dangling relation is to click on the dangling sketch point once. It will turn red. Next, drag the point onto an entity that you want to reattach the relation to.

12. **Exit the sketch.**

13. **Drag the rollback bar to just before CutExtrude1. Edit 3DSketch1.** This sketch is over-defined. If the Sketch Relations are not selected at this point, then select them again.

Tip

Because selecting and deselecting the display of the sketch relations in the graphics window is a task that you will perform many times, this is a good opportunity to set up a hotkey for this function. As a reminder, to set up a hot-key, choose Tools ⇨ Customize ⇨ Keyboard, and in the Search box type relations. In the Shortcut column for this command, select a hotkey to use. ∎

14. **Double-click any of the relation icons; the Display/Delete Relations PropertyManager appears.** Notice that one of the sketch relations is a Fixed relation. Delete the Fixed relation, and exit the sketch.

15. **Right-click anywhere in the FeatureManager and select Roll To End.**

16. **Click CutExtrude1 in the FeatureManager so that you can see it in the graphics window and then click a blank space to deselect the feature.**

FIGURE 6.22

Fixing dangling errors

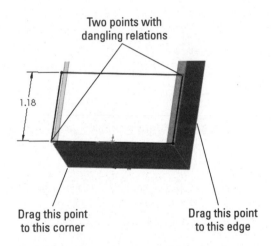

Two points with
dangling relations

1.18

Drag this point
to this corner

Drag this point
to this edge

17. **Ctrl+drag any face of the cut feature, and drop it onto another flat face.** The Ctrl+drag function copies the feature and the sketch, but the external dimensions and relations become detached. This will only work if Instant3D is unselected.

18. **Click Dangle in response to the prompt.** This means that you will have to reattach some dangling dimensions rather than re-creating them. Edit the newly created sketch, which now has an error on it.

19. **Two of the dimensions that went to external edges now have the olive dangling color.** Select one of the dimensions; a red handle appears. Drag the red handle and attach it to a model edge. Do this for both dimensions. The dimensions update to reflect their new locations. Exit the sketch and verify that the error flag has disappeared.

20. **Expand CutExtrude1, and select Sketch5 under it.** Ctrl+select a flat face on the model other than the one that Sketch5 is on. In the menu, choose Insert ⇨ Derived Sketch. You are now in a sketch editing the derived sketch.

21. **The sketch is blue, and so you should be able to resize it, right?** No, it doesn't work that way for derived sketches. You can test this by dragging the large circle; it only repositions the entire sketch as a unit.

22. **Dimension the center of the large circle to the edges of the model.**

23. **Drag the smaller circle, and notice that it swivels around the larger circle.** Create an angle dimension between the construction line between the circle centers and one of the model edges. Notice that the sketch is now fully defined.

24. **Exit the sketch, and look at the name of the derived sketch in the FeatureManager.** The term *derived* appears after the name, and the sketch appears as fully defined.

25. **Right-click the sketch and select Underive Sketch.** Notice that the sketch is now under-defined. The Underive command removes the associative link between the two sketches.

Tutorial: Controlling Pictures, Text, Colors, and Styles

This tutorial guides you through some of the miscellaneous functions in sketches, and shows you what they are used for and how they are used. Follow these steps to learn how to control these items:

1. **Open a new part using a template with inches as units.** Open a sketch on the Front plane and draw a construction line starting from the origin 12 inches down (negative Y) away from the Origin.

2. **Insert a sketch picture in this sketch.** Use Sketch Picture 1.tif from the DVD for Chapter 6.

3. **Resize the image so that the endpoints of the construction line are near the centers of the holes on the ends of the part.** To move the image, just double-click it first, and then drag it. To resize it, drag the corners.

4. **In the Transparency panel of the Sketch Picture PropertyManager, select the Eyedropper tool and click in the white background of the image.** Make sure that the color field next to the Eyedropper tool changes to white.

5. **Slide the Transparency and Matching Tolerance sliders all the way to the right, or type 1.00 in the number boxes.**

6. **Close the sketch, and rename it** Sketch Image Front View.

7. **Put the image** Sketch Picture 2.tif, **also from the DVD, in a sketch on the Right plane, and resize it to fit with the first image.** Center it symmetrically about the Origin. Also, set the transparency to the same setting as the first image.

8. **Open a new sketch, also on the Front plane, and draw two circles to match the features on the ends.** Extrude them using a Mid Plane extrusion to match the image in the other direction (about 2.5 inches), as shown in Figure 6.23.

9. **Open another new sketch on the Front plane and draw the tangent lines to form the web in the middle of the part. Use the automatic relations to draw the lines tangent to the two cylinders. It is easiest if you the Front View for this.** Close the sketch to make a solid extrusion. Extrude this part .5 inches Mid Plane.

10. **Open a new sketch on the face of the large flat web that you created in the previous step, and offset the arc edge of the larger circular boss by 2.10 inches.**

FIGURE 6.23

Using sketch pictures

11. **Change the arc to a construction arc and drag its endpoints to approximately the position shown in Figure 6.24.** The endpoints of the arc are blue after you drag them. Give them a Horizontal relation, and then dimension them.

    To create the 2.10 dimension as shown, select the arc and circle with the Dimension cursor while pressing down the Shift key.

FIGURE 6.24

Creating an offset arc

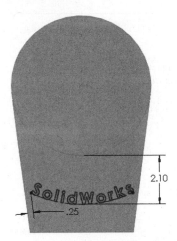

12. **Choose File ⇨ Properties.** Make sure the Custom tab is active, and type **Sketch Text** in the first open box of the Property Name column. Make sure the Type is set to Text, and in the Value field, type **SolidWorks**. Click OK when you are done.

13. **Choose Tools ⇨ Sketch Entities ⇨ Text to initiate the creation of sketch text.**

14. **Select the construction arc to go into the Curves window.**

 15. **Below the Text window, click the Link to Property button. Select Sketch Text from the drop-down list. Select the Full Justify option, then click the green check mark icon to accept it.**

16. **Deselect the Use Document Font option, click the Font button, and then set the Units to .50 inches.** Click the Bold button to make the text thicker. Click OK to exit the dialog box. Click the green check mark icon to exit the sketch text, and then exit the sketch.

17. **Extrude the text to a depth of .050 inches with 3 degrees of draft.** The part at this point resembles Figure 6.25.

Performance

Sketch Text is a real performance killer. The more text that you use, the longer it takes to extrude. Draft on the extrusion adds to the time required. ■

FIGURE 6.25

Creating extruded text

18. **Select the flat face on the other side of the part from where you just extruded the text, and open a sketch.**

19. **Select the face and click the Offset button to make a set of sketch entities offset to the inside of the face by .50 inches.** Remember that you may have to reverse the offset to get it to work properly.

20. **Open the Line Format toolbar (right-click any toolbar other than the CommandManager and select Line Format).**

21. **Select all the sketch lines and change their color using the Line Color tool.** Change the line thickness and the line style using the appropriate tools. The sketch now looks something like Figure 6.26.

22. **When you click the Color Display Mode tool, the colors return to regular sketch colors.** When you exit the sketch, the line weight and style also return to normal.

FIGURE 6.26

Using line thickness and line style

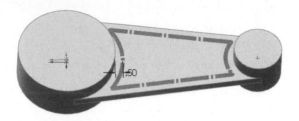

Tutorial: Using Metadata

If you integrate the use of metadata into your company's modeling process, your SolidWorks models can be a resource for much more than just geometrical data. In this tutorial, discover the hidden treasure of extra information stored as metadata in this model.

1. **Open the part from the DVD called** `Chapter 6 - Dial Cover.sldprt`.

2. **Check the Custom Properties in this file by choosing File ⇨ Properties.** Notice the Thickness and Process properties in particular. All the metadata entry interfaces are shown in Figure 6.27.

FIGURE 6.27

Metadata entry interfaces

3. **Add a Custom Property with the Property Name Material, type Text, and value ABS.** The Custom Property interface is located at File ⇨ Properties.

4. **Check the Comments in this part.** Notice that a Comments folder exists near the top of the FeatureManager. Inside it is a list of the features for which I have written comments.

5. **Add a Comment by right-clicking the VarFillet3 feature, selecting the Comment flyout arrow, clicking the Add Comment option, clicking the Date/Time Stamp button, and adding a comment that uses the word Blend.**

6. **Check the Tags for the part by clicking the small yellow tag in the lower-right corner of the Status Bar, then click any feature, and double-click in the Tags interface box.**

7. **Add a Tag by selecting the Cut-Extrude1 feature and adding the tag** pilar.

8. **Right-click any item in the FeatureManager and select Go To from the options.**

9. **Type** 37 **in the box and click the Find Next button.** The FeatureManager should highlight a feature near the bottom of the tree named Fillet37.

10. **Click Fillet37 in the Feature Manager and select the Zoom to Selection tool.** Zoom to Selection is a magnifying glass with an equal sign in it. The display zooms and pans to a fillet on one end of the part.

11. **Right-click a face of Fillet37 on the model and select Go To Feature (In Tree), which will select the FeatureManager if necessary and scroll to show Fillet37.** This sequence of tools shows the importance and interdependence of feature names and the actual geometry.

12. **Type the word** Thickness **in the filter at the top of the FeatureManager.** Figure 6.28 shows the result. Notice how quickly the results appear. Notice also that the metadata item that caused the feature to show in the list can be shown in a tool tip by hovering the mouse over the feature.

FIGURE 6.28

Using the FeatureManager Filter to search for metadata

13. **Click the X at the right end of the filter to restore the FeatureManager to its original state, and type the word** Pilar **instead.** Now filter for Thermoform.

Tutorial: Sketching Calculator

Sketches can be used as geometrical calculators. Parametrics can be extremely powerful when you can define relationships between geometry. In this tutorial, you will set up a sketch to calculate the complex size and location relationships between the rings of a child's stacking toy.

1. **Open a new part document with inch units.**

2. **Draw a pyramid with the base centered on the origin, as shown in Figure 6.29.** Do not use dimensions, but use sketch relations and construction geometry to enable it to change symmetrically.

3. **Draw three circles to the right of the pyramid.** The bottom circle should be tangent to the bottom and the angled side of the pyramid. The middle and top circles should be tangent to the lower circle and the angled side of the pyramid, respectively. Figure 6.30 shows this process partially completed.

FIGURE 6.29

Build a pyramid without dimensions.

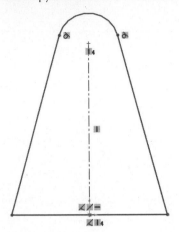

FIGURE 6.30

Sketching stacking rings

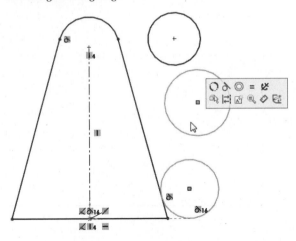

4. **Put a diameter dimension on each circle.** In the PropertyManager for each dimension, rename the dimension for **ring1dia@Sketch1**, **ring2dia**, and so on. This is shown in Figure 6.31.

5. **Place a dimension from the center of the bottom circle to the construction line, and place the dimension on the far side of the construction line from the circle.** This creates a diameter dimension.

6. Place a dimension for the middle circle in the same way as the bottom circle, but this time, make the dimension value about 75 percent of the first diameter.

Naming dimensions

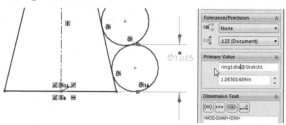

7. Complete the sketch as shown in Figure 6.32, with all the dimensions and sketch relations.

The finished sketch

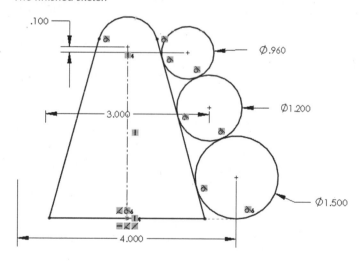

8. **Make changes to the sketch to see which changes it will allow and which it will not.**
   Double-click dimensions and use the wheel in the middle of the Modify dialog box to apply changes smoothly. Try changing each dimension.

Summary

Many tools that are available in sketches are not commonly covered in the most popular sources of information, including official training manuals. The difference between a good CAD tool and a great communication tool can be minor functions that just make life a little easier, or the presentation or editing of data a little better. When you explore the capabilities of SolidWorks, it usually rewards you with functionality that is not immediately obvious.

Modeling with Primary Features

The most frustrating part of a complex modeling job is to be able to envision a result, but not be able to create it because you do not have the tools to get it done. Worse yet is to actually have the tools but either not understand how to use them or not even realize that you have them. Getting the job done is so much more satisfying when you use the right tools and get the job done right — not just so that it *looks* right, but so that it really *is* right.

SolidWorks offers so many tools that it is sometimes difficult to select the best one, especially if it is for a function that you do not use frequently.

This chapter helps you identify which features to use in which situations, and in some cases, which features to avoid. It also helps you evaluate which feature is best to use for a particular job. With some features, it is clear when to use them, but for others, it is not. This chapter guides you through the decision-making process.

I have split the list of SolidWorks features into two groups: primary features and secondary features. Primary features are, of course, the ones you use most frequently, and secondary features are used less frequently. Of course, my definition of primary and secondary may be different from yours, and this subject is too big for a single chapter.

Identifying When to Use Which Tool

I am always trying to think of alternate ways of doing things. It is important to have a backup plan, or sometimes multiple backup plans, in case a feature doesn't perform exactly the way you want it to. You may find that the more complex features are not as well behaved as the simple features. You may be able to get away with only doing blind extrudes and cuts with simple chamfers and fillets for the rest of your career, but, even if you could, would you really want to?

As an exercise, I often try to see how many different ways a particular shape might be modeled, and how each modeling method relates to manufacturing methods, costs, editability, efficiency, and so on. You may also want to try this approach for fun or for education.

As SolidWorks grows more and more complex, and the feature count increases with every release, understanding how the features work and how to select the best tool for the job becomes ever more important. If you are only familiar with the standard half-dozen or so features that most users use, your options are limited. Sometimes simple features truly are the correct ones to use, but using them because they are the only things you know is not always the best choice.

Using the Extrude feature

 Extruded features can be grouped into several categories, with extruded Boss and Cut features at the highest level. When you use Instant 3D, extruded bosses can be transformed into cuts by simply dragging them with the Instant 3D handle in the other direction. It is unclear what advantage this has in real-world modeling, but it is an available option. As a result, the names of newly created extrude features are simply Extrude1 where they used to be Extrude-Boss1 or Extrude-Cut1.

The "Base" part of the Extruded Boss/Base is a holdover from when SolidWorks did not allow multi-body parts, and the first feature in a part had special significance that it no longer has. This is also seen in the menus at Insert ➪ Boss/Base. The Base feature was the first solid feature in the FeatureManager, and you could not change it without deleting the rest of the features. The introduction of multi-body support in SolidWorks has removed this limitation.

Cross-Reference
Multi-body parts are covered in detail in Chapter 19. ■

Creating a solid feature

In this case, the term *solid feature* is used as an opposite of *thin feature*. This is the simple type of feature that you create by default when you extrude a closed loop sketch. A closed loop sketch fully encloses an area without gaps or overlaps at the sketch entity endpoints. Figure 7.1 shows a closed loop sketch creating an extruded solid feature. This is the default type of geometry for closed loop sketches.

Creating a thin feature

The Thin Feature option is available in several features, but is most commonly used with Extruded Boss features. Thin features are created by default when you use open loop sketches, but you can also select the Thin Feature option for closed loop sketches. Thin features are commonly used for ribs, thin walls, hollow bosses, and many other types of features that are common to plastic parts, castings, or sheet metal.

Even experienced users tend to forget that thin features are not just for bosses, but that they can also be used for cuts. For example, you can easily create grooves and slots with thin feature cuts.

Figure 7.2 shows the Thin Feature panel in the Extruded Boss PropertyManager. In addition to the default options that are available for the extrude feature, the Thin feature adds a *thickness* dimension, as well as three options to direct the thickness relative to the sketch: One-Direction, Mid-Plane, and Two-Direction. The Two-Direction option requires two dimensions, as shown in Figure 7.2.

A closed loop sketch and an extruded solid feature

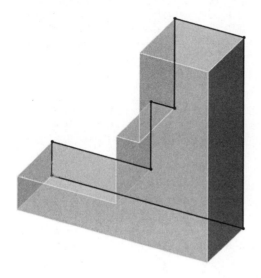

The Thin Feature portion of the Extrude PropertyManager

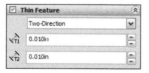

You can create the simplest cube from a single sketch line and a thin feature extrude. However, because they are more specialized in some respects, thin features may not be as flexible when the design intent changes. For example, if a part is going to change from a constant width to a tapered or stepped shape, thin features do not handle this kind of change. Figure 7.3 shows different types of geometry that are typically created from thin features.

Exploring sketch types

You may see the words *loop, contour, region,* and *profile* used interchangeably in various areas of the software. In this book I try to standardize some of the more confusing terminology, but in this case, each of the four terms tends to be used in different situations.

FIGURE 7.3

Different types of geometry created from thin feature extrudes

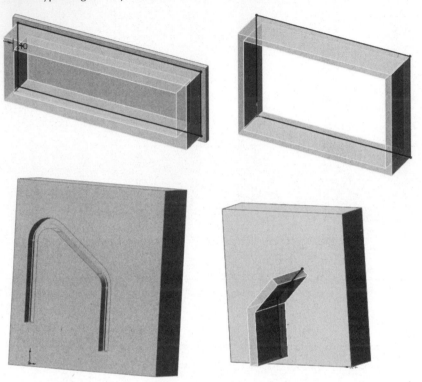

A loop is a selection of edges or sketch entities that touch end-to-end without gaps or overlaps. A contour can mean the same thing as a loop or it may also mean an area enclosed by a loop of sketch entities that may not meet the "touch end-to-end without gaps or overlaps" part of the definition. Contours can also refer to an enclosed area selected for a feature such as an extrude or revolve, as you will see later in this chapter. A region is typically the same thing as a contour, but the term is only found in error messages and is probably nonstandard terminology left over from previous versions of SolidWorks. Technically, a profile is only found in a loft or sweep feature, but various sources of documentation might use it to refer to any sketch or selection of entities that are used to create a feature.

I have already mentioned several sketch types, including closed loop and open loop. Closed loop sketches make solid features by default, but you can also use them to make thin features. Open loop sketches make thin features by default, and you cannot use them to make solid features. A nested loop is one closed loop inside another, like concentric circles. Self-intersecting sketches can be any type of sketch where the geometry crosses itself. SolidWorks also identifies sketches where three or more sketch elements intersect at a point by issuing an error if you try to use the sketch in a feature. Figure 7.4 illustrates these different types of sketches. Some of these examples are errors and some are just warnings.

FIGURE 7.4

Identifying different types of sketches in SolidWorks

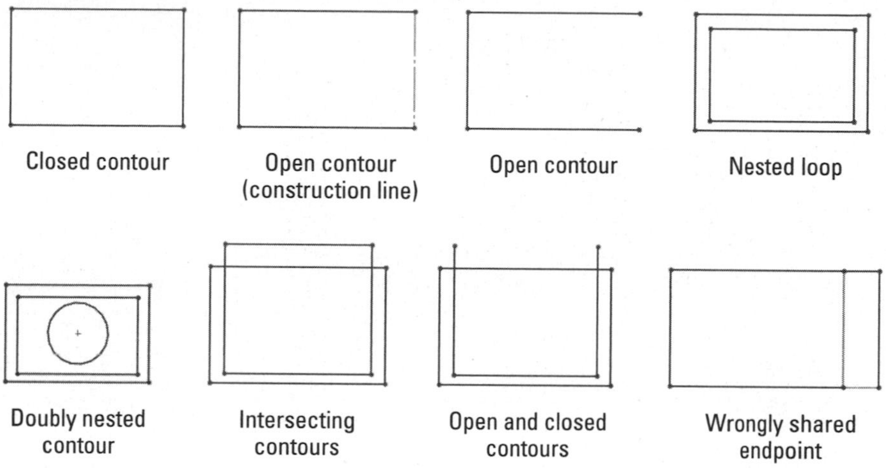

Closed contour

Open contour
(construction line)

Open contour

Nested loop

Doubly nested
contour

Intersecting
contours

Open and closed
contours

Wrongly shared
endpoint

Sketch contours

 Sketch contours enable you to select enclosed areas where the sketch entities themselves actually cross or otherwise violate the usual sketch rules. One of these conditions is the self-intersecting contour.

Best Practice

SolidWorks works best with well-disciplined sketches that follow the rules. Therefore, if you plan to use sketch contours, you should make sure that it is not simply because you are unwilling to clean up a messy sketch.

When you define features by selecting sketch contours, they are more likely to fail if the selection changes when the selected contour's bounded area changes in some way. It is considered best practice to use the normal closed loop sketch when you are defining features. Contour selection is best suited to "fast and dirty" conceptual models, which are used in very limited situations. ■

There are several types of contour selection, as shown in Figure 7.5.

3D sketch

You can make extrusions from 3D sketches, even 3D sketches that are not planar. While not necessarily the best way to do extrudes, this is a method that you can use when needed. You can establish direction for an extrusion by selecting a plane (normal direction), axis, sketch line, or model edge.

When you make an extrusion from a 3D sketch, the direction of extrusion cannot be assumed or inferred from anything — it must be explicitly identified. The default extrusion direction from a 2D sketch is always perpendicular to the sketch plane unless otherwise specified.

Non-planar sketches become somewhat problematic when you are creating the final extruded feature. The biggest problem is how you cap the ends. Figure 7.6 shows a non-planar 3D sketch that is being extruded. Notice that the end faces are, by necessity, not planar, and are capped by an unpredictable method, probably a simple Fill surface. This is a problem only if your part is going to use these faces in the end; if it does not, then there may be no issue with using this technique. If you would like to examine this part, it is included on the DVD as Chapter 7 Extrude 3D Sketch.sldprt.

FIGURE 7.5

Types of contour selection

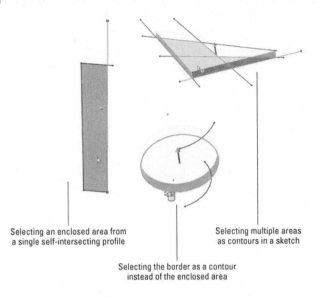

Selecting an enclosed area from
a single self-intersecting profile

Selecting multiple areas
as contours in a sketch

Selecting the border as a contour
instead of the enclosed area

FIGURE 7.6

Extruding a non-planar 3D sketch

If you need to have end faces with a specific shape, and you still want to extrude from a non-planar 3D sketch, then you should use an extruded surface feature rather than an extruded solid feature.

One big advantage of using a 3D sketch to extrude from is that you can include profiles on many different levels, although they must all have the same end condition. Therefore, if you have several pockets in a plate, you can draw the profile for each pocket at the bottom of the pocket using planes offset at different levels, and extrude all the profiles Through All; as a result, they will all be cut to different depths.

Three-dimensional sketches also have an advantage when all the profiles of a single loft or boundary are made in a single 3D sketch. This enables you to drag the profiles and watch the loft update in real time.

Cross-Reference
Surfacing features are covered in detail in Chapter 20. Chapter 4 contains additional details on extrude end conditions, thin features, directions, and the From options.■

Understanding the workflow
The Extrude feature workflow offers several options:

1. From within an active sketch with appropriate geometry, click the Extrude toolbar icon.
2. Set the Extrude feature options.
3. Click OK.

Or:

1. With no sketch active, click the Extrude toolbar icon.
2. Select an existing sketch with appropriate geometry.
3. Set the Extrude feature options.
4. Click OK.

Or:

1. With no sketch active, click the Extrude toolbar icon.
2. Select a plane on which to create a sketch to extrude.
3. Create your sketch.
4. Exit the sketch using the Confirmation Corner icon.
5. Set the Extrude feature options.
6. Click OK.

Understanding Instant 3D

 Instant 3D is the tool that enables you to use the mouse to pull arrows or handles on the screen to establish various dimension parameters for features like extrude, revolve, fillet, and even move face. Not every dimension feature parameter is editable in this way. In some cases Instant 3D offers you convenient ways to edit geometry without needing to figure out which feature is responsible for which faces. With Instant 3D, you simply pull on handles on the screen to move and resize sketches, and features including fillets.

Creating extrudes with Instant 3D
Instant 3D enables you to select a sketch or a sketch contour and drag the Instant 3D arrow to create either a blind extruded boss or cut. The workflow when using this function requires that the sketch

be closed. Instant 3D cannot be used to create a thin feature, and any sketch or contour that it uses must be a closed loop. Sketches must also be shown (not hidden) in order to be used with Instant 3D.

Note

Even though the words "Instant 3D" suggest that you should be able to instantly create 3D geometry from a sketch that you may have just created, you do have to close the sketch first to get instant functionality. In this case, Instant 3D requires the sketch to be closed (as in not active) and closed (as in not an open loop). ■

Figure 7.7 shows Instant 3D arrows for extruding a sketch into a solid and the ruler to establish blind extrusion depth. These extrusions were done from a single sketch with three concentric circles, using contour selection.

Identifying Instant 3D interface elements

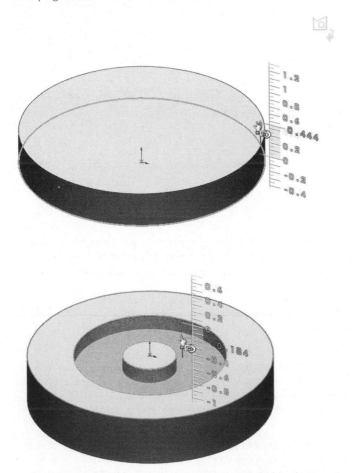

Even after you create an extruded boss, you can use Instant 3D to drag it in the other direction to change the boss into an extruded cut. When you do this, the symbol on the feature changes, but the name does not.

If you have a sketch that requires contour selection, SolidWorks automatically hides the sketch, and to continue with Instant 3D functionality using additional contours selected from that sketch, you will have to show the sketch again. This interrupts the workflow and makes using this functionality less fluid than it might otherwise be. I only mention it here so that you are aware of what is happening when the sketch disappears and the Instant 3D functionality disappears with it.

You can also continue to create extrudes using contours of a consumed sketch by just clicking on the sketch so that it displays highlighted, and is only shown temporarily. This is a shortcut so that you don't have to repeatedly show the sketch every time — you just select it.

If geometry already exists in the part, and you drag a new feature into the existing solid, SolidWorks assumes you want to make a cut. However, maybe you are really trying to make a boss that comes out the other side of the part. These context toolbars enable you to do this. Options include boss, cut, and draft. The draft option enables you to add draft to a feature created with Instant 3D.

While Instant 3D can only create extruded bosses and cuts, it can edit revolves. If you create a revolved feature revolving the sketch, say, 270°, the face created at the angle can be edited by Instant 3D dragging. You can also drag faces created by any under-defined sketch elements.

Editing geometry with Instant 3D

Instant 3D enables you to edit 2D sketches and solid geometry. You can also edit some additional feature types using Instant 3D, such as offset reference planes. It can neither create nor edit surface geometry or 3D sketches in some situations. To edit solid geometry, click a face, and an arrow appears. Drag the arrow, and SolidWorks automatically changes either the sketch or the feature end condition used to create that face. If a dimensioned sketch was used to create that face, SolidWorks will not allow you to use the Instant 3D arrow to move or resize the face. An option exists that enables Instant 3D changes to override sketch dimensions at Tools ⇨ Sketch Settings ⇨ Override Dims on Drag.

Caution

Be careful with the Override Dims on Drag option. If you accidentally drag a fully defined sketch, this setting enables Instant 3D to completely resize the sketch by dragging, even though the sketch is fully defined. For working conceptually, it can be a great aid, but for final production models, you may do better to leave this option off. The Override Dims on Drag option is off by default. ∎

Instant 3D offers different editing options depending on how a sketch is selected.

- **A sketch is selected from the graphics window.** The pull arrow appears, enabling you to create an extruded boss or cut.

- **A sketch is selected from the FeatureManager.** If the sketch has relations to anything outside of the sketch, the sketch is highlighted with no special functionality available. If no external relations exist, a box with stretch handles enable scaling the sketch, and a set of axes with a wing enables you to move the sketch in X or Y or X and Y. Figure 7.8 shows this situation.

When Instant 3D is activated, double-clicking a sketch in either the FeatureManager or on a sketch element in the graphics window opens that sketch. While you are in a sketch, if you double-click with the Select cursor in blank space in the graphics window, you close the sketch. This only works for 2D sketches; 3D sketches can be opened, but not closed, this way.

FIGURE 7.8

Sketch scaling and moving options with Instant 3D.

Ruler for hole diameter

Drag handles and web for hole location

Drag handle for hole depth

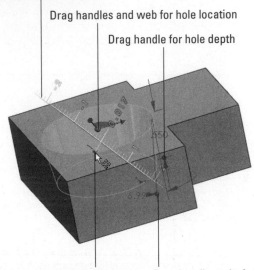

Drag handle for hole diameter   Drag handle to draft dimension

Working with the Revolve feature

 Like all other features, revolve features have some rules that you must observe when choosing sketches to create a revolve:

- **Draw only half of the revolve profile.** (Draw the section to one side of the centerline.)
- **The profile must not cross the centerline.**
- **The profile must not touch the centerline at a single point.** It can touch along a line, but not at a point. Revolving a sketch that touched the centerline at a single point would create a point of zero thickness in the part.

You can use any type of line or model edge for the centerline, not just the centerline/construction line type.

Understanding end conditions

There are five Revolve end conditions. Some of the following options are new in SolidWorks 2011:

- Blind
- Up to Vertex
- Up to Surface
- Offset from Surface
- Midplane

There is no equivalent for Up to Next or Up to Body with the Revolve feature. Figure 7.9 shows the new Revolve feature PropertyManager for SolidWorks 2011.

FIGURE 7.9

Using the Revolve PropertyManager in SolidWorks 2011

SolidWorks 2011 changes the way that you create two-direction revolves. The options in the end conditions list used to be One Direction, Two Directions, or Midplane. Starting in 2011 the end conditions for revolve are more similar to the end conditions for extrude, with the five options listed for revolve, and controls for separate directions.

Workflow

The workflow for the Revolve feature is exactly the same as for the Extrude feature.

Using contour selection

Like extrude features, revolve features can also use contour selection; and as with the extrude features, I recommend that you avoid using contours for production work.

Introducing loft and boundary

 Loft and boundary are known as *interpolated* features. That means that you can create profiles for the feature at certain points, and the software will interpolate the shape between the profiles. You can use additional controls with loft, such as guide curves or centerlines, and establish end conditions to help direct the shape. A loft with just two profiles is a straight line transition. If you have more than two profiles, the transition from one profile to another works more like a spline.

Many users struggle when faced with the option to create a loft, boundary, or sweep. Some overlap exists between the three features, but as you gain some experience, it becomes easier to choose between them. Generally, if you can create the cross-section of the feature by manipulating the dimensions of a single sketch, a sweep might be the best feature. If the cross-section changes character or severely changes shape, loft or boundary may be best. If you need a very definite shape at both ends and/or in the middle, loft and boundary are better choices because they enable you to explicitly define the cross-section at any point. However, if the outline is more important than the cross-section, you should choose a sweep. In addition, if the path between ends is important, choose a sweep.

Both types of features are extremely powerful, but the sweep has a tendency to be fussier about details, setup, and rules, while the loft and boundary can be surprisingly flexible. I am not trying to dissuade you from using sweeps, because they are useful in many situations. However, in my own personal modeling, I probably use about ten lofts or boundary features for every sweep. For example, while you would use a loft or combination of loft features to create the outer faces of a complex laundry detergent bottle, you would use the sweep to create a raised border around the label area or the cap thread.

A good example of the interpolated nature of a loft is to put a circle on one plane and a rectangle on an offset plane and then loft them together. This arrangement is shown in Figure 7.10. The transition between shapes is the defining characteristic of a loft, and is the reason for choosing a loft instead of another feature type. Lofts can create both Boss features and Cut features.

FIGURE 7.10

Interpolation inside a loft

Notice how the cross-sectional shape of the loft transitions from the circle to the rectangle. The default setting, shown in Figure 7.10, is for the interpolated transition to happen evenly across the loft, but the distribution of change from one end to the other could be altered, which might result in the transitions shown in Figure 7.11.

FIGURE 7.11

Adding end conditions to a loft alters how the interpolation is distributed.

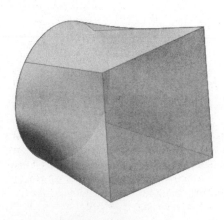
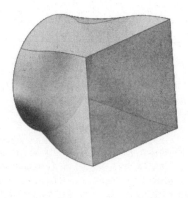

Both shapes are two-profile lofts. The two-profile loft with default end conditions always creates a straight transition, which is shown in the image to the left. A two-point spline with no end tangency creates a straight line in exactly the same way. By applying end conditions to either or both of the loft profiles, the loft's shape is made more interesting, as seen in the image to the right in Figure 7.11. Again, the same thing happens when applying end tangency conditions to a two-point spline: it goes from being a straight line to being more curvaceous, with continuously variable curvature.

The Loft PropertyManager interface is shown in Figure 7.12.

FIGURE 7.12

The Loft PropertyManager

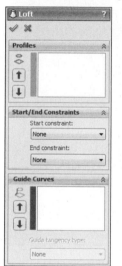
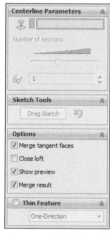

Comparing the Loft and Boundary features

 The Boundary feature is relatively new to SolidWorks. The Boundary surface feature was added first, and was a big hit in surfacing applications, so boundary solid was added later. In my view, the solid feature is not as effective as the surface feature, and solid loft probably offers fewer advantages over boundary than surface loft does. Chapter 20 has more information on the surfacing functionality.

An important difference between boundary and loft is that there are more options for setting up boundary features in terms of the geometrical layout of profiles and guide curves. A second major difference is that there is no such thing in boundary as profiles and guide curves — the two directions are treated equally, and are simply called Direction 1 and Direction 2. In the Loft feature, you don't have as much continuity control across the guide curve direction. This is less meaningful with solid features than with surfaces.

The geometrical layout of profiles is the most important difference between boundary and loft. With loft, you must have a profile at the beginning and end of the feature. With boundary, you can lay out the profile sketch planes like an X. You could also lay the feature out like a T, which would act like a sweep. Using a layout shaped like an F actually combines the functionality of a loft with that of a sweep. So boundary is a very powerful feature, with new options for creating interpolated solid shapes. Face-by-face control, however, still has to come from using surfacing features.

Figure 7.13 shows the boundary PropertyManager and features made with F and X layouts of sketches. These two features represent functionality that doesn't exist with the Loft feature.

FIGURE 7.13

Using different profile arrangements for boundary solid features

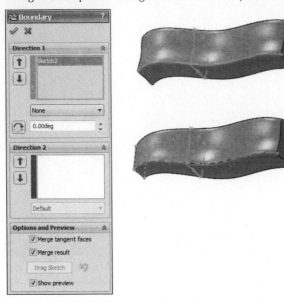

Using entities in a loft

For solid lofts, you can select faces, closed loop 2D or 3D sketches, and surface bodies. You can use sketch points as a profile on the end of a loft that comes to a point or rounded end. For surface lofts, you can use open sketches and edges in addition to the entities that are used by solid lofts, but you cannot combine open and closed contours.

Some special functionality becomes available to you if you put all the profiles and guide curves together in a single 3D sketch. In order to select profiles made in this way, you must use the SelectionManager, which is discussed later in this chapter.

The Sketch Tools panel of the Loft PropertyManager enables you to drag sketch entities of any profile made in this way while you are editing or creating the Loft feature, without needing to exit and edit a sketch.

Cross-Reference

I discuss 3D sketches in more detail in Chapter 6.■

Comparing lofts and splines

The words *loft* and *spline* come from the shipbuilding trade. The word *spline* is actually defined as the slats of wood that cover the ship, and the spars of the hull very much resemble loft sections. With the splines or slats bending at each spar, it is easy to see how the modern CAD analogy came to be.

Lofts and splines are also governed by similar mathematics. You have seen how the two-point spline and two-profile loft both create a straight-line transition. Next, a third profile is added to the loft and a third point to the spline, which demonstrates how the math that governs splines and lofts is also related to bending in elastic materials. Figure 7.14 shows how lofts and splines react geometrically in the same way that bending a flexible steel rod would react (except that the spline and the loft do not have a fixed length).

FIGURE 7.14

Splines, lofts, and bending

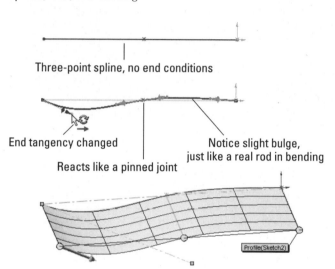

With this bit of background, it is time to move forward and talk about a few of the major aspects of loft features in SolidWorks. It is possible to write a separate book that only discusses modeling lofts and other complex shapes. This has in fact been done. The *SolidWorks Surfacing and Complex Shape Modeling Bible* (Wiley, 2008) covers a wide range of surfacing topics with detailed examples. In this single chapter, I do not have the space to cover the topic exhaustively, but coverage of the major concepts will be enough to point you in the right direction.

Understanding the need for surfaces

In this chapter, I deal exclusively with solid modeling techniques because they are the baseline that SolidWorks users use most frequently. Surfaces make it easier to discuss complex shape concepts because surfaces are generally created one face at a time, rather than by using the solid modeling method that creates as many faces as necessary to enclose a volume.

From the very beginning, the SolidWorks modeling culture has made things easier for users by taking care of many of the details in the background. This is because solids are built through automated surface techniques. Surface modeling in itself can be tedious work because of all the manual detail that you must add. Solid modeling as we know it is simply an evolutionary step that adds automation to surface modeling. The automation maintains a closed boundary of surfaces around the solid volume.

Because surfaces are the underlying building blocks from which solids are made, it would make sense to teach surfaces first, and then solids. However, the majority of SolidWorks users never use surfacing, and do not see a need for it; therefore, surface functions are generally given a lower priority.

Cross-Reference

Refer to Chapter 20 for surfacing information. For a comprehensive look at surfacing and complex shapes, see the SolidWorks Surfacing and Complex Shape Modeling Bible (Wiley, 2008). ■

Exploring loft end constraints

Loft end conditions control the tangency direction and weighting at the ends of the loft. Some of the end constraints depend upon the loft starting or ending from other geometry. The optional constraints are covered in the following sections.

None

The direction of the loft is not set by the None end constraint, but the curvature of the lofted faces at the ends is zero. This is the default end constraint for two-section lofts. This means that at the ends of the loft using the None end constraint, the loft has no curvature, and is tangent to some direction controlled by the location of the previous profile.

Default

The Default end constraint is not available for two-section lofts, only for lofts with three or more sections. This end constraint applies curvature to the end of the loft so that it approximates a parabola being formed through the first and last loft profiles.

Tangent to Face

The Tangent to Face end constraint is self-explanatory. The Tangency to Face option includes a setting for tangent length. This is not a literal length dimension, but a relative weighting, on a scale from 0.1 to 10. The small arrow to the left of the setting identifies the direction of the tangency. Usually, the default setting is correct, but there are times when SolidWorks misidentifies the intended tangency direction, and you may need to correct it manually.

The Next Face option is available only when lofting from an end face where the tangency could go in one of two perpendicular directions. This is shown in Figure 7.15.

Apply to All refers to applying the Tangent Length value to all the tangency-weighting arrows for the selected profile. When you select Apply to All, only one arrow displays. When you deselect it, one arrow should display for each vertex in the profile, and you can adjust each arrow individually.

Curvature to Face

The difference between tangency and curvature is that tangency is only concerned with the direction of curvature immediately at the edge between the two surfaces. Curvature must be tangent and match the radius of curvature on either side of the edge between surfaces. This is often given many names, including curvature continuity and c2 or g2. Lofted surfaces do not usually have a constant radius; because they are like splines, they are constantly changing in local radius.

Direction Vector

The Direction Vector end constraint forces the loft to be tangent to a direction that you define by selecting an axis, edge, or sketch entity. The angle setting makes the loft deviate from the direction vector, as shown in Figure 7.15. The curved arrows to the left identify the direction in which the angle deviation is going.

FIGURE 7.15

Examples of end constraints

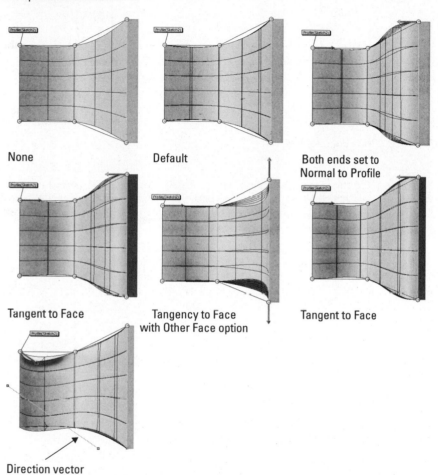

None

Default

Both ends set to Normal to Profile

Tangent to Face

Tangency to Face with Other Face option

Tangent to Face

Direction vector

Displaying isoparameter U-V lines

The mesh or grid shown in the previous images appears automatically for certain types of features, including lofts. The grid represents *isoparameter* lines, also known as NURBS mesh or U-V lines. This mesh shows the underlying structure of the faces being created by the feature. If the mesh is highly distorted and appears to overlap in places, then it is likely that the feature will fail.

You can show or hide the mesh through the right mouse button (RMB) menu when editing or creating a Loft feature, unless the SelectionManager is active. In this case, you can see only SelectionManager commands in the RMB menu. In addition, planar faces do not mesh, only faces with some curvature.

Using guide curves

Guide curves help to constrain the outline of a loft between loft profiles. Although it is best to try to achieve the shape you want by using appropriately shaped and placed loft profiles, this is not always possible. The most appropriate use of guide curves for solid lofts is at places where the loft is going to create a hard edge, which is usually at the corners of loft profile sketches. Guide curves often (but not always) break up what would otherwise be a smooth surface, and you should avoid them in these situations, if possible.

Best Practice

Do not try to push the shape of the loft too extremely with guide curves. Use guide curves mainly for tweaking and fine-tuning rather than coarse adjustments. Use loft sections and end constraints to get most of the overall shape correct. Pushing too hard with a guide curve can cause the shape to kink unnaturally.■

Although guide curves can be longer than the loft, they can not be shorter. The guide curve applies to the entire loft. If you need to apply the guide curve only to a portion of the loft, then split the loft into two lofts: one that uses the guide curve and one that does not. The guide curve must intersect all profiles in a loft.

If you have more than one guide curve, the order in which they are listed in the box is important. The first guide curve helps to position the intermediate profiles of the loft. It may be difficult to visualize the effects of guide-curve order before it happens, but remember that it does make a difference, and depending on the difference between the curves, the difference may or may not be subtle.

Guide curves are also used in sweeps, which I address later in this chapter. Figure 7.16 shows a model that is lofted using guide curves. The image to the left shows the sketches that are used to make the part. There are two sketches with points; you can use points as loft profiles. The image in the middle shows the Loft feature without guide curves, and the one to the right is the part with guide curves. If you would like to examine how this part is built, you can find it on the DVD with the filename `Chapter 7 Guide Curves.sldprt`.

FIGURE 7.16

A loft with and without guide curves

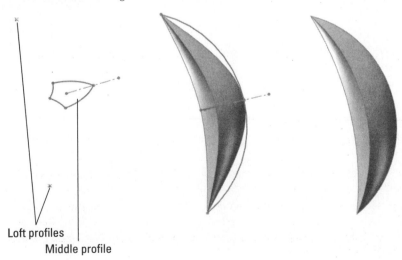

Loft profiles
Middle profile

Using centerline lofts

The Centerline panel of the Loft PropertyManager is used to set up a centerline loft. You can use the centerline of a loft in roughly the same way that you use a sweep path. In fact, the Centerline loft resembles a sweep feature where you can specify the shape of some of the intermediate profiles. Centerline lofts can also create intermediate profiles. You may prefer to use a centerline loft instead of either a sweep or a regular loft because the profile may change in ways that the Sweep feature cannot handle, and the loft may need some guidance regarding the order of the profiles, or how to smooth the shape between the profiles. While most of the functionality you find in the Loft feature can be duplicated and improved upon by the Boundary solid feature, the Boundary feature cannot do anything like the Centerline loft.

I cover sweep features in this chapter. If you are creating a centerline loft, you may want to examine the sweep functionality as well.

You can use centerlines simultaneously with guide curves. While guide curves must touch the profile, there is no such requirement for a centerline; in fact, the centerline works best if it does not touch any of the profiles.

The slider in the Centerline Parameters panel enables you to specify how many intermediate sections to create between sketched profiles.

Using the SelectionManager

The SelectionManager simplifies the selection of entities from complex sketches that are not necessarily the clean, closed loop sketches that SolidWorks works with most effectively.

The SelectionManager has been implemented in a limited number of features. Selection options in the SelectionManager include the following:

- **OK.** Accepts the selection. This feature is also available on the RMB menu.

- **Cancel.** Quits the SelectionManager.

- **Clear All.** Clears the current selection set.

- **Push Pin.** Keeps the SmartSelection window available, even when it is not required for sketch entity selections.

- **Select Closed Loop.** You can select two different types of loops with this tool:
  - A parametric closed loop in a 2D or 3D sketch
  - A parametric loop of edges around a surface

- **Select Open Loop.** Selects a chain (end-to-end sketch entities).

- **Select Group.** Selects entities individually. If you click the Propagate symbol, all tangent edges are selected.

- **Select Region.** Works like the Contour Selection described earlier in this chapter.

- **Standard Selection.** Disables special functions of the SelectionManager. This feature works like a regular selection tool.

- **Auto OK Selections.** Becomes enabled when you use the Push Pin. Auto OK Selections works for closed and open loop selection.

Choosing loft options

You can choose from the following Loft options, as shown in Figure 7.17:

FIGURE 7.17

Loft options

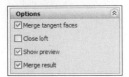

- **Merge tangent faces.** Merges model faces that are tangent into a single face. This is done behind the scenes by converting profiles into splines, which make approximations but are smoother than sketches with individual tangent line and arc entities.
- **Close loft.** The loft is made into a closed loop. At least three loft profiles must exist in order to use this option. Figure 7.18 shows a loft where the Close Loft option is used, and the loft sections are shown. This model is on the DVD with the filename `Chapter 7 – Closed Loft.sldprt`.

FIGURE 7.18

A closed loft

- **Show preview.** Selecting and deselecting this option turns the preview of the Loft feature on or off, respectively, if the feature is going to work. All the following loft preview options are system options and remain selected until you deselect them.
  - **Transparent/Opaque Preview** is available from the RMB menu when you edit a loft, if the SelectionManager is not active.
  - **Mesh Preview** is also available on the same RMB menu.
  - **Zebra Stripe Preview** is also available on the same RMB menu, and is covered in more depth in Chapter 12.

- **Merge result.** Merges the resulting solid body with any other solid bodies that it may contact.

Workflow

The workflow for the Loft feature is as follows:

1. Create or have available a set of profiles, including sketches or faces. All sketches must be closed loop and not active.
2. Select profiles and guide curves as necessary.
3. Select the required options as the situation requires.
4. Click OK to accept the feature.

Controlling Sweep features

The Sweep feature uses multiple sketches. A sweep is made from a profile (cross-section) and a path, and can create a boss or a cut feature. If you want, you can also use guide curves. Sweeps can run the gamut from simple to complex. Typical simple sweeps are used to create wire, tubing, or hose. Sweeps that are more complex are used for creating objects such as bottles, involutes, springs, and corkscrews.

The main criteria for selecting a sweep to create a feature are that you must be able to identify a cross-section and a path. The profile (cross-section) can change along the path, but the overall shape must remain the same. The profile is typically perpendicular to the path, although this is not a requirement.

Using a simple sweep

An example of a simple sweep is shown in Figure 7.19. The paper clip uses a circle as the profile and the coiled lines and arcs as the path.

FIGURE 7.19

The sweep profile follows the path.

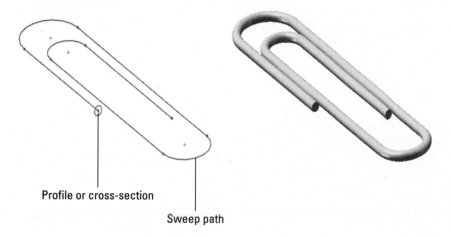

Profile or cross-section

Sweep path

Using a sweep with guide curves

Sweeps that are more complex begin to control the size, orientation, and position of the cross-section as it travels through the sweep. When you use a guide curve, several analogies can be used to visualize how the sweep works. The cross-section/profile is solved at several intermediate positions along the path. If the guide curve does not follow the path, the difference between the two is made up by adjusting the profile. Consider the following example. In this case, the profile is an ellipse, the path is a straight line, and there are guide curves that give the feature its outer shape. Figure 7.20 shows all these elements and the finished feature.

FIGURE 7.20

The sweep profile follows the path and is controlled parametrically by guide curves.

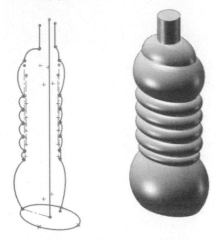

On the DVD

The part shown in Figure 7.20 is on the DVD with the filename Chapter7 Bottle.sldprt. ∎

The PropertyManager for the Sweep function includes an option for Show Sections, which in this case creates almost 200 intermediate cross-sections. These sections are used behind the scenes to create a loft. You can think of complex sweeps with guide curves or centerlines as an automated setup for an even more complex loft. It is helpful to envision features such as this when you are troubleshooting or setting up sweeps that are more complex. If you open the part mentioned previously from the DVD, you can edit the Sweep feature to examine the sections for yourself.

In most other published SolidWorks materials that cover these topics, sweeps are covered before lofts because many people consider lofts the more advanced topic. However, I have put lofts first because understanding them is necessary before you can understand complex sweeps, as complex sweeps really are just lofts.

Using a Pierce relation

The Pierce sketch relation is the only sketch relation that applies to a 3D out-of-plane edge or curve without projecting the edge or curve into the sketch plane. It acts as if the 3D curve is a length of string and the sketch point is the hole in the center of a bead where the string pierces the hole in the bead. The Pierce relation is most important in the Sweep feature when it is applied in the profile sketch between endpoints, centerpoints, or sketch points and the out-of-plane guide curves. This is because the Pierce relation determines how the profile sketch will be solved when it is moved down the sweep path to create intermediate profiles.

Figure 7.21 illustrates the function of the Pierce relation in a sweep with guide curves. The dark section on the left is the sweep section that is sketched. The lighter sketches to the right represent the intermediate profiles that are automatically created behind the scenes and are used internally to create the loft.

FIGURE 7.21

The effects of the Pierce relation

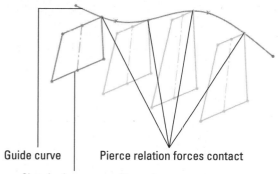

Guide curve   Pierce relation forces contact

Sketched sweep profile

Figure 7.21 shows what is happening behind the scenes in a sweep feature. The sweep re-creates the original profile at various points along the path. The guide curve in this case forces the profile to rebuild with a different shape. Pierce constraints are not required in simple sweeps, but when you start using guide curves, you should also use a pierce.

Tip

If you feel that you need more profile control, but still want to create a sweep-like feature, try a centerline loft. The centerline acts like a sweep path that doesn't touch the profiles, but unlike a sweep, you can use multiple profiles with it. ∎

Figure 7.22 shows a more complicated 3D sweep, where both the path and the guide curve are 3D curves. I cover 3D curves in Chapter 8; you can refer to these sections to understand how this part is made.

On the DVD

The part shown in Figure 7.22 is on the DVD with the filename `Chapter 7 3D Sweep.sldprt`.∎

This part is created by making a pair of tapered helices, with the profile sketch plane perpendicular to the end of one of the curves. The taper on the outer helix is greater than on the inner one, which causes the twist to become larger in diameter as it goes up.

FIGURE 7.22

A 3D sweep

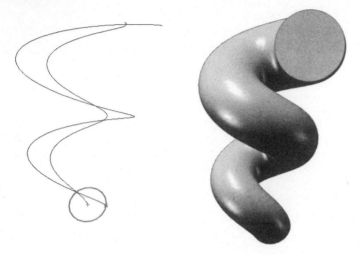

To make the circle follow both helices, you must create two pierce relations, one between the center of the circle and a helix, and the other between a sketch point that is placed on the circumference of the circle and the other helix. This means that the difference in taper angles between the two helices is what drives the change in diameter of the sweep.

Using a cut sweep with a solid profile

The Cut Sweep feature has an option to use a solid sweep profile. This kind of functionality has many uses, but is primarily intended for simulating complex cuts made by a mill or lathe. Figure 7.23 shows a couple of examples of cuts you can make with this feature. The part used for this screen shot is also on the DVD.

FIGURE 7.23

Cuts you can make with the Cut Sweep feature using a solid profile

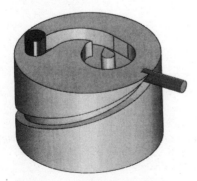

The solid profile cut sweep has a few limitations that I need to mention:

- It uses a separate solid body as the cutting tool, so you have to model multi-bodies.
- The path must start at a point where it intersects the solid cutting tool body (path starts inside or on the surface of the cutting tool).
- The cutting tool must be definable with a revolved feature.
- The cutting tool must be made of simple analytical faces (sphere, torus, cylinder, and cone; no splines).
- You cannot use a guide curve with a solid profile cut (cannot control alignment).
- The cut can intersect itself, but the path cannot cross itself.

You can create many useful shapes with the solid profile cut sweep, but because of some of the limitations I've listed, some shapes are more difficult to create than others. For these shapes, you might choose to use regular cut sweep features. Figure 7.24 shows an example of a cam-like feature that you may want to create with this method, but may not be able to adequately control the cutting body.

FIGURE 7.24

Controlling a cam cut can be a challenge.

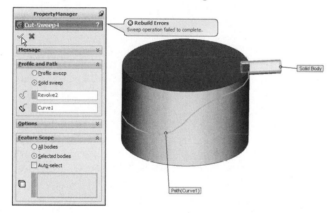

Workflow

Use the following general steps to create sweep features:

1. Create the path first. It may be tempting to create the profile first, but as a general rule, things work out better if you make the path first.
2. Create guide curves. Again, these work out better if you create them before the profile.
3. Create the profile (sweep cross-section) and relate it to the path with a Pierce sketch relation. Select a point in the sweep profile that you want to be driven down the path, like a bead follows a string.
4. Make sure that, as the profile is driven down the path (with the profile sketch plane maintaining its original relationship with the path), the profile has the flexibility to change the way it needs to. The sketch is re-evaluated at each point along the path. Use relative relations (parallel, perpendicular, and so on) instead of absolute ones (horizontal, vertical, fixed).

5. Start the Sweep feature from the toolbar or menu (all sketches must be closed).

6. Select the profile first, then the path. SolidWorks automatically toggles from the profile selection box to the path selection box as soon as a profile is selected, so take advantage of this automation to help you work quickly. Pay attention to any tool tip warnings or error messages that come up. If you are not able to select something, it is usually because there is something about that entity that is inappropriate for the purpose you are trying to assign to it.

7. Use the preview to check that it is performing the way you want it to. Click OK when you are satisfied with the result.

Understanding Fillet Types

SolidWorks offers very powerful filleting functions. The Fillet feature comprises various types of fillets and blends. Simple fillets on straight and round edges are handled differently from variable radius fillets, which are handled differently from the single or double hold line fillet or setback fillets. Once you click the OK button to create a fillet as a certain type, you cannot switch it to another type. You can switch types only before you create an established fillet feature.

Many filleting options are available, but most of them are relatively little used or even known. In fact, most users confine themselves to the constant radius or variable radius fillets. The following section describes all the available fillet types and options:

- Constant radius fillet
  - Multiple radius fillet
  - Round corners
  - Keep edge/Keep surface
  - Keep feature
- Variable radius fillet
- Face fillet
  - Curvature continuous fillet
  - Face fillet with Help Point
  - Single hold line fillet
  - Double hold line fillet
  - Constant width fillet
- Full round fillet
- Setback fillet
- Setback fillet with variable radius

Figure 7.25 shows the Fillet PropertyManager. Other options affect preview and selection of items, and these options are discussed in this section.

FIGURE 7.25

The Fillet PropertyManager

Creating a constant radius fillet

Constant radius fillets are the most common type that are created if you select only edges, features, or faces without changing any settings. When applying fillets in large numbers, you should consider several best practice guidelines and other recommendations that come later in this chapter.

There are still some longtime users who distinguish between fillets and rounds (where fillets add material and rounds remove it). SolidWorks does not distinguish between the two, and even two edges that are selected for use with the same fillet feature can have opposite functions; for example, both adding and removing material in a single feature.

Selecting entities to fillet

You can create fillets from several selections, including edges, faces, features, and loops. Edges offer the most direct method and are the easiest to control. Figure 7.26 shows how you can use each of these selections to create fillets on parts more intelligently.

Tip

To select features for filleting, you must select them from the FeatureManager. The Selection Filter only filters edges and faces for fillet selection. You can select loops in two ways: through the right-click Select Loop option or by selecting a face and Ctrl+selecting an edge on the face.

Another option for selecting edges in the Fillet command is the Select Through Faces option, which appears on the Fillet Options panel. This option enables you to select edges that are hidden by the model. This can be a useful option on a part with few hidden edges, or a detrimental option on a part where there are many edges due to patterns, ribs, vents, or existing fillets. You can control a similar option globally for features other than fillets by choosing Tools ➪ Options ➪ Display/Selection, Allow Selection In HLR [Hidden Lines Removed], and Shaded Modes. ∎

Selection options for fillets

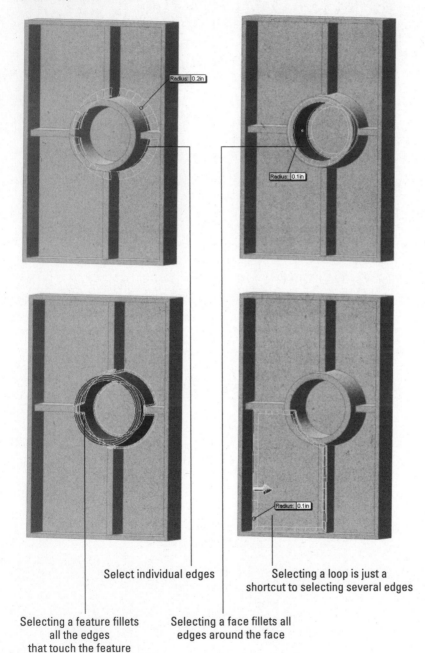

Select individual edges

Selecting a loop is just a
shortcut to selecting several edges

Selecting a feature fillets
all the edges
that touch the feature

Selecting a face fillets all
edges around the face

Faces and Features selections are useful when you are creating fillets where you want the selections to update. In Figure 7.27, the ribs that are intersecting the circular boss are also being filleted. If the rib did not exist when the fillet was applied, but was added later and reordered so that it came before the Fillet feature; then the fillet selection automatically considers the rib. If the fillet used edge selection, this automatic selection updating would not have taken place.

Using tangent propagation

By default, fillets have the Tangent Propagation option turned on. This is usually a good choice, although there may be times when you want to experiment with turning it off. Tangent propagation simply means that if you select an edge to fillet, and this edge is tangent to other edges, then the fillet will keep going along tangent edges until it forms a closed loop, the tangent edges stop, or the fillet fails.

FIGURE 7.27

Deselecting the Tangent Propagation option

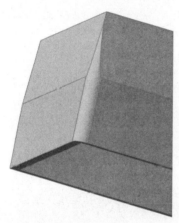

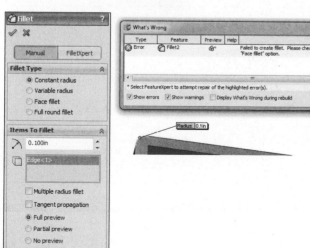

If you deselect Tangent Propagation, but there are still tangent edges, you may see different results. One possible result is that it could fail. One of the tricks with fillet features is to try to envision what you are asking the software to do. For example, if one edge is filleted and the next edge is not, then how is the fillet going to end? Figure 7.27 shows two of the potential results when fillets are asked not to propagate. The fillet face may continue along its path until it runs off the part or until the feature fails.

Tip

This may sound counterintuitive, but sometimes when fillet features fail, it may be useful to deselect propagation and make the fillet in multiple features. There are times when creating two fillets like the one shown in Figure 7.27 will work, and making the same geometry as a single feature will not. This may be due to geometry problems where the sharp edges come together and are eliminated by the fillet. ■

Best Practice

In general, fillets should be the last features that are applied to a model, particularly the small cosmetic or edge break fillets. Larger fillets that contribute to the structure or overall shape of the part may be applied earlier.

Be careful of the rock-paper-scissors game that you inevitably are caught up in when modeling plastic parts and deciding on the feature order of fillets, draft, and shell. Most fillets should come after draft, and large fillets should come before the shell. Draft may come either before or after the shell, depending on the needs of the area that you are dealing with on the part. In short, there is no single set of rules that you can consistently apply and that works best in all situations. ■

Dealing with a large number of fillets

Figure 7.28 shows a model with a bit of a filleting nightmare. This large plastic tray requires many ribs underneath for strength. Because the ribs may be touched by the user, the sharp edges need to be rounded. Interior edges need to be rounded also for strength and plastic flow through the ribs. Literally hundreds of edges would need to be selected to create the fillets if you do not use an advanced technique.

FIGURE 7.28

A plastic tray with a large number of fillets

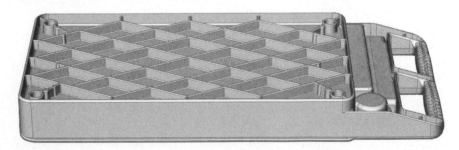

Selecting entities

Some of the techniques outlined previously, such as face and feature selection, can be useful for quickly filleting a large number of edges. Another method that still selects a large number of edges, but is not as intuitive as the others, is window selection of the edges. To use this option effectively, you may want to first position the model into a view where only the correct edges will be selected, turn off the Select Through Faces option, and use the Edges selection filter.

Using the FilletXpert

The FilletXpert is a tool with several uses. One of the functions is its capability to select multiple edges. A part like the one shown in Figure 7.28 is ideal for this tool. To use the FilletXpert, click the FilletXpert button in the Fillet PropertyManager. Figure 7.29 shows this. When you select an edge, the FilletXpert presents a popup tool bar giving you a choice of several selection options. Notice that Figure 7.29 shows the majority of the edges selected that are needed for this fillet.

FIGURE 7.29

Using the FilletXpert selection technique

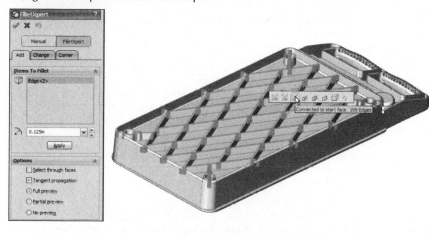

The FilletXpert is also a tool that automatically finds solutions to complex fillet problems, particularly when you have several fillets of different sizes coming together.

The Corner tab of the FilletXpert enables you to select from different corner options, which are usually the result of different fillet orders. To use the CornerXpert, make sure the FilletXpert is active; then click the corner face, and toggle through the options.

Using preview

I like to use the fillet preview. It helps to see what the fillet will look like, and perhaps more important, the presence of a preview usually (but not always) means that the fillet will work.

Unfortunately, when you have a large number of fillets to create, the preview can cause a significant slowdown. Deselecting and using the Partial Preview are both possible options. Partial Preview shows the fillet on only one edge in the selection and is much faster when you are creating a large number of fillets.

Performance

For rebuild speed efficiency, you should make fillets in a minimum number of features. For example, if you have 100 edges to fillet, it is better for performance to do it with a single fillet feature that has 100 edges selected rather than 100 fillet features that have one edge selected. This is the one case where creating the feature and rebuilding the feature are both faster by choosing a particular technique. (Usually if it is faster to create, it rebuilds more slowly.) ∎

Best Practice

Although creation and rebuild speed are in sync when you use the minimum number of features to create the maximum number of fillets, this is not usually the case. (There had to be a downside.) When a single feature has a large selection, any one of these edges that fail to fillet will cause the entire feature to fail. As a result, a feature with 100 edges selected is 100 times more likely to fail than a feature with a single edge. Large selection sets are also far more difficult to troubleshoot when they fail than small selection sets that fail. ∎

Using folders

When you have a large number of fillet features, it can be tedious to navigate the FeatureManager. Therefore, it is useful to place groups of fillets into folders. This makes it easy to suppress or unsuppress all the fillets in the folder at once. Separate folders can be particularly useful if the fillets have different uses, such as fillets that are used for PhotoWorks models and fillets that are removed for FEA (Finite Element Analysis) or drawings.

Making multiple fillet sizes

The Multiple radius fillet option in the Fillet PropertyManager enables you to make multiple fillet sizes within a single fillet feature. Figure 7.30 shows how the Multiple radius fillet feature looks when you are working with it. You can change values in the callout flags or in the PropertyManager.

FIGURE 7.30

Using the Multiple radius fillet option

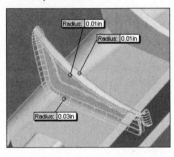

This may seem like an attractive way to group several fillets into as small a space on the FeatureManager as possible, but I cannot think of a single reason that would drive me to use this option. While there may be a small performance benefit to condensing several features into one, many more downsides adversely affect performance:

- Loss of control of feature order.
- A single failed fillet causes the whole feature, and thus all the fillets, to fail.
- Troubleshooting is far more difficult.
- Smaller groups of fillets cannot be suppressed without suppressing everything.
- You cannot change the size of a group of fillets together.

Best Practice

While this may be more personal opinion than best practice, I believe that there are good reasons to consider using techniques other than single features that contain many fillets, or single features that drive fillets of various sizes. Best practice would lean more toward grouping fillets that have a similar use and the same size. For example, you may want to separate fillets that break corners on ribs from fillets that round the outer shape of a large plastic part.

Another consideration is feature order when it comes to the fillet's relationship to draft and shell features. If the fillets are all grouped into a single feature, then controlling this relationship becomes impossible. ■

Rounding corners

The Round corners option refers to how SolidWorks handles fillets that go around sharp corners. By default, this setting is off, which leaves fillets around sharp corners looking like mitered picture frames. If you turn this setting on, the corner looks like a marble has rolled around it. Figure 7.31 shows the resulting geometry from both settings.

FIGURE 7.31

The Round corners option, both on and off

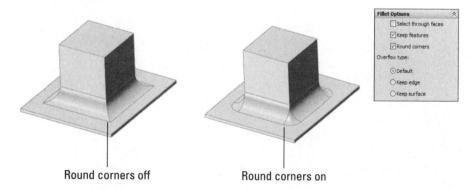

Round corners off   Round corners on

Using the Keep edge/Keep surface toggle

The Keep edge/Keep surface toggle determines what SolidWorks should do if a fillet is too big to fit in an area. The Keep edge option keeps the edge where it is and tweaks the position (not the radius) of the fillet to make it meet the edge. The Keep surface option keeps the surfaces of the fillet and the end face clean; however, to do this, it has to tweak the edge. There is often a tradeoff when you try to place fillets into a space that is too small. Sometimes it is useful to try to visualize what you think the result should look like. Figure 7.32 shows how the fillet would look in a perfect world, followed by how the fillet looks when cramped with the Keep edge option and how it looks when cramped with the Keep surface option.

FIGURE 7.32

The Keep edge option and the Keep surface option

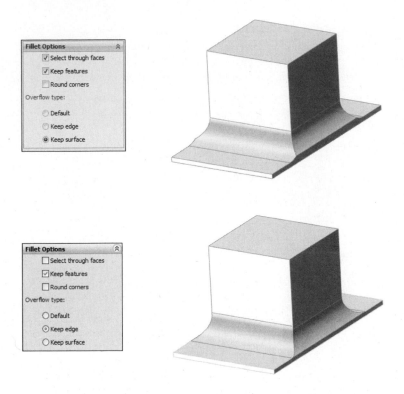

The Default option chooses the best option for a particular situation. As a result, it seems to use the Keep edge option unless it does not work, in which case it changes to the Keep surface option.

Using the Keep Feature option

The Keep Feature option appears on the Fillet Options panel of the Fillet PropertyManager. By default, this option is turned on. If a fillet surrounds a feature such as a hole (as long as it is not a through hole) or a boss, then deselecting the Keep Feature option removes the hole or boss. When Keep Feature is selected, the faces of the feature trim or extend to match the fillet, as shown in Figure 7.33.

FIGURE 7.33

The Keep Feature option, both selected and unselected

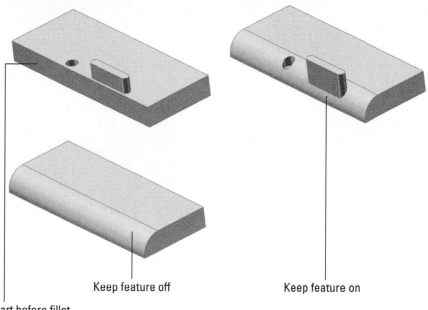

Keep feature off

Keep feature on

Part before fillet

Creating variable radius fillets

Variable radius fillets are another powerful weapon in the fight against boring designs; they also double as a useful tool to solve certain problems that arise. Although it is difficult to define exactly when to use the variable radius fillet, you can use it when you need a fillet to round an edge, and it has to change in size to fit the available geometry.

Best Practice

It may be easier to identify when not to use a variable radius fillet. Fillets are generally used to round or break edges, not to sculpt a part. If you are using fillets to sculpt blocky parts and are not actively trying to make blocky parts with big fillets, you may want to consider another approach and use complex modeling, which gives the part a better shape and makes it more controllable. Other options exist that give you a different type of control, such as the double hold line fillet. ■

In some ways, variable radius fillets function like other fillets. For example, they offer propagation to tangent edges and preview options.

Applying the values

When you first select an edge for the variable radius fillet, the endpoints are identified by callout flags with the value *unassigned*. A preview does not display until at least one of the points has a radius value in the box. You can also apply radius values in the PropertyManager, but they are easier to keep track of using the callouts. Figure 7.34 shows a variable radius fillet after the edge selection, after one value has been applied, and after three values have been applied. To apply a radius value that is not at the endpoint of an edge, you can select one of the three colored dots along the selected edge. The preview should show you how the fillet will look in wireframe display.

FIGURE 7.34

Assigning values to a variable radius fillet

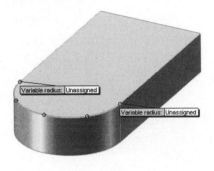

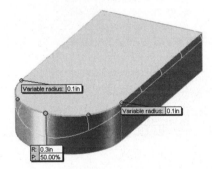

By default, the variable radius fillet puts five points on an edge, one at each endpoint, one at the midpoint, and one each halfway between the ends and middle. If you want to create an additional control point, there are three ways to do it:

- Ctrl+drag an existing point.
- Select the callout of an existing point and change the P (percentage) value.
- Change the Number of Instances value in the Variable Radius Parameters panel of the PropertyManager.

If you have selected several edges, and several unassigned values are on the screen, then you can use the Set Unassigned option in the PropertyManager to set them all to the same value. The Set All option sets all radius values to the same number, including any values that you may have changed to be different than the rest. Figure 7.35 shows the Variable Radius Parameters panel.

FIGURE 7.35

The Variable Radius Parameters panel of the Fillet PropertyManager

Another available option with the variable radius fillet is that you can set a value of zero at an end of the fillet. You need to be careful about using a zero radius, because it is likely to cause downstream problems with other fillets, shells, offsets, and even machining operations. You cannot assign a zero radius in the middle of an edge, only at the end. If you need to end a fillet at a particular location, you can use a split line to split the edge and apply a zero radius at that point. (Chapter 8 covers split lines.) Figure 7.36 shows a part with two zero-radius values.

The image on the right shows Instant3D being used to edit a variable radius fillet. Select the face of the fillet with Instant3D turned on, and blue dots appear where ever radius values are assigned. You can move these dots to dynamically edit the corresponding value of the variable radius.

FIGURE 7.36

Zero-radius values in the variable radius fillet

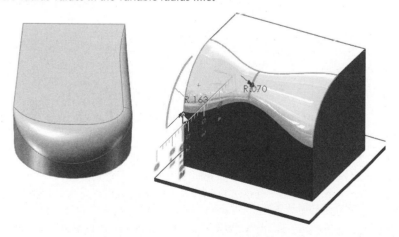

Using straight versus smooth transitions

Variable radius fillets have an option for either a straight transition or a smooth transition. This works like the two-profile lofts that were mentioned earlier in this chapter. The names may be somewhat misleading because both transitions are smooth. The straight transition goes in a straight line, from one size to the next, and the smooth transition takes a swooping S-shaped path between the sizes. The difference between these two transitions is demonstrated in Figure 7.37.

Straight versus smooth transitions of a variable radius fillet

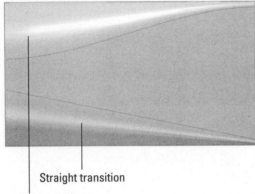

Straight transition

Smooth transition

Recognizing other uses for the variable radius fillet

Variable radius fillets use a different method to create the fillet geometry than the default constant radius fillet. Sometimes using a variable radius fillet can make a difference where a constant radius fillet does not work. This is sometimes true even when the variable radius fillet uses constant radius values. It is just another tool in the toolbox.

Using face fillets

Face fillets may be the most flexible type of fillet because of the range of what they can do. Face fillets start as simply an alternate selection technique for a constant radius fillet and extend to the extremely flexible double hold line face fillet, which is more of a blend than a fillet.

Under normal circumstances, the default fillet type uses the selection of an edge to create the fillet. An edge is used because it represents the intersection between two faces. However, there can sometimes be a problem with the edge not being clean or being broken up into smaller pieces, or any number of other reasons causing a constant radius fillet using an edge selection to fail. In cases like this, SolidWorks displays the error message, "Failed to create fillet. Please check the input geometry and radius values or try using the 'Face Fillet' option."

Users almost universally ignore these messages. In the situation shown in Figure 7.38, the Face Fillet option suggested in the error message is exactly the one that you should use. Here the face fillet covers over all the junk on the edge that prevents the fillet from executing.

FIGURE 7.38

A face fillet covering a bad corner

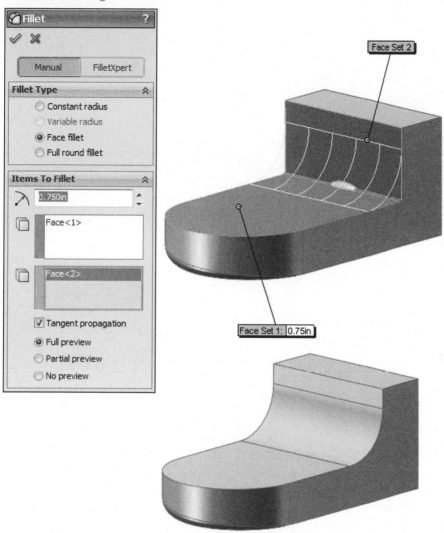

Face fillets are sometimes amazing at covering over a mess of geometry that you might think you could never fillet. The main limitation on fillets of this type is that the fillet must be *big* enough to bridge the gap. That's right, I said *big* enough. Face fillets can fail if they are either too small or too large. Figure 7.39 shows a complex fillet situation that is completely covered by a face fillet.

FIGURE 7.39

A face fillet covering complex geometry

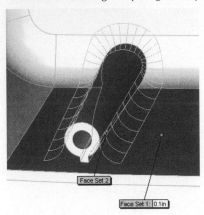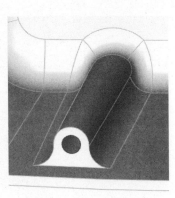

On the DVD

The model used for this image can be found on the DVD, with the filename `Chapter 7 Plastic Cover Fillets.sldprt`. ∎

Using continuous curvature face fillets

Curvature continuity refers to the quality of a transition between two curves or faces, where the curvature is the same or continuous at and around the transition. The best way to convey this concept is with simple 2D sketch elements. When a line transitions to an arc, you have non-continuous curvature. The line has no curvature, and there is an abrupt change because the arc has a specific radius.

Note

Radius is the inverse of curvature, and so $r = 1/c$. For a straight line, $r = \infty$, in which case $c = 0$. ∎

To make the transition from $r = \infty$ to $r = 2$ smoothly, you would need to use a variable radius arc if such a thing existed. There are several types of sketch geometry that have variable curvature, such as ellipses, parabolas, and splines. Ellipses and parabolas follow specific mathematical formulas to create the shape, but the spline is a general curve that can take on any shape that you want, and you can control its curvature to change smoothly or continuously. Splines, by their very definition, have continuous curvature within the spline, although you cannot control the specific curvature or radius values directly.

All this means that continuous curvature Face fillets use a spline-based variable-radius section for the fillet, rather than an arc-based constant radius. Figure 7.40 illustrates the difference between continuous curvature and constant curvature. The spikes on top of the curves represent the curvature (1/r, and so the smaller the radius, the taller the spike). These spikes are called a *curvature comb*.

FIGURE 7.40

Using curvature combs to evaluate transitions

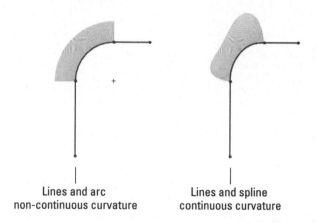

Lines and arc
non-continuous curvature

Lines and spline
continuous curvature

In comparison to Figure 7.41, notice how the curvature comb immediately jumps from no curvature to the constant arc radius, but the spline image ramps up to a curvature that varies.

Using face fillets with the Help Point

The Help Point in the Face Fillet PropertyManager is a fairly obscure option. However, it is useful in cases where the selection of two faces does not uniquely identify an edge to fillet. For example, Figure 7.41 shows a situation where the selection of two faces could result in either one edge or the other being filleted (normally, I would hope that both edges would be filleted). The fillet will default to one edge or the other, but you can force it to a definite edge using the Help Point.

In some cases, the Help Point is ignored altogether. For example, if you have a simple box, and select both ends of the box as selection set 1, and the top of the box as selection set 2, then the fillet could go to either end. Consequently, assigning a Help Point will not do anything in this case, because multiple faces have been selected. The determining factor is which of the multiple faces is selected first. If this were a more commonly used feature, the interface for it might be made a little less cryptic, but because this feature is rarely, if ever, used, it just becomes a quirky piece of trivia.

FIGURE 7.41

Using a Help Point with a face fillet

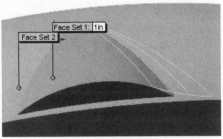

Face fillet defaults
to the right side

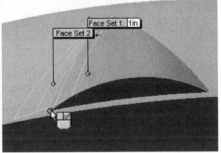

Selecting the Help point
forces it to the other side

Applying a single hold line fillet

A single hold line fillet is a form of variable radius fillet. Rather than the radius being driven by specific numerical values, it is driven by a hold line, or edge, on the model. The hold line can be an existing edge, forcing the fillet right up to the edge of the part, or it can be created by a split line, which enables you to drive the fillet however you like. Figure 7.42 shows these two options, before and after the fillets. Notice that these fillets are still arc-based fillets; if you were to take a cross-section perpendicular to the edge between filleted faces, it would be an arc cross-section with a distinct radius.

However, in the other direction, hold line fillets do not necessarily have a constant radius, although they may if the hold line is parallel with the edge between faces.

You can select the hold line in the Fillet Options panel of the Face Fillet PropertyManager, as shown in Figure 7.43. The top panel, Fillet Type, is available only when the feature is first created. When you edit it after it has been created, the Fillet Type panel does not appear. As a result, you cannot change from one top-level type of fillet to another after it has been initially created.

FIGURE 7.42

Single hold line fillets

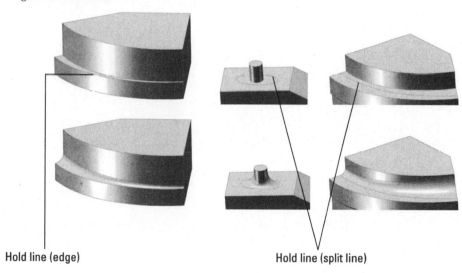

Hold line (edge)   Hold line (split line)

FIGURE 7.43

The PropertyManager interface for the hold line face fillet

Using a double hold line fillet

There are times when a single hold line does not meet your needs. The single hold line controls only one side of the fillet, and in order to control both sides of the fillet, you must use a double hold line fillet. SolidWorks software does not specifically differentiate between the single and double hold line fillets, but they are radically different in how they create the geometry. When both sides of the fillet are controlled, it is not possible to span between the hold lines with an arc that is tangent to both sides unless you were careful about setting up the hold lines so that they are equidistant from the edge where the faces intersect. This means that the double hold line fillet must use a spline to span between hold lines, as shown in Figure 7.44.

To get this feature to work, you need to use the curvature continuous option in the Fillet Options panel. Remember that this option creates a spline-based fillet rather than an arc-based fillet, which is exactly what you need for a double hold line fillet. This makes the double hold line fillet more of a blend than a true fillet. This requirement is not obvious to most users and may not even be documented in the SolidWorks Help, nor is it exactly intuitive. To get the double hold line fillet to work, you must use the curvature continuous option. Figure 7.45 shows examples of the double hold line fillet.

FIGURE 7.44

A double hold line uses a spline, not an arc.

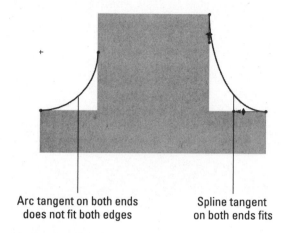

Arc tangent on both ends
does not fit both edges

Spline tangent
on both ends fits

FIGURE 7.45

Examples of the double hold line fillet

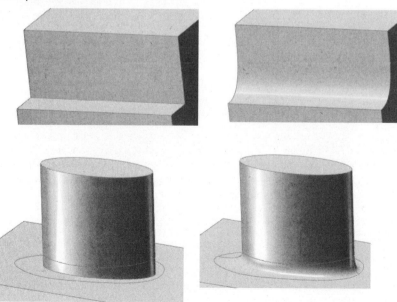

Using a constant width fillet

The Constant width option of the Face Fillet PropertyManager drives a fillet by its width rather than by its radius. This is most helpful on parts where the angle of the faces between which you are filleting is changing dramatically. Figure 7.46 illustrates two situations where this is particularly useful. The setting for constant width is found in the Options panel of the Face Fillet PropertyManager. The part shown in the images is on the DVD as `Chapter 7 Constant Width.sldprt`.

FIGURE 7.46

The constant width fillet

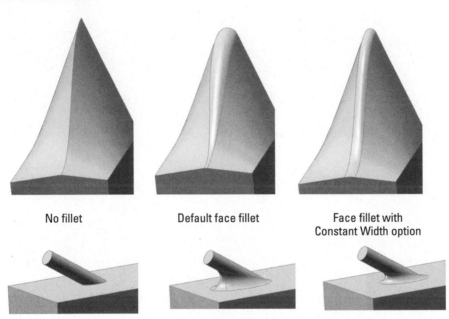

No fillet   Default face fillet   Face fillet with
                                                   Constant Width option

Applying a full round fillet

The full round fillet is very useful in many situations. In fact, it may actually work in situations where you would not expect it to. It does require quite a bit of effort to accomplish the selection, but it compensates by enabling you to avoid alternate fillet techniques.

To create a full round fillet, you have to select three sets of faces. Usually one face in each set is sufficient. The fillet is tangent to all three sets of faces, but the middle set is on the end and the face is completely eliminated. Figure 7.47 shows several applications of the full round fillet. Notice that it is not limited to faces of a square block, but also propagates around tangent entities and can create a variable radius fillet over irregular lofted geometry.

FIGURE 7.47

A full round fillet

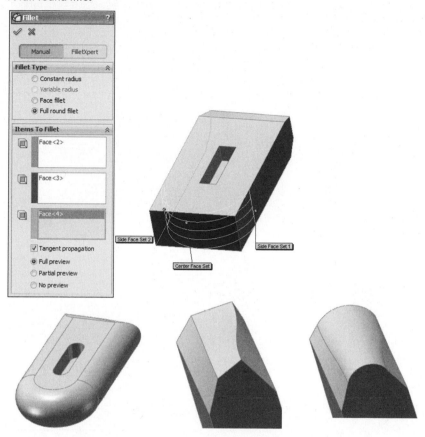

Note

Be aware that special workflow assisting options exist for the full round fillet. After selecting a face, you can click the right mouse button to advance to the next selection box, or if you are already at the last selection box, you can click OK and finish the feature. You might instinctively reach for the Tab key, but remember to look at the cursor to find that backwards green L-shaped arrow or the check mark. ∎

Building a setback fillet

The setback fillet is the most complex of the fillet options. You can use the Setback option in conjunction with constant radius, multiple radius, and variable radius fillet types. A setback fillet blends several fillets together at a single vertex, starting the blend at some "setback" distance along each filleted edge from the vertex. At least three, and often more, edges come together at the setback vertex. Figure 7.48 shows the PropertyManager interface and what a finished setback fillet looks like. The following steps demonstrate how to use the setback fillet.

FIGURE 7.48

The Setback Fillet interface and a finished fillet

Setback vertices: All edges coming
to these vertices will be filleted

Setting up a setback fillet can take some time, especially if you are just learning about this feature. You must specify values for fillet radiuses, select edges and vertices, and specify three setback distances for every vertex. If you are using multiple radius fillets or variable radius fillets, then this becomes an even larger task. The steps are as follows:

1. **Determine the type of fillet to be used:**
   - Constant radius fillet
   - Multiple radius fillet
   - Variable radius fillet
2. **Select the edges to be filleted.** Selected edges must all touch one of the setback vertices that will be selected in a later step.
3. **Assign radius values for the filleted items.** Figure 7.49 shows a sample part that illustrates this step.

FIGURE 7.49

The setback fillet setup for Steps 1 through 3

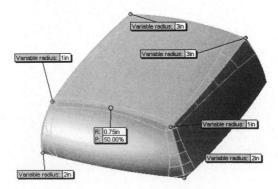

4. **Select the setback vertices.** In the Setback Parameters panel of the PropertyManager, with the second box from the top highlighted, select the vertices. Although this box looks like it is only big enough for a single selection, it can accept multiple selections.

5. **Enter setback values.** As shown in Figure 7.50, the setback callout flags have leaders that point from a specific value to a specific edge. Alternately, you could use the Set All or Set Unassigned options in a similar way to how they are used with the variable radius fillet interface. The dimensions refer to distances, as shown in the image to the right in Figure 7.50. The setback distance is the distance over which the fillet will blend from the corner to the fillet.

FIGURE 7.50

Entering setback values

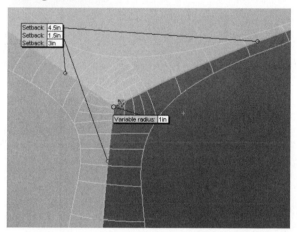

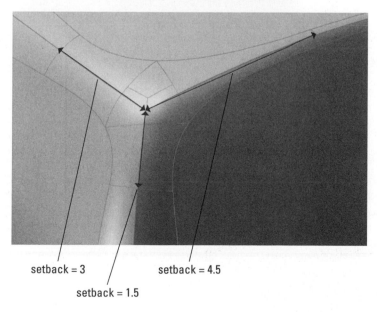

setback = 3

setback = 4.5

setback = 1.5

Caution

When you select multiple vertices, the preview arrows that indicate which edge you are currently setting the set-back value for may be incorrect. The arrows can only be shown on one vertex; therefore, you may want to rely on the leaders from the callouts to determine which setback distance you are currently setting. ■

6. **Repeat the process for all selected setback vertices.** If you are using a preview, then you may notice that the preview goes away when starting a second set of setback values. Don't worry. This is probably not because the feature is going to fail. Once you finish typing the values, the preview will return. When you have spent as much time setting up a feature as you will spend on this, seeing the preview disappear can be frustrating; however, persevere, and it will return.

Using Chamfers

Chamfers in SolidWorks are not as flashy as fillets, but they do have some useful functionality. Some similarities exist between chamfers and fillets, such as the propagation to tangent edges, selecting faces to select the loop of edges around the face, and the ability to see full, partial, or no preview of the finished feature. Many of the best practice ideas you can apply to fillets also apply to chamfers. Figure 7.51 shows the PropertyManager for chamfers.

FIGURE 7.51

Working with chamfer features

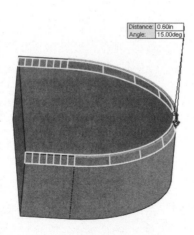

You can specify a chamfer using either an angle and a distance or two distance values. For most common situations, these methods are adequate. The situation becomes less definite if you are creating a chamfer between faces that are not at right angles to one another or may not even be planar. These situations require some experimentation to find the correct geometry.

When you create chamfers at angles other than 45 degrees, you can use the Flip Direction option to control the feature. It is important to note the difference between having direct control (angle the chamfer from *this* face) and indirect control (angle the chamfer from *the other* face). Indirect control is essentially trial and error. If you don't like what you are given automatically, you can try the other option.

The Flip Direction option flips the direction of all of the chamfers being created by a particular feature. This is obviously only important when you have chamfers that are made at an angle that is not 45 degrees, or unequal distances in the case of a distance-distance chamfer. So in some situations, where the default directions of more than a single edge are going in opposite directions, your only recourse is to create multiple chamfer features and control them independently.

One of the most interesting functions of the Chamfer tool is the vertex chamfer, shown in Figure 7.52. You can chamfer a corner with equal distances or distances along each edge. This feature can only be used at corners where three edges come together — standard block corners.

FIGURE 7.52

Applying a corner chamfer

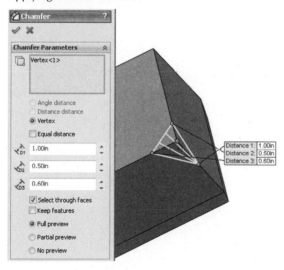

On the DVD

Check the DVD for video content for this chapter including video tutorials for Extrude options and Fillet options.

Tutorial: Bracket Casting

When you follow this tutorial, you are encouraged to follow the directions the first time to make sure that you understand the concepts involved, and then to go through it again, this time deviating from the Instructions to see If you can expand your understanding by experimentation. To try bracket casting, follow these steps:

1. Open a new part using an inch-based template.

2. On the Right plane, draw a circle centered at the origin with a diameter of 1.50 inches, and a second circle placed 4.000 inches vertically from the first, with a diameter of 2.250 inches.

3. Exit the sketch, and make sure Instant 3D is selected. The Instant 3D icon is on the Features toolbar, and looks like a ruler with an arrow. Click the sketch in the graphics window, and pull the Instant 3D arrow to create a solid. Edit the feature (right- or left-click the feature either in the graphics window or in the FeatureManager and click the Edit Feature icon, which is the yellow and green block with a hand pointing to it). Now enter numbers by hand so that you extrude the sketch 1.000 inch using a From condition of Offset by 1.000 inch, such that the offset and the extrude depth are in the same direction. Rename this feature **Bosses in the FeatureManager**. Figure 7.53 shows the results of these steps.

FIGURE 7.53

The results of Steps 1 to 3

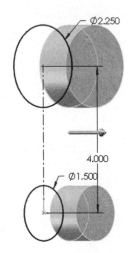

Note

These steps produce multiple bodies that will be merged in a later step. Multi-body parts are covered in more detail in Chapter 19. You can tell that there are multiple bodies by looking at the Solid Bodies folder near the top of the tree and expanding the folder. The bodies are listed in the folder. ∎

4. On the Top plane, open a new sketch and draw a horizontal construction line across the cylinder, from the midpoint of one side to the midpoint of the other side. To pick up the automatic relations for the midpoints more easily, it is recommended that you orient the view, normal to the sketch, or use the Top view. It does not matter if you make the relations to the top or bottom cylinder, because the midpoints of the sides are in the same place when they are projected into the sketch plane.

5. Next, draw an ellipse (Tools ⇨ Sketch Tools ⇨ Ellipse) centered at the midpoint of the construction line and that measures .700 inches horizontally and 1.375 inches

vertically. You may want to assign a relation between the center of the ellipse and one of the control points to prevent the ellipse from rotating and fully define the sketch Exit the sketch when you are satisfied with the result.

6. **Show the sketch for the Bosses feature.** Click the plus icon next to the Bosses extrude to show the sketch, and then right-click the sketch and select Show.

7. **Create a plane parallel to the Top plane at the center of the larger circle.** You can access the Plane creation interface by choosing Insert ⇨ Reference Geometry ⇨ Plane. If you pre-select the Top plane from the flyout FeatureManager and the center of the larger sketch circle from the graphics window, the interface automatically creates the correct plane. Click OK to create the plane. Rename this plane **Top Boss Plane.**

8. **Draw a second ellipse on the Top Boss Plane.** Do not draw a construction line as you did for the first ellipse; instead, you can just make the centerpoint of the second ellipse directly on top of the first ellipse's centerpoint. The dimensions should be 1.000 inch horizontal by 1.750 inches vertical. Figure 7.54 shows the results up to this point.

FIGURE 7.54

The results up to Step 8

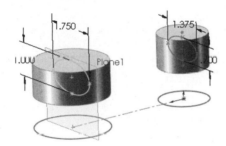

Tip

When you are sketching on parallel planes that are separated by some distance and trying to pick up automatic relations, it is often very helpful to be looking "normal to" the sketch, so that you can see how other entities are projected into the sketch plane. ■

9. **Use the Loft feature to loft between the two ellipses.** Be sure to select the ellipses in approximately the same location so that they do not twist. If the loft preview accidentally twists, then use the connectors (light-blue square dots on the sketches that are connected by a straight line) to straighten out the loft.

Note

Notice that this feature joined together the other two disjoint bodies with the body that was created by the loft into a single body. This is a result of selecting the Merge Result option in the Options panel. ■

Tip

If you want to experiment, expand the Start/End Constraints panel and apply end conditions for the loft. This causes the loft to change from a straight loft to a curved loft. ■

10. **Right-click all sketches that are showing, and select Hide.** Do the same for the Top Boss Plane. This cleans up the display to prevent it from becoming confusing. However, if you prefer to see the sketches, then you can leave them displayed.

Tip
You can either hide or show different types of entities in groups by using the View menu. Hide All Types hides everything, and disables the options for individual entity types to be used. ∎

11. **Open a sketch on the Right plane.** Sketch an ellipse such that the center is oriented 1.750 inches vertically from the Origin, and the ellipse measures .750 inches horizontally and 1.500 inches vertically.

12. **Extrude this ellipse using the Up To Next end condition.** If Up To Next does not appear in the list, then change the direction of the extrude and try it again.

13. **Show the sketch of the Bosses feature by expanding the feature (click the "+" next to it), right- or left-clicking the sketch icon, and clicking the Hide/Show icon (eyeglasses).** Next, open a sketch on the Right plane. Sketch two circles that are concentric with the original circles, with the dimensions of .875 inches and 1.250 inches. Exit the sketch.

14. **Use Instant 3D to create an extruded cut that goes through the large circular bosses.** This feature will look like a boss extrusion at first, so when you have finished dragging its depth, a small toolbar with two icons appears. One of the icons enables you to add draft; the other enables you to turn the boss into a cut. Figure 7.55 shows the state of the model up to this step.

FIGURE 7.55

The results up to Step 14

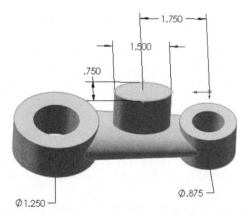

15. **Start a fillet feature, and select the face of the Loft feature.** Assign a radius of .200 inches.

Note

Although this fillet is created by selecting a face, it is not a face fillet. Selecting a face for a regular constant radius fillet simply fillets any edge that is on the face. ∎

16. **Create a mirror feature, using the Right plane as the mirror plane.** In the Mirror PropertyManager, expand the Bodies To Mirror panel, and select anywhere on the part. Make sure that the Merge Solids option is selected. Click OK to accept the mirror.

17. **Orient the view to the Front view, and then turn the view on its side (hold down Alt and press the left- or right-arrow key six times).**

18. **Open a new sketch on the Front plane.** From the View menu, make sure that Hide All Types is not selected, and show Temporary Axes. Draw and dimension a horizontal construction line, as shown in Figure 7.56.

The results up to Step 18

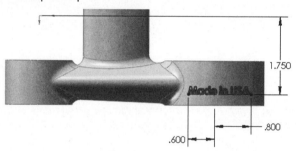

19. **With the construction line selected, start the Sketch Text command (Tools ⇨ Sketch Entities ⇨ Text).** Make sure that the line appears in the Curves selection box.

20. **Click in the text box, and type** Made in USA **(or your name or company name).** Select the text and click the Bold button. Deselect the Use Document Font option, change the font to use units, and set the height to .175 inches.

21. **Click OK to exit the Sketch Text PropertyManager, and click OK again to exit the sketch.** You can turn off the Temporary Axis display.

22. **Choose Insert ⇨ Features ⇨ Wrap.** You should be prompted to select a plane or a sketch. Use the Flyout FeatureManager to select the sketch that you just created with the sketch text in it. Next, select the cylindrical face of the boss to see a preview of the text wrapped onto the face. If the text appears backward, then select the Reverse Direction option in the Wrap PropertyManager.

23. **Select the Emboss option, and assign a thickness of .025 inches.** Click in the Pull Direction selection box and select the Front plane. Click OK to accept the feature.

24. **Save the part and close it.** If you would like to examine the reference part, you can find it on the DVD with the filename `Chapter 7 Tutorial Bracket Casting.sldprt`. The finished part is shown in Figure 7.57.

FIGURE 7.57

The finished part

Summary

SolidWorks has a wide selection of feature types to choose from, ranging from simple extrudes and revolves to more complex lofts and sweeps. Some features have so many options that it may be difficult to take them all in at once. You should browse through the models on the DVD for this chapter and use the Rollback bar (described in detail in Chapter 12) to examine how the parts were built. You can then try to create a few on your own. The best way to learn these features is to use them on practice parts, and through experimentation. Curiosity is your greatest teacher.

Selecting Secondary Features

When you need to create features that are somewhat outside of the mainstream, you may need to reach deeper into the depth of the SolidWorks toolbox. SolidWorks has a lot of functionality that lies out of the public eye that in certain situations may be just what you are looking for. You will probably not use the tools you find in this chapter every day, but knowing about them may mean the difference between having capability and not having it.

Creating Curve Features

Curves in SolidWorks are often used to help define sweeps and lofts, as well as other features. Curves differ from sketches in that curves are defined using sketches or a dialog box, and you cannot manipulate them directly or dimension them in the same way that you can sketches. Functions that you are accustomed to using with sketches often do not work on curves.

The curve features that this chapter deals with are:

- Projected curve
- Helix and Spiral
- Curve Through XYZ Points
- Curve Through Reference Points
- Composite curve
- Imported curve

Several features that carry the curve name are actually sketch-based features:

- 3D sketch
- Equation driven curve
- Intersection curve
- Face curves

IN THIS CHAPTER

Defining and creating curves in SolidWorks

Choosing an occasional specialty feature

Creating a wire-formed part tutorial

Split Line is another feature that can create edges on faces that can be used like curve features. Split Lines are not even remotely considered curves, but they can function in the same way in some situations, so this section discusses the Split Line along with the rest of the curve and other curvelike features.

Of these, the Projected and Helix curves are by far the most used, but the others may be important from time to time. Curve functions do not receive much attention from SolidWorks. Updates to curve features are few, and in some cases the functions are buggy. The usefulness of curve features is limited in the software, but in some cases there is not another good way to achieve the same result.

Tip

When you come across a function that does not work using a curve entity, but that works on a sketch (for example, making a tangent spline), it may help to use the Convert Entities function. Converting a helix into a 3D sketch creates a spline that lies directly on top of the helix and enables you to make another spline that is tangent to the new spline. ■

You can find all the curve functions on the Curves toolbar or by choosing Insert ➪ Curve from the menu.

Curve features in general have several limitations, some of which are serious. You often have to be prepared with workaround techniques when using them. When curves are used in features, you often cannot reselect the curve to reapply sketch broken sketch relations. (The workaround for this is to select the curve from the FeatureManager, or if that doesn't work, you may need to delete the feature and re-create it). In addition, curves cannot be mirrored, moved, patterned, or manipulated in any way. (A workaround for this may be to use Convert Entities to create a sketch from the curve, or to create a surface using the curve, and pattern or mirror the surface, using the edge of the surface in place of the curve feature.)

Working with Helix curve features

 The Helix curve types are all based on a circle in a sketch. The circle represents the starting location and diameter of the helix. Figure 8.1 shows the PropertyManagers of the Constant Pitch and Variable Pitch helix types.

You can create all the helical curve types by specifying some combination of total height, pitch, and the number of revolutions. The start angle is best thought of as a relative number. It is difficult to predict where zero degrees starts, and this depends on the relation of the sketch plane to the Origin. The start angle cannot be controlled outside of the PropertyManager and cannot be driven by sketch geometry. The term *pitch* refers to the straight-line distance along the axis between the rings of the helix. Pitch for the spiral is different and is described later.

Using the Tapered Helix panel

The Tapered Helix panel in the Helix PropertyManager enables you to specify a taper angle for the helix. The taper angle does not affect the pitch. If you need to affect both the taper and the pitch, then you can use a Variable Pitch helix. Figure 8.2 shows how the taper angle relates to the resulting geometry.

FIGURE 8.1

The Helix PropertyManager

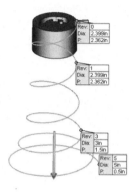

FIGURE 8.2

The Tapered Helix panel

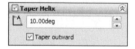
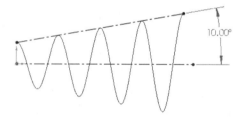

Using the Variable Pitch helix

You can specify the Variable Pitch helix either in the chart or in the callouts that are shown in Figure 8.3. Both the pitch and the diameter are variable. The diameter number in the first row cannot be changed but is driven by the sketch. In the chart shown, the transition between 4 and 4.5 revolutions is where the pitch and diameter both change.

SolidWorks 2011 adds functionality that allows you to double-click a Helix feature and it displays the dimensions on the screen, which you can then double-click and change, rather than going back through the Helix PropertyManager interface. These dimensions can also be configured, which is a new function for helix features. This makes the Helix feature more standardized with other SolidWorks features. Figure 8.4 shows the variable helix with dimensions displayed from double-click. Simpler helix features have fewer dimensions on the screen.

FIGURE 8.3

The Variable Pitch helix

	P	Rev	H	Dia
1	1in	0	0in	1.24in
2	1in	4	4in	1.24in
3	0.5in	4.5	4.375	0.75in
4	0.5in	10.5	7.375	0.75in
5				0.75in

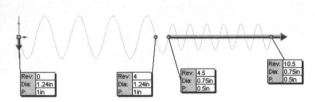

FIGURE 8.4

Double-click dimensions on a helix feature

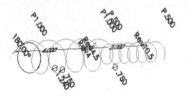

Workflow

The workflow for all of the Helix type curves is as follows:

1. Draw a circle, or select an existing circle.
2. Start the Helix command.
3. Set the options.
4. Click the green check to accept the feature.

Using the Spiral

A spiral is a flattened (planar) tapered helix. The pitch value on a spiral is the radial distance between revolutions of the curve.

Creating projected curves

The two types of projected curves are:

- Sketch On Faces
- Sketch On Sketch

These names can be misleading if you do not already know what they mean. In both cases, the word *sketch* is used as a noun, not a verb, so you are not actively sketching on a surface; instead, you are creating a curve by projecting a sketch onto a face.

Using Sketch On Faces

The Sketch On Faces option is the easiest to explain, so I will describe this one first. With this option set, the projected curve is created by projecting a 2D sketch onto a face. The sketch is projected normal (perpendicular) to the sketch plane. This is like extruding the sketch and using the Up To Surface end condition. The edge at the end of the surface would be the projected curve. The sketch can be an open or closed loop, but it may not be multiple open or closed loops, nor can it be self-intersecting. Figure 8.5 shows an example of projecting a sketch onto a face to create a projected curve.

A projected curve using the Sketch On Faces option

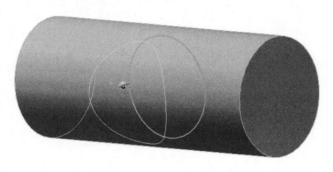

Using Sketch Onto Sketch

This is the concept that most frequently causes difficulty for users. The Sketch Onto Sketch Projected Curve option can be visualized in a few different ways.

Picturing reverse 2D drawing visualization method

One way to visualize Sketch Onto Sketch projection is to think of it as being the reverse of a 2D drawing. In a 2D drawing, 3D edges (you can think of the edges as curves) are projected onto orthogonal planes to represent the edge from the Front or Top planes. The Sketch Onto Sketch projection takes the two orthogonal views, placed on perpendicular planes, and projects them back to make the 3D edge or curve. This is part of the attraction of the projected curve, because making 3D curves accurately is difficult if you do it directly by using a tool such as a 3D sketch spline; however, if you know what the curve looks like from two different directions, then it becomes easy. Figure 8.6 illustrates this visualization method.

When you think of describing a complex 3D curve in space, one of the first methods that usually comes to mind is describing it as two 2D curves from perpendicular directions, exactly in the same way as you would if you created projected drawing views from it. From this, it makes sense to see the creation of the curve as the reverse process, drawing the 2D views first, from which you can then create the 3D curve.

Intersecting surfaces visualization method

A second method used for visualizing Sketch On Sketch projected curves is the intersecting surfaces method. In this method, you can see the curve being created at the intersection of two surfaces that are created by extruding each of the sketches. This method is shown in Figure 8.7.

FIGURE 8.6

The reverse 2D drawing visualization method for projected curves

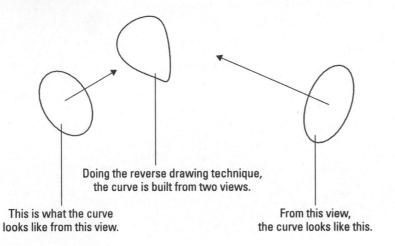

Doing the reverse drawing technique,
the curve is built from two views.

This is what the curve
looks like from this view.

From this view,
the curve looks like this.

FIGURE 8.7

Using intersecting surfaces to visualize a Sketch On Sketch projected curve

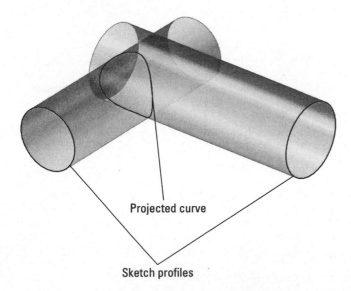

Projected curve

Sketch profiles

Using the Curve Through XYZ Points feature

The Curve Through XYZ Points feature enables you to either type in or import a text file with coordinates for points on a curve. The text file can be generated by any program that makes lists of numbers, including Excel. The curve reacts like a default spline, so the teeter-tottering effect may be noticeable, especially because you cannot set end conditions or tangency. To avoid this effect, it may be a good idea to overbuild the curve by a few points on each end, or have a higher density of points.

If you import a text file, the file can have an extension of either `*.txt` or `*.sldcrv`. The data that it contains must be formatted as three columns of X-, Y-, and Z-coordinates using the document units (inch, mm, and so on), and the coordinates must be separated by comma, space, or tab. Figure 8.8 shows both the Curve File dialog box displaying a table of the curve through X, Y, and Z points, and the `*.sldcrv` Notepad file. You can read the file from the Curve File dialog box by clicking the Browse button, but if you manually type the points, then you can also save the data out directly from the dialog box. Just like any type of sketch, this type of curve cannot intersect itself.

FIGURE 8.8

The Curve File dialog box showing a table of the curve through X, Y, and Z points, and a Notepad text file with the same information

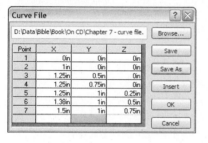
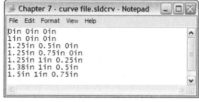

Using the Curve Through Reference Points feature

The Curve Through Reference Points feature creates a curve entity from selected sketch points or vertices. The curve can be an open or closed loop, but a closed loop requires that you select at least three points. You cannot set end conditions of the curve, and so this feature works like a default spline in the same way as the XYZ curve.

The most common application of this feature is to create a wire from selected points along a wire path. Another common application is a simple two-point curve to close the opening of a surface feature such as Fill, Boundary, or Loft. One drawback in that regard is that the end tangency directions cannot be controlled on curve features. If a 3D sketch spline is used, end tangency direction is controlled easily through the use of spline handles and tangency to construction geometry. Curve Through Reference Points is largely unused, probably because 3D sketch splines are so much more powerful.

Putting together a composite curve

The composite curve joins multiple curves, edges, or sketches into a single curve entity. The spring shown in Figure 8.9 was created by using a composite curve to join a 3D sketch, Variable Pitch helix, and a projected curve. You can also use model edges with the composite curve. The curve is shown on half of the part; the rest of the part is mirrored. Curves cannot be mirrored.

Composite curves overlap in functionality with the Selection Manager to some extent. In some ways, the composite curve is nicer because you can save a selection in case the creation of the feature that uses the Selection Manager fails. (If you can't create the feature, you can't save the selection.) On the other hand, composite curves don't function the same way that a selection of model edges do for settings like tangency and curvature.

FIGURE 8.9

A part created from a composite curve

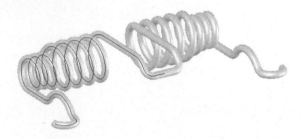

Using Split lines

 Split lines are not exactly curves; they are just edges that split faces into multiple faces. Split lines are used for several purposes, but are primarily intended to split faces so that draft can be added. They are also used for creating a broken-out face for a color break or to create an edge for a hold line fillet, discussed in Chapter 7.

There are some limitations to using split lines. First, they must split a face into at least two fully enclosed areas. You cannot have a split line with an open loop sketch where the ends of the loop are on the face that is to be split; they must either hang off the face to be split or be coincident with the edges. If you think you need a split line from an open loop, try using a projected curve instead.

The SolidWorks 2010 version removed some other long-standing limitations, such as splitting on multiple bodies, using multiple closed loops, and using nested loops. These much-needed improvements will help users avoid workarounds.

Caution

A word of caution is needed when using split lines, especially if you plan to add or remove split lines from an existing model. The split lines should go as far down the tree as possible. Split lines change the face IDs of the faces that they split, and often the edges as well. If you roll back and apply a split line before existing features, you may have a significant amount of cleanup to do. Similarly, if you remove a split line that already has several dependent features, many other features may also be deleted or simply lose their references. ∎

Using the equation driven curve

 The equation driven curve is not really a curve feature; it is a sketch entity. It specifies a spline inside a 2D sketch with an actual equation. Even though this is a spline-based sketch entity, it can only be controlled through the equation, and not by using spline controls. This feature is covered in more detail in Chapter 3, with other sketch entities.

Selecting a Specialty Feature

SolidWorks contains several specialty features that perform tasks that you will use less often than some of the standard features mentioned in Chapter 7. Although you will not use these features as frequently as others, you should still be aware of them and what they do, because you never know when you will need them.

These features include:

- Scale
- Dome
- Wrap
- Flex
- Deform
- Indent

Other types of less commonly used features fall into specialty categories such as sheet metal, multibodies, surfacing, plastics, or mold design. This includes features such as Freeform, Combine, Cavity, Scale, and several others. I placed the discussion about these features in chapters devoted to those specialized topics. The features treated in this chapter are more general use features.

Using Scale

The Scale feature, found at Insert ⇨ Feature ⇨ Scale, is mainly used for preparing models of plastic parts to make mold cavity geometry; however, it can be used for any purpose on solid or surface geometry. Scale does not act by scaling up dimensions for individual sketches and features; rather, it scales the entire part at the point in the FeatureManager history at which it is applied. The Scale PropertyManager is shown in Figure 8.10.

FIGURE 8.10

Applying the Scale feature

The Scale feature only becomes available when the part contains at least one solid or surface body. You can scale multiple bodies at once and can select from one of three options for the "Scale About" or fixed reference: the part origin, the geometry centroid, or a custom coordinate system. Of these, it is generally preferable to select the part origin because it is most often the case that you would want the standard planes moving with respect to the rest of the part as little as possible. If you needed to scale about a specific point on the geometry, you would need to create a custom coordinate system at that point and use that as the reference.

The Scale Factor works like a multiplier, so if you want to double all the dimensions, you would enter the Scale Factor 2. This does not work like the Scale function in the Cavity feature, which is less commonly used. Scale within Cavity uses a scale factor that is shown as a percentage, so to double the linear dimensions of a part would require a scale factor of 100%. The Cavity feature is only available in the context of an assembly, and has fallen out of favor with most mold designers.

Scale is also configurable, starting with SolidWorks 2011, meaning that different configurations can use different scale factors. Configurations are covered in Chapter 11.

An interesting aspect of the Scale feature is that you can disable the Uniform Scaling option. This allows you to apply separate scale factors for the X, Y, and Z directions. In mold making, this can be used if you have a fiber-filled material and the mold requires differential shrink compensation based on the direction of plastic flow, and thus of fiber alignment (the part will shrink less in the direction of fiber alignment). But you could also use it to size any general part. Just remember that if you apply differential scale, circles may be distorted. To get around this, you may be able to reorder the features to apply the Scale feature before the circular features are added.

Because Scale is simply applied to the body rather than to dimensions, it can be applied to imported parts as well as SolidWorks native parts. Sometimes people use the Scale feature to compensate for improper imported units. For example, if a part was originally built in inches, and translated in millimeters, you might want to scale the part by a factor of 25.4. You can also enter an expression in the Scale Factor box so that if the import units error went the other way, you could scale a part down by 1/25.4. The limitation to the scale feature is that the SolidWorks modeling space for a single part is approximately a box of between 500 and 700 meters centered around the origin. There appears to be some difference between sketching limits and 3D solid limits.

Using the Dome feature

The Dome feature in SolidWorks is generally applied to give some shape to flat faces, or an area of a flat face. A great example of where a Dome fits well is the cupped bottom of a plastic bottle, or a slight arch on top of buttons for electronic devices.

Until SolidWorks 2010, another very similar feature existed, which was called Shape. You can no longer make Shape features, but you may find one from time to time in old parts. If you find a Shape feature on an old part, it will continue to function unless any of its parent geometry changes. Shape features will not update in SolidWorks 2010 or later. SolidWorks recommends you re-create the geometry as another feature, possibly a Dome or Freeform feature.

Best Practice

Dome features are best used when you are looking for a generic bulge or indentation and are not too concerned about controlling the specific shape. Occasionally, a dome may be exactly what you need, but when you need more precise, predictable control over the shape, then you should use the Fill, Boundary, or Loft feature. ■

The Dome feature has several attributes that will either help it qualify for a given task or disqualify it. These attributes can help you decide if it will be useful in situations you encounter:

- The Dome feature can create multiple domes on multiple selected faces in a single feature, although it creates only a single dome for each face.
- Using the Elliptical Dome setting, Dome can create a feature that is tangent to the vertical.
- Dome can use a constraint sketch to limit its shape.
- Dome works on non-planar faces.
- Dome cannot establish a tangent relationship to faces bordering the selected face.
- Dome cannot span multiple faces.
- Dome displays a temporary untrimmed four-sided patch that extends beyond the selected face when you use it on a non-four-sided face.
- Dome functions only on solids, not on surfaces.

The error caused by a Shape feature being forced to update in SolidWorks 2010 or later is shown in Figure 8.11.

FIGURE 8.11

Shape features may fail in SolidWorks 2010 and later

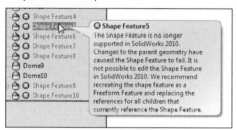

The Dome feature has two notable settings: the Elliptical Dome and Continuous Dome.

The Elliptical Dome is available only on flat faces where the boundary is either a complete circle or an ellipse. The cross-section of the dome is elliptical and does not account for draft, which means that it is always tangent to the perpendicular from the selected flat face.

The Continuous Dome is a setting for any noncircular or elliptical face, including polygons and closed-loop splines. The setting results in a single unbroken face. If you deselect the Continuous Dome setting, it functions like the Elliptical Dome setting. Figure 8.12 shows the most useful settings for the Dome feature.

The workflow for the Dome feature is as follows:

1. Select an area to be domed, or use a split line to create an area to be domed on an existing face.
2. Initiate the Dome feature, set a height, tell it to add or remove material, and set the other settings including the constraint sketch.
3. Accept the feature with the green check mark.

FIGURE 8.12

Examples of various types of domes

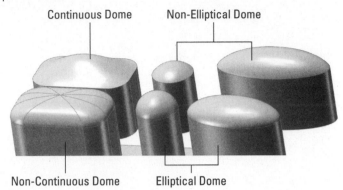

Continuous Dome Non-Elliptical Dome

Non-Continuous Dome Elliptical Dome

Using the Wrap feature

The Wrap feature enables you to wrap 2D sketches around cylindrical and conical faces. However, trying to wrap around 360 degrees can cause some difficulties, although all the available documentation from SolidWorks on the Wrap feature says that you can wrap onto a conical surface.

The Wrap feature works by flattening the face, relating the sketch to the flat pattern of the face, and then mapping the face boundaries and sketch back onto the 3D face. The reason why it is limited to cylindrical and conical faces is that these types of geometry are *developable*. This means that the faces can be mapped to the flat pattern through some relatively simple techniques that happen behind the scenes. Developable geometry can be flattened without stretching. You will see in a later chapter that sheet metal functions are limited in the same way and for the same reasons.

SolidWorks does not wrap onto other types of surfaces, such as spherical, toroidal, or general NURBS surfaces, because you cannot flatten these shapes without distorting or stretching the material. The distinguishing characteristic is that Wrap works on faces with curvature in only one direction and will not work with compound curvature. There is software that can flatten these shapes, but it is typically done for sheet metal deep-drawing applications, which highly deform the metal. Figure 8.13 shows the Wrap PropertyManager interface.

The Wrap feature has three main options:

- Emboss
- Deboss
- Scribe

Using Scribe

Scribe is the simplest of the options to explain, and understanding it can help you understand the other options. Scribe creates a split line–like edge on the face.

FIGURE 8.13

The Wrap PropertyManager interface

Several requirements must be met in order to make a wrap feature work:

- The face must be a cylindrical or conical face.
- The loop must be a closed loop or nested closed loop 2D sketch.
- The sketch must be on a plane that is either tangent to or parallel to another plane that is tangent to the face.
- Wrap supports multiple closed loops within a single feature.
- Wrap supports wrapping onto multiple faces.
- The wrap should not be self-intersecting when it wraps around the part. (Self-intersection will not cause the feature to fail, but on the other types, Emboss and Deboss, it may produce unexpected results.)

Scribes can be created on solid or surface faces. Scribed surfaces are frequently thickened to create a boss or a cut. Figure 8.13 shows a scribed wrap.

Using Emboss

The Wrap Emboss option works much like the scribe, but it adds material inside the closed loop sketch, at the thickness that you specify in the Emboss PropertyManager. Embossing can only be done on solid geometry. If the feature self-intersects, then the intersecting area is simply not embossed and is left at the level of the original face. One result is that creating a full wraparound feature, such as the geometry for a barrel cam, requires a secondary feature. This is because the Wrap feature always leaves a gap, regardless of whether the sketch to be wrapped is under or over the diameter-multiplied-by-pi length.

Tip

To work around this problem, you can use a loft, extrude, or revolve feature to span the gap. ■

When you use the Emboss option, you can set up the direction of pull and assign draft so that the feature can be injection molded. This limits the size of the emboss so that it must not wrap more than 180 degrees around the part.

Using Deboss

Deboss is just like emboss, except that it removes material instead of adding it. Figure 8.14 demonstrates all these options. The part shown in the images is available on the DVD with the filename `Chapter 8 Wrap.sldprt`. For each of the demonstrated cases, the original flat sketch is shown to give you some idea of how the sketch relates to the finished geometry.

FIGURE 8.14

The Wrap feature options

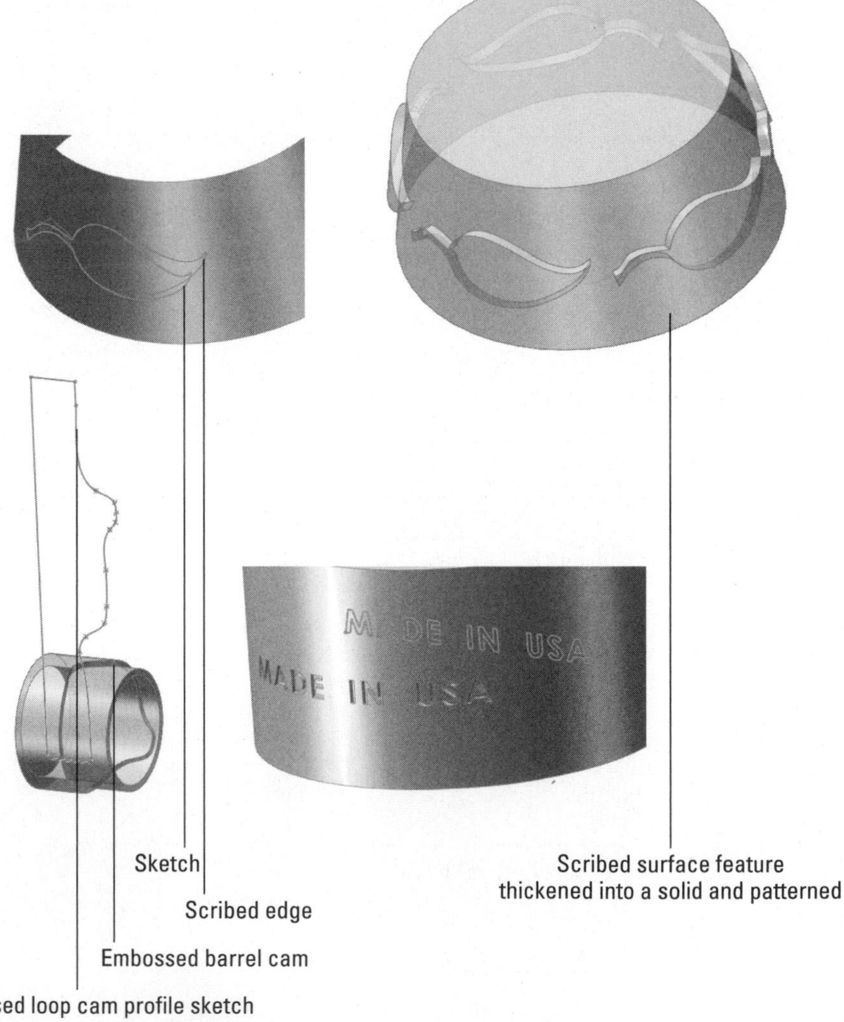
MADE IN USA
MADE IN USA
Sketch
Scribed edge
Embossed barrel cam
Closed loop cam profile sketch
Scribed surface feature
thickened into a solid and patterned

Keep in mind that this feature is not like the projected sketch. A projected sketch is not foreshortened on the curved surface, but is projected normal from the sketch plane. A sketch that is 1-inch long when flat will measure 1 inch when wrapped along the curvature of the surface and will measure less than 1 inch linearly from end to end.

The scribed part in the previous figure was created on a conical surface body. The surface was then thickened as a separate body and patterned.

Cross-Reference

Chapter 19 covers working with multi-bodies, and Chapter 20 covers surfaces. ∎

The embossed cam employed a workaround with a revolve feature to close the gap that is always created when wrapping all the way around a part.

The example with the debossed text employs a direction of pull and draft so that the geometry can be molded.

Using the Flex feature

The Flex feature is different from most other features in SolidWorks. Most other features create new geometry, but Flex (and Deform, which follows) takes existing geometry and changes its shape. Flex can affect the entire part, or just a portion of it. Flex works on both solid and surface bodies, as well as imported and native geometry.

Figure 8.15 shows the Flex PropertyManager interface. Flex has four main options and many settings. The four main options are as follows:

- **Bending.** Establishes two trim planes to denote the ends of the bent area and specifies an angle or radius for the bend.
- **Twisting.** Establishes two trim planes to limit the area of the twist and enters the number of degrees through which to twist.

FIGURE 8.15

The Flex PropertyManager interface

- **Tapering.** Establishes two trim planes to limit the area of the taper. The body will be larger toward one end and smaller toward the other end.
- **Stretching.** Establishes two trim planes to limit the area to be stretched. You can stretch the entire body by moving the trim planes outside of the body.

Best Practice

Flex is not the kind of feature that you should use to actually design parts, but it can be extremely valuable when you need to show a flexible part in an "in use" state. A simple example would be a rubber strap that stretches over something when it is used, but that is designed and manufactured in its free state. The geometry that you can create by using the flex functions is not generally production-model quality, but it is usually adequate for a looks-like model. ∎

Figure 8.16 shows examples of each flex option using a model of a rubber grommet. The part shown in the figure can be found on the DVD with the filename Chapter 7 Flex.sldprt.

FIGURE 8.16

A rubber grommet in various flex states

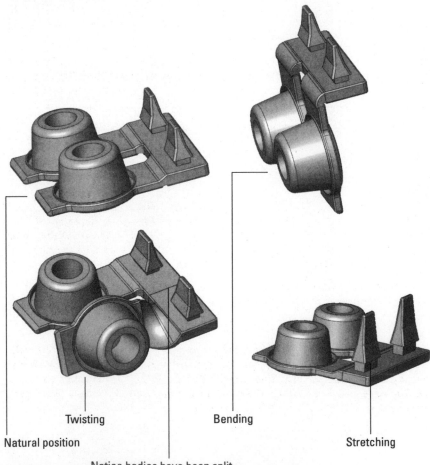

Twisting   Bending

Natural position

Notice bodies have been split

Stretching

In some cases, the triad and trim planes are slightly disoriented. The best thing to do in situations like this is to simply reorient the triad using the angle numbers in the Triad panel of the PropertyManager. This is also a solution if the planes are turned in such a way that the axis of bending is not oriented to the bend that the part requires.

The Flex feature is very conscious of separate bodies. In some cases this can be helpful, but in default situations when there is only one body in the part, it can be annoying. Remember to select the body to be affected in the very first selection box at the top of the PropertyManager.

Tip

If you want to bend only one of the tabs on the grommet, then the best solution is to split the single body into two bodies and flex only one of the bodies. The examples shown for twisting and stretching use this technique. ∎

Cross-Reference

Splitting a single body into multiple bodies is covered in Chapter 19. ∎

You can place the trim planes by selecting a model vertex, by dragging the arrow on the plane, or by typing in a number. Be careful when dragging the plane arrows because dragging the border of the plane drags the flex value for the feature. (Dragging the plane in a bending operation is like changing the angle or radius for the bend.)

Using the triad can be very tricky. Moving the triad in the bending option moves the axis of the bend, and so it determines whether the bend will compress or stretch the material. The position of the triad also determines which side of the bent body will move or stay stationary, or if both sides will move. Placing the triad directly on a trim plane causes the material outside the bend on that side of the trim plane to remain stationary.

I highly recommend taking a look at the models that are provided with this chapter to examine the various functions of the Flex feature more carefully. The model uses configurations, which are covered in Chapter 11.

Applying the Deform feature

Like the Flex feature, the Deform feature changes the shape of the entire model without regard to parametrics, features, history, or dimensions. Some software packages call this technique *global shape modeling*. Also like Flex, Deform works on surface bodies as well as solids. Deform can also handle imported geometry as well as SolidWorks native parts. Model complexity is not an issue unless the part runs into itself during deformation.

The Deform feature is also another feature type that you may not use to actually design anything, but that you may use to show a model in a deformed state.

Best Practice

Typically, if you want a model to have a certain shape, then you need to intentionally and precisely model it with that shape. The problem with using deform and flex geometry for actual design data is that they both create fairly approximate geometry, and this process yields a result that is not completely intentional. The shape that you finally achieve is the result of arbitrary uncontrolled function of the feature, not necessarily creating a shape that you had clearly envisioned beforehand. ∎

Deform has three types:

- **Point.** This type deforms a portion of the model by pushing a point and the geometry around it.
- **Curve to curve.** The most precise and useful deform type, this type selects an existing edge and forces the edge to match a curve.
- **Surface push.** This type of deform, while conceptually a very interesting function, is nearly unusable in practice. The part is deformed into a shape vaguely resembling an intermediate shape between the existing state of the part and a "tool" body.

Figure 8.17 shows the PropertyManager interface for the Deform feature. The interface is different for each of the three main types, and also changes, depending on selections within the individual types. The interface shown is for the Curve to curve type because I believe this to be the most useful type.

FIGURE 8.17

The PropertyManager interface for the Curve to curve deform

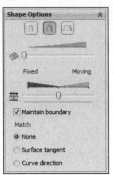

Looking at Point deform

The Point deform option enables you to push a point on the model, and the model deforms as if it were rubber. Figure 8.18 shows the PropertyManager, as well as a before-and-after example of the Point deform function. The key to using this feature is to ensure that the Deform region option is unselected. Aside from that, you just have to use trial and error when applying the Point deform option. The depth, diameter, and shape of the deformation are not very precise. Also, you cannot specify the precise location for the point to be deformed. Again, this is best used for "looks-like" models, not production data.

In the model from Figure 8.18, two Point deform features are used, one to apply some shape to the back and one to apply some shape to the seat.

FIGURE 8.18

The Deform Point PropertyManager and a before-and-after example

Looking at Curve to curve deform

Because the Curve to curve uses curve (or sketch or edge) data, it is a more precise method than the other deform types. The main concept here is to transform a curve on the original model to a new curve, thus deforming the body to achieve the new geometry.

The model shown in Figure 8.19 has been created using the Curve to curve deform. The part starts as a simple sweep (sweep an arc along an arc), and then a split line is created to limit the deform to a specific area of the model. The model is on the DVD with the filename Chapter 8 Deform Curve to Curve.sldprt.

Looking at Surface push deform

I do not go into much detail on the Surface push deform type because it is not one of the more useful functions in SolidWorks. In order to use it, you must have the body of the part that you are modeling and a tool body that you will use to shape the part that you are modeling. The finished shape does not fit the tool body directly, but looks about halfway between the model and the tool body, blended together in an abstract sort of way. It looks like the dent that would result from an object being thrown very hard at a car fender, in that neither the thrown part nor the fender is immediately recognizable from the result.

Using the Indent feature

The Indent feature is what the Surface push deform is trying to be, or should try to be. Indent uses the same ingredients as the Surface push, but it produces a result that is both intelligible and useful. For

example, if you are building a plastic housing around a small electric motor, then the Indent feature shapes the housing and creates a gap between the housing and the motor. Figure 8.20 shows the PropertyManager interface for the Indent feature, as well as what the indent looks like before and after using the feature.

FIGURE 8.19

Using the Curve to curve deform option

FIGURE 8.20

Using the Indent feature

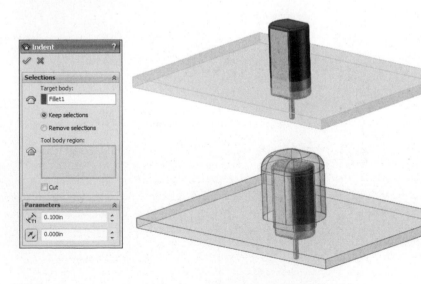

In this case, the small motor is placed where it needs to be, but there is a wall in the way. Indent is used to create an indentation in the wall by using the same wall thickness and placing a gap of .010 inches around the motor. The motor is brought into the wall part using the Insert ⇨ Part command. This is a multi-body technique. Multi-bodies are examined in detail in Chapter 20.

Tutorial: Creating a Wire-Formed Part

Follow these steps to create a wire-formed part:

1. **Open a new part using an inch-based template.**

2. **Open a sketch on the Right plane and sketch a circle that is centered on the Origin with a diameter of 1.500 inches.**

3. **Create a Helix, Constant Pitch, Pitch, and Revolution, where the Pitch = .250 inches, Revolutions = 5.15, and Start Angle = 0.** The Helix command is found at Insert ⇨ Curve ⇨ Helix/Spiral.

4. **Create a sketch on the Front plane, as shown in Figure 8.21.** Pay careful attention when adding the construction line, as shown. This line is used in the next step to reference the end of the arc.

The results up to Step 4

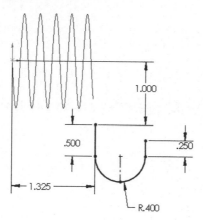

5. **Open a sketch on the Right plane and use Figure 8.22 to add the correct relations and dimensions.** Be aware that the two sketches shown are on different sketch planes, which makes it difficult to depict in 2D. You can also open the part from the DVD for reference.

6. **Exit the sketch and create a projected curve.** The Projected Curve function is found at Insert ⇨ Curve ⇨ Projected Curve. Use the Sketch On Sketch option.

7. **Open a 3D sketch.** You can access a 3D sketch from the Insert menu. Select the helix and click Convert Entities on the Sketch toolbar. Then select the projected curve and click Convert Entities again. You now have two sections of a 3D sketch that are unconnected in space.

FIGURE 8.22

The sketch for Step 5

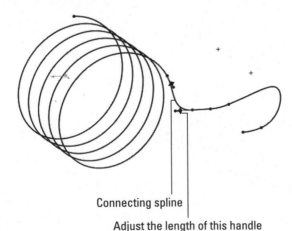

Coincident

Dimension references
end of construction line

Vertical relation

R.750

.100

8. **Draw a two-point spline to join the ends of the 3D sketch entities that are closest to one another.** Assign tangent relations to the ends to make the transition smooth. Figure 8.23 illustrates what the model should look like at this point.

FIGURE 8.23

The results up to Step 8

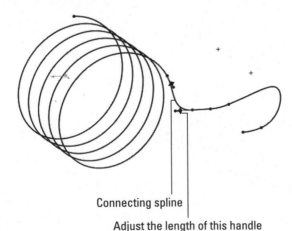

Connecting spline

Adjust the length of this handle

Tip

You may have to adjust the length of one of the spline tangency length arrows to keep the spline from remaining inside the cylinder of the helix. ∎

9. **Open a sketch on the Right plane, and draw an arc that is centered on the Origin and coincident with the end of the 3D sketch helix.** The 185-degree angle is created by activating the dimension tool and clicking first the center of the arc and then the two endpoints of the arc. Now place the dimension. This type of dimensioning allows you to get an angle dimension without dimensioning to angled lines. Exit the sketch.

10. **Create a composite curve (Insert ⇨ Curve ⇨ Composite) consisting of the 3D sketch and the new 2D sketch.**

11. **Create a new plane using the Normal to Curve option, selecting one end of the composite curve.**

12. **On the new plane, draw a circle that is centered on the end of the curve with a diameter of .120 inches.** You need to create a Pierce relation between the center of the circle and the composite curve.

13. **Create a sweep feature using the circle as the profile and the composite curve as the path.** To create the sweep, you must first exit the sketch.

14. **Hide any curves that still display.**

15. **Choose Insert ⇨ Cut ⇨ With Surface.** From the Flyout FeatureManager, select the Right plane. Make sure that the arrow is pointing to the side of the plane with the least amount of material. Click OK to accept the cut. The finished part is shown in Figure 8.24.

FIGURE 8.24

The finished part

Summary

SolidWorks has a wide range of features beyond the basic extrudes and revolves. You saw the depth of the standard features in Chapter 7, and now in Chapter 8 you have seen the breadth of some of the less-used, but still useful operations. Not all of these secondary features measure up in terms of value for general modeling, but it is nice to know that if you need to show a model in a flexed in-use state, you at least don't have to directly model the deformed part manually.

Patterning and Mirroring

P atterning and mirroring in SolidWorks are great tools to help you improve your efficiency. SolidWorks software provides many powerful pattern types that also help you accomplish design tasks. In addition to the different types of patterns, there are options that enable functionality that you may not have considered. A solid understanding of patterning and mirroring tools is necessary to be able to build the maximum amount of parametric intelligence into your models, and to open up the possibilities of your design objectives.

Patterning in a Sketch

You can use both pattern and mirror functions in sketch mode, although sketch patterns are not a preferred choice. The distinction between patterning and mirroring in sketch mode is important when it comes to sketch performance.

Performance

Although there are many metrics for how software performs, in SolidWorks, the word performance means the same thing as speed. Sketch patterns have a very adverse effect on speed and do not offer the same level of control as feature patterns. ■

You might hear a lot of conflicting information about which features are better to use in different situations. Users coming from a 2D background often use functions such as sketch patterning because it's familiar, without questioning whether there is a better approach, and often without having any way of measuring how it performs. When in doubt, you can perform a test to determine which features work best for a given situation.

To compare the performance of various types of patterns, I made a series of 20-by-20 patterns using circles, squares, and hexagons. The patterns are both sketch patterns and feature patterns, and I created them with both Verification on Rebuild and Geometry Pattern turned on and off. Verification on Rebuild is an error-checking setting that you can access through Tools ⇨ Options ⇨ Performance, and Geometry Pattern is a setting that is applicable only to feature patterns that disables the intelligence in patterned features.

Table 9.1 shows the rebuild times (in seconds) of solid geometry created from various types of patterns as measured by Feature Statistics (found at Tools ⇨ Feature Statistics). Sketch patterns are far slower than feature patterns, by a factor of about ten. The biggest speed reduction occurs when you use sketch patterns in conjunction with the Verification on Rebuild setting, especially as the number of sketch entities being patterned increases.

Generally, the number of faces and sketch relations being patterned has a significant effect on the speed of the pattern. The sketch pattern times are taken for the entire finished model, including the sketch pattern and a single extrude feature, using the sketch with the pattern to do an extruded cut. The sample parts are on the DVD for reference. Look for the filenames beginning with Reference1 through Reference7.

TABLE 9.1

Pattern Rebuild Times

Pattern Type	Default	Geometry Pattern	Verification on Rebuild
20 × 20 sketch circle	.87	n/a	5.52
20 × 20 sketch square	4.5	n/a	60
20 × 20 sketch hex	9.6	n/a	126
20 × 20 feature circle	.06	.53	.08
20 × 20 feature square	.23	.53	.23
20 × 20 feature hex	.36	.55	.36

The most shocking data here is the difference between a sketch pattern of a hex when a patterned sketch cuts into a flat plate compared to a feature pattern of a single extruded hex with each using the Verification on Rebuild option — 0.36 seconds compared to 126 seconds.

Always keep this general information about sketch patterns in mind:

- Sketch patterns are bad for rebuild speed.
- The more faces created by any pattern, the longer it takes to rebuild.
- The more sketch relations a sketch pattern has, the longer it takes to rebuild.
- Geometry pattern does not improve rebuild speed (unless a special end condition like Up to Surface has been used).
- Verification on Rebuild dramatically increases rebuild time with the number of faces but is far less affected by feature patterns than extruded sketch patterns.

Figure 9.1 shows one of the parts used for this simple test.

FIGURE 9.1

A pattern part used for the test

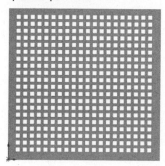

One interesting result of this test was that if a patterned extruded feature creates a situation where the end faces of the extruded features have to merge into a single face, the feature could take ten times the amount of time to rebuild as a pattern with unmerged end faces. This was an inadvertent discovery. I'm sure you would make your own discoveries if you were to investigate rebuild speeds for end conditions for cuts such as Through All, Up to Face, Up to Next, and so on, as well as the difference between cuts and boss features. Further, using Instant 3D can be an impediment when you're editing very large sketches simply due to the effects of the preview.

You should also note that the situation this simple test covers is very limited in scope. Because the plate is a constant thickness, the Geometry Pattern option actually works, which it wouldn't if the plate varied in thickness (with the through holes). It also only tests the Through All end condition, and the Geometry Pattern is best used to simply disable intelligent end conditions. I get the impression that many people use it as a random toggle trying to get patterns to work that SolidWorks would otherwise not allow to work.

I discuss the Geometry Pattern option in more detail later in this chapter. I wanted to start the chapter with a discussion that called attention to the misperception that some people have that sketch patterns are somehow better than feature patterns.

Debunking more sketch myths

People often say that it is best practice to define your sketches fully. I completely agree with this statement. However, I have heard people go to the extent to say that fully defined sketches solve faster, with the rationale being that SolidWorks has to figure out how to solve the under-defined sketch, but the fully defined sketch is already spelled out. Let's find out.

In this example, I created a sketch pattern of 4 × 4 rectangles and used the Fully Define Sketch tool to add dimensions. Then I copied and pasted the sketch and removed all the dimensions and relations. Figure 9.2 shows the Feature Statistic results.

It is safe to say that fully defined sketches are best practice, but it is not due to rebuild speed. Sketch relations are costly from a rebuild time point of view. Patterning sketch relations are even more costly. The rebuild time does not even come close to the time that it takes the Fully Define Sketch tool to create all the dimensions and relations in the first place. This combination of geometry, software, and hardware took about 30 seconds of CPU time to add the relations and dimensions.

FIGURE 9.2

Comparing rebuild times of a fully defined sketch to a completely undefined sketch

 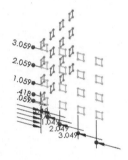

For most models that have fewer than 50 features, you may never notice this rebuild time, and the price you pay is certainly worth the peace of mind you get from having the stability of a fully defined sketch. For large models where you have hundreds of features, or features that use a lot of very busy sketches, you should pay attention to how much information you put into the sketch, and try to limit sketch patterns and even elements such as sketch fillets, using feature fillets instead where possible.

Patterning a sketch

I used the first part of this chapter to debunk some SolidWorks myths about sketches and sketch patterns. In this section, I will discuss how to use sketch patterns. Sketch patterns are an available tool, they are valid, and in a few cases, they are truly necessary.

It is best to pre-select the sketch entities that you want to pattern before using the Sketch Pattern tool. If you do not pre-select, then after the PropertyManager is open, you can only select entities to pattern one by one, because the window select is not available for this function. The right mouse button selection options, such as Select Chain, are also not available in this interface, reinforcing the need to treat sketch patterns as a pre-selection feature.

Tip

When creating a linear sketch pattern, be sure to select the Add Spacing Dimension check boxes. If these dimensions are not added, then editing the pattern becomes more difficult. ■

Using the Linear Sketch Pattern

The Linear Pattern PropertyManager is shown in Figure 9.3.

Unlike other PropertyManagers, the selected entities for the sketch pattern functions are found at the bottom of the PropertyManager instead of at the top. This is a little confusing. Sketch tool PropertyManagers, such as Convert Entities and Mirror, place the selection box at the top.

The Direction 1 panel works predictably by establishing the direction and spacing, and then the number. The Angle setting enables you to specify a direction that does not rely on anything outside of the sketch.

FIGURE 9.3

The Linear Pattern PropertyManager

The Direction 2 panel works a little differently. You must first specify how many instances you want, and then the other information becomes available. The spacing is grayed out until you tell it you want more than one instance in Direction 2.

Using the Circular Sketch Pattern

The Circular Sketch Pattern defaults to the sketch Origin as the center of the pattern. You can move and position this point using the numbers in the PropertyManager, but you cannot dimension it until after the pattern is created. Again, this is another feature where you need to pre-select because window selection is not available (patterned sketch entities must be selected one by one to go into the Entities to Pattern panel). Figure 9.4 shows the Circular Pattern PropertyManager.

FIGURE 9.4

The Circular Pattern PropertyManager

Mirroring in a Sketch

Mirroring in a sketch is a completely different matter from patterning in a sketch. It offers superior performance, and the interface is better developed. Mirrored entities in a sketch are an instrumental part of establishing design intent.

Two methods of mirroring items in a sketch are discussed here, along with a method to make entities work as if they have been mirrored when in fact they were manually drawn.

Using Mirror Entities

Mirror Entities works by selecting the entities that you want to mirror along with a single centerline, and clicking the Mirror Entities button on the Sketch toolbar. You can use this simple and effective tool on existing geometry. This method is the fastest way to use the tool, but there are other methods. You can pre-select or post-select, using a dialog box to select the mirror line, which does not need to be a centerline.

One feature of Mirror Entities may sometimes cause unexpected results. For example, in some situations, Mirror Entities will mirror a line or an arc and merge the new element with the old one across the centerline. This happens in situations where the mirror and the original form a single line or a single arc. SolidWorks may delete certain relations and dimensions in these situations.

Figure 9.5 shows the Mirror Entities PropertyManager.

If you are a longtime user, you should note that there are some relatively new ways to use functions such as Mirror Entities, which can now involve a selection box in a PropertyManager window. Longtime users are used to operating tools such as Mirror, Offset, and Convert Entities without an interface. In more recent versions of SolidWorks, these functions have had PropertyManagers that enable a selection list window.

FIGURE 9.5

Selecting items in the Mirror Entities PropertyManager

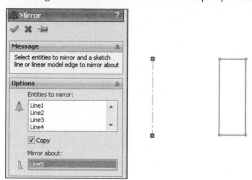

Some longtime users find the PropertyManager disruptive to their workflow. Other people may appreciate the benefit of the selection list window. Here are three workflows for this function that allow you to use a range of techniques:

- **Traditional method.** To continue to work with the Mirror Entities tool using the traditional method without an interface, click the Mirror Entities button on the Sketch toolbar and disable the pushpin. The pushpin is shown disabled (pointing to the left instead of into the screen) in Figure 9.5. Now when you use the function, pre-select your sketch geometry, including the centerline you want to mirror about. You do not see the interface; your sketch geometry is just mirrored for you. This is actually the fastest way to work.

- **New method.** To always make sure that you see the new Mirror Entities PropertyManager with the selection list box, make sure the pushpin is enabled (where the pin is pointing into the screen). This allows you to always see the list of selected entities and to make sure that the line you want to mirror about is selected. One of the hidden benefits of using the Mirror Entities PropertyManager is that you can select a non-centerline to mirror about — a convenient and useful option. Overall, this method is slower and more deliberate, but it offers more control, and it's there if you need or want it. If you pre-select sketch entities before activating the tool, you are still presented with the PropertyManager.

- **Hybrid method.** To some extent, you can have it both ways. If you unpin the Mirror Entities PropertyManager, you can pre-select your geometry, as in the traditional method, and the PropertyManager never appears, or you can select the geometry afterwards using the new method, and you are presented with the PropertyManager to be more deliberate about the selections. To me, this is the method that makes the most sense because you can determine what you need as you perform the operation. Both the fast and the more deliberate methods are available to you on the fly.

Notice also that the Mirror Entities PropertyManager has a Copy check box. This option is activated by default, and in this configuration, it works as you usually intend the Mirror function to work. If you disable this option, then the entities you want to mirror are simply flipped to the other side of the mirror line, and the entities in the original location are removed.

I have heard many people complain about these new PropertyManagers. It is possible that people are just reacting to the interruption of the old workflow without stopping to see what benefits it offers. In my opinion, the new options add functionality, and if you understand how to use them, they will not interrupt your fast workflow.

Using Dynamic Mirror

 As the name suggests, Dynamic Mirror mirrors sketch entities as they are created. You can activate it by selecting a centerline and clicking the Dynamic Mirror button on the Sketch toolbar. Dynamic Mirror is not on the toolbar by default; you need to choose Tools ⇨ Customize ⇨ Commands to add it to the toolbar. You can also access Dynamic Mirror by choosing Tools ⇨ Sketch Tools ⇨ Dynamic Mirror from the menu.

When you activate this function, the centerline displays with hatch marks on the ends and remains active until you turn off or exit the sketch. Figure 9.6 shows the centerline with hatch marks. Dynamic Mirror has no other interface.

The Dynamic Mirror function remains active until you turn it off. You can use the same toolbar icon you used to turn it on. The icon remains depressed until you release it or exit the sketch.

FIGURE 9.6

The Dynamic Mirror centerline with hatch marks

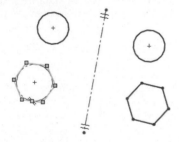

Using Symmetry sketch relation

 I have covered the Symmetry sketch relation in previous chapters on sketching, but I mention it again here because it offers you a manual way to mirror sketch entities. There are editing situations when you may not want to create new geometry, but instead use existing entities with new relations driving them. To create the Symmetry sketch relation, you must have two similar items (such as lines or endpoints) and a centerline selected.

To add the symmetry relation after you have made the proper selection, use the popup toolbar interface, the Sketch PropertyManager, or the Add Relation toolbar button. These three options are shown in Figure 9.7.

You can find more information on manipulating sketch relations in Chapter 3.

FIGURE 9.7

Three ways to add a symmetric sketch constraint

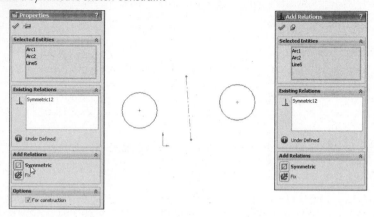

Using Mirroring in 3D sketches

Chapter 8 deals with 3D sketches in more detail, but I discuss the mirror functionality here to connect it with the rest of the mirroring and patterning topics. Three-dimensional sketches can contain planes, and if you are sketching on a plane in a 3D sketch, you can mirror items on it. You cannot mirror general 3D sketch entities.

Sketch patterns are also unavailable in the 3D sketch, but you can use the Move, Rotate, and Copy sketch tools on planes in 3D sketches. Combining one questionable function (planes in 3D sketches) with another (sketch patterns) does not usually improve either one.

Exploring the Geometry Pattern Option

The SolidWorks Help file says that the Geometry Pattern option in feature patterns results in a faster pattern because it does not pattern the parametric relations. This claim is valid only when there is an end condition on the patterned feature such that the feature will actually pattern the end condition's parametric behavior. The part shown in Figure 9.8 falls into this category. The improved rebuild time goes from .30 to .11 seconds. Although a 60 percent reduction is significant, the most compelling argument for the use of the Geometry Pattern has nothing to do with rebuild time. It is to avoid the effect of patterning the end-condition parametrics.

In fact, the Geometry Pattern option's main intent is to pattern existing geometry without the parametric intelligence. The main mission of Geometry Pattern has nothing to do with rebuild speed.

Under some conditions, Geometry Pattern will not work. One example is any time a patterned face merges with a face that cannot be patterned. Figure 9.9 shows two patterns, one that can use Geometry Pattern and one that cannot.

FIGURE 9.8

A geometry pattern test

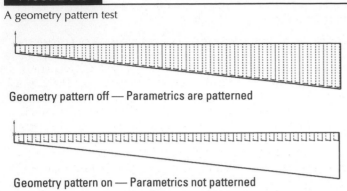

Geometry pattern off — Parametrics are patterned

Geometry pattern on — Parametrics not patterned

The pattern of the rectangular bosses cannot use Geometry Pattern because the face that is merged is not merged in all pattern instances. The pattern of truncated cylinders shown on the same part as the pattern of rectangular bosses can use Geometry Pattern because the flat face is merged in every pattern instance. The circular pattern in the image to the right in Figure 9.9 also allows Geometry Pattern for the same reason.

FIGURE 9.9

Merged faces

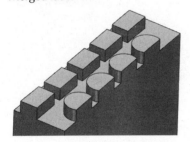

In some situations, SolidWorks error messages may send you in a loop. One message may tell you that the pattern cannot be created with the Geometry Pattern turned on, so you should try to turn it off. When you do that, you may get another message that says the pattern will not work, and that you should try to use the Geometry Pattern setting. In cases like this, you may try to use a different end condition for the feature that you want to pattern, or change the selection of features patterned along with the feature, such as fillets. You may also try to pattern bodies or even faces rather than features. These last two options are covered in the following sections.

Patterning Bodies

I cover multi-bodies in depth in Chapter 20, but I will briefly discuss the topic here. Any discussion of patterning is not complete without a discussion of bodies because using bodies is an available and highly useful option with all the pattern and mirror types.

SolidWorks parts can contain multiple *solid* or *surface* bodies. A solid body is a solid that comprises a single contiguous volume. A surface body is different — think of it as a sheet knitted together from several faces — but it can also be patterned and mirrored as a body.

There are both advantages and disadvantages to mirroring and patterning bodies instead of features. The advantages can include the simplicity of selecting a single body for mirroring or patterning. In cases where the geometry to be patterned is complex or there is a large number of features, patterning bodies also can be much faster. However, in the example used earlier with patterning features in a 20-by-20 grid of holes, when done by patterning a single body of 1" × 1" × .5" with a .5" diameter hole, patterning bodies gives a rebuild time of about 60 seconds with or without Verification on Rebuild. The function combines the resulting bodies into a single body that takes most of the time. This says that for large patterns of simple features, patterning bodies is *not* an efficient technique. Although I do not have an experiment in this chapter to prove it, it seems intuitive that creating a pattern of a smaller number of complex bodies using a large number of features in the patterned body would show a performance improvement over patterning the features.

Another disadvantage of patterning or mirroring bodies is that it does not allow you to be selective. You cannot mirror the body minus a couple of features without doing some shuffling of feature order in the FeatureManager. Another disadvantage is that if the base of the part has already been mirrored by a symmetrical sketch technique, then body mirroring is not going to help you mirror the subsequent features. In addition, the Merge Bodies option within the mirror feature does not work in the same way that it works for other features. It merges only those bodies that are part of the mirror to bodies that are part of the mirror. Pattern Bodies does not even have an option to merge bodies. Both of these functions are often going to require an additional combine feature (for solid bodies) or knit (for surface bodies) to put the final results together.

Some of these details may seem obscure when you're reading about them, but when you begin to work patterning bodies and begin trying to merge them into a single body, read over this section again. The inconsistency between the Merge option existing in Mirror but not in Pattern, as well as the functional discrepancy between the Merge in Mirror and the Merge Result in, say, Extrude is unexplainable, and a possible opportunity for an enhancement request.

Cross-Reference

Bodies modeling are discussed in more detail in Chapter 19. Surface modeling is covered in Chapter 20. ■

Patterning Faces

Most of the pattern types have an option for Pattern Faces. This option has a few restrictions, the main limitation being that all instances of the pattern must be created within the boundaries of the same face as the original. Figure 9.10 shows an example of the Pattern Faces option working with a Circular Pattern feature.

To get around the same face limitation, you can knit faces together and pattern the resulting surface body, as shown in Figure 9.11.

Cross-Reference

Working with surface bodies is covered in Chapter 20. ■

FIGURE 9.10

A circular pattern using the Pattern Faces option

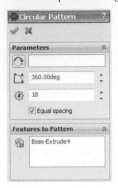

Patterning faces is another way of patterning geometry within SolidWorks without patterning the feature intelligence that was built into the original. It is also a way to make patterns on imported parts from existing geometry. Chapter 23 addresses this topic briefly in the discussion on imported geometry and direct edit techniques.

Patterning faces is not a widely used technique; however, it should be somewhere in your toolbox of tricks. Although it may be lurking near the bottom of the pile, it is still useful in special circumstances.

FIGURE 9.11

Patterning a surface body

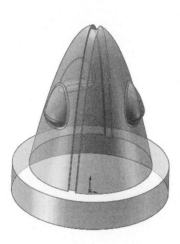

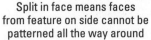
Split in face means faces
from feature on side cannot be
patterned all the way around

Patterning Fillets

You may hear people argue that you cannot pattern fillets. This is only partially true. It is true that fillets as individual features cannot be patterned. For example, if you have a symmetrical box and a fillet on one edge and want to pattern only the fillet to other edges, this does not work. However, when fillets are patterned with their parent geometry, they are a perfectly acceptable candidate for patterning. This is also true for the more complex fillet types, such as variable radius and full radius fillets. You may need to use the Geometry Pattern option, and you may need to select all the fillets affecting a feature, but it certainly does work.

Understanding Pattern Types

Up to now, I have discussed patterns in general; differentiated sketch patterns from feature patterns, face patterns, and body patterns; and looked at some other factors that affect patterning and mirroring. I will now discuss each individual type of pattern to give you an idea of what options are available.

Using the Linear Pattern

The Linear Pattern feature has several available options:

- **Single direction or two directions.** Directions can be established by edge, sketch entity, axis, or linear dimension. If two directions are used, the directions do not need to be perpendicular to one another.

- **Spacing.** The spacing represents the center-to-center distance between pattern instances, and can be driven by an equation.

- **Number of Instances.** This number represents the total number of features in a pattern, which includes the original seed feature. It can also be driven by an equation. Equations are covered in detail in Chapter 9.

- **Direction 2.** The second direction works just like the first, with the one exception of the Pattern Seed Only option. Figure 9.12 shows the difference between a default two-direction pattern and one using the Pattern Seed Only option.

FIGURE 9.12

Using the default two-direction pattern and the Pattern Seed Only option

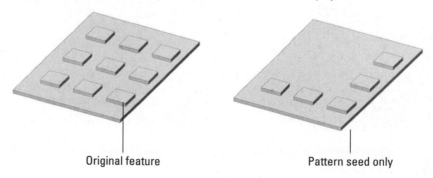

Original feature   Pattern seed only

- **Instances to Skip.** This option enables you to select instances that you would like to leave out of the final pattern. The pink dots are the instances that remain, and the red dots are the ones that have been removed. Figure 9.13 shows the interface for skipping instances. You may have difficulty distinguishing the red and pink colors on the screen.

FIGURE 9.13

Using the Instances to Skip option

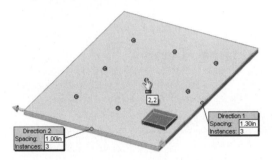

- **Propagate visual properties.** This option patterns the color, texture, or cosmetic thread display, along with the feature to which it is attached.

- **Vary Sketch.** This option in patterns is often overlooked and not widely used or understood. While it may have a niche application, it is a powerful option that can save you a lot of time and open up design possibilities you may not have considered before.

  Vary Sketch allows the sketch of the patterned feature to maintain its parametric relations in each instance of the pattern. It is analogous to Geometry Pattern. Where Geometry Pattern disables the parametric end condition for a feature, Vary Sketch enables the parametric sketch relations for a pattern.

  To activate the Vary Sketch option, the Linear Pattern must use a linear dimension for its Pattern Direction. The dimension must measure in the direction of the pattern, and adding the spacing for the pattern to the direction dimension must result in a valid feature.

  The sketch relations must hold for the entire length of the pattern. Figure 9.14 shows the sketch relations and the resulting pattern. This feature does not have a preview function.

On the DVD

To better understand how this feature works, open the sample file from the DVD called Chapter 9 Vary Sketch.sldprt, **and edit Sketch2.** ■

Edit the .40-inch dimension. Double-click it and use the scroll arrow to increase the dimension; watch the effect on the sketch. If a sketch does not react to changes properly, then it cannot be used with the Vary Sketch option. In this case, the .40-inch dimension is used as the direction, because that is the dimension that will drive the sketch down the pattern. When using this option, the feature sketch must be driven by a single dimension. If the .48-inch dimension were anchored to the origin or the edge of the part like the .40-inch dimension, the pattern would not work properly. The direction dimension has to be able to drive the sketch in the same way that this one does. These dimensions cannot pass through the Zero value and cannot flip directions or move into negative values.

FIGURE 9.14

Using the Vary Sketch option

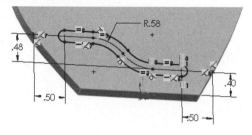

To make the sketch react this way to changes in the dimension, the slot was created using the bidirectional offset that was demonstrated in an earlier chapter, which means that the whole operation is being driven by the construction lines and arcs at the centerline of the slot. Sketch points along the model edges are kept at a certain distance from the ends of the slots using the .50-inch dimensions. The arcs are controlled by an Equal Radius relation and a single .58-inch radius dimension. The straight lines at the ends of the slots are controlled by an Equal Length relation.

This type of dimensioning and relation creation is really what parametric design is all about. The Vary Sketch option takes what is otherwise a static linear pattern and makes it react parametrically in a way that would otherwise require a lot of setup to create individual features. If you model everything with the level of care that you need to put into a Vary Sketch pattern feature sketch, then your models will react very well to change.

Using the Circular Pattern

The Circular Pattern feature requires a circular edge or sketch, a cylindrical face, a revolved face, a straight edge, an axis, or a temporary axis to act as the Pattern Axis of the pattern. All the other options are the same as the Linear Pattern — except that the Circular Pattern does not have a Direction 2 option and the Equal Spacing option works differently.

Equal Spacing takes the total angle and evenly divides the number of instances into that angle. The name *equal spacing* is a bit misleading because all Circular Patterns create equal spacing between the instances, but somehow everyone knows what they mean.

Without using the Equal Spacing option, the Angle setting represents the angular spacing between instances.

The Vary Sketch option is available in Circular Pattern as well. The principles for setup are the same, but you must select an angular dimension for the direction. The part shown in Figure 9.15 was created using this technique.

FIGURE 9.15

A Circular Pattern vary sketch

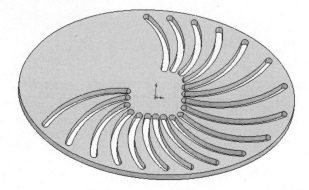

If you are creative with the sketch relations you apply to a sketch, you can get some pretty exotic results from patterns using the Vary Sketch option.

Using the Curve Driven Pattern

A Curve Driven Pattern does just what it sounds like: it drives a pattern along a curve. The curve could be a line, an arc, or a spline. It can be an edge, a 2D or 3D sketch, or even a real curve feature. An interesting thing about the Curve Driven Pattern is that it can have a Direction 2, and Direction 2 can be a curve. This pattern type is one of the most interesting and has many options.

For an entire sketch to be used as a curve, the sketch must not have any sharp corners — all the entities must be tangent. This could mean using sketch fillets or a fit spline. The example shown in Figure 9.16 was created using sketch fillets. This pattern uses the Equal Spacing option, which spaces the number of instances evenly around the curve. It also uses the Offset Curve option, which maintains the patterned feature's relationship to the curve throughout the pattern, as if an offset of the curve goes through the centroids of each patterned instance. The Align to Seed option is also used, which keeps all the pattern instances aligned in the same direction.

FIGURE 9.16

The Curve Driven Pattern using sketch fillets

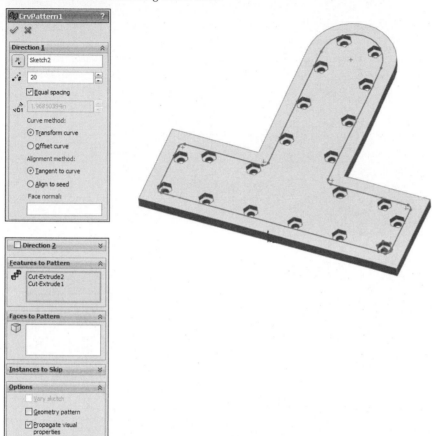

Figure 9.17 shows the same part using the Transform Curve positioning option and Tangent to Curve alignment option.

Instead of an offset of the curve going through the centroids of each patterned feature instance, in the Transform Curve, the entire curve is moved rather than offset. On this particular part, this causes a messy pattern. The Tangent to Curve option gives every patterned instance the same orientation relative to the curve as the original.

The Face Normal option is used for a 3D pattern, as shown in Figure 9.18. Although this functionality seems a little obscure, it is useful if you need a 3D curve-driven pattern on a complex surface. If you are curious about this example, it is on the DVD with the filename Reference 3d Curve Driven. sldprt.

FIGURE 9.17

Using the Transform Curve and Tangent to Curve options

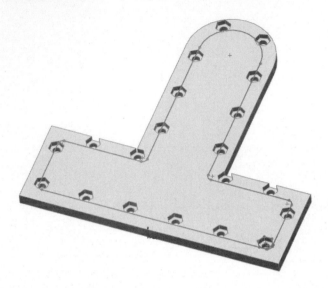

Using a Direction 2 for a Curve Driven Pattern creates a result similar to that in Figure 9.19. This is another situation that, although rare, is good to know about.

The rest of the Curve Driven Pattern works like the other pattern features that have already been demonstrated.

FIGURE 9.18

Using a 3D Curve Driven Pattern

FIGURE 9.19

Using Direction 2 with a Curve Driven Pattern

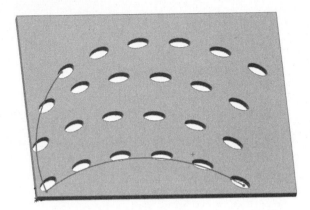

Using the Sketch Driven Pattern

 Sketch Driven Patterns use a set of sketch points to drive the locations of features. The Hole Wizard drives the locations of multiple holes using sketch points in a similar way. However, the Sketch Driven Pattern does not create a 3D pattern in the same way that the Hole Wizard does. Figure 9.20 shows a pattern of several features that has been patterned using a Sketch Driven Pattern. A reference point is not necessary for the first feature.

FIGURE 9.20

Using a Sketch Driven Pattern

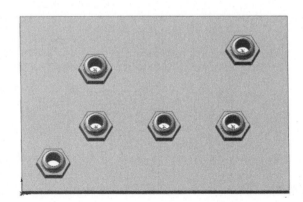

The Centroid option in the Reference Point section is fine for symmetrical and other easily definable shapes such as circles and rectangles, where you can find the centroid just by looking at it, but on more complex shapes, you may want to use the Selected Point option. The Selected Point option is shown in Figure 9.21.

FIGURE 9.21

Using the Selected Point option in a Sketch Driven Pattern

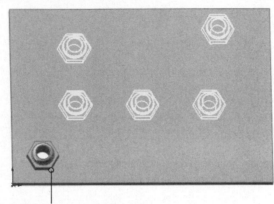

Selected point corresponds to the sketch points in the pattern

Using the Table Driven Pattern

 A Table Driven Pattern drives a set of feature locations, most commonly holes, from a table. The table may be imported from any source with two columns of data (X and Y) that are separated by a space, tab, or comma. Extraneous data will cause the import to fail.

The X, Y Origin for the table is determined by a Coordinate System reference geometry feature. The XY plane of the Coordinate System is the plane to which the XY data in the table refers.

You can access the Coordinate System command by choosing Insert ⇨ Reference Geometry ⇨ Coordinate System from the menu. You can create the Coordinate System by selecting a combination of a vertex for the Origin and edges to align the axes. Like the Sketch Driven Pattern, this feature can use either the centroid or a selected point on the feature to act as the reference point.

The fact that this feature is still in a floating dialog box points to its relatively low usage and priority on the SolidWorks upgrade schedule. The interface for the feature is rather crude in comparison to some of the more high-usage features. This interface is shown in Figure 9.22.

FIGURE 9.22

The Table Driven Pattern dialog box

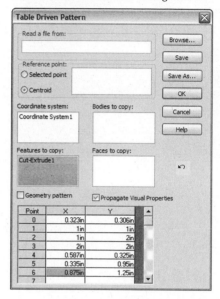

Using the Fill Pattern

 The Fill Pattern feature fills a face or area enclosed by a sketch with a pattern of a selected feature. The type of pattern used to fill the area is limited to one of four preset patterns that are commonly used in gratings and electronics ventilation in plastics and sheet metal. These patterns and other options for the Fill Pattern are shown in Figure 9.23.

The Pattern Layout panel enables you to control spacing and other geometrical aspects of the selected pattern layout, as well as the minimum gap from the fill boundary. This is most useful for patterns of regularly spaced features with an irregular boundary.

FIGURE 9.23

Using the Fill Pattern feature

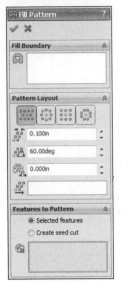

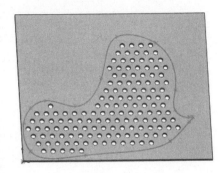

Using Cosmetic Patterns to Create an Appearance

Cosmetic Patterns are not patterns in the same sense as all the other pattern types in SolidWorks. Cosmetic Patterns do not actually create any geometry, just the appearance of geometry. They are applied using RealView functionality, which may or may not be available to you depending on your hardware, in particular your video card.

Note

More information is available on RealView-capable video cards from the SolidWorks corporate Web site, at www.solidworks.com/sw/support/videocardtesting.html. ■

Cosmetic Patterns are appropriate if your manufacturing method does not require actual geometry. For example, rapid prototyping requires explicit geometry in order to build a part, but a perforated sheet metal panel or a knurled cylindrical handle may require only a note on a drawing for the shop to set up a manufacturing process to create the geometry.

To apply a Cosmetic Pattern to a face, feature, body, or entire part, click the Appearances, Scenes, and Decals tab from the Task pane, and choose Appearances ⇨ Miscellaneous ⇨ Pattern or Appearances ⇨ Miscellaneous ⇨ RealView Only Appearances. Drag and drop the desired pattern onto the model, and use the popup menu to apply it to a face, feature, body, or the entire part. Figure 9.24 shows the Appearances, Scenes, and Decals tab of the Task Manager with some of the Cosmetic Pattern options.

Cross-Reference

You can find more details about appearances in Chapter 5. ■

FIGURE 9.24

Cosmetic Pattern options in the Appearances, Scenes, and Decals tab of the Task Manager

Mirroring 3D Solids

 Because symmetry is an important aspect of modeling parts in SolidWorks, mirror functions are a commonly used feature. This is true whether you work on machine parts, sheet metal, injection-molded, cast, or forged parts. I discussed sketch-mirroring techniques earlier in this chapter, and now I will discuss 3D mirroring techniques.

Mirroring bodies

Earlier in this chapter, I discussed patterning bodies. I mentioned that the patterning and mirroring tools in SolidWorks do not have adequate functionality when it comes to body management (specifically the merge options). Neither tool allows the patterned or mirrored bodies to be merged with the main body if the main body is not being patterned or mirrored. Figure 9.25 shows the Options panels for both the Linear Pattern (on the left) and the Mirror (on the right) features. Here you can see that the pattern function has no provision whatsoever for merging bodies. The Mirror appears to have the functionality, but it applies only to bodies that are used or created by the Mirror feature and ignores any other bodies that may exist in the part.

FIGURE 9.25

Options panels from the Linear Pattern and Mirror PropertyManagers

 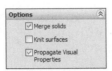

Best Practice

Mirroring bodies is the fastest and simplest method when a part has complete symmetry. However, this may not be an option if the part is not completely symmetrical. In addition, the decision to mirror must often be made when you are creating the first feature. If the first feature is modeled as a sketch that is built symmetrically around the Origin, then you may need to cut the part in half to mirror it. This is an adequate modeling technique, although it is not very efficient. ■

Mirroring features

Features can be mirrored across planes or flat faces used as the plane of symmetry. If you are mirroring many features, then it is best to mirror them all with a single mirror feature rather than to make several mirror features. You may have to do this by moving the mirror feature down the tree as you add new features. Depending on your part and what you are trying to accomplish, it may be better to mirror bodies than features, but you should not go too far out of your way or model in a contrived manner to make this happen.

Mirroring entire parts

Often when modeling, you are required to have a left- and a right-handed part. For this, you need to use a method other than body or feature mirroring. The Mirror Part command creates a brand-new part by mirroring an existing part. The new part does not inherit all the features of the original, and so any changes must be created in the original part. If you want different versions of the two parts, you need to use Configurations.

Cross-Reference

Configurations are covered in detail in Chapter 11. ■

You can use the Mirror Part command by pre-selecting a plane or planar face. You should be careful when choosing the plane because the new part will have a relationship to the part Origin, based on the plane on which it was mirrored. The Mirror Part command is one of the few remaining features without a PropertyManager that relies completely on pre-selection techniques.

The Mirror Part command is found in the Insert menu. When mirroring a part, you can bring several entity types from the original file to the mirrored part. These include axes, planes, sketches, cosmetic threads, and surface bodies. You can also bring over features and even break the link to the original file.

Mirror Part invokes the Insert Part feature, which is covered in more detail in Chapters 19, on multibodies and Master Model techniques, respectively.

One of the options available when you make a mirrored part is to break the link to the original part. This option brings forward all the sketches and features of the original part, and then adds a Move/Copy Body feature at the end of the tree that simply mirrors the body. Figure 9.26 shows the PropertyManager for the Insert Part feature.

FIGURE 9.26

Selecting items to bring into the mirrored part

Note

Under normal circumstances, you cannot get the Move/Copy Body feature to mirror a body. SolidWorks has applied some magic pixie dust behind the scene to make this happen. ■

Tutorial: Creating a Circular Pattern

Follow these steps to get practice with creating circular pattern features:

1. **Draw a square block on the Top plane centered on the Origin, 4 inches on each side, .5-inch-thick extruded Mid Plane with .5-inch chamfers on the four corners.**

2. **Pre-select the top face of the block and start the Hole Wizard.** Select a counterbored hole for a 10-32 socket head cap screw, and place it as shown in Figure 9.27.

FIGURE 9.27

Start drawing a plate with holes.

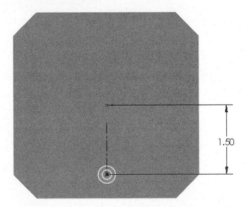

3. **Create an axis using the Front and Right planes.** Choose Insert ⇨ Reference Geometry ⇨ Axis. Select the Two Planes option, and select Front and Right planes from the flyout FeatureManager. (Click the bar that says Axis at the top of the PropertyManager to access the flyout FeatureManager.) This creates an axis in the center of the rectangular part.

4. **Click the Circular Pattern tool on the Features toolbar.** Select the new Axis in the top Pattern Axis selection box in the Circular Pattern PropertyManager. Select the Equal Spacing option and make sure that the angle is set to 360°. Set the number of instances to 8.

5. **In the Features to Pattern panel, select the counterbored hole.** Make sure that Geometry Pattern is turned off.

6. **Click OK to finish the part, as shown in Figure 9.28.**

The finished circular pattern

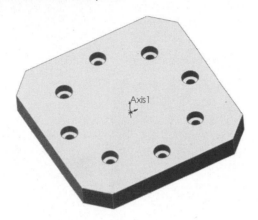

Tutorial: Mirroring Features

Follow these steps to get some practice with creating mirror features:

1. **Open the file from the DVD called** Chapter9 Tutorial2.sldprt.
2. **Open a sketch on the side of the part, as shown in Figure 9.29.** The straight line on top is 1.00 inch long, and the angled line ends 2.70 inches from the edge, as shown.

The sketch for the Rib feature

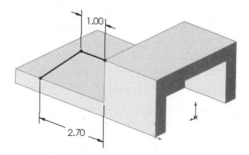

3. **Click the Rib tool on the Features toolbar or select it from the menu at Insert ⇨ Features ⇨ Rib.** Set the material arrow to go down toward the block, and the thickness setting to go to the inside by .375 inches. The PropertyManager and the preview should look like Figure 9.30.

FIGURE 9.30

Applying the Rib feature

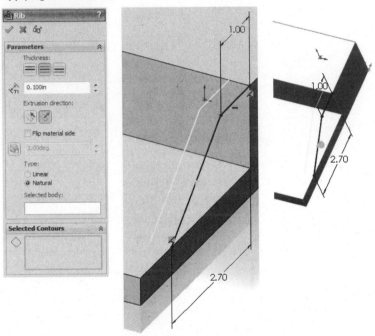

4. **Create a linear pattern using the rib, making the pattern reaches 2 inches into the part.**
5. **Create a chamfer on the same side of the part as the original rib, as shown in Figure 9.31.** The chamfer is an Angle-Distance using 60° and .5 inches.
6. **Create a round hole, sized and positioned as shown.**
7. **Mirror the hole and the chamfer about the Right plane.** The parametrics of the chamfer will have difficulty patterning, and so you need to use the Geometry Pattern option. The finished part is shown in Figure 9.32.

FIGURE 9.31

FIGURE 9.31

Additional features on the part

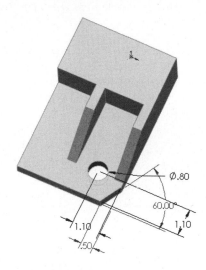

FIGURE 9.32

The finished part

Tutorial: Applying a Cosmetic Pattern

Follow these steps to practice creating a cosmetic pattern:

1. **Open the file from the DVD for Chapter 9 called** Chapter 9 – tutorial – cosmetic pattern.sldprt.

2. **Click the Appearances tab in the Task Pane.** These steps will work whether or not you have RealView actually selected.

3. **Expand the Appearances heading, then the Metal heading, then Steel, and then drag the Sandblasted Steel icon from the lower panel onto the part.** When the popup menu appears, select the Part icon to apply the appearance to the entire part. Figure 9.33 shows the Task Pane and the popup menu.

Applying an appearance to a part

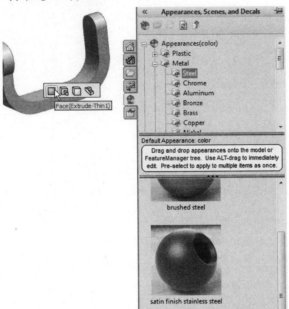

4. **Expand the Miscellaneous listing (under Appearances) and the Pattern heading.** Drag the Waffle Pattern onto the large cylindrical face of the part, and then Alt-click the Face icon in the popup toolbar. Using the Alt key while dragging or to select face, feature, body, or part automatically activates the PropertyManager to edit the appearance. Figure 9.34 shows the Appearances PropertyManager.

5. **In the Mapping tab of the Appearances PropertyManager, select the cylindrical mapping under the Mapping Style section of the Mapping Controls panel.**

6. **Change the Rotation to 45 degrees, and choose the smallest Mapping Size.**

FIGURE 9.34

FIGURE 9.34

The Appearances PropertyManager

Summary

Feature patterns and mirrors are powerful tools, but you need to have some discipline to benefit from their usefulness. Patterns in particular are extremely flexible, with many types of functions and options available. You should avoid sketch patterns if possible, not only because of performance considerations but also because complex sketches (sketches with a lot of entities and relations) tend to fail more often than simple sketches.

Using Equations

P arametric sketch relations are not the only way to drive dimensions with intelligence. You can also use equations, link values, and global variables. Equations help you create simple or complex mathematical relations between dimensions. Link values are essentially a quick way of making two dimensions equal. Global variables can be used in equations like other dimension names. These three techniques are all very similar and related to one another in the interface, but are used in different ways in different situations.

Equations can cause problems if used incorrectly, but if you are familiar with how they work, you can avoid the common pitfalls and get maximum benefit by adding intelligence to your designs.

Understanding Equations

 You can use equations to create mathematical relations between dimensions. You can find the Equations tool on the Tools toolbar or by choosing Tools ⇨ Equations from the menu. Equations are stored in a folder at the top of the FeatureManager. Figure 10.1 shows the Equations main interface along with the Add Equation window. As I have noted with other areas of the interface, Equations still uses a floating dialog box. SolidWorks has put most functions in the PropertyManager, but equations tend to be more horizontal than vertical, while the PropertyManager is more vertical than horizontal.

FIGURE 10.1

The Equations interface

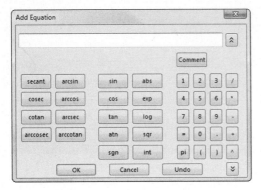

Using the Equations interface, you can turn off individual equations temporarily by deselecting the Active check box to the left of the equation. Equations can also be deactivated by a design table. I will discuss design tables in more detail in Chapter 11, where I also discuss configurations.

Caution

Although I do not cover configurations until Chapter 11, I will mention part of the relationship between equations and configurations here. Equations and configurations (particularly those that are driven by a design table) should probably not be mixed. This is not because they do not work together, but is more for the sake of organization. Add to this the fact that starting in SolidWorks 2011, Global Variables are now configurable, and it certainly opens up new possibilities, but it also creates potential problems for users, as they can control dimensions from both configurations and equations. Also, equations in Excel are far more powerful than the comparatively limited equation functionality offered in SolidWorks. Of course, every user will have her own reasons for working one way or another; I am just offering a warning of a potential source of conflict. ■

Creating equations

Equations are easy to create and useful for many purposes. A common situation where you would use an equation is to space a pattern of holes evenly along an edge, including the gap on both ends, where the gap at the ends is half of the regular spacing. Before you write an equation, you need to take care of a few organizational details.

Naming dimensions

It is not necessary to name every entity in every SolidWorks document, but you should get in the habit of naming important features, sketches, and even dimensions. Named dimensions become particularly important when you use them in equations, configurations, and design tables. Under most circumstances, you do not use or even see dimension names, but with equations, you do.

Named dimensions make a huge difference when you want to recognize the function of an equation by simply reading it. A most obvious example would be the difference between D3@Sketch6 and Length@WindowExtrusionSketch. The first name means nothing, but the second one is descriptive if you are familiar with the part.

To name a dimension, click the dimension and go to the PropertyManager. In the Primary Value panel shown in Figure 10.2, type the new name for the dimension in the Name text box. You cannot use the symbol @ in dimension names because it is used as a delimiter between the name of the dimension and the feature or sketch to which it applies. Also, be aware that even though the software allows you to change the name of the sketch or feature in the Dimension PropertyManager, it will not accept this change.

FIGURE 10.2

Renaming a dimension

Best Practice

You should keep dimension names as short as possible while still making them unique and descriptive. This is because space in the interface is often limited, and when combined with sketch or feature names (and even part names when used in an assembly), the names can become difficult to display in a readable fashion. Also keep in mind that spaces in dimension names can be misinterpreted by Excel. ■

Tip

You can show dimension names as a part of the actual dimension; make sure the option that you access by choosing View⇨Dimension Names is selected. It's also helpful to know the FeatureManager Filter filters dimension names, which makes named dimensions easy to find. Figure 10.3 shows the filter displaying features and sketches that contain a dimension containing the filtered word "height." Other filtered words display in tool tips, but dimension names appear not to. ■

FIGURE 10.3

Using the FeatureManager Filter to filter dimension names

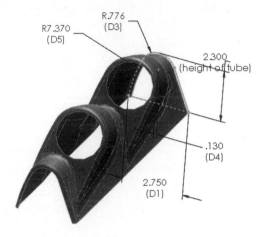

Building the equation

When creating an equation in SolidWorks, it is often a good idea to write it out on paper first to make sure you have the concept correct. Examine the part shown in Figure 10.4, where the relevant dimensions have been named and displayed. The number of holes — called Instances here — is the driving variable. From that number, the spacing of the holes is calculated over the length of the part. There is also a gap on each end of the pattern of holes. This gap (measured between the center of the last hole and the end of the part) always needs to be half of the spacing between the holes. The sigma symbols to the left of the dimensions indicate that an equation is driving it. Dimensions driven by equations cannot be directly edited.

FIGURE 10.4

Variables for the hole pattern

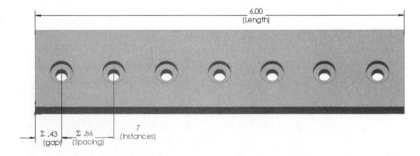

In this case, a more sophisticated equation has not been implemented to account for the diameter of the holes possibly interfering with one another when there are a large number of holes. In other words, because there are two values that need to be calculated (the spacing and the gap), you need to create two equations. Because the gap dimension is always half of the spacing, the spacing needs to be calculated first, as follows:

```
Spacing = Length / ((Instances-1)+1)
```

The *Instances –1* term stands for the number of spacings. If you have two holes, then there is only one spacing. The *+1* term stands for the two half-spacings for the two ends. The second equation is simpler and looks like this:

```
Gap = Spacing / 2
```

The order of the equations is important. SolidWorks solves the equations in the order in which they are listed in the Equations dialog box. Because the gap is dependent on the spacing, the spacing must be calculated before the gap. If it is done the other way around, you can get into a situation where it takes two rebuilds to finalize a set of equations, or even a situation where in every rebuild all the numbers change. This is called a circular relation, and is a common error in order or history dependent functions, not just in SolidWorks but in many CAD applications. Figure 10.5 shows the resulting set of equations.

FIGURE 10.5

Equations for the hole pattern

Before beginning to build the equation, you should first display the dimensions that you need to use to create the equation. You can add dimensions to the equation by clicking them from the graphics window. To do this, right-click the Annotations folder at the top of the FeatureManager, and select Show Feature Dimensions, as shown in Figure 10.6. You should also select the Display Annotations option if it is not already selected. When you have done this, all the dimensions that you need to create every feature are displayed. Also, be sure to turn on the Show Dimension Names option by choosing View ⇨ Dimension Names.

Tip

For models that have more than a few features, showing all the dimensions in the entire model may overload the screen with information. In this case, you can double-click a feature from the FeatureManager to show all the dimensions on that feature. ∎

To build the equation, first click the Equation button on the Tools toolbar to open the Equations dialog box. Then click the Add button to display the Add Equation dialog box. To add dimensions to the equation section, just select the dimension. You can use the keypad on the dialog box or on your keyboard to add operators and syntax. All standard rules of syntax apply for the order of operations, use of parentheses, and driving versus driven sides of the equation.

FIGURE 10.6

Showing all of the dimensions in a part

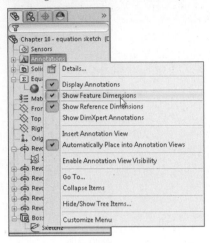

Using comments

Notice the comment to the right of the first equation in Figure 10.5. Comments can be very useful for annotating equations for yourself or others. Two important reasons to annotate are to remember the significance of variables or dimensions and to add special notes about the logic of the equation that may not be obvious.

You can make comments for equations by using a single quote after the end of the equation, or by clicking the Comment button in the Add Equation dialog box. In the following example, the comment, "This must be solved first," is applied to the equation using the single quote before the comment.

```
"Spacing@LPattern1" = "Length@Sketch1" / ("Instances@LPattern1")
     'This must be solved first
```

To expand on the earlier discussion about projected changes to the Equation interface, several standard selection functionalities do not work in the Edit Equation dialog box. These include triple-clicking to select all (although double-clicking works to select a single word) and pressing Ctrl+A to select all.

Tip

You can make general comments for the model in the Design Journal, a Microsoft Word document that is embedded into the SolidWorks file. The Design Journal is found in the Design Binder folder near the top of the FeatureManager. ■

On the DVD

You can find the part used in this section on the DVD with the filename `Chapter 10 Equations.sldprt`. ■

Using driven dimensions

Sometimes it is more convenient to use a driven (reference) dimension in an equation. This is particularly true when using geometry is the best way to calculate a number. For example, if you are manufacturing a helical auger in 90-degree sections from flat steel stock, then you need to design the auger in 3D but begin to manufacture it in 2D.

What is the shape of the auger when flat? The best way to figure this out (aside from lofted bends, which are discussed in Chapter 21) is to use a little high school geometry, a construction sketch, and some simple equations.

Figure 10.7 shows a 90-degree section of an auger blade. The outside diameter is 12 inches, and the blade width is 3 inches. The overall height is 4 inches. In this case, the auger is represented as a surface because the thickness is ignored. Surface features can be useful in situations like this (used as construction geometry) and are discussed in Chapter 20.

FIGURE 10.7

A representation of the auger

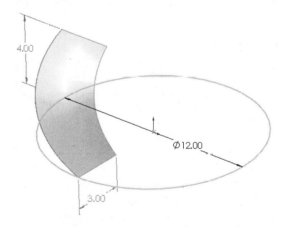

On the DVD

You can find the part for Figure 10.7 on the DVD with the filename `Chapter 10 Auger.sldprt`. ∎

With this information, you can calculate the lengths of the 3D edges using a sketch and a simple equation. In Figure 10.8, the hypotenuses of the triangles represent the helical edges of the inside and outside of the auger. By making the triangles the same height as the auger section, and by making the horizontal side of the triangle the same length as a quarter of the inside or outside diameter by using simple equations, the geometry and sketch relations automatically calculate the flat lengths of the inside and outside edges of the auger (length of triangle side = diameter of circle × pi / 4). In this way, the triangle is used to simplify the calculation, and give it a visual result.

FIGURE 10.8

Triangles calculate the length of the helical edge.

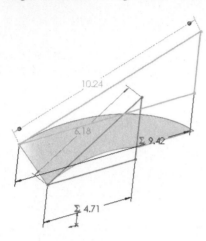

From this point, you can calculate the flat pattern again, using SolidWorks' sketch-solving capabilities as the calculator. Think of the auger as being the cardboard tube inside a roll of paper towels. If you examine one of these tubes closely, you see that it is simply a straight and flat strip of cardboard that has been wound around a cylinder. What was the flat, straight edge of the original board is wound into a helix. This method simply reverses that process.

This example requires the little-used arc-length dimension to drive the size of the arc. The hypotenuse dimensions are shown by driven or reference dimensions, and these are used to drive the arc-length dimensions, as shown in Figure 10.9. Remember that you can create arc length dimensions by using the Smart Dimension tool to click both endpoints of the arc and then the arc itself.

The reasoning behind this example may be a little difficult to grasp, but the equations and the sketches are certainly simple.

Caution

Using reference dimensions on the driving (independent or right) side of the equation can, in some situations, require more than one rebuild to arrive at a stable value (meaning a value that does not change with the next rebuild). SolidWorks issues a warning when it sees that you are using a reference dimension in an equation, but it does allow it. ∎

 Equations are listed in the Equations folder in the FeatureManager. You can edit, add, or delete them through the right mouse button (RMB) menu.

FIGURE 10.9

Figuring the flat pattern of the auger

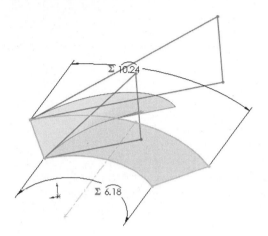

Using equation tricks

Some functions that are permitted in SolidWorks equations are often viewed as parlor tricks, but they actually do have some practical applications. The two functions that fall into this category are IIF and SWITCH. If you are familiar with any programming language, you may already be familiar with these two functions.

IIF

In words, this is how an IIF statement is used:

If some relationship is fulfilled, then the IIF function returns a value. If the relationship is not fulfilled, then it returns a different value.

A more technical description is

```
IIF(expression, value if true, value if false)
```

In practice, you could use it like this:

```
IIF(x>5, x-1, x+1)
```

which reads, "if x is greater than 5, then subtract 1 from x; if not, then add 1 to x." One of the reasons why this is considered a parlor trick is that this function causes the value of x to oscillate between two numbers (depending on the number that it starts with) with each rebuild. It may be difficult to imagine an application where this sort of behavior would be desirable, but when you combine it with a macro that simply rebuilds a model a number of times, you can use it to create a certain animation effect.

On the DVD

A simple example of the `IIF` function can be found on the DVD with the filename `Chapter 10 Oscillate.sldprt`. The equation is shown in Figure 10.10. ∎

FIGURE 10.10

An equation using `IIF`

Tip

You can find some great examples of this function at `www.mikejwilson.com`, along with many other extremely creative examples of SolidWorks modeling. The model on this site called `Ship in a Bottle.sldprt` also includes a macro that will rebuild the model a certain number of times, which is useful for animations that are created in this way. ∎

You can use an IIF statement to control the suppression state of features and components. This function is described in detail later in this chapter.

SWITCH

The `SWITCH` function enables you to have a list of relationships with associated values. The value of the first relationship in the list that is satisfied is returned by the `SWITCH` function. For example,

```
switch (x>2, 1.5, x>1, .5 x<1, 2.5)
```

reads as follows: "if x is greater than 2, then the answer is 1.5; if x is not greater than 2 but greater than 1, then the answer is .5; if x is less than 1, then the answer is 2.5."

As you can see, this function does not cover all situations, but it does create a condition where the value cycles through three different numbers in a specific order. Is this useful? Possibly. Again, the main application for this function would be a simple animation for changing the size or shape of SolidWorks components that cannot be changed in other more conventional ways.

Using Link Values

Link values are simply a way to link several dimensions together, making them equal. A link value is not exactly like an equation that sets the dimensions equal, because it does not depend on order like an equation does. All dimensions are set to the same value simultaneously.

A special relationship and overlap of functionality exists between Link Values and Global Variables. I cover this relationship in this chapter.

Link values are available by right-clicking on a dimension. You can also get to link values by clicking the down arrow on the right side of the Modify dialog box. Unfortunately, they are not available from the RMB menu when the dimension tool is active. To apply a link value to a new dimension, you must place the dimension, exit the dimension tool, right-click the dimension, and select Link Value.

Link values are listed under the Equations folder in the FeatureManager. Figure 10.11 shows the link values in a listed part, and the drop-down list from which you can select them or type them. Notice again that the Link Values feature also operates from a dialog box instead of the PropertyManager.

FIGURE 10.11

Link values listed in the FeatureManager, and the Shared Values interface

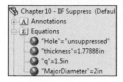 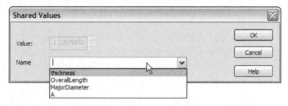

Note

Another way to access link values is through the Modify dialog box. If you click the down arrow at the right end of the dimension value box, you can select between Link Values and Equations. In fact, if you press the Down Arrow key on the keyboard, the Equation interface becomes available. There is no similar trick to get Link Values to appear. ■

You must type in the first link value that is assigned in a part. After you add the first one, you can link other dimensions to this link value by using the drop-down arrow shown in Figure 10.11. You cannot edit link values directly, which means that you cannot change a dimension from linking to a value called "height" and instead link it to a value called "length." In order to change the value to which a dimension is linked, you must first unlink the value and then relink it. The Unlink function is available from the RMB menu in the same way that you assign link values. Dimensions that have a link value have the small chain symbol displayed to the left of the dimension. Figure 10.12 shows the Unlink option in the RMB menu.

FIGURE 10.12

Unlinking a link value

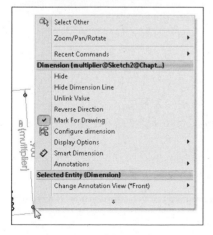

To link several dimensions to the same value at the same time, you can Ctrl+select multiple dimensions and then right-click one of them and select Link Value. It will link all the dimensions selected at once. (Thanks to Brian McElyea for this suggestion!)

Tip

One link value name has a special significance. If you use the name thickness, then a Link To Thickness option appears in all extrude dialog boxes. This is intended to reflect sheet metal functionality, but it is useful for models of various manufacturing techniques.

To take this one step further, you can save a part template with a thickness link value; all your new parts will also have this functionality right from the start. To save the template with a link value, you must create at least one dimension to assign the link value, and then delete the geometry (and the dimension); however, the link value will remain. ■

Link values of different types are not necessarily interchangeable. You cannot use angular dimension link values on radius, diameter, or linear dimensions. You can use linear and diameter link values interchangeably, but not angle link values.

Using Global Variables

Global variables are assigned in the Equations dialog box as simply the variable name equaling an expression or a value. Figure 10.13 shows a list of equations, link values, and global variables. When you type in a variable name, you do not need to add the quotation marks; they are added automatically. The global variable named "multiplier" uses an expression to calculate its value. The global variable shown in Figure 10.13 called "global variable" is simply assigned a value directly.

Equations, link values, and global variables

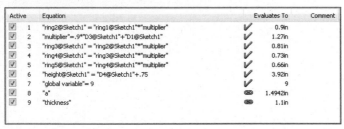

Active		Equation	Evaluates To		Comment
☑	1	"ring2@Sketch1" = "ring1@Sketch1"*"multiplier"	✔	0.9in	
☑	2	"multiplier"=.9*"D3@Sketch1"+"D1@Sketch1"	✔	1.27in	
☑	3	"ring3@Sketch1" = "ring2@Sketch1"*"multiplier"	✔	0.81in	
☑	4	"ring4@Sketch1" = "ring3@Sketch1"*"multiplier"	✔	0.73in	
☑	5	"ring5@Sketch1" = "ring4@Sketch1"*"multiplier"	✔	0.66in	
☑	6	"height@Sketch1" = "D4@Sketch1"+.75	✔	3.92in	
☑	7	"global variable"= 9	✔	9	
☑	8	"a"	⚊	1.4942in	
☑	9	"thickness"	⚊	1.1in	

Global variables can be used as values in other equations, or they can be used as link values. The link value functionality has been available since SolidWorks 2007. Figure 10.14 shows the Shared Values dialog box enabling the user to select either global variables or link values when assigning a link value. Note that link values cannot be assigned through the Equations interface; they must be assigned through the Shared Values dialog box, while global variables can only be assigned in the

Equations interface, not in the Shared Values dialog box. Notice that the items with the $VAR syntax are the global variables.

FIGURE 10.14

Assigning a link value or a global variable as a link value

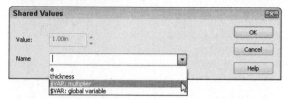

You can use custom and file properties to drive equations. If you right-click your Equations folder and select Show Properties, you see that the default file properties already exist in the list, shown in Figure 10.15:

Global Variable

Custom Property

Default File Property

FIGURE 10.15

Equations and properties

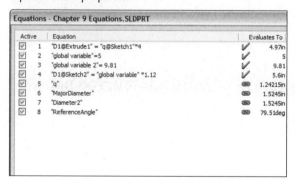

In the equation editor shown on the right in Figure 10.15, you can expand the list of global, custom, and default properties for easy selection and placement into equations. Any custom properties you add that are of the type "number" are automatically added to this list and can be used in equations. Notice that the custom property "cost" is a property saved in my template and gets picked up for use here.

Note that you can assign both a custom property and a global variable with the same name. The global variable will take precedence over the custom property to evaluate an equation.

Starting in SolidWorks 2011, global variables are now configurable. Chapter 11 covers this feature in more detail, but the syntax for using a design table to drive a global variable is as follows:

$VALUE@*global_variable_name*@equations

Using Expressions

Expressions, unlike all the previous variables, values, and equations, can be entered directly into dimension dialog boxes in the Modify dialog box and PropertyManager value boxes. The expressions have to be composed of numbers and mathematical operators. An expression such as

```
2.375+(4.8/3) -1.1
```

is perfectly acceptable, as is

```
1+1/2
```

or

```
1 1/2
```

In the second case in this example, the plus symbol is understood.

Other types of operations are also available, such as ones for changing units in a dimension box. For example, if you are editing a part in inches, and enter 40mm, then SolidWorks does the conversion for you. You can even mix units in a single expression such as 4.875+3.5mm, where the inch part is assumed as the document units.

SolidWorks does not remember the expression itself, only the final value. Expressions can be entered into any place where you enter dimensions for SolidWorks features.

Controlling Suppression States of Features

You can use the IIF statement described earlier in this chapter to control suppression states of features and components. An example of the syntax is:

<feature name> = iif(*expression, value if true, value if false*)

Figure 10.16 shows this type of equation in use. Keep in mind that the quotes are important.

On the DVD
The part used in Figure 10.16 is on the DVD with the filename `Chapter 10 - IIF Suppress.sldprt.` ∎

You can also use this equation in assemblies to control suppression states of components (parts and subassemblies).

FIGURE 10.16

Using IIF to control suppression states

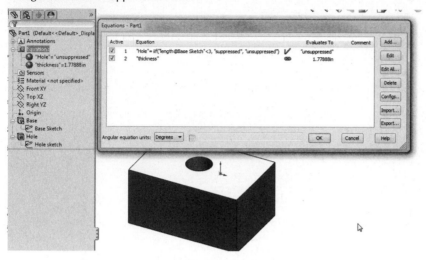

Linking to External Equations

You can use externally saved equations to share equations between models. To export an equation, click the Export button in the lower-right corner of the Equations dialog box, as shown in Figure 10.16. To link the current model to the externally saved equation, make sure the Link To File option is checked at the bottom of the Equation Export dialog box, as shown in Figure 10.17.

FIGURE 10.17

Saving an equation to an external file

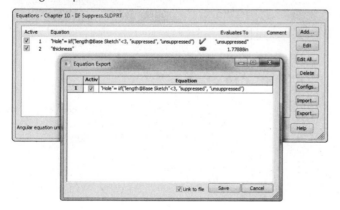

The equation is saved to a simple *.txt file. The default name for the external equation text file is equations.txt. You can change the name if you like, but remember that if you use Windows Explorer to change the name or change it with the referencing file closed, SolidWorks will not know that the filename has been changed. At the bottom of the Equations dialog box is a path for a linked equation file. You can only link to one equation file at a time.

To link to an existing equation from a SolidWorks model, use the Import button in the Equations dialog box.

Also be aware that only equations and global variables can be shared in this way. Link values cannot be shared.

Tutorial: Using Equations

Follow these steps to get some practice with using equations:

1. **Start from the part on the DVD with the filename** Chapter10 Tutorial Start. sldprt, **shown in Figure 10.18.**

Starting the Equations tutorial

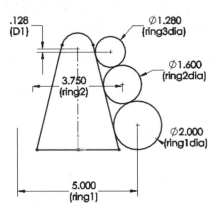

2. **Show the dimension names.** Choose View ⇨ Show Dimension Names to find this setting.

3. **Double-click the Circular Pattern feature to display the angle and number of instances of the feet and related features.** You may have to move the angle dimension to see the pattern instance number.

4. **Click the instance number.** Change the name of the dimension to # (pound or number sign) in the Dimension PropertyManager. Make sure that Instant3D is unselected when doing this.

5. Double-click the first feature, which is the revolve, and rename the 3.60-inch dimension CapRad, **again by selecting it and using the PropertyManager.**

6. **Write an equation that drives the number of legs by CapRad/7.**

   a. Open the Equations dialog box by choosing Tools ⇨ Equations.

   b. Click Add to add an equation.

   c. Double-click the Circular Pattern and click the # dimension. Make sure that the name of the dimension is listed in the equation box, and type an equal sign.

   d. Double-click the Revolve feature and select the CapRad dimension; then type the characters **/1.5**.

   e. Add a comment to the equation to reflect which dimension is driving which dimension.

7. **Click Rebuild, press Ctrl+B or Ctrl+Q to rebuild the model, and observe whether any update takes place.**

8. **Rename the 6.00-inch dimension for the height of the revolved feature to** DomeHt.

9. **Create a second equation that drives the DomeHt dimension at the current ratio of the height to the radius.**

   a. Create a global variable called Ratio = 6/3.6 (1.66667) in the Equations dialog box.

   b. Create the equation. The equation will take the form of DomeHt = (Ratio) × CapRad. You can use the drop-down list under the calculator pad to select the Ratio variable from the list.

10. **Use a link value to make the radii of Fillet1 and Fillet2 the same.**

11. **Double-click the revolve feature.** Change the CapRad dimension to 5 and rebuild. You should observe 3 feet. Change it again to 6 and you should see 4 feet.

12. **Give the part a new name, including your initials or the date, and save and close it.**

Summary

SolidWorks equations and related dimension-management tools are powerful but often leave you wishing for a little more flexibility and control. The interface is not up to date with the rest of the SolidWorks interface, and so I would look to see an updated equation interface soon that integrates dimension input, link values, and global variables.

Be careful about crossing SolidWorks native equation functionality with configurations; you may end up with dimensions that are controlled by both tools. Remember that the calculation capability of Excel is far greater than what is found in SolidWorks equations.

Working with Part Configurations

Configurations, also known as simply *configs*, are variations of a part in which dimensions are changed, features are suppressed (turned off), and other items such as color or custom properties may be controlled. Configurations enable you to have these variations within a single part file, which is both convenient and efficient.

This chapter deals only with part configurations, but assemblies can also have configurations. Assembly configurations can use different part configurations, among other things. This will mean more to you as you learn about part configurations.

Cross-Reference

Assembly configurations are discussed in the *SolidWorks 2011 Assemblies Bible* (Wiley, 2011). ■

One example of configurations is having many sizes of a fastener within a single part file. Socket Head Cap Screws have thousands of potential sizes, and you could very efficiently reuse the same sketches and features to create all of those sizes based on a table. Configured parts can also have features that you can turn off and on (suppress and unsuppress, respectively), such as a cross drive or a slotted drive. Changing dimensions and suppressing or unsuppressing features are the most commonly used techniques available through configurations.

There is some overlap between the topics of configurations and display states, with colors and hide/show states being controlled by both methods. When you have an option, it is best to control visual properties using display states because they require fewer resources (they're faster). Display states for part documents are covered in more detail in Chapter 5.

IN THIS CHAPTER

Controlling part configurations

Exploring design tables

Creating a design table

Examining the benefits of using the Configuration Publisher

Working with configurations and design tables tutorial

Controlling Items with Configurations

With every new release of SolidWorks software, it seems that more items become "configurable"; that is, able to be driven by configurations. Configurable items for parts include the following:

- Feature dimensions, tolerances, driving/driven state
- Suppression of features, equations, sketch relations, and feature end conditions
- Sketch plane used by a sketch
- Configuration-specific custom properties
- Part, body, feature, and face colors
- Derived configurations
- Properties that can be assigned, such as mass and center of gravity
- Configuration of base or split parts
- Sketch pattern instances
- Sketch text
- Scale feature sizes
- Cosmetic threads
- Global variables
- Helix feature parameters
- Size of Hole Wizard holes

You can control configurations in several ways:

- Making changes manually to dimensions and features
- Using the Configure Feature/Modify Configurations table
- Using an Excel-based design table
- Using the Configuration Publisher

Finding configurations

 SolidWorks lists configurations in the ConfigurationManager. This is a tab at the top of the FeatureManager area, shown in Figure 11.1.

Tip

You can split the FeatureManager interface into two by dragging the splitter bar at the top of the panel. This very useful function is shown in Figure 11.1, and it enables you to see the ConfigurationManager in the upper panel and the FeatureManager in the lower panel. Also remember that you can detach the PropertyManager from the left-side panel area. ■

FIGURE 11.1

Locating the ConfigurationManager tab

Deleting configs

Each part has a default config named "Default." There is nothing special about this config; you can rename it and even delete it. At least one config must always remain in the tree, and you cannot delete the configuration that is currently active. If you would like to remove a config, then you need to switch to another config (by double-clicking the other configuration in the ConfigurationManager), and then delete the one you want to remove.

If you have used the software for a while, you may remember not being able to delete or rename configurations that are referenced by open documents. This limitation (at least for renaming configurations) was removed. Being able to rename configurations referenced by open documents such as assemblies or drawings is an important change that new users will probably take for granted and veteran users need to be aware of.

Cross-Reference

The *SolidWorks 2011 Assemblies Bible* (Wiley, 2011) deals with configurations of assemblies in depth. This chapter deals only with configurations of parts. Configurations of drawings do not exist, although drawings can reference both part and assembly drawings. ∎

> If you try to delete a part configuration being used by an open assembly, SolidWorks simply issues the message "None of the selected entities could be deleted" without explanation.

If you delete a configuration of a part that is used in an assembly, but the assembly is not currently open, the next time the assembly is opened it issues the message "The following component configurations could not be found . . . . If the configuration was renamed the same configuration will be used, otherwise the last active configuration will be substituted for each instance."

You can delete groups of configs by window select, Shift+select, or Ctrl+select in the ConfigurationManager. You can also use the right mouse button (RMB) menu, much like regular features in the FeatureManager. None of the configurations selected for deletion may be active, or referenced by other open and resolved documents.

Sorting configs

In the ConfigurationManager, configs are listed alphabetically, not in the order in which they are created. This has several advantages, especially when you have a large number of configs. For example, if configs are named by size in a part that you are working with, then when you select a configuration you can type in a number and the selection scrolls to that place in the list of configs. This makes it easier to select the one you are looking for, much the same as it works in Windows Explorer.

Enhancing alphabetization

This alphabetized order is significant because many other sections of the SolidWorks interface are not alphabetized, which causes problems when you are browsing for items in larger lists. Sections that are not alphabetized include Help/Contents, Files of Type lists in Open and Save dialog boxes, and the File Locations settings (Tools ⇨ Options ⇨ File Locations), Entity Color list, and several others. If you are inclined to submit an Enhancement Request to SolidWorks, alphabetization of lists is one topic that would benefit everyone and should be easy for SolidWorks to implement.

Naming configs

In order for this sorting and alphabetization to work, you must first name the configs properly. For example, if you have a list of sizes or config names from 1 to 100, then you should use 001, 002...100 as your syntax. This makes the config names easier to browse and type in. Syntax becomes most important when you place a part with many configs into an assembly, because you must select a config from the list, and typing in the first few numbers is often faster and easier than scrolling to it.

On the DVD

The DVD contains a part called `Chapter 11 Config Names.sldprt`**, which illustrates proper naming and alphabetization. ■**

To understand this technique better, you can open the part called `Chapter 11 Config Names.sldprt` from the DVD, split the FeatureManager area, and change one of the panes to display the ConfigurationManager. Click one of the configuration names, and type in a number between 001 and 100. The highlight scrolls to the number that you typed in. Thoughtful selection of the configuration names can save you and your co-workers a lot of time when you need to insert select configs into an assembly. Figure 11.2 shows this arrangement.

Cross-Reference

The splitter bar and other portions of the FeatureManager interface appear in Chapter 2. ■

FIGURE 11.2

The split FeatureManager, displaying the ConfigurationManager

Activating configurations

Within a part file, to change the display from one configuration to another, you must first switch to the ConfigurationManager panel, and then either double-click the desired config or right-click it and select Show Configuration.

Alternatively, you can right-click the config in the ConfigurationManager and select Show Preview, as shown in Figure 11.3. A small preview thumbnail displays in the PropertyManager panel. However, not all configurations will have previews. For example, in a part with many configs that have been generated automatically by a design table, the configurations may not have previews because the config itself has never actually been rebuilt. Previews exist only when the configuration has been activated at least once, the image on the screen generated, and the part then saved. SolidWorks stores both the body (geometry) and the preview image of the part so that next time you access the configuration, the software does not have to rebuild everything again. Storage space is cheaper than rebuild time.

You can even select a configuration while opening a file. This enables you to save time by avoiding rebuilding the model. To take advantage of this option, you must use the File ➪ Open interface, which is shown in Figure 11.4. You can select the config from the lower-right drop-down Configurations list.

FIGURE 11.3

Showing a configuration preview

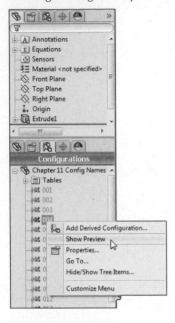

FIGURE 11.4

Selecting a configuration from the Open dialog box

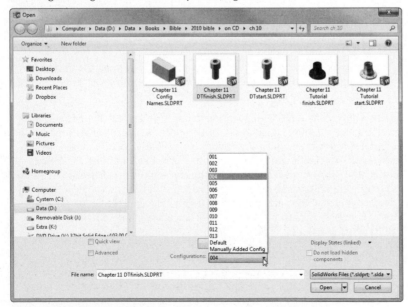

Creating configurations

You can create configs manually using the Modify dialog box, using the Configure Feature/Modify Configurations table, or through Excel-driven design tables. Design tables are extremely useful for situations where there are more than a few configs or more than a few items are being controlled. You should use design tables because they keep things very organized within the spreadsheet grid.

For now, I am going to focus on creating and manipulating configs manually so that you can become familiar with them without also worrying about Excel and design table syntax. I talk about design tables near the end of this chapter.

Creating a new config

To make a new config, you can right-click the top-level icon in the ConfigurationManager, which displays a part symbol and the name of the part, and select Add Configuration. If you right-click an existing configuration, SolidWorks will make a derived config, which I discuss later in this chapter. Figure 11.5 shows the RMB menu and the Properties dialog box that you can use to set up the new config.

Creating a new configuration

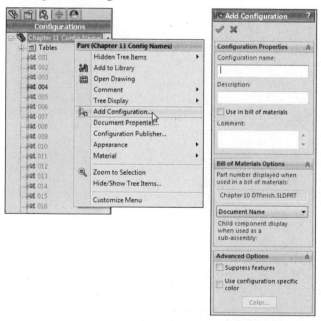

Using Configuration properties and options

The name of the config is important mainly for quick access and organization purposes. The configuration description is also important, because it can display in the ConfigurationManager, and even in the Assembly tree. (You can also use the FeatureManager Filter to search configuration descriptions.) This is important when the name of the config is numerical rather than descriptive, and you would like to also have a description but not include it in the name. The config description can also appear in place of the filename in the Assembly tree display. Config descriptions can be driven manually through the Configuration Properties dialog box or through a design table if you have many configs to manage. You can display config descriptions through the RMB menu, as shown in Figure 11.6.

Enabling configuration descriptions

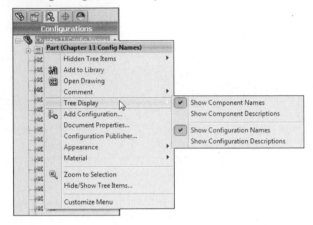

The Bill of Materials (BOM) option is set in the Configuration Properties to use the filename, the configuration name, or a custom name that the user specifies. You can save this setting with a template. You achieve control over configurations through the combination of the Configuration Properties and the Advanced Options, which I discuss next.

Best Practice

Although you can change the preferred settings at any time, it is definitely a best practice to make a template early on when you are using SolidWorks to model parts. SolidWorks remembers the BOM options and Advanced options that you set for the Default configuration and uses them in document templates. This is true for both part and assembly templates. ■

Using Advanced options

Two advanced configuration options are found in the bottom panel of the Configuration Properties PropertyManager: Suppress features and Use configuration specific color. While the second option is self-explanatory, the first one is not and often catches new and even experienced users off-guard.

Suppress features refers to how inactive configurations should handle new features that are added to the part. For example, if you have two configs, 1 and 2, and config 1 is active and you add a new Fillet feature, what happens to that feature in config 2? If this option is turned on, the new features are suppressed in the inactive configs. If it is turned off, the new features will be unsuppressed when the inactive configs are activated. This creates a much bigger challenge for manually created configurations than for design table-driven configs because changing suppression states for several features across multiple configs is much easier in a design table than in manual config management.

Using the Modify dialog box

The Modify dialog box enables you to change dimensions by just double-clicking the dimension and changing the value. When you change a dimension using the Modify dialog box in a part that has more than one configuration, an additional button appears on the Modify dialog box, shown in Figure 11.7.

FIGURE 11.7

The Modify dialog box

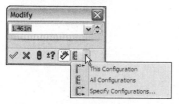

Modify has three options for configuring dimensions: This Configuration, All Configurations, and Specify Configurations. The All Configuration is the default option. Choosing the Specify Configurations option opens a dialog box, which is shown in Figure 11.8.

FIGURE 11.8

Using the Specify Configurations dialog box to change a dimension in multiple configurations

Using Negative dimensions

A negative dimension serves only to change the direction of the dimension, and then the negative dimension is discarded; it does not stay with the dimension. An equation that results in a negative dimension will flip the sense of the dimension every time it is rebuilt. This may be a useful trick, but will probably serve as an annoyance for most modeling situations. When you put a negative dimension in a Modify dialog box, the dimension changes sense (direction) and the negative sign disappears after one rebuild. If you put a negative dimension into a Modify Configurations dialog box, it will also disappear, and change the direction of the dimension for all configurations. When you enter a negative dimension into a design table, the negative is retained (until the next time you open the design table), and the sense of the dimension is retained only for the configs to which you assigned negative dimension values.

Note

This design table functionality is something that arouses my suspicion. I would not build a design intent scenario based on negative dimensions in design tables. The functionality seems unintentional, unstable, or otherwise subject to change. ■

Negative dimensions can only be assigned to sketch dimensions, not to feature dimensions. You cannot change the extrusion direction by making the blind depth negative. If you use Instant 3D to change the direction of an extrude, be careful, because this may change a boss to a cut in addition to making it go in the other direction.

Using the Modify Configurations dialog box

The Modify Configurations dialog box, shown in Figure 11.9, enables you to create and modify configured features and dimensions in a more organized way than by using the simple manual methods described earlier, but without getting involved in an Excel-based design table, described later in this chapter. Do not confuse the Modify Configurations dialog box with the Modify dialog box, which is used to change dimensions.

FIGURE 11.9

Using the Modify Configurations dialog box to configure a feature

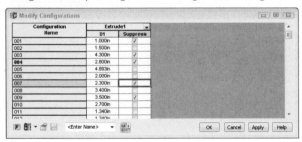

You can access the Modify Configurations dialog box by right-clicking a dimension or feature you want to drive via configurations and selecting Configure Dimension or Configure Feature.

With the Modify Configurations dialog box active, double-click a dimension to add it to the configured features list. You can add configurations on the fly by typing in the appropriate box, and change values or states of features by double-clicking and entering numbers or selecting the check box in the appropriate column.

The Modify Configurations interface is still a relatively new part of the software. I still tend to use either the manual or Excel-based techniques. I have not yet found a use for the middle ground offered by the Modify Configurations dialog box, but I can see where it might be valuable for people who might want to configure a couple of features without getting involved in a big spreadsheet. It might also be valuable to people who do not have Excel available on their computer but want to create a more structured way to manage configuration data.

In addition, I should mention that much folklore exists surrounding what is perceived as a problematic relationship between Excel and SolidWorks. Some users claim that Excel often causes SolidWorks to crash. Beyond that, many workplaces may not have Excel available to them, either because of the cost or because they use a non-Microsoft solution for spreadsheet applications. These users still want the functionality of design tables even if Excel is not installed on their machines.

The icons in the lower left of the Modify Configurations dialog box enable you to use the dialog box for more than just dimensions and feature suppression. Figure 11.10 shows that you can also use it to control custom properties. Some of these changes are relatively recent, so even if you are familiar with this dialog box from a previous release, you might want to have another look at it to see whether there is some new functionality that you can take advantage of.

Using Modify Configurations to control dimensions, features, and custom properties

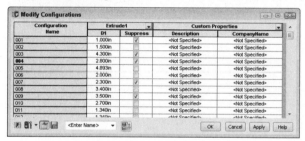

The Modify Configurations dialog box does not give you control over everything. Some things that you can configure, you cannot drive from this dialog box, such as part color. Design tables are still the most powerful way to go, but Modify Configurations offers a lot of flexibility and immediacy.

Using Table Views

The Modify Configurations dialog box adds significantly to your options for creating and editing configurations. Two very nice tools that add to the convenience and power of SolidWorks configurations are called Table Views and Hide/Show Custom Properties.

Table Views enable you to keep a small table of only the parameters that you want to show. The Parameters drop-down list enables you to select which Table View you want to display, or to create a new one. Using drop-down lists on the parameter headings, you can suppress the display of any parameter in a new Table View.

Dividing what might otherwise be a large design table into several Table Views helps to keep your data organized and easy to access. Figure 11.11 shows the ConfigurationManager of a part with configurations managed with Table Views.

Displaying Table Views in the ConfigurationManager of a configured part

Adding custom properties with the Modify Configurations dialog box

 The second nice option in the Modify Configurations dialog box is the Hide/Show Custom Properties option. When this button is depressed, the Modify Configurations dialog shows columns for existing custom properties, as well as a drop-down list that enables you to add more custom property columns. This makes it very easy to control configuration-specific custom properties within a configured part.

Figure 11.12 shows these tools in action.

Using Modify Configurations to control configuration-specific custom properties

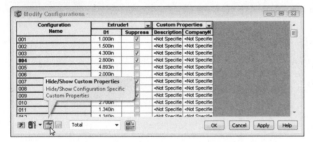

Using custom property managers

The Property Tab Builder enables an administrator to create special Task Pane tabs that are used to control custom properties and configuration-specific custom properties. As an administrative function, the Property Tab Builder is covered in more detail in the *SolidWorks Administration Bible* (Wiley, 2009). Configuration-specific custom properties can be controlled through design tables, Custom Property tabs, or the regular SolidWorks configuration-specific custom property interface. Select the method that works best for the way you and your company use the software.

Figure 11.13 shows the Property Tab Builder interface. You can access the Property Tab Builder by clicking the Windows Start button and choosing SolidWorks ⇨ SolidWorks Tools from the menu. This is the place where you actually construct the interface that shows up in the Properties tab of the Task Pane on the right side of the SolidWorks graphics window.

Using the Property Tab Builder to construct a Custom Properties tab for the Task Pane

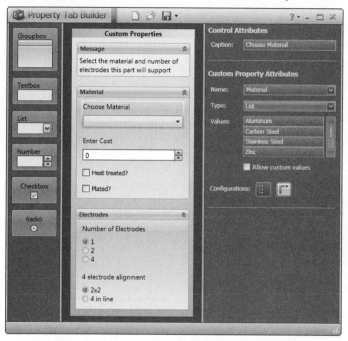

Using this type of interface enables the administrator to standardize custom properties values due to spelling or difference in interpretation. The Task Pane interface is easy to use and highly customizable. Notice that you can create regular custom properties or configure custom properties, and that option can be set independently for each property value entered using this interface.

Once you create a Property Tab file (called templates), save it to the location indicated at Tools ⇨ Options ⇨ File Locations ⇨ Custom Property Files. If you only have one template for a document type (part, assembly, or drawing), it will automatically appear when you display the Custom Properties tab of the Task pane. If you have multiple templates established, the Custom Properties tab will give you the option of which one to use. Figure 11.14 shows a Custom Properties tab in use within the SolidWorks Task Pane interface.

Using the Custom Properties tab to assign custom properties

Using derived configurations

Derived configurations are configs that are dependent on other configs. You can create them from the RMB menu on a configuration, and they appear indented underneath the parent config. Figure 11.15 shows the RMB menu and the position of the derived config in the tree.

Creation and placement of the derived config

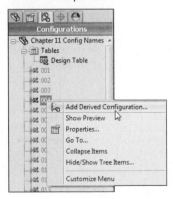

Derived configurations maintain the same values and properties of the parent config unless you break the link to the child (derived) config by explicitly changing a value in the child config. For all other values, the child config value changes when the parent config value changes.

One very nice application of derived configs is to use them for simplified configurations, and set the properties so that any features that are added to the parent config are also added to the derived config. You can do this by deselecting the Advanced Option Suppress Features to Off in the PropertyManager for the configuration. This causes the derived config to inherit *only* features that are added to the parent, and not to other configs. You can use the simplified configs for Finite Element Analysis (FEA), making drawings of models where all of the edge breaks have actually been modeled. You can also use them for the reverse (a complex config rather than a simple one) to have a config that includes fillets for rendering purposes that are otherwise not there. In addition, you can create and maintain derived configs using design tables, which are discussed in the next section.

Understanding how file size affects speed

A long-standing dispute has raged over the effects of file size on speed. Here are the facts: When SolidWorks creates a configuration, it stores information about the 3D geometry and a preview thumbnail of the configuration inside the part file. This makes it faster to access the configuration the next time because it has only to read the data, rather than read other data and then recalculate the new data. As a result, saving the stored data makes the file larger but also enables you to avoid having to recalculate it.

Many people assign more importance to file size than I do, and use it as a criterion on which to base decisions about which features or techniques to use or not use. If I can use a single file instead of multiple files by using configurations, I prefer the single file technique, even though it is guaranteed to produce larger files, and in some cases *much* larger files. Libraries of parts can often be made more manageable by using configured parts rather than many individual parts. Large hard drives for storage are cheaper and easier to upgrade than processors. In the end, reading stored data rather than recalculating it is faster. This is why when SolidWorks can store data that will probably be needed again at some point, it is useful to take advantage of the single-file technique. Storage space is cheaper than rebuild time. The result is that configurations definitely increase file size.

The ideal situation would be if SolidWorks would give users control over which data is stored in model files. This is a good place for an enhancement request.

Performance

File size has a negative effect on speed when you are sending data across the Internet or working across a network. If the data is on your hard drive, then storing data instead of calculating it offers a big benefit. If you are sending data across a slow network connection, you should take measures to decrease the size of the file before sending it, such as using a zip or compression utility. ■

Controlling dimensions

Controlling dimensions with configurations is simple. You need only three things to start: one dimension and two configurations. Because you already know how to create these elements, you are ready to start. Configurations require that you spend some time developing "design intent" for parts. Configurations drive changes in models, and if they are properly modeled, you can avoid feature or sketch failures due to dimension changes.

I will start with the example of a simple block. A fully dimensioned block has three dimensions. Make sure that you have manually created at least two configurations. Double-clicking a model face opens all the dimensions, and double-clicking one of the dimensions opens the familiar Modify dialog box.

Figure 11.6 shows that there is a small difference in the Modify dialog box. It now has a drop-down list where you can specify whether this change applies only to this config, to all configs, or to specified configs. If you select specified configs, then a dialog box shown on the top in Figure 11.16 appears, where you can select which configs this dimension change applies to.

FIGURE 11.16

Specify Configurations supplies a list of configs from which to choose

Once you are finished, you can toggle back and forth between the configs by double-clicking each of the configs in the ConfigurationManager. Although this is simple, if you forget to change the drop-down list from the All Configurations setting to either the This Configuration or the Specify Configurations setting, then you apply the change to all of the configurations. This shows that building a configuration manually is fine for a few simple changes, but it can become unwieldy if you are changing more than a few dimensions in this way. You would then have to remember which dimensions were changed to what. As you can see, using design tables is a better method for multiple dimensions.

Controlling suppression

 Suppressing a feature is just like turning it off; the feature appears as grayed-out text in the FeatureManager. With configurations, you can suppress a feature in one config and unsuppress it in another. Also, while a feature may be suppressed, the sketch associated with it is not necessarily suppressed. When dealing with manual configuration techniques, there are two methods for controlling suppression: manually suppressing features and creating configurations with the appropriate options for the inclusion of new features, which I discussed previously in this chapter.

In addition to the Suppress toolbar button, you can also use the Unsuppress and Unsuppress buttons with Dependents functions. When you suppress a feature, any feature that is dependent on it is also suppressed. If you then use the Unsuppress feature, it unsuppresses only the feature itself. However, Unsuppress with Dependents brings back all the dependent features, as well.

Performance

Suppressing complex features is a great way to improve performance. Experienced users often create a configuration of a part that they use as a simplified config, where patterns, fillets, and extruded text features are suppressed. This becomes more important as you start working with assemblies. For reasons I discuss in the assemblies chapters, it can be a great advantage to make a configuration for each part called "simplified." You can make a second configuration in template files so that new parts and assemblies automatically have this built in to them. ∎

Generally, SolidWorks users employ a combination of these methods, mainly because configurations are not usually started on a complete model; they are often added when the model is still in progress, and so features are added after the users create the configurations.

On the left side of Figure 11.17, you can see a feature that is alternately unsuppressed and suppressed in the tree. The text and icon for the suppressed feature are grayed out. You can suppress features from the RMB menu on the feature, from the Edit menu, or through a tool on a toolbar. The Suppress button is not on a toolbar by default, but you can find it in the Commands dialog box (Tools ⇨ Customize ⇨ Commands), along with the other buttons for the Features toolbar. Only the Edit menu offers the options of Unsuppress With Dependents and This Configuration ⇨ All Configurations ⇨ Specify Configurations options for each of the Suppress, Unsuppress, Unsuppress With Dependents functions.

FIGURE 11.17

Suppressing a feature

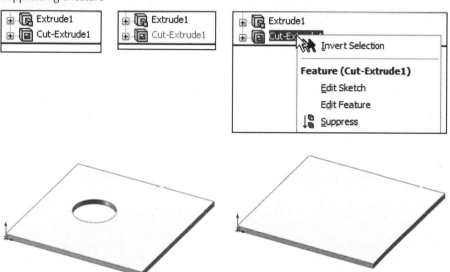

Using Unsuppress With Dependents can save you a lot of time or the hassle of looking for all the features dependent upon a feature that has been suppressed. Because it is not available on the RMB menus, this function is used less than it might otherwise be.

You may also need more control than the use of the simple suppress and unsuppress features. Figure 11.18 shows a section of the Edit menu related to suppression. All three options (Suppress, Unsuppress, and Unsuppress with Dependents) each in turn have three options: This Configuration, All Configurations, and Specified Configurations. This is a case where the drop-down menu options offer more detailed functionality than you can find in the RMB menus.

FIGURE 11.18

Accessing more precise suppression functionality through the Edit drop-down menu

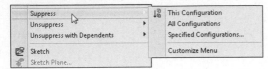

Controlling custom properties

Several reasons may compel you to use custom properties, including integration with searches for a Product Data Management system, automatically filling out drawing title blocks, or adding information to the BOM.

When you are using custom properties with configurations, you must use the Configuration Specific Custom Properties interface (or an appropriately configured custom property tab or the Modify Configurations dialog box), which enables you to have custom properties that change with each configuration. Standard custom properties apply to the top-level part and keep the same value for all configurations. The configuration-specific functionality is useful for situations such as different part numbers for configurations, and many other situations that are limited mostly by your use of configs. The Custom tab of the Summary Information dialog box, shown in Figure 11.19, still applies custom properties that do not change with the configurations to the part.

The interface for managing custom properties manually is shown in Figure 11.19. You can access this dialog box by choosing File ➪ Properties from the menu.

FIGURE 11.19

The Configuration Specific tab in the Summary Information dialog box

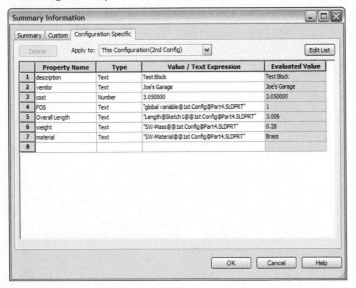

	Property Name	Type	Value / Text Expression	Evaluated Value
1	description	Text	Test Block	Test Block
2	vendor	Text	Joe's Garage	Joe's Garage
3	cost	Number	3.050000	3.050000
4	FOS	Text	"global variable@1st Config@Part4.SLDPRT"	1
5	Overall Length	Text	"Length@Sketch1@@1st Config@Part4.SLDPRT"	3.006
6	weight	Text	"SW-Mass@@1st Config@Part4.SLDPRT"	0.28
7	material	Text	"SW-Material@@1st Config@Part4.SLDPRT"	Brass
8				

You can also link custom properties to mass properties, model dimensions, link values, sketch text, and global variables by selecting from the drop-down list under the Value/Text Expression column, which appears when you select a cell in the column, as shown in Figure 11.19. To link a custom property to a model dimension, simply place the cursor in the Value/Text Expression box that you want to populate and click a dimension in the graphics window. Again, managing this data for a single config or only a few configs is easy enough; however, it can quickly become unwieldy, which is where using design tables can make a huge difference.

Controlling sketch relations

You can individually suppress or unsuppress sketch relations using configurations. Figure 11.20 shows the Display/Delete Relations PropertyManager interface, at the bottom of which is the Configurations panel. To suppress a relation, select it from the list and select the Suppressed option in the Relations section above the Delete buttons.

FIGURE 11.20

The Display/Delete Relations dialog box for configuring sketch relations

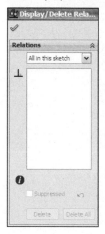

Tip

This is another situation where Delete is not used as an editing option. Using this technique, you can save sketch relations or activate different sets of relations in different configs; this technique allows a single sketch to react to changes differently. ■

Controlling sketch planes

You cannot configure the Offset distance in the From option for extrudes, but you *can* configure the sketch plane for the sketch that is used in the feature. The Sketch Plane PropertyManager interface expands when configurations are present, as shown in Figure 11.21.

FIGURE 11.21

The Sketch Plane PropertyManager interface for configuring a sketch plane

Tip

Another way to change the sketch plane is to put the sketch on an offset plane or a plane that can otherwise be driven by a dimension (for example, using reference sketch geometry). Actually moving a sketch to another plane can cause the sketch to rotate or flip. Moving the plane it is on is a better option that does not cause the sketch to rotate or flip. ■

Caution

Changing sketch planes indiscriminately can have serious consequences for your model. "Face/Plane Normals" sometimes point in different directions and can cause a sketch to flip, rotate, or mirror when you change it from one plane to another. One strange result is that changing it back to the original location can cause the sketch to flip again, but in a different way so that it does not go back to its original location/orientation. As a result, every time you change the configuration, the sketch could appear in a new and unexpected location or orientation. ■

Controlling configurations of inserted parts

 Inserted parts have a long history in SolidWorks. They have had several names in the past, and some sources (including SolidWorks documentation such as training documents and even help files) still use some of these legacy names out of habit or precedence. For example, you will sometimes hear inserted parts called *derived* or *base* parts. Both of these terms are obsolete.

Cross-Reference

Inserted parts are discussed in detail in the *SolidWorks 2011 Assemblies Bible* (Wiley, 2011), which describes master model techniques. ■

Inserted parts use one part as the starting point for another part. The inserted part sits as a feature in the FeatureManager of the child part. You can insert just the body geometry itself, or you can bring forward reference geometry, sketch data and all features, and break the link to the original part if you wish to.

The role of configurations with inserted parts is that the configuration of the inserted part can be controlled from the child component. For example, you may have designed an engine block for an automobile. This engine block is a casting, and using configurations, you have both the six-cylinder and the eight-cylinder blocks in a single-part file. This model represents the "as-cast" engine block. The next step is to make the block with all the secondary machining operations, such as facing mating surfaces, boring cylinders, drilling and tapping holes for threaded connections, and so on. As a result, the as-cast part is inserted into the as-machined part, and the configuration is selected before you add the cut features. As the name suggests, you add inserted parts by choosing Insert ⇨ Part from the menu.

The interface for assigning the configuration is shown in Figure 11.22. Simply right-click the inserted part feature and select List External References. It would seem to make more sense if the configuration could be selected when the part is first inserted, but it does not work this way; you have to select the configuration after the part is inserted.

FIGURE 11.22

Assigning the configuration of an inserted part

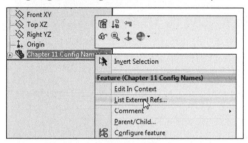

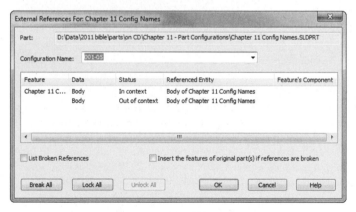

Using Library features

Library features can have configurations, and they carry those configurations with them into the part in which they are placed. Unfortunately, part configs cannot reference different library feature configs.

Cross-Reference

Chapter 13 discusses library features. ∎

Configurations for library features are created in exactly the same ways that configurations are created for other parts. The technique for saving the configs to the library feature is discussed in Chapter 13.

Identifying unconfigurable items

As important as it is to know what you *can* do, it is equally important to know what you *cannot* do. The following is a list of items that are not configurable. Although this list is not complete, it contains many of the more relevant items that cannot be configured:

- Library feature configs
- Blocks
- Extrude direction or From Offset dimension or direction
- Most of the values in features such as Deform, Freeform, and Twist

While Library Features can be configured, once you drop them into a part and click OK, the configurations are no longer accessible (unless you have selected Link To Library Part), so a part's configurations cannot select the configuration of a Library feature. A part's configurations can change the dimensions of a library feature.

Using Design Tables

In addition to describing some of the basic concepts involved with configurations, the first part of this chapter presents reasons for using design tables. For example, while manual configuration management can be haphazard, and is highly prone to mistakes, design tables lay everything out in an Excel spreadsheet. Although many new users ask whether they can use a different replacement spreadsheet program, you must use Excel for design tables.

Note

Excel is a format that is easy to read and print out, and even non-SolidWorks users can understand and work with it. Although there is some special syntax that you need to use with design tables, for most uses, SolidWorks can create the syntax automatically for you; therefore, there is minimal manual data entry. If you are careful to name dimensions, features, and configurations properly, design tables should be easy to understand and manage. In Excel, you can also color cells, rows, and columns in such a way that large amounts of tabulated data are easier to sort through. In addition, because design tables use Excel, they can also use all of Excel's calculation capabilities. ∎

Best Practice

When using equations and design tables, it is considered best practice to name dimensions, sketches, features, and other configured items. However, it is not recommended to mix design tables with SolidWorks equations. Besides the fact that Excel equations are far more sophisticated than those of SolidWorks, driving dimensions from too many locations can be confusing when you edit the part after you have forgotten the details of how the part was built.

It is a great idea to document design intent using comments in the features or the Design Journal. You should also add comments to design tables as needed. ∎

Identifying what can be driven by a design table

Just because something can be configured does not necessarily mean that it can also be driven by a design table. Here is a small list of items that fit into this category:

- Sketch plane configuration
- Suppressed sketch relations
- Suppressed dimensions (suppressed dimensions become driven dimensions)

However, the good news is that there are many items that can be driven by a design table. Table 11.1 lists these items, along with their associated syntax.

TABLE 11.1

Items That Can Be Driven by a Design Table

Item	Syntax (Goes in Column Header)	Possible Values (Goes in Field Cell)	Default Value If Field Is Blank
Configs of Inserted Parts	$configuration@<*part name*>	<*config name*>	not evaluated
Configs of Split Parts	$configuration@<*split feature name*>	<*config name*>	not evaluated
Comment Column	$comment	comment text	blank
Configuration Description	$description	description text	<*config name*>
BOM Part No.	$partnumber	$d, $document = document name $p, $parent = parent config name $c, $configuration = config name <*text*> = custom name	config name
Feature Suppression State	$state@<*feature name*>	suppressed, s unsuppressed, u	present suppression state
Dimension Value	dimension@<*feature name*> dimension@<*sketch name*>	allowed numerical values	not evaluated
Parent Config (creates a derived config)	$parent	parent config name text	not evaluated
Config Specific Custom Property	$prp@<*property name*>	property name text	not evaluated
Equation State	$state@<*equation number*>@equations	suppressed, s unsuppressed, u	unsuppressed
Light Suppression State	$state@<*light name*>	suppressed, s unsuppressed, u	unsuppressed
Sketch Relation Suppression	$state@<*relation name*>@<*sketch name*>	suppressed, s unsuppressed, u	unsuppressed

continued

TABLE 11.1 *(continued)*

Item	Syntax (Goes in Column Header)	Possible Values (Goes in Field Cell)	Default Value If Field Is Blank
User Notes (same as comment)	$user_notes	Text	blank
Part or Feature Color	$color $color@<feature name>	see SolidWorks Help, Colors, Parameters in design tables	0, black
Assigned Mass	$sw-mass	allowed numerical values	value from Mass properties
Assigned Center of Gravity X, Y, Z Coordinates	$sw-cog	allowed numerical values in the format of x, y, z	value from Mass properties
Dimension Tolerance	$tolerance@<dimension name>	see SolidWorks Help, Tolerance Keywords, and Syntax in Design Tables	none

Creating a Simple Design Table

When you prepare to create a design table, you generally need to give appropriate names to dimensions, sketches, and features. Remember that while the feature is the most visible item and the easiest to rename, most of the dimensions probably belong to the sketch, which you may also need, or want, to rename. Names should reflect the function or location of the item. It is a good idea to show dimension names when renaming items (remember that you can show dimension names by selecting the Dimension Names option by choosing View ⇨ Dimension Names). Figure 11.23 shows the result of renaming the feature and dimension.

You can use one of the following three techniques to add a design table to a SolidWorks part by choosing Insert ⇨ Tables ⇨ Design Tables from the menus:

- **Insert Blank Design Table.** This method starts from a blank template that contains the underlying framework, but no values.
- **Auto-create Design Table.** This method populates the new design table with any existing configurations and items that are different between the configs.
- **From file.** This method enables you to create a design table externally and then import it.

Although I prefer the Auto-create method, it is most appropriate for when you have existing configurations. The From file method is best when a design table has been exported from another part, saved externally, and brought into the current part. For the following example, I am using the Insert Blank Design Table method.

FIGURE 11.23

Renamed features and dimensions

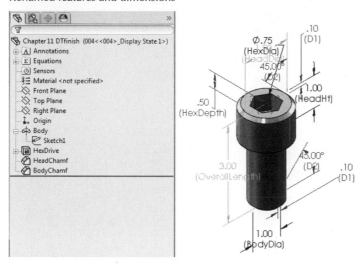

On the DVD

If you would like to follow along with these steps to create the design table, you can use the part from the DVD with the filename `Chapter 11 DTstart.sldprt.` ■

Figure 11.24 shows the results of starting with the new blank design table. You may notice that the window title bar at the top says SolidWorks, but the toolbars look a lot like the Excel interface. This is because Excel is actually running inside of SolidWorks. Clicking outside of the Excel window can cause the Excel window to close, although there are several items outside of the Excel window that you can select without the window closing, such as features in the FeatureManager and dimensions in the graphics window. You can also rotate and pan the view in the graphics window without closing the Design Table window. If you are very careful, you can also drag the thin hatched border of the Excel window to adjust its size or location.

You can also edit Design Tables in a separate window, which makes editing easier but makes adding dimension and feature names more difficult. To edit the table in its own window, right-click on the Design Table in the FeatureManager and select Edit Table In New Window.

Figure 11.25 shows a fully developed design table, with some complexity. Although your first design table does not need to be this complex, this example demonstrates what you can do with this feature.

FIGURE 11.24

The interface where you can create the design table, and the resulting blank design table

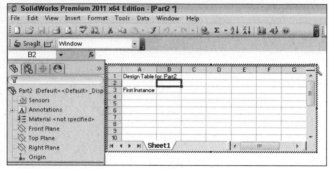

FIGURE 11.25

A fully populated design table

Config Names   Feature or Property Syntax from Table

	A	B	C	F	G	N	S	T	U
		$PARTNUMBER	$PRP@DESCRIPTION	MajorDia@Sketch1	MinorDia@Cosmetic Thread1	ThreadLength@Sketch1	HeadSideHeight@Sketch1	HeadHeight@Sketch1	HexWidth@Sketch2
3	0-80 X .125 Button Head-Soc-SS	54383-0-AAHA	SCR,BHS,0-80X1/8,SOC,SS	0.0600	0.046	0.1250	.010	.032	.035
4	0-80 X .187 Button Head-Soc-SS	54383-0-ABHA	SCR,BHS,0-80X3/16,SOC,SS	0.0600	0.046	0.1875	.010	.032	.035
5	0-80 X .25 Button Head-Soc-SS	54383-0-ACHA	SCR,BHS,0-80X1/4,SOC,SS	0.0600	0.046	0.2500	.010	.032	.035
6	0-80 X .312 Button Head-Soc-SS	54383-0-ADHA	SCR,BHS,0-80X5/16,SOC,SS	0.0600	0.046	0.3125	.010	.032	.035
7	0-80 X .375 Button Head-Soc-SS	54383-0-AEHA	SCR,BHS,0-80X3/8,SOC,SS	0.0600	0.046	0.3750	.010	.032	.035
8	0-80 X .437 Button Head-Soc-SS	54383-0-AFHA	SCR,BHS,0-80X7/16,SOC,SS	0.0600	0.046	0.4375	.010	.032	.035
9	0-80 X .5 Button Head-Soc-SS	54383-0-AGHA	SCR,BHS,0-80X1/2,SOC,SS	0.0600	0.046	0.5000	.010	.032	.035
10	0-80 X .562 Button Head-Soc-SS	54383-0-AHHA	SCR,BHS,0-80X9/16,SOC,SS	0.0600	0.046	0.5625	.010	.032	.035
11	0-80 X .625 Button Head-Soc-SS	54383-0-AJHA	SCR,BHS,0-80X5/8,SOC,SS	0.0600	0.046	0.6250	.010	.032	.035
12	0-80 X .687 Button Head-Soc-SS	54383-0-AKHA	SCR,BHS,0-80X11/16,SOC,SS	0.0600	0.046	0.6875	.010	.032	.035
13	0-80 X .75 Button Head-Soc-SS	54383-0-ALHA	SCR,BHS,0-80X3/4,SOC,SS	0.0600	0.046	0.7500	.010	.032	.035
14	0-80 X .812 Button Head-Soc-SS	54383-0-AMHA	SCR,BHS,0-80X13/16,SOC,SS	0.0600	0.046	0.8125	.010	.032	.035
15	0-80 X .875 Button Head-Soc-SS	54383-0-ANHA	SCR,BHS,0-80X7/8,SOC,SS	0.0600	0.046	0.8750	.010	.032	.035
16	0-80 X 1.0 Button Head-Soc-SS	54383-0-APHA	SCR,BHS,0-80X1,SOC,SS	0.0600	0.046	1.0000	.010	.032	.035
17	1-72 X .125 Button Head-Soc-SS	54383-0-BAHA	SCR,BHS,1-72X1/8,SOC,SS	0.0730	0.058	0.1250	.010	.039	.050
18	1-72 X .187 Button Head-Soc-SS	54383-0-BBHA	SCR,BHS,1-72X3/16,SOC,SS	0.0730	0.058	0.1875	.010	.039	.050
19	1-72 X .25 Button Head-Soc-SS	54383-0-BCHA	SCR,BHS,1-72X1/4,SOC,SS	0.0730	0.058	0.2500	.010	.039	.050
20	1-72 X .312 Button Head-Soc-SS	54383-0-BDHA	SCR,BHS,1-72X5/16,SOC,SS	0.0730	0.058	0.3125	.010	.039	.050
21	1-72 X .375 Button Head-Soc-SS	54383-0-BEHA	SCR,BHS,1-72X3/8,SOC,SS	0.0730	0.058	0.3750	.010	.039	.050

The config names go in the first column and the feature or property names go in the second row. The first row is reserved for the name of the table. All this is automatically set up by SolidWorks.

Note

Because you are actually working in Excel when working with design tables, you can use Excel formatting, which is how the text in Figure 11.25 is rotated 90 degrees for the column headers. (To rotate text in a table, right-click the cell, group of cells, or row; select Format Cells; and then select the Alignment tab.) ■

In the new design table, the next step is to type in some configuration names. Because you are working in Excel, all the fill functionality is available. In the example shown in Figure 11.26, I have typed in the first three values of 001, 002, and 003, then window-selected the cells, and dragged the fill handle on the selection window to fill the number pattern to populate a larger area. To find more information about this technique, look for Fill or Automatically Number Rows in the Excel Help files.

FIGURE 11.26

Filling in configuration names

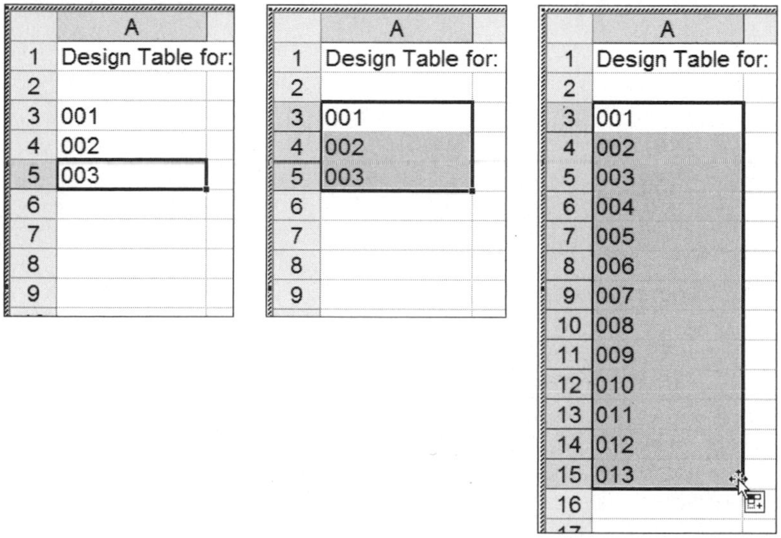

The next step is to fill in some feature and dimension names in the second row. The first thing that you do is to suppress the HexDrive feature. To make this the first feature in the list, click in cell B2, and then double-click the HexDrive feature in the FeatureManager. The name of the feature and its current suppression state are added to the design table with all the necessary syntax and correct spelling.

To rotate the text in this row vertically, right-click row number 2, select Format Cells, click the Alignment tab, and turn the orientation to 90 degrees. The word *unsuppressed* displays in all capitals and fully spelled out, while all you need is a U or an S. Replace the word with an S, and double-click the line between the column heading letters B and C at the top of the Excel window to condense column B as much as possible. Alternate the rest of the rows between *U*s and *S*s to either suppress or unsuppress the HexDrive feature in various configurations. Figure 11.27 shows the current state of the design table.

FIGURE 11.27

Building the design table

	A	B	C
1	Design Table for: Chapter 10		
2		$STATE@HexDrive	
3	001	s	
4	002	u	
5	003	s	
6	004	u	
7	005	s	
8	006	u	
9	007	s	
10	008	u	
11	009	s	
12	010	u	
13	011	s	
14	012	u	
15	013	s	

Close the Design Table window, and click OK on the message box that lists the new configurations created by the Design Table. Now split the FeatureManager, set the lower pane to the ConfigurationManager, and double-click some configurations. Notice that in the configs where you specified an S, the HexDrive is suppressed and no longer appears in the model.

You can now add a dimension to the design table. To add a dimension, it is most convenient to display the dimensions on the screen at all times. To show all the dimensions in the part, right-click the Annotations folder in the FeatureManager and select Display Annotations. If the dimensions do not display, you may have to go back and select Show Feature Dimensions. Arrange the dimensions so that you can clearly see them all, as shown in Figure 11.28.

To display the design table again, locate it in the ConfigurationManager, right-click it, and select Edit Table. Editing the feature changes the settings used for the design table. Edit Table in New Window is an option that you will use later because it simplifies many things; however, for now, the Edit Table option makes it easiest to add new items to the design table.

FIGURE 11.28

Dimension and annotation display settings

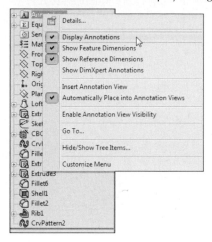

Note

If a window appears with the name Add Rows and Columns, just click OK for now. This window lists parameters that have changed in its lower pane, and it is asking you if you would like to add any of the changed parameters to the design table. If you would like to add them, just select the parameter in the lower pane and click OK. If not, just click OK. ■

If the design table displays on top of your model, you can either move the model or move the design table. Moving the design table is a bit tricky and involves dragging the striped-line border of the Excel window; remember not to grab it at the corners or midpoints, because this will simply resize it. If you click inside the border, nothing happens. If you click outside of the border, the Excel window closes. Moving the model may be easier. To do this, Ctrl+drag in blank space in the graphics window; it pans the display so that you can see the part dimensions.

With cell C2 selected, or whatever the next available cell is in the second row, double-click the OverallLength dimension in the graphics window. SolidWorks adds the proper syntax to the design table, along with the current value for the first configuration in the list. Fill in values for the rest of the configurations. You can then calculate these values in Excel using any of the available techniques.

Exit the design table and toggle through the various configurations to see their different lengths. These examples should get you started on more complex configurations and design tables. Any dimensions that are controlled by the design table (and that are therefore locked) display in pink on the screen.

Editing design table settings

Figure 11.29 shows the PropertyManager for design tables. After you have created the table, you can edit the table settings by right-clicking the table and then selecting Edit Feature. Edit Feature enables you to edit the settings for the table only; it does not enable you to edit values within the table.

Linked design table

By selecting the From File source option, you can create a design table from an external file; you can also link the table to the external file. When you use the other two options, Blank and Auto-Create, SolidWorks stores the Excel file within the SolidWorks document. Linking to an external file may be useful if you have a non-SolidWorks user who is entering data into the design table, or if a single table controls multiple parts.

Edit control

The Edit Control panel has two options, which act as a toggle. The Allow model edits to update the design table option is self-explanatory, as is its opposite, the Block model edits that would update the design table option. If the Allow model edits option is selected, and you make a manual change to the model, the next time you open the design table SolidWorks warns you about the change and that it will update the design table. Likewise, if you try to make a manual change and the Block model edits option is selected, you receive a warning that the value cannot be changed.

Options

The Options settings determine the behavior when you are using the Allow model edits option and a new item has been configured. For example, the design table may already exist and you manually add a configuration and suppress a feature.

Configurations that have been added manually are displayed somewhat differently from configs that are being managed by the design table. Figure 11.29 shows the two configurations at the bottom of the tree with square symbols, while the design table configs have Excel symbols.

FIGURE 11.29

Manually created configs versus design table–created configs

After you manually add the config and suppress the feature, the next time you open the design table, the Add Rows and Columns dialog box appears. Many users are simply annoyed by this, but that may be because they do not understand what it does or why it appears. In the example shown in Figure 11.30, a new configuration has been manually added; it appears in the Configurations box as ManuallyAddedConfig, and in the Parameters box it looks like a feature named BodyChamfer has been either suppressed or unsuppressed manually. The appearance of this dialog box means that SolidWorks is asking you if you would like to include these items in the design table. If so, simply select the items you would like to add to the design table and click OK. If you do not want to include the items in the design table, then simply click OK or Cancel. If you click OK, you will not be offered these choices again; if you click Cancel, the next time you open the table, the dialog box with the same choices will reappear. If you never want to see this dialog box again, then make sure that all the options in the Options panel shown in Figure 11.24 are deselected.

FIGURE 11.30

The Add Rows and Columns dialog box

Editing the design table

As I mentioned earlier, when you open the design table inside the SolidWorks window, it can some-times be difficult to work with. One way to handle this problem is to only edit the design table inside SolidWorks when you want to add new features to the column headers, and when adding new config-urations or editing the field values, edit the table in a separate window. This option appears on the RMB menu as Edit Table In New Window. It gives you much more flexibility in resizing the Excel win-dow, changing zoom scale, and other operations, but it does not enable you to double-click a dimen-sion so that it is added automatically to the column header.

Caution

When working on design tables, it is a good idea to avoid conflicts with other sessions of Excel by closing any other Excel windows. The combination of operating Excel spreadsheets inside both SolidWorks and Excel has been known to cause crashes, or the "Server Busy" warning message. If you are diligent about having only one session of Excel active at a time when you are working on design tables (or Excel BOMs), there is less likelihood of a crash or conflict. ■

Using the Configuration Publisher

The Configuration Publisher enables you to create an interface that creates configurations on the fly based on rules that you establish. The interface that you create appears when you put the part into an assembly, enabling you to create a custom size and a new configuration to go with it. This is similar to putting a Toolbox part into an assembly, and getting a special interface to specify sizes and create new configurations if necessary. In order to create a Configuration Publisher for a part, the part must contain a Design Table with at least a single row. You can use an auto-created Design Table if you need to.

You access the Configuration Publisher by right-clicking the name of the part at the top line of the ConfigurationManager and selecting Configuration Publisher from the menu.

Figure 11.31 shows the Configuration Publisher interface. It is like the Property Tab Builder in that you use it to place interface controls on a PropertyManager that will pop up when the part is placed into an assembly.

FIGURE 11.31

The Configuration Publisher helps you build an interface to create configurations as you place a part into an assembly.

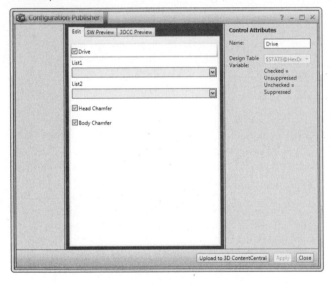

Aside from users putting parts into assemblies, the interface you create using the Configuration Publisher can also be used in 3D Content Central to specify a new component size. If you are a supplier and make parts in a wide variety of sizes, instead of creating all the sizes and uploading to 3D Content Central, you can just create the rules in the Configuration Publisher interface and allow the configurations to be created automatically according to the rules.

When the interface has been created, a PropertyManager entry shows up under the name of the part in the ConfigurationManager, as shown in Figure 11.32.

When the part is placed into an assembly, the PropertyManager shown in Figure 11.33, which is the one created in the Configuration Publisher, appears and enables you to access options to size and configure the new instance. A similar interface is also used if you have uploaded the part to 3D Content Central to allow other people to download the part.

FIGURE 11.32

The PropertyManager entry in the ConfigurationManager

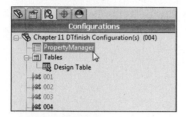

FIGURE 11.33

A custom PropertyManager makes it easy to size and configure a part as it is inserted into an assembly.

Tutorial: Working with Configurations and Design Tables

Throughout this book, parts that I use for one purpose may also be useful for other purposes. For example, the part used in this tutorial uses a loft with guide curves where both guide curves are created in the same sketch. The guide curve sketch is made from symmetrical splines where I have used the spline handles to change the shape smoothly and in a controlled way. I have also used a curve-driven pattern to go around an elliptical shape.

Tip

If at some point you decide that you have made mistakes from which you cannot recover, or you would simply like to start over again, you can choose File ⇨ Reload. This is the same as exiting the part without saving and then reopening the part to start from the beginning. ∎

To start working with configurations and design tables, follow these steps:

1. **From the DVD, open the part called** `Chapter 11 Tutorial start.sldprt`. Take a moment to become familiar with this part by using the rollback bar to see how it was made. In particular, look at the two patterns, which need to be parametrically linked. Figure 11.34 shows the part.

FIGURE 11.34

The Chapter 11 Tutorial start.sldprt file

2. **Manually create a configuration for the part called Size 1.** Remember that to create a configuration, you must show the ConfigurationManager tab in the FeatureManager area, and right-click the name of the part at the top level. It is better to do this by splitting the FeatureManager window and setting the lower pane to the ConfigurationManager.

3. **Set the Advanced option by selecting both Suppress Features and Use Configuration Specific Color.**

4. **Before closing the Add Configuration PropertyManager, click the Color button on the Advanced Options panel of the Configuration PropertyManager and select a different color for the Size 1 configuration.** The color does not change immediately. It will change after you close the PropertyManager.

5. **Choose View ⇨ Dimension Names.**

6. **Double-click the feature CrvPattern1 in the FeatureManager.** A number 6 with a D1 under it will appear on one of the holes in the pattern. If you have changed your part to a blue color, it may be difficult to see because the text will also be blue.

7. **Change the name of the dimension to Hole# by clicking the dimension and using the PropertyManager.**

8. **Change the value of the number to 8, and be careful to also change the drop-down setting to This Configuration Only instead of All Configurations.** If you forget to do this, then you will have to go to the other configuration and set it back to 6.

9. **Click the Rebuild symbol (which resembles a traffic light) to show the changes before exiting the Modify dialog box.** Notice that the CrvPattern2 fails after rebuilding CrvPattern1 with eight instances. Click the green check mark icon to exit the Modify dialog box, and then make the same changes to the CrvPattern2: change the dimension name and the number of patterned instances to eight (remember to use the This Configuration Only setting). The part should now look like Figure 11.35.

FIGURE 11.35

The model after Step 9

10. **When you double-click to change configurations, the SolidWorks interface now shows a part with a different color and a different number of holes and ribs.** After the first change between configurations, the changes should happen quickly because SolidWorks has stored the geometry.

11. **Choose File ⇨ Properties and select the Configuration Specific tab.** Set the Apply To drop-down list to Default, and type a Property Name of **description** and a Value of **Gray Vent Cover**. Now change the Apply To drop-down setting to Size 1 and type a description for the new configuration using the name of the color that you applied to this config. Figure 11.36 shows the two states of the data.

FIGURE 11.36

Setting the Configuration Specific custom properties

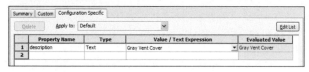

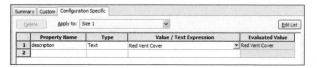

12. **Exit the Custom Properties dialog box.** Now that you have made a few changes manually, the following steps guide you through bringing these changes into a design table and using the design table to make additional changes.

13. **Choose Insert ⇨ Tables ⇨ Design Table from the menus.** Use Auto-create as the Source, allow model edits, and select all three options in the Option panel. Click OK to create the design table. Figure 11.37 shows the design table that you have automatically created.

FIGURE 11.37

The automatically created design table

	A	B	C	D	E	F
1	Design Table for: Chapter 10 Tutorial start					
2		$DESCRIPTION	$COLOR	$PRP@description	Hole#@CrvPattern1	Rib#@CrvPattern2
3	Default	Default	12632256	Gray Vent Cover	6	6
4	Size 1	Size 1	255	Red Vent Cover	8	8

14. **Use the striped border to move the window without closing it.** This may take some practice. If the window closes, right-click the design table in the FeatureManager and select Edit Table. Move the window to a place where you can see the model clearly.

15. **If a cell in the second row of the design table is selected, select a different empty cell that is not in the second row (this prevents data from automatically populating cells until you have the correct data).** Now double-click the Extrude1 feature in the FeatureManager. Find the .500" (D1) dimension on the screen. Right-click the dimension and rename it **BaseThk**.

16. **Click the next open cell in the second row, and double-click the .500" dimension that you just renamed.** You may have to use the handles at the corners and side midpoints to resize the Excel window to see everything. Add another configuration row and the additional values in the cells, as shown in Figure 11.38. The color number is determined by a formula that you can find in the help section under the topic Color Parameter.

17. **Remember that this part needs to have the number of ribs always equal to the number of holes.** This is simple to do in Excel. Click in the first row value for the Rib# number. This is cell F3 in Figure 11.39. Type the equal sign and then click in the cell to the left, E3. You can also simply type **=E3** in this cell. This links the Rib# cell to the Hole# cell.

18. **Use the Window Fill feature by selecting the dot at the lower-right corner of the selected F3 cell and dragging it down to include cells F4 and F5, as shown in Figure 11.39.**

FIGURE 11.38

Make additions to the design table

	A	B	C	D	E	F	G
1	Design Table for: Chapter 10 Tutorial start						
2		$DESCRIPTION	$COLOR	$PRP@description	Hole#@CrvPattern1	Rib#@CrvPattern2	BaseThk@Extrude1
3	Default	Default	12632256	Gray Vent Cover	6	6	0.5
4	Size 1	Size 1	255	Red Vent Cover	8	8	0.8
5	Size 2	Size 2	16711680	Blue Vent Cover	10	10	1
6							

FIGURE 11.39

Copying the equation to other cells

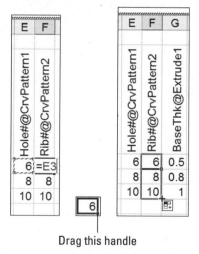

Drag this handle

19. **Click in a blank space to exit the design table.** Double-click through the configurations in the ConfigurationManager to see the results of your efforts.

Summary

Configurations are a powerful way to control variations of a design within a single part file. Many aspects of the part can be configured, while a few cannot. Manually created configurations are useful for making a small number of variations and a small number of configurations, but they become unwieldy when you need to make more than a few variations of either type.

Design tables are recommended because they enable you to see all the changes more clearly that have been made for all the configurations. Having the power of Excel available enables you to access many functions that are not shown here, such as using lookup tables and Concatenate functions to build descriptions or configuration names.

Editing, Evaluating, and Troubleshooting

When you use CAD programs, you typically create a part once but edit it many times. *Design for change* is at the core of most of the modeling work that you will do in SolidWorks, and deletion is not an editing option.

The initial stages of modeling are the most crucial. This is when you set up parametric relations between the features and sketches that form the foundation for an assembly or complex part. For this reason, editing often quickly turns into repair. Granted, some changes are simply unavoidable, but a thorough knowledge of editing — and repairing — can help you to understand the how, what, and why of modeling best practice.

This chapter starts with some very basic concepts of editing, which you may have picked up if you have been reading this book from the beginning. It also contains a summary of part modeling best practice techniques and a set of model evaluation tools that can help you evaluate the manufacturability and aesthetic properties of parts. I have included these evaluation tools in a chapter on editing because the create-evaluate-edit-evaluate cycle is one of the most familiar in modeling and design practice.

Using Rollback

Rolling back a model simply means looking at the results of the design tree up to a certain point in the model history. In SolidWorks, you can actually change history — that is, you can change the order in which operations are completed. The order in which you create features is recorded, and if you change this order, you get a different geometric result.

You can use several methods to put the model in this rolled-back state:

- Dragging the Rollback bar with the cursor.
- Right mouse button (RMB) clicking and selecting one of the Rollback options.

IN THIS CHAPTER

Using Rollback to look at the results of the design tree

Reordering features in the design tree

Reordering all features as a folder

Selecting items using the Flyout FeatureManager

Summarizing best practice suggestions for modeling parts

Applying evaluation techniques to plastic parts and complex shapes

Diagnosing errors

Editing and evaluation techniques tutorial

- Editing a feature other than the last one in the design tree. (SolidWorks rolls back the model automatically.)
- Choose Tools ⇨ Options ⇨ FeatureManager ⇨ Arrow key navigation to control the Rollback bar with the arrow keys.
- Saving the model while editing a feature or sketch, and then exiting the model. When the part is opened again, it is rolled back to the location of the sketch that was being edited.
- Pressing Esc during a long model rebuild. This method is supposed to roll you back to the last feature that was rebuilt when you pressed Esc; however, in practice, I have rarely seen it do this, and it usually rebuilds the entire model anyway.

Using the Rollback bar

The Rollback bar, which typically appears at the bottom of the FeatureManager in SolidWorks part documents, enables you to put the part into almost any state in the model history. This is not the same as the Undo command, but is the equivalent of going back in time to change your actions, and then replaying everything that you did after that point. Figure 12.1 shows the Rollback bar in use. Notice how the cursor changes into a hand icon when you move it over the bar.

FIGURE 12.1

Using the Rollback bar

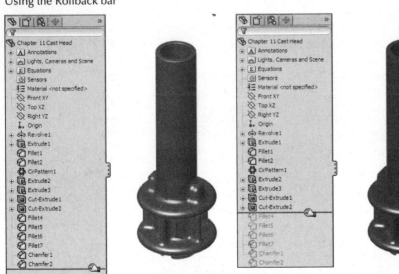

Understanding consumed features

When you use a sketch for a feature such as a Sketch Driven Pattern, the sketch is left in the design tree, in the place where it was created. However, most other features, such as extrudes, *consume* the sketch, meaning that the sketch disappears from its normal order in the FeatureManager and appears indented under the feature that was created from it. Consumed sketches are sometimes also referred to as *absorbed* sketches.

Examining the parent-child relationship

In genealogical family tree diagrams, the parent-child relationship is represented with the parent at the top, and the children branched below the parent. In SolidWorks, parent-child relationships are tracked differently. Figure 12.2 shows the difference between a genealogical family tree and the SolidWorks design tree.

Different interpretations of the structure of parent-child relationships

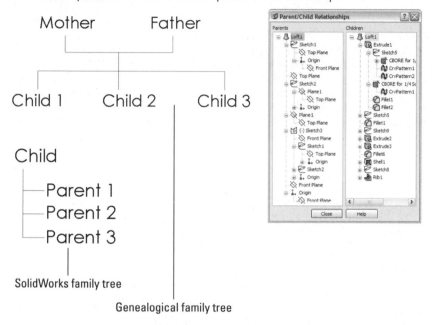

You can display the parent-child relations between SolidWorks features, as shown in Figure 12.2, by right-clicking on any feature and selecting Parent/Child. This helps you determine relationships before you make any edits or deletions because you can see which features will be removed or go dangling (lose their references).

When SolidWorks puts the child feature at the top, it is, in effect, turning the relationship upside down. In the SolidWorks FeatureManager, the earlier point in history is at the top of the tree, but the children are listed before the parents. The SolidWorks method stresses the importance of solid features over other types of sketch or curve features.

For example, you create an extrude from a sketch, and, therefore, the sketch exists before the extrude in the FeatureManager. However, when you create the extrude, SolidWorks places the sketch underneath the extrude. This restructuring can become more apparent when a sketch (for example, Sketch1) is created early in the part history, and then not used to create a feature (for example, Extrude5) until much later. If you roll down the FeatureManager feature by feature, you arrive at a point at the end of the design tree where Extrude5 appears and Sketch1 suddenly moves from its location at the top of the tree to under Extrude5 at the bottom of the tree.

This scenario may cause a situation where many sketches and other features that are created between Sketch1 and Extrude5 are dependent on Sketch1, but where Sketch1 suddenly appears after all these other features. This can be difficult to understand but is key to effectively editing parts, especially parts that someone else created.

The main point here is that SolidWorks displays many relationships upside down. You need to understand how to navigate and manage these history-bound relationships.

One way to get around difficulties in understanding the chronological order of features when compared against the relationship order of features is to roll back a model tree item by item. This can help you sort through the issues. Also remember that from SolidWorks's point of view, the solid feature is the most important item in the tree and is what the rest of the items in the tree support. SolidWorks has made the solid features easily visible and accessible in the tree.

Rolling back features with multiple parents

Take an example such as a loft with guide curves. If you create the guide curves first, and then you create the loft profiles by referencing the guide curves, the loft automatically reorders these sketches when they display under the loft feature such that the profiles are listed in the order in which they were selected, followed by the guide curves in the order in which they were selected. This is shown in Figure 12.3. This restructuring can be confusing if you want to go back and edit any of the relationships between the sketches. You can find this example on the DVD with the filename Chapter 12 Loftwgc.sldprt.

FIGURE 12.3

Multiple parents and sketch reordering

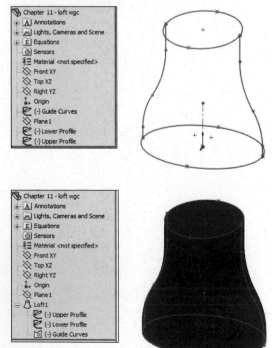

Note

In this example, the two guide curves were created as part of a single sketch, and the SelectionManager was used to select them as individual open curves. This is why the Guide Curves sketch is represented with the contour symbol rather than a regular sketch symbol. ∎

Viewing consumed features in their original order

If you want to view consumed sketches in their original order — for example, the sketches in the loft feature in Figure 12.3 — you must first expand the feature by clicking the plus (+) symbol next to it so that you can see the consumed sketches, and then roll back between the feature and the first sketch. At this point, a warning message appears, stating that the sketches will be temporarily unabsorbed during editing. You can then move the Rollback bar again to show the sketches.

This maneuver can become complicated when you have two sketches absorbed by a projected curve, the projected curve absorbed by a composite curve, and the composite curve absorbed by a sweep feature. To isolate the original projected sketches, you need to repeat the technique with the Rollback bar as described earlier, once for each parent/child relationship. This is shown in Figure 12.4, and the steps to accomplish it are as follows.

FIGURE 12.4

Rollback of nested, absorbed features

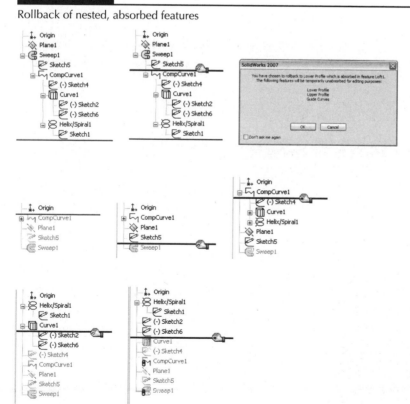

To view consumed sketches in their original order, follow these steps:

1. **Expand the sweep.**
2. **Roll back between the sweep and the profile sketch.**
3. **Answer the prompt that appears.**
4. **Roll down so that you can see the unabsorbed sketches and curves.**
5. **Expand the composite curve.**
6. **Roll back to just after the composite curve.**
7. **Roll back so that you can see the contents of the composite curve.**
8. **Expand the projected curve.**
9. **Roll back to just after the projected curve.**
10. **Roll back so that you can see the contents of the projected curve.**

Using other Rollback techniques

The Rollback feature is located on the RMB menu. Simply right-click a feature and select either Rollback or Roll to Previous. If you are already rolled back and you right-click below the Rollback bar, you can access additional options to Roll Forward and Roll to End.

Editing any feature other than the last feature also serves to roll back the model while you are in Edit mode. As soon as you rebuild the feature or sketch, SolidWorks rebuilds the entire design tree.

The Tools ➪ Options ➪ View setting for Arrow Key Navigation enables you to use the up- and down-arrow keys to manipulate the Rollback bar. Under normal circumstances, the arrow keys control the view orientation, but after you have moved the Rollback bar once using the cursor, the up- and down-arrow keys control the Rollback bar, thereby, inactivating the arrow keys. The left- and right-arrow keys have no effect on the Rollback bar.

Caution

The one situation where this technique does not work as expected is when you are working on a part in the context of the assembly, with the design tree rolled back. The down arrow simply causes the Rollback bar to roll immediately to the end of the design tree. ■

Reordering Features

The ability to reorder features is one that offers SolidWorks users control over the modeling process and its outcome. Without this capability, editing would not be one of the strengths of the software. As you already know, feature order can make a difference in the final shape of a part. For example, this order:

Extrude

Cut

Fillet

Shell

gives you a very different part from this order:

Extrude

Shell

Cut

Fillet

The results of these different orders are shown in Figure 12.5. (The part is split and partially transparent for demonstration purposes only.) You can view this part on the DVD; it is filename `Chapter 12 Reorder.sldprt`.

FIGURE 12.5

Parts that use a different feature order

On the part in the example shown in Figure 12.5, it is fairly simple to reorder the Shell feature by dragging it up the design tree. As a result, the well created by the Cut feature is not shelled around (to create a tube) if the cut comes after the shell. Also, notice the effect of applying the fillets after the shell rather than before it. The corners inside the box are sharp, while the outside corners have been filleted. When you apply the fillet before the shell, fillets that have a radius larger than the shell thickness are transferred to the inside of the shell.

 When you are reordering the features, a symbol may appear on the reorder cursor that says that you cannot reorder the selected feature to the location you want. In this case, you may want to select the Parent/Child option from the RMB menu to investigate. Sketch relationships, feature end conditions, and faces or edges selected for features such shell, patterns, and mirror can cause relationships that prevent reordering.

If two adjacent features are to swap places, it generally does not matter whether you move one feature up the design tree or you move the other one down. However, there are isolated situations that are usually created by the nested, absorbed features discussed earlier, where one feature cannot go in one direction, but the other feature can go in the opposite direction, achieving the exact same result. If you run into a situation where you cannot reorder a feature in one direction even though it appears you should be able to, try moving another feature the other direction.

Note

While this behavior may appear to be a bug, it is more likely just a product of parent/child relationships hidden by the way SolidWorks reorders consumed parent sketches and other types of features. If you were able to stretch the FeatureManager out into a straight line from earliest to latest, the difficulties in reordering would become apparent. ∎

Reordering Folders

There are times when, regardless of which features you choose to move and which direction you choose to move them in, you are faced with the task of moving many features. This can be time-consuming and tedious, not to mention have the potential to introduce errors. To simplify this process, you can put all the features to be moved into a single folder, and then reorder the folder. Keep in mind that the items in the folder need to be a continuous list (you cannot skip features), and you can only reorder the folder if each individual feature within the folder can be reordered.

Best Practice

Folders are frequently used for groups of features that go together and that may be suppressed or unsuppressed in groups. You can also use folders in assemblies. Folders are frequently used to group cosmetic fillet features that are often found at the end of design trees for plastic parts or for groups of whole features. ∎

To create a folder, right-click a feature, or a selected group of features, and select Add to New Folder. Folders should be renamed with a name that helps identify their contents. You can reorder folders in the same way as individual features. When you delete a folder, the contents are removed from the folder and put back into the main tree; they are not deleted.

You can add or remove features to or from the folders by dragging them in or out. If a folder is the last item in the FeatureManager, the next feature that is created is not put into the folder; you must place it in the folder manually. You cannot drag features out of a folder and place them immediately after it, because they will just go back into the folder. If you want to pull a feature out of a folder and place it after the folder, there must be another feature between the feature that you are moving and the folder. However, you can pull a feature out of the folder and place it just *before* the folder.

Using the Flyout and Detachable FeatureManagers

The Flyout FeatureManager resides at the top-left corner of the graphics window. The PropertyManager goes in the same space as the FeatureManager and is sometimes too big to allow this area to accommodate both managers in a split window.

The Flyout FeatureManager enables you to select items from the design tree when the regular FeatureManager is not available because it is covered by the PropertyManager. It usually appears collapsed, so that you can only see the name of the part and the part symbol. To expand it, click the plus icon next to the name of the part in the Flyout FeatureManager.

You can use the Flyout FeatureManager in parts or assemblies. However, you cannot use the Flyout FeatureManager to suppress or roll back the tree.

You can access the settings for the Flyout FeatureManager by choosing Tools ⇨ Options ⇨ FeatureManager ⇨ Use Transparent Flyout FeatureManager in Parts/Assemblies.

You may prefer not to work with the flyout FeatureManager because it interrupts your workflow by covering the regular FeatureManager with a PropertyManager; this inhibits your access to items you may have to select from the FeatureManager such as features and reference planes. If this is the case, you can use the detachable PropertyManager instead. Detaching the PropertyManager removes the need for the flyout. I often dock the detachable PropertyManager where the flyout FeatureManager would go, or even use it undocked on a second monitor. The main advantage of using the detachable PropertyManager instead of the flyout FeatureManager is that with the detachable PropertyManager you don't have to re-locate features in the FeatureManager that were already in view.

Figure 12.6 shows the difference between the flyout FeatureManager on the left and the detachable PropertyManager on the right. My preference is clearly the detachable PropertyManager. When you use the PropertyManager, you don't have to go hunting for features that are listed right in front of you when you do something that opens a PropertyManager. You can put the PropertyManager on a second monitor, in the graphics area, or outside the SolidWorks window. This works best on a wide aspect monitor or multiple monitors.

FIGURE 12.6

Comparing the flyout FeatureManager with the detachable PropertyManager

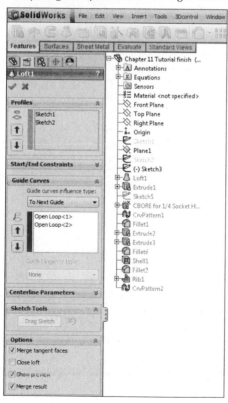
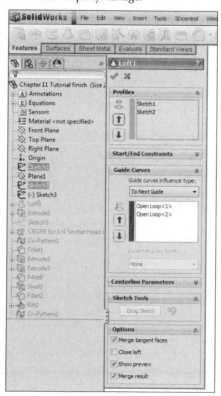

You may correctly ask "What's the difference?" The difference is that when you do something like editing a sketch plane, the current state of the FeatureManager is covered and replaced by the PropertyManager. You may have had the new plane you wanted to use in view. Especially with long FeatureManagers, in both parts and assemblies, when the flyout appears, you have to again scroll to find the plane that was right in view. However you use the detachable PropertyManager, I think you will find it an improvement over the flyout.

On the downside of the detachable PropertyManager, its implementation appears to be incomplete. It does not always automatically expand when needed, and it seems to experience some graphics or display problems, such as target areas for the check and X controls not being directly over the graphics for the control.

Summarizing Part Modeling Best Practice

This section is a summary of best practice suggestions for modeling parts. Best practice lists are important because they lay the groundwork for usage of the software, which is helpful for new users and users who are trying to experiment with the limits of the software.

I believe that it is only after you respect the rules and understand why they are so important, that you know enough to break them. However, best practice lists should not be taken too seriously. They are not inflexible rules, but conservative starting places; they are concepts that you can default to, but that can be broken if you have good reason. Following is a list of suggested best practices:

- Always use unique filenames for your parts. SolidWorks assemblies and drawings may pick up incorrect references if you use parts with identical names.
- Using Custom Properties is a great way to enter text-based information into your parts. Users can view this information from outside the file by using applications such as Windows Explorer, SolidWorks Explorer, and Product Data Management (PDM) applications.
- Learn to sketch using automatic relations.
- Use fully dimensioned sketches when possible. Splines are often impractical to fully dimension.
- Limit your use of the Fixed constraint.
- When possible, make relations to sketches or stable reference geometry, such as the Origin or standard planes, instead of edges or faces. Sketches are far more stable than faces, edges, or model vertices, which change their internal ID at the slightest change and may disappear entirely with fillets, chamfers, split lines, and so on.
- Do not dimension to edges created by fillets or other cosmetic or temporary features.
- Apply names to features, sketches, and dimensions that help to make their function clear.
- When possible, use feature fillets and feature patterns rather than sketch fillets and sketch patterns.
- Combine fillets into as few fillet features as possible; this also enables you to control fillets that need to be controlled separately — such as fillets to be removed for Finite Element Analysis (FEA), drawings, and simplified configurations — or added for rendering. The trade-off is that troubleshooting is more difficult with fillets that use more edges.

- Create a simplified configuration when building very complex parts or working with large assemblies.

- Model with symmetry in mind. Use feature patterns and mirroring when possible.

- Use link values or global variables to control commonly used dimensions.

- Do not be afraid of configurations. Control them with design tables where there are more than a few configs, and document any custom programming or automated features in the spreadsheet for other users.

- Use display states when possible instead of configurations.

- Use multi-body modeling for various techniques within parts; it is not intended as a means to create assemblies within a single part file.

- Cosmetic features — fillets, in particular — should be saved for the bottom of the design tree. It is also a good idea to put them all together into a folder.

- Use the Tools ➪ Options ➪ Performance ➪ Verification on Rebuild setting in combination with the Ctrl+Q command to check models periodically and before calling them "done." The more complex the model, or the more questionable some of the geometry or techniques might be, the more important it is to check the part.

- Always fix errors in your part as soon as you can. Errors cause rebuild time to increase, and if you wait until more errors exist, troubleshooting may become more difficult.

- Troubleshoot feature and sketch errors from the top of the tree down.

- Do not add unnecessary detail. For example, it is not important to actually model a knurled surface on a round steel part. This additional detail is difficult to model in SolidWorks, it slows down the rebuild speed of your part, and there is no advantage to actually having it modeled (unless you are using the model for rapid prototype or to machine a mold for a plastic part where knurling cannot be added as a secondary process). This is better accomplished by a drawing with a note. The same concept applies to thread, extruded text, very large patterns, and other features that introduce complex details.

- Do not rely heavily on niche features. For example, if you find yourself creating helices by using Flex/Twist or Wrap instead of Sweep, then you may want to rethink your approach. In fact, if you find yourself creating a lot of unnecessary helices, then you may want to rethink this approach as well, unless there is a good reason for doing so.

- File size is not necessarily a measure of inefficiency.

- Be cautious about accepting advice or information from Internet forums. You can get both great and terrible advice from people you don't know, along with everything in-between. Sometimes even groups of people can be dead wrong. Get someone you trust to verify ideas, and as always, test them on copied data to determine if they're effective.

If you are the CAD Administrator for a group of users, you may want to incorporate some best practice tips into standard operating procedures for them. The more users that you manage, the more you need to standardize your system.

Cross-Reference

Best practice development is covered at length in the SolidWorks Administration Bible (Wiley, 2009). ■

Using the Skeleton Approach

The term *Skeleton* in Pro/ENGINEER has a different significance than the way it is being used here. SolidWorks does not have any feature or function named "skeleton." The term just refers to a technique and a set of sketches, planes, axes, and reference points used to lay out the major faces and features of a part.

The SolidWorks Help files, tutorials, and training curricula have encouraged users in some respects to take a "fast and loose" approach to modeling, which is great for initial modeling speed but not so good for design for change. The main consideration seems to be the simplest way to do something, or how it *could* be done rather than how it *should* be done. This mentality fit well with the initial several releases of the SolidWorks software, which at that time was marketed as being simple and fast.

The software has progressed immensely since those days. It is now entirely plausible to create complex castings and plastic parts with many hundreds of features, weaving in and out of surface and solid techniques, multi-bodies, and external references. This is a far cry from the typical tutorial or training part, which still tend to have fewer than 15 features, half of which may be fillets. With the simpler parts, you hardly give a thought to parent/child relationships, rebuild times, or the consequences of making changes that cause a feature to fail, because the whole part can be rebuilt from scratch in ten minutes anyway.

SolidWorks users have traditionally been taught to build each feature linearly, on top of the one that came before. This is the genealogical equivalent of each generation having a single child, and then that child having a single child, and so on. The family tree, or FeatureManager, winds up looking like a long staircase, with each generation related only to the generation immediately before it. In the SolidWorks world, this creates long, linear, daisy-chained relationships between consecutive features. The main downside to this is that when a single feature fails, everything below it also fails.

It turns out that this is not a great idea, especially as the parts begin to get more complex. When each feature is dependent upon the one before it, all the features must be solved in a particular order, and if one feature fails, so do all the features that come after it. This also slows down the rebuilding process. Especially as we move into the age of parallel multi-threaded processing, a linear set of commands or features must be executed in order one after the other, and there is really little room for parallel processes.

The sophistication of the documentation provided with SolidWorks has not kept pace with the sophistication of either the software or its users, which I suppose is why you are reading this book rather than the help files provided with the software. The documentation is still based on the simple scenarios, and the advanced user is left to figure things out on his or her own.

As the software gets more sophisticated, the models created with the software can become more sophisticated, and the methods used to build the models must become more sophisticated, as well. It's time to leave the linear modeling approaches behind.

Rather than using a linear daisy-chain modeling scenario, it is better practice to base features on entities that are less likely to fail or change in such a way that dependent downstream features also fail. In earlier chapters, I have suggested that you make sketch relations to other sketches when possible instead of model edges for this very reason.

Taking that scenario one step further, what if a handful of sketch and plane features were used to centralize control of all of the rest of the features? What if every feature, to the extent possible, related back to these "skeleton" features? Features such as fillets, shell, and draft by design require selections from solid geometry, but other features, such as any feature created from sketches, could be made with only reference to those original skeleton sketches and planes. The parent/child relationship would look very different for a model made in this way.

Instead of looking like a long staircase, this tree would look more like a tree that gets wide very quickly. There would be fewer "generations," but each generation would be more populated. The main upshot of this is that if any feature fails, the dependent features that fail should be minimized.

The first thing to notice is that errors in features at the top of the tree do not cascade down the tree as they do in the "stairstep" model. Second, it is always much easier to find how a model is constructed, because all the reference geometry used to build it is set up in the first few features. This scenario also has the potential to make better use of multi-threaded processing because the logic is less linear and more parallel.

On the DVD

Examine the part on the DVD for Chapter 12 called `Chapter 12 Sketleton.sldprt`. **Roll back the FeatureManager and examine it. Notice that sketches do not reference faces or edges of the part, but other sketches and planes.** ■

Using Evaluation Techniques

You can use evaluation techniques to evaluate geometry errors, demonstrate the manufacturability of a given part, or to some degree quantify aesthetic qualities of a given part, or section of a part. I discuss evaluation techniques here because the design cycle involves iterations around the combination of create-evaluate-edit-evaluate functions. I discuss the following techniques in this section:

- Verification on rebuild
- Check
- Zebra Stripes/RealView/Lights and specularity
- Curvature display
- Deviation analysis
- Tangent Edges as Phantom
- Geometry Analysis
- Feature statistics
- Curvature comb
- DFMXpress (Design For Manufacturability)
- SimulationXpress

Many of these techniques apply specifically to plastic parts and complex shapes, but even if you do not become involved in these areas of design or modeling, these tools may help you to find answers on other types of models as well.

A special tab called Evaluate appears in the CommandManager; this tab has much of the functionality that is discussed in this chapter. You can use the commands on this tab to evaluate parts in several ways. Some focus on plastic parts or thin-walled parts or symmetric parts, and so on. Most of these tools are from the Tools toolbar but are found on the Evaluate tab in the Command Manager.

Using Verification on rebuild

Verification on rebuild is an option that you can access by choosing Tools ⇨ Options ⇨ Performance ⇨ Verification on rebuild. Under normal circumstances (with this setting turned off), SolidWorks checks each face to ensure that it does not overlap or intersect improperly with every adjacent face. Each face can have several neighbors. This option is shown in Figure 12.7.

The Verification on rebuild option

With the setting selected, SolidWorks checks each face with every other face in the model. This is a better check than with the setting off but greatly increases the workload. The switch is deselected by default to prevent rebuild times from getting out of control. For most parts, the default setting is sufficient; however, when parts become complex, you may need to select the more advanced setting.

If you are having geometry or rebuild error problems with a part and cannot understand why, then try turning Verification on rebuild on and pressing Ctrl+Q. Ctrl+Q applies the Forced Rebuild command and rebuilds the entire design tree. Ctrl+B, or the Rebuild command, only rebuilds what SolidWorks determines needs to be rebuilt.

If you see additional errors in the design tree that were not there before, then the combination of Verification on rebuild and Forced Rebuild has identified problem areas of the model and the features that caused the errors failed. If not, then your problem may be elsewhere. You still need to fix any errors found this way.

Performance

For speed reasons, it is normal practice to turn Verification on rebuild off, and to use it selectively to check models with potential errors. The type of speed degradation that you can see is dependent on the number of faces and bodies in the model. Some of the performance degradation as relates to patterns is documented in Chapter 9. ∎

Using the Check tool

Check is a tool that checks geometry for invalid faces and other similar geometry errors. It is also often used to find open edges of surface bodies, short edges, and the minimum radius on a face or entity. I usually apply the Check tool before selecting the Verification on rebuild option. The Check tool points to specific face or edge geometry (not features or sketches) that is the cause of the problem. When the Check tool finds general faults, the locations it points to may or may not have something obvious to do with a possible fix.

Much of the time, the best tool for tracking down geometry errors is the combination of experience and intuition. It is not very scientific, but you come to recognize where potential problems are likely to arise, such those that occur when you attempt to intersect complex faces at complex edges, sharp or pointy geometry, and geometry or faces that vary significantly from rectangular with 90-degree corners. Figure 12.8 shows the Check Entity dialog box.

The Check Entity dialog box

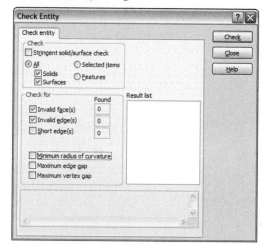

Evaluating geometry with reflective techniques

Evaluating complex shapes can be difficult. A subjective evaluation requires an eye for the type of work you are doing. An objective evaluation requires some sort of measurable criteria for determining a pass or fail, or a way for you to assign a score somewhere in the middle.

One way to subjectively evaluate complex surfaces, and in particular the transitions between surfaces around common edges, is to use reflective techniques. If you look at an automobile's fender, you can tell whether it has been dented or if a dent has been badly repaired by seeing how the light reflects off of the surface. The same principle applies when evaluating solid or surface models. Bad transitions appear as a crease or an unwanted bulge or indentation. The goal is to turn off the edge display and not be able to identify where the edge is between surfaces for the transition to be as smooth as if the whole area were made from a single surface.

With all of the RealView functionality in SolidWorks that emphasizes reflective finishes and backgrounds that emphasize the reflections, sometimes the RealView Appearance and Scenes are all you need to employ reflective evaluation techniques. Chapter 5 covers all of the display information you need to make the most of RealView, Appearances, and Scenes.

Using Zebra Stripes

 Zebra Stripes can be activated one of two ways, by choosing View ➪ Display ➪ Zebra Stripes from the menus or by clicking a toolbar button on the View toolbar. Zebra Stripes place the part in a room that is either spherical or cubic, where the walls are painted with alternating black-and-white stripes (although you can change the colors and the spacing of the stripes). The part is made to be perfectly reflective, and the way that the stripes transition over edges tells you something about the qualities of the faces on either side of the edge. Four conditions are of particular interest:

- $c0$ = faces contact at edge
- $c1$ = faces are tangent at edge
- $c2$ = curvature of each face is equal at the edge and the transition is smooth
- $c3$ = rate of change of curvature of each face is equal at the edge

The Zebra Stripes tool can only help you identify $c0$, $c1$, and $c2$, and only subjectively. This feature is of most value between complex faces. Figure 12.9 illustrates how the Zebra Stripes tool shows the differences between these three conditions.

FIGURE 12.9

Contact, tangency, and curvature continuity

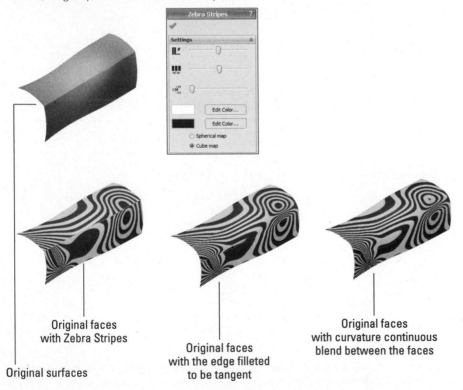

Original surfaces

Original faces
with Zebra Stripes

Original faces
with the edge filleted
to be tangent

Original faces
with curvature continuous
blend between the faces

Notice how on the Contact-only model, the Zebra Stripe lines do not line up across the edge. On the Tangent example, the stripes line up across the edges, but the stripes themselves are not smooth. On the Curvature Continuous example, the stripes are smooth across the edges. The part shown in Figure 12.9 is a surface model and can be found on the DVD with the filename `Chapter 12 Zebra Stripes.sldprt`.

Tip

You should rotate the model a lot when you are using the Zebra Stripes tool. Changing the density of the lines can also help, as can increasing the image quality (Tools ⇨ Options ⇨ Document Properties ⇨ Image Quality). Turning off the edge display may also help. ∎

Using RealView

RealView Graphics display is only available to users with certain types of video cards. To see whether your card supports RealView, consult the system requirements on the SolidWorks Web site.

RealView causes reflections that can be used in a way similar to the reflections in Zebra Stripes. Rotate the part slowly and watch how the reflections flow across edges. Instead of black and white stripes, it uses the reflective background that is applied as part of the RealView Scene.

Cross-Reference

RealView techniques and usage are covered in more depth in Chapter 5. ∎

Using Curvature display

Model curvature can be plotted onto the model face using colors, as shown in Figure 12.10. The accuracy of this display leaves a bit to be desired, but it does help you identify areas of very tight curvature on your part. Areas of tight curvature can cause features such as fillets and shells to fail.

FIGURE 12.10

Curvature display

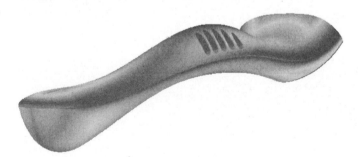

Using Deviation Analysis

Deviation Analysis measures how far from tangent the surfaces on either side of a selected edge actually are. For example, the edges shown in Figure 12.11 are found to be fair, but not very good. I prefer deviations of less than 0.5 degrees. Often with some of the advanced surface types such as Fill and Boundary, SolidWorks can achieve edges with less than 0.05-degree maximum deviation.

While Deviation Analysis helps to quantitatively measure how close to tangent the faces on either side of the selected edge are, it does not tell you anything about curvature, so you must still run Zebra Stripes to get the complete picture of the flow between faces. Both tests have to return good results to have an acceptable face transition.

An example of Deviation Analysis

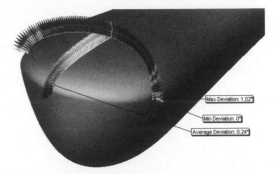

Using the Tangent Edges as Phantom setting

Using the Tangent Edges as Phantom setting is an easy way to evaluate a large number of edges visually. This function does not do what the Zebra Stripes tool does, but it gives you a good indication of the tangency across a large number of edges very quickly. Again, it only represents tangency, and tells you nothing about curvature continuity. Nor does it give you as detailed information as the Deviation Analysis; it only tells you whether SolidWorks considers the faces to be tangent across the edge. Several releases ago, SolidWorks widened the tolerance of what it considers to be tangent, which is both good and bad news. It's good because features that require tangency will work more frequently, and it's bad because if fractional tangency degrees matter to you, "close" is not close enough. If you use Tangent Edges as Phantom as an analysis technique, you should also follow it up with Deviation Analysis to find out how close you actually are.

I have not seen this function deliver false positives (edges displayed as tangent when in fact they were not), but I have seen many false negatives (edges that display as non-tangent when in fact they were). Figure 12.12 shows a situation where the edges are displayed with solid edges, but Deviation Analysis shows them to have a zero-degree maximum deviation.

Using the Tangent Edges as Phantom setting

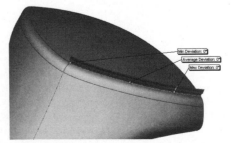

The measure of tangency has some tolerance. Users cannot control the tolerance, nor does the documentation say what it is. If SolidWorks says two faces are *not* tangent at an edge, you can believe that, but if SolidWorks says that the faces *are* tangent, you still have to ask *how* tangent. That is the question that Deviation Analysis can answer.

Using Geometry Analysis

 Another tool that is fairly new is the Geometry Analysis tool. You can find it in the Tools menu or the new Evaluate tab in the Command Manager. It is an extremely useful tool for troubleshooting problematic geometry. The PropertyManager, shown in Figure 12.13, allows you to look for several specific items:

- Short edges
- Small faces
- Sliver faces
- Knife edges/vertices
- Discontinuous faces or edges

FIGURE 12.13

Using Geometry Analysis to find typical problem spots

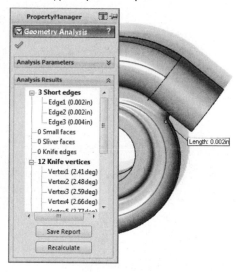

These specific types of geometry typically cause problems with other features, such as shells or fillets. If you are having difficulty with a feature failing for a reason that you can't explain, use the Geometry Analysis tool to point out potential problem spots. This is not a tool that will do your job for you, but it is a tool that gives you useful information to help you do your job better with less guesswork.

Geometry analysis is only available with SolidWorks Professional and higher.

Using Feature Statistics

 The Feature Statistics tool has been used previously in this book to measure rebuild times for individual features in parts. You can find it either in the Tools menu or the Evaluate tab of the Command Manager.

Feature Statistics lists the rebuild times of each individual feature in a part. This is useful for researching features, benchmarking hardware or versions of SolidWorks, and developing best practice recommendations for different tools and techniques. Figure 12.14 shows the Feature Statistics interface.

Feature Statistics helps you analyze rebuild times for features.

Overall, I do not recommend relying too heavily on the data the Feature Statistics tool provides; this is not because it is inaccurate but because rebuild time is not always the best way to evaluate a model. You can certainly use the information, but you also need to keep it in perspective. A feature that takes a long time to rebuild but gives the correct result is always better than any feature that does not give the correct result, regardless of rebuild time.

Using the Curvature Comb

 The Curvature Comb is a graphical tool you can apply to a spline, circle, arc, ellipse, or parabola to indicate the curvature along the length of the curve. You cannot apply a Curvature Comb to a straight line because a straight line has no curvature. The height of the comb indicates the curvature. Curvature is defined as the inverse of radius ($c=1/r$), so that as the radius gets smaller, the curvature gets bigger.

Figure 12.15 shows a curvature comb applied to a spline. Notice that the spline continuously changes curvature. An arc has constant curvature.

FIGURE 12.15

A Curvature Comb shows the constantly changing curvature of the spline.

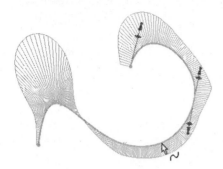

When the comb crosses the spline, it means that the direction of curvature has changed. When the comb intersects the spline, it means that the spline at that point has no curvature.

Cross-Reference

The Curvature Comb is discussed in depth in the SolidWorks Surfacing and Complex Shape Modeling Bible (Wiley, 2008). ■

Using DFMXpress to catch manufacturability problems

DFMXpress is a free add-in to the software that may entice you to buy a higher functionality product. DFMXpress may provide some first-level manufacturability guidance for novice designers and engineers or those unfamiliar with one of the four processes that DFMXpress supports.

DFMXpress checks various rules for parts to be manufactured using the following processes:

- Mill/Drill
- Turn with Mill/Drill
- Sheet Metal
- Injection Molding

For each process, the user must establish some rule parameters. For example, for injection molding, the parameters are minimum and maximum wall thickness. It makes no mention of draft or undercuts. For Sheet Metal, you must set various thickness ratios for minimum hole diameter, bend radius, standard hole sizes, and so on. The evaluation tool requires some minimum setup, and some input from an experienced person in your operation. It is certainly not complete, or a replacement for an expert, but it offers a great first look at the geometry to check that the most obvious errors are caught before it leaves your desk.

You can activate DFMXpress from the Tools menu, and it runs in the Task Pane. Figure 12.16 shows DFMXpress in action on an injection-molded part. The results point to specific faces that fail specific rules, so when it fails, you know exactly where and why.

FIGURE 12.16

Reading results in DFMXpress

Analyzing with SimulationXpress

SimulationXpress (formerly COSMOSXpress) is a limited version of SolidWorks Simulation (formerly COSMOS Works) that is bundled with SolidWorks to acquaint users with FEA. The full version of SolidWorks Simulation does a wide range of analysis, from vibrations to large deformations. SimulationXpress is a very quick and easy wizard for simple stress analysis on stand-alone parts with simple constraints. It does simple linear stress analysis on a single part with a single material using only fixed constraints and a load. You can also use SimulationXpress to do a simple stress/weight optimization based on dimensions that you select to be altered.

You can start SimulationXpress through the Tools menu, or from the Evaluate tab of the CommandManager. The interface guides you through a very simple wizard. If you have any familiarity with FEA applications, you will find SimulationXpress easy to understand and use, but possibly lacking in flexibility or capability.

SimulationXpress uses a combination of the Task Pane on the right of the graphics window and the PropertyManager on the left side of the graphics window. In this book, I am using the detached PropertyManager, so I can position it for more compact screen shots.

SimulationXpress is intended as a quick and dirty analysis run to see whether you are even close to having a part that will stand up to the loads you apply to it. As with any type of analysis, the results are only of value if the setup was correct and if you are able to interpret the results.

In this chapter I do not aim to teach analysis theory or best practice; this is simply a quick overview of how to use the tool. FEA is a field of study unto itself, and you should learn it from a dedicated resource. Analysis is a field that depends on approximations and simplifying assumptions. Knowing how and when to make the correct approximations and assumptions along with being able to interpret approximated results are some of the keys to success not provided by this book.

As you step through the process, the notes in the Task Pane seem to continually prompt you that various conditions will require the next level higher (not free) in order to correctly solve the model.

SimulationXpress is clearly a sales and marketing tool, but if your needs are simple, and you understand the process, you may be able to get useful information from it.

Welcome to SolidWorks SimulationXpress

When you start SimulationXpress, an image welcomes you to the tool and lets you know what to expect from the process. It also issues a disclaimer that seems to downplay the value of this tool. There is also a link here for some valuable Web-based training if you are new to analysis or simulation. Figure 12.17 shows the new Welcome screen.

Welcoming you to the SimulationXpress software

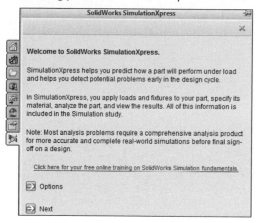

If you are a veteran SimulationXpress user, most of what you see here may be new, including the order of the steps and some of the terminology.

Applying Fixtures

Every analysis must have at least one face that is held stationary in order for the analysis to work. These are usually faces on the bottom of the part.

In the past, Fixtures were referred to as Restraints. You must apply Fixtures to the part to be analyzed as the first step in the process. A PropertyManager appears to collect the faces you select. Fixtures are fixed, meaning they are the faces in the analysis that remain perfectly stationary. These are usually some sort of mounting location or a welded area.

On this part, I have used the Split Line feature to split out areas of the bottom face around the bolt holes to represent sections of the part that will not move regardless of how much force is applied to the part.

The dark blue underlined text in the Task Pane offers links to simple animations showing some possibilities for assigning Fixtures. Clicking the Add a fixture link in the Task Pane brings up the Fixture PropertyManager, shown in Figure 12.18.

FIGURE 12.18

Assigning fixed faces using the Fixture PropertyManager

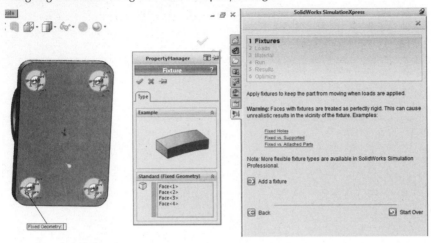

Applying Loads

You can apply forces or pressures to model faces. Forces are normal to selected faces by default, but you can select an axis, edge, or sketch element to specify a selected direction for the force. Again links in the Task Pane enable you to see small video hints or tool tips. Figure 12.19 shows the Loads interfaces.

FIGURE 12.19

Applying loads to the model in SimulationXpress

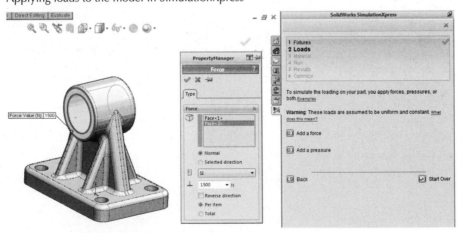

Selecting a material

The third step in setting up SolidWorks SimulationXpress is to assign a material. Once you have made your selection, click Apply. Figure 12.20 shows some of the materials selection. Materials can be created or customized in the same way that you would create or customize standard SolidWorks materials.

Assigning a material in SimulationXpress

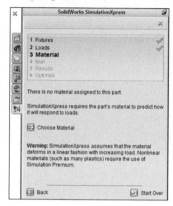 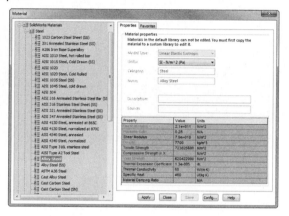

Tip

My experience with the early versions of SimulationXpress in SolidWorks 2010 sp0.0 has been that much of the tool did not work properly the first time. It took several tries to get a material to apply, the loads appeared to be applied incorrectly, and the initial screen did not appear when I first started the software. ∎

Running the analysis

Analyzing simple parts on modern computers usually takes a matter of seconds. Because SimulationXpress is limited to single parts, most analyses you run will not take very long. You need to make sure that you have green check marks to the right of Fixtures, Loads, and Material before you can run the analysis. Figure 12.21 shows the analysis of this part in the process of running.

Visualizing the results

SimulationXpress makes three different types of results available to you:

- vonMises stress plot
- Displacement plot
- Factor of Safety (FOS) plot

FIGURE 12.21

Running the analysis

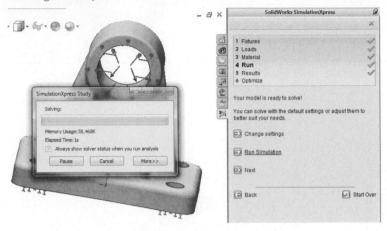

Each of these can be animated. The deformation shown by the model is exaggerated by a deformation scale factor, which is shown as part of the legend on the screen. It is typically around 1000x. Deformation is exaggerated to make it easier to visualize how the structure flexes under load.

Figure 12.22 shows a deformed vonMises stress plot.

FIGURE 12.22

Visualizing the results of the stress analysis

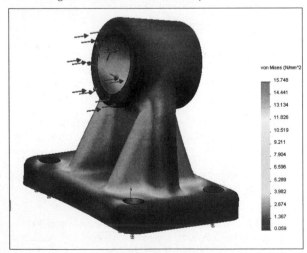

All the values that you enter and faces that you select are stored in the SimulationXpress Study panel, which shows up by default on the bottom in a split PropertyManager, as shown in Figure 12.23. This is saved with the part and is displayed any time you have the SolidWorks SimulationXpress panel open in the Task Pane.

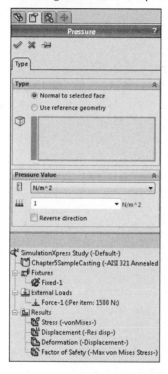

FIGURE 12.23

Accessing the results and inputs for the study in the lower panel of the PropertyManager

Optimizing the design

The final step in the Simulation process, if you choose to use it, is the Optimization. Optimization enables you to vary a dimension of the part and run multiple studies to determine what value for that dimension produces the best result.

Optimization displays another panel at the bottom of the graphics window that enables you to establish a range for the dimension that will be varied during the optimization. This panel is shown in Figure 12.24.

When you run the optimization, SolidWorks will change the model dimension within the range that you specified and run an analysis for each dimension value. For this to be most successful, you must have a robust model where all the features can adapt to the range of dimensions for the feature being changed.

FIGURE 12.24

Entering a range of sizes for the optimized feature

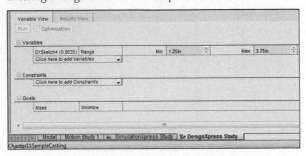

Troubleshooting Errors

You will encounter many types of errors in SolidWorks. Improper installation or even bad computer hygiene can cause errors that might look like bugs in the software. Software bugs can cause errors that look like training issues. Operator errors can cause problems that are very difficult to sort out. In this book, I do not have the space to go into all of the possible errors and how to work around or fix them, but I will focus on feature-related errors that happen in the course of working on models. If you are interested in debugging errors caused by installation, maintenance, or administrative issues, refer to the *SolidWorks Administration Bible* (Wiley, 2009).

When you get an error in SolidWorks, figuring out what caused the error and how to fix it is the goal of troubleshooting. Error messages appear in several places, including in message boxes in the graphics window, in the Task Bar, in tool tip bubbles next to the PropertyManager, and in small symbols within the FeatureManager window.

Interpreting rebuild errors

Chapter 3 discusses sketch colors and troubleshooting errors in sketches. You can apply much of what you learned from troubleshooting sketches to troubleshooting features in parts. The FeatureManager displays yellow triangles with black exclamation marks that point out some sort of warning. A warning means that there is a problem, but that the feature has not failed. The red circle with an X in it is a failure symbol, and it means that the feature does not create any geometry.

Figure 12.25 shows a portion of a feature tree of a part from which a feature in the middle of the tree was deleted. Unless you are very careful about how you set up your part, a deletion of this kind will result in a lot of errors.

Notice the tool tip balloon in Figure 12.25. Many users get in the habit of clicking out of any sort of warning or error message. You shouldn't be afraid of errors. Once you know how to deal with them, you will think of errors as a tool to help you investigate your model. The first thing you should do with an error message is read it. Eventually, you will be able to recognize error messages and their meanings very quickly.

FIGURE 12.25

Deleting a feature in the middle of a tree can cause a lot of errors.

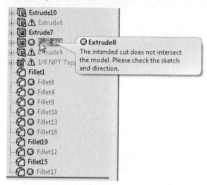

This error message says, "The intended cut does not intersect the model. Please check the sketch and direction." This means that you have a cut that is cutting air. This is because the feature it was cutting was deleted. You may know the cause of errors or you may not. If you had inherited this part from someone else who did not explain the state of the model to you, you might have to figure it out yourself. Most of the time, it is not difficult to figure out what is going on.

When you inherit a model with errors, the first thing you should do is look for the error that is highest in the tree. When you make a change that causes errors, these errors are almost always lower in the tree than the change. Special situations can arise where a change causes an error up the tree, but they are rare.

Here are some common error messages and what they are really trying to tell you:

- **Some Items are no longer in the model. You can reselect the items using the Edit Definition in the FeatureManager design tree.** The first thing to know here is that Edit Definition has been gone for several releases now. Edit Feature is the name of the command you will be looking for. You can get this message when an edge or a face for a selected feature no longer exists. A number of things can cause it, but the culprit is usually changes to the model upstream. As a result, if you roll back the model, and make changes (especially if you delete something, but adding features can also cause errors of this sort), you can expect some problems when you unroll the model.

- **Operation failed due to geometric condition.** This is one that frustrates a lot of users, because "geometric condition" is vague and could mean just about anything related to geometry. It can sometimes mean that a selection set is incomplete — the feature requires another face or another edge to be selected in order to work, or a fillet cannot work because an edge flips convexity, or a sketch line does not cut all the way across a solid body. There are too many possibilities to list, but it is a clue that you need to check either the selections for the feature or the body on which the feature is operating. In more complex cases, it might mean that the part has some geometrical errors that you need to figure out by using the Check tool or Verification on Rebuild.

- **Warning: This sketch contains dimensions or relations to model geometry which no longer exists...** This is one of the better messages that SolidWorks provides. It is fairly self-explanatory and goes on to give you a couple of useful suggestions as to how you might fix the problem.

- **Some filleted items are no longer in the model. Edit the feature to reselect the items.** When all of the edges selected in a fillet feature are suddenly not there, the entire fillet feature fails because there is nothing to do. This warning displays the red circle with the X in it. Some edges may remain selected, and the fillet feature can still work. In these cases, you will get the next message, which is just a warning rather than an error.

- **Warning: Edge for fillet/chamfer does not exist.** In this case, you see the yellow triangle warning, and the fillet still creates some fillets, but one of the selected edges is missing, and the feature can't create all of the fillets it created originally. The fastest way to fix this warning is to right-click it, select Edit Feature, and then immediately click the green check icon. SolidWorks displays a message to make sure that you want to just remove the references to the missing edge, but will continue to create fillets on the selected edges. Another option is to find the missing edge in the selection box and reselect an edge to take its place.

Many more types of errors exist, and rather than going through an exhaustive list, which would require another book of its own, I would like to impart to you some guidelines to help you find a useful answer. Hopefully you only have to figure out an error once, and you will remember it the next time you see it. Here are some general guidelines for troubleshooting errors with causes that aren't obvious:

- **CAD in general does not like line-on-line geometry.** In SolidWorks, you don't get extra points for being close. Most features require you to be exact or so close that it looks exact. It is often a good idea to "overbuild" geometry so that it is bigger than it needs to be if it is going to merge with other geometry.

- **Zero thickness errors.** Zero thickness errors can be some of the most difficult for users that are new to 3D to diagnose. Much in the same way that CAD doesn't like line-on-line geometry, it doesn't like edges that create a section of a single body where there is air on two sides of an edge. If you were to extrude two rectangles that touch at a point, SolidWorks would create two separate bodies from that point, because it physically would fall apart if it were a single body. If the two touching rectangles were also trying to merge with an existing solid body, you would get an error.

- **Planar means planar.** If you click on a face, and it just won't let you open a sketch, maybe the face is not planar. Errors of this sort can happen in surfacing applications and imported geometry quite often. I use the Sketch icon as a quick test for whether or not a face is planar. SolidWorks doesn't really give you another way to measure this. Non-planar faces can also cause a lot of trouble with assembly mates.

- **Even if it's planar, is it square to the coordinate system?** If you work with plastic parts or castings, or anything else that requires draft, you can and probably do have faces that are not perpendicular or parallel to the standard reference planes. This can cause problems with projections (a circle projected at an angle becomes an ellipse, and an ellipse projected at an angle becomes a spline) and extrusion directions.

- **If it doesn't like one method, try another that produces similar results.** One common example of this is when a constant radius fillet will not work, and you think it should work. In this case, try to use a variable radius fillet with all the same radius values.

For most errors, a rational reason exists. Belief in supernatural forces is not likely to be useful when troubleshooting errors in SolidWorks. If you are using very common features such as extrudes and cuts and you run into errors, it is very unlikely that you have found a bug (although bugs in sketches are quite common). Generally speaking, the more traffic a feature sees, the less likely you are to find bugs with it. Sometimes just determining whether the problem is with the software or with something you are doing is the toughest thing to troubleshoot. In general, users are far too eager to assign blame to the software.

Using SolidWorks RX and Performance Benchmark

SolidWorks provides a couple of automated troubleshooting tools: SolidWorks RX and Performance Benchmark. SolidWorks RX troubleshoots your system, or at least records facts about your system so someone trained in how to view the results can diagnose the problem.

Using SolidWorks RX

SolidWorks RX is a diagnostic tool that SolidWorks provides to help support techs solve your problem or to help you solve it yourself. You can access SolidWorks RX through the Windows Start menu ⇨ All Programs ⇨ SolidWorks 2011 ⇨ SolidWorks 2011 Tools ⇨ SolidWorks RX. Figure 12.26 shows the Home page of the interface.

FIGURE 12.26

Using SolidWorks RX

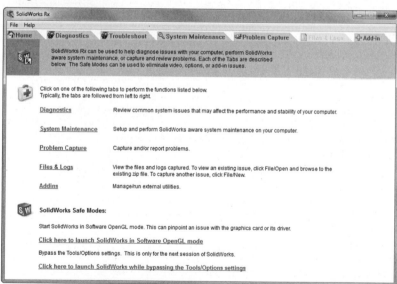

Using the Diagnostics tab

The first tab in the SolidWorks RX interface is a self-help diagnostics list, shown in Figure 12.27. This points out that my computer is a less common brand (Xi), that it is compatible with my video card, and that the driver is out of date (it gives me the option to download the correct driver); it also lists other information related to system maintenance.

FIGURE 12.27

Using the SolidWorks RX Diagnostics tab

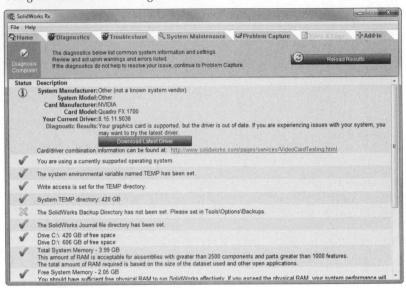

The items in the Diagnostics tab are things that a support tech might ask you about if you were to call with a crash problem or some other problem that might be related to general system issues. Running SolidWorks RX before calling tech support could save you time and make you more self-reliant.

Using the Troubleshoot tab

The Troubleshoot tab contains mostly links to the SolidWorks Knowledge Base, for which you will need a subscription login. These links are useful, and it is a good idea to check them out before calling tech support.

Using the System Maintenance tab

The System Maintenance tab contains paths to critical SolidWorks and system folders. If you click the Start Maintenance button in the upper-right corner, SolidWorks RX clears all the files from the listed paths. If you use the Browse buttons, you can clear paths individually. These are generally temporary and backup folders, so make sure you do not need any of the files before clearing them. Figure 12.28 shows the System Maintenance tab.

Using the Problem Capture tab

Often when you call your reseller tech support, and you are having some sort of difficulty that is not readily explained, the technician will ask you to submit a SolidWorks RX log file. This log file includes the information from the other tabs, along with an optional description of the problem, SolidWorks files that were in use when the problem occurred, and a video of the problem actually happening. Figure 12.29 shows the Problem Capture tab.

FIGURE 12.28

Clearing temp files with the System Maintenance tab

FIGURE 12.29

Collecting information in the Problem Capture tab

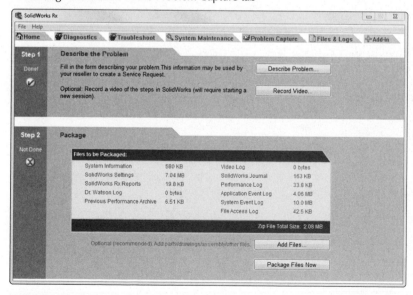

Using the Files & Logs tab

The Files & Logs tab shows a summary of the issue and a list of all of the files included in the RX package. You can click on the files that have been added to view their contents before sending the package. The Files & Logs tab is shown in Figure 12.30.

FIGURE 12.30

Listing the files to be sent in the RX package

Using Performance Benchmark

SolidWorks RX has an Add-in tab that allows add-ins to be developed to extend the RX functionality. New for SolidWorks 2011 is the Performance Benchmark add-in. This benchmark runs your installation of SolidWorks through some automated display and rebuild exercises and measures the time for various operations such as zoom, rotate, rebuild, for a part and an assembly. Figure 12.31 shows the interface for the Performance Benchmark test.

This benchmark is similar to an older benchmark application called SPECapc, which was available several years ago and could be used across several different CAD systems. SPECapc still exists (and is available from the Web site www.spec.org), but the SolidWorks benchmark was last updated in 2007. The point of benchmarks like this is to measure hardware capabilities.

Other less formal benchmarks exist, such as Mike Wilson's Ship-in-a-Bottle (www.mikejwilson. com), which is just a surface model with a rebuild macro, where you use Feature Statistics to measure the results. Anna Wood (www.solidmuse.com) also has an informal benchmark with a model of Scooby Doo and a punch plate. None of the informal benchmark models are particularly good at measuring all aspects of the software. There are no assemblies among them, and a couple of them are heavy in surfacing, which makes better use of multi-threading than solid models.

The models for the SolidWorks RX Performance Benchmark are a small, stamped part and an injection-mold die set. Figure 12.32 shows the benchmark in action.

FIGURE 12.31

Running Performance Benchmark

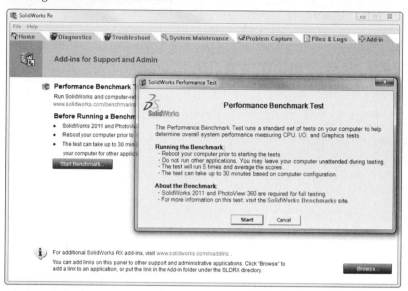

FIGURE 12.32

Putting the computer through its paces with Performance Benchmark

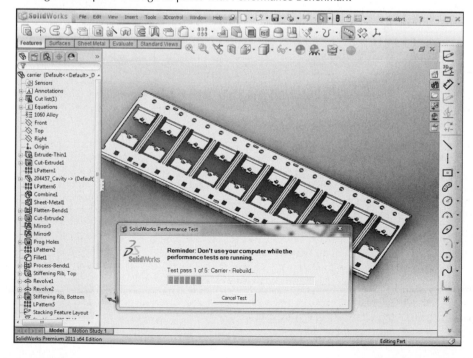

The results of the benchmark test are measured in two ways. One way is in the average number of seconds each test took (where a lower score is better), and the other way is to simply reuse the Windows Experience Index (where a higher score is better), which you can find in the Windows Control panel.

Finally, you can submit your results to the SolidWorks Web site, where they are posted immediately for comparison. This is used to help people make decisions about what hardware to buy. Figure 12.33 shows the local results, and Figure 12.34 shows accumulated results from many users.

FIGURE 12.33

Evaluating your hardware with a SolidWorks RX Performance Benchmark test

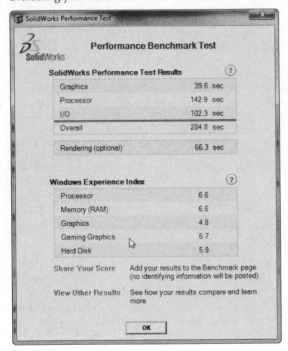

You can check out the compared scores at www.solidworks.com/sw/support/shareyour-score.htm. Look through the list to see which kind of hardware receives a consistently high score and which is not represented in the top results. It's nice that these test results are now more formalized, as previously the closest thing to a database of benchmark scores was a spreadsheet on Anna Wood's Web site.

You can find more information on benchmarking and SolidWorks at www.solidworks.com/sw/support/benchmarks.htm.

FIGURE 12.34

Comparing your score against other submitted scores

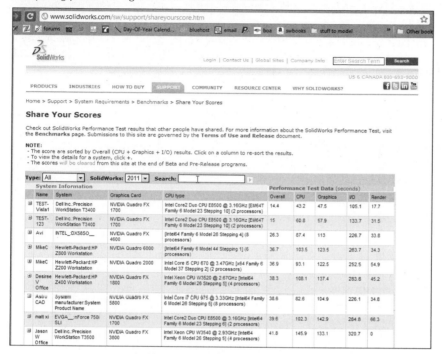

Tutorial: Making Use of Editing and Evaluation Techniques

Using this tutorial, you make some major edits to an existing part. You use some simple loft and spline commands and work with the rollback states and feature order, as well as some evaluation techniques. Please follow these steps:

1. **Open the existing part with the filename** Chapter 12 Tutorial Start.sldprt. Roll the part back and step through it feature by feature to see how it was made. Edit the loft feature to see which sketches were used to create it. This can help you to understand how the part was built. Exit the loft command and move the rollback bar back to the bottom of the tree.

2. **Open the Deviation Analysis tool (Tools ⇨ Deviation Analysis).** Select the edges, as shown in Figure 12.35.

FIGURE 12.35

Deviation analysis of an existing part

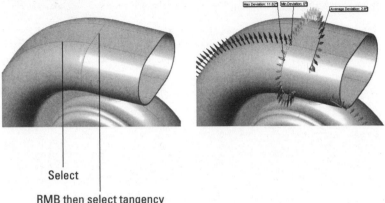

Select

RMB then select tangency

The maximum deviation is about ten degrees, which is far too much. This part needs to be smoothed out, which you can do using splines in place of lines and arcs.

3. **The first step is to make the outlet all one piece with the spiral.** You can do this with a Fit Spline. You need to create the Fit Spline before the loft profiles and after the spiral.

   Expand the loft, and roll back between the loft feature and the first sketch. Click OK in response to the prompt, and then roll back to just after the spiral, as shown in Figure 12.36.

FIGURE 12.36

Rolling back to just after the spiral

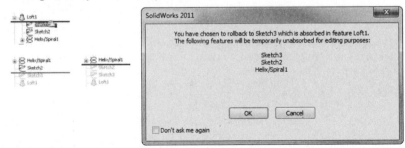

4. **Right-click the spiral in the FeatureManager and show it.** Open a new sketch on the Top plane.

5. **Try to draw a horizontal line from the outer end of the spiral.** You will notice that you cannot reference the end of the spiral.

Tip

Curves that are absorbed into other features are notoriously difficult to work with. Generally, you need to select them from the FeatureManager to do anything at all with them. Also, if you need to reference an end of an absorbed curve, you are better off using Convert Entities to make it into a sketch entity. ■

6. **Notice that you cannot select the spiral from the graphics window.** Even when selected from the FeatureManager, it appears not to be selected in the graphics window. Ensure that it is selected in the FeatureManager, and then click the Convert Entities button on the sketch toolbar.

7. **Draw a horizontal line from the outer end of the spiral and dimension it to be 3 inches long, as shown in Figure 12.37.**

FIGURE 12.37

Preparing for the Fit Spline

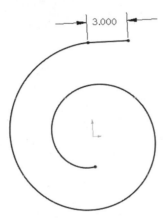

3.000

8. **Select both the converted spiral and the line, and click Tools ⇨ Spline Tools ⇨ Fit Spline.** Set the Tolerance to .1 and make sure that only the Constrained option is selected. Click OK to accept the Fit Spline. Test to make sure that a single spline is created by moving your cursor over the sketch to see whether the whole length is highlighted.

Note

The Fit Spline feature fits a spline to a set of sketch entities within the specified tolerance. It can be a useful tool for smoothing out sketch geometry. ■

Caution

Do not exit the Fit Spline by pressing the Enter key as you do with other commands, because it simply exits you out of the command without creating a spline. ■

9. **Right-click on spline and select the Curvature Comb.** Notice how the comb is affected by the transition from the spiral to the straight line.

10. **Exit the sketch, and create a new plane.** Choose Insert ⇨ Reference Geometry ⇨ Plane from the menus. Select the Right plane from the Flyout FeatureManager as the first reference and the outer end of the Fit Spline that you have just created as the second reference. Click OK to accept the new plane. This is illustrated in Figure 12.38.

FIGURE 12.38

Creating a new plane

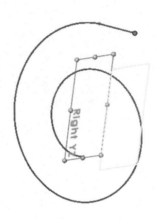

12. **Drag the Rollback bar down between Sketch3 and Loft1.** If it goes beyond Loft1, then you need to navigate back to this position again.

12. **Right-click Sketch3 and select Edit Sketch Plane.** Select the newly created Plane1 from the Flyout FeatureManager, and click OK to accept the change.

13. **Notice that the loft profile has moved to a place where it does not belong.** This is because the sketch has a Pierce constraint to the spiral, and there are multiple places where the spiral pierces the sketch plane.

    Edit Sketch3 and delete the Pierce constraint on the sketch point in the middle of the construction line. Create a Coincident relation between the sketch point and the outer end of the Fit Spline, as shown in Figure 12.39. Do not exit the sketch.

14. **One of the goals of these edits is to smooth out the part.** Remember that the Deviation Analysis told you that the edges created between the lines and arcs in Sketch3 were not very

tangent. For this reason, it would be a good idea to replace the lines and arcs in Sketch3 with another Fit Spline.

Right-click one of the solid sketch entities in Sketch3, and click Select Chain.

FIGURE 12.39

Sketch3 in its new location

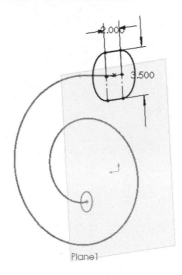

Plane1

15. **Create another Fit Spline using the same technique as in Step 8.** Exit the sketch.

16. **Drag the Rollback bar down one feature so that it is below the Loft.** Notice that the Loft feature has failed. If you hold the cursor over the feature icon, the tooltip confirms this by displaying the message, "The Loft Feature Failed to Complete."

17. **Edit the Loft feature.** Expand the Centerline Parameters panel if it is not already expanded, and delete the Spiral from the selection box. In its place, select the Spiral Fit Spline.

18. **If the loft does not preview, check to ensure that the Show Preview option is selected in the Options panel, at the bottom.**

19. **If it still does not preview, right-click in the graphics window and select Show All Connectors.** Position the blue dots on the connector so that it looks like Figure 12.40.

20. **Click OK to accept the loft.** The loft should be much smoother now than it was before. In addition, the spiral feature should no longer be under the loft; it should now be the first item in the design tree.

21. **Drag the Rollback bar down to just before the Shell feature.** Notice that Fillet5 has failed. Move the mouse over Fillet5. The tool tip tells you that it is missing some references. Edit Fillet5 and select edges in order to create fillets, as shown in Figure 12.41.

FIGURE 12.40

Positioning the connectors

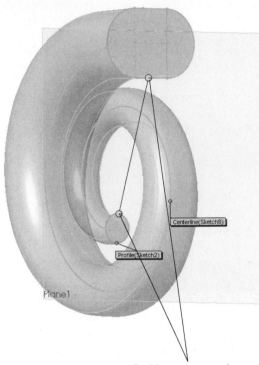

Position connector dots
in approximately corresponding
locations on the two loft profiles

FIGURE 12.41

Repairing Fillet5

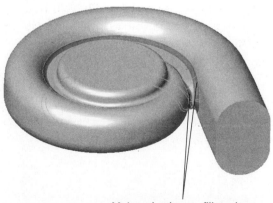

Make selections to fillet edges

22. **Right-click in the design tree and select Roll To End.** This causes the FeatureManager to become unrolled all the way to the end.

23. **The outlet of the involute is now longer than it should be.** This is because the original extrude was never deleted from the end. Right-click the Extrude1 feature and select Parent/ Child. The feature needs to be deleted, but you need to know what is going to be deleted with it.

24. **The Shell is listed as a child of the extrude because the end face of the extrude was chosen to be removed by the Shell.** Edit the Shell feature and remove the reference to the face. (A Shell feature with no faces to remove is still hollowed out.)

25. **If you right-click Extrude1 and select Parent/Child again, the Shell feature is no longer listed as a child.**

26. **Delete Extrude1, and when the dialog box appears, press Alt+F to select Also Delete Absorbed Features.**

27. **Edit the Shell feature and select the large end of the loft.** Exit the Shell feature. The results up to this step are shown in Figure 12.42.

FIGURE 12.42

The results up to Step 27

28. **Drag a window in the design tree to select the four fillet features.** Then right-click and select Add to New Folder. Rename the new folder Fillet Folder.

29. **Click the Section View tool, and create a section view using the Front plane.**

30. **Reorder the Fillet folder to after the Shell feature.**

31. **At this point, you should notice that something does not look right.** This is because creating the fillets after the Shell causes the outside fillets to break through some of the inside corners. The fillets should have failed, but have not, as shown in Figure 12.43.

32. **Choose Tools ⇨ Options ⇨ Performance, and select Verification on rebuild.** Then click OK to exit the Performance menu and press Ctrl+Q. The fillets should now fail.

33. **Click Undo to return the feature order to the way it was.**

34. **Save the part.**

FIGURE 12.43

Fillets that should have failed

Summary

Working effectively with feature history, even in complex models, is a requirement for working with parts that others have created. When I get a part from someone else, the first thing that I usually do is look at the FeatureManager and roll it back if possible to get an idea of how the part was modeled. Looking at sketches, relations, feature order, symmetry, redundancy, sketch reuse, and so on are important steps in being able to repair or edit any part. Using modeling best practice techniques helps ensure that when edits have to be done, they are easy to accomplish, even if they are done by someone who did not build the part.

Evaluation techniques are really the heart of editing, as you should not make too many changes without a basic evaluation of the strengths and weaknesses of the current model. SolidWorks provides a wide array of evaluation tools. Time spent learning how to use the tools and interpret the results is time well spent.

Using Hole Wizard and Library Features

The SolidWorks Hole Wizard is an automated tool that helps you place standard-sized holes in parts

Library features are user-defined, and you might use them in a similar way to how you use the Hole Wizard. They can be automated to some extent, and can make use of configurations. This chapter contains the information you need to decide how to implement and use the Hole Wizard and library features in your work.

IN THIS CHAPTER

Working with the Hole Wizard

Exploring library features

Creating library features

Examining Dissection feature

Working with library features tutorial

Using the Hole Wizard

The Hole Wizard enables you to place holes for many types of screws with normal, loose, or close fits. You can create Hole Wizard holes as assembly features in an assembly or as features in individual parts that are built in the context of an assembly using the Series Hole functionality. This tool is called a *wizard* because it guides you through the process step by step. A summary of the workflow of creating a Hole Wizard hole is as follows:

1. **Pre-select the face to put the holes on, although this is not required.** Versions after SolidWorks 2010 no longer require pre-selection to avoid 3D placement sketches; the Hole Wizard uses 2D sketches by default.

2. **Select the type of hole; for example, counterbored, countersunk, drilled hole, tapped hole, pipe tap, or legacy.**

3. **Set the standard to be used, such as ANSI** (American National Standards Institute) **inch, ANSI metric, or ISO** (International Organization for Standardization).

4. **Select the type of screw.** For example, a counterbored hole can accommodate a socket head cap screw or a hex head screw, among others.

5. **Select the size of the screw.** This is not the size of the hole. If you select a ¹/₄-inch hole, the hole will not measure .250 inch; it will have the nominal diameter to fit a ¹/₄-inch screw. You also have the option to select Show Custom Sizing to enter in custom dimensions for the hole directly, in case the hole is meant to accommodate something other than a standard-sized fastener.

6. **Select the fit of the screw into the hole, such as normal, loose, or close.**

7. **Select the end condition of the hole.**

8. **Select options for clearance and countersinks or edge breaks.**

   Alternatively, you can use or assign a favorite. A favorite is a hole with settings that you use frequently and want to save. I discuss these later in this chapter.

   You can use Custom Sizing when you need a hole with nonstandard dimensions.

9. **Locate the center of the hole or holes.** Switch to the Positions tab of the Hole Wizard PropertyManager to do this. You can place multiple holes in a single Hole Wizard feature, even on different faces and curved faces. I address the specifics of this step later in this chapter. Note that if you want to place holes on multiple faces, non-planar faces, or at different heights, you will need to do this with a 3D Sketch, on the Positions tab.

10. **Click OK to accept the type, size, and placement of the hole.** Figure 13.1 shows the Hole Wizard PropertyManager interface.

FIGURE 13.1

The Hole Wizard PropertyManager interface

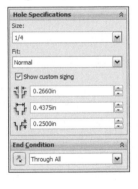

Defining the anatomy of a Hole Wizard hole

Hole Wizard holes are made of two sketches: a center placement sketch and a revolved cut profile. Figure 13.2 shows a simple part with an expanded Hole Wizard feature. Notice that the feature is named for the size and type of the hole.

FIGURE 13.2

A design tree containing a Hole Wizard hole

Using the placement sketch

The placement sketch is listed first under the Hole Wizard feature. It contains one or more sketch points marking the hole centers. It may also contain construction geometry with relations and dimensions to parametrically locate the hole centers. The placement sketch may be a 2D or a 3D sketch. A 3D sketch is more powerful, but also more complex and prone to difficulties. I discuss placement sketches in more detail in the next section.

Using the hole sketch

The revolve profile sketch is not on an identifiable sketch plane that you can reuse for other features. You can change the sketch dimensions outside of the wizard interface, and if you later use the wizard to edit it, then the changes appear in the Custom Sizing panel. Figure 13.3 shows the Custom Sizing panel with the changed counterbore diameter highlighted.

FIGURE 13.3

The Custom Sizing area of the Hole Specifications panel

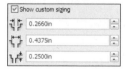

If you change any of the options in the Options panel, the revolved sketch profile is altered to accommodate the change. For example, if you select the check box for a near side countersink, the sketch changes to add a line for the countersink; a separate chamfer feature is not added.

Using 2D versus 3D placement sketches

In SolidWorks 2010, SolidWorks changed the Hole Wizard so that it defaults to a 2D sketch. Preselection of a plane or planar face is still recommended because it eliminates a step later on, but it is no longer required in order to avoid being forced into a 3D placement sketch. Three-dimensional placement sketches are still available and still useful, but because they are so much more difficult to use and rarely truly needed, SolidWorks decided to change the default to a 2D sketch.

Three-dimensional placement sketches are needed for Hole Wizard holes if you have a set of similar holes that are placed on different levels or are always perpendicular to non-planar surfaces. If you need 3D placement sketches, they are still available, but they are no longer the default. To use a 3D placement sketch in a new Hole Wizard feature, just click the 3D Sketch button on the Positions tab. There is no way to change an existing 2D sketch to a 3D sketch. You would have to delete the feature and re-create it.

For most people who have learned SolidWorks software prior to the 2010 version, it may already be instinctive to pre-select a face before opening the Hole Wizard; this change will have no effect. It will have a positive effect on new users and those who frequently forget to pre-select.

Understanding the advantages and limitations of the 2D sketch

The main advantages of the 2D sketch method are the simplicity and completeness of the available tools. Everyone knows how to manage 2D sketches, sketch planes, dimensions, and construction geometry.

A limitation of the 2D sketch is that the holes that you create through this method are limited to a single planar face, and the holes will all be perpendicular to that face. Sometimes this creates a great limitation, while other times it does not matter.

Understanding the advantages and limitations of the 3D sketch

The obvious advantage of the 3D placement sketch is that it can put a set of holes on any set of solid faces, regardless of whether they are at different levels, are non-parallel, or are even non-planar. This function offers multiple holes, multiple faces, and multiple directions. In situations where that is what you need, nothing else will do.

A limitation of the 3D sketch is that it can be fairly cumbersome. Dimensions work very differently in 3D sketches compared to 2D sketches. For example, to create and place a hole in a specific position on a cylinder, you need to follow these steps:

1. **Begin with a circle with a diameter of 1 inch, drawn on the Top plane and extruded using the Mid-plane option 1 inch.**

2. **Start the Hole Wizard without any pre-selection, either through the Features toolbar or by choosing Insert ⇨ Features ⇨ Hole ⇨ Wizard.**

3. **Set the interface to use an ANSI inch, one-quarter-inch, and counterbored hole for a socket head cap screw.** Use a Normal fit and Through All for the End Condition, with a .100-inch head clearance (in the Options panel) and no custom sizing changes. These settings are shown in Figure 13.4.

4. **Click the Positions tab, which is located at the top of the PropertyManager window.** The interface asks you to select a face where you would like to put the holes or to select the 3D sketch option. In this case, click the 3D Sketch button.

Note

Be careful with clicking when the Point tool is turned on. For example, if you click in a blank space, the Point tool places a point off the part. SolidWorks will try to use the point later to create a hole in empty space, which usually causes an error. ∎

FIGURE 13.4

The Hole Wizard settings for the socket head cap screw

5. **Click the cylindrical surface of the part.** The surface appears orange when you move the cursor over it to indicate that an UnSurface sketch relation will be created between the sketch point and the cylindrical surface.

6. **The hole should be positioned from one end of the cylinder.** Using the SmartDimension tool, click one flat end face of the cylinder and the sketch point. Place the dimension and give it a value of .300 inches, as shown in Figure 13.5.

   Locating the point angularly around the cylinder is more difficult. You can use several methods to do this, but this example shows one using construction sketch geometry.

FIGURE 13.5

Dimensioning the 3D Placement sketch point

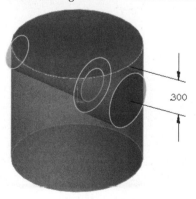

Tip

To force a 3D dimension to have a certain orientation, dimension from a plane or planar face rather than from an edge, vertex, or sketch entity. A dimension from a plane is always measured in a direction perpendicular to the plane, but a dimension from a line or point is always measured by the shortest distance between the entities. Two-dimensional sketches can force dimensions to be horizontal or vertical, but 3D sketches cannot. ■

7. **With the Line tool activated while still in the 3D sketch, Ctrl+click the flat end face that the previous dimension referenced.** This moves the red "space handle" origin to the selected face and constrains any new sketch entities to that face. You are still in the 3D sketch but are constrained to the selected plane and still must play by all the 3D sketch rules. The elements of 3D sketches are described in detail in Chapter 6.

8. **Select the Temporary Axes view by choosing View ⇨ Temporary Axes.**

9. **Place the cursor near the center of the activated end face; a small, black circle appears, indicating that the end point of the line will pick up a coincident relation to the temporary axis.** Draw the line so that it picks up an AlongX sketch relation. The cursor shows the relations about to be applied, just like in a 2D sketch.

10. **Draw a second line again from the center, but this time do not pick up any automatic relations. This line should also be on the flat end face.**

Note

Although you can set these lines to display as construction lines if you like, this is not required for the feature to work; the lines also work as regular solid lines. ■

11. **Put an angle dimension between the lines and change the angle to 30 degrees.** To be thorough (which is always recommended in 3D sketches, which have a tendency to handle underconstrained sketch geometry unpredictably), constrain the ends of the lines to the circular edge of the cylinder. At this point, the part looks like Figure 13.6.

FIGURE 13.6

The example part at the end of Step 11

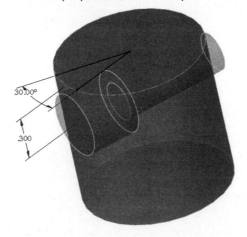

12. **Create an AlongY sketch relation between the points indicated in Figure 13.7.** The hole centerpoint on the cylindrical face is one of the points, as well as the endpoint of the angled line. Change the angle dimension to ensure that it is controlling the sketch point as expected. Click the green check in the upper-right corner of the graphics window to accept the result and exit the command.

FIGURE 13.7

Control the placement of the 3D sketch point around the cylinder.

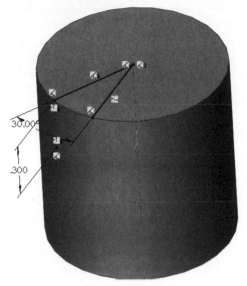

On the DVD

You can find the finished part from this example on the DVD with the filename Chapter 13 3D Hole Placement.sldprt. ∎

Cross-Reference

Chapters 6 and 8 contain more information on general 3D sketch tools and techniques. ∎

Making and using favorites

Hole Wizard Favorites store types of holes that you use frequently so that you can simply recall a favorite, rather than manually making all the changes every time you use the same hole. Favorites are saved to a database named Default.mdb as you create them, and are immediately available from all other part documents connected to that database. You can also save favorites to a special file type with the extension *.sldhwfvt. Other users can then load these files and add your favorites to their Default.mdb databases. This is a convenient way to create company standards for hole features.

Shared Toolbox installations share a SWBrowser.mdb between several users, making Hole Wizard Favorites available to everyone. I cover how to set up shared Toolbox installations later in this chapter.

Creating a Hole Wizard Favorite

To create a Hole Wizard Favorite, set up a Hole Wizard hole as you normally would, and then use the Add Favorite button to add it to the Favorites database. The Hole Wizard Favorite panel contains five buttons:

 • **Apply Defaults/No Favorites.** Removes favorite settings from the current interface, setting all values back to their defaults.

 • **Add or Update Favorites.** Either adds a new favorite to the database or changes the name or other settings for an existing favorite.

 • **Delete Favorite.** Removes a favorite from the database.

 • **Save Favorite.** Saves a favorite to an external file with the extension `*.sldhwfvt`, which can be loaded by other users and added to their databases.

 • **Load Favorite.** Loads a saved favorite file.

Storing custom holes

You can use Hole Wizard Favorites to store custom holes. Create the hole with its custom sizes, and then add the favorite and give it a recognizable name. The custom hole will now be available to anyone who connects to the same database file.

Administering Hole Wizard Favorites

The database file is typically found in the `Data` subdirectory of the SolidWorks installation directory, but an option in Tools ➪ Options ➪ File Locations ➪ Hole Wizard Favorites Database theoretically enables you to move the file to somewhere else.

Further, the `*.sldhwfvt` files do not have an entry in the File Locations list, but seem to always default to the `lang\english` subdirectory of the SolidWorks installation directory. Neither this location nor the `Data` directory makes sharing among multiple users very convenient, but both file types can be copied to other installations.

Best Practice

It is a best practice to create a folder for library type files that you want to save and use with a future version of SolidWorks. You can specify the locations for these files by choosing Tools ➪ Options ➪ File Locations. I recommend a location such as `D:\Library`. This moves the file off of the same drive as the operating system, in case you need to reformat, and it keeps it out of the Program Files area to prevent it from being lost or overwritten when SolidWorks is installed, uninstalled, upgraded, or changed in other ways ■

Confronting favorites quirks

Hole Wizard Favorites seem to have a couple of quirks that are possibly "suboptimal," as they say. First, you can only see the favorites for a specific type of hole when that type of hole is activated in the interface. For example, if you have a number of favorites for countersunk holes, but you currently have the counterbored hole icon activated, you will not be able to see the countersunk favorites until you switch to the countersunk icon.

If you have a lot of favorites, this may be beneficial, but if you have only a few favorites, or you do not use favorites frequently, it may be confusing and can create some unnecessary steps to find all your favorites.

A second quirk occurs when you allow SolidWorks to name the favorites and you have fractional values such as $^1/_4$ — which happens now and then in hole sizes — and then try to save the favorites. Each favorite is saved as a separate file, using the name that was automatically assigned to it by SolidWorks as the filename. Unfortunately, the character "/" is not allowed in a filename, so it fails.

Using the Hole Series

The Hole Series enables you to make a series of in-context hole features in individual parts that are connected by a Hole Series assembly-level feature. It is intended for a stack of parts where, for example, the top part has a counterbored hole, the middle part has a clearance through hole, and the final part has a blind threaded hole.

The Hole Series functionality is covered in more detail in the *SolidWorks 2011 Assemblies Bible* (Wiley, 2011), as it is only used when you have an assembly.

Using Library Features

Library features are features that you create once and reuse many times. They are intended to be parametrically flexible to fit into many types of geometry, but they can also be of a fixed size and shape. You will use all the information that you have learned in previous chapters about designing for change, and design intent, as well as learn how to create, use, and store library features.

Library features reside in the Design Library, which is located in the Task Pane to the right of the graphics window.

Tip

You can detach the Task Pane from its docking location and move it wherever you want, leave it undocked, or move it to a second monitor. ■

You can use library features for snap ring grooves, custom holes, mounting bosses for plastics, mounting hole patterns, electrical connector holes, and much more.

One very useful aspect of library features is that they can be driven by configurations and design tables. Once the feature is in the part, the configurations are still available, and so you can change the config of an applied library feature at any time.

You can also link a library feature to an external file. This enables you to change a feature or a set of features in several parts at once if they are all externally linked to the file.

Getting started with library features

Library features are simple to use and only slightly less simple to set up. For that reason I discuss using them first, so that you know what kind of behavior you are trying to create when you go to make your own features. As a result, setting them up should make a little more sense.

To use a library feature, you just drag-and-drop it from the Design Library onto the appropriate geometry. You are then prompted to select references in the new part that match the base geometry that the library feature is attached to. You can be fairly creative with references, but one of the goals when creating the feature is to make it work with as few references as possible, in order to make it easy, fast, and reliable to use.

SolidWorks software installs with several sample library features in the Design Library. The following demonstration uses some of these standard library features. Later, you can add library features from the DVD to your Design Library.

Applying the library feature interface

Library features work best if they go from a certain type of base geometry to a similar type of base geometry; for example, from rectangular to rectangular or from circular to circular. This is because the relations or dimensions that link the feature to the rest of the part tend to be dimensions from straight edges or concentric sketch relations. Of course, there are other ways of applying library features, but these are the most prevalent. Library features can be applied unconstrained and then constrained or moved later, but the process is cleanest when it all just falls together correctly the first time.

Using the Task Pane

You do not have to save the part or do anything special before applying a library feature. All you need to do is find the Task Pane. The Task Pane is the window that flies out from the right when you open SolidWorks. You may have turned it off and forgotten about it, in which case you can turn it back on by choosing View ⇨ Task Pane from the menu.

The Task Pane automatically closes when you click outside of it unless you pin it open using the push-pin icon in the upper-right corner of the window. When you do this, any toolbars that appeared on the right side of the Task Pane control tabs are moved out and positioned between the graphics window and the Task Pane, which now remains open by default.

You can also detach the Task Pane by dragging the bar at the top of the pane. Figure 13.8 shows the Task Pane docked to the right side of the SolidWorks window.

Tip

If you are using dual monitors, you can drag the detached Task Pane onto the second monitor, which enables you to use the Task Pane and at the same time gives you more room in the graphics area. You must do this for each session; the Task Pane does not remember positions on a second monitor. ■

Using Design Library

 The Design Library tab displays an image of a stack of books. It is the overall library area for all sorts of elements in SolidWorks, which I discuss later in this chapter. The only part of the Design Library of concern right now is the Features folder. If you expand this folder, you can see that it is populated with some sample features.

Open a new part and create a cylinder using any method you want (for example, extrude, revolve). Make the diameter 3 inches and the length a little more than 1 inch.

FIGURE 13.8

The Task Pane docked to right side of the SolidWorks window

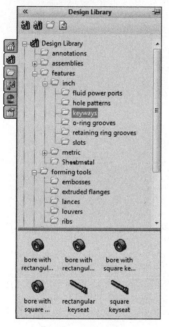

In the Inch features folder, click the folder called o-ring grooves. The first feature in the list is called *face static – gas*. Drag-and-drop this feature onto the end flat face of the cylinder. As shown in the image to the left in Figure 13.9, the PropertyManager displays a yellow information panel explaining the process.

The next step is to select the configuration, as shown in the image to the right in Figure 13.9. Not all library features have multiple size configurations, but these do. The configs in this case are driven by design tables. Select configuration 330.

FIGURE 13.9

Placing the feature and selecting the configuration

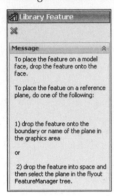

When you select the configuration, the interface changes. In this case, only a sketch relation locates the feature; it is not located by dimensions. Notice that in the References panel shown in Figure 13.10, there is an Edge entry with a question mark, which becomes a check mark after you select the edge. This means that the library feature needs a circular edge to locate it. Notice that a small window appears, displaying the library feature. You may not be able to distinguish it in Figure 13.10, but the circular edge around the face that the library feature is on is highlighted in green. This indicates that you need to select an edge that has the same relation to the library feature as the highlighted edge. Pick the circular edge of the part on the end of the cylinder where you want to place the library feature.

FIGURE 13.10

Locating the library feature

Next, use a rectangular part where the library feature is located by using dimensions rather than sketch relations. Create a rectangle 1.5 inches by 2 inches and extrude it to about 2 inches in depth.

In the Design Library, browse to features, then inch, and then the fluid power ports folder and drag the sae j1926-1 feature onto the end of the extruded rectangle. Select the 38-24 size from the configurations list. A window appears, prompting you for reference selections, as shown in Figure 13.11.

Placing a library feature with dimensions

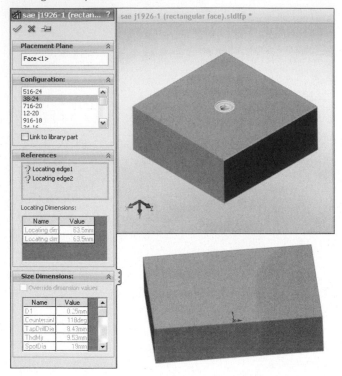

Tip

It is often helpful to orient the part that is receiving the library feature in the same way as the part shown in the preview window. This helps you to visualize which edges to select. ■

After the locating edges have been identified, the Locating Dimensions box becomes active and you can change the values of the dimensions to locate the feature. Further, in the Size Dimensions pane at the bottom of the PropertyManager, selecting the Override dimension values option enables you to change dimensions of the feature itself.

When you use a library feature with a design table, the design table is not brought into the part with the library feature. If the part already had a design table, this would cause multiple tables, which is not currently possible in SolidWorks. The configurations in the design table are brought forward, however.

If you override the feature dimensions using the Override Dimension Values option in the Size Dimensions panel of the Library Feature PropertyManager when feature configurations already exist, then a new configuration called Custom Configuration is created in the list of feature configurations. It appears that multiple custom configurations are not allowed, and so if you have to make changes, then you must ensure that they are right before you use the library feature in a part.

Exploring other Design Library functions

The Design Library has other functions besides library features. For example, you can use it as a repository for other items that you use frequently.

Storing annotations

You can store commonly used annotations in the Design Library. If you look at the Annotations folder with the default sample annotations, you see a combination of symbols and blocks. You can use symbols and notes in 3D models, but you can only use blocks in sketches or 2D drawings. Keep in mind that not all annotation types can be used in all places.

Annotations can be stored in the library as favorites or blocks. Many file extensions are used for different types of favorites, but they typically begin with *.sld and end with fvt, as in *.sldweldfvt. Figure 13.12 shows the default location of the Design Library and the Thumbnail view of the favorites and blocks in the Annotations folder.

FIGURE 13.12

The Annotations folder in Windows Explorer

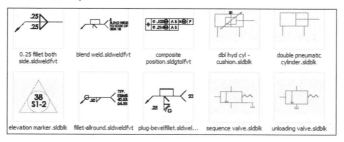

Note

The screen capture with the thumbnails displayed was taken in Windows XP. The capture of the folders was taken in Windows 7. I am not able to get thumbnail images of the favorites to display in Windows 7 with SolidWorks 2011 sp0.0 installed, but thumbnails for the blocks appear to work okay. This issue is not resolved as of this writing. ■

Location of the Design Library folder

If you frequently work with different types of annotations, then you should organize the library into subfolders to separate symbols, annotations, and blocks, and move these folders to a different location. By default, the Design Library folders are found at C:\ProgramData\SolidWorks\SolidWorks 2010\design library\. You should store them in another location, not in the SolidWorks installation directory, but in an area that you have selected to maintain SolidWorks data between releases. For example, I have a folder at D:\Library that contains folders for macros, templates, library features, library parts, favorites, and so on. You can easily back up or copy these files from one computer to another, although you must quit SolidWorks before making these changes. Keeping the data off the operating system drive is also a good idea because if you ever have to reinstall the OS, you will not lose your SolidWorks library data.

After moving the library, you have to point SolidWorks to the new location. To do this, choose Tools ⇨ Options ⇨ File Locations ⇨ Design Library. Delete the old location and browse to the new location. You should move other items in this list and redirect any items that you use, such as the templates and any other items you use frequently. Once you have specified the settings, they should be retained when you install service pack upgrades or future versions.

Storing library parts

The Design Library can also store commonly used library parts. One of the advantages of using the library for parts is that on placement into the assembly, if configurations are available in a part, then a window pops up, enabling you to select which configuration to place into the assembly.

Note

In many cases, using the Design Library for library parts is considered an acceptable replacement for the automated function of Toolbox. If you use Toolbox to make the parts and populate them with configurations, and then save the parts out of Toolbox and into the Design Library, many options, including naming conventions, and a more flexible use of custom properties that are not available through Toolbox become available. ■

Figure 13.13 shows the configuration selection window. Note that the configurations are alphabetically listed, and you can type in the box to go to the configuration that you want.

![FIGURE 13.13]

Inserting library parts with configurations

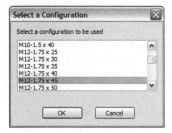

Parts inserted from the library parts folder can also take advantage of the Mate References functionality in the same way as Toolbox, by allowing parts to snap into place.

Using sheet metal forming tools

I only mention sheet metal forming tools here as a part of the library. They work much like other library features, but they do so within the specialized functions of sheet metal parts in SolidWorks. I discuss sheet metal forming tools in Chapter 21. Forming tools folders have special properties. If you want to use the parts in a folder as forming tools, you must right-click the folder in the Design Library and choose Forming Tool Folder. The only other library type that needs special folders is library assemblies.

Using assemblies

You can use library assemblies in SolidWorks in the same ways that you use library parts because they are inserted into the top-level assembly as a subassembly. For subassemblies that require motion, such as universal joint subassemblies, you can set the subassembly to solve as flexible or simply dissolve the subassembly into the upper-level assembly, through a RMB option.

Tip

When saving assemblies to the library, it is recommended that you put the parts in a separate folder to segregate the parts of different assemblies. ■

Using routing

Routing is a separately purchased add-in that is included with SolidWorks Office Premium. It includes piping, tubing (rigid and flexible), and wiring. Routing makes extensive use of libraries and automation but is not part of the scope of this book. The documentation on routing at this time is rather sparse, but SolidWorks offers a reseller training class, and at this time, it's your best bet for information on this add-in.

Using Smart Components

Smart Components are components that resize by automatically selecting configurations, depending on the size of the geometry onto which they are being dropped. They do this from a design table–like interface that you set up to enable it to automatically select part configurations based on mating part sizes. For example, a clamp with many sizes driven by configurations would select the correct config when dropped onto different sizes of cylinders.

Creating Library Features

When you save library features to the library, they use the file extension *.sldlfp (library feature part). They must contain some base geometry, which simulates the part onto which the feature will be dropped. The base geometry is not transferred to the new part; only features that are marked with the "L" in the FeatureManager (for Library) are transferred to the new part. Figure 13.14 shows the FeatureManager of a library feature part.

FIGURE 13.14

The FeatureManager of a library feature part

Creating a library feature

When creating a library feature, the first problem that you need to solve is how the feature will be located on a new part. Does it need to be placed on cylindrical parts, rectangular parts, other types of shapes, or does this matter at all? Will the feature be located by using dimensions or sketch relations, or will it just be placed underdefined and later fully defined manually rather than automatically?

You may have noticed in one of the earlier examples that the sample fluid power ports had two versions of the same feature. One version is intended for the feature to be placed on the flat end of a cylinder, and the other version is intended for the feature to be placed on a rectangular face.

Understanding library limitations

Library features can contain multiple features of different types. They may add and remove material, even within a single library feature. However, a few limitations exist. For example, they require a base feature, and multi-body features and external references are not allowed, nor are surfaces, sheet metal, weldments, or molds-related features. In addition, you cannot add a scale feature (a feature that affects the entire body) to the library, nor can you apply library features to an assembly.

Creating a new library feature

To start a new feature, the first decision that you need to make is what shape to make the base. Is the feature a type that is usually going to go onto a single shape or multiple shapes? Regardless of your decision, you or whoever ends up using the feature will have the flexibility to change, or simply not use, the relations when you place the feature.

For this example, I use a rectangular base. The library feature that I want to create consists of two boss extrudes, a cut extrude, and several fillets. Here is how it works.

First, you need to create a rectangular extrusion. The size should be bigger than the feature that goes on it and representative of the face of the end part onto which this feature will typically be placed.

Next, in beginning to create the features that you want to reuse, it is very important that you pay attention to any references outside of the sketch; these include absolutely *anything* outside the active sketch, such as the sketch plane, references to edges, the Origin, other planes, other sketches, and axes. Although these references are allowed, each reference to anything that is not already part of the library feature must be reconnected when you place the feature on a new part. The ideal situation is obviously a single drag-and-drop, but generally speaking, at least one other step is usually needed. The initial drag-and-drop determines the face for the feature to start from, and from there, you usually need to locate features, either by using relations or dimensions. A concentric relation locates the feature in a single reference selection of a circular edge (although it may also need to be rotated), and dimensions typically require one dimension in the X dimension and another one in the Y dimension.

Figure 13.15 shows the base feature and the first feature of the library feature. The only relations between the sketch of the library feature and the base feature are the sketch plane and the two dimensions.

Note

Notice that names have been assigned to all the dimensions, sketches, and features. This is because the dimension names all display in the interface. If you look back to Figure 13.4, in the Size Dimensions pane, dimension names make it easy to know which dimension to change, whereas the D1 dimension leaves you guessing as to what it applies. ∎

FIGURE 13.15

Creating a library feature

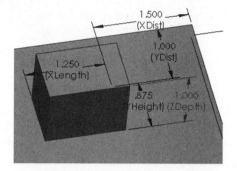

You should ensure that subsequent features after the first one reference only the first feature of the library feature (which is the second feature in the part). This is not a mandatory requirement, but a helpful guideline. You can make additional references, but they should be limited to the same items that were already referenced if possible. Users who model carelessly or do not pay attention to what they are doing typically have trouble making library features that function and are easy to use. Successful modeling of library features is like planning a strategy in a game of chess.

Now you can add the second extruded feature, being careful to reference only geometry that is going to move with the library feature. Figure 13.16 shows the newly added feature. If you would like to follow along as I detail how this feature is built, you can open the part from the DVD under the filename `Chapter 13 First Library Feature.sldlfp`.

FIGURE 13.16

Adding the next feature to the library feature

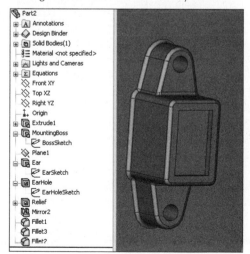

Notice that a plane has been added. The plane is made to only reference geometry that is internal to the library feature; it is perpendicular to an edge at the midpoint, which simultaneously locates and orients the plane correctly to enable it to be used to mirror the Ear feature.

Also, notice that the EarSketch uses the same face reference from the base feature. This will appear in the Reference list as a single reference.

Saving the library feature

You can use two methods to save a library feature. You can either drag-and-drop it into a Design Library folder or use the Save As method. Because Save As is a little more common, I describe it first.

The first step in saving the library feature is to select all the features in the FeatureManager that are intended to be a part of the library feature. Collapse the features first so that the sketches belonging to features are not selected. If the sketches are selected, you may get a warning message saying that no selected features can be used in the library feature. Do not worry; the sketches still will be included.

Tip

Remember that you can Ctrl+select individual features, Shift+select a range, or click-and-drag a selection box in the FeatureManager to select multiple features. Also keep in mind that if you do not select a feature (other than the base feature), then it will not be placed into the part when you insert the library feature. If there were any relations to the omitted feature, they may display as errors or warnings when you place the feature. ∎

With the features selected, click File, click Save As, and under Files of Type drop-down list, select the `*.sldlfp` file type. Browse to the Design Library folder and save the part. Figure 13.17 shows the FeatureManager of the finished library feature.

FIGURE 13.17

The finished library feature part

Changing the display of the library feature thumbnail

During the Save As process, a new folder was added to the Design Library named Bosses, as shown in Figure 13.17. Notice the new icon for the library feature in the lower window. You may notice that some of the default library features saved in the Design Library have a bluish background. This occurs because of the SolidWorks viewport background color, which you can set by choosing Tools ➪ Options ➪ Colors. Even if you never see that color because you are using a gradient background or a scene, SolidWorks still uses the color specified by that setting as the background when saving thumbnails and previews. I always set this color to white for this reason, so that document backgrounds in previews do not have the blue color.

You may want to orient and zoom the library feature before saving it so that it displays clearly in the panel. One of the techniques that I like to use is to make the base feature a different color than the library feature itself; this helps you to more easily determine what is the geometry that will be transferred and what is just dummy material.

Tip

Figure 13.18 shows various settings for displaying the icons in the Design Library. Which one you select will depend on your screen resolution, the number of icons that you want to display, and the quality of the preview images. ■

FIGURE 13.18

Display modes for the Design Library

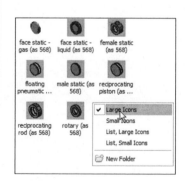

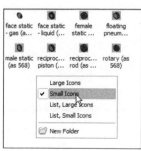

The real test for a library feature comes when you actually use it. This feature is re-created perfectly on the new part, but I have noticed one problem. When the feature was placed, it was 90 degrees away from the orientation that I wanted it to be in. It seems that the only way to make the feature rotatable is to create it with parallel and perpendicular relations rather than horizontal and vertical ones, so that one of the references can act as a rotation reference. Figure 13.19 shows the completed library feature placed on a part.

The completed library feature placed on a part

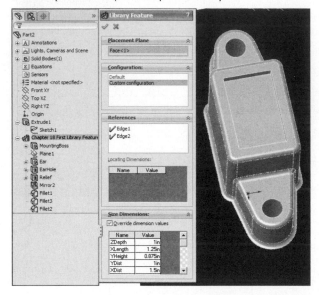

Once you place a library feature on a part, it can be edited unless you select the Link to library part option in the Configuration pane, in which case the feature is driven externally from the `*.sldlfp` file. The Link to library part option is only available when the feature is first placed; it is not available when you edit an existing library feature in a part.

One of the available RMB menu options is to dissolve the library feature so that all the constituent features become regular features in the main part. Doing this on a configured library feature will destroy the configurations.

Creating a library feature from an existing part

When creating a library feature from an existing part, you use essentially the same process, but it is somewhat more difficult to achieve the correct results. It is best to remove all the features that do not either form the base feature or go into the library feature itself. This can cause many broken references. Most parts are not modeled with creating a library feature in mind, and creating library features with effective references, as I mentioned earlier, is like a chess match and requires some forethought. It may be better to use a different technique, such as creating a new part with only the base feature. You can then Ctrl+drag the desired features from the existing part to the new part, set up the rest of the library feature, and save it with a *.sldlfp extension.

You can also create a library feature by dragging and dropping, although there are some limitations with this technique that seem to override the convenience. However, there is a workaround for the biggest limitation. If you select faces from features and drag them into the lower Design Library window, an Add to Library PropertyManager interface appears to enable you to start creating a library feature. The Add to Library PropertyManager interface is shown in Figure 13.20. You must select the features from the flyout FeatureManager. This is the source of one of the limitations. In the example, the plane cannot be selected by this method. The workaround for this is to complete the feature without the plane, right-click the icon in the Design Library window, and then select Open. With the library feature open in its own window, right-click the plane feature and select Add to Library; that individual feature is then added.

FIGURE 13.20

The Add to Library PropertyManager interface

Adding folders to the library

You can add folders to the library in two ways, either by right-clicking in the Design Library window and selecting New Folder or by using the Windows Explorer interface. Another RMB menu option is Add Existing Folder, which enables you to add a folder from another location to the library. The folder is not moved or copied, but a shortcut is added to the Design Library and the contents appear in the lower pane.

Tip

After a library feature has been edited, or folders or documents have been added to the library using Windows Explorer, you can press F5 in either the lower or the upper window to update the display for that window or use the Refresh icon located at the top of the Task Pane. ■

Locating and Internal dimensions

When you create a library feature, SolidWorks adds two folders to the FeatureManager: the References folder and the Dimensions folder. In turn, the Dimensions folder has two more folders: Locating Dimensions and Internal Dimensions. All these folders are shown in Figure 13.21.

The References folder shows the entities you used to reference the library feature. These are the features you are prompted to select upon placing the library feature in a new part. No additional work on your part is required with this folder.

The Dimensions folder lists all the dimensions in the library feature. Some of these dimensions are used to locate the feature to the dummy block and some are meant to size the feature itself. When you make a library feature, it is recommended that you separate the locating features from internal features by dragging the dimensions into the separate folders. The Locating Dimensions can be changed while placing the library feature, but the Internal Dimensions cannot be accessed. You might want to limit user access to some dimensions if you have standard tooling for the library feature that you are creating.

FIGURE 13.21

References, Locating Dimensions, and Internal Dimensions in a library feature

Understanding Dissection

Dissection is a process that SolidWorks goes through by which it examines all the parts on your computer and makes Design Clipart of the sketches and features. People who might get some use from this function are those who have not modeled a lot of parts and will tend to reuse the same features over and over again. The types of data it will try to recycle for you are extrudes and cuts, sketches, blocks, and tables from drawings.

The first interaction most people have with this function is learning how to turn it off. If you notice your computer starting to run small SolidWorks windows in the background starting at about 11 pm daily, you may have Dissection turned on. To select or deselect Dissection, choose Tools ⇨ Options ⇨ Search. Dissection is connected to SolidWorks Search, another function many users prefer to deselect.

Tutorial: Working with Library Features

This tutorial guides you through customizing a Hole Wizard hole to use as a specialty library feature, then storing it in the library, editing it, and placing it in a part. Follow these steps:

1. **Open a new part, and create a rectangular base feature, about 3 inches high by 3 inches wide and 3 inches deep.**

2. **Pre-select a flat face and start the Hole Wizard.**

3. **Create a counterbored hole for a Heavy Hex Bolt, ½-inch, Normal Fit, Blind, 1.2 inches deep.** Locate the hole with dimensions from two perpendicular edges, as shown in Figure 13.22. Click the green check mark icon twice to accept the hole settings.

FIGURE 13.22

Placing a hole

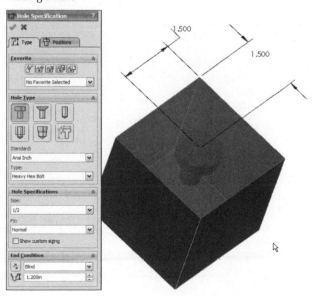

4. **Turn on the setting at View ▷ Dimension Names.**

5. **Double-click the counterbored hole feature in the FeatureManager to show the dimensions.** Make sure Instant3D is unselected for the next step.

6. **Click one of the dimensions that you created to locate the center of the hole and rename the dimension in the Dimension PropertyManager (Primary Value panel) using names that will have meaning when you place the dimension, such as XDir, or YDir.** Do this for both dimensions.

7. **Edit the second sketch of the hole.** Figure 13.23 shows what the sketch should look like before and after the edit.

Caution

Do not delete any of the named dimensions in a normal or revised Hole Wizard hole. SolidWorks has a checking mechanism that looks for these names and will display an error if any of the named dimensions is not there. If there is no use for the dimension, it still has to be there, although it does not need to be used for its original use. You could rename another dimension with the name or simply dimension the length of the centerline or an otherwise unused construction line. It does not matter about the function of the dimension, as long as there is a dimension with that name in the sketch. ■

Tip

You should also name any new dimensions that you may want to change. These dimensions will have more meaning when you are placing the feature if they have names. Be aware that the two angled lines are parallel and equal length. This will enable you to get a fully defined sketch. ■

FIGURE 13.23

Reconfiguring the hole

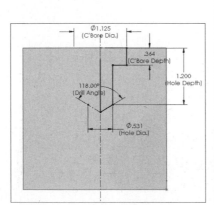
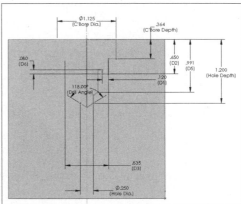

Tip

Remember that to get the diameter dimensions shown in Figure 13.15 (instead of radius dimensions), you must use the dimension tool to select the centerline (construction line) and the line or endpoint on one side, and then move the cursor to the other side of the centerline to place the dimension (the order of selection does not matter). When the cursor crosses the centerline, the dimension will display as a diameter instead of a radius. ■

8. **When you are done editing the sketch and renaming dimensions, exit the sketch.**

9. **Click the CBORE feature twice, or click it once and press F2 to rename it as** SpecialHole.

10. **Pre-select the same flat face that the first hole feature was placed on and then start the Hole Wizard again.**

11. **Place a #8-32 tapped hole, accept the default depth, and specify a center-to-center distance of .75 inches between it and the SpecialHole in the Horizontal or Vertical direction.** Rename the radial dimension as **MountRad**.

12. **Using a cylindrical face of the SpecialHole, make a circular pattern of the new tapped hole, creating a total of four instances of the tapped hole.** Make the SpecialHole Feature red and the tapped hole and pattern yellow.

13. **Split the FeatureManager window into two by using the splitter bar at the top.** Change the lower panel to the ConfigurationManager.

14. **Rename the Default configuration** Size1.

15. **Create a new configuration called Size2.** Double-click the SpecialHole feature and change the dimension named C'Bore Dia to 1.5 inches. Be sure to change to This Configuration Only using the drop-down menu.

16. **Make a dimension change for the MountRad dimension to 1 inch.** The results to this point are shown in Figure 13.24.

FIGURE 13.24

The results after Step 16

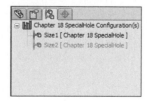

17. **Auto-create a design table by choosing Insert ⇨ Design Table and then selecting the Auto-Create option.** Edit the design table to look like Figure 13.25. Hide or delete extra columns that don't match the data shown.

FIGURE 13.25

The design table for the SpecialHole feature

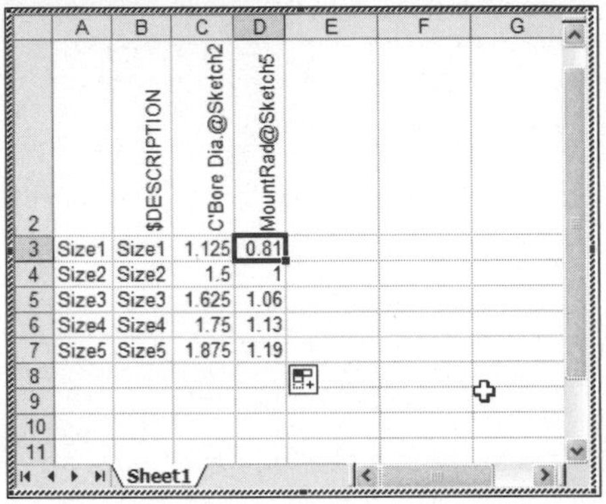

Tip

Remember that to fill the first two columns up to Size5, you can make the two-by-two selection of the Size1 and Size2 entries in the first two columns and pull down the handle in the lower-right corner of the selection box until the appropriate boxes are filled. ∎

18. **Manually fill in the C'Bore Dia values, but in cell D3, type the equation** =C3/2+.25. Then use the same Fill technique to populate cells D3 to D7. Click outside of the Design Table to close it.

19. **Test the configurations to make sure that they all work.**

20. **In the Design Library, browse to a folder where you would like to put this library feature.** (Make sure that it is not used by assemblies or sheet metal forming tools.) Click a face created by the SpecialHole feature and drag the feature into the lower pane of the Design Library. The Add to Library PropertyManager should appear on the left.

21. **Although you selected a feature and dragged it into the library, the Items to Add field appears blank.** Select the SpecialHole, tapped hole, and circular pattern features using Ctrl+select for multiple selections, either through the detachable PropertyManager, the split FeatureManager, or the flyout FeatureManager. Selecting the features from the graphics window does not work.

22. **Position and zoom the view of the part so that when it is saved, you see a good preview of the library feature.** Also, if you have not changed your background color from blue to white, this would be a good time to do so.

23. **In the Save To pane, make sure that you select the correct folder, then fill in a filename and click OK.** Figure 13.26 shows the completed PropertyManager interface for this function.

Tip

You may notice that there are two library entries in the window. This is because an additional path has been added in Tools ➪ Options ➪ File Locations ➪ Design Library. ∎

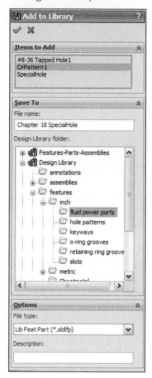

FIGURE 13.26

Saving the library feature

24. **If the new library feature does not appear in the Design Library, then click in the Design Library and press F5.** If you do not like the way that it displays, then right-click in a blank space inside the lower library window and select one of the other three options.

25. **To edit the preview image of the feature, right-click the feature in the Design Library window, select Open, reposition or zoom the view, and save it. Click in the Design Library and press F5 again.**

Tip

It is recommended that when placing a library feature, you should close the original library feature window. The workflow proceeds much more smoothly if the part is closed before you use it. ∎

26. **Open the part from the DVD called** `Chapter 13 Tutorial Blank.sldprt`. If you would like to examine the version of the SpecialHole part that I created, it is saved as `Chapter 13 – SpecialHole.sldlfp`. Notice that this is a library feature part file, not a regular SolidWorks part file.

27. **Drag the SpecialHole library feature from the Design Library onto the face of the blank part.** Place the feature near the squared-off end. Select a configuration from the list in the PropertyManager.

Tip

Although there is no prompt, when the Library Feature interface hesitates and there are configurations in the library feature, it is waiting for you to select a configuration. A prompt actually does exist, but it appears in the lower-left corner of the screen on the status bar in a tiny font and most users probably do not notice it. ■

28. **Try to orient the part in the same way that it appears in the preview window, as shown in Figure 13.27.**

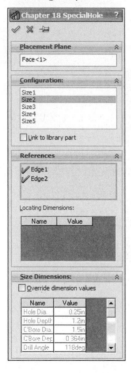
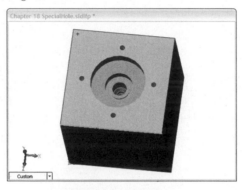

FIGURE 13.27

Orienting the part and selecting references

29. **Select edges on the Blank part that correspond to the preview window.** Click OK to accept the placement of the feature.
30. **Double-click the SpecialHole feature and change the X and Y placement dimensions to place it 1 inch from the edges in both directions.**

Note

You may remember from Chapter 11 that library feature configurations cannot be controlled by part configurations. In order to show different library feature configurations in different part configurations, you need to suppress one library feature and insert another. This is the best available workaround. It may be time to visit that enhancement request site again. ■

31. **Place another library feature onto the blank part.** Select a configuration, and click the green check mark icon without selecting edges for the references.

32. **Notice that the feature in the FeatureManager appears with an exclamation mark.** If you investigate the cause of this, then you can see that the two dimensions that should be attached to edges are dangling because you did not select the references while placing the library feature. This was done on purpose to show a different technique.

33. **Expand the library feature and the SpecialHole feature, and edit the first sketch in the Special Hole.** This is the placement sketch. Delete the two dimensions that appear in dangling colors.

34. **Add a concentric sketch relation between the placement point and the arc edge of the Blank part. Exit the sketch.** The error message should now be gone and the hole should now be placed in the center of the arc.

35. **Right-click the second library feature and select Dissolve Library Feature.** Figure 13.28 shows the finished part and FeatureManager. Good job!

FIGURE 13.28

The finished part

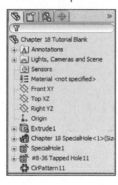 

Note

When you dissolve a library feature, you lose any access to any configurations. Some users insist on dissolving every library feature so that they can see regular features in the FeatureManager. This technique may also be useful if you would like to reorder some of the individual features within the library feature. ∎

Summary

The Hole Wizard can make holes based on 2D or 3D sketches. The type of hole that you create is up to you. Two-dimensional sketches are far easier to use than 3D sketches.

Library features are very useful in automating frequent design tasks. They are easy to create, store, apply, and automate. Setting up the features for the most flexibility often takes careful planning and attention to the detail of the references that you use. The more data you reuse, the more time you will save by automating and centralizing your libraries.

Part III

Creating Part Drawings

Automating Drawings: The Basics

Engineering drawings include a lot of repetitious information from one drawing to the next. The information is not always exactly the same, but it is usually in the same format and of the same type. For example, part drawings always include information about who made the drawing, when the person made it, what the material and surface finish of the part are, and some basic notes that depend on the use of the drawing (manufacturing, assembly, or inspection).

All this information needs to appear consistently on each drawing, every time. However, humans are not always good at following dull routines, which is why we have computers to help with these boring or difficult tasks.

SolidWorks drawing templates and formats enable you to automate some of these tasks. SolidWorks can insert information on a drawing's creator and the materials to be used, and start similar types of drawings from a consistent starting point. Drawing templates and formats also save settings that you may want to reuse.

Comparing Templates and Formats

Simply put, *templates* are collections of document-specific settings and default views saved in the *.prtdot (part template), *.asmdot (assembly template), and *.drwdot (drawing template) file types. In this chapter, I cover the *.drwdot file type.

Formats, more formally called "sheet formats," are exclusive to drawing documents and contain the sheet size, the drawing border-line geometry, and the text/custom property definitions that go with the text in the drawing border. You can think of a sheet format as an underlay beneath a clear drawing sheet. Formats can also include company logo images.

You can save formats in drawing templates; in fact, this is the method that I use and recommend. Using SolidWorks' default drawing templates, the templates and formats are initially kept separate. You specify the size and the format when creating a new drawing from a blank template. However, when the format is already in the template, the size has already been determined, and so the templates end up being saved as sizes. Of course, you can change formats later if you need to use a larger drawing sheet, but you cannot change templates.

A SolidWorks drawing template can have multiple sheets, which can be the same or different sizes. You can use a different format for each sheet. For example, if you want a default two-page drawing, you can save it as a template, with different formats for the first and second sheets.

Changing existing templates

Currently, once you create any kind of document from whatever kind of template, you cannot change the underlying template. However, you can change all the settings, which is for the most part equivalent.

SolidWorks offers custom drafting standards, which provide some of the functionality that the ability to swap templates would achieve. You can take a drafting standard such as ISO (International Organization for Standardization) or ANSI (American National Standards Institute), make adjustments to it, and save the standard out to a file that you can distribute to other users. You can change the standard by choosing Tools ➪ Options ➪ Document Properties ➪ Drafting Standard from the menus. You can load and save standards from the same location. More details on what you can actually change within the drafting standard come later in this chapter.

While *templates* cannot be reloaded, *formats* can be. You might want to reload a format (drawing border and associated annotations) if you have made changes to the information or line geometry. You can also reload a format to change the sheet size for a drawing.

Maintaining different templates or formats

Different formats must be maintained for different sheet sizes. If you do contract design or detailing work, then you may need to maintain separate formats for different customers. Some people also choose to have different formats for the first sheet of a drawing and a simplified format for the following sheets.

If you put formats on the templates, then you are making separate templates for various sized drawings. Also, separate templates are frequently created for different units or standards because templates contain document-specific settings. I also keep a blank drawing template with a blank format on it just to do conceptual scribbles or to make an informal, scalable, and printable drawing without the baggage that typically accompanies formal drawings.

Caution

SolidWorks can install with default document templates that use different standards. Be careful of the difference between drawings with ANSI and ISO standards or, more importantly, the use of Third Angle Projection versus First Angle Projection. Figure 14.1 shows the difference between a Third Angle and First Angle Projection. Third Angle is part of the ANSI standard used in the United States, whereas First Angle is part of the ISO standard used in Europe. ∎

If you work for a company that does a lot of work for manufacturing in Europe, then you may have to deal this issue more frequently. The setting that controls the projection angle is not in Tools ➪ Options (where you might expect it to be) but in the Sheet Properties, which you can access by right mouse button (RMB)+clicking anywhere on the blank drawing sheet and selecting Properties.

Third Angle versus First Angle Projection

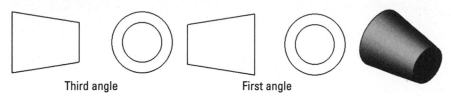

Third angle   First angle

Creating custom drafting standards

In my experience, in companies that work in the real world, very few companies follow any of the single drafting standards perfectly. Each company seems to have its own interpretation of, or exceptions to, the standards. SolidWorks is coming to grips with this in a practical way. In SolidWorks, you can create your own custom drafting standards, equivalent to the established ISO and ANSI standards. These standards allow you to save all the settings found in Tools ➪ Options ➪ Document Properties to a single standard that you can then transfer to other users.

To make your own custom standard, make changes to the various settings for annotations, symbols, dimensions, and so forth, and then go back to the Drafting Standard page of the Document Properties tab, rename the Overall Drafting Standard, and save the standard to a file. I have created a new standard, which is shown in Figure 14.2.

Creating a new customized drafting standard

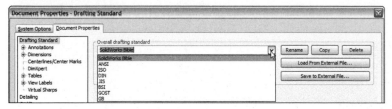

The drafting standard file type has the extension of *.sldstd. If someone else has sent you a standard file, you can read it in to your drawing using the settings shown on the right of Figure 14.2 and assign it as the active standard; your drawing will assume all the customized properties.

On the DVD

I have saved a custom standard file and put it on the DVD for Chapter 14. You can load this file into an open drawing by choosing Tools ➪ Options ➪ Document Properties ➪ Drafting Standard and using the interface. ∎

Creating Drawing Formats

Creating drawing formats can be either simple or difficult, depending on your requirements. Generally, copying existing drawing borders from other drawings imported through DXF (Data eXchange Format) or DWG format is the easiest way to go. Trying to edit an existing border into a different size is usually much more difficult. Adding all the automated annotation information is much easier than editing the lines in the border and title block. What's difficult about it is that SolidWorks is not very good at handling very large sketch data, which is what it considers a drawing format to be. If you disable sketch relations, moving sketch entities correctly can be difficult, and if you enable sketch relations, the performance is very slow.

Customizing an existing format

The simple solution is to customize an existing format of the size or sizes you require for your own use. This generally works well, and you can usually finish the task in a few minutes, depending on your requirements. The easiest option is to take the existing SolidWorks sample formats and add a few things such as a company name, logo, and tolerance block to them. You can also use formats from other drawings, editing and saving them out as your own. If you really need to make extensive edits to a format or create a new one from scratch, I would consider using DraftSight, a free 2D AutoCAD clone provided by Dassault Systèmes, the parent company of SolidWorks.

Using sample formats

The sample formats installed with SolidWorks include ANSI sizes A through E, and ISO sizes A0 through A4. You can probably find enough space on the formats to place a company logo and some standard notes. These templates are located in different directories in Windows XP, Windows Vista, and Windows 7. Choose Tools ➪ Options ➪ File Locations to locate the path for your templates.

You cannot open a format directly — it must be on a drawing — and, so, to get a closer look at the format, you must make a new drawing using the format.

Note

Templates that have been saved with a format already on them skip the step of prompting you to select a format. This enables you to create new drawings more quickly. If you select one of the default SolidWorks templates, these do not have formats on them, so you are prompted to select a format immediately. Figure 14.3 shows the interface for selecting a format that displays after you have selected the template for a drawing. ∎

FIGURE 14.3

Selecting a format

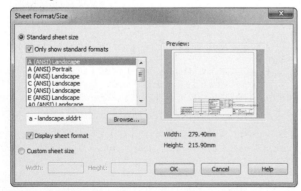

Editing a format

In the drawing, you are either editing the sheet or editing the format. You can think of the sheet as being a piece of transparent Mylar over the top of the drawing border format. In order to get to the format, you have to peel back the Mylar layer. Drawing views go onto the sheet, so when you edit the format, any drawing views that may be there disappear.

To peel back the sheet and gain access to the format, right-click a blank area of the sheet and select Edit Sheet Format. Alternatively, you can also access the sheet format by right-clicking on the sheet tab in the lower-left corner of the SolidWorks window. This RMB menu is shown in Figure 14.4. Be careful of the terms here, which include Sheet and Sheet Format. The sketch lines of the format light up like a sketch becoming active, and the "Editing Sheet Format" message appears at the lower-right corner on the status bar.

FIGURE 14.4

Selecting the edit sheet format

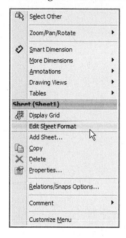

The lines in the format border are regular SolidWorks sketch entities, but they display a little differently. Also, sketch relations are sometimes disabled in formats because solving the relations causes the software to be a bit sluggish. Typically, Trim, Extend, and Stretch functions are the best sketch tools for editing lines.

You can use most common image types to insert logo or other image data onto your drawing or format by choosing Insert ➪ Picture. Not all compression styles are supported, however. I have had difficulty with compressed TIFF (Tagged Image File Format) images. Be aware of the file size of the image when you put it into the format, as images can be large, and all that extra information will travel around with each drawing that you create from the format. Figure 14.5 shows a bitmap placed in the format.

You can resize the image by dragging the handles in the corners and move it by simply dragging it. The bottom image in Figure 14.5 was taken from the Print Preview window. I included it here to show that the outline around the image that displays while you are working in SolidWorks does not print out.

FIGURE 14.5

Placing an image

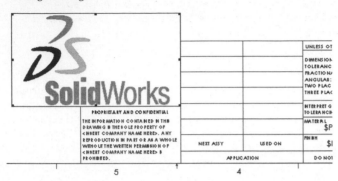

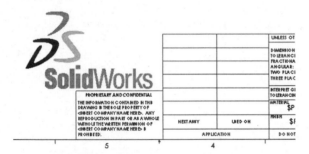

Managing text

SolidWorks allows you to make a text box of a specific size that causes text to wrap. This is particularly useful in drawings. The upper image in Figure 14.6 shows a new annotation being added. The lower image shows the same text box after the corner has been dragged.

FIGURE 14.6

Adding an annotation and wrapping the text

Tip

When dragging the text box, it may seem intuitive to drag the middle handle on the end, thinking that shortening the box will cause it to wrap. However, that only works if the box has some space on the bottom to wrap. SolidWorks does not automatically reduce the text box down the way PowerPoint does. You are better off dragging the lower-right corner handle of the text box to get the wrap to work. ∎

Using custom properties

The most important part of the drawing format is the custom properties. While the rest of the format is just for display, custom properties use automation to fill out the title block using matching custom properties in either the model or the drawing document. Custom properties can pull items such as filenames, descriptions, materials, and other properties from the model associated with the sheet, or they can pull data from the drawing itself, such as the sheet scale, filename, sheet number, and total sheets. If you are seriously looking to automate drawings, you cannot overlook custom properties.

Entering custom property data

Custom property data entry happens at the part or assembly level. This information is then reused in the drawing format and in tables such as BOMs (Bills of Materials) and revision tables, as well as searches using the FeatureManager filter, and all PDM (Product Data Management) systems make use of SolidWorks custom properties. You can enter the data several ways, but the two most prominent ways are through the Summary Information dialog box and through the Custom Properties Tab in the Task Pane.

Using the Summary Information dialog box

Figure 14.7 shows the Summary Information dialog box. This functionality has existed in SolidWorks for several releases. You access this dialog box by choosing File ⇨ Properties from the menus. You can select Property Names from a drop-down list or type in your own, assign types of data, and enter in a specific value for the property. The Value/Text Expression column also has a drop-down list from which you can select several preset variables, such as mass, density, and even link values used in the part.

FIGURE 14.7

The Summary Information dialog box

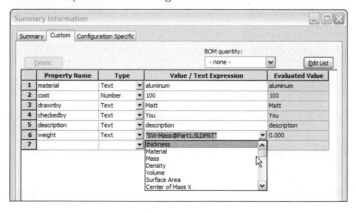

This is a perfectly functional way of entering data, but the fact that it is somewhat out of the way, hidden in the menus, means that it does not get used as much as it should. So SolidWorks came up with another way of entering data.

Using the Custom Properties tab

The Custom Properties tab of the Task Pane enables you to quickly and easily access and assign custom properties within a document. Figure 14.8 shows the process of building your own Custom Properties tab. You can start the Custom Property Tab Builder by either clicking the Create button on the Custom Properties tab or choosing Start ⇨ Programs ⇨ SolidWorks ⇨ SolidWorks Tools ⇨ Property Tab Builder from the menus.

FIGURE 14.8

Using the Custom Properties Builder and Custom Properties tab

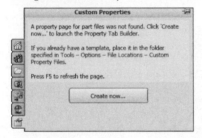

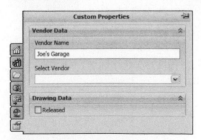

Cross-Reference

Chapter 11 contains more detailed information on the Custom Property Tab Builder and how to create, use, and share Custom Property tabs. ■

The interface enables you to add drop-down lists, toggles, and text entry boxes. This gives you a lot of flexibility with custom property data entry and is a very nice addition to the software.

Displaying property links

Figure 14.9 shows the existing custom property formatting in the default format being used for this example.

Custom property formatting in the title block

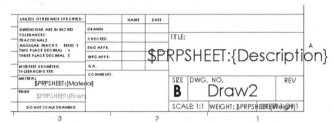

The syntax `$PRP` or `$PRPSHEET` indicates that the property that follows the syntax is to be pulled from either the current document (drawing) or from the model specified in the Sheet Properties, respectively. This is an important distinction to make. Most of the time, you can type custom properties in at the part or assembly level so that you can reuse the data by drawing properties, BOM, or even design tables.

Notice that all the notes in the format that are showing raw syntax are pulling data from the model. "Draw2" and the Scale notes are driven by the drawing. When no value exists for the property to display, you have an option of what to show. The top portion of Figure 14.10 shows the settings in the View menu that control the display of syntax of the custom property links. In general, it is common to deselect the error display and to show the link variables.

The link variable's display options and effects

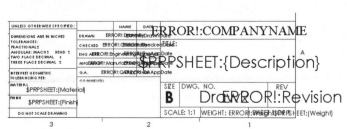

Displaying errors and link variables

The errors in Figure 14.10 are caused by links to the local document for which there is no corresponding property. For example, the "ERROR!: COMPANYNAME" message is linked to "$PRP: COMPANYNAME," but the local custom property COMPANYNAME does not exist. If it existed but had a null or space value, the error would disappear.

Likewise, with the option to display link variables selected, the syntax that calls model custom properties displays until there is some value for it to pull from. If a part is put onto the drawing, then some of the properties are filled in because properties and values exist to pull from, and the rest of the properties simply disappear to make space. Notice in Figure 14.11 that the Material property has been filled in, but the Finish property has not. This is because either there is no Finish property in the part on the drawing or there is a null value in the Finish property.

FIGURE 14.11

Custom properties filled in by a part

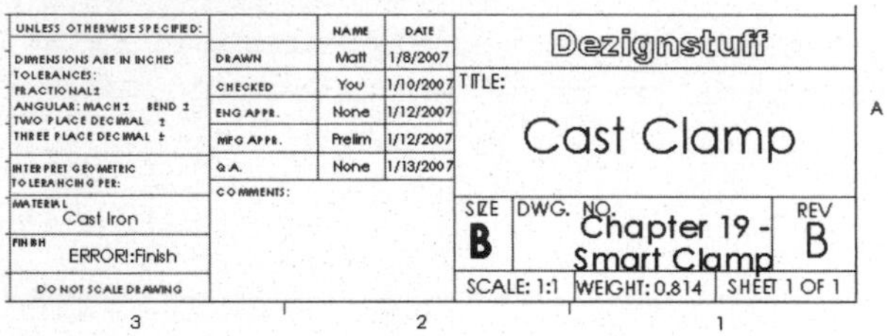

Tip

When initially setting up the format, it can be useful to have a dummy model already on the drawing. The dummy model should have all the custom properties in it that you intend to use in your drawings. This prevents the blank fields or error messages from appearing during setup. ■

Note

If you drag-and-drop a part onto a drawing while editing in the Sheet Format, the views may appear for a split second and then disappear again. This is because you cannot display drawing views while editing the Sheet Format. Once you exit the Sheet Format and go back to editing the sheet, the views can display once more. ■

Creating linked properties

It is easy to create annotations that are linked to properties. Begin as if you are creating a note:

1. **Click the Note toolbar button on the Annotations toolbar, or choose Insert ➪ Annotations ➪ Note.**

2. **Place the note on the drawing.** The Formatting toolbar appears.

3. **Click the Link to Property button in the Text Format pane of the Note PropertyManager.** This displays the Link to Property dialog box, as shown in Figure 14.12, which gives you the option of linking to a custom property in the current (drawing) document or in the model (part or assembly) that is on the drawing.

FIGURE 14.12

The Link to Property dialog box

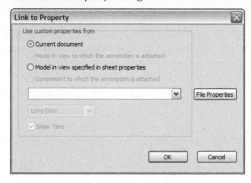

4. **If the desired custom property is not in the drop-down list shown to the right, then you can type it into the text box or click the File Properties button to edit the properties.** If the property is added to the part file or a part file with that property is used on the drawing, this linked annotation will pick it up. This button is not available for the model if there is no model on the drawing, in which case you must type in the name of the property manually.

Using the Title Block function

The Title Block enables the person who sets up the sheet format to specify an area that contains notes that are easy to access without editing the format. (Many CAD administrators prefer that the users not have to deal with the details inside the Sheet Format.) You can even cycle through these notes in a specific order by pressing Enter or Tab. Figure 14.13 shows the resizable black border of the Title Block, the Title Block PropertyManager, and where the Title Block sits in the drawing FeatureManager.

FIGURE 14.13

Using the Title Block function

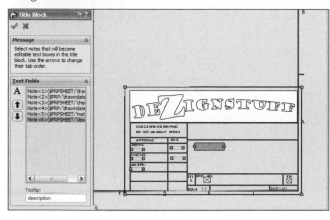

You can access the Title Block to edit or define it by right-clicking in the Sheet Format (while editing the Sheet Format, not the sheet) and selecting either Define Title Block or Edit Title Block, as the situation requires.

The Title Block can be any size you like, but it must remain rectangular, and you can only create one Title Block area per sheet format. The area bounded by the Title Block box is used to zoom the display to make it easier to fill in the text boxes. If you want to include areas in different corners of the drawing in the Title Block area, you will need to make the Title Block box as big as the entire sheet, and the user will have to manually zoom to each corner.

Select each Note item to add it to the list in the PropertyManager selection box. Use the arrows to the left of the box to assign the order in which the user cycles through the boxes. The idea is that the user clicks in a box within the Title Block area, fills it in, then presses Enter or Tab to get to the next box. The order will loop if the user does not start on the first box listed in the PropertyManager.

On the DVD

You will find a sample template with a format with a Title Block definition added to it on the DVD. The file is called `title block.drwdot`. Add it to your template library folder and try it out. ■

Creating a format from a blank screen

SolidWorks is not good at manipulating a lot of 2D sketch-line data, such as what you find when drawing title blocks. I have gone through the process of making my own formats, as well as the process of importing DWG data from which to create them. If you choose to custom build one size and then use it to create the rest of the sizes, you need to be patient. SolidWorks typically turns off the most useful parametric sketch functions when working with a format (what SolidWorks considers a large sketch) because of speed problems. If you would like to turn on these settings, you can find them by choosing Tools ⇨ Sketch Settings.

If you insist on creating your own borders and title blocks, set aside some time for it and have an idea of what you are trying to achieve, maybe sketched out by hand or in a printout of a title block that you would like to replicate. You can also use the free 2D tools DWG Editor or DraftSight, which are much better suited to this kind of work.

The Modify Sketch tool may be useful for moving entities around the screen, and even scaling them. You can also access a useful hidden command by right-clicking the name of the drawing in the FeatureManager and selecting Move from the menu, as shown in Figure 14.14. A small dialog box appears that enables you to move the entire format by a specified distance.

Tip

If you need to use construction geometry to help you size or locate objects or text while manually creating your Sheet Format, then you do not need to delete the geometry when you are done. You can put all the construction geometry on a specially created drawing layer and turn the layer off. ■

FIGURE 14.14

The Move Drawing dialog box

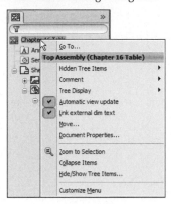

Creating a format from an imported DWG/DXF file

If you want to create your format from an imported DWG or DXF file, choose File ➪ Open to locate the file that you would like to import and then click to open it. The DXF/DWG Import screen appears, as shown in Figure 14.15.

FIGURE 14.15

The DXF/DWG Import screen

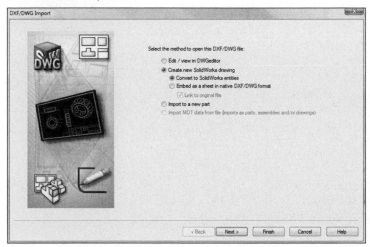

You can find the sample files used for this example on the DVD for Chapter 14 if you are interested in following along. You will find five * . dwg format files. You can use any of them to create a format, but I suggest either the A or B size. To make a drawing format, you can select the Create New SolidWorks drawing and Convert to SolidWorks entities options. Although one of the other options contains the word *format*, it is not being used in the same sense, so do not be misled. When this selection is complete, click Next. Figure 14.16 shows the next screen.

FIGURE 14.16

The Drawing Layer Mapping screen

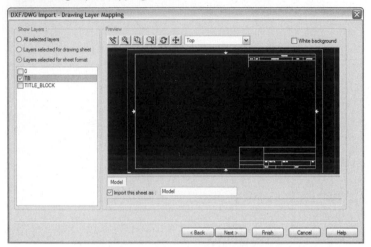

Select the Layers selected for sheet format option. Select the TB layer, leaving the other layers unselected. Every imported file will be different in this respect, because layers used by title blocks vary widely. Click Next when you have made these selections. Figure 14.17 shows the Document Settings screen.

FIGURE 14.17

The Document Settings screen

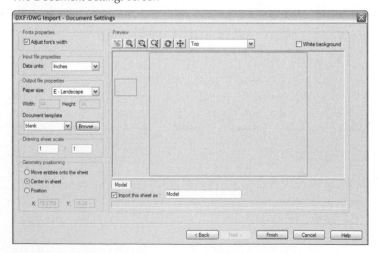

The important features in the Document Settings screen are the Document template selection and the Geometry positioning options.

Document template selection is only important if you plan to save the format with a template. Be sure to select a template that does not already have a format saved in it. In the Geometry positioning section, if you can get the software to center the title block for you, definitely take advantage of this functionality and use the Center in sheet option. Once you are happy with these settings, click Finish. The resulting format is shown in Figure 14.18.

The finished imported format

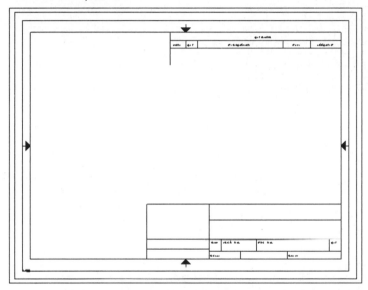

From here, you can add the links to custom properties as described earlier, as well as logo images, loading favorites, and blocks. You can now save the format as described in the next section.

 Tip

The Color Display Mode button on the Line Format toolbar toggles the display between using the layer color to using the SolidWorks sketch colors. Another setting that affects sketch display in drawings is found at Tools ⇨ Options ⇨ System Options ⇨ Drawings ⇨ Display Sketch Entity Points, which shows endpoints and arc center points in the same way that they are shown in feature sketches. ■

Saving the format

You can save drawing formats in two ways: either with the template or separate from the template. You cannot edit formats separate from a template, but they do have their own file type, `*.slddrt`.

Note

If you are wondering how the extension *.slddrt relates to a sheet format, what is now known as sheet format used to be called a drawing template (thus, the drt of slddrt). What is now called a template did not exist in 1997. The shift in architecture and, more importantly for users, the shift in terminology still leave many people a bit confused. ∎

Saving templates is covered in the next section. To save a format, choose File ⇨ Save Sheet Format. You can do this with or without the format being active. Save the format into a location with other formats and give it a descriptive but unique name. If you have not yet done so, this is a good opportunity to create a separate folder, outside of your SolidWorks installation folder, that contains your most frequently used files. Remember also to tell SolidWorks where this library location is by choosing Tools ⇨ Options ⇨ System Options ⇨ File Locations ⇨ Sheet Formats.

Even if you have saved a format with a template, it is a good idea to also save the format on its own. This is because you might want to use that format on an existing drawing that has a different format on it or use it on a second sheet.

Using second sheet formats

When you have multi-sheet drawings, it is often important to have a simplified or specialized format for the second sheet. Figure 14.19 shows sample page-one and page-two formats side by side.

FIGURE 14.19

First and second sheet formats

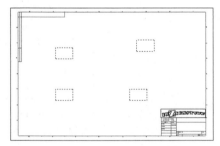 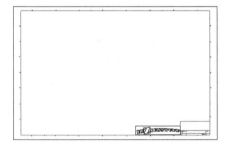

Adding new sheets

 You can add sheets to a drawing by clicking the Add Sheets icon to the right of the sheet tabs at the bottom of the SolidWorks window or through the RMB menu of the sheet tab at the lower-left corner of the drawing window. If you right-click the first sheet tab, the sheet that is added gets the format that is used on the first sheet. If you right-click the second sheet tab, the added sheet gets the second sheet format.

Reloading formats

If a format has been changed, and you would like to update a drawing to the new format, this option is available in the Sheet Properties, as shown in Figure 14.20.

Updating a format through the Sheet Properties

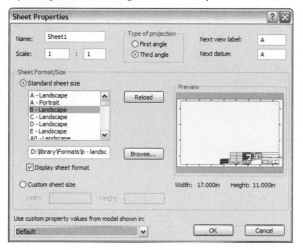

Creating Drawing Templates

Document-specific settings are an important part of the template, and it is probably best to get one drawing size completely set up the way you want it, and then create the other sizes from this drawing. This helps to ensure that the settings, such as bent leader length, font, and line weight, are the same for all the templates. Uniform settings on drawings give them a consistent look and make them easier to read. An in-depth discussion of document-specific settings at Tools ➪ Options ➪ Document Properties can be found in Appendix B. Drafting standards are also controlled by drawing templates.

Using Pre-defined Views in drawing templates

When I use drawing templates, one of my favorite techniques to get to a multi-view drawing quickly is to put one Pre-defined View on the template along with appropriate views projected from the Pre-defined View. A Pre-defined View establishes an orientation and location on the drawing sheet. You can add multiple Pre-defined Views and align them with one another on the drawing sheet so that a drawing is automatically populated by the model, but this is not recommended because if you decide to change the orientation of the drawing, you have to change each Pre-defined View independently. If you set up a single Pre-defined View and make the rest of the views with Projected Views, changing the orientation of the Pre-defined View causes all the Projected Views to update associatively. You cannot directly change the orientation of a Projected View. Pre-defined Views and views projected from Pre-defined Views appear blank until they are populated with model geometry. The *pre-defined* part of a Pre-defined View is the orientation and placement of the view.

Figure 14.21 shows a template using Pre-defined and Projected Views. You can access Pre-defined Views on the Drawings toolbar; although it is not there by default, you can place it on the toolbar by choosing Tools ⇨ Customize ⇨ Commands and using the interface. You can also access Pre-defined Views by choosing Insert ⇨ Drawing Views ⇨ Pre-defined. Projected Views are also accessed from the Drawings toolbar.

FIGURE 14.21

Pre-defined Views on a template

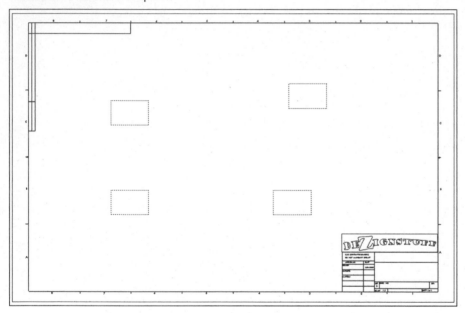

Once a Pre-defined View has been placed, you can select an orientation for it from the PropertyManager. Figure 14.22 shows the Drawing View PropertyManager. The orientation for a view is set in the top Orientation panel. In addition to orthogonal views, you can also create isometric and other custom views as Pre-defined Views.

After the view has been oriented, you may want to create more views on the drawing that also become populated by model geometry. This is where the Projected Views are used. Make sure that the drawing properties are set to the correct projection angle.

Because the rest of the views have been created relative to the Front view, none of the views needs to be rotated as it would if, for example, the Top view was placed above the Back or Right view.

Although it is not on this drawing, many drawing templates include a Third Angle Projection symbol as a part of the Title Block, which is in the format. Figure 14.23 shows First and Third Angle Projection symbols. These are included as blocks with the sample data in the SolidWorks installation. Blocks are discussed in more detail in Chapter 16.

FIGURE 14.22

The Drawing View PropertyManager

FIGURE 14.23

Projection angle symbol blocks

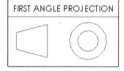
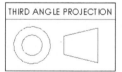

Aligning Pre-defined Views

You can align views to one another through a view's RMB menu, as shown in Figure 14.24. Projected Views are aligned to one another automatically, but if you chose to use a Pre-defined View rather than a Projected View to one side of the original Pre-defined View, you can use the Align Vertical by Origin or the Align Horizontal by Origin command. This ensures that the parts in each view are aligned. Aligning by center should not be used for Projected Views on an engineering drawing, because it is not guaranteed to line up edges in adjacent views.

FIGURE 14.24

Selecting view alignment options

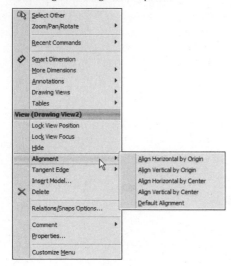

Populating a drawing with Pre-defined Views

Four methods exist to populate a drawing with Pre-defined Views:

- **Drag-and-drop.** Drag a part or assembly from the FeatureManager and drop it in the drawing window. All Pre-defined Views are automatically populated.

- **Insert Model.** Right-click a view and select Insert Model. From the interface, browse for the model to be displayed in all the related (projected) views.

- **PropertyManager.** Select a Pre-defined View, and from the PropertyManager, select Browse in the Insert Model panel.

- **Make Drawing from Part/Assembly.** Click the Make Drawing From Part/Assembly button in the Standard toolbar and select a template that uses Pre-defined Views.

Scaling Pre-defined Views

When Pre-defined Views are created, they are set to follow the sheet scale by default; however, you can manually set them to have a custom scale. If you are using the automatic scaling option (found at Tools ⇨ Options ⇨ System Options ⇨ Drawings ⇨ Automatically Scale New Drawing Views), the sheet scale is automatically changed when the drawing views are populated to make a nice fit of the model geometry on the drawing. The scales used by the automatic feature are all standard multiples of two, so you do not have to worry about odd scale factors on your drawings.

Understanding the limitations of Pre-defined Views

The function and expectations of Pre-defined Views are fairly straightforward, although there are a few things that could be improved. For example, SolidWorks does not allow you to create pre-defined section or detail views. Also, the View Palette does not preview the populated Pre-defined Views.

Using styles and blocks in templates

The functionality formerly known as *favorites* is now known as *styles* in certain parts of SolidWorks, although you will find other parts where the term favorites is still used. In SolidWorks, styles function like styles and formatting in Microsoft Word, or other word-processing software, by adding under-lines, bold formatting, and even items such as tolerances and symbols. Hole Wizard Styles are described in Chapter 13, and work similarly to Dimension and Note Styles (described in Chapter 16). This chapter addresses the fact that styles can be saved to files and loaded to documents. In particular, they can be loaded to documents that can be saved as templates, thus maintaining the loaded styles. Several types of styles can be loaded into and saved with drawing templates, including dimension, note, GD&T, weld, and surface finish symbols.

When a style is loaded into a template, any document that you create from that template can use any of the loaded styles. The many file types for styles exist mainly to transfer styles from one document to another, but they are not needed once the style is loaded. As a result, before saving a template, you should gather together your styles into your library folder and load them into the template.

You can load styles by going to the interface for the type of favorite; for example, dimensions or notes. Figure 14.25 shows the top of the Note PropertyManager interface, which contains the Styles panel.

FIGURE 14.25

The Styles panel for the Note PropertyManager

The buttons in the Styles panel of the Note PropertyManager interface have the following functions, from left to right:

 • Apply the default attributes to the selected notes

• Add or update a style

• Delete a style

• Save a style

• Load a style

This section is concerned with the last function, Load a style. After clicking this button, you can load multiple styles at once by Shift+selecting them through the Open dialog box that appears.

Even symbol types that can be applied by dragging-and-dropping from the Design Library can also be loaded as styles. However, I prefer dragging from the Design Library because you get a preview of the symbol; with the styles, you just see a text tag.

Blocks can also be loaded into a template or used from the Design Library as drag-and-drop items.

Using custom properties in templates

Part of the usefulness of templates is that you can do work once and have it replicated many times. This is an excellent example of process automation. One of the ways that you can take advantage of this feature is by putting default custom properties in your templates. In many cases, simply having a default value for something is better than no value, and a default value may even prompt you to put a value with real significance in the property. For example, the Description of a document is extremely important, especially if you are using sequential part numbers for your filenames. A custom property named Description can be added to your template, and the default value is used unless it is changed when the template is used in a document.

You have already seen how custom properties used in parts can be instrumental in filling out a title block on a drawing. Custom properties in part and assembly documents work exactly the same as they do in drawings. The custom properties interface is shown in Figure 14.26.

FIGURE 14.26

The custom properties Interface

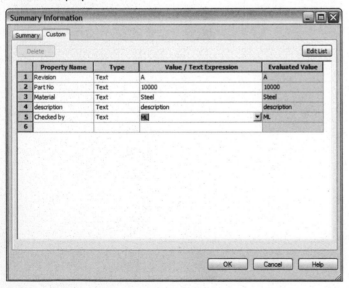

Saving a template

To save drawing templates, choose Save As ➪ Files of Type and then select Drawing Templates from the drop-down list. This automatically takes you to the folder for the templates, as specified in Tools ➪ Options ➪ File Locations ➪ Templates.

In the case where a template and format have been saved together and are being saved together, but the format also needs to be saved to its own file, saving the template with the changed format only changes the format for documents that are made from that point forward with that template.

You may also save out the format to its own file from the edited template. Formats are needed in their own file (in addition to existing within a template) for situations when you have an existing drawing and want to change the size of the sheet and then need a format to put on the sheet. Another situation is when a drawing may come in to your organization from an outside contractor, and they have not used your format; in this case, you can simply replace their format with yours, or you can send them your format (and template, for that matter), from which the contractor can create all drawings for you.

Separate formats are important for when you have multi-sheet drawings. When adding a sheet, you also need to add a format. You can save multi-sheet drawing templates in which the first and second sheets have different formats on them.

Creating Blocks

Blocks are an important aspect of automating drawing creation. They enable you to combine text and sketch geometry and to annotate common features on drawings. Blocks are discussed in Chapter 4 and also in Chapter 16 (creation, editing, and placement). Blocks can be used for many purposes, including the following:

- Tolerance blocks on drawings that might change with the process (if you do not have separate formats that already contain this information)
- Electrical or pneumatic schematic symbols that can be snapped together
- Flowchart type symbols
- Fluid flow-direction arrows
- Special markers calling attention to a specific detail
- Sheet formats that can be created as a block, enabling you to move it around as a single entity much more easily

You can create blocks by selecting a group of sketch entities, annotations, or symbols and then choosing Tools ➪ Block ➪ Make.

Cross-Reference

For more information on creating, editing, managing, and placing blocks, see Chapter 22. For more information on general CAD Administration and specific recommendations for templates and formats, please refer to the SolidWorks Administration Bible (Wiley, 2009). ■

Summary

Getting your templates and formats correct creates an excellent opportunity to save some time with drawings by automating many of the common tasks using templates, Pre-defined Views, multiple formats, blocks, favorites, and linked custom properties. Setup becomes more important when you are administering a larger installation, but is also important if it is just for yourself. One of the most important things that you can do is to establish a file library and direct your Tools ⇨ Options ⇨ File Locations paths to the files. There is nothing quite as productive as having something that works right the first time, and every time.

Working with Drawing Views

I n SolidWorks drawings you do not create lines to create views. The drawing view is a snapshot of the 3D model from a particular point of view. To change the lines on the view, you have to change the 3D model; you do not just move lines around the view.

If you are coming from AutoCAD, this might seem a little bit confining. However, this method will become liberating rather than confining. It means that you do not have to worry about the drawing views being inconsistent or incorrect. All you have to worry about is the 3D model being correct.

SolidWorks automatically maintains the views better than you could do it manually. It can update any type of view from any point of view of even the most complex model or assembly geometry perfectly.

Creating Common View Types

The previous chapter discussed Pre-defined Views in templates. Pre-defined Views make it faster to automatically create drawings with consistently placed, simple views. However, sometimes you may need to create views on templates that do not have Pre-defined Views, or you may need a special arrangement of views. SolidWorks has a good assortment of view types to make practically any type of view that you may need.

Note
When creating or changing either the geometry or the settings that control how a view is displayed, the view may become cross-hatched, indicating that the model needs to be rebuilt. To resolve this problem, press Ctrl+B to rebuild the drawing. ■

IN THIS CHAPTER

Using common view types

Exploring other view types

Assigning hotkeys to View items

Sketching in a view versus sketching on a sheet

Working with view types, settings, and options tutorial

Using the View palette

The View palette is shown in Figure 15.1. It is activated automatically if you use the Make Drawing From Part tool, unless the drawing template that you select has Pre-defined Views on it. In this case, the Pre-defined Views are populated and the View palette is not activated.

FIGURE 15.1

The View palette

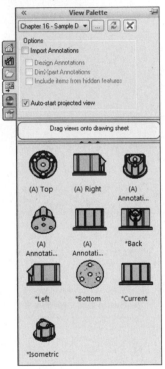

The View palette contains all the standard named views, the current view of the model, custom named views, and any annotation views (views that the model was in when annotations were added to it). You can drag-and-drop these views on the drawing.

If multiple parts are available, they are listed in the drop-down list at the top of the panel. You can also browse, refresh, or cancel out of the view from this same area.

 To activate the View palette without using the Make Drawing From Part tool, simply create a new drawing document, ensure that the Task Pane is available, and click the View Palette tab in the Task Pane. Then use the ellipsis button (...) to browse to a part. After you select a part, the palette window is populated with views of the model. This method has the advantage of enabling you to see the views before you put them down. It does not link views in the same way that the Predefined and projected views are linked, however. I find this interface somewhat difficult to use, and prefer to set up the Pre-defined Views in templates or to use the Multiple Views option in the Model Views PropertyManager, which is shown later in this chapter.

Using Model Views

Model Views are one of the few types of views that are not dependent on another view. Everything has to start from somewhere, and most drawings have to start with either a named or Pre-defined View. A Model View starts from a named view in the model.

You can place named views by clicking the Model View button on the Drawings toolbar or by choosing Insert ⇨ Drawing View ⇨ Model. Using the Model View PropertyManager is a two-step process, and is shown in Figure 15.2. In the first step, you select the model, and in the second step, you set the options for the view. Views dragged from the View palette are also Model Views.

The Model View PropertyManager

The Model View PropertyManager has seen several changes in SolidWorks 2010, some of which are shared with the Drawing View PropertyManager and other view creation PropertyManagers. This has to do with Display States and annotations to import to the drawing view.

Open documents

The large selection box in the Part/Assembly to Insert panel displays any models that are open in SolidWorks at the moment. If the model that you are looking for is not in the list, then you can use the Browse button to look for it.

I typically use Create Drawing From This Part/Assembly if the part is open, and if not, I drag-and-drop the part onto a new drawing created from a template with Predefined and projected views on it. This combination saves a lot of extra steps.

If you click in the drawing window for some reason (for example, if you are expecting it to simply place a view), then a prompt appears, stating that you have selected a drawing document, and that only parts and assemblies can be inserted into drawings.

Thumbnail Preview

This is a nice option that shows the part that you selected in the Open Documents window. It is a useful feature, but because it is collapsed by default, it is easy to miss. After it is used the first time, it remembers the expanded setting.

Start Command When Creating New Drawing option

The Start Command When Creating New Drawing option causes this PropertyManager to open immediately when a new drawing is created. If you click in the drawing window, then the prompt appears, telling you that you are not paying attention.

Reference Configuration

The Reference Configuration list enables you to select which configuration of the part to show in the view. This shows up not only when creating new views, but also in the generic Drawing View PropertyManager that shows up when you select any view.

Select Bodies

When a part has multiple bodies, a button called Select Bodies also shows up in this panel. If the part does not have multiple bodies, you will not see this button, When you click the button, it immediately takes you out to another PropertyManager, the smaller one shown in Figure 15.3 called Drawing View Bodies, where you are sent back to the model window to select a body. Clicking the green check after selecting a solid body in Drawing View Bodies then sends you back to the drawing to place the view. It does not send you back to the Model View PropertyManager.

If you click the red X in the Drawing View Bodies PropertyManager, SolidWorks leaves you in the part window, and you will have to press Ctrl+Tab to get back to the drawing window.

Cosmetic Thread Display

Many people see the High and Draft quality options and assume that the option refers to the quality of the view, while in fact it refers to the quality of the cosmetic thread display. Cosmetic threads can display in either high or draft quality. The distinction is made for performance reasons. The difference in terms of display is that in high-quality mode, hidden cosmetic threads (cosmetic threads that are behind a face) do not display in shaded mode.

Number of Views and Orientation

To create multiple views, toggle multiple view creation on in the Orientation panel of the Model View PropertyManager. Next, select all views from the Standard Views icons that you want to be displayed, including choices from the More Views list such as Current Model View and any named or annotation views that exist. These views are indicated on the drawing as boxes (representing view borders), as shown in Figure 15.3.

This is really useful functionality. It makes view selection and placement very easy and is visually clear. Unfortunately, the Single View setting is the default setting, and the PropertyManager does not remember the last setting that was used. Still, the combination of Multiple Views and Orientation is far better, in my opinion, than the View palette.

FIGURE 15.3

Placing multiple views

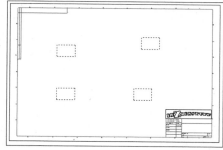

Import Options panel

The Import Options panel is for bringing annotations into the drawing view that is being created. You should find it an advantage, being able to select these items quickly from the PropertyManager while the view is being created.

Display State

On the drawing you can now select the Display State. This is probably meant for situations like using Display States for hide and show operations, but remember that there is a lot more to Display States than just hide and show. You can also change display styles and colors, and transparency, which you might think do not have any place on a technical drawing.

Display Style

You can set the default Display Style by choosing Tools ➪ Options ➪ System Options ➪ Drawings ➪ Display Style. This panel provides an override for views being placed. This panel also enables you to control High or Draft quality views, which are described later in this chapter.

Scale

SolidWorks drawings always default to showing views at the overall sheet scale unless the System Option on the Drawings page called Automatically Scale New Drawing Views is selected. If this setting is selected, the sheet scale saved with the drawing template is overridden. For example, a 1:1 sheet scale can be changed automatically by the setting to 1:4.

You can change the sheet scale through the sheet properties, which were discussed in Chapter 14. Controlling views with the sheet scale makes it much easier to change the size of a drawing and to scale all the views together. Individual views can be displayed at the view scale, and detail views are typically created at a different scale automatically. To locate the scale setting, choose Tools ➪ Options ➪ System Options ➪ Drawings ➪ Detail View Scaling. Detail Views, covered later in this chapter, automatically get a note showing the custom scale for the view.

You can automatically add a label or note to an orthogonal drawing view displayed at a scale different than the sheet scale. You access this setting at Tools ⇨ Options ⇨ Document Properties ⇨ View Labels ⇨ Orthographic. Enable the Show Label If View Scale Differs From Sheet Scale option, and specify the rest of the settings shown in Figure 15.4 as appropriate.

FIGURE 15.4

Displaying a label to show the view scale when it is different from the sheet scale

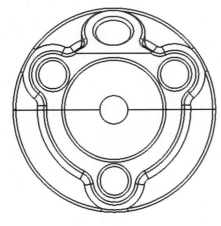

SCALE 1 : 2

Tip

You could consider creating a note style or block for a note that automatically links to the scale of a drawing view. ■

Dimension Type

Even in non-orthogonal (isometric) views, true dimensions should be used for most drawing views. Projected dimensions depend on the angle of the edge to the view plane.

Cosmetic Thread Display

If something is worth having, it is worth having twice. This panel appears in both steps, just in case you missed it in the first step.

Using the Projected View

The Projected View type simply makes a view that is projected in the direction that you dragged the cursor from the selected view. Be aware that first-angle and third-angle projections result in views that are opposite from one another. For example, if you drag at a 45-degree angle, the result is an isometric view. When placing an isometric view that you have created in this way, SolidWorks constrains the new view to a 45-degree-angle line through the Origins of the two views. To place the view somewhere other than along this line, press the Ctrl key while placing the view to break the alignment. The PropertyManager for the Projected View is shown in Figure 15.5.

The Projected View PropertyManager

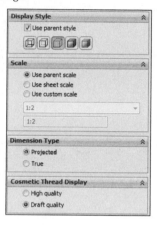

When you use the pushpin on the Projected View PropertyManager, you can place multiple projected views from the originally selected view or select a new view to project views from. Display properties and scale of the projected views are taken from the parent view.

Using Standard 3 View

You can access the Standard 3 View tool on the Drawings toolbar by choosing Insert ⇨ Drawing View ⇨ Standard 3 View. This places a Front view, and projects Top and Right views for third-angle projection drawings. Figure 15.6 shows the PropertyManager for the Standard 3 View function.

Use the PropertyManager to select open models that you want to place on the drawing. Also select configuration and body or bodies to place here as well.

Using Detail View

You activate the Detail View from the Drawings toolbar or by choosing Insert ⇨ Drawing View ⇨ Detail. Either way, you can use the function in two different ways: one that is fast and easy and the other that gives you more control but is not quite as fast.

Placing three Standard Views

Pre-drawing a detail circle

You can draw the detail "circle" before you initiate the Detail View command. When you pre-draw a detail circle, you must ensure that you are sketching in the view and not on the sheet. To draw in the view, the view must be activated. You can activate a view by clicking in the view or by bringing a sketch cursor inside the boundary of the view. When you activate a view, the status bar in the lower-right corner of the SolidWorks window displays the message, Editing Drawing View, as shown in Figure 15.7.

Activated drawing views

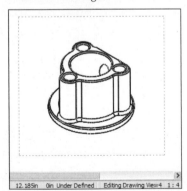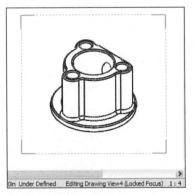

The dotted border in the image to the left shows that the view is selected, and the status bar shows that it is activated. The image to the right with the solid corners indicates that the view has Locked Focus. You can lock focus on a drawing view by double-clicking it or by right-clicking and selecting Lock View Focus from the menu.

If a view is not activated or the focus is not locked on the view, then any sketch elements that you draw will be placed on the drawing sheet. While sketching in a drawing view, it is a good practice to watch the status bar.

The point of all of this is to sketch a closed loop in the view so that it can be used for a Detail View. The closed loop can be a circle, ellipse, spline, series of lines, or any other shape, as long as it is a closed loop. SolidWorks refers to a closed loop as a *circle* with the Detail View.

A setting controls how the circle displays, in particular whether it displays as drawn or as an actual circle. This setting is found in the Detail Circle PropertyManager. If the setting is grayed out, the Style option may be set *per standard*, and the standard you are using does not allow for non-circular detail circles. You could choose With Leader instead or change the drafting standard you are using. The different results are shown in Figure 15.8.

Drawing a closed loop with the Display Detail Circle as Circles option both on and off

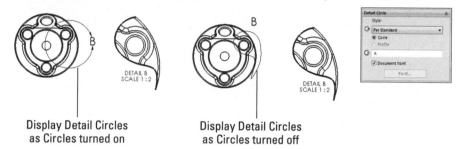

Display Detail Circles
as Circles turned on

Display Detail Circles
as Circles turned off

Once you create the loop, you can click the Detail View toolbar button and place the view. The view is automatically scaled by the factor set at Tools ➪ Options ➪ Drawings ➪ Detail View Scaling. By default, this scale is set to twice the parent view scale, but you can reset the default to whatever you like.

Drawing a detail circle in-line

A faster way to complete the Detail View is to simply click the Detail View toolbar button without pre-selecting or pre-drawing the loop. This activates the Circle sketch tool immediately, which activates the view as soon as you bring the cursor over the view, so that when you draw the circle, it is sure to be in the view rather than on the sheet.

Alternatively, you could swap the circle tool for an ellipse or spline; this works just as well, but offers more flexibility. Regardless of the sketch tool, when you close the loop, SolidWorks prompts you to place the view. The workflow for this in-line method is better than the old-school pre-drawn loop technique.

Editing a Detail View

You can edit a Detail View by dragging the circumference of the detail circle to a new diameter, dragging the center of the detail circle to a new location, or by selecting Edit Sketch from the detail circle right mouse button (RMB) menu. This method enables you to edit sketch relations or otherwise edit the sketch that you used for the detail. When you are done with the sketch, you can use the Confirmation Corner to click OK.

You can delete Detail Views by selecting and deleting the detail circle. Deleting the detail circle gives you the option to delete the resulting view as well as the original sketch. Also, deleting the Detail View gives you the option to delete the detail circle and the original sketch.

Working with Section Views

Section Views in SolidWorks offer many options, such as Default Section View, Partial Section View, Aligned Section View, and Editing a Section View.

Using a Default Section View

The Default Section View has the same in-line and pre-drawn optional techniques as the Detail View, as well as the same advantages and disadvantages.

Section Views may have a straight line that may go through the center of a cylindrical feature. Even though you are in a drawing and not in a model sketch, you may still benefit from model sketching techniques. For example, to draw a straight vertical line through the model shown in Figure 15.9, in the images on the left, you can hover the cursor over a circular edge to wake up the center, and then pick up the inference lines to the center. Another technique is to show the temporary axes (using the View menu), just sketch the line, and then assign a sketch relation in the same way that you would in a feature sketch. This technique is shown in the images on the right.

FIGURE 15.9

Aligning a line in a Section View sketch

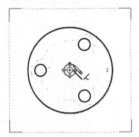
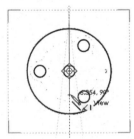
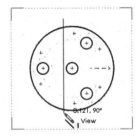

You can also use jogged section lines with the default section tool. Similar sketch relation techniques are more common in jogged sections because there are more sketched lines. The results are shown in Figure 15.10.

Default and jogged Section Views

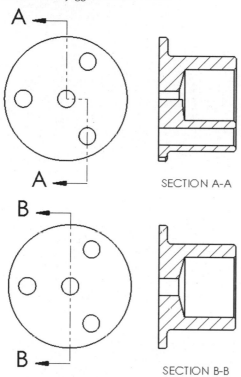

SECTION A-A

SECTION B-B

You can also tell a Section View how deep you want the section view to see into the part. In the PropertyManager of the Section View, you can set a depth with a number or you can select a face, edge, or vertex to determine the depth. When you select the check box at the top of the Section Depth panel, a graphic handle becomes available on the drawing view, which enables you to visually drag the depth as well. This functionality is shown in Figure 15.11.

Setting a depth for a Section View

 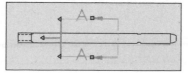

Using a Partial Section View

A Partial Section View is created when the section line does not cut all the way across the model. In Figure 15.12, the line that is drawn to create the Partial Section View was the vertical section line. The prompt that appears enables you to confirm that you intended to create a partial section cut. If you answer No to the prompt, the result is an error, with the new view displayed in the dangling color.

FIGURE 15.12

A Partial Section View requiring only a single sketched line

Sketched line

You can use another technique to create a section that looks like a partial section but is not considered a partial section by SolidWorks. You can create it by drawing perpendicular lines and selecting the line to be used as the projection direction for the section before clicking the Section View tool. This differs from a true partial section in that it shows half of the model unsectioned. It is also similar to the Aligned Section View, but it does not unfold the second sectioned side. When the prompt shown in Figure 15.12 displays, clicking Yes causes the resulting view to look like the view on the left in Figure 15.12. Clicking No causes the view shown in Figure 15.13 to appear. Creating the view shown in Figure 15.12 requires only a single sketched line, while Figure 15.13 requires perpendicular sketched lines.

FIGURE 15.13

A Section View requiring perpendicular sketched lines

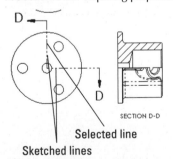

Using an Aligned Section View

The Aligned Section View takes two separate sections at right angles to one another and lays them out flat on the page. It is essentially two partial sections that display side by side. The section lines look identical to those shown in Figure 15.11, but the resulting view is different, as shown in Figure 15.14. The finished view aligns with the selected sketch element.

FIGURE 15.14

The Aligned Section View

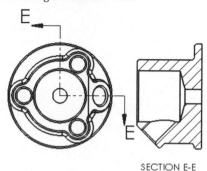

SECTION E-E

Editing a Section View

Section Views are edited in the same way as Detail Views. You can edit the section lines directly by dragging, or the section line sketch through the RMB menu. You can click the RMB menu and select the Edit Sketch command to edit sketch relations, or to add to or remove sketch elements from the sketch.

Section Views are also deleted in the same way as detail views, with the option to also delete the underlying sketch for the section. When you delete one segment of the section line, the resulting view, as well as the underlying sketch, is also deleted.

Creating Other View Types

SolidWorks is able to create any type of view that you need. If you can define what the view should look like, then SolidWorks can create it. The only limit is your creativity.

Using a Crop View

 The Crop View is simply a view that looks like a Detail View without requiring a parent view. This feature enables you to reduce the number of views on a sheet and save some room. However, a cropped view may be confusing if it is not clear which area is being detailed in the cropped view.

Unlike Detail Views, in Crop Views the closed loop must be sketched in the view before you invoke the command. To make the Crop View, draw the closed loop as shown in Figure 15.15 in the image to the left, and then click the Crop View button on the drawing toolbar or access the command by choosing Insert ➪ Drawing View ➪ Crop.

To edit a Crop View, right-click the view, expand the arrow next to Crop View, and select either Edit Crop or Remove Crop. Removing the crop does not delete the sketch that the crop was created from.

FIGURE 15.15

A sketch loop and a Crop View

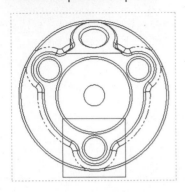

Using a Broken-out Section View

The Broken-out Section View is another view type that alters an existing view rather than creating a new view. It also requires a closed loop sketch. The Broken-out Section View is very useful in assembly views where parts are obscured by other parts, in particular when a set of parts is inside a housing and you want to show the inside parts without hiding the housing. Of course, you can also use Broken-out Section Views on parts with internal detail.

Broken-out Section Views act like a cut that is created from the drawing view. Any faces created by the cut are hatched. Figure 15.16 shows a casting part view using a Broken-out Section View. You can create Broken-out sections on parts or assemblies. You cannot create Broken-out Section Views using existing Detail, Section, or Alternate Position Views.

FIGURE 15.16

A Broken-out Section View

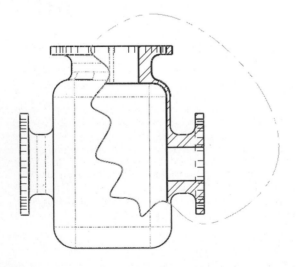

Notice that in Figure 15.16 the temporary axes for the flange holes are showing and cannot be turned off. This is probably a display bug and is present in SP0 of SolidWorks 2011.

The hatch pattern is associated with the materials assigned for each part. You can change the hatch scale by double-clicking a hatched region and using the settings in the dialog box shown in Figure 15.17. To change the hatch size, you have to deselect the Material Crosshatch option.

Changing the hatch pattern on a broken-out section

Broken-out Section Views require you to specify a depth for the break. You can use an edge selected from a different view or a distance to specify the depth. In the case of the broken-out section, the depth is into the screen, while with the regular section the section depth is measured as a distance perpendicular to the section line.

Drawing the closed loop

Broken-out Section Views are initiated from an existing view either with or without a pre-drawn closed loop. If the loop is pre-drawn, then you must select it before clicking the Broken-out Section toolbar button on the Drawings toolbar or accessing the command by choosing Insert ⇨ Drawing View ⇨ Broken-out Section.

If the view has no pre-drawn, pre-selected loop, then initiating the function activates the spline sketch tool. It is not necessary to use a spline as the closed loop for this view type, but Broken-out Section Views are traditionally created with a freehand sort of boundary, even when drawn manually.

If the loop is closed in an uninterrupted workflow, then after the last spline point is drawn, joining the spline back to itself, the Section Scope dialog box appears. This enables you to select any parts that are not to be sectioned if an assembly is in the sectioned view. It is customary to avoid sectioning shafts, screws, or other cylindrical components. Using the Section Scope, the image on the right in Figure 15.16 would be altered to look like the image on the right in Figure 15.18.

FIGURE 15.18

Using the Section Scope

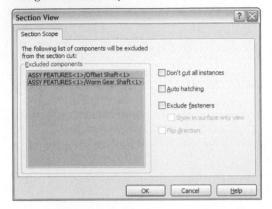

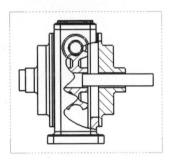

The recommended workflow is to initiate the function from the toolbar, use the spline to create the closed loop, and to not pre-draw a loop. This makes everything flow more smoothly, and you create the view surprisingly quickly. If you must use a sketch tool other than the spline, then you must pre-draw it. Even if you simply change sketch tools when the Broken-out Section View automatically activates the spline, because the workflow has been broken, creating the closed loop does not automatically display the Section Scope interface.

Selecting the depth

After you make the Section Scope selections, the next step is to set the depth of the cut. You can do this in one of several ways. Broken-out Section Views are usually applied to the center of a hole if available, or in other ways that show the view as cleanly as possible. If you know the depth of the cut that you want to make, then you can type it in as a distance value. Of course, that raises the question "Distance from *what*?" to which the answer seems to be "from the geometry in the view that would come the farthest out of the screen toward the user." Users most often choose the distance when it does not matter *exactly* how deep the cut goes or exactly *where* it cuts, but it gives a relative position.

In situations when you want to cut to the center of a particular feature or up to an edge, it is far easier and less bothersome to simply select the geometry from a drawing view. For example, Figure 15.19

shows the PropertyManager interface where the depth of the cut is set. In this example, the edge of the shaft in the view to the right has been selected. This tells SolidWorks that the cut should go to the center of the shaft. Another possibility is to show the temporary axes, as shown in Figure 15.19, and to select an axis through the center of the shaft.

FIGURE 15.19

Setting the depth of the Broken-out Section View

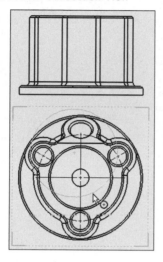
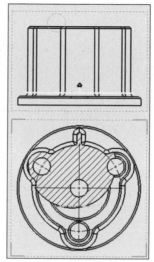

Editing the view

At this point the view is finished. Now you may choose to edit the view in some way, such as by changing the sketch, the depth, the section scope, and so on. Figure 15.20 shows how the Broken-out Section View is positioned in the Drawing FeatureManager. It is listed as a modification to an existing drawing view. The Broken-out Section RMB menu is also shown. Selecting Edit Definition displays the PropertyManager, shown in Figure 15.19. Selecting Edit Sketch enables you to change the section spline shape. Selecting Properties displays the dialog box shown to the right in Figure 15.20. This contains options for the underlying original view as well as the broken-out section modification to the original view. Only the Section Scope tab is added by the Broken-out Section View. The rest of the options are for normal view properties.

Using a Break View

 Break Views are typically used to display parts that are very long in one dimension on a drawing in such a way that you can see both ends or other important features. You can break views more than once in the same direction, or even in opposite directions. Figure 15.21 shows the full view of a part and a view that was broken twice. Notice that the dimensions are correct, and any dimension that includes a broken length has a special dimension line.

FIGURE 15.20

Editing the Broken-out Section View

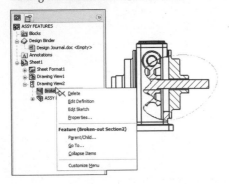

FIGURE 15.21

Dimensions on a Break View

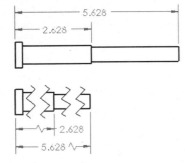

The PropertyManager in Figure 15.18 shows a bit of a discrepancy in terminology. Using "Break" as the name of the view seems a little awkward, and I much prefer it as "Broken View," as it is shown here in the PropertyManager. It is inconsistent, but you get the idea anyway.

To create a Break View, click the Break toolbar button on the Drawings toolbar, or choose it at Insert ⇨ Drawing View ⇨ Break. You need to place break lines in pairs, and you can choose from one of four break symbol styles, as shown in Figure 15.22. You can change the style from the RMB menu or from the PropertyManager.

The Broken View PropertyManager also enables you to set the gap size and the style of the break. The gap refers to the gap between the break lines in the finished broken view. The setting here overrides the default for this view only. The default setting is a template setting found in Tools ⇨ Options ⇨ Document Properties ⇨ Detailing. Other options that you can set in this location are the break line extension (the distance the lines extend past the model edges) and the break line font (on the Line Font page of the Document Properties tab). The setting that enables the broken symbol on a dimension is found on the Dimensions page and is named Show Dimensions As Broken In Broken Views.

FIGURE 15.22

Selecting the break symbol

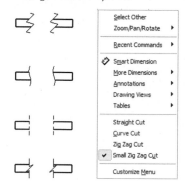

You can remove individual breaks in a broken view by selecting one of the break lines and pressing Delete. You can add breaks by applying the Break command and adding more breaks to a view. You can alter breaks by simply dragging the break lines. In past versions, it was possible to get the view very confused by dragging one set of breaks to interfere with another set of breaks. That problem has been fixed by not allowing break lines to be dragged past one another.

Broken views enable you to dimension the break lines themselves so that when the model changes, you can control the location of the break lines relative to part geometry.

Consider using the Unbreak option from the RMB menu to temporarily unbreak a view to make dimensioning more convenient.

Using an Auxiliary View

 An Auxiliary View is a view that is projected from a non-orthogonal edge. This type of view is often necessary to view features (such as holes drilled at an angle) square on, so that they appear circular in the view rather than foreshortened and elliptical. An Auxiliary View is shown in Figure 15.23 in the image to the left. If the edge that the view was created from is updated, then the Auxiliary View will reorient itself. The image to the right shows an Auxiliary View projected from an arbitrarily drawn sketch line. The line or edge used to project an Auxiliary View cannot be reselected; however, if a sketch is used to project the view, then the Edit Sketch option is available through the view arrow RMB menu.

Two Auxiliary Views

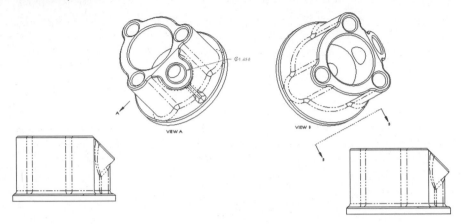

Using an Alternate Position View

 While assemblies are dealt with in detail in the *SolidWorks 2011 Assemblies Bible* (Wiley, 2011), this assembly-only view type is introduced here only to offer all of the drawing view types in a single location. (Additional information on this and other assembly functionality is located in the above referenced book.) The Alternate Position View is only available for views of an assembly and shows the assembly in two different positions (not from different viewpoints; this requires an assembly that moves). This is another view type that does not create a new view but alters an existing view. Figure 15.24 shows the PropertyManager interface for the Alternate Position View, a sample view that it creates, and the way that it is represented in the drawing FeatureManager.

The Alternate Position View

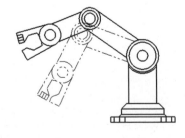

To create an Alternate Position View, ensure that you have an assembly on the active drawing that can have multiple positions, and click the Alternate Position View button from the Drawings toolbar, or choose Insert ➪ Drawing View ➪ Alternate Position and then select the Alternate Position View.

Next, click in the drawing view to which you want to add the alternate position. The PropertyManager shown in Figure 15.24 prompts you to select an existing configuration for the alternate position or to create a new configuration. If you choose to create a new config, then the model window appears, a new config is created, and you are required to reposition the assembly. The alternate position is shown in a different line font on the same view, from the same orientation as the original.

Tip

The best way to create this view is to either create two configurations used exclusively for the Alternate Position View or to have two configurations where you know that parts will not be moved, suppressed, or hidden. The main idea is that you need to ensure that these configurations remain in the same position or are changed intentionally, knowing that it will alter this drawing view. ■

To delete an Alternate Position View, select it in the drawing FeatureManager, and press Delete.

Using a Pre-defined View

Pre-defined Views are discussed in depth in Chapter 14, and are primarily used as views on drawing templates.

Using an Empty View

Empty Views are just that — empty. The reasons for creating an Empty View can include making a view from a sketch, making a schematic from blocks, or combining several elements — such as blocks, sketches, imported drawing geometry, annotations, and symbols — into an entity that can be moved as a group on a drawing.

Using a Custom View

You can create Custom Views by orienting the view in the model document and saving the view. Remember that views can be saved in the View Orientation window, which you can access by pressing the spacebar. Custom Views are placed on the drawing using the Named View functionality.

While not appropriate for showing dimensions, views using perspective are most useful for pictorial or illustrative views. The only way to get a perspective view on a drawing is to save a custom view in the model with perspective turned on. You can access the Perspective option by choosing View ➪ Display ➪ Perspective, and you can edit the amount of perspective by choosing View ➪ Modify ➪ Perspective.

Using a Relative View

The Relative View enables you to create a view that does not necessarily correspond to any of the standard orthogonal views or named views. This type of view is very similar to using the Normal To tool. First select the face that is to be presented square to the view, and then select the face that represents the top of the view. When this view type is initiated, SolidWorks opens the 3D model window to allow you to select the faces needed to define the view.

This type of view is particularly useful when a part has a face that is at an odd angle to the standard planes of the part. It is in some ways similar to the Auxiliary View, except that in the Auxiliary View you cannot select which face is the top.

The Relative View has a special function that is important for drawings of multi-body parts. If both faces used to establish the view are from the same body, then all the rest of the bodies in the part can be hidden with an option in the Relative View PropertyManager, which is shown in Figure 15.25. Multi-body modeling is covered in Chapter 19.

FIGURE 15.25

The Relative View PropertyManager

Using the 3D Drawing View Mode

 3D Drawing View Mode is not technically a drawing view type. It is a mode that enables you to select faces or edges of the model that may need to be selected for some purpose, but cannot be seen from the orientation of the drawing view. You can invoke the 3D Drawing View Mode from the 3D Drawing View toolbar button, which is on the View toolbar and can be accessed by choosing View ⇨ Modify ⇨ 3D Drawing View from the menus.

Ironically, this mode does not work for the Relative View, which would be a perfect application for it. Instead, Relative View makes you go to the model window. 3D Drawing View Mode is intended for views such as the Broken-out Section View where a depth must be selected for the cut.

In Figure 15.26, notice the small toolbar above the drawing view. This toolbar is available while the 3D Drawing View Mode is turned on. Clicking OK on the small toolbar turns off the mode and returns the view to its previous state.

FIGURE 15.26

3D Drawing View Mode

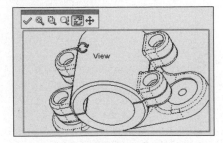

Changing view orientation and alignment

Although you may have selected the Top view, and it displays the correct geometry, you may want to spin the view in the plane of the paper, or orient it in a particular way. You can do this using two methods. The easiest way to reorient the view is to use the Rotate View tool on the View toolbar. This rotates the view in the plane of the paper much like it rotates the model in 3D.

Another option is to select an edge in the view and assign the edge to be either a horizontal or vertical edge. Figure 15.27 shows how a view can be reoriented using this tool, which you can locate by choosing Tools ⇨ Align Drawing View ⇨ Horizontal or Vertical Edge.

FIGURE 15.27

Rotating a drawing view to align an edge

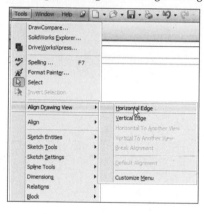 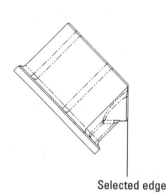

Selected edge

Another option for view alignment is to align it relative to another view; this involves stacking one view on top of another or placing them side by side. You can do this by selecting the second pair of options in the menu shown in Figure 15.27, Horizontal to Another View and Vertical to Another View. These are grayed out in the figure, but preselecting a linear edge before selecting this option in the menus will activate them.

Situations may arise where a view is locked into a particular relationship to another view, and you need to disassociate the views. The Break Alignment option, which is grayed out in the menu in Figure 15.27, serves that purpose.

Using Display Options in Views

Some important display options and settings are not listed in the Tools ⇨ Options menu; they are only available through the menus, and in particular the View menu. You can effectively deal with most items in the View menu by assigning a hotkey that can be toggled on or off. For example, Axes and Temporary Axes are things you often want to be visible when you're sketching something, but not visible when printing a drawing. You can easily assign the display for Axes and Temporary Axes to hotkeys, making them ready at your fingertips. You can assign hotkeys by choosing Tools ⇨ Customize ⇨ Keyboard.

Using Display States

You can use Display States in drawing views, but unless you are only hiding and showing parts with the Display States (that is, you are not changing colors or display styles with Display States), they only have an effect when a drawing view is set to Shaded Display style. You can control Display States for drawing views in the View PropertyManager. The Drawing View Properties dialog box appears, as shown in Figure 15.28.

FIGURE 15.28

The View PropertyManager

One of the limitations of the Display States functionality in drawing views is that when wireframe display is used, the drawing edges appear in black rather than using the color settings to show wireframe in the same color as shaded. The necessary color settings are found in two places, and you need to set both. The System Options setting is on the Colors page and is called Use Specified color for shaded with edges mode. The second setting is in the part Document Properties (not assembly), again on the Colors page, and is called *Apply Same Color to Wireframe, HLR (Hidden Lines Removed), and Shaded*.

Using Display styles

The 2D drawing world is becoming less and less black-and-white, and SolidWorks has the capability to apply shaded views to drawings. This is probably most useful in isometric, perspective, or pictorial views on the drawings. The shading and color may be distracting for dimensioned and detailed views, but it can also be indispensable when you need to show what a part actually looks like in 3D. Not everyone can read engineering prints, and even for those who can, nothing communicates quite like a couple of shaded isometric views.

The more standard 2D drawing display modes are Wireframe, HLR, and HLV (Hidden Lines Visible), which work in the same way as they do in the model environment. Unless you override it on a per part basis, the Display mode is set for all the components in the view.

Selecting a Component Line Font

Individual components within an assembly can be shown in different fonts, similar to the display in the Alternate Position View. You can access this function by right-clicking the component to access the RMB menu and selecting Component Line Font. Figure 15.29 shows the Component Line Font dialog box, along with a drawing view in which a couple of part line fonts have been changed. The part can only be changed in the view where it was selected, or it can be changed across the board in all views in the active drawing where it appears. This is useful if you want to emphasize or de-emphasize certain parts in the assembly view.

FIGURE 15.29

The Component Line Font dialog box

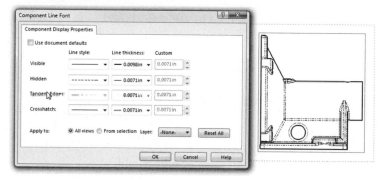

Using layers

Yes, SolidWorks drawings *can* use layers. You can place individual parts onto layers, and the layers can have different colors and line fonts. Most entities can be put into layers, including edges, annotations, and sketch items. Hidden layers are often used for reference information or construction entities on a drawing. Figure 15.30 shows the Layers dialog box on a SolidWorks drawing.

FIGURE 15.30

Using the Layers dialog box in SolidWorks

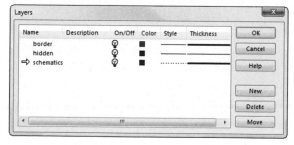

Working with tangent edge display options

SolidWorks drawings and models offer some options for displaying tangent edges. Many users find it distracting when tangent edges (which in a physical part are not edges at all) are given as much visible weight as the sharp edges of, say, a chamfer. To find the settings, shown in Figure 15.31, choose View ➪ Display, or select them from the RMB menu. The Tangent Edges Removed option may be appropriate for parts with few fillets, but it causes a part to look oversimplified and makes details of the shape difficult to distinguish.

Edge display options

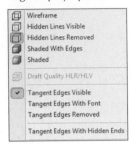

| Wireframe |
| Hidden Lines Visible |
| Hidden Lines Removed |
| Shaded With Edges |
| Shaded |
| Draft Quality HLR/HLV |
| ✓ Tangent Edges Visible |
| Tangent Edges With Font |
| Tangent Edges Removed |
| Tangent Edges With Hidden Ends |

Tangent edges shown   Tangent edges in front   Tangent edges with font and ends removed   Tangent edges removed

Additional options are available, including applying a color to the tangent edges by choosing Tools ➪ Options ➪ Color list for Tangent Edge display, and the Hide/Show Edges options.

 You can use the Hide/Show Edges tool for specific selected edges, or just click the tool with nothing selected to activate the Hide/Show Edges PropertyManager, shown in Figure 15.32. Hide/Show Edges functionality is only available with high-quality views. View quality is addressed in the next section. Hide/Show Edges is available from the left-click context toolbar or the RMB menu.

The PropertyManager indicates that Hide/Show Edges works from a selection, although it has no list box to show the edges selected. The tools offered here may not have a wide general appeal, but they will be most useful probably to people documenting complex shapes or plastic parts. Hide Non-Planar Edges is meant to simplify the display of complex parts with a lot of curvature. Hide Blend Edges limits the filtering to edges with curvature continuity across the edge, which is usually found only in more sophisticated surfaced parts. Hide Edges Shorter Than gives you the ability to filter the edge display again. These settings apply only to the current view, not to the entire drawing.

Take note of the options in the Hide/Show Edges PropertyManager message box shown in Figure 15.32:

- Box selection toggles the active edge selections
- Shift+box selection selects all edges, including previous selections
- Alt+box selection clears all selected edges

These mass selection options can be important if you have used one of the Tangent Edge Filters, Hide Non-Planar Edges, Hide Blend Edges, or edges shorter than a given value.

FIGURE 15.32

The Hide/Show Edges PropertyManager offers tangent edge display options.

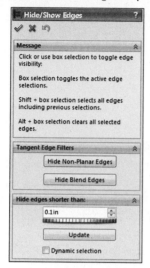

Choosing view quality settings

You have the choice between two options for drawing view quality: High quality and Draft quality. The quality that you choose influences the performance of the software. Draft quality views are noticeably rough when viewed closely, but from a distance, they are at least recognizable. However, Draft quality is becoming less accessible, and so I would not recommend relying on this option. Although new Draft quality views can be created, once they are set to High quality, they cannot be set back to Draft quality.

All views are created as High quality unless the view quality setting is overridden. To find this setting, choose Tools ➪ Options ➪ System Options ➪ Drawings ➪ Display Style ➪ Display Quality For New Views. The only other way that you can create Draft quality views is if you open a drawing from an older version of SolidWorks that used Draft quality views.

In Figure 15.2 earlier in the chapter, the image to the right shows the Display Style pane. This PropertyManager has been taken from a High quality view. A Draft quality view enables you to toggle between Draft and High quality, as shown in Figure 15.33. This means that you can switch a view from Draft to High, but not from High to Draft. Also notice in Figure 15.33 that the cursor over a Draft quality view displays a lightning bolt symbol, indicating draft quality.

You can access the Cosmetic Thread Display setting in both the Step 1 PropertyManager and the Step2 PropertyManager. However, you need to be careful not to misread the interface by thinking that either of these interfaces controls the View Quality.

FIGURE 15.33

The Draft quality options and cursor

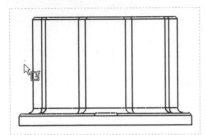

Distinguishing Views from Sheets

It is sometimes difficult for new users to understand the difference between being *in* a sketch and being *out of* a sketch, or the difference between editing the *sheet* as opposed to the *sheet format*. In the same way, confusion frequently surrounds the difference between sketching in a view and sketching on a sheet. The easiest way to determine if a sketch will be associated with a view or with the drawing sheet is to look at the prompt in the lower-right corner of the SolidWorks window, on the status bar, which displays the message, Editing Sheet, Editing Sheet Format, or Editing View.

This issue becomes especially important when you want to do something with a sketch entity, but it is grayed out and unavailable. This means that whatever entity is active is *not* the one that the sketch entity is on. Drawing views expand to contain all the sketch entities that are associated with the view, and so if you see a view that is extended on one side, larger than it should be, then it could be extended to contain the grayed-out sketch entity. Activate the sheet and the suspected views; when the sketch entity turns from gray to black, you have found the place where it resides.

Tutorial: Working with View Types, Settings, and Options

This tutorial is intended to familiarize you with many of the view types, settings, and options that are involved in creating views. To begin, follow these steps:

1. **From the DVD, open the part called** Chapter 15 – Tutorial Part.sldprt.

2. **Move the drawing template named** Inch B Bible Template.drwdot, **also found on the DVD, to your templates folder.** If you do not know where your templates are located, choose Tools ⇨ Options ⇨ System Options ⇨ File Locations ⇨ Document Templates.

3. **From the window with the open part, click the Make Drawing from Part button from the toolbar.** The drawing becomes populated with three standard views and an isometric view, as shown in Figure 15.34.

4. **In the drawing document, select the display of the Origins.** This will help you to align a section view. You can display Origins through the menus by choosing View ⇨ Origin.

5. **Click the Section View tool on the Drawings toolbar.** This activates the Line sketch tool.

FIGURE 15.34

Using a template with Pre-defined Views

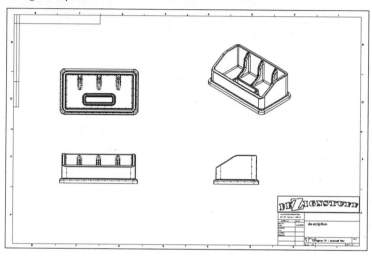

6. **In the Top view (in the upper-left section of the drawing), draw a vertical line that picks up the inference from the Origin.** You may have to run the cursor over the Origin to activate the inference lines. Make sure that the line goes all the way through the model geometry in the view, as shown in Figure 15.35. When you finish the line, the section view is ready to be placed. Place it to the right of the parent view.

FIGURE 15.35

Creating a section view

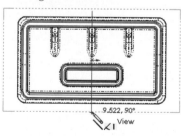

When sketching, remember to make sure that you are sketching in the view rather than on the sheet. A section view cannot be created from a sketch entity if it is not in a view. A glance at the status bar in the lower-right corner of the window lets you know if you are in Editing View or Editing Sheet.

To change the letter label on the drawing, click the section line and change the label in the top panel of the Section View PropertyManager.

Note that you may see a Section Scope dialog box asking you to omit rib features. Ribs are usually not hatched in section views.

7. **Bring the cursor over the corner in the section line until the cursor looks like the image to the left.** Double-click the cursor; the section arrows flip to the other direction, and the drawing view becomes cross-hatched. The cross-hatching indicates that the view needs to be updated.

8. **Press Ctrl+Q; the view updates, removing the cross-hatching.**

9. **Click the section line and press Delete.** Answer Yes to the prompt. You may also need to separately delete the sketched section line.

10. **Create a new section view using a jogged section line, as shown in Figure 15.36.** In order to do this, you must pre-draw the jogged section line, and press the Section View button with the part of the line that you want to use to project the new view.

FIGURE 15.36

Creating a jogged section view

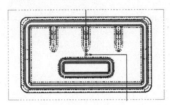 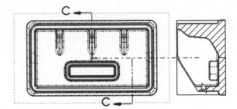

11. **Next, click the Detail View button on the Drawings toolbar.** This activates the Circle sketch tool.

12. **Sketch a circle in the Front view, located in the lower-left section of the drawing.** Try not to pick up any automatic relations to the center of the circle. One way to prevent this is to hold down the Ctrl key when creating the sketch.

13. **Place the view when the circle is complete.** Note that the view was created at a scale of 1:2. The sheet scale is 1:4, and so the detail is two times the sheet scale. The Detail View is shown in Figure 15.37.

FIGURE 15.37

Creating a Detail View

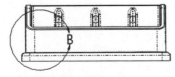

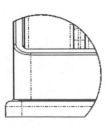

DETAIL B
SCALE 1 : 2

14. **Drag the circumference of the circle and watch the view dynamically resize.**

15. **Leave the Detail circle selected so that the center of the circle is highlighted.** Drag the center of the circle around the view. The effect is like moving a magnifying glass over the part. If you drag the center with the Ctrl key pressed, then you will not pick up any automatic sketch relations when you drop it somewhere.

16. **Click the Broken-out Section View tool on the Drawings toolbar.** Draw a spline on the Right View similar to the one shown in the image to the left in Figure 15.38. Use a section depth of 1 inch; splines take a little practice.

FIGURE 15.38

Creating a Broken-out Section View

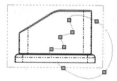 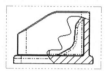

17. **Click inside the view border but outside of the part in the Top view (in the upper-left section of the drawing).** Press Ctrl+C.

18. **Click the Add Sheet icon to the right of the sheet tab in the lower-left corner of the drawing that says Sheet1, and select Add New Sheet.** If you used the template that I provided, a message may appear, saying that SolidWorks cannot find the format. This is because I only supplied you with the template file, not the format as a separate file. In any case, switch to the B size format and accept.

19. **Click any spot inside the sheet and press Ctrl+V.** SolidWorks pastes the copied view from the other sheet. Delete the section line. You may also need to delete the sketch lines separately.

20. **Click the Projected View tool from the Drawings toolbar, and then click the pasted view.** Practice making a couple of projected views, including dragging one off at a 45-degree angle to make an isometric. Make sure that one of the views is a side view showing the angled edge, as shown in Figure 15.39. Once you create the views, click model edges in the views and drag them around to a better location.

21. **Select the angled edge from one of the side views and click the Auxiliary View toolbar button.** While placing the view, press and hold the Ctrl key to break the alignment. You can resize the view arrow by selecting the corners and dragging. If you drag the line itself, then you can move it between the views. Alternatively, with the view arrow selected and the PropertyManager displayed, you can deselect the green check mark icon in the Arrow panel at the top of the window to turn off the arrow.

22. **Create a new drawing from the New dialog box.** Select a template without predefined views on it, so the Inch B Bible Template (no Views).drwdot will work. If you select a default SolidWorks template, you need to verify that the template uses Third Angle rather than First Angle Projection. An easy way to do this is to switch the drafting standard from ISO to ANSI in Tools ⇨ Options ⇨ Document Properties ⇨ Drafting Standard. If the automatic Model View interface appears in the PropertyManager, click the red X icon to cancel out of it.

FIGURE 15.39

Projecting views

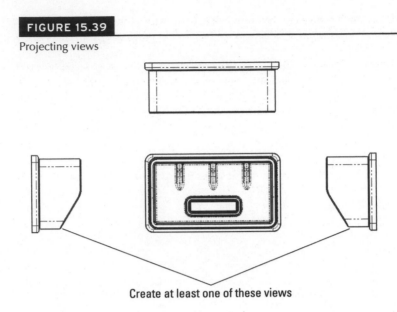

Create at least one of these views

23. **Expand the Task pane and activate the View palette (the tab that looks like a drawing icon).** Click the ellipsis button (...) and browse for the assembly named Chapter 15. SF casting assembly.sldasm. This is shown in Figure 15.40.

FIGURE 15.40

The View palette

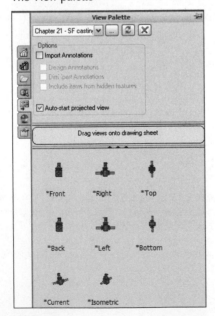

24. **Drag the Back view onto the drawing.** Notice that when you use this technique, the views do not resize automatically, regardless of the setting at Tools ➪ Options ➪ Drawings ➪ Auto matically Scale New Drawing Views.

25. **Delete any view that you have created using this method.** Open Windows Explorer, browse to the assembly, and drag it into the drawing. The views that you create using this method are equivalent to the Standard 3 View tool. This time, the views auto-size.

26. **Select the Front view and change it to the Back view.** Notice that the rest of the views change to reflect the new parent view. You will get a warning about this change.

27. **Zoom in on the Back view.** Change the view to show Tangent Edges With Font through View ➪ Display. You can also change this from the view RMB menu.

28. **Click the Alternate Position View toolbar button.** Type a name in the PropertyManager for a new configuration and click the green check mark icon. SolidWorks opens the assembly model window.

29. **Rotate the handle 90 degrees and click the green check mark icon.** SolidWorks returns to the drawing and shows the new position in a dashed font, as shown in Figure 15.41.

FIGURE 15.41

Creating an Alternate Position View

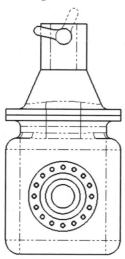

30. **Place an isometric view on the drawing.** Change the Display Mode to make it a shaded view.

31. **Right-click inside the view but away from the parts, and select Properties.** The dialog box appears, as shown in Figure 15.42. Make sure that the view is set to use the Default configuration, and also select the Show in exploded state option.

FIGURE 15.42

The Drawing View Properties dialog box

Summary

SolidWorks has the capacity to make many different types of views of parts. In addition to the tools for projecting views, custom views saved in the model document can be saved and used on the drawing. The associative nature of the drawing to the model helps ensure that drawing views, regardless of how unusual the section angle or view orientation, are displayed in the correct size, location, and geometry.

It is sometimes better to create some of the views that require sketches by pre-sketching. Make use of workflow enhancements when possible; for example, the Broken-out Section automated workflow works well, but forcing it to be a manual process makes it awkward to use.

Using Annotations and Symbols

Annotations and symbols are a major component of communicating a design through a drawing. SolidWorks has several tools available to help you manage these entities to make engineering drawings look good and communicate effectively.

Using Notes

Notes are the workhorse of SolidWorks annotations. You can use notes in many different configurations and mix them with links to custom properties, hyperlinks, and text wrapping boxes. You can also use them with styles, leaders, symbols, and balloons; and you can even embed balloons into notes.

Setting up a workflow for placing notes

Sometimes users have difficulty working through some of the interfaces in SolidWorks. This is not necessarily the fault of the software, but is often because users may not fully understand how the workflow of a particular feature is designed to function. The Model View interface from the last chapter is one that can be confusing until you have been through it a few times and gain a more intuitive feel for how it works.

Understanding the workflow is paramount to being able to use the software efficiently. I sometimes find myself using the annotations clumsily, and sometimes wind up with blank notes, double notes, or extra lines at the ends of notes. After using the tool a few times, I get back in the groove.

For these reasons, I have added an outline of the workflow here to help you create annotations more efficiently.

Follow these steps to create a note:

1. **Click the Note toolbar button on the Annotations toolbar.**

2. **Click in the graphics window where you want to create the note** *or* **click an entity that you want the note leader to point to, and** *then* **click where you want the note.**

3. **Type the note.** Press Enter at the end of a line, or, if you intend to force the note to wrap later, just allow the line of text to be as long as it wants to be. While you create the note, the text box expands to the right until you press Enter, and it expands down every time a line is added.

   At the end of the last line of the note, *do not* press Enter again (this creates extra lines), but you may press Esc. Esc gets you out of the note and ready to place a new note. When you press Esc twice, you get out of the note you were typing, and then get out of the Note command altogether.

4. **Another way to finish the note is to click the mouse outside of the text box. After that, if you are done, press Esc.** If you want to continue with another note, click again to place it, and start typing. If you want to place the same note as the first one again, the text is already there, so click a second time.

Making use of fonts

SolidWorks can make use of any TrueType fonts that Windows will accept. This includes symbol, non-English, and Wingding fonts. SolidWorks does not use true monofonts like AutoCAD because they do not have width information and thus do not print like fonts with widths. Some AutoCAD monofont look-alike fonts are installed with SolidWorks that do have a very narrow width, and are shaped like some of the monofonts.

In the Customize dialog box (Tools ⇨ Customize), the Fonts toolbar displays as the Formatting toolbar. The Formatting toolbar also appears in the graphics area immediately over your text every time you either insert a new note or edit an existing note, unless the toolbar is already docked somewhere. The Formatting toolbar is shown in Figure 16.1.

FIGURE 16.1

The Formatting toolbar

Using text boxes and wrapping

Text boxes enable you to limit the size, particularly the width, that a note can occupy. This enables notes to wrap in tight spaces on title or revision blocks, as well as other places.

You can size text boxes immediately after placement, even while they are blank; the text then wraps to fit the box width as you type it. The text box expands downward automatically. Blank text boxes can be left on the drawing to provide a placeholder for future text. The blank text box has a rectangular border that contains an X, both of which are removed when you add text. If spaces are added to a text box, the text box becomes invisible, although you can select it if you know where it is. When you move the cursor over the text box, the cursor displays the note symbol.

While typing a note, it is not possible to make the note box smaller using the middle handle on the right end of the box; you can only stretch it larger. Using any corner handle, as shown in Figure 16.2, you can make the box taller, wider, or narrower. The note box will not resize smaller if the text string it contains does not contain spaces.

FIGURE 16.2

Resizing a text box using the lower-right corner handle

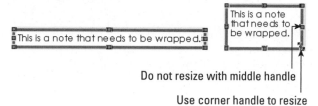

Do not resize with middle handle

Use corner handle to resize

If a custom property value is used to populate a note and you select the Annotation Link Variables option in the Views dialog box, when you activate the text box to resize it, the text value will go away and the link variable will be displayed. This makes it difficult to dynamically resize the box to fit the note, so it might be best to deselect the Annotation Link Variable option before placing and sizing notes.

Using Fit Text in notes

 The Text Format panel of the Note PropertyManager, shown in Figure 16.3, contains the justification buttons for note text, but also has a Fit Text option. When the Fit Text button is depressed, changing the width of the text box changes the width of the individual characters.

FIGURE 16.3

Stretching the characters in note text by using Fit Text

Figure 16.3 shows the Note Property Manager when you are editing text. When you are creating the note, the vertical justification buttons (to the left of the Fit Text tool tip) are not displayed. These are called (from left to right) Top Align, Middle Align, and Bottom Align. They work differently from most vertical justification tools that you find in Microsoft Word or PowerPoint. In Microsoft applications, this feature justifies the text within the text box, but SolidWorks vertical justification justifies the text box on the placement point. So if you click a spot on the drawing sheet and use Bottom Align, the bottom of the text box will go to that point. It winds up working almost backwards from what you might be used to if you use Microsoft applications. Figure 16.4 shows what this justification does. Selecting the Bottom Align option actually makes the text move up, even though the graphic on the icon definitely shows it going down.

FIGURE 16.4

Using the vertical justification options in a note

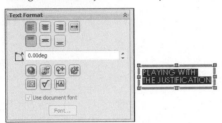
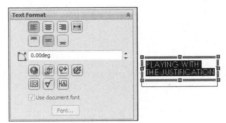

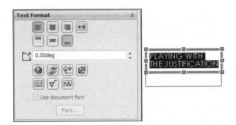

Patterning notes

Starting in SolidWorks 2011, you are now able to pattern notes in linear and circular patterns. Both commands are in the Annotation tool set, but are not on the toolbar by default. To put them on the toolbar, go to Tools ➪ Customize ➪ Commands ➪ Annotations, and drag them from the dialog box to the toolbar area. Figure 16.5 shows the Linear Note Pattern PropertyManager. It looks very similar to the sketch pattern PropertyManager.

Once the note is patterned, you can change individual pattern instances. I have to mention, though, that changing a patterned note does not work the same as changing a regular note. In a regular note, you double-click to activate it and type to replace the note contents. With a patterned note, you have to activate it, click again to deselect the text, press Delete or Back to remove the text, and then type new text.

Circular patterns work similarly to linear patterns, and also work like circular sketch patterns, with the same editing limitations.

FIGURE 16.5

Patterning a note

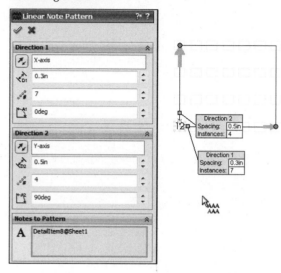

Placing notes and leaders

When you start to place a note, a preview shows the text box with or without a leader depending on the position of the cursor. If the cursor is over a blank section of the drawing, the note is placed without any leader. If the cursor is over a face, edge, or vertex, then a leader is added using the arrow found in the Attachment dialog box at Tools ⇨ Options ⇨ Document Properties ⇨ Arrows ⇨ Attachments. By default, a leader attached to a face uses a dot as an arrow, and a leader attached to an edge, sketch entity, or nothing at all uses a regular arrow. You can change these defaults at the options location mentioned previously, and you can change individual note leaders in the PropertyManager that becomes available when you select a note. These settings can also become part of a custom drafting standard.

Figure 16.6 shows the preview that is displayed by the cursor when you place a note over a face, an edge, and blank space on the drawing.

FIGURE 16.6

Placing a note with a leader

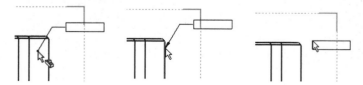

You can also change settings for bent leaders by choosing Tools ⇨ Options ⇨ Document Properties. It is recommended that you use the same bent leader lengths for all annotations, and save them in the templates that you use.

Single-clicking inside an active text box places the cursor between letters, as expected. Double-clicking inside an active text box selects the entire word that you click, again as expected. Ctrl+A selects all the text inside a text box. If you double-click an existing note to activate it, the entire contents are highlighted immediately. You also cannot drag-and-drop selected text to move it within a text box. However, you can Ctrl+C, Ctrl+X, and Ctrl+V the text.

To format the entire note, do not activate the text box; instead, only select the border of the note, and apply the setting to the entire note rather than to selected text within the note.

Adding a leader to a note

To add a leader to a note that was created without a leader, click the note and select the leader options in the Leader panel of the PropertyManager, as shown in Figure 16.7. After you add the leader, you can reposition the handle at the end of the leader to attach it to an entity on the drawing.

FIGURE 16.7

Adding a leader to a note

Using multiple leaders

You can also attach multiple leaders to notes. To create a new note with multiple leaders, pre-select the entities that the leaders are to be attached to, and then click the Note toolbar button.

To add a leader to an existing note, first click the note, and then Ctrl+drag the handle or small dot on the end of a leader to the second location. A note with multiple leaders is shown in Figure 16.8. To remove one of multiple leaders from a note, click the handle at the end of the arrow and press Delete.

FIGURE 16.8

A note with multiple leaders

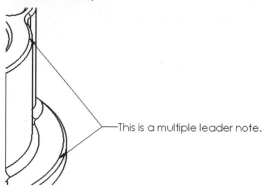

This is a multiple leader note.

Using jogged leaders

Jogged leaders have come a long way since their introduction many releases ago. You can switch a regular leader to a jogged leader by selecting an option in the PropertyManager. In Figure 16.7, the middle icon in the top row is the Jogged Leader icon. The icon to the left simply turns on the default leader, and the icon to the right turns off leaders altogether.

Once you activate the jogged leader option, you can add a jog from the leader right mouse button (RMB) menu. Notice in Figure 16.9 that two options give you control over the jogged leader — Insert New Branch and Add Jog Point.

FIGURE 16.9

Jogging a leader

Adding a jog point

Selecting the Add Jog Point command adds a new handle to the leader that you can move around. You can add multiple jog points to the leader.

Inserting a new branch

The Insert New Branch command enables you to create a new jogged leader that ends in another arrow from the selected point. This arrangement with multiple branches in a jogged leader is shown in Figure 16.10.

The results of adding a new branch to a jogged leader

Multi-branch
Jogged
Leader

Adding styles

For notes, a style can apply a font, an underline, bold formatting, or any other setting from the Formatting (Fonts) toolbar to a note.

To create a note that uses the style setting from another existing note, pre-select the existing note with the style to be copied before starting the Note command; SolidWorks applies the style to the new note.

Caution

Sometimes adding a style to a note can make other changes that you may not expect, such as turning off the leaders if a note has multiple leaders. In particular, if the style is made from a note with a jogged leader, then it turns off leaders for regular multiple leaders. Styles that are created from regular leader notes do not turn off jogged leaders.

Making a change to the leader of a note after you apply the style removes the style from the note, although the formatting remains. This does not apply to adding multiple leaders, only to changing the type of leader.

Applying a style may also remove the ability of the text to wrap, as well as any changes to the text box shape. You cannot move the corner of a text box of a note to which you have applied a style. ■

Styles exist only in the document in which they were created, but they can be shared to other documents by saving the style out as a separate file. Note styles use the extension *.sldnotestl. Once you save the style, you can load it into other documents. The Style panel of the Note PropertyManager interface is shown in Figure 16.11.

FIGURE 16.11

The Style panel of the Note PropertyManager interface

Annotation types that can use styles are

- Note
- Dimension
- Weld Symbol
- Surface Finish
- Datum Feature
- Datum Target
- Balloon
- Auto Balloon
- Stacked Balloon
- Center Mark

Note

Styles before the 2009 release were called Favorites, and some functions still retain the old name. The file type for note favorites was `*.sldnotefvt`. If you run across any of these legacy file types, you will at least know what they are. When loading styles, the Open dialog box will recognize and use both the new file type and the legacy file type. ■

The Style panel contains the following buttons:

  • **Apply Defaults/No Styles.** Removes style settings from the current interface, setting all values back to the defaults.

 • **Add or Update Styles.** Either adds a new style to the database or changes the name or other settings for an existing style.

 • **Delete Style.** Removes a style from the database.

 • **Save Style.** Saves a style to an external file (`*.sldhwfvt`), which can be loaded by other users and added to their databases.

 • **Load Style.** Loads a saved style file.

Styles can be loaded into document templates so that for every document created from the template, those Styles will be available.

Linking notes to custom properties

You can link notes to custom properties. The custom properties can be from the drawing or from the model that is referenced by the drawing. I mention this kind of link briefly in Chapter 20, but discuss it more thoroughly here.

Figure 16.12 shows a note on a drawing with custom property links pulling data from the model shown on the drawing. To add these links, driven by the syntax $PRPSHEET:"material", click the icon indicated in the image to the right in Figure 16.12.

Linking notes to custom properties

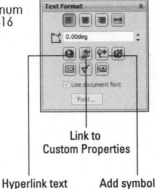

Material: $PRPSHEET:"material"
Part Weight: $PRPSHEET:"weight"

Material: aluminum
Part Weight: 2.616

Link to
Custom Properties

Hyperlink text   Add symbol

In this case, text has been combined with custom properties, but custom properties can also appear alone. To access the Custom Properties interface, choose Tools ➪ Properties.

When you activate the note, you may want to see the syntax, or you may want to see the actual text value of the custom property. You can find the setting that controls which one is displayed by choosing View ➪ Annotation Link Variable.

Hyperlinking text

Hyperlinking text is sometimes useful on drawings to provide a link to reference documentation, specification, test results, and so on. The first button in the third row of the Text Format panel of the Note PropertyManager enables you to add a hyperlink to text in the note. Figure 16.12 shows this panel. Either copy the URL to the hyperlink dialog box that appears or browse to it from the dialog box.

Note that there is a bug in SW (which has been around for years!), including SW2011 SP0 where you cannot un-hyperlink a box. Once you type "http://" into a note, it automatically turns the entire note into a hyperlink. According to the Knowledge Base you are supposed to right-click on the note, and then select the hyperlink button in the FeatureManager, where you can then delete the link and click

OK to remove the link. Unfortunately, this just produces an error. If you want to put a Web address into your drawing note without it turning into a hyperlink, you have to trick Solidworks into not recognizing it as a Web link. I suggest putting a space between the : and the // of the link, which will not be obvious on a printed drawing.

Adding notes and symbols

Notes and symbols are regularly combined in SolidWorks. Symbols are discussed more fully later in this chapter, but are mentioned here because of the frequency with which they are used with notes. In reference to Figure 16.12, the image to the right shows the Text Format panel, which contains a button to the interface where you can add symbols.

Using Blocks in Drawings

Blocks in SolidWorks can contain sketch elements and notes. When used in drawings, blocks have several common uses, including the following:

- You can use standard note blocks for tolerances, disclaimers, or default requirements.
- You can put together a mechanism in 2D where each block represents a part.
- You can use flow direction for fluid systems.
- You can use drawing stamps such as "Not For Release," "Preliminary," "Obsolete," and so on.
- You can use symbols for schematics that can be snapped together.
- You can save drawing formats as blocks to make them easier to place as a single entity.

Like styles, blocks reside in the document in which they are created, but you can save them out to a *.sldblk file, load them into other documents, and save them as a part of a document template.

Inserting blocks

 You can apply blocks in several ways, including by dragging from Windows Explorer and by using the Block menus (Insert ⇨ Annotations ⇨ Block). However, the most efficient way is to access them from the Design Library. Library folders can be established specifically for blocks. Check the setting by choosing Tools ⇨ Options ⇨ File Locations ⇨ Blocks, and redirect this setting to a library area outside of the SolidWorks installation directory. Figure 16.13 shows the Design Library with a folder containing blocks that are selected. The blocks do not show previews in the window, but the tool tip displays large previews. You can drag blocks from the Design Library onto the drawing sheet.

Each block has an insertion point, which snaps to any sketch entity point, even if it is in another block. This makes schematics easy to snap together. If the default insertion point is not the point that you need to snap to the other geometry, then you can place the block anywhere on the drawing and drag the point that needs to snap.

Once blocks are snapped together, to detach them from one another, you can click the point at which they touch; a Coincident sketch relation displays in the PropertyManager. Deleting the sketch relation enables you to drag the block away from the other geometry.

FIGURE 16.13

Blocks in the Design Library

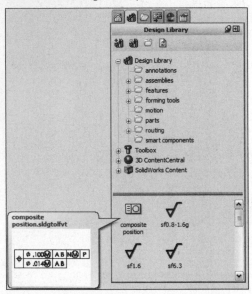

When blocks are inserted, you can control several options in the PropertyManager. This function may be somewhat hidden because it does not appear automatically when you place the block. After you place the block, SolidWorks wants you to place another copy of the block. If you press Esc to cancel out of placing additional blocks, the first placed block is not selected, so the PropertyManager does not display. Figure 16.14 shows the Block PropertyManager.

FIGURE 16.14

The Block PropertyManager

Following is a list of sketch relations linked to the block:

- **Existing Relations.** This panel lists the sketch relations that are linked to the block. These may cause the block to not move properly when you drag it. This feature is most helpful when the block is being used as a representation of a part in a simulated 2D mechanism.

- **Add Relations.** This panel enables you to quickly select sketch relations to apply when placing blocks.

- **Definition.** Blocks can be linked to an external file, which enables all linked instances of a block to be updated at once, even if they are being used in other drawing documents. The path box for the Link to File option only displays if you select the check box.

- The Edit button refers to editing the block. A toolbar button also exists for editing blocks. Clicking the Leader & Insertion Points button enables you to edit both of the controls. You can select the For Construction option to change the entire block to construction entities.

- **Parameters.** The top field with the two circles to the left controls the scale of the block. This number affects the entire block, including the text. You also have the option to scale dimensions, so that the dimension text size (not the dimension value) increases with the overall block scale.

- The Lock Angle option refers to the rotation of the block. If the Lock Angle option is not selected, then you can rotate the block if one point on it is coincident to a stationary object, such as a vertex in a drawing view.

- **Leader.** You will recognize these options from the Notes leaders. The leader is attached to the block where the angled black handle was placed when you created the block. You can edit the leader connection and insertion points by clicking the Leader & Insertion Points button on the Definition panel.

- **Text/Dimension Display.** The Display Dimensions option controls whether or not any notes and dimensions in the block are displayed or hidden.

- **Layer.** You can assign most entities on drawings to layers, which in turn have controls for items, such as line type, color, and visibility.

Creating blocks

 You can create blocks by selecting the sketch and annotation elements and clicking the Make Block toolbar button in the Blocks toolbar, or by accessing the command by choosing Tools ⇨ Block ⇨ Make from the menus.

By default, when you create a block, the Insertion Point panel of the PropertyManager does not expand. If you expand this panel, the blue Origin symbol represents the insertion point that is attached to the cursor during block insertion, as shown in Figure 16.15. The angled line hanging off the left side of the block is the leader attachment point for the block. You can also drag this line around the block and snap it to sketch geometry. By default, this block does not use a leader, but if one is required, then you can select it when you place the block.

Cross-Reference
Sketch blocks are covered in some detail in Chapter 3. This chapter is limited to a discussion of blocks that may be found on drawings rather than those used in model sketches or layouts. ■

FIGURE 16.15

Creating a block

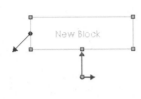

Editing blocks

 Although you do not have many options when creating blocks, many more options become available when you edit them. You can access editing options for a block from four locations:

- The Edit Block toolbar button on the Blocks toolbar
- The Edit button in the Block PropertyManager
- Choosing Tools ➪ Block ➪ Edit from the menus
- From the RMB menu of the block in the Blocks folder in the drawing FeatureManager

The standard edit function gives you access to the sketch and note elements that make up the block.

 - **Add/Remove Entities.** While you are editing the block, the Add/Remove Entities button on the Blocks toolbar becomes available. This enables you to add or remove sketch or note entities from the block definition.

 - **Rebuild.** Rebuild Blocks reapplies sketch relations within the block, without exiting Edit Block mode.

 - **Explode.** Explode is available when you are not editing the block, but when it is selected. Explode returns the contents of that particular instance of the block to the drawing, removing them from the block. This removes any leaders that are attached to the block, as well as sketch relations. This is not technically an edit option, but it certainly does change things.

Using Symbols

SolidWorks symbols are different from symbols that are a part of a font family. SolidWorks symbols fall into several categories, including weld, surface finish, hole, modifying symbols, GD&T (geometric dimensioning and tolerancing), and several flag symbols. You can also construct custom symbols.

Using symbols in notes and dimensions

You can use symbols in notes and dimensions. They also are an intrinsic part of weld symbols and surface finish symbols. Hole Callouts use symbols extensively, as do GD&T frames.

Figure 16.16 shows the Text Format panel from the Note PropertyManager and the Dimension Text panel from the Dimension PropertyManager. Both of these interfaces give you access to the symbol library.

FIGURE 16.16

Accessing symbols and the symbol library

  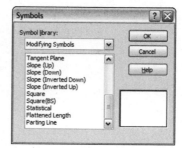

Creating custom symbols

You can create custom symbols in SolidWorks, but creating them may not be as simple as you expect. In the `lang\english` subfolder of the SolidWorks installation directory is a file called `Gtol.sym`. This file stores the representations of all the SolidWorks symbols. It is also where you can create symbols of your own. You can edit the file in Notepad.

Be warned, however. Unless you enjoy writing scripts for the command line, or you are a fan of DOS 5.0, you may not want to create custom symbol projects. The format for creating symbols is simple enough, but it is what you might call somewhat arcane. It is effective at creating line-art symbols that can be used with text and can even be used to contain text. If you are a little inventive with this, you can create interesting shapes that integrate with your notes and dimensions.

Keep in mind that this topic does not appear in the Help files, but all the instructions you need are inside the file itself. You may have to experiment a little to discover what the rules are in terms of making shapes outside of the limits of the 1X1 matrix. It is probably easier to create the geometry using Blocks functionality, but blocks cannot be inserted into text notes as easily as symbols.

Also note, if you modify the gtol.sym file, anyone who uses the drawings you create must also have the same custom gtol.sym file. So if you actually do this and work in a group environment, make sure everyone uses the same file and it is available to others.

Using Center Marks and Centerlines

You can apply center marks either manually or automatically to edges that project as circular in the drawing view. To find the settings that control automatic insertion, choose Tools ⇨ Options ⇨ Document Properties ⇨ Drafting Standard ⇨ Centerlines/Center Marks. The size of the mark at the center and the use of lines extending to the actual circular edge are also controlled on this tab, in the Center Marks section. Figure 16.17 shows some of the options available for center marks.

FIGURE 16.17

Options available for center marks

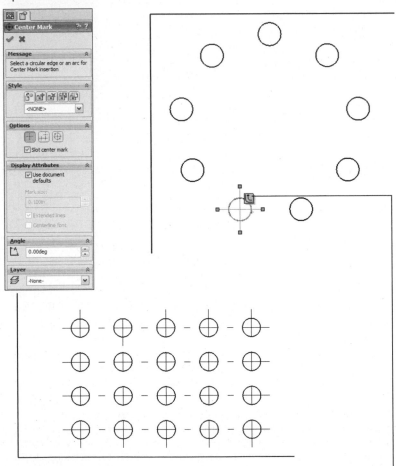

Select symbol to propagate
center mark to pattern

Center marks propagate well to patterns, and you can dimension to them individually. You can rotate center marks in views where they need to be referenced from an edge that is not horizontal. You can also place center marks into layers.

 You can apply centerlines to any geometry that has a temporary axis that is perpendicular to the view. Centerlines can also be placed automatically when you place the part into the drawing. You can create centerlines by selecting a face or a pair of parallel lines or concentric arcs. Centerlines may be displayed improperly on parts that are created by mirroring, as shown in Figure 16.18. This bug was originally printed here in the 2007 version and is still active for 2011 sp0.0.

FIGURE 16.18

Centerlines can display improperly on a mirrored part.

Tutorial: Using Annotations

This tutorial shows you how to use some of the tools that were discussed in this chapter. It does not cover every feature, so you should explore a little on your own and not necessarily follow the instructions exactly. Start here:

1. **From the DVD, open the file named** Chapter 16 - Tutorial.slddrw**. This is a** drawing file with views of the part from Chapter 21, but it does not contain dimensions or annotations.

2. **Click the Center Mark tool on the Annotations toolbar.** (If the button is not there, then choose Tools⇨Customize⇨Commands to place it on the toolbar, along with the Centerline tool.) Click one of the holes in the pattern of three, and click the Propagate symbol to propagate the center marks to all three holes in the pattern. The view should look like Figure 16.19 when you are done.

3. **Activate the Centerline tool to add two centerlines to the right view, in the lower-left area.** Change the view display style to Hidden Lines Visible. Select the cylindrical faces for each feature to place the centerlines. Click the vertical centerline and drag the ends past the edges of the part.

4. **Select the edge that is indicated in Figure 16.20, and initiate a note from the Annotations toolbar.** Type the text shown, all in one line. You can place the degree and diameter symbols from the symbol library, which you can access using the indicated button in the PropertyManager. Both symbols are in the Modifying Symbols library, also shown in Figure 16.20. Drag the lower-right corner of the text box to make the text wrap as shown.

FIGURE 16.19

Center marks and centerlines on a part

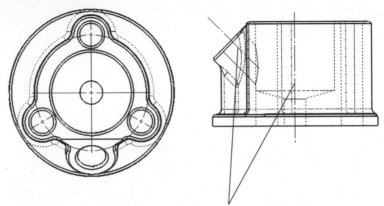

Add centerlines by clicking cylindrical faces

FIGURE 16.20

Placing symbols in an annotation

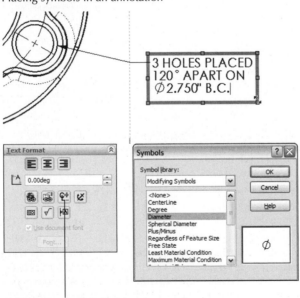

3 HOLES PLACED
120° APART ON
⌀2.750" B.C.

Access the symbol library

5. **Draw an arrow with a text note inside it, as shown in Figure 16.21.** Make the sketch and text into a block by window-selecting all of it and clicking Make Block from the Blocks toolbar, or by choosing Tools ⇨ Block ⇨ Make. Make sure that the end of the arrow is its insertion point. You have to expand the Insertion Point panel in the PropertyManager to access this option. When the block is set up, accept it by clicking the green check mark icon. When the block is created, delete it from the drawing.

FIGURE 16.21

Creating a block

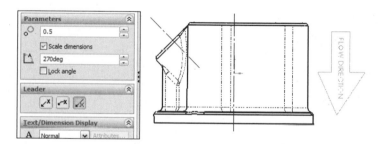

6. **Place the block using the Insert Block function, so that the block is to the right of the right view.** Once you place it, press Esc to cancel the placement of more blocks. Then select the block to activate the PropertyManager. Deselect the Lock Angle option, and set the angle to 270 degrees.

Summary

Annotations and symbols in SolidWorks have many options for connection, creation, and display. Recent releases have brought major improvements to text box–driven annotations. Custom properties and hyperlinks enable the user to populate drawing annotations with content and links to content. Sharing styles in templates is a great idea for readily available note styles.

Blocks have several flexible uses and can be updated from external files across many documents. Their use for simulating mechanisms, piecing together schematics, and annotating drawings, in addition to the Belts functionality discussed in Chapter 3, make blocks one of the most flexible functions available.

Dimensioning and Tolerancing

D imensioning and tolerancing is an art form as much as a science. People become very passionate when discussing the right way to perform these tasks. In truth, the techniques are not so black and white, but are highly dependent on the industry, the means of manufacture, and the purpose of the drawing. Drawings might be used for quotes, manufacturing, inspection, assembly, testing, and so on; and the drawings, as well as the dimensioning and tolerancing used, for each purpose might need to be somewhat different in each circumstance.

While it is important to follow standards and use drawing conventions properly, this is not an argument that I want to reignite here. In this chapter, I will focus on how the available tools work. You will need to decide for yourself how to apply them in each situation. Refer to the *SolidWorks Administration Bible* (Wiley, 2009) for more information on standards and conventions.

Putting Dimensions on Drawings

The debate on how to get the dimensions from the model to the drawing is much like the "tastes great/less filling" debate. Each side of the issue has valid points, and the question is not likely to be resolved any time soon.

At the center of this debate is whether you should place the dimensions that you use to create the model directly on the drawing or whether you should use reference dimensions created on the drawing. In the following sections, I examine each method for its benefits and drawbacks.

Using Insert Model Items

Insert Model Items takes all the dimensions, symbols, annotations, and other elements that are used to create the model and puts them onto the drawing. Because these dimensions come directly from the sketches and features of the model, they are *driving* dimensions. This means that you can double-click and change them from the drawing the same way you can change sketch and feature dimensions, and with the same effect. As a result, changing these dimensions even from the drawing causes the parts and assemblies in which they are used to be changed.

You can insert the model items in several ways: on a per-feature basis, bringing only the items that are appropriate into the current view, or bringing items into all views. Insertion can be further broken down by type of item, and it can become as specific as pattern counts, Hole Wizard items, specific symbol types, and reference geometry types. To use Insert Model Items, you can choose Insert ⇨ Model Items or can access this command from the Annotations toolbar. The Model Items PropertyManager interface is shown in Figure 17.1.

The Model Items PropertyManager interface

Often, the dimensions need to be rearranged to some extent, although SolidWorks does try to arrange them so that they do not overlap. Figure 17.2 shows the result of bringing dimensions into all views for the part. The part is on the DVD in the Chapter 17 materials.

Figure 17.2 contains duplicate dimensions, overlapping dimensions, unnecessarily long leaders, radius dimensions pointing to the wrong side of the arc, and a lot of awkward placement. This is what you can expect from using the automatic functions. At best, these dimensions require rearranging, and at worst, they probably require that you delete and replace some of them or move them to new views where they make more sense.

To move a dimension to another view, you can Shift+drag it from one view to the other (make sure that the dimension is appropriate in the destination view). To copy a dimension, you can Ctrl+drag it. If you cannot place the dimension in the view that you have dragged it to, then the cursor will indicate this with a special cursor symbol.

FIGURE 17.2

The default placement of dimensions into all views

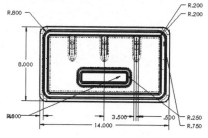
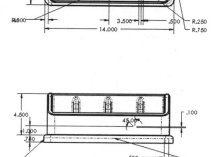
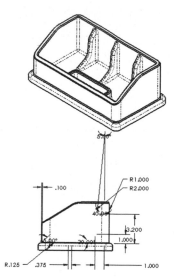

If you approach this task by placing dimensions on a per-feature or per-view basis, it does not change the number of dimensions that you will have to move; it just means that you will insert fewer dimensions several times. Keep in mind that if you choose this method, there is a significant amount of cleanup and checking that you must do. The convenience of having the dimensions put into the views for you and the ability to actually change the model from the drawing are quite useful, but you may not save very much time or effort by doing things this way.

Using reference dimensions

One alternative to automatically inserting all model dimensions is to manually place reference dimensions. You create reference dimensions by using the regular Smart Dimension tool. At first, this appears to be simply re-creating work that you have already done, and this is somewhat true, but there is more to the story.

These dimensions are not duplicates of the model items. In fact, the reference dimensions that you manually place on the drawing are completely different from the dimensions that are used in the model. The dimensions serve completely different purposes in the two settings.

When modeling, I tend to dimension symmetrically, but only on one side, which would not be shown on a manufacturing or inspection drawing. I frequently use workarounds to avoid some special problem that forces a different model dimensioning scheme than I would prefer to use. Often, a feature is located from the midpoint of an edge, which involves no dimensions whatsoever. Sketch entities may have Equal relations, which also leave sketch elements undimensioned. Dimensions may lead to faces or edges that are not in the final model or to faces that are later changed by scale, draft, or fillets.

Beyond that, when draft is involved, as is the case with plastic or cast parts, the dimensions of the sketch that you used to create the feature often have little to do with the geometry that is dimensioned on a print for inspection or mold building. Dimension schemes in models reflect the need for the model to react to change, while dimension schemes in drawings reflect the manufacturing or inspection methods, in order to minimize tolerance stack-up, and to reflect the usage of the actual part.

Although there are strictly technical reasons for dimensioning drawings independently from the way the model was dimensioned, there are other factors such as time, and the neat and orderly placement of dimensions. Time is an issue because by the time you finish rearranging dimensions that were inserted automatically from the model — checking and eliminating duplicates and then manually adding dimensions that were left out or that had to be eliminated because they were inappropriate for some reason, as well as ensuring that all the necessary dimensions are on the drawing — it would have been much quicker to manually dimension the drawing correctly the first time using reference dimensions.

In most cases, inserting model dimensions into the drawing is impractical for manufacturing or inspection drawings unless you have simple plates with machined holes. This is because of the amount of time required to rearrange and check the dimensions, the need to ensure that you have placed the necessary dimensions and taken geometric tolerancing into account, and the simple fact that the dimensioning and sketch relations needed for efficient modeling are usually very different from the dimensioning needed for manufacturing or inspection.

I recommend that you use the manual dimension placement option, which works much in the same way as when dimensions are added to sketches. Dimensions that you place in the drawing in this way are called *driven*, or *reference*, dimensions. In drafting lingo, reference dimensions are usually shown with parentheses around them. In SolidWorks, reference dimensions are simply driven rather than driving dimensions. To find the setting that controls the parentheses around reference dimensions, choose Tools ⇨ Options ⇨ Document Properties ⇨ Dimensions ⇨ Add Parentheses By Default.

Rapid Dimension

Rapid Dimension offers a manipulator wheel that shows the possible locations of a dimension you are trying to place. Rapid Dimension works for dimensions inside drawing views, not on dimensions on the sheet. It enables you to choose from either two or four options, and you can move between the options with the Tab key, making your selection with the Spacebar. You can also left-click on the manipulator to select an option The Rapid Dimension manipulator wheel is shown in Figure 17.3 in the placement of diameter and linear dimensions.

The tool does have some limitations, however. It does not seem to be capable of handling combined aligned dimensions and horizontal and vertical dimensions. For example, if you dimension an angled line, Rapid Dimension would only allow a dimension that is aligned to the angled line. If you dimension between the diagonal corners of a rectangle, it would not allow you to place the diagonal dimension, only the horizontal and vertical dims.

You can disable the Rapid Dimension manipulator and control some of the other dimensioning assistance tools in the Dimension PropertyManager. This might lead to some confusion, because it seems that there are three separate Dimension PropertyManagers. The one I am talking about here is the PropertyManager that appears when the Dimension tool is active in the drawing. You see a different

PropertyManager when the Dimension tool is active in the part, and another one when you select an existing dimension on the drawing.

FIGURE 17.3

Placing dimensions with the Rapid Dimension manipulator wheel

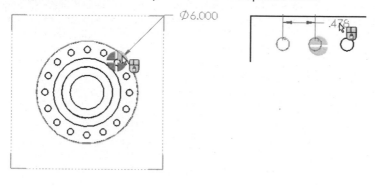
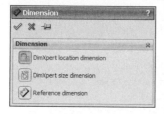

Figure 17.4 shows the Dimension PropertyManager that gives you some control over automatic dimension tools (on the right).

FIGURE 17.4

The Dimension PropertyManager for choosing DimXpert or Reference dimensions

Reference dimensions and the DimXpert

You can apply reference dimensions to the 3D model or to the drawing. In this chapter, I talk mainly about adding them to the 2D drawing, but I do want to take a moment to talk about how reference dimensions *in the model* relate to the DimXpert functionality, which you will find later in this chapter.

Reference dimensions on the solid model

By default, when you go to add new reference dimensions *to a solid model*, you may see some error messages you aren't accustomed to seeing and some odd toolbars. If you are not expecting it, the DimXpert can interfere with reference dimension functionality.

When you activate the Smart Dimension tool in the part environment, a PropertyManager appears, giving you the option to use dimensions to drive the DimXpert (the default) or use it to place reference dimensions. Figure 17.4 shows this Smart Dimension PropertyManager for parts on the left and for drawings on the right.

Reference dimensions on the drawing

I've already made the case for why I think it is better to use reference dimensions on the drawing than model dimensions. This is opinion, of course, and I realize that for many simple parts, you actually *can* model them the way you would detail them, so the model items make more sense in that case. Many respectable power users use model items on drawings. I mostly model complex plastic parts, which are often only annotated with a handful of critical inspection dimensions that you can measure with available instruments.

Using the DimXpert

 The DimXpert is a tool to apply reference (driven) dimensions with tolerances to models and drawings. DimXpert employs feature and topology recognition so it can work on either native data or imported data. Use the DimXpert tab at the top of the part Feature manager, and click the Autodimension Scheme button (the first button on the left) to apply dimensions to the entire model based on selected datums. The goal of DimXpert is to comply with ANSI Y14.41, which deals with 3D annotated models. The general consensus on this is that neither the standard nor the DimXpert tools are up to the rigors of daily production use at this time. The concept seems compelling, but the implementation is not yet practical.

When you use the dimensions and tolerances created with the DimXpert in conjunction with the TolAnalyst, you are able to do simple stack-up analysis. TolAnalyst is outside the scope of this book, because it is part of the Premium package and I confined this book to SolidWorks Standard. A limitation of this system is that you can only apply location or size dimensions; you cannot apply non-dimensional geometric form tolerancing such as parallelism, cylindricity, or flatness. All controls must drive size or location, and have associated dimensions.

When you use the DimXpert on a drawing, it first places a datum at a vertex or centerpoint. After that, it automatically dimensions the entire feature in the view that is the parent of the edge you select. Figure 17.5 shows the Dimension PropertyManager when DimXpert is activated. The image on the right shows a few dimensions applied by the DimXpert, along with the datum used for the dimensions in the view.

You can choose to place the DimXpert dimensions on the drawing when placing the views either through the second page of the Model View PropertyManager or on the Import Options panel (which is closed by default). No, it's not your imagination, this is about as obscure as SolidWorks could possibly make this functionality. Apparently they didn't really expect anyone to use it. Both pages of the Model View (Insert ⇨ Drawing View ⇨ Model, or click Model View from the View Layout tab on the Command Manager) are shown in Figure 17.6. The Import Options panel is shown at the bottom of the second page, although I have cut the second page off about halfway down.

You can find this functionality in one other place: when you drag views from the View Palette in the Task Pane. This interface appears in the image on the right in Figure 17.6.

FIGURE 17.5

Dimension PropertyManager for DimXpert in drawing

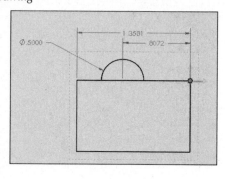

FIGURE 17.6

The setting to import DimXpert annotations is buried well.

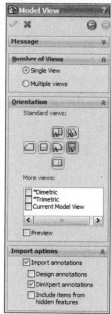
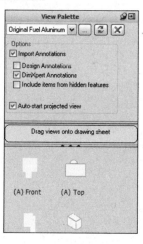

Consensus on this functionality is that it is a work in progress, and while it may offer some interesting functionality, you may not find that it is ready to save you a lot of time when you are dimensioning and tolerancing parts on a drawing. It seems that it has particular difficulty with molded or cast parts, which typically don't have parallel faces.

Annotation views

Annotation views are views in the model in which annotations have been added. You can access annotation views from the Annotations folder in the model FeatureManager. They are created automatically when you add dimensions or notes to the part. You can use the annotation view in the model to show the note or dimension in the view in which it was created or on the drawing to help parse the dimensions into views where they are easily read.

Annotation views can be inserted manually or automatically. You can access the settings for annotation views through the right mouse button (RMB) menu of the Annotations folder of the model, shown in Figure 17.7. The image on the right shows part of the PropertyManager you get when inserting a named view on a drawing. It shows that the Front and Top views of the model have annotations associated with them (indicated by the A on the view symbol).

FIGURE 17.7

The Annotations folder RMB menu and the Model View orientation panel

Driven dimension color

Driven dimensions on the drawing display in gray, and this can be a problem when the drawing is printed out. There are two methods that you can use to deal with this printing problem. The first method is to set the Page Properties of the drawing to force it to print in black and white rather than color or grayscale. To find the Page Properties, choose File ➪ Page Setup. The Page Setup dialog box is shown in Figure 17.8.

The second method is to set the color for driven dimensions to black rather than gray. You find this color setting by choosing Tools ➪ Options ➪ Color ➪ Dimensions Non-Imported (Driven).

FIGURE 17.8

The Page Setup dialog box

Ordinate and baseline dimensions

Ordinate and baseline dimensions are appropriate for collections of linear dimensions when you have a number of items that can all be dimensioned from the same reference. Flat patterns of sheet metal parts often fall into this category. When you apply ordinate dimensions, a zero location is selected first, followed by each entity for which you want a dimension. When dimensions become too tightly packed, SolidWorks automatically jogs the witness lines to space out the dimensions adequately. You can create jogs manually by using the RMB menu. Once you create a set of ordinate dimensions, you can add to the set by selecting Add To Ordinate from the RMB menu.

Baseline dimensions are normal linear dimensions that all come from the same reference and are stacked together at a defined spacing. To find the default settings for baseline dimensions, choose Tools ⇨ Options ⇨ Dimensions ⇨ Offset Distances.

Tip

Baseline dimensions work best either when they are horizontal or when the dimension text is aligned with the dimension line (as is the default situation with the International Organization for Standardization, or ISO, standard dimensioning). Vertical dimensions where the text is horizontal do not usually stack as neatly because the dimension text runs over the dimension line of the adjacent dimensions. Figure 17.9 shows ordinate and baseline dimensions in the same view. ∎

You can access ordinate and baseline dimensions from the Dimensions/Relations toolbar or by right-clicking in a blank space, selecting More Dimensions, and then selecting the type of dimension that you want to use.

Autodimensioning

If the Insert Model Items feature is not likely to produce dimensions that are usable in a manufacturing drawing, then the Autodimension feature is even less likely to do so. However, if you use autodimensioning in a controlled way, in the right situations, it can be a valid way to create selected dimensions. The Autodimension PropertyManager is shown in Figure 17.10. Autodimension is only available in the drawing environment. In the part environment, similar functionality for sketches is part of the Fully Define Sketch tool. To access Autodimension, click the Smart Dimension toolbar icon and click the Autodimension tab in the PropertyManager.

FIGURE 17.9

Ordinate and baseline dimensions in the same view

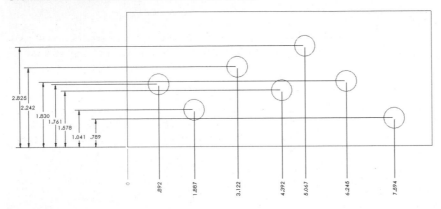

FIGURE 17.10

The Autodimension PropertyManager interface

The Autodimension function can fully dimension the geometry in a drawing view. This is best for ordinate or baseline dimensioning where many dimensions are derived from a common reference, as is often the case with sheet metal parts or a plate with many holes drilled in it. You should limit the use of this option to cases where that type of dimensioning is what you would choose, having the choice of all available types of dimensions — do not allow the software to dictate the dimensioning scheme for your drawing.

Reference sketches

For some types of dimensions, you may need to create additional reference sketch entities. For example, with angle dimensions, it may be desirable to add construction lines to help define the angle. You can add centerlines as separate axis-like entities, as discussed in Chapter 16, but you can also sketch in centerlines manually if needed. This type of sketch is most often attached to the view rather than the drawing sheet.

Tip

Remember that, if necessary, you can create angle dimensions by selecting three points (vertex of the angle first) instead of two lines. When you do this, sketch lines are typically drawn to indicate the vertex of the angle. ∎

Understanding dimension options

The Dimension PropertyManager contains settings, default overrides, tolerances, styles, and several other important settings for use with dimensions. The PropertyManager for driven dimensions is shown in Figure 17.11. I cover styles and tolerances specifically later in this chapter; the other tabs of the Dimension PropertyManager are as follows.

FIGURE 17.11

The Dimension PropertyManager interface

Dimension Text

The Dimension Text panel enables you to add text to the dimension. You can add lines of text both above and below the dimension value itself, and you can also add text before and after the DIM value on the same line. The DIM field is what places the actual value; if this syntax is somehow deleted, you can type it back in and the dimension will still work.

The Dimension Text panel includes some formatting tools, such as justification settings and a setting for the position of the dimension line. The last two rows of buttons include the more commonly used symbols, with access to the complete library, such as any custom symbols that you may have made for the library.

Primary Value Override

The most famous bad habit former AutoCAD users use is overriding dimension values. Apparently due to popular demand, the Primary Value Override is now available in SolidWorks, in the Dimension PropertyManager, as shown in Figure 17.11. This option was added to the software mainly to enable the creation of dimensions with words instead of numbers, as shown in Figure 17.12.

FIGURE 17.12

Using the Override Dimension value

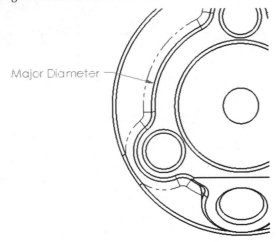

Display Options

You can control the default setting for parentheses around driven (reference) dimensions in the Add Parenthesis By Default dialog box by selecting the choosing Tools ➪ Options ➪ Document Properties ➪ Dimensions ➪ Add Parentheses By Default.

Although you can also control dual dimension defaults in the Options dialog box by choosing Tools ⇨ Options, you can turn them on and off from this interface for individual dimensions. When you enable the Dual Dimension option, SolidWorks uses the settings from the Tools ⇨ Options menu.

Note

The Display Options now appear on the RMB menu. The options shown in Figure 17.11 are different depending on what type of dimension you have selected. In the images in this chapter, a diameter dimension was used. ■

The foreshortened radius is only valid for individual radial dimensions. A foreshortened radius is shown in Figure 17.13. Foreshortened radius dimensions are typically used for large radii when dimensions to the centerpoint are not important. The Foreshortened radius function does not work on diameter dimensions. The inspection dimension is shown in Figure 17.13 with an oval around the dimension.

You cannot foreshorten a diameter; however, you can dimension a diameter and then hide the extension line and dimension line in one direction. This option is found by right-clicking on both the extension line and dimension line, and there is an option in the RMB menu for hide extension line and hide dimension line. This is useful if you have a diameter dimension in a detail view where the opposite side of the diameter is outside the detail view. This can also be used for linear dimensions that terminate to a known end outside the drawing view.

FIGURE 17.13

Λ foreshortened radius

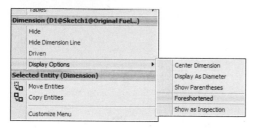

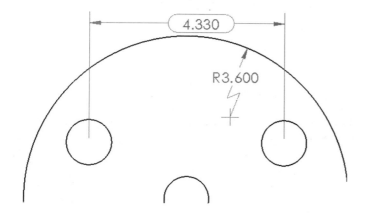

Witness/Leader Display

This panel enables you to set the arrows and dimension lines to be placed inside the witness lines. You can perform this function more easily by using the handles on the arrowheads. From this panel, you can also change the display type of individual arrowheads.

Break Lines

When you select the Use document gap option in this panel, the witness, or extension, lines of the selected dimension are broken by other crossing dimension lines, witness lines, or arrows. This is shown in Figure 17.14.

FIGURE 17.14

Broken witness lines

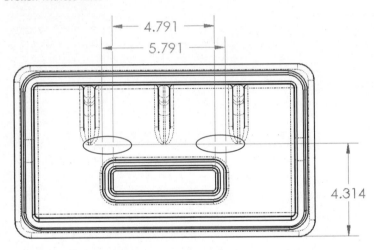

Cross-Reference

Layers are discussed in detail in Chapter 18. ∎

Formatting dimensions with the Dimension Palette

When you select a dimension on a drawing (the dimension can be a model item or a reference dimension), a small symbol appears above and to the right of the dimension. If you click the symbol, the Dimension Palette expands. The Dimension Palette enables you to:

- Add tolerances
- Specify dimension precision

- Assign styles (favorites)
- Apply parentheses
- Center the dimension between the witness lines
- Apply inspection dimension
- Offset the text with a leader
- Establish horizontal and vertical justification
- Add text on top, before, after, and below the dimension value

The Dimension Palette appears when you select a dimension and disappears when you move the cursor away from it. The Dimension PropertyManager still appears, but the Dimension Palette pops up right next to the dimension, making it very easy to use. Figure 17.15 shows the Dimension Palette.

Adding text and tolerances to dimensions using the Dimension Palette

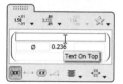

The Dimension Palette seems to be the most convenient place to make these alterations to the basic dimension itself.

Adding Tolerances

You can add dimension tolerances in the Dimension PropertyManager, which you can activate by selecting the dimension that you want to modify. Available tolerance types include:

- Basic
- Bilateral
- Limit
- Symmetric
- MIN
- MAX
- Fit
- Fit with tolerance
- Fit (tolerance only)

Note

You can also add tolerances to dimensions in models; the tolerance is brought in with the dimension if you use the Insert Model Items feature. ∎

Refer to the Tolerance/Precision panel shown in Figure 17.11. The appropriate number entry fields are activated when you assign the corresponding tolerance type to the dimension. The tolerance types that are available in SolidWorks are shown in Figure 17.16.

FIGURE 17.16

The available tolerance types in SolidWorks

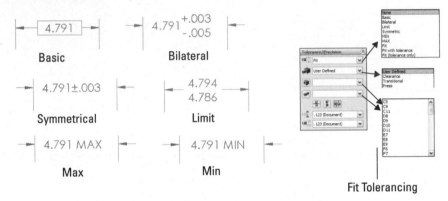

Fit Tolerancing

Changing precision values

In SolidWorks, *precision* means the number of decimal places with which dimensions are displayed. Typically, SolidWorks works to eight places with meters as the default units. You can create templates that use up to eight places as the default setting, and then change the number of places for individual dimensions as necessary. The first of the two boxes under Precision is used for the dimension precision, and the second is used for tolerance precision.

You can change Precision values for individual dimensions in the PropertyManager for the dimension as well as the entire document by choosing Tools ⇨ Options ⇨ Document Properties ⇨ Units.

Using Geometric Tolerancing symbols

The full range of Geometric Tolerancing symbols is available for control frames, datums, datum targets, and so on. You can use the Geometric Tolerance dialog box to build control frames. This dialog box is shown in Figure 17.17. For commonly used Geometric Tolerance symbols, you may want to create and use styles.

FIGURE 17.17

The Geometric Tolerance settings

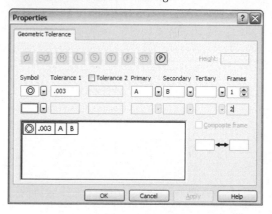

Using Dimension Styles

You can use dimension styles to apply many items to dimensions. Styles were formerly known as *favorites* in SolidWorks. Unlike notes, this is not limited to fonts and formatting. Some of the most common uses of dimension styles are

- To add standard tolerances to dimensions
- To set precision values for dimensions
- To add text, such as TYP, to a dimension
- To add a commonly used GD&T (geometric dimensioning and tolerancing) reference

You can save styles from one document and load them into another document, even between document types. For example, you can load part dimension styles into a drawing.

When a style is updated from an external file, any document that it is linked to also updates. In addition, you can break links to external styles (with the appropriate button on the Styles panel). Otherwise, dimension styles have very similar functions to the other types of styles; the functions of all the buttons on the Styles panel are the same.

Aligning Dimensions and Annotations

When you place dimensions and annotations on a drawing, it is nice to have them lined up in an orderly way. Drawings contain a lot of information, and that information needs to be easy to read. Keeping items lined up in horizontal and vertical alignment is one of the keys to making the information on a drawing easily accessible.

SolidWorks has a toolbar just for the alignment of dimensions and annotations. The toolbar is shown with labels for individual icons in Figure 17.18. To add the Align toolbar to the CommandManager, right-click one of the CommandManager tabs, and select Customize CommandManager. Then click the new tab that appears and select the Align toolbar from the list.

FIGURE 17.18

Using the tools from the Align toolbar

Using the alignment tools

The alignment tools are all pre-select tools, and so it is best to box-select (or Ctrl+select) the dimensions and annotations you want to align first, and then click the toolbar icon. For example, to align a set of balloons to the right, you would drag a box around the balloons, Ctrl+select any balloons you could not select with the box, and then click the Align Right button. These tools work best with larger selections of dimensions or annotations. For aligning individual dimensions or pairs of dimensions, it might be better to use the drag methods discussed in the section "Inferencing alignment and grid snapping."

Using the alignment tools Align Collinear/Radial and Align Parallel/Concentric creates persistent relationships, so those dimensions aligned with the tools will maintain that alignment. The other tools on the Align toolbar do not work this way. To break an alignment created by these tools, select Break Alignment from the RMB menu.

Using the Group tool allows a set of dimensions and annotations within a single view to maintain the spatial relationships for dimensions that were not aligned with the alignment tools, until they are ungrouped.

Inferencing alignment and grid snapping

When you drag individual dimensions on a drawing, they are snapping to a grid. (Annotations do not snap to the grid.) This is one way that SolidWorks helps you to align them. If you drag one dimension level with another, either horizontally or vertically, a line appears and the dimension inferences the position of the other dimension, just like lines snapping in model sketches.

Annotations will inference other annotations, but they won't inference dimensions, and they won't snap to the grid.

If you want to disable both kinds of snap (grid and inference) on the fly, just hold down the Alt key while dragging, and the dimension or annotation will slide freely. To permanently disable the snapping, go to Tools ➪ Options ➪ Drawings ➪ Disable Note/Dimension Inference. To disable the snap, make sure this option is selected. You should be aware that this option controls both the snap to the grid and the inferencing of one dimension or annotation to another. You cannot separate the grid from the inferencing.

If you like the snaps and want to change the spacing, you can do that by selecting Tools ⇨ Options ⇨ Document Properties ⇨ Dimensions ⇨ Offset Distances and changing the appropriate numbers for the distance of the dimension from the edge of the part and the distance between dimensions.

If you are used to older versions of SolidWorks, you will remember that the snapping used to depend on where you selected the dimension — from the top, middle, or bottom — and it would line up with other dimensions using the same references. Newer versions of SolidWorks are more simplified, and I think they work better.

If you want a group of dimensions or annotations that you have aligned to maintain their current alignment, box-select them and use the Group function from the Align toolbar. All of the selected dimensions and annotations must belong to the same view.

Using Dimension Palette alignment options

The Dimension Palette, mentioned earlier in this chapter, enables you to surround a dimension with all of the necessary information, such as additional text, tolerances, symbols, justification, leader control, dual dimension display, and other useful information. It can also perform some alignment functions. If you multi-select dimensions, and activate the Dimension Palette, you see what is shown in Figure 17.19. In this case, the Dimension Palette is used to apply the Align Stagger function to a set of vertical dimensions to pack them in close to one another. This function is not found on the Align toolbar. However, notice that it also has some of the Align toolbar functionality, including bottom, top, left, and right justification. The functions have different names and symbols in the Dimension Palette than in the Align toolbar, but they appear to do the same thing.

FIGURE 17.19

Selecting alignment options from the Dimension Palette

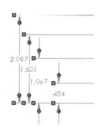

The Dimension Palette is one of my favorite tools in SolidWorks drawings because it consolidates a lot of functionality into a small space that is available right where you need it. When it was originally released, many users thought that it got in the way, but the small activation icon solved that problem, and the functionality has only improved.

Arranging dimensions automatically

Every few releases, SolidWorks improves the automatic dimension-arranging tools. But to me, they have a long way to go before I will trust them to arrange dimensions on a large drawing, where they would offer the most benefit. Sometimes they do a good job on simple rectangular parts, but they don't save much time on the complex parts.

When you put Model Items onto a drawing, SolidWorks automatically arranges the dimensions. The alignment option on the left side of the Dimension Palette is called Auto Arrange Dimensions. Also, when you use the Autodimension function mentioned earlier in this chapter, SolidWorks automatically arranges the dimensions for you.

The best auto-arrange functionality probably comes with balloons. The Auto Balloon functionality is shown in Figure 17.20. Balloons are part of assembly drawings, and as such, they are covered in more detail in the *SolidWorks 2011 Assemblies Bible* (Wiley, 2011).

FIGURE 17.20

Using options for automatic ballooning in an assembly drawing

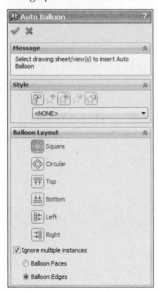

The best way to use these tools with dimensions and general annotations is probably in small, controlled situations until you learn how they react to the type of work you tend to do frequently. Selecting items in groups that are close to where they need to go may help the automatic tools do a better job.

Tutorial: Working with Dimensions and Tolerances

In this tutorial, you can use a single part in several different ways to demonstrate different dimensioning and tolerance functions. Follow these steps to learn more about these topics:

1. **Open the part from the DVD called** Chapter 17 Tutorial.sldprt.

2. **Open the drawing from the DVD called** Chapter 17 Drawing.slddrw.

3. **Tile the windows by choosing Window ⇨ Tile Vertically, and drag the part from the top level of the FeatureManager into the drawing window.** This automatically populates the four drawing views.

4. **Delete the Top view, leaving the views as shown in Figure 17.21.**

FIGURE 17.21

The drawing after Step 4

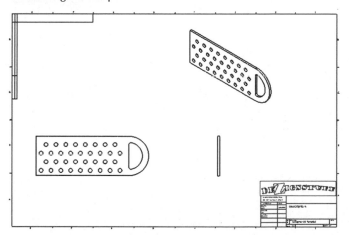

5. **Choose Insert ⇨ Model Items, and ensure that the Select All option is selected for Annotations and the Marked for drawing option is selected for Dimensions.** Also make sure that the Source/Destination drop-down list is set to Entire Model. Click the green check mark icon and watch the drawing populate.

6. **The resultant drawing is quite cluttered.** Delete and move dimensions so that the drawing looks like Figure 17.22.

FIGURE 17.22

The drawing after dimensions have been deleted and moved

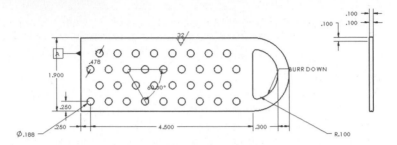

7. **Shift+drag the surface finish symbol to the Right view, and do the same with the 1.900-inch dimension.** You may have to first Shift+drag it into the other view, and then drag it again to correctly attach or position it.

8. **Create a set of horizontal ordinate dimensions from the left end of the part, and dimension the X position of each column of holes.** Do the same for rows of holes, using the bottom edge of the Front view as the zero reference. Remember that you can create ordinate dimensions by starting a normal Smart Dimension, right-clicking to display the More Dimensions list, and then selecting your choice.

9. **If necessary, add center marks and centerlines to the view for clarity.**

10. **Select the.188 diameter dimension, and in the Dimension Text box, type** TYP **after the <DIM> text, and add a bilateral tolerance of +.003, –.005.** Save this as a style by clicking the Add Style icon.

11. **Apply the newly created dimension style to the R.100 dimension.** The results up to this step are shown in Figure 17.23.

FIGURE 17.23

Dimensions and tolerances after Step 11

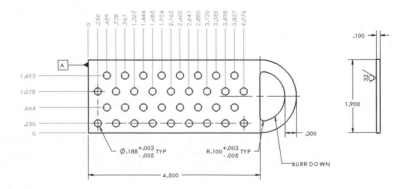

12. **Make one of the dimension leaders for either the .188 or the R.100 dimensions cross the extension lines of the 4.500 dimension.** Then select the 4.500 dimension, and in its PropertyManager select the Use Document Gap option in the Break Lines panel, on the Leaders tab.

13. **Place a B datum marker on the circumference of the smaller arc on the left end of the part.** Create a Geometric Tolerance control frame, as shown in Figure 17.24.

FIGURE 17.24

Creating a Geometric Tolerance control frame

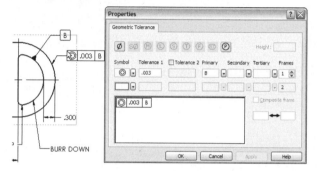

14. **In the Right view that shows the thickness, select the .100 dimension, and add a tolerance and a note below the text using the Dimension Palette, as shown in Figure 17.25.**

FIGURE 17.25

Using the Dimension Palette

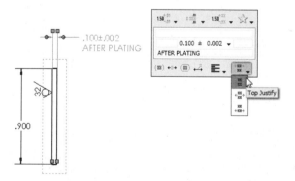

15. **Delete the last two dimensions of the horizontal ordinate group (3.837 and 4.076).** Start a new Detail view that includes the holes those dimensions called out, as shown in Figure 17.26. Place the detail view above the main view.

16. **Right-click the zero for the horizontal ordinates and select Add To Ordinate.** Place the two ordinate dimensions in the detail view.

17. **Use the Geometric Tolerance tool to make a Flatness call out of .002.** Add a leader to the control using the PropertyManager, and attach the leader to the .100 thickness dimension in the Right view.

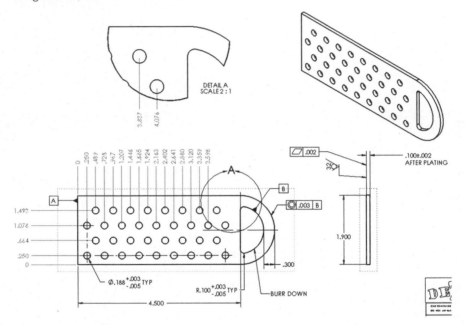

FIGURE 17.26

Adding more dimensions and annotations

Summary

The argument about how to set up and use dimensions on drawings is as old as the process of creating geometrical plans from which objects are built. It is often difficult to separate fact and best practice from opinion. Although I leave it up to you to decide these issues for yourself, this chapter is intended to help you understand how to create the type of drawing that you want.

The biggest conflict in this subject arises over whether to place live model dimensions on the drawing or to allow the requirements of the drawing to specify which dimensions are placed where. I am by no means impartial when it comes to this question, but again, you must make the choice for yourself.

Using Layers, Line Fonts, and Colors

AutoCAD has left its mark on CAD users of all kinds in the form of the default expectations users have about CAD software. A few common expectations are that layers, the Command Line, and paper space/model space need to exist in order for graphical software to be considered CAD, and printing should be really difficult.

When former AutoCAD users make the switch to SolidWorks, the questions start: Where is the Command Line? How do I put parts on layers? How do I change the background color to black? And my personal favorite, Where is the zero-radius trim?

This chapter addresses AutoCAD-like functions in the SolidWorks drawing environment. The goal is not to make the functions look or work or compare in any way to AutoCAD, but to simply make them useful in the context of the SolidWorks software. It is never productive to try to use SolidWorks as if it were AutoCAD. If you are making the transition, you will be much further ahead if you just embrace SolidWorks for what it is, and accept that it does not work like AutoCAD. You will be even further ahead if you do not assume that AutoCAD functionality is universal.

Controlling Layers

Layers are only available in SolidWorks drawing documents, not in 3D modeling or even sketching at all. Even in drawings, layers do not see a lot of use. This is not to say that they serve no purpose, just that the software does not depend on them.

Working with layers in imported 2D data

When you import data through DXF (Data eXchange Format) or DWG format files, the layers that exist in the original data are brought forward into SolidWorks, and you can use them in a similar way to the original AutoCAD usage. For example, you can turn layers on or off (visible or hidden), and you can change layer names, descriptions, color, line thickness, and line style.

The way you intend to use the imported data determines how you should open the file. If you only intend to view and print the drawing, then I would suggest using DraftSight, a free download from the Dassault Systèmes or SolidWorks Web sites, or the DWG Editor, which is installed with SolidWorks and enables you to do much of what you can do with basic AutoCAD. These tools offer a familiar interface for the AutoCAD user.

If you need to integrate data from the imported document into a native SolidWorks drawing, you can open the DWG file from the normal Open dialog box in SolidWorks.

Tip

If you want to make a 3D part from the 2D data in the DWG file, you may want to import the drawing into the part sketch environment. This usually leads to some speed issues. If you prefer, sketch entities can also be copied from the drawing to the model sketch. You can even copy entities from DWG Editor to the SolidWorks sketch. The sketch needs to be open in order to paste the sketch entities. In the case where imported 2D data is brought into the model sketch, you lose all the layer information because part and assembly documents do not allow layers. ■

The colors assigned to layers in data coming from AutoCAD are often based on a black background, and so they can be difficult to see on a white background. The two ways of dealing with this are to change the SolidWorks drawing sheet color to something dark or to change the individual layer colors to something dark. Either method is easy, although if you have to send the 2D data back to its source, it may be best to temporarily change the drawing sheet color.

Figure 18.1 shows the layer interface with an imported drawing in the background. To open the Layers dialog box, click the Layer Properties button, which is found on both the Layer and Line Format toolbars.

FIGURE 18.1

The Layers dialog box and the Layer toolbar

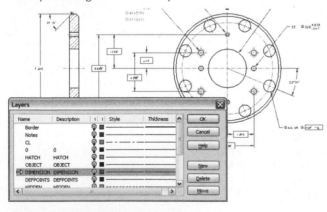

Be aware that many items in an imported drawing may come into SolidWorks as blocks. These items may need to be exploded before you can work with them. This is often the case with the drawing border, title block, or format. To explode a block, right-click on the block and choose Explode.

Working with layers on the sheet format

One of the most obvious uses of layers is for the drawing border sketch lines on the sheet format. The sketch lines used to create the border often have a heavier line weight and a different color that easily distinguishes them from model geometry.

You can assign layers in one of three ways:

- Select existing items, and then select a layer from the drop-down list on the Layer toolbar.
- Set the active layer and create new items.
- While creating items such as sketch entities and annotations, select the layer for the new entity directly from the PropertyManager.

To set a layer to the active layer, double-click it from the Layers dialog box, as shown in Figure 18.1, or change it from the drop-down list on the Layer toolbar. When you assign an active layer, other newly created entities are also placed on the layer, not just sketch entities. Symbols, annotations, blocks, and other elements can also be put onto layers. If you are not particular about the layering scheme on a drawing, then it may be advisable to set the active layer to None, which is a valid option in the Layer toolbar drop-down list.

When you create a new layer in SolidWorks, the new layer becomes the active layer, and any new items that are added are automatically placed on that layer.

Another option when building a sheet format, or any other drawing function that requires sketching, is to use a special layer for construction geometry. This enables you to hide the layer when it is not being used, but it still maintains its relations. Hidden layers can be used in several other ways (for example, as standard notes on the drawing), and they can be easily turned on or off.

Adding dimensions and notes to layers

SolidWorks drawings have a tendency to be drab black-and-white drawings in contrast to AutoCAD drawings, which often seem to take on a plethora of contrasting colors. Drawings are often a little easier to comprehend when different types of items are colored differently, but to do this effectively, you must apply the coloring scheme consistently. Dimensions and annotations can also be placed on layers in the three ways described in the previous section (active layer, from the PropertyManager during creation, and through the drop-down list on the Layer toolbar). However, the line styles do not affect dimensions and notes, only the color and visibility settings.

Working with components on layers

Assembly drawings probably suffer the most from the monochromatic nature of most SolidWorks drawings because individual components can be difficult to identify when everything is the same color. This is why SolidWorks users typically color parts in the shaded model assembly window. It only makes sense that they would want to do the same thing on the drawing.

Using assembly colors on drawings

Starting in SolidWorks 2011, you can now use assembly part colors on drawings. This is a document-specific setting, so it will only apply to the documents where you want it to apply, not to all drawings. If you use this setting, you may also need to be more careful in how you choose part colors in your assemblies. You will generally want to choose darker and more saturated colors, and avoid the yellows, grays, and light colors that will not contrast with the white or gray color of the default SolidWorks drawing sheet.

You can find the setting to use assembly part color on your drawing at Tools ⇨ Options ⇨ Document Properties ⇨ Detailing ⇨ Use Model Color for HLR/HLV in Drawings. HLR stands for *hidden lines removed*, and HLV stands for *hidden lines visible*. These are the two wireframe display modes that are most frequently used on drawings. Of course, another way to display part color on drawings is to use shaded views, but for traditional drawings, shaded views are often considered nonstandard. Figure 18.2 shows the setting in the Document Properties dialog box.

FIGURE 18.2

Using assembly part colors on your drawing

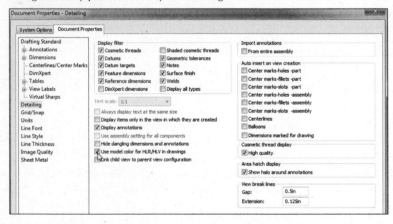

The setting mentioned for shaded drawing views is available by selecting the view on the drawing, and clicking the Shaded display style toolbar icon from the Heads Up View toolbar on the drawing, or from wherever the View toolbar is displayed. You could do the same thing by selecting the view and then choosing View ⇨ Display ⇨ Shaded or Shaded With Edges.

Using assembly parts on layers

Another option to display the components of an assembly in different colors while using a wireframe display mode that wouldn't rely on colors assigned to parts in the assembly is to use the Component Line Font options. (Line Fonts are covered in the section "Controlling Line Format.") The Component Line Font dialog box contains a Layer setting, which you can use to put a part on a layer. If the layer is set up with a color, then the part displays with that color in all views of the drawing or in just the current view, depending on your settings. It does take a little time to set up the individual layers for each part and then to set the parts to the layers.

You can access the Component Line Font dialog box by right-clicking a component in a drawing view. The Component Line Font dialog box is shown in Figure 18.3.

FIGURE 18.3

The Component Line Font dialog box

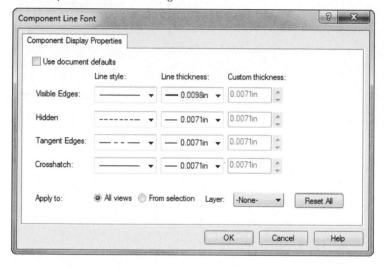

In normal use, the Use document defaults option is selected and all the settings in the dialog box are grayed out. To gain access to these settings, you must deselect the Use document defaults option, as shown in Figure 18.3.

Controlling Line Format

The Line Format toolbar contains the Layer tool and four additional tools that control lines: Line Color, Line Thickness, Line Style, and Color Display Mode. These settings can be controlled separately from layers; therefore, they can be used in model sketches as well as on drawings. In the model, the line font can only be displayed for inactive sketches. Any sketch that is both closed and shown can be displayed with the Line Format settings.

Cross-Reference

For more information on using line styles in the model, see Chapter 6. ■

Figure 18.4 shows the Line Format toolbar along with the interfaces for Line Color, Line Thickness, and Line Style.

FIGURE 18.4

The Line Format toolbar and related interface options

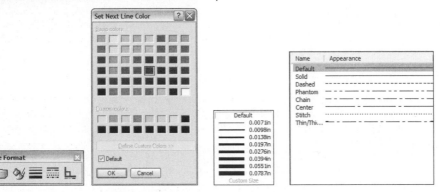

Note

The term line font refers to a combination of style, end cap, and thickness. To set line fonts, choose Tools ⇨ Options ⇨ Document Properties ⇨ Line Font and use the document-specific settings. ■

Using the Line Format settings

You can specify the Line Format settings using two different methods. In the first method, you can set them with nothing selected, in which case they function like System Options (the new setting takes effect for all documents that are opened on the current computer). In the second method, if they are set with sketch entities or edges selected, then the settings apply only to the selected entities.

Caution

If you change these settings with nothing selected, then the Line Format settings for color, thickness, and style function as system options. ■

Setting the End Cap Style

Another option for the Line Font settings is the End Cap Style. This offers an important option, especially for thick lines. The three options are flat, round, and square. Of these, the square style is usually most appropriate. In the past, flat was the default style. To find this setting, choose Tools ⇨ Options ⇨ Document Properties ⇨ Line Font. You may want to change this setting and update your drawing template files.

Figure 18.5 shows the difference between the three options of End Cap Style.

FIGURE 18.5

The End Cap Style setting options

Notice the small notches at the sharp corners of the style to the left, which is the flat style. These can be very distracting on a drawing, and in my opinion they don't look very professional. This notched effect is most pronounced on thicker lines.

Setting the line thickness

The Line Thickness settings are Default, Custom, and eight width settings. Interestingly, the different thicknesses are named in the interface where you set the actual thicknesses, but not in the interface where you set lines to thicknesses. Figure 18.6 shows the Line Thickness page (Tools ➪ Options ➪ Document Properties ➪ Line Thickness).

FIGURE 18.6

The Line Thickness settings in Tools ➪ Options

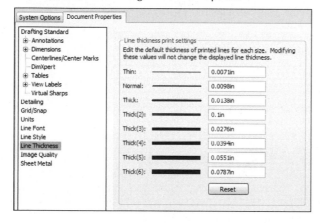

The way the line thickness is shown in the drawing does not have anything to do with the numerical width that is assigned to it. For example, in Figure 18.6, notice that Thick(2) is set to 0.1 inch, which is much wider than Thick(3), which, in this case, is set to 0.0275 inch. Changing the numbers only affects printed line thickness; it does not affect the display at all.

Caution

The Line Thickness settings are document options, not system options. As a result, two drawings with the same line type assignments may have different numerical widths; thus, the two drawings would print differently on the same computer. This can be a benefit or a trap, so pay attention when you change the settings. ■

Setting the line style

You can create custom line styles using the syntax shown on the Line Style page (Tools ⇨ Options ⇨ Document Properties ⇨ Line Style). This is a document-specific setting; therefore, if you make a custom line style and want to use it in another document, you have to save it out (as a `*.sldlin` file) and load it into the other document. Also, if you save your templates with this line style loaded, then you will not have to load the styles for any document made from that template.

Changing the Color Display mode

 Color Display mode toggles between the display of assigned colors and standard sketch state colors. This is primarily used in drawings when you are making sketches where sketch relations are important. This setting is used to control the display of sketch entities only.

Hiding and Showing Edges

 Sometimes, for illustrative purposes, it is desirable to hide certain edges in drawing views. The Hide/Show Edge toolbar button is on the Line Format toolbar, although it may not be on the toolbar by default. You can choose Tools ⇨ Customize to put it on a toolbar.

To use the Hide Edge tool, simply select the edges that you would like to hide, and click the Hide Edge toolbar button. To show the edges, click the Show Edge toolbar button; the cursor will now be able to select the hidden edges.

Be aware that if your view is in Draft Mode, edges that you hide will still be shown until the view is made into a High Quality view.

Note

Hide/Show Edges was formerly two separate toolbar buttons. In SolidWorks 2010, they became a single button. ■

Tutorial: Using Drawing Display Tools

Some of the functions described in this chapter are difficult to understand until you actually use them. This tutorial guides you through the functions step by step so that you can see them in action. Start here:

1. **From the DVD, open the drawing called** Chapter 18 – Tutorial.slddrw. **Make sure that the Layer and Line Format toolbars are active and that the Hide/Show Edges buttons are available on the Line Format toolbar.**

2. **Right-click a blank space and select Edit Sheet Format from the menu.**

3. **Window+select everything on the format and use the drop-down list on the Layers toolbar to assign the selection to the Border layer.** Notice that this changes the color and the thickness of the sketch lines.

4. **Right-click a blank space and select Edit Sheet.**

5. **Click the Layer Properties button on either the Layer or Line Format toolbar.** Add new layers for each of the part groups, bracket, clevis, pins, and blocks, assigning different colors to each layer. Figure 18.7 shows the Layers dialog box with these layers created.

The Layers dialog box

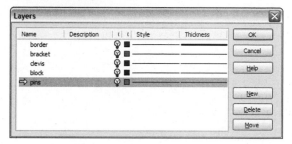

Caution

Be aware that creating new layers leaves the last layer that you created active, as indicated by the yellow arrow in Figure 18.6. There is no way to set the active layer to None from the Layers dialog box; you have to do this using the drop-down list in the Layer toolbar. ■

6. **Set the active layer to None in the Layer toolbar drop-down list.**

7. **Right-click the Bracket part in one of the views and select Component Line Font.** Deselect the Use Document Defaults option, and select the Bracket layer from the drop-down list in the lower-right corner of the dialog box, as shown in Figure 18.8. Make sure that the Drawing View option is set to All views.

The Component Line Font dialog box

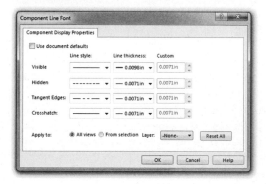

8. **Repeat Step 7 for all the components, assigning each component to its own layer.** Notice how this makes the parts easier to identify.

Note

Alternatively, you could simply change the line style and thickness for each component. This saves you creating the layers, but you lose the color settings. The way SolidWorks handles line thickness and thickness values has changed significantly in SolidWorks 2010. The line thickness assignments in the Print dialog are still the old format. ■

9. **Open the Component Line Font dialog box for the Bracket part again.** This time, set the Line thickness to 0.0787, and click OK. You may have to rebuild the drawing to show the change (Ctrl+B or Ctrl+Q). Figure 18.9 shows a detail of the corners that are created by the thick lines. Notice the notches created at the corners.

FIGURE 18.9

Applying thick edges

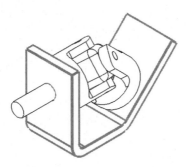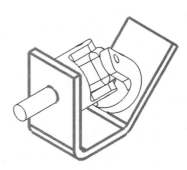

10. **These notches are supposed to be fixed using the End Cap setting at Tools ⇨ Options ⇨ Document Properties ⇨ Line Font.** Set the End Cap Style to Square. Click OK to exit the Document Properties. In the drawing, select inside the view where you are working and make sure that it is set to High Quality. (The setting is found in the PropertyManager for the view in the Display Style panel. If it is already set to High Quality, then there will be no other view option; if it is not, then there will be an option that is set to Draft Quality.)

   The image to the left in Figure 18.8 is the old setting with the draft-quality view, and the image to the right is the new setting with the high-quality view.

11. **In the Component Line Font dialog box, set the Line Weight setting back to Default for the Bracket part, but keep it on the Bracket layer.**

12. **In the isometric view, Ctrl+click all the tangent edges on the Bracket part, as shown in Figure 18.10.** Click the Hide/Show Edges toolbar button on the Line Format toolbar.

FIGURE 18.10

Hiding edges

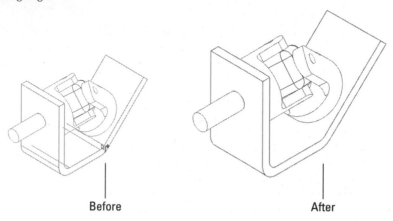

Before   After

13. **Click the Hide/Show Edges toolbar button.** The PropertyManager message changes to indicate that you can now select hidden edges, and the hidden edges are shown. Ctrl+select the hidden edges and right-click when you are done.

Summary

While SolidWorks is not primarily built around the strength of its 2D drawing functionality, it offers more capabilities than most users take advantage of. Layers, colors, and line styles can make your drawings clearer and easier to read.

Part IV

Using Advanced Techniques

Modeling Multi-Bodies

SolidWorks allows multiple solid bodies within a single part at the same time. There are many uses for this type of functionality, but it can also sometimes cause problems that you need to be aware of. This chapter aims to help you take advantage of the benefits of multiple bodies while avoiding some of the potential traps.

You could work with SolidWorks in such a way that you would never need to use multiple bodies inside a single part, ever. Almost everything that average users normally do can be done with a single solid body and without any knowledge of multi-body functionality whatsoever.

However, to access some more powerful functionality, and options that offer more flexibility, multi-body modeling is necessary. In fact, if you want to move on to surface modeling, multi-body knowledge is mandatory because in surface modeling, multi-body is the default.

Multi-body modeling is the gateway from basic solid modeling mainly described in the book up until now into the more advanced functionality that follows. The gateway can lead in two directions: it can lead to more power, more flexibility, more options, more advanced functionality, or it can lead to sloppy, bad habits that could get you or those who work with your data into some modeling hot water down the road. This chapter will help you tell the difference and avoid the pitfalls.

Using Powerful Tools Effectively

The SolidWorks software is so filled with powerful functionality that you will find many ways to create any given piece of geometry. In SolidWorks, the geometry itself is not the only measure of success. What is also important is *how* you arrived at that geometry. Multi-body modeling is one area that is prone to misuse. This is not because some SolidWorks style police pass judgment on your technique, like a panel of judges rating an Olympic diver, but rather because your models will be passed on to other people who will need to understand how you got your results, and because your model has to be able to react predictably to changes. This is how multi-body modeling became such a hot topic for best-practice issues.

It is not always easy to remember how you executed a particular model six months and 100 models ago. Other users may have to edit your work, and if errors appear (and they will appear), then you have to be able to navigate the design intent without destroying the relationships in the FeatureManager or completely rebuilding it. This is the reason for trying to standardize best-practice issues, particularly with advanced functionality and in larger organizations where more users may work with the data.

If you are an independent contractor and do not share your models with other SolidWorks users, then you have more flexibility to model how you like. As long as you can come back to the model and change it when you need to, more power to you.

Comparing multi-body modeling with assembly modeling

I cover assembly modeling in the companion to this book, the *SolidWorks 2011 Assemblies Bible* (Wiley, 2011). There is some overlap of the issues between the two books. This is one topic that bridges the worlds of part and assembly modeling. If you are a new user, you may not understand what the big deal is; after all, you just make bodies within a part, right? By the end of this chapter, you should be able to recognize that the issue is more complicated than that. If you are an experienced user, you may have already run into some problems with multi-body modeling or may be having difficulty figuring out where to draw the line between parts and assemblies. This chapter will also offer you some answers.

Multi-body modeling is not assembly modeling. Many times when new users are introduced to the capabilities of multi-body modeling, the first thought that comes to mind is, "This is far easier than making assemblies." However, multi-body modeling should not be treated as a replacement for assembly modeling. This is not just because I say so; there are practical reasons for the distinction.

Several assembly type functions are missing or more difficult to obtain from multi-bodies. They include the following:

- Interference detection
- Dynamic assembly motion
- Exploded views
- Configs for separate parts
- Drawings for individual parts
- Center-of-gravity calculations for individual parts
- Feature lists for individual parts
- Custom Property information for individual parts
- Mass property calculations for individual parts

To say that these functions are missing from or difficult in multi-bodies does not imply that they should or will be there someday. In fact, I believe that the distinction between multi-body and assembly modeling techniques should be kept as clear as possible. Simply because a technique is easier does not make it *better*. Above all, remember that modeling multi-body parts puts *all* the data for *all* the bodies in a *single* part file, in a *single* FeatureManager; there is no easy way to separate out the parametric features into individual parts later on, regardless of how complex the part becomes.

You may find parallels between making multi-body parts and making virtual components (parts that are saved within an assembly file). While both these techniques offer shortcuts or make some basic tasks easier, good reasons exist for being mindful of the "one part, one file" mentality, including:

- Segmenting rebuild times (the ability to rebuild one part instead of several)
- Segmenting large data sets (being able to work on one part at a time)
- Switching out parts
- Using multiple instances of parts
- Reusing parts
- Bills of Materials (BOMs)

Further, creating drawings of individual bodies of a multi-body part is more difficult than creating drawings of individual parts, not that it cannot be done (remember that starting in SolidWorks 2010 you can now specify bodies from a part to be used in a drawing view), just that it is more difficult. Also, editing the features of individual bodies is not as easy as if the individual body were an individual part. When you create several bodies in a single part, you constantly have to carry the feature and design intent overhead of *all* the features used to create *all* the bodies to edit any individual body.

Using multi-body techniques appropriately

You need to have a healthy respect for the problems that you can create for yourself and others by using multi-body modeling in inefficient or inappropriate ways. Still, appropriate uses for multi-body modeling do exist. You may hear people recommend that at the end of the FeatureManager, only a single solid body should remain, with the rest of the bodies either absorbed or deleted. On the other extreme, for some people, anything they can create is allowable. I recommend that if you decide to use multi-bodies, then you should be at least able to articulate *why* you have chosen to do so in a way that does not sound like you are making excuses for careless work.

Appropriate uses for multi-body modeling include (but are not limited to):

- As an intermediate step on the way to a single-body solid.
- As multiple or inserted bodies for reference (reference bodies may be deleted at the bottom of the FeatureManager).
- As over-molded parts.
- As parts that need to be assembled into a single, smooth shape, such as a computer mouse or an automobile body where the shape is impossible (or at least far more difficult) if done in-context.
- When the end shape of the finished product is known, but the separation occurs between parts due to manufacturing methods, and materials have not been decided yet; in this case, multi-body techniques can save a lot of time compared to modeling an assembly.

- As captive fasteners and purchased inseparable subassemblies.
- When SolidWorks weldments result in a multi-body part.
- When features require tool bodies, such as the Indent feature.
- When the Mold Tools result in a single multi-body part representing the plastic part and the major mold components.

If you are administering a SolidWorks installation of multiple users, then you may be looking for a "bright line" test to clearly define for users which types of multi-body modeling are allowable and which are not. So many possibilities exist that it is difficult to say definitively what really *should not* be done, but here is a short list that you can modify for your needs:

- Do not use multi-body modeling simply to avoid making an assembly.
- Do not leave a part in a multi-body state that should be joined together into a single body.
- Hiding a body is sometimes appropriate, and deleting a body is sometimes appropriate — understand the difference.

Okay, the lecture is over. The message that you should take from all this is not to use multi-body techniques just because you can; use them only when you have a solid reason to do so. This is the criterion that I use for my own modeling, what I would like to see in models that I inherit from other SolidWorks users, and a philosophy that will serve you well if you are conscientious about it.

Multi-body modeling is powerful, and for complex parts can even increase rebuild speed compared with single body modeling or assembly modeling. You can develop and use many powerful techniques based on multi-bodies, but as I mentioned earlier, sometimes you pay a price for the shortcut.

Understanding Multi-Body Techniques

To complicate the issue somewhat, nearly all surface modeling is also multi-body modeling. In this chapter, I am referring to solids unless I specifically state otherwise. Still, most solid body techniques have some sort of equivalent in surface body techniques. Surface bodies are discussed in Chapter 20.

Multi-body techniques cover a wide range of functionality, and as soon as someone creates a list of what you can do with them, someone else will come up with a new technique. Still, here is a short list of techniques where multi-body functionality makes things either easier or simply possible:

- Complex shapes across multiple parts
- Tool bodies/Boolean operations
- Local operations
- Patterning
- Simplifying very complex parts
- As a bridge between solids
- Undetermined manufacturing methods
- Manipulating imported geometry

In the remainder of this chapter, I illustrate each technique using an example model and discuss the positives and negatives of each technique. As you get deeper into SolidWorks, you will find that the more complex functions tend to come at a price. A given feature might be the only way to accomplish a particular task, but it rebuilds slowly, might only work in special conditions, might crash from time to time, or might not make sense to other users if they have to edit it.

Creating complex shapes across bodies

When creating a part such as a computer mouse, you encounter complex shapes that span several parts. It makes the most sense to model the entire shape as a single part, and then to break it up into separate bodies, making parts from the bodies, adding detail to individual piece parts, and then bringing the parts back together as an assembly.

Cross-Reference

This method also uses the Master Model techniques discussed in the SolidWorks 2011 Assemblies Bible (Wiley, 2011). ■

A part that uses this technique is shown in Figure 19.1. This part seems to contradict what I said earlier about not being able to use exploded views with multi-body parts, but this part uses the Move/Copy Bodies feature to move bodies within the part. This function remains in the part as a history-based feature in the FeatureManager and is much more labor-intensive to create than an assembly exploded view because each body is moved by a separate feature.

FIGURE 19.1

A multi-body part with a complex shape across bodies

The part shown in Figure 19.1 is not complete, but the starting point for each part has been formed. This part was created from surface features that are discussed in detail in Chapter 20. The part is named `Chapter 19 – Mouse Base Part.sldprt` and is located on the DVD. You may find it interesting to open the part to see how it has been modeled.

From here, each body is saved out to individual parts to complete the detailing, and then the parts are brought back together to create an assembly. The separate bodies in this case were created using the Split feature, which enables you to use surfaces, sketches, or planes to split a single body into multiple bodies. This is described in more detail later in this chapter.

The entire process for creating a finished assembly of finished parts is detailed in Figure 19.2. This flow chart shows conceptually how the overall shape created as a single part has moved from a single part/single body to a single part/multiple body to individual parts to an assembly of individual parts.

FIGURE 19.2

A Master Model workflow

The image to the left in Figure 19.3 depicts how this part was modeled. The first step was to create the shape as a single body within the part. As shown in the FeatureManager, this is all contained inside the Overall Shape Features folder. This folder is presented here as a *black box* because surface features were used to create the part. It really doesn't matter at this point *how* the part was created, and these features are not discussed until Chapter 20.

The image to the right in Figure 19.3 shows transparent surface bodies that were used to split the model into separate bodies using the Split features shown in the tree. Using this technique, you can create the overall shape as a single piece and then split it into separate parts. It is also possible to apply this technique in the context of an assembly, but this method is far more direct.

To go from the multi-body part created here to a set of separate parts uses a Master Model function, which is described in the *SolidWorks 2011 Assemblies Bible* (Wiley, 2011).

FIGURE 19.3

Splitting the part into bodies

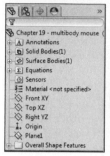   

Using tool bodies and Boolean operations

Some features require multiple bodies within a part, such as the Indent and Combine features, among others. Using one body to create a shape in another is a common use for bodies within a part.

Using the Indent feature

 The Indent feature is covered briefly in Chapter 8 before multi-bodies are introduced, so it is fitting that I revisit it here so that you can better understand the multi-body aspect of its use. The Indent feature *indents* the *target* body with the *tool* body. It can also use another part in the context of an assembly as the tool. The indentation can exactly fit the form of the tool, or there can be a gap around the tool. You can also control the thickness of the material around the indent. A further option is to simply cut the target with the tool instead of indenting.

Figure 19.4 shows the target part as transparent, and the tool as opaque, before and after the Indent feature has been applied. The Indent PropertyManager is also shown.

On the DVD

To take a closer look at this part and the Indent feature, look at the part on the DVD named Chapter 19 – Indent Part.sldprt. ∎

FIGURE 19.4

The Indent feature using a tool body

The Indent feature can be problematic if it breaks into multiple areas as it does in this part, due to the ribbing on the underside of the target body. Notice that in the PropertyManager in Figure 19.4, two selections were made in the Tool body region selection box. The tool body is selected on either side of the rib that bisects the tool. This concept is not very intuitive, and you may have to play with the part and the options to understand what it is doing.

The Keep selections and Remove selections options are equally unintuitive, but they determine which side of the target body is indented. For example, if the part of the tool body that is outside of the target body (flat side) were selected instead of the two inside regions, then the resulting part would look as it does in Figure 19.5, where the tool body has been hidden. You can achieve the same result by toggling the Keep selections and Remove selections options. These options exist because sometimes it is difficult or impossible to select the correct areas of a body that is embedded in another body.

FIGURE 19.5

Using the Keep and Remove selections options

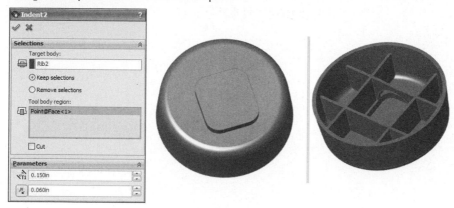

Tip

Also notice that toggling the Keep and Remove selections options means that only one region of the tool body needs to be selected to create the original result shown in Figure 19.4. ■

Using the Move/Copy Bodies and Combine features

The Move/Copy Bodies and Combine features can be demonstrated using the same part. The body that was used in the previous example to indent the main body is moved and then added to the main body in this example.

Figure 19.6 shows the starting and ending points of the process, as well as the PropertyManagers of the two features used to get from one point to the other. Keep in mind that both the Move/Copy Bodies and the Combine features are history-based features listed in the FeatureManager.

In this case, the Move/Copy Bodies feature uses mates. These mates enable you to locate bodies in a way similar to the way they are used in assemblies. One important difference is that with bodies, you must use the actual body geometry of the body that is moving; you cannot use reference geometry such as planes. By clicking the Translate/Rotate button at the bottom of the PropertyManager, you can also position bodies using distances and angles.

In the Combine PropertyManager, you will notice that common Boolean operations, such as union (add), difference (subtract), and intersection (common), are available through this interface.

Tip

You can use an interesting technique in this part. The features creating the smaller tool body and the Move/Copy Bodies and Combine features can be put together into a folder, and the folder itself reordered before the Shell feature. This means that the combined body is also shelled out, and the rib goes down inside of it. This produces an odd error message and unexpectedly places several features into the folder, but it does work.

You may want to open this part in SolidWorks to see exactly how all this was done instead of relying on the figure illustrations. The part used for Figure 19.7 is on the DVD and is named Chapter 19 – Move Body.sldprt. ■

FIGURE 19.6

Using the Move/Copy Bodies and Combine features

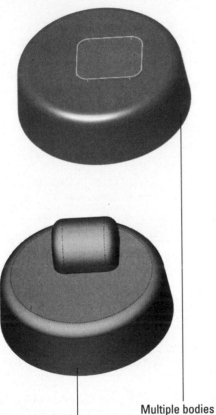

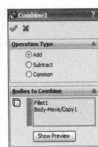

Multiple bodies

Repositioned and combined into a single body

FIGURE 19.7

Reordering features

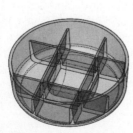

Using local operations

If you have ever had a modeling situation where you needed to shell out a portion of a part but not the entire part, or you had a fillet that would work if only certain geometry were not there, then you may have been able to benefit from multi-body techniques to accomplish these tasks.

Using the Flex feature

The part shown in Figure 19.8 first appears in Chapter 7, where I demonstrate the Flex feature. This is a rubber plug for an electronic device. In order to make one side of the part flex without flexing the other side, multiple bodies were used. The part was split into two bodies using the Split feature and a plane. One side of the part was then twisted, and the two bodies were combined back together. The Features folder contains the features that were used to build the original part geometry, which could just as easily have been either native or imported.

FIGURE 19.8

Splitting a part to perform a local operation

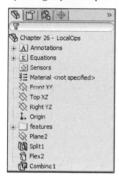

Using the Shell feature

The Shell feature hollows out one solid body at a time. If there are multiple solid bodies, then you must select one to be shelled. Any face of the solid that you select will be removed during the shelling. You can select a body without selecting a face by using the small Solid Body selection box under the larger Faces to Remove selection box in the PropertyManager. If you do not select any faces to be removed, then the body will be hollowed out with no external indication that the part is hollow unless you view it in section view, transparency view, or wireframe view. Single or multiple faces can be removed. This feature works by offsetting the faces of the outside of the model, and the feature may fail if this causes problems with the internal geometry.

The Multi-thickness Shell option enables you to select faces that will have a different thickness from the overall shell thickness. This is one method that you can sometimes use to limit the scope of the Shell feature to a certain area of a body, but it is somewhat limited. Faces with different thicknesses cannot be tangent to one another.

Because the Shell feature only works on one body at a time, splitting a part into multiple bodies can be an effective way to limit the scope of the feature. The part shown in Figure 19.9 has been split in half, and one-half has been made transparent for visualization purposes; as a result, you can see that the part is shelled on the bottom on one end and on the top on the other end. The Shell feature has no option for doing this with existing geometry. The only ways that you can do this are either through feature order or by using multi-bodies. You can find the part shown in Figure 19.9 on the DVD with the name Chapter 19 – LocalOps Shell.sldprt.

FIGURE 19.9

Shelling locally

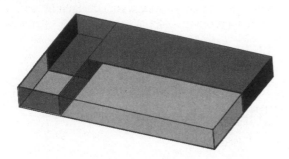

To shell the part this way with feature order, you create one block and shell it, and then create the other block and shell that. In order for this technique to work, the second shell needs to be as big as, or bigger than, the first shell. If it is smaller, then it will (or may) hollow out areas that are not intended to be hollow.

To shell the part with multi-bodies, you can use two methods. One method is to build the first block, and then build the second block but turn off the Merge option. This creates bodies that are side by side. You then shell one block on the bottom and the other on the top. To avoid a double-thickness wall between them, the end face can be removed along with either the top or bottom face. If you edit the part, then you may notice that one of the Shell features has two faces removed.

The second method is to build a single block, then split it using a sketch line, a plane, or a surface, and then proceed in the same way as the first method.

Patterning

Patterns of bodies are fast, powerful, and commonly used alternatives to patterning features. Chapter 8 discusses feature patterns and mirroring, and examines, at least in part, how different types of patterns affect model rebuild speeds. When appropriate, patterning bodies can also be a big rebuild time-saver. When patterning a body, none of the parametrics or intelligence is patterned with it, but you must pattern the entire body. Another odd thing about patterning bodies in SolidWorks is that there is no option to join the bodies either to one another or to a main body. This requires an extra step that involves adding a Combine feature. Mirroring is the same, except that it has an option to merge bodies, but it only merges the original body to the mirrored body. It will not merge either the original or the mirrored body to a central main body.

In this example, an imported part has a "feature" that needs to be reused around the part. The technique used here is to split away the feature as a separate body and then pattern the body around the part and join it all back together. This function can be used with native geometry as well as imported. This process is shown in Figure 19.10. This function does use a simple planar surface. A plane could have been used to split off the body to be patterned, but the plane would have also split off a part of the globe at the top, so a planar surface (which can be limited in extent where a plane cannot) was used.

The image on the left in Figure 19.10 is the raw imported part. The middle image shows a planar surface created on the face of the part, where the planar surface has been used with the Split feature to cut the leg off the part. The image on the right shows the split leg patterned around an axis that was created from the intersection of two planes.

FIGURE 19.10

Splitting away a body and patterning it

If you would like to practice with this part, it is on the DVD for Chapter 19; the imported Parasolid file is named Chapter 19 – Pattern import.x_t.

Performance

In some situations, patterning bodies is a performance advantage, and in some situations it is not. You get an advantage from patterning bodies when the geometry used to create the pattern seed is complex, uses many features, or does not work well or at all for a feature pattern.

On the other hand, if you repeat the experiments from Chapter 9 using a small body with a hole in it instead of patterning a hole feature, you find that the body pattern is far slower than the feature patterning because of the necessary step of combining bodies. ■

Simplifying very complex parts

Certain types of parts work better when they're built in sections as separate parts than when they are built as a single feature tree. For very complex parts with a lot of features, this sometimes makes sense from the point of view of segmenting the rebuild times for parts with hundreds of features. The example used to demonstrate this technique is a large plastic part built entirely from ribs, and making use of literally hundreds of solid bodies, and is shown in Figure 19.11 and Figure 19.12.

This part is molded using tooling pulls in five directions. Two of these directions are symmetrical, and the core block pulls in a single direction; as a result, in the end, the modeling has to account for three directions.

The rebuild time for a model like this can easily reach several minutes, and the feature count can be in the hundreds, or in this case, well over one thousand. To minimize the rebuild time, a different workflow was established for this part. First, the major inside and outside faces were created with surfaces. Next, the surfaces were saved into several other parts. Each of these parts represents the part geometry that will pull in a particular direction from the mold. Enough information exists in the Master Model to align the features in each part.

The ribs on this part were created by making a single extrusion (the Rib feature could not be used because there was no geometry to serve as a boundary for the ribs), and then the extrusion was patterned and the pattern was mirrored. After all the ribs were created, they had to be shaped, and so the surfaces from the Master Model were used to cut the ribs to shape.

The ribs could not be extruded with a draft or with fillets because the outer and inner surfaces were non-planar. The draft had to be built as a Parting Line draft for the same reason, and the fillets had to be applied after the draft. Further, draft and fillets can only be applied to a single body at a time; as a result, a separate draft feature and a separate fillet feature had to be applied to each body, and each rib was a separate body. Once the draft and fillets were applied, the bodies were joined into a single body.

I recognize that this description of how I made the part is a lot to follow. The point is not to show in detail how the parts were built, but to demonstrate how you can get to a part with 1,200 features or more. It is precisely on parts with this level of complexity that you need to think about modeling the part in this modular fashion — build each part separately and bring each separate section of the part together as individual bodies.

Figure 19.11 shows two of the separate pull direction parts being separated from one another in the same way that the mouse part was shown exploded in the previous example. Here the frame is also modeled as a separate part, again because it was not so intimately related to the other parts and was easily separated out.

Once this was complete for each direction, the separate parts were put together as bodies into a single part and again joined together using the Combine feature. Having all those features in separate parts enables you to segment the rebuild time. This is the opposite of building all the parts of an assembly in a single part, where you are simply compounding your rebuild time. Figure 19.12 shows bodies joined together as a single body.

This is probably a technique that you will not use very often, but when you do, it can save you a lot of rebuild time. I use it whenever I have a model that takes more than 20 to 30 seconds to rebuild and I know that I am going to be working on it a lot; it must also lend itself to segmenting in the way that this one did, with easily definable areas.

FIGURE 19.11

A complex model created as separate parts and brought together as bodies in a single part

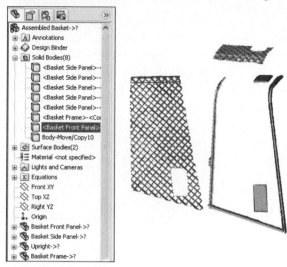

FIGURE 19.12

Bodies all joined together as a single body

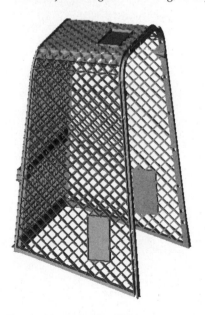

Bridging between solids

Often when modeling, you "build what you know" and "fill in as you go." An example of this would be modeling a duct between end connections that are well defined. The duct in between is defined only by the ends, which must exist first. Another example is a connecting rod where you know the diameter of each end and the distance between the ends, and the connection between them is of secondary importance.

Figure 19.13 shows a connecting rod made in this way. In this case, the bearing seat at one end was created, and the other end was created by copying the body of the first one. From there, the link between bearing seats was created, which joined the separate bodies together into a single solid body.

FIGURE 19.13

Connecting disjoint bodies

This part contains some interesting features. First is the Thin Feature extrude that is used to make the first bearing seat, which is combined with a Mid-plane extrude to make it symmetrical at the same time. Then comes the Move/Copy Bodies feature, which copies the body in the same way that the feature in previous examples has moved bodies. Next is the use of the Extrude From option, which extrudes from a face, and then the use of the end condition Up To Next, which ends the feature neatly. The part also incorporates fillets that use faces and features to form the selection.

If you are not familiar with these options, I recommend that you open up the part from the DVD and have a look at it. It is a simple part that takes advantage of nice but simple productivity-enhancing options that have been available for some time in the SolidWorks software. The part filename is `Chapter 19 – Bridge.sldprt`.

By default, Solid features have the Merge option selected, and they automatically combine with any bodies that they touch. At the same time, they do not display errors if the Merge option is selected but the new body does not touch any existing bodies.

Modeling for undetermined manufacturing methods

Sometimes you must start a design before you know exactly how the product will be manufactured. This is an example of where the geometry of the finished product exists first and is then broken up into manufacturable parts. The initial model, shown in the image at the top in Figure 19.14, is created as a single part as a result of input from marketing, but when it comes time for manufacturing input, the part count and processes keep changing. Where the parts break from one another keeps changing as well. When that kind of change is happening, having the parts created as individual parts is a big liability because it is difficult to change. Changing which bodies are merged together is much easier.

A towel rack, modeled as a single part and broken into individual parts in an assembly

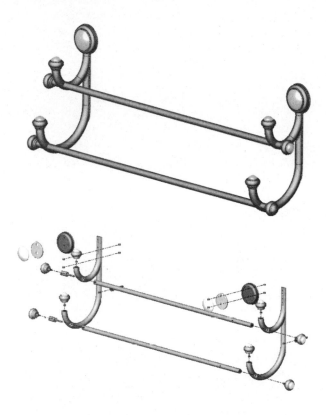

It is worth mentioning two potential difficulties that you may run into with methods like this. The first is that if you have people making drawings from parts that have been derived from bodies in a single part, then they are forced into the Reference Dimension scheme of dimensioning parts because the feature dimensions do not survive being moved from the multi-body part. This may or may not be an issue, depending on how the people doing the drawings are accustomed to working.

The second potential issue is what you do in situations where there are multiple instances of a part that has been modeled this way. Notice in the towel rack in Figure 19.14 that there are several finials, spacers, rails, and other parts that are duplicated. This requires some manual assembly modeling. You can make the assembly directly from the multi-body part, but if you need to make multiple instances of particular parts, you need to do this manually rather than automatically.

Creating Multi-Bodies

In the first section in this chapter, I raised the questions of *if* or *when* multi-bodies should be used, and in the second section, I raised the question of *why* multi-bodies should be used. In this section, I simply ask, or rather answer, *how* they should be used.

Using disjoint sketches

The easiest way to create multiple bodies is to simply create what SolidWorks classifies as multiple disjoint closed contours. What that means is simply two circles or rectangles that do not touch or overlap. If these are created in the same sketch, then when extruded, they will create as many bodies as there are closed loops in the sketch.

If the part has an existing solid, then creating a sketch that does not touch the solid can also create a separate body. You cannot make Multiple Thin features in a single sketch. This is presumably because the interface has no way to identify different thickness directions for different open profiles. This holds true whether or not the Multiple Thin features create multiple bodies.

If a solid feature other than a mirror or pattern touches a solid body, then the new and the old bodies will be merged into a single body.

Turning off the Merge Result option

You can prevent a feature from automatically combining with other bodies by deselecting the Merge Result option. This holds true between features, but not across all bodies in a part. For example, if an extrude feature uses the Merge result option, all the bodies that it touches become merged together, but if the original extrude feature does not touch a body, it will not be merged. This option is shown in Figure 19.15 and is found on all features that create new solid bodies except for the Patterns, Rib, and Move/Copy Bodies features.

FIGURE 19.15

The Merge result option

Applying the Feature Scope to bodies

The Feature Scope used for multi-bodies is not the same as the Feature Scope used for assembly features, but it does function in a similar way. In assemblies, the Feature Scope identifies which parts are affected by the current assembly feature. In parts, it only applies to bodies and can be used for features that add material as well as features that remove material (assembly features can only remove material).

The Feature Scope is a way to make the Merge result option more selective. The Merge result option by default does not discriminate; it causes the feature to merge with any other solid body that it touches. However, the Feature Scope enables the user to select which bodies to merge with or otherwise affect. Feature Scope also applies to additional feature types such as cuts. The Feature Scope becomes available in the PropertyManager whenever there are multiple bodies in the part and an eligible feature is used. The Feature Scope panel is shown in Figure 19.16.

FIGURE 19.16

The Feature Scope panel

The default setting for the Feature Scope is to use the Selected bodies option with the Auto-select option. The All bodies option is essentially the same as using the Merge result option. When the Selected bodies option is selected and Auto-select is unselected, as is shown in Figure 19.16, you must select bodies for the current feature to affect them. New bodies that are added to the model are not automatically added to the list; you need to manually edit the feature and add additional bodies to the list as appropriate.

Using the Rib feature

The Rib feature is hypersensitive to changes to the number of bodies. A rib only automatically merges with a body if it is the only body in the part. If a rib is created in a single body part and then the model is rolled back and an additional body is created before the rib, then the Rib feature will fail when the tree is unrolled. The error that this causes reads, "The rib is not bounded properly. The extension of the rib does not intersect the part model." Technically speaking, this is true, but like other SolidWorks error messages, that does not make it helpful. The cause of the error is that suddenly the body that the rib is supposed to merge with is no longer identified. The Rib feature does not have an Auto-select option. You can fix this problem by going to the Feature Scope in the Rib PropertyManager to select a body for it to merge with. The Rib feature does not use the normal Feature Scope, because the Feature Scope is intended to select multiple bodies, and the Rib feature requires a single body. There is a simple Selected Body selection box in the Rib PropertyManager.

After you have selected the target body, deleting the new bodies that caused the problem in the first place, thankfully, does not make the problem reoccur. However, if the body that the rib is merged with is split using the Split feature, then that *does* cause a problem. As a result, the two things that cause the Rib feature problem are rolling back and either adding bodies or splitting the body to be ribbed.

Caution

As you encounter more specialized situations with multi-bodies and dependencies, you may notice more quirks in the SolidWorks internal body management. The next section on managing bodies addresses some of these quirks directly. ■

Using the Delete Solid/Surface feature

If you have created many ribs in a casting or plastic part, then it may be tedious to go through and repair them all every time the body count changes. This sort of thing happens even if the other body is just a reference body or an unused leftover.

In cases like this, you can use the Delete Solid/Surface feature. This is alternatively called Delete Body, depending on where you look. Delete Solid/Surface removes the body from the body folder (discussed in the section on body folders). This is a *history-based delete*, which means that before the Delete Body feature in the tree, the body exists, and after the Delete Body feature in the tree, the body does not exist. This feature has no effect on file size, because the data for the body must still exist, and it has little, if any, effect on rebuild time. What is happening is that the body is still there; you just cannot see it and have no access to it.

Delete Solid/Surface is often used for other purposes as well, primarily to clean up a model at the end of the tree. The reasoning is that multiple bodies in a part confuse people. My recommendation here is to remove bodies if they are getting in the way, either for a hyper-sensitive feature like the Rib feature or if they are causing visualization problems.

Creating multi-bodies with the Cut feature

A Cut feature may create multi-bodies, either intentionally or unintentionally. When it does happen, the Bodies to Keep dialog box appears, enabling you to select which bodies you intend to keep. The Bodies to Keep dialog box is shown in Figure 19.17. This dialog box was formerly called Resolve Ambiguity, which was not as descriptive as Bodies to Keep.

FIGURE 19.17

The Bodies to Keep dialog box

Notice that the Bodies to Keep settings are also configurable; therefore, different bodies can be kept in different configurations, which is very useful.

Managing bodies with the Split feature

The Split feature has essentially three functions:

- To split a single solid body into multiple solid bodies using planes, sketches, or surface bodies
- To save individual solid bodies out to individual part files
- To reassemble individual part files that are saved out into an assembly where the parts are all positioned in the same relative position as their corresponding bodies

The part of the Split feature that concerns this chapter is the first function mentioned, which is splitting a single solid body into multiple bodies using a sketch, a plane, or a surface body.

The Split feature cannot be used to split surface bodies. In fact, nothing in SolidWorks can split surface bodies. Only solid bodies can be split. Surface bodies can only be trimmed, so the effective workaround for not being able to split surface bodies is to copy the body, then trim and keep one side of the copy and the other side of the original. This seems like a functionality oversight, and would make a great enhancement request if you have ever come across the need for this functionality.

Splitting with a sketch

When you are using a sketch to split a single solid body into multiple bodies, the Split process works like this:

1. **Create a sketch with an open or closed loop; even a mixture of open and closed profiles will work.** If it is open, then the endpoints have to either be on an exterior edge or hanging off into space; they cannot actually be inside the boundaries of the solid.

2. **Initiate the Split feature from the Features toolbar or from the menus by choosing Insert ⇨ Features ⇨ Split.** You can do this with the sketch active, with the sketch inactive but selected, or with nothing selected at all.

3. **Click the Cut Part button.** This does not actually cut anything; it only previews the split. When this is done, the resulting bodies appear in the window below and callout flags are placed on the part in the graphics window. These flags are often useless because they tend to point to the borders between two different bodies in such a way that it is completely ambiguous as to which body they are indicating. However, in the example shown in Figure 19.18, the result is very clear.

Check marks next to the body in the list indicate that the body will be split out. The lack of a check mark does not necessarily mean anything. For example, in Figure 19.18, notice that two boxes are checked, but this will result in a total of four bodies. If only Body 1 were selected, then the result would be only two bodies.

Clicking the Save All Bodies button simply puts check marks in all the boxes. If the Resulting Bodies box contains more than ten bodies, then the interface changes slightly, as shown in the image to the right in Figure 19.18. The Consume cut bodies option removes, or consumes, any of the bodies that have a check mark.

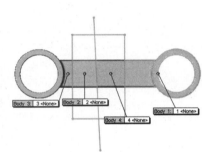

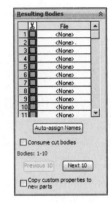

FIGURE 19.18

Using the Split feature

Splitting with a plane

Splitting with a plane provides the same type of results, and uses the same options, as splitting with a sketch. However, you never have to worry about the plane being extended far enough, because the cut is made from the infinite extension of the plane. The only thing you have to worry about with a plane is whether it intersects the part.

Splitting with a surface body

Surface bodies are used to split solid bodies for a couple of reasons. In the part shown in Figure 19.10, a surface body was used to make the split instead of a sketch or a plane, because both of those entities split everything in an infinite distance either normal to the sketch plane or in the selected plane. A surface body only splits to the extents of the splitting surface body. If you look closely at the part, you will notice that a plane or sketch would lop off one side of the sphere on top of the object, but the small planar surface is limited enough in size to only split what is necessary.

Another advantage to using a surface body is that it is not limited to a two-dimensional cut. The surface itself can be any type of surface, such as planar, extruded, revolved, lofted, or imported. Taking this a step further, the surface is not limited to being a single face, or a body resulting from a single feature; it could be made from several features that are put together as long as it is a single body and all the outer edges of the surface body are outside the solid body. If you examine the mouse part shown in Figure 19.1, you will notice that it has splits made from multi-feature surface bodies.

I mention splitting with surface bodies here because this is where I discuss the Split function, even though I haven't covered the surfacing functions yet. It may be useful to read parts of this book out of order; given how the topics interrelate, it is impossible to order them in such a way that some sections will not refer to a topic that has not yet been covered.

Cross-Reference

For more information about surface bodies, see Chapter 20. ■

Adding bodies using the Insert Part feature

 The Insert Part button can be found on the Features toolbar, or you can access this feature by choosing Insert ⇨ Part from the menus.

Insert Part enables you to insert one part into another part. When inserting the part, you have the option to insert solid bodies, axes, planes, cosmetic threads, surface bodies, and several other types of entities, including sketches and features. The PropertyManager interface for the Insert Part feature is shown in Figure 19.19.

FIGURE 19.19

The Insert Part PropertyManager

This feature has two major functions: inserting a body as the starting point for a new part and inserting a body to be used as a tool to modify an existing part. Notice that the basket part shown in Figure 19.11 and Figure 19.12 also uses Insert Part to put together bodies to form a finished part.

When you use Insert Part, there is no Insert Part feature that becomes part of the tree. Instead, a part icon is shown with the name of the part being inserted as a feature.

Also notice in Figure 19.19 that the Launch move dialog option appears near the bottom and is selected by default. This option launches the Move dialog box after you insert the part. This Move feature is the same as the Move/Copy Bodies feature, with the same options (translate or rotate by distance or angles, or use assembly-like mates to position bodies). Insert Part is used in many situations, some of which are covered in Chapter 11.

Working with secondary operations

One commonly used technique has to do with secondary operations. For example, you may have designed a casting that needs several machining operations after it comes from the foundry. The foundry needs a drawing to produce the raw casting, and the machine shop needs a different drawing to tap holes, spot face areas, trim flash, and so on.

You can use configurations to do this by using Insert Part in another way. This has nothing to do with multiple body techniques, but this is the only place where Insert Part is covered in much detail. One of the advantages of using Insert Part is that you no longer carry around the overhead of all the features in the parent part. It is as if the inserted part were imported. The configurations method forces you to carry around much more feature overhead. Of course, the downside is that now there is an additional file to manage, but this can be an advantage because many companies assign different part numbers to parts before and after secondary operations.

Starting point

Looking back to the mouse shown in Figure 19.1, the main part has been split into several bodies. You can use Insert Part to insert the whole mouse into a new part where all the bodies except one are deleted, and then the remaining body serves as the starting point for a new part. Many additional features are needed on all the bodies that make up the mouse, such as assembly features, cosmetic features, functional features, and manufacturing features.

Managing Bodies

Managing bodies in SolidWorks is not as clean a task as managing parts in an assembly. As you work with bodies, you may discover some surprises in how bodies are managed. This section prepares you for the challenges involved in managing bodies in SolidWorks.

Using Body folders

The top of the FeatureManager includes a pair of folders: one called Solid Bodies and the other called Surface Bodies. These folders are only there if you have solids or surfaces in the model, and they reflect the state of the model at the current position of the Rollback bar. As a result, the folders can change and even disappear as you roll the tree back and forth in history. Figure 19.20 shows the top of a FeatureManager that has both solid and surface body folders. Notice that the number in parentheses after the name of the folder shows how many bodies are in that particular folder.

FIGURE 19.20

Body folders in the FeatureManager

An odd fact about these folders is that you are allowed to rename the folders, but the name changes never remain. If you go back to rename the folder again, the name that you previously assigned will display.

You may encounter another problem with the display of FeatureManager header items in general when they are set to Automatic display (display only when they contain something). This does not guarantee that the folder is going to display when it should. A more direct way of saying this is that the Automatic setting works incorrectly from time to time. For this reason, I suggest using the Show option to display important folders. Figure 19.21 shows the Options page (Tools ➪ Options) that controls the visibility of folders.

FIGURE 19.21

Control the visibility of FeatureManager items

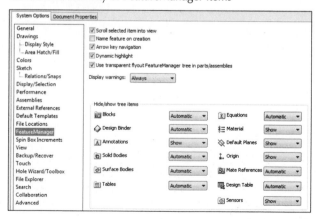

By right-clicking either of the bodies folders, you can select the Show Feature History option, which shows the features that have combined to create the bodies in an indented list under the body name. This view of the FeatureManager is shown in Figure 19.22. This option is very useful when you are editing or troubleshooting bodies.

Using the Show Feature History option

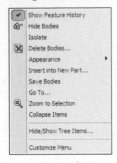
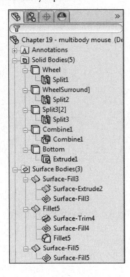

Figure 19.22 also shows the other options in the right mouse button (RMB) menu. All the bodies in the folder can be alternately shown or hidden from this menu, as well as deleted. While the Hide or Show state of a body does not create a history-based feature in the tree, the Delete feature does, as discussed previously.

You can expand the Display pane in parts to show display information for bodies. In Figure 19.23, the Display pane shows the colors assigned to the solid bodies, as well as the fact that several surface bodies exist but are hidden.

Also in Figure 19.23, the DisplayManager tab shows colors assigned to specific bodies. This is helpful when trying to decipher appearance overrides, which are more common on multi-body parts than on single body parts. The DisplayManager is new in SolidWorks 2011.

The folders also make bodies easier to identify, especially when combined with the setting found at Tools ➪ Options ➪ Display/Selection ➪ Dynamic Highlight From Graphics View. This setting quickly turns the body outline red if you move the mouse over the body in the body folder.

FIGURE 19.23

The Display pane showing information about solid and surface bodies

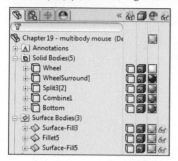

Hiding or showing bodies

You can hide or show bodies in one of several ways. I have already described the method of using the bodies folders to hide or show all the bodies at once, but you can also right-click individual bodies in the folders to hide or show them using the RMB menu. Remember that with the context bars, you have the option to use them with the RMB menu as well as with left-click selections. I include all context bar options in the RMB menu generically.

If you can see a body in the graphics area, then you can right-click the body and select Hide under the Body heading. This works for both solids and surfaces. The Display Pane, shown to the right of the FeatureManager in Figure 19.23, can also be used to hide or show bodies, change body transparency and appearance, as well as change the display mode of bodies. Display Pane is a handy tool for visualization options.

When you are hiding or showing bodies from the FeatureManager, but not using the bodies folders and using the features themselves instead, things get a little complicated. If you want to hide or show a solid body, then you can use any feature that is a parent of the body to hide or show the body. For example, you can use the Shell feature in the mouse model to hide or show all the bodies of which it is a parent.

Other facts that you need to know about bodies and their hide or show states are that the Hide or Show feature is both configurable and dependent on the rollback state. As a result, if you hide a body, and then roll back, it may appear again and you will have to hide it. Then, if you roll forward, the state changes again. Also, a body can be hidden in one configuration, and then when you switch configurations, it remains hidden. This makes it rather frustrating to work with bodies. To me, it would be nice if bodies had simple on/off switches.

SolidWorks 2010 adds the Display State functionality from assemblies to multi-body parts. This is extremely handy, and a very fast way to change color, transparency, or display modes for individual bodies. The best way to handle this is to expand the Display Pane and control Hide/Show, Display Mode, Appearance, and Transparency directly from the Display Pane. Figure 19.24 shows the Display Pane in action on a multi-body part.

FIGURE 19.24

Using the Display Pane to control multi-body Display States

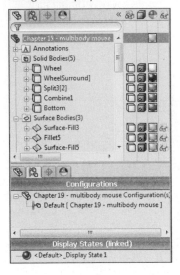

In Figure 19.24, the FeatureManager panel is split so you can see the configurations and Display State information alongside the bodies folder and display pane. If you are familiar with Display States in assemblies, it is the same as for bodies.

You are able to assign different materials to each body. If different parts are made of different materials, the only situations in which I would model this way would be overmolds, where multiple materials are molded onto one another, and inseparable subassemblies, like purchased components such as screws with captive washers or a circuit board with rivets. If you need to manufacture something that has different materials, you need to have each material in a separate file for manufacturing purposes. Computer Numerical Control (CNC) software operators generally do not want parts that need to be machined separately given to them as multi-body single parts. To apply materials to bodies, right-click the body in the Solid Bodies folder and select Material.

Caution

Some features exclude bodies if the bodies are hidden when you edit the feature. Be careful of this, and be sure to show all the bodies that are used in a particular function before you edit it. For example, if a body is hidden and you create a new extrude that touches the hidden body, then the new body does not merge with the hidden one even if the Merge option is on. If the hidden body is then shown and you edit the second body, then the bodies will merge upon the closing of the second body. ■

Deleting bodies

 I have already mentioned that you can delete bodies using the Delete Solid/Surface feature, and that this feature exists in the tree of the part. This feature used to be called Delete Bodies.

Delete Solid/Surface does not affect file size or rebuild speed. In fact, I find it difficult to come up with examples of when you should use it, other than the situation already mentioned with the Rib feature, or if a throwaway body somehow remains in the part. Some people use this feature to clean up the organization of the tree, which could be useful if there are many bodies in the part. Other users insist on keeping the tree free of extraneous bodies and immediately delete bodies that have been used. To me, this technique replaces one kind of clutter with another, and means that tools that should be available to you (solid or surface bodies) are not available unless you reorder the Delete Body feature down the tree and/or roll back. In any case, this is really a matter of personal working style and not of any great importance.

Some export filetypes will export all the bodies without warning. Thus the easiest way to make sure that a file does not have extra bodies for the export is to just add a delete bodies feature that removes the extraneous bodies that are not included in the final part. Also, always make sure to re-import any exported bodies to make sure they were exported correctly.

Renaming bodies

Notice that the bodies that you see in the folders have been named for the last feature that touched a given body. That naming scheme is as good as any, except that it means that the body keeps changing names. If you deliberately rename a body, it will retain the name through future changes. You should follow the same rules of thumb for naming bodies as you do for naming features. It is not necessary to rename every body, but if you will use one body frequently and need to select it from the FeatureManager, renaming it is very useful.

Using Multiple Bodies with Sheet Metal, Weldments, and Molds

Various types of special SolidWorks documents require that you work with multi-body data. Those are sheet metal, weldments, and molds. Sheet metal and Weldments are SolidWorks files with special properties, and the molds are simply created from a separate set of specialized Mold Tools.

Introducing multi-body functionality in weldments

Weldments are a special type of SolidWorks document that require the use of multiple bodies. Each structural member in a weldment frame is created as a separate solid body. So if you are getting involved in using the Weldment tools in SolidWorks, you will need to also master the multi-body tools.

Introducing multi-body functionality in sheet metal

SolidWorks sheet metal parts do not require the use of multiple bodies, but they do allow it, which is useful when you have sheet metal parts together with welded parts or special fasteners as a part of an inseparable subassembly, such as PEM fasteners. SolidWorks added the multi-body functionality to sheet metal mainly to accommodate weldments. Sheet metal is covered in Chapter 21, and the details of multi-body modeling as it relates to sheet metal are also covered there. Again, I include the multi-body capabilities of sheet metal in this chapter as an introduction to the idea. Weldments are covered in the companion to this book, *SolidWorks 2011 Assemblies Bible* (Wiley, 2011).

Introducing multi-body functionality in molds

Creating mold geometry using SolidWorks Mold Tools is another multi-body function. Other mold creation software that works within SolidWorks uses assemblies to do this, but SolidWorks has chosen to use bodies. You can also do the same kind of work without using the specialized tools if you choose, and can even work exclusively in solids or in a hybrid solid and surface workflow. Unless you choose to create geometry for various types of molding or casting manufacturing methods using assemblies, you are probably going to need to do it using multi-body parts. SolidWorks Mold Tools are discussed in the companion book *SolidWorks 2011 Assemblies Bible* (Wiley, 2011).

Tutorials: Working with Multi-Bodies

This tutorial contains various short examples of multi-body techniques in order from easy to more difficult.

Merging and local operations

This tutorial gives you some experience using the Merge Result option and using features on individual bodies to demonstrate the local operations functionality of multi-body modeling. Try these steps:

1. **Start a new part, and sketch a rectangle centered on the origin on the Top plane.** Size is not important for this exercise.

2. **Extrude the rectangle to roughly one-third of its smaller dimension.**

3. **Open a second sketch on the Top plane.** Hide the first solid body by right-clicking it in either the FeatureManager or the graphics window.

4. **Show the sketch for the first feature, and draw a second rectangle on the far side of the rectangle from the Origin.** Make sure that the second rectangle gets two coincident relations to the first sketch at two corners so that the rectangles are the same width. When the sketch is complete, hide the sketch that was shown.

5. **Extrude the second rectangle to about two-thirds of the depth of the first rectangle.**

Note

Notice that the Merge option was not changed from the default setting (On) for the second extrude, but because the first extrude was hidden, the second extrude did not merge with it. Be careful of subsequent edits to either of the features if the first body is shown, because this may cause the bodies to merge unexpectedly. In this tutorial, the bodies are later merged intentionally. Ideally, what you should do is deselect the Merge option of the second extrude. ∎

6. **Shell out the second extrusion by removing two adjacent sides, as shown in Figure 19.25.** One of the sides is the top and the other is the shared side with the hidden body. The body that should be hidden at this point is shown as transparent in the image for reference only. The body was made transparent to make it easier to select the face of the second body.

FIGURE 19.25

Shelling two sides of a block

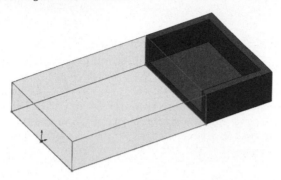

7. **Show the first body either from the Solid Bodies folder at the top of the tree or from the RMB menu of the first solid feature in the tree.**

8. **Shell the bottom side of the first body, so that the cavities in the two bodies are on opposite sides.**

9. **Combine the two bodies using the Combine tool you can find by choosing Insert ⇨ Features ⇨ Combine.** This feature is also available via the RMB menu in the solid body folder. Select the Add option and select the two bodies. Click OK to finish the feature. Figure 19.26 shows the finished part.

FIGURE 19.26

The finished part

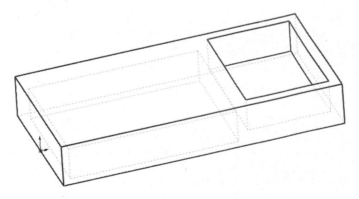

Splitting and patterning bodies

This tutorial guides you through the steps to delete a pattern of *features* from an imported body, separate one of the features, and then pattern it with a different number of features. This introduces some simple surface functions in preparation for Chapter 20. Follow these steps:

1. **Open the Parasolid file from the DVD called** Chapter 19 – Bonita Tutorial.x_t.

2. **Using the Selection Filter set to filter Face selection (the default hotkey for this is X), select all the faces of the leg.** You can use window selection techniques to avoid clicking each face.

3. **Click the Delete Face button on the Surfaces toolbar, or access the command by choosing Insert ➪ Face ➪ Delete from the menus.** Make sure that the Delete and Patch option is selected. The selected faces and the Delete Face PropertyManager should look like Figure 19.27. Click OK to accept the feature.

FIGURE 19.27

The Delete Face PropertyManager

4. **Repeat the process for a second leg, leaving the third leg to be separated from the rest of the part and patterned.**

5. **After the two legs have been removed, click the outer main spherical surface, and then choose Insert ➪ Surface ➪ Offset from the menus.** Set the offset distance to zero. Notice that a Surface Bodies folder is now added to the tree, near the top.

Tip

A zero distance offset surface is frequently used to copy faces. ■

6. **Hide the solid body.** You can do this from the Solid Bodies folder, from the FeatureManager, or from the graphics window.

7. **Hiding the solid leaves the offset surface, and there should be three holes in it.** Select one of the edges of the hole indicated in Figure 19.28 and press the Delete key. The Choose

Option dialog box appears. Select the Delete Hole option rather than the Delete Feature option. The Delete Hole operation becomes a history-based feature in the model tree. Before moving on to the next step, remember that you may need to turn off the Selection Filter for faces.

FIGURE 19.28

Using the Delete Hole option

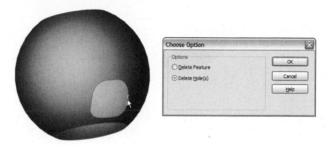

Note

Delete Hole is really a surface feature called Untrim. Untrim is discussed more in Chapter 20, but you can use it to restore original boundaries to a surface. ■

8. **Once you delete the hole from the surface body, change the color of the surface body the same way you changed the colors of parts, faces, and features.**

9. **Click the surface body in the Surface Bodies folder and either press the Delete key or select Delete Body from the RMB menu.** Then click OK to accept the feature. This places a Delete Body feature in the tree. It keeps the body from getting in the way when it is not needed. This is not a necessary step, but many people choose to use it. (Suppress the Delete Body feature, since this body is needed again later.)

Tip

If you delete a body in this way and then need it later down the tree, you can delete, suppress, or reorder the Delete Body feature later in the tree. ■

10. **Now show the solid body.** You will notice the color of the surface conflicting with the color of the solid. This mottled appearance is due to the small approximations made by the rendering and display algorithms.

11. **Initiate the Split feature by choosing Insert ⇨ Features ⇨ Split from the menus or clicking the Features toolbar.** Use the surface body to split the solid body. Click the Cut Part button, and select the check boxes in front of both bodies in the list. Click OK to accept the feature. Notice now that the Solid Bodies folder indicates that there are two solid bodies.

12. **From the View menu, select the display of Temporary Axes.** Initiate a Circular Pattern feature, selecting the temporary axis as the axis, and the split-off leg in the Bodies to Pattern selection box. Set it to four instances, as shown in Figure 19.29.

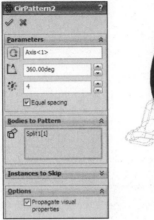

FIGURE 19.29

Patterning a body

13. **Use the Combine feature to add together all five bodies.** You can access this feature by choosing Insert ⇨ Features ⇨ Combine from the menus.

Summary

Beginning to understand how to work with multiple bodies in SolidWorks opens a gateway to a new world of modeling possibilities. Like in-context design, multi-body modeling is definitely something that you have to go into with your eyes open. You will experience difficulties when using this technique, but you will also find new possibilities that were not available with other techniques. The key to success with multi-body techniques is understanding the capabilities and limitations of the tools.

When using a model with the multi-body approach, make sure that you can identify a reason for doing it this way rather than using a more conventional approach. Also keep in mind the list of applications or uses for multi-body modeling mentioned in this chapter. For some types of work, you cannot avoid multi-body modeling, such as using the SolidWorks Mold Tools and Weldments.

Working with Surfaces

With *surface modeling* you build a shape face by face. Faces made by surface features can be knit together to enclose a volume, which can become a solid. With solid modeling, you build all the faces to make the volume at the same time. In fact, solid modeling is really just highly automated surface modeling. Obviously there is more detail to it than that, but this definition will get you started.

You can drive a car without knowing how the engine works, but you cannot get the most power possible out of the car by only pressing harder on the gas pedal; you have to get under the hood and make adjustments. In a way, that is what working with surfaces is really all about — getting under the hood and tinkering with the underlying functionality.

The goal of most surface modeling is to finish with a solid. Some surface features make faces that will become faces of the solid, and some surface features only act as reference geometry. Surface modeling is inherently multi-body modeling because most surface features do not merge bodies automatically.

Introducing Surfaces

In the end, you may never really *need* surfaces. It is possible to perform work-arounds using solids to do most of the things that most users need to do. However, many of these workarounds are inefficient, cumbersome, and raise as many difficulties as they solve. Although you may not view some of the typical things you now do as inefficient and cumbersome, once you see the alternatives, you may change your mind. The goal for this chapter is to introduce surfacing functions to those of you who do not typically use surfaces. I am not showing how surfaces are used in the context of creating complex shapes, just how you can use them for various general 3D modeling tasks.

The word *surfacing* has often been used (and confused) to signify complex shapes. Not all surface work is done to create complex shapes, and many complex shapes can be made directly from solids. Many users think that because they do not make complex shapes, they never need to use surface features. This chapter shows mainly examples that do not require complex shapes, in situations where surfaces make it easier, more efficient, or simply possible to do the necessary tasks.

While some of the uses of surfaces may not be immediately obvious, by the end of this chapter you should have enough information and applications that you can start experimenting to increase your confidence in surfacing techniques.

Understanding Surfacing Terminology

When dealing with surfaces, you may hear different terminology than the terminology typically used with solid modeling. This special terminology also often exists for surfaces because of important conceptual differences between how solids and surfaces are handled.

These terms are fairly universal among all surfacing software. The underlying surface and solid construction concepts are generally uniform between the major solid and surface modeling packages. What varies from software to software is how the user interacts with the geometry through the software interface. You may never see some of these terms in the SolidWorks menus, Help files, training books, or elsewhere, but it becomes obvious as you use the software that the concepts are relevant.

Exploring the Knit function

 Knit is analogous to the solid feature Combine in that it joins multiple surface bodies into a single surface body. Unlike Combine, Knit does not perform the subtract or intersect Boolean operations. It also has an option to create a solid if the resulting surface body meets the requirements (a fully enclosed volume without gaps or overlaps). However, unlike the solid bodies in Combine, which may overlap volumetrically, surface bodies must only intersect edge to edge, more like sketch entities that can only touch end to end.

Knit is also sometimes used in the same way that the zero-distance offset is used, to copy a set of solid faces to become a new surface body.

You can find one nice option that enables you to quickly see where the boundaries of a surface body lie by choosing Tools ⇨ Options ⇨ Display/Selection ⇨ Show Open Edges Of Surfaces In Different Color. By default, this color is a medium blue, and you can change it by choosing Tools ⇨ Options ⇨ Colors ⇨ Surfaces ⇨ Open Edges.

Using the Trim function

 The Trim function in SolidWorks is analogous to the solid Cut. You can use sketches, planes, or other surface bodies to trim a surface body. The underlying surface is defined by a two-dimensional mesh, and for this reason, it is usually four-sided, but may be other shapes. When the underlying surface is trimmed, the software still remembers the underlying shape, but combines it with the new boundary, which is typically how face shapes (especially non-four-sided shapes) are created.

Using the Untrim function

 Untrim is predictably the opposite of Trim. It removes the boundary from a surface. It can remove the boundary selectively (one edge at a time, interior edges only, and so on) or remove all the edges at once. Untrim even works on imported geometry, as described in the tutorial in Chapter 19. Figure 20.1 shows how Untrim works.

FIGURE 20.1

Untrimming a surface

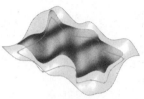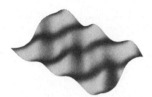

Surface created native in SolidWorks by lofting

Surface trimmed by a sketch, trimmed away portion shown as transparent

Trimmed surface with an Untrim feature applied to it

Untrim works on native and imported geometry. It is not truly like feature history in imported geometry, but it does help to uncover the underlying original shape of the face.

Exploring hybrid modeling

Modeling software has long divided itself along Solid/Surface lines with products such as Rhino (strictly surface modeling) and early versions of SolidWorks (strictly solid modeling). However, modelers are now increasing functionality in both methods and allowing them to interact. This hybrid modeling is a combination of solid and surface modeling. Surface modeling is now better understood by people who are doing general modeling, so combining the techniques is also more popular.

Surface modeling tends to be slower than solid modeling because you model each face individually, and then manually trim and knit. Cutting a hole in a surface model is much more involved than cutting a hole in a solid. To cut a hole in a surface model, you first trim a hole on one side, then the other side, then make the face of the hole, and then knit it together as a single, enclosed volume.

Solid modeling is essentially highly automated surface modeling; however, as any software user knows, automation almost always comes at the expense of flexibility, and this situation is no different. Surface modeling puts the compromised power back into your hands.

Solid modeling strengths are predisposed to a type of part with square ends or a flat bottom because solids are creating all sides of an object at once, and capping off a solid feature with a domed shape is difficult. For example, think about an extrusion: regardless of the shape of the sketch, you have two flat ends. Even lofts and sweeps typically end up with one or two flat ends because the section sketches are often planar. Surfaces enable you to create one side at a time. Another way of looking at it is that using surfaces *requires* you to build parts in sections.

You will find times when, even with prismatic modeling, surfacing functions are extremely useful. I do not propose that you dive into pure surface modeling just to benefit from a few of the advantages, but I do recommend that you consider using surface techniques to help define your solids. This hybrid approach is sensible and opens up a whole new world of capabilities. I have heard people say after taking a SolidWorks surfacing class that they would never look at the software in the same way again.

Understanding Non Uniform Rational B Spline

NURBS stands for Non Uniform Rational B Spline. NURBS is the technology that most modern mechanical design modelers use to create 3D geometry. NURBS surfaces are defined by curves called isoparameter lines in perpendicular directions (referred to as U and V directions), which form a mesh. The fact that perpendicular directions are used means that the surfaces have a tendency to be four-sided. Of course exceptions exist, such as three-sided or even two-sided patches. Geometry of this kind is referred to as *degenerate* because one or more of the sides has been reduced to zero length. Degenerate geometry is often, but not always, the source of geometrical errors in SolidWorks and other CAD packages.

Figure 20.2 shows some surfaces with the mesh displayed on them. You can create the mesh with the Face Curves sketch tool.

FIGURE 20.2

Meshes created with the Face Curves sketch tool

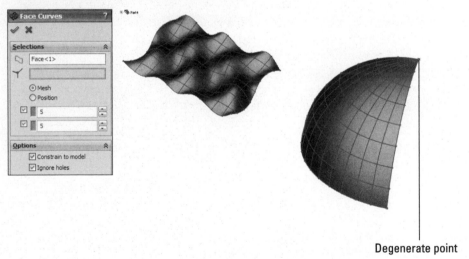

Degenerate point

An example of a competitive system to NURBS surface modeling is point mesh data. This comes from systems such as 3DSMax, which create a set of points that are joined together in triangular facets, and can be represented in SolidWorks as an STL (stereolithography) or VRML (virtual reality markup language) file. When displayed in SolidWorks, this data looks very faceted or tessellated into small, flat triangles, but when viewed in software that is meant to work with these kinds of meshes, it looks smooth. Many advantages come with this type of data, especially when it comes to applying colors and motion. However, the main disadvantage is that the geometrical accuracy is not very good. Point mesh data is typically used by 3D graphic artists, animators, and game developers.

By using a SolidWorks add-in such as ScanTo3D (available only in SolidWorks Premium), it is possible to take point mesh data and create a NURBS mesh over it. This is not a push-button solution, but it offers capabilities where none previously existed. ScanTo3D is beyond the scope of this book, but you should find it useful if you are interested enough to read about NURBS and point meshes.

Using developable surfaces

Developable surfaces can be flattened without stretching. They are also surfaces that you can extend easily in one or both directions. These include planar, cylindrical, and conical shapes. It is not a coincidence that these are the types of shapes that can be flattened by the Sheet Metal tools.

Using ruled surfaces

Developable surfaces are a special type of a broader range of surface called ruled surfaces. SolidWorks has a special tool for the creation of ruled surfaces that is described in detail in the next section. Ruled surfaces are defined as surfaces on which a straight line can be drawn at every point. A corollary to this is that ruled surfaces may have curvature in only one direction. Ruled surfaces are far less limited than developable surfaces, but are not as easily flattened.

Ruled surfaces are used frequently in plastic parts and plastic mold design where draft and parting surfaces from 3D parting lines are needed.

Defining Gaussian curvature

Gaussian curvature is not referred to directly in SolidWorks software, but you may hear the term used in more general CAD or engineering discussions. It can be defined simply as curvature in two directions. As a result, a sphere would have Gaussian curvature, but a cylinder would not.

Surfacing Tools

Surface feature equivalents are available for most solid features such as extrude, revolve, sweep, loft, fillet, and so on. Some solid features do not have an equivalent, such as the Hole Wizard, shell, and others. Several surface functions do not have solid equivalents, such as trim, Untrim, Extend, Thicken, Offset, Radiate, Ruled, and Fill.

This is not a comprehensive guide to complex shape modeling, but it should serve as an introduction to each feature type and some of the details about how it operates.

Classifying the Extruded Surface

 The Extruded Surface works exactly like an extruded solid, except that the ends of the surface are not capped. It includes all the same end conditions, draft, contour selection, sketch rules, and so on that you are already familiar with. Figure 20.3 shows the PropertyManager for the Extruded Surface.

FIGURE 20.3

The Extruded Surface PropertyManager

You can also create extruded surfaces from open sketches, and, in fact, that is probably a more common situation than creating a surface with a closed sketch.

When two non-parallel sketch lines are joined end to end, the result of extruding the sketch is a single surface body that is made of two faces with a hard edge between them. If the sketch lines were disjointed, then the extrude would result in disjoint surface bodies. If the sketch lines were again made end to end, but done in separate sketches, then the resulting surface bodies would be separate bodies; the second body would not be automatically knit to the first one as happens with solid features. This is an important quality of surfaces to keep in mind. If you create surfaces in different features and want them knitted into a single body, then you will have to do that manually.

Starting in SolidWorks 2011, there is a new method you can use to extrude surfaces. If you have a split line on a surface, you can select the surface and start the Extruded Surface command. You then need to select a plane or axis to define the extrusion direction, and specify the depth of the extrusion. Figure 20.4 shows the PropertyManager and result of this new function.

This technique is special because of the additional options: Cap End, Delete original faces, and Knit result. The Cap End option has existed for some time, but the ability to remove the face inside the extrude and to knit it all together is new. It would be nice for these functions to exist with regular sketch-based extrudes and other surface features as well.

You can find a similar function in the Surface Extrude's ability to extrude a 3D sketch. You can also use a regular solid Extrude to extrude a 3D sketch, and it caps the ends for you. While I find all of these extrude options interesting, I have yet to find an application for them. The new ability to extrude a 3D surface duplicates the Ruled surface, although the additional options must be selected manually.

FIGURE 20.4

Extruding a 3D surface

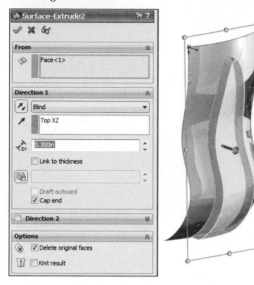

Using Revolved Surface

The Revolved Surface functions like its solid counterpart, right down to the rules for how it handles entities that are touching the axis of revolution; nothing can cross the axis. A single sketch entity is allowed to touch it at a single point, but multiple sketch entities cannot touch it at the same point.

Using Swept Surface

Swept Surfaces work much like their solid counterpart, and the sketch rules and available entities are the same. The main difference here is going to be that Swept Surfaces usually use an open contour for the profile, while swept solids use closed contours.

Identifying the Lofted Surface

The main difference between Lofted Surfaces and lofted solids is that the surfaces can use edges and curve features as profiles, rather than simply sketches and faces.

Using Boundary Surface

The Boundary Surface was created as a higher quality replacement for the Loft feature, but certain limitations mean that Loft has not been removed from the feature list. The Boundary Surface most resembles a loft, but has elements of the sweep. Loft also does a few things that Boundary cannot, such as a closed loop loft without a direction 2 curve, and most importantly, a centerline loft. Boundary Surface can use sketches, curves, or edges in several arrangements, such as curves arranged in an X, F, E, T, L, and other shapes. Figure 20.5 shows some of these shapes.

FIGURE 20.5

Using different curve arrangements with the Boundary Surface feature

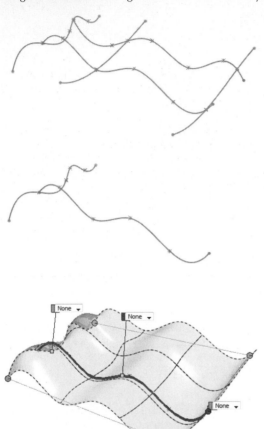

If several edge or sketch segments combine to form a curve in one direction, then you must use the SelectionManager to form the edge segments into a group. SelectionManager enables you to select portions of a single sketch or to combine elements such as sketch, edge, and curve into a single selection for use as a profile or guide curve for Boundary or Loft features.

The interface for the Boundary Surface is shown in Figure 20.6.

The types of models where you end up using the Boundary Surface are highly curvy models that are modeled mainly with surface features and require a four-sided patch.

The main advantage of Boundary Surface over Loft is that Boundary Surface can apply a Curvature boundary condition all the way around, while Loft cannot apply curvature continuity across the guide curves. Fill Surfaces also can apply a Curvature boundary condition all the way around.

Unlike the Sketch Offset function — and as v
zero distance. This is usually done to copy ei
Zero-distance offset and Knit are sometimes surface, only the small arrows that indi-
you are selecting a surface body that is comp ed to switch the arrows to the other side,
knit one body to another, and so, by default, ■
you cannot knit a body to itself. Because Kni
tool when copying faces to make a new surfa
for the offset distance, the Offset PropertyM always results in an incorrect result,

Knit does have two functions that Sketch Of p. As long as individual edges are listed
from the knit body if it forms a closed body.
the ability to select all faces on one side of a
in this chapter in the Knit Surface section. resting usage is when you combine it
                                                 s a part surrounded by a Radiate
When talking about copying surface bodies, faces to one side of the radiated sur-
which is described in Chapter 19. When sim r that contains Face<1> is called a *seed*
issues a warning that asks whether you real the same side of the model as the
annoying and pointless message. Also, the M es completely around the model and
only a part of a body (selected faces) or to n ces on the other side of the Radiate.
Surface features.   ly useful for mold creation.

All things considered, I recommend using th
parts of bodies unless your goal is to immed
the Knit feature) or when using a Radiated s

Using Radiate Surface

The Radiate Surface is not one of the more (
seded by the Ruled Surface. This is because
Surface does, as well as a lot more, and is al
reference plane, and a distance. The newly (
parallel to the selected plane, and the set di
ating molds or other net shape tooling such
ing, and so on. Figure 20.7 shows the Proper

The Radiate Surface PropertyManager

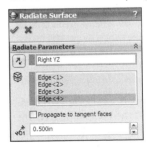

minology section as well as in the

orm solid option turns the volume
other functions. The Fill Surface has
e body; if the knit surface body is
y nice, complete interface design,
s described in more detail later in

The Gap Control panel, shown in Figure 20.9, shows the gap between the edges of surfaces to be knit, and enables you to see the gaps in a certain range and force gaps of less than a specified tolerance value, called the Knitting Tolerance, to knit. This replaces the old Minimal Adjustment option in Knit, which SolidWorks did not go to any great length to help users understand. The Knitting Tolerance tools are easier to understand and more powerful when it comes to forcing knit features to work.

FIGURE 20.9

Knitting Surfaces with gaps using tolerances

With all powerful tools the possibility of misusing the tool always exists. The ability to play with tolerances is a double-edged sword. On one hand it gives you the ability to force surfaces to knit that may have otherwise not knit at all. On the other hand, if you allow a larger tolerance, SolidWorks may force together surfaces or edges that have problems that should be solved in other ways. such as removal and remodeling. Gap tolerances can cause problems during import operations to other software that doesn't have the capability to adjust tolerances. Certainly use the Gap Control options, but also be aware of the potential problems you might see with data downstream.

Using Thicken Surface

The other function that also creates a solid from a surface is the Thicken feature. If a surface body that encloses a volume is selected, then the option Create solid from enclosed volume appears on the Thicken PropertyManager, as shown in Figure 20.10. You can access the Thicken feature by choosing Insert ⇨ Boss/Base ⇨ Thicken from the menus.

FIGURE 20.10

The Thicken PropertyManager

Using Planar Surface

Planar Surfaces can be created quickly and are useful in many situations, not just for surfacing work. Because they are by definition *planar*, you can use them to sketch on and for other purposes that you may use a plane for, such as mirroring.

However, more commonly, Planar Surfaces are created from a closed sketch such as a rectangle. You can create multiple Planar Surfaces at once, and the surfaces do not need to all be on the same plane or even parallel. This is commonly done to close up holes in a surface model, such as at the bottom of cylindrical bosses on a plastic part, using a planar circular edge. A good example of this is the bike frame part in the material for Chapter 20 on the DVD, named Chapter 20- bike frame.sldprt.

Remember that a Planar Surface was used in Chapter 19 with the Split feature to split the leg off of an imported part. This was more effective than a sketch or a plane because the split was limited to the bounds of the Planar Surface, not infinite like the sketch or the plane.

The Planar Surface does not knit itself into the rest of the surface bodies around it automatically; you have to use the Knit feature to do this.

Using Extend Surface

The Extend Surface feature functions much in the same way that the Extend function works in sketches. Figure 20.11 shows the PropertyManager interface and an example of the feature at work.

The only item here that requires explanation is the Extension Type panel. The Same surface option means that the extended surface will simply be extrapolated in the selected direction. A Planar Surface is the easiest to extend because it can go on indefinitely without running into problems. A cylindrical surface can only be extended until it runs into itself. Complex lofted or Swept Surfaces are often difficult to extend. Extrapolating a complex surface is not easy to do and often results in self-intersecting faces, which cause the feature to fail.

When the Same surface setting works, it creates a nice result because it does not create an edge where the extension begins; it smoothly extends the existing face.

FIGURE 20.11

The Extend Surface PropertyManager

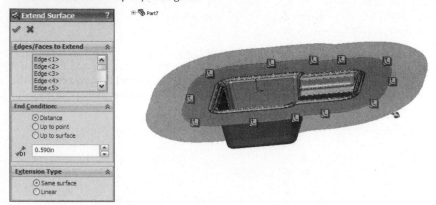

The Linear option is more reliable than the Same surface option because it starts tangent to the existing surface and keeps going in that direction, working much like a Ruled surface, which is covered later in this chapter. It does not rely on extending the existing surface. This option creates an edge at the starting point of the new geometry.

Using Trim Surface

 The Trim Surface feature is described briefly earlier in this chapter, but it warrants a more complete description here. Surfaces can be trimmed by three different types of entities:

- Sketches
- Planes
- Other surfaces

When you use surface bodies to trim one another, you must select one of two options: Standard or Mutual Trim. The Standard option causes one surface to act as the Trim tool and the other surface to be trimmed by the Trim tool. When you select the Mutual Trim option, both surfaces act as the Trim tool, and both surfaces are trimmed.

For an example of trimmed surfaces, open the mouse example from Chapter 19 and step through the tree. This shows examples of a couple of types of trimmed surfaces, as well as extended surfaces and others.

Many people overlook the ability to trim a surface with a plane, which can be very handy sometimes. Planes are infinite, which means you have less to worry about when it comes to changes that affect features rebuilding correctly.

Finally, trimming with 2D sketches is well known, but trimming with 3D sketches is less known. There is a 3D sketch tool called Spline on Surface that enables you to draw a spline directly on any surface body. An option exists in the Trim Surface PropertyManager to trim a surface with this type of sketch. This is very useful in many situations if you can remember that it is available.

Using Fill Surface

The Fill Surface is one of my favorite tools in SolidWorks. I often refer to it as the "magic wand" because it is sometimes amazing what it can do. It is alternately referred to by the SolidWorks interface and documentation as either Fill or Filled, depending on where the reference is made. You will find it listed as both in the SolidWorks interface.

The Fill Surface is intended to fill in gaps in surface bodies. It can do this either smoothly or by leaving sharp corners. You can use constraint curves to drive the shape of the fill between the existing boundaries. It can even knit a surface body together into a solid, all-in-one step. Beyond this, you can use the Fill Surface directly on solid models and integrate it directly into the solid automatically (much like the Replace Face function, which is described later in this chapter).

Several rather complex examples of the Fill Surface are found in the bike frame example. One of these fills is shown in Figure 20.12.

FIGURE 20.12

The Fill Surface PropertyManager and the results of applying it

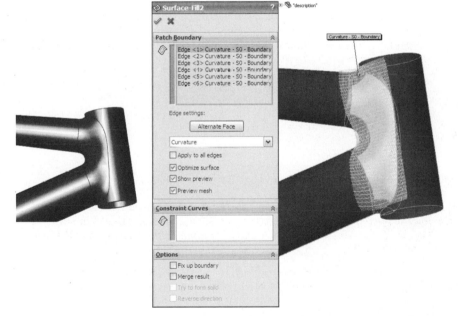

The first thing you should notice about the Fill Surface is that it is creating an oversized, four-sided patch and trimming it to fit into the available space. This is one of the reasons why I consider this to be such a magical tool. The four-sided patch I referred to earlier in the section on NURBS is shown very clearly in this feature preview. Also, the trimmed surface concept is illustrated nicely by this feature. Not surprising, if you untrim the Fill Surface, then you return to the surface that is previewed here. In this one function, SolidWorks gives you some useful insight about what is going on behind the scenes.

When using the Fill Surface, it is best to have a patch completely bounded by other surfaces, as shown in Figure 20.11. Fill Surface can work with a boundary that is not enclosed, but it works better with a closed boundary.

You can set boundary conditions as Contact, Tangent, or Curvature. Contact simply means that the faces touch at an edge. Tangent means that the slopes of the faces on either side of the edge match at all points along the edge. Curvature means curvature continuous (or C2), where the Fill Surface matches not only tangency, but also the curvature of the face on the other side of the boundary edge. This results in a smoother transition than a transition that is simply tangent.

When you select the Optimize Surface option, SolidWorks tries to fit the four-sided patch into the boundary. Notice that on this part, even though the Optimize surface option is selected, it is clearly being ignored because the boundary is a six-sided gap and cannot be patched smoothly with a four-sided patch. It is not necessarily an improvement to make a Fill Surface optimized, even when it works.

Constraint curves can influence the shape of the Fill Surface. An example of this is shown in Figure 20.13. The construction splines shown on the faces of the part were created by the Intersection Curve tool and enabled the spline used for the constraint curve to be made tangent to the surface.

FIGURE 20.13

The Fill Surface feature with constraint curves

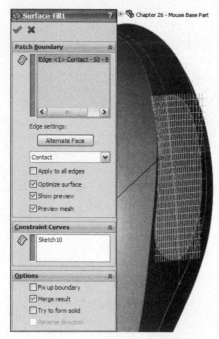

Using MidSurface

 The MidSurface feature is not used very often. It was probably originally intended to be used in conjunction with analysis tools to create plate elements for thin-walled structures. It works on parallel faces of a solid, creating a surface midway between the faces. If the faces have opposing draft (such that a wall is wider at the bottom than at the top), then the MidSurface will not work. It works on linear walls and cylindrical walls, but not on elliptical or spline-based shapes. The PropertyManager for the MidSurface is shown in Figure 20.14.

The MidSurface PropertyManager

Similar to the Planar Surface, you can also use the MidSurface to create a surface that can be used like a plane. No plane type can create a symmetrical plane, but using a MidSurface, you can create a symmetrical Planar Surface between parallel walls.

Using Replace Face

 The Replace Face feature does not create new surface geometry, but it does integrate existing surface geometry into the solid. It replaces selected faces of a solid or surface body with a selected surface body. Replace Face is one of the few tools that can add and remove material at the same time with a single feature.

If you were to manually perform the functions that are done by Replace Face, then you would start by deleting several faces of the solid, then extending faces, and then trimming surface bodies, and finish by knitting all the trimmed and extended faces back into a single solid body.

This is a very powerful and useful tool, although it is sometimes difficult to tell which situations it will work in. Figure 20.15 shows a part before and after a Replace Face feature has been added. The surface used to replace the flat face of the solid has been turned transparent. The first selection box is for the original face or faces, and the second selection box is for the surface body with the new faces. The tool tips for each of the boxes are Target Faces For Replacement and Replacement Surface(s), which seem a little ambiguous. I like to think of them as Old (top) and New (bottom).

Using Replace Face

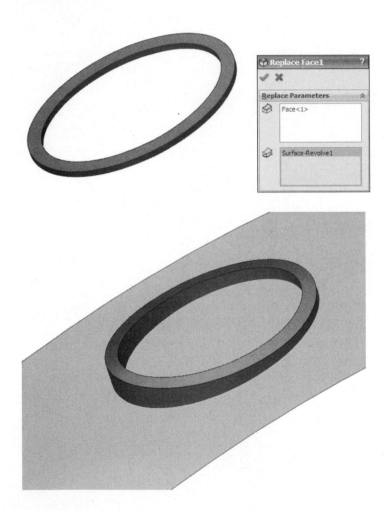

Using Untrim Surface

The Untrim Surface is discussed in the terminology section of this chapter. You can use it either selectively on edges or on the entire surface body.

Using Parting Surface

The Parting Surface is part of the SolidWorks Mold Tools. The Mold Tools are addressed in the companion to this book, the *SolidWorks 2011 Assemblies Bible* (Wiley, 2011).

Using Ruled Surface

Ruled Surfaces are discussed in general in the section on terminology. Here I discuss the topic in more detail, and specifically with regard to the SolidWorks interface for creating Ruled Surfaces.

The Ruled Surface feature in SolidWorks is one of those features that you may never have missed until you see it in action. It is extremely useful for constructing faces with draft, extending faces tangent to a direction, making Radiate Surface types, building molds, and many other applications.

Figure 20.16 shows the PropertyManager interface for the Ruled Surface.

FIGURE 20.16

The Ruled Surface PropertyManager interface

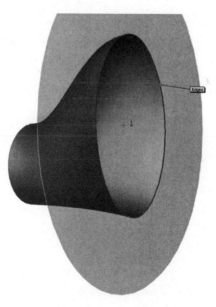

The Ruled Surface works from the edge of a solid or surface body. The feature has five basic types of operations that it can perform:

- Tangent to Surface
- Normal to Surface
- Tapered to Vector
- Perpendicular to Vector
- Sweep

The Tangent to Surface setting is self-explanatory. The Alternate Face option would be available if the base shape had been a solid, with a face filling the big elliptical hole. This would make the Ruled Surface tangent to the bottom face instead of the side.

With the Normal to Surface setting, it tilts up five degrees from the horizontal because the surface is lofted with a five-degree draft angle at the big end, making a Ruled Surface that is normal. Be careful of using this setting because it looks close to what you may be hoping for, but is slightly off. One of the other options may be a better choice, depending on what you are looking for.

The Tapered to Vector setting needs a plane or axis selection to establish a direction, and then the Ruled Surface is created from that reference at the angle that you set. With a combination of the Alternate Side button and the arrow direction toggle button next to the plane selection, you can adjust the cone created by this setting. The interface to make the changes is not exactly clear unless you use this function often, but it does work.

The Perpendicular to Vector setting is a better option than the Normal to Surface setting when the surface has been created with some sort of built-in draft angle. This is also the setting that looks most like the Radiate Surface feature, although it works much better than Radiate Surface.

The Sweep setting makes a face that is perpendicular to the surface created by Perpendicular to Vector. It is as if a straight line were swept around the edge. This is actually a great way to offset an edge or 3D sketch: using the edge of the surface as the offset of the original.

Using Surfacing Techniques

This section serves as a brief overview of some of the techniques commonly used among people who model using surfaces. This section could be the topic for an entire book on its own. In fact, it is the topic of an entire book that goes into far greater detail. You may want to use the *SolidWorks Surfacing and Complex Shape Modeling Bible* (Wiley, 2008) to continue your SolidWorks education in far greater detail and depth.

Using Up To Surface/Up To Body

Cross-Reference

Chapter 7 contains more information on end conditions such as Up To Surface and Up To Body. ∎

Some modeling situations seem to require elaborate workarounds until you think of doing them with a combination of solid and surface features, such as the part shown in Figure 20.17. This geometry could be made completely with solids, but it would be more difficult. In this case, a surface is revolved, representing the shape at the bottom of the hole, and the cut is extruded up to it. You can follow along with the part from the DVD at `Chapter 20 - square hole.sldprt`.

Another familiar situation is when you have a feature to place and you want to use an Offset from Surface end condition, but the feature spans two faces. In that situation, you can knit the necessary faces together (or use offset), and then extrude offset from that surface body.

FIGURE 20.17

Using the Up To Body setting

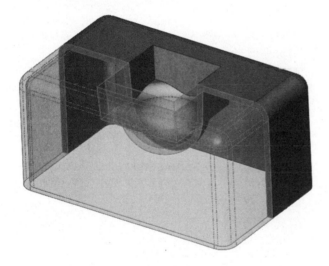

Tip

Using Up To or Offset From Body rather than Face often avoids the common error message, "The end face cannot terminate the extruded feature," especially if the feature that is extruded spans more than one face. ∎

Figure 20.18 shows a part using an Offset Surface to extrude text up to where the text spans more than a single surface. This is a very common application, even if it is not text that is being extruded. The part that was used in Figure 20.17 is on the DVD in the materials for Chapter 20, and is called `Chapter 20 - Up To Body.SLDPRT`.

FIGURE 20.18

Extruding text

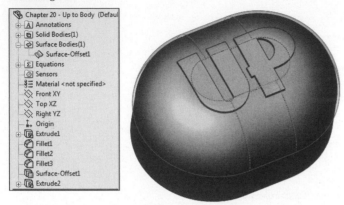

Using Cut With Surface

 Sometimes you may need to make a cut that is more complex than what a simple extrude can do. For example, the cut may need to have shape in multiple directions. You could make the cut with multiple cut features, or even with a surface. Figure 20.19 shows a part that is cut with a surface.

FIGURE 20.19

Using the Cut With Surface feature on a part

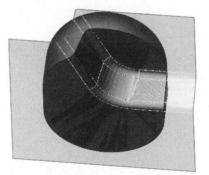

When cutting with a surface, the edges of the surface must be outside of the body that is being cut. With sketches, it is advisable to have more sketch than you need so that you are not trying to cut line-on-line. The same applies to cutting with a surface, where it is advisable to have more surface than you need to make the cut.

Using Replace Face

 The Replace Face feature can be used on imported or native geometry. You can use it to add or remove material from a part. When it adds material, it must be able to extend faces adjacent to those that are being replaced, which can be a limitation. A face or faces do not need to be replaced with the same kind or same number of faces, but the entire face that is being replaced must be removed. If you only want to replace a part of a face, then you can use a Split line to scribe the face, and then replace the part you want.

Figure 20.20 shows that the multiple faces of the letter U on this part have been replaced with a surface from an inserted part. Replace Face is a fantastic tool that you can use in a number of situations, although it is a little particular sometimes and you cannot always predict when it will or will not work.

Using Fill Surface

The Fill Surface feature is one of my favorites in the SolidWorks software. It can get you out of modeling binds easily, and is often used to cover over nasty modeling mistakes or areas you just can't get right by any other method. In addition to its duty in the complex shapes department, it can also be used as a fast way to create a Planar Surface in some situations. If you do much surface modeling, the Fill feature will become a staple of your diet.

FIGURE 20.20

Using Replace Face

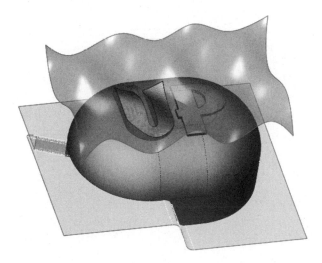

Note

The Fill Surface is an advanced surfacing function. Sometimes, when talking about advanced surfacing functions, or indeed any software function, users have a tendency to sound a little cynical. This is because the tool is often expected to work on very complex geometry. It is not always the software's fault when it cannot perform a particular task, or does not do what you imagine you want it to do. Sometimes, the tool is simply not meant to perform certain tasks, there may be an unseen flaw in the geometry that prevents it from working, or the user does not understand the settings completely. The more complex the work, the more frequently you need to find workarounds to get something done. Avoiding problems does not make them go away. In this book, I have chosen to take a realistic look at most of the features. ∎

Figure 20.21 shows the Fill Surface blending an intersection between tubes. The image to the left shows the before condition with the tubes coming together at an edge. The center image shows the edge trimmed out using the Trim feature, and the right image shows the hole blended over by the Fill Surface feature.

In Figure 20.22, a solid starts with a Split line on the surface. A sketch is then added, and a Fill Surface is created using the sketch as a constraint and the Split line as the boundary. The Merge Result option in the Fill PropertyManager has a different significance than it does in a solid feature PropertyManager, but the end result is the same. Remember that this is a surface function, and if it does not merge, then it is left as a surface feature.

FIGURE 20.21

Blending with the Fill Surface

The Fill PropertyManager for merging a Fill Surface directly into a solid

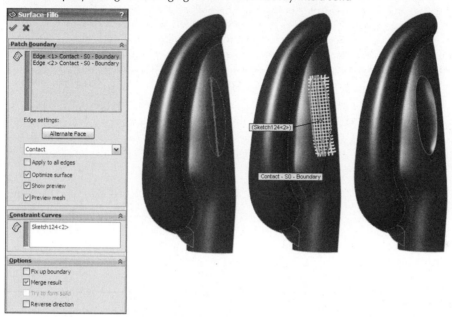

If you had to go through these steps manually, then you would use the Replace Face feature to integrate the surface into the solid. The key to integrating the Fill Surface directly into the solid without any additional features is the Merge Result option in the Fill PropertyManager.

Using a memory surface

A *memory surface* is not another new type of feature that you can select from the menu or a toolbar; it is just the name that I gave to a technique that I use from time to time. A memory surface is just a Knit or Offset Surface that is made at one point in the feature tree when a particular face is whole, and reused later when the face has been broken up, but you still need to reference the entire original face. An example of this technique is shown in Figure 20.23. In this case, extra material is created around the opening, and a surface that was created in a Rollback state is used to remove it.

FIGURE 20.23

Using the memory surfaces technique to cut away unwanted geometry

Tutorial: Working with Surfaces

This is another chapter that contains many important ideas, and yet there is only so much space for tutorials. The best way to learn is to experiment. I recommend that you closely follow the tutorial steps once, and then, when you understand the concepts involved, that you go back and experiment.

Using Cut With Surface

Follow these steps to gain some experience with the Cut With Surface feature:

1. **Start by creating a new part and drawing a rectangle on the Top plane, centered on the Origin, about 4 inches by 6 inches, with the 4-inch dimension in the vertical direction.**

2. **Extrude the rectangle Mid-plane, by 2 inches.**

3. **From the Surface toolbar, select Lofted Surface, and select one 4-inch edge as a loft profile.** Then select a second 4-inch edge diagonal from the first one. This is shown in Figure 20.24.

4. **Expand the Start/End Constraints panel, and set both ends to use the Direction Vector setting, selecting the plane that is in the middle of the long direction in each case.** In the part shown, the Right plane is used. Click OK to accept the feature. This is shown in Figure 20.24.

FIGURE 20.24

Lofting a surface from the edges of a solid

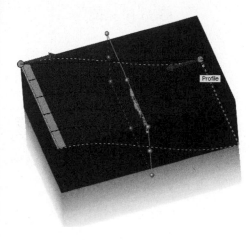

5. **From the menus, choose Insert ⇨ Cut ⇨ With Surface.** Select the surface from the flyout FeatureManager, and toggle the arrow direction so that the top is cut off. (The arrow points to the side that is cut off.)

Using Offset Surface

Follow these steps to gain some experience with the Offset Surface:

1. **Open the part from the DVD called** Chapter 20 – Offset Tutorial.sldprt.

2. **Right-click a curved face of the part and click Select Tangency in the menu.**

3. **With the faces still selected, from the Surfaces toolbar, click Offset Surface, and set the surface to offset to the outside of the part by .060 inches.** You can tell when the surface is offsetting to the outside when the transparent preview appears. If you do not see the transparent preview, toggle the Flip Offset Direction arrow button. Click OK to accept the feature when you are satisfied.

4. **Look in the Surface Bodies folder at the top of the FeatureManager tree, expand the folder, and select the Offset Surface.** Then use the Appearances toolbar button to change the transparency of the surface body to about .75. You can also do this through the Display

Pane, by clicking in the column following the surface body in the bodies folder that is far-thest to the right, as shown in Figure 20.25. This is done so that you can see the part under-neath the surface, without mistaking the surface for the actual part.

FIGURE 20.25

Using the Display Pane to change transparency

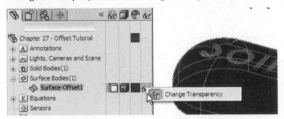

Tip

It is a common practice to change surface colors to something that contrasts with the part color. I usually use a color like yellow, which suggests temporary status or construction. Some users take this a step further and set the template colors for surface types by choosing Tools ⇨ Options ⇨ Document Properties ⇨ Colors. These settings do not always work; in some cases, they turn surface features to a different color, and in other situations they do not. ∎

5. **Select Sketch2, and select Extruded Boss/Base from the Features toolbar.** Do not mis-take the Extruded Surface for an Extruded Solid. Set the end condition to Up To Body, acti-vate the body selection box, and select the Offset Surface body from the Surface Bodies folder. The result is shown in Figure 20.26.

FIGURE 20.26

Extruding with the Up To Body setting

Tip

It is preferable to select the surface from the Surface Bodies folder, rather than the feature list or the graphics window. In this case, you want to extrude up to a body. If you make the selection from the feature list, then you are likely to select a feature (which is okay in this situation, but not in all situations). If you make the selection from the graphics window, then the selection is likely to be interpreted as a face. It is best to be as explicit as possible when making selections because SolidWorks may interpret your selection literally. In this case, it is probably a better idea to use Up To Body for the end condition than Up To Surface, because the goal is really to use the surface body as the end of the feature. ■

6. **To invert the lettering so that it sits below the surface rather than above the surface, you can make a few simple changes.** First, edit the Offset Surface feature and flip the direction of the offset so that the surface is now inside the solid rather than outside the solid. You will not be able to see it unless the solid is either transparent or in wireframe mode.

7. **Next, delete the extrude that you created to extrude the text.** There is no way to change an extrude into a cut in this context.

8. **Re-create the extrude as an extruded cut.** Use the From settings at the top of the PropertyManager window. The settings and results are shown in Figure 20.27.

FIGURE 20.27

An extruded cut

Another way to accomplish this would be to use the Move Face tool, select the faces of the letters, and move them .120 of an inch into the solid.

Using Fill Surface blend

Sometimes fillets do not meet your needs. Blends, such as those shown in the bike frame example, are smoother and can blend just about anything. However, the technique is not exactly straightforward. Follow these steps to gain familiarity with this technique:

1. **Open the part from the DVD for Chapter 20 called** Chapter 20 - Blend.SLDPRT. **Box select all the features from the DeleteFace1 to the Shell, and suppress them.**

2. **On the Top plane, draw a square 2 inches on a side and centered on the Origin.**

3. **Use the Split Entities tool found on the Sketch toolbar or choose Tools ⇨ Sketch Tools ⇨ Split Entities from the menus.** Divide each line of the rectangle into three pieces, with the two outer pieces of each line being .6 inches (use an Equal sketch relation). The sketch should be fully defined when you are done. This arrangement is shown in Figure 20.28. This is done because the edges of the tubes need to be broken into sections.

   With the lines split, now use the Split Line tool at Insert ⇨ Curves ⇨ Split line to split the faces of all tubes.

FIGURE 20.28

Using split entities to split lines

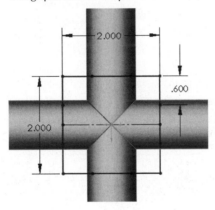

4. **Use Delete Face to delete the ends of the four tubes.** Set the option to Delete, not the default option of Delete and Patch. This converts the solid into a surface body.

5. **Use the sketch with the split entities to trim out the center section of the tubes, keeping the outer section and leaving four surface bodies.** This divides each tube end into four segments where they have been trimmed, as shown in Figure 20.29.

6. **Initiate the Lofted Surface feature, and select the nearest edge segments from adjacent tubes.** If the loft preview twists, use the light-blue handles to straighten it out or deselect and reselect one of the edges in approximately the same location as the other edge was selected. Expand the End Conditions panel and set each edge to use the Curvature setting. You may adjust the End Tangent Length option if you want, but keep in mind that this may make the part asymmetrical.

FIGURE 20.29

Split ends after trimming

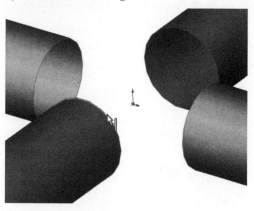

As a note, you may choose to use the Boundary Surface in the place of the loft. For this function, the two are similar enough.

7. **Create Lofted Surfaces all the way around the part, linking all the tubes.** Figure 20.30 shows the part with three of the lofts already completed and the last one in progress.

FIGURE 20.30

Adding Lofted Surfaces

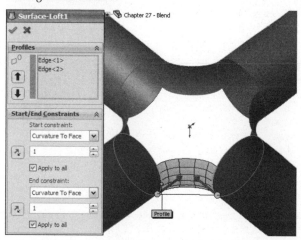

8. **Start a Planar Surface feature, and select the open ends of each tube where the faces were deleted in Step 4.**

Note

Not all features allow you to operate from multiple bodies, but the Loft and Planar Surface features do. Features such as Fillet and Draft restrict you to creating features that are associated with one body at a time. ∎

9. **Start a Knit Surface feature, and Shift+select all the bodies in the Surface Bodies folder (select the first body in the list and Shift+select the last body).** When you click OK to accept the feature, notice that the number of surface bodies changes to one. Selecting bodies in this way is much faster for large numbers of bodies than selecting them one at a time from the graphics window.

Note

Notice that the open edges of the surface body are shown in a different color. At this point, there are two open edges around the holes at the intersection of the tubes. ∎

10. **This is a situation that the Fill Surface is really meant for.** In fact, this technique was created specifically to take advantage of the Fill Surface capabilities. Right-click any of the open edges and choose Select Open Loop. Initiate the Fill Surface. Change the Edge setting option to Tangent, and make sure that the Apply to all edges option is selected. Select the Merge result option, but leave the Try to form solid option unselected. The model at this point is shown in Figure 20.31, along with the PropertyManager settings that are used.

FIGURE 20.31

Creating a Fill Surface patch

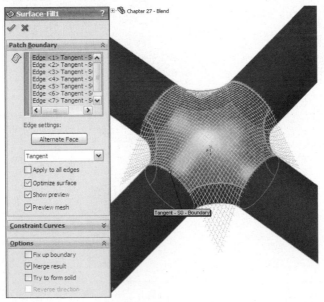

Note

The Optimize surface option is ignored for this part because the opening is eight-sided rather than four-sided. Also note that you may have to change the resolution control slider to get the surface to remain convex instead of going concave in the center. ■

11. **Click OK to accept the feature.**

12. **Start another Fill Surface, turning the part over to use the same selection on the back and the same settings as the first fill.** However, on this one, also use the Try to form solid option. Click OK when the selections and settings are complete.

13. **For the last feature, apply a Shell feature, selecting the flat ends of the tubes and shelling to .100 inches.** The final state of the model is shown in Figure 20.32.

FIGURE 20.32

The finished model

Summary

Surface functions have a wide range of uses other than for complex shape parts, but thinking about your models in terms of surface features requires a slightly different approach. Becoming comfortable with the terminology, and the similarities and differences between solids and surfaces, is the first step toward embracing surfacing tools for everyday work.

You can think of surfaces as being reference geometry — stand-alone faces that you can use to complete various tasks.

Part V

Working with Specialized Functionality

Using SolidWorks Sheet Metal Tools

SolidWorks contains two completely separate methods for working in sheet metal. In one method you can use dedicated sheet metal features from the start, and in the other method you build a part using thin features and other generic modeling tools, and then tell SolidWorks it is sheet metal so you can flatten it.

The reason for two methods is that the generic modeling method came first, and then SolidWorks introduced a more powerful set of dedicated sheet metal features. You can use these tools together or separately, and either way you get an accurately flattened part at the end. Situations where you might want to use one or the other are covered in this chapter.

Sheet metal tools do not always represent real-world sheet metal manufacturing processes 100 percent accurately because some shapes that result from bending processes are too complex to easily represent in a CAD model. So there are times when you still have to use your imagination a little bit, particularly where bends intersect or overlap. The main point is that the Flat Patterns are always accurate because sheet metal is usually fabricated using 2D data.

Using the Base Flange Features

The features used in the Base Flange method are easy to grasp conceptually, and they have many individual controls. These are the tools that represent the newer method of building sheet metal parts from dedicated sheet metal features. You can edit many of the features by pulling handles, by using spin arrows, or by typing in specific numbers or dimensions. Maybe best of all, SolidWorks knows to change the thickness for the entire part at once.

The SolidWorks sheet metal Base Flange method works on a straight brake-press basis. This means that you can place straight bends of a constant radius. The software does not behave well when bends intersect, and does not allow bends to cross. SolidWorks does not flatten anything where the material deforms or does anything other than a straight bend. The exceptions to this are the Lofted Bends and Edge Flange on a curved edge. You should use these two features sparingly, and you should always verify the results before depending on the flat patterns you get from these features.

You will most often design a part in 3D and then flatten it for manufacturing, but SolidWorks also offers a workflow where you start with a flat pattern and add bend lines to it. Both methods work, but designing in 3D is most effective when you are trying to make a sheet metal part fit together with other parts.

Understanding sheet metal manufacturing processes is very helpful for using SolidWorks sheet metal tools to design functional and manufacturable parts. SolidWorks helps you by not allowing you to create a part that cannot be flattened, but it is still easy enough to model a part that cannot be manufactured, or cannot be manufactured economically. You may find it useful to rely on the expertise of either designers with experience or shop personnel to help you learn how to design for sheet metal processes.

You can access the Sheet Metal features by clicking the tool you need in the Sheet Metal toolbar or by choosing Insert ⇨ Sheet Metal from the menus and selecting the appropriate tool.

Using the Base Flange/Tab feature

The first feature you add to a sheet metal part is the Base Flange feature. In addition to letting SolidWorks know that the part is a dedicated sheet metal part, the Base Flange/Tab tool has three functions:

- By drawing an open contour in the first feature, the Base Flange creates a thin feature-like extrusion that includes the rounded corners of the bends.
- By drawing a closed contour in the first feature, the Base Flange creates a flat pattern sheet that is shaped like your sketch for you to start from.
- When the Base Flange is used at any time other than the first feature, it functions as a tab.

Figure 21.1 shows these three functions of the Base Flange/Tab feature.

Notice that the sketch of the part shown in preview in Figure 21.1 has all sharp corners, and that the bend radius is automatically added to each corner by the software. SolidWorks automatically adjusts when bend directions are combined to make sure that the inside radius is always the same, regardless of bend direction.

The bends are shown as BaseBend features in the FeatureManager. You can change individual bend radii from the default setting by editing the BaseBend feature, as well as by assigning custom bend allowances on a per-bend basis. You cannot change the bend angle for these particular bends because the angle is controlled through the sketch. However, for other types of bends (such as those created by Edge Flanges), you can adjust the bend angle through the feature PropertyManager.

If you need to, you can reorder all the bends from a list that you can access from the right mouse button (RMB) menu selection Reorder Bends on the Flat Pattern. This dialog box is shown in Figure 21.2.

FIGURE 21.1

The three functions of the Base Flange/Tab feature

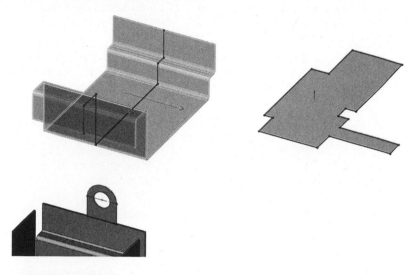

FIGURE 21.2

The Reorder Bends dialog box

The BaseBend features can be suppressed, but the only effect that this has is to prevent the associated bend from flattening when the Flat Pattern feature is unsuppressed.

Using the Sheet Metal feature

 The FeatureManager is shown for the Base Flange with all the bends in Figure 21.3. The Sheet-Metal1 feature is automatically added to sheet metal parts as a placeholder for default sheet metal settings such as material thickness, default bend allowance settings, and Auto Relief options, as well as the default inside bend radius.

FIGURE 21.3

The FeatureManager after the Base Flange is added

Gauge Table

Gauge Tables are a legacy table type, which is simply an Excel spreadsheet. The data from gauge tables was consolidated with other types of flat pattern calculation into what is now called Bend Calculation Tables, which are described in more detail later in this chapter.

Cross-Reference

Bend tables are described in more detail later in this chapter. ■

Gauge Tables enable you to assign a thickness and available inside-bend radii, which limits the choices that the user has for those settings in the table. Each K-Factor has a separate table, and the choices listed in the table appear in the drop-down lists in the Sheet Metal PropertyManager. Figure 21.4 shows the top few lines of a sample Gauge Table and a Sheet Metal PropertyManager when a Gauge Table is used.

If necessary, you can override the values that are used in the Gauge Table by using the override options in the thickness, bend radius, and K-Factor fields of the PropertyManager.

The Bend Allowance options (Allowance, Deduction, and K-Factor) are explained in more detail later in this chapter.

On the DVD

Sample tables with both gauge and bend data are provided on the DVD that accompanies this book. ■

FIGURE 21.4

A sample Gauge Table and Sheet Metal PropertyManager

Type:	Steel Gauge Table				
Process	Steel Air Bending				
Bend Type:	Bend Allowance				
Unit:	inches				
Material:	Steel				
Gauge No.	Gauge 5				
Thickness:	0.2092				
				Radius	
Angle					
		0.25	0.50	0.75	1.00
15		0.40	0.41	0.42	0.43
30		0.40	0.41	0.42	0.43
45		0.40	0.41	0.42	0.43
60		0.40	0.41	0.42	0.43
75		0.40	0.41	0.42	0.43
90		0.40	0.41	0.42	0.43

Bend Radius

This option specifies the default inside bend radius for all bends in the part. You can override values for individual bends or individual features.

Thickness

The part thickness is grayed out in the Sheet Metal PropertyManager. You can change the value by double-clicking any face of the model and then double-clicking the thickness dimension displayed in the graphics area. The thickness displays as a blue dimension rather than a black dimension. It is easier to identify if you have dimension names selected, because it is assigned the link value name Thickness and has a red link symbol to the left of the dimension value.

All features in sheet metal parts that use the thickness value use a link value to link all the feature thicknesses. This makes it easy to globally change the thickness of every feature in the entire sheet metal part.

To save these settings to a template file, you can create a Sheet Metal feature, specify the settings, delete the Sheet Metal features, and then save the file to a template with a special name that represents the settings that you used.

Tip

When a link value is named Thickness, the Extrude dialog box always shows a Link To Thickness option to link the depth of an extrusion to the Thickness link value. If you save a template where Thickness has been created as a link value, then the option is always available to you, regardless of whether or not you are making sheet metal parts. ■

Bend Allowance

You can control the Bend Allowance by using one of four options:

- Bend Table
- K-Factor
- Bend Allowance
- Bend Deduction

Bend Table

Two general types of Bend Tables are available, text-based and Excel-based. The first few rows of each type of table are shown in Figure 21.5. Each table can use K-Factor, Bend Allowance, or Bend Deduction.

FIGURE 21.5

Sample text- and Excel-based Bend Tables

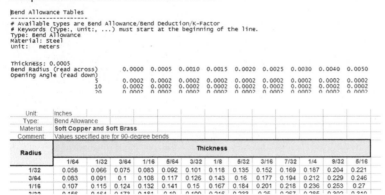

Sample Bend Tables can be found in the `lang\english\Sheetmetal Bend Tables` subdirectory of the SolidWorks installation directory. While the values may not be what you need, the syntax and organization are correct. You may want to contact your sheet metal fabrication shop to see what they are using for a table or equations.

Note

Data from Gauge Tables and Bend Tables have been consolidated, but both legacy types can still be read. ■

K-Factor

When sheet metal is formed from a flat sheet, bending the metal causes it to stretch slightly on the outside part of the bend and to compress slightly on the inside part of the bend. Somewhere across the thickness of the sheet is the Neutral Plane, where there is no stretching or compression. This Neutral Plane can be at various places across the thickness, depending on the material, tooling, and process. The ratio of the distance from the inside bend surface to the Neutral Plane to the thickness is identified as the K-Factor, where .5 means halfway, 0 means on the inside face, and 1 means on the outside face. Typically, you can expect values between .5 and .3.

Bend Allowance and Bend Deduction

Bend Allowance and Bend Deduction are specific length values, not a ratio like the K-Factor. The Bend Allowance is essentially the arclength of the Neutral Plane through the bend region. The Bend Deduction is the length difference between a sharp corner and the radius corner, as expressed by the formula in Figure 21.6.

The three values are related, as shown in Figure 21.6. The dark rectangle represents the bend area. Material outside of the bend area really does not matter, although it is usually shown and used in the generally accepted formulas about bend calculations for sheet metal.

FIGURE 21.6

Calculating the Bend Deduction from the Bend Allowance and K-Factor

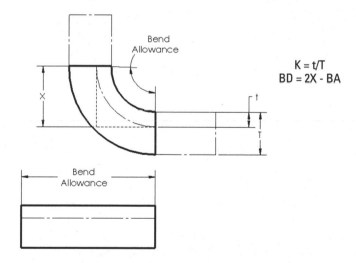

$$K = t/T$$
$$BD = 2X - BA$$

You usually use a ratio t/T (the K-Factor) from a published table or by asking your sheet metal vendor what values they typically use. The values from the tables have been developed experimentally by bending a piece of metal of known length and then measuring the arclength of the inside of the bend and the arclength of the outside of the bend. By comparing these numbers to the original linear length of the bent area, you can find the t value and thus the K value. From the K value, the BA (Bend Allowance) value can be calculated, and from that, the BD (Bend Deduction) value is easy to find.

The specific formulas for finding these numbers are not as important as an intuitive grasp of what the numbers mean and how they are used, at least in relation to using SolidWorks to model sheet metal parts. The numbers used to fill out Bend Tables using K, BA, or BD values are typically taken from experimentally developed tables.

Bend Calculation Tables

Bend Calculation Tables are Excel spreadsheets that enable you to divide bend angles into ranges and assign flat (also referred to as developed) length equations for each range. You can also assign an equation for the K-Factor.

The Excel table must be set up like the example shown in Figure 21.7 in several respects.

FIGURE 21.7

Setting up the Bend Calculation Table

	A	B	C
1	bend type:	bend calculation	
2	unit:	inches	
3	material thickness:	t	
4	radius	r	
5	k-factor	0.65+0.5*lg(r/t)	
6	bend angle	180-a	
7			
8	**Angular Range**	**Equation**	**Use Tangent Length**
9	0<=b<=90	v=pi*((180-b)/180)*(r+((t/2)*k))-2*(r+t)	yes
10	90<b<=165	v=pi*((180-b)/180)*(r+((t/2)*k))-2*(r+t)*tan((180-b)/2)	no
11	165<b<=180	v=0	no

The declarations in the first several rows must include the following items in the first column (capitalization is not important, but the colon must be as shown). Although the first column may also contain other declarations, it must have at least the ones shown here:

> bend type:
>
> unit:
>
> material thickness:
>
> radius
>
> k-factor
>
> bend angle

The first three items listed must have colons, and the last three items must not have colons or you will get an error saying that the first improperly formatted item is invalid. It works this way in SolidWorks 2011 SP 0, and because this looks like a bug, it may change in later releases.

The available options for Bend Type are Bend Allowance, Bend Deduction, K-Factor, and Bend Calculation.

The available options for Unit are Inch, Millimeter, Meter, and Centimeter (although it looks like plurals are also allowed, such as *inches*, but abbreviations such as *in* are not).

The material thickness can be any variable letter you choose. The radius can also be any variable letter you choose.

The F-Factor can be an equation or a specific value. In the SolidWorks Web Help, the equation shown as a sample is k = 0.65+.5*lg(r/t). The *lg* in this case is assumed to mean logarithm. After some research, the DIN 6935 standard says that the formula for the k-factor is k = (0.65+log(r/t)/2)/2, which differs from the SolidWorks-provided equation by a /2 term. K is sometimes approximated as 0.447*T. You should note that K-Factors are usually determined experimentally, and it is a good idea for designers not intimately familiar with the process details to work with a manufacturing expert to learn the ropes of calculating sheet-metal flat patterns.

Caution

The equation given in the SolidWorks Web Help for 2011 SP 0 for the K-Factor in the Bend Calculation Table example may be incorrect. It is different from what is referenced by a DIN standard. You should verify all equations independently before using them to create manufacturing data. ■

The headers shown in Row 8 of the Excel spreadsheet in Figure 21.7 must be spelled as shown without embellishment.

The equations in cells B9 to B11 can use the variables for thickness and radius from the parameters specified in the declarations at the top of the table. It may seem odd, but the equations are just entered as text into the cells of the spreadsheets. These are not active Excel equations. They must be read into SolidWorks and evaluated there, not in Excel. I have not verified these equations for accuracy. As demonstrated with the K-Factor equation, it is best for you to verify the equations yourself or with help before depending on them for production data. ■

The variable *v* used on the left side of the equations represents the length of the flattened (developed) bend area. The Web Help (which is the most complete source of information available for this feature as of this writing) refers to a β (beta) variable, which in the equations appears to be replaced with the letter *b*.

So you have to assume that *b* stands for bend angle, and the equation for bend angle (180 – *a*) includes the variable *a*, which is shown in the Help diagrams as a linear dimension, but which you have to assume is the angle through which the sheet metal must bend. So when *a* is 45, *b* is 135, which corresponds to bending the sheet metal 45 degrees, but the bend angle is 135 degrees. Figure 21.8 shows how these variables relate to actual geometry.

FIGURE 21.8

Assigning variables to geometry in Bend Calculation Tables

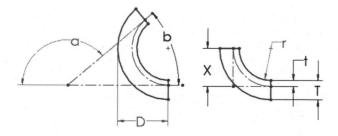

Notice that the tangent length option can only apply when the bend angle is 90 degrees or less. For more than 90 degrees, you have to use the virtual sharp method.

Also, just be aware that the angles here are measured in degrees. In design tables, you have the option to use degrees or radians.

Auto Relief

When a bend does not go all the way across a part, some sort of feature is needed at the end of the bend. In real manufacturing processes, the metal may just transition smoothly from the bent area to the flat area, but in SolidWorks, the software cannot create that smooth transition, or it could, but it would add significantly to sheet metal rebuild times. For this reason, all bends in SolidWorks sheet metal must terminate cleanly, with some sort of a cut, or as they are called here, a relief. SolidWorks allows three kinds of reliefs: Rectangular, Tear, or Obround.

Auto reliefs were formerly called Bend reliefs. You can specify three different Auto relief options to be applied automatically to bends that end in the middle of material. These options are illustrated in Figure 21.9.

The three Auto relief configurations: Rectangular, Tear, and Obround

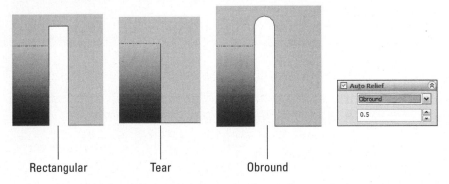

Rectangular   Tear   Obround

For the Rectangular and Obround types, you can control the width and the distance past the tangent line of the bend through the Relief Ratio selection box, which is immediately below the type selection box in the Sheet Metal PropertyManager. This ratio is the width of the relief divided by the part thickness. For the Rectangular relief, a ratio of .5 and a thickness of .050 inches means that the relief is .025 inches wide and that it goes .025 inches deeper into the part beyond the tangent line of the bend. The Obround relief goes slightly deeper because it has a full radius after the distance past the tangent line of the bend, and so it essentially goes a total of one full material thickness past the tangent line.

The Tear relief is simply a face-to-face shear of the material with no gap.

Using the Flat Pattern feature

 The Flat Pattern feature is added automatically to the end of the tree when the Base Flange feature is added. This feature is used to flatten the sheet metal part when the feature is unsuppressed. The Flatten toolbar button acts as a toggle to unsuppress or suppress the Flat Pattern feature in the tree.

It may be a little confusing, but the Flatten toolbar button and the flat-pattern feature in the FeatureManager refer to the same functionality. As mentioned earlier, the Flat Pattern has a couple of special properties that are not seen in other features. The first is that it remains at the *bottom* of the FeatureManager when other Sheet Metal features are added.

The second property of the Flat Pattern feature is that it is added in the *suppressed* state. When it is unsuppressed, it flattens out the sheet metal bends.

Notice also that the Flat Pattern PropertyManager allows you to select an edge, axis, or sketch line to denote the grain of the material.

By editing the Flat Pattern feature, you can set a few options. The Flat Pattern PropertyManager is shown in Figure 21.10.

FIGURE 21.10

The Flat Pattern PropertyManager

The Fixed face parameter determines which face remains stationary when the part is flattened out. Generally, the largest face available is selected automatically, but if you want to specify a different face to remain stationary, you can do that here.

When the Merge faces option is selected, it causes the Flat Pattern to form a single face rather than being broken up by the tangent lines around the bends. This does a few things. First, selecting the face of the flattened part and clicking Convert Entities (found on the Sketch toolbar) makes an outline of the entire flattened part, which is easier to use for certain programming applications. Second, the edges around the outside are not broken up. Third, the tangent edges around the bends are not shown. The differences between Flat Patterns with this option selected and unselected are shown in Figure 21.11.

Bend lines are shown in both examples in Figure 21.11.

When you turn on the Simplify Bends option, it simplifies curved edges that are caused by flattening bends to straight lines from arcs or splines. When the option is off, the complex edges remain complex. Simple edges can be cut by standard punches and do not require Computer Numerical Control (CNC) controlled lasers or abrasive water jets.

The Corner Treatment option controls whether or not a corner treatment is applied to the Flat Pattern of a part. The corner treatment is illustrated in Figure 21.12. The model used to create this corner used a Miter Flange around the edges of a rectangular sheet.

FIGURE 21.11

The Merge Faces option showing on and off

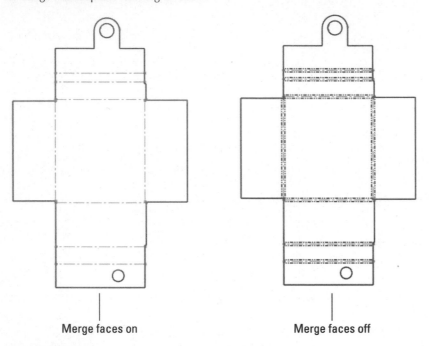

Merge faces on   Merge faces off

FIGURE 21.12

Using the Corner Treatment setting in the Flat Pattern PropertyManager

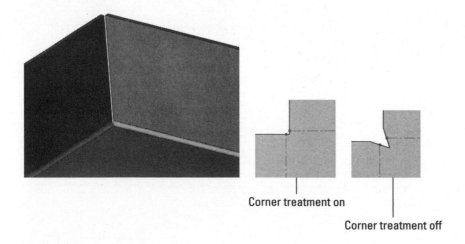

Corner treatment on

Corner treatment off

Note

You can export a `*.dxf` file of the Flat Pattern directly from the model without creating a drawing by right-clicking the Flat Pattern feature and selecting Export to DXF/DWG. ■

Using the Edge Flange feature

Edge Flange is intended to turn a 90-degree flange from a selected straight edge in the direction and distance specified using the default thickness for the part. The default workflow for this feature is that you select the tool, select the edge, and then drag the distance, clicking a distance reference such as a vertex at the end of another flange of equal length or typing a distance value manually. You can select multiple edges from a part that do not necessarily need to touch one another. That is all there is to a simple default flange, although several options give you some additional options for angle, length, and so on. Figure 21.13 shows the Edge Flange PropertyManager, as well as a simple flange.

FIGURE 21.13

The Edge Flange PropertyManager and a simple flange

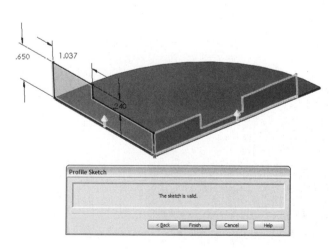

Edit Flange Profile

The Edit Flange Profile button in the Edge Flange PropertyManager enables you to edit a sketch to shape the flange in some way other than rectangular, or to otherwise edit the shape of the flange. Notice in Figure 21.13 that both of the flanges made by a single flange feature have been edited. You can do this by selecting the flange for which you want to edit the profile before clicking the Edit Flange Profile button.

Note

If you have added dimensions to the sketch, as shown in Figure 21.13, then you will no longer be able to use the arrow to drag the length of the flange. To edit the length, you will need to edit the sketch or double-click the feature, and then double-click the dimensions that you want to change. ■

You can add holes to the flange profile as nested loops. This enables you to avoid creating additional hole features but does not enable you to control suppression state independently from the flange feature.

You can make flanges go only part of the way along an edge by pulling one of the end lines back from the edge. This works even though the end lines appear black and fully defined. A situation where the sketch has been edited this way is shown in the image to the right in Figure 21.13.

Use default radius

This option enables you to override the default inside bend radius that is set for the entire part for this feature. The bend radii for individual bends within an Edge Flange that has multiple flanges cannot be set; the only override is at the feature level. If you need individual bends to have different bend radii, then you need to do this using multiple Edge Flange features.

Gap distance

The gap distance is illustrated in Figure 21.14. The Gap Distance selection box is only active when you have selected multiple edges in the main selection box for this feature. The gap refers to the space between the inside corners of the perpendicular flanges.

FIGURE 21.14

Specifying the gap distance

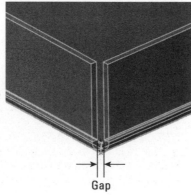

Gap

Angle

Because the Edge Flange is not dependent on a sketch for its angle like the Base Flange is, you can set the angle in the Angle panel of the PropertyManager. The values that this selection box can accept range from any value larger than zero to any value smaller than 180. Of course, each flange has practical limits. In the flange shown in Figure 21.15, the limitation is reached when the bend radius runs into the rectangular notch in the middle of the flange to the right, at about 158 degrees. The angle affects all the flanges that are made with the feature. To create a situation where different flanges have different angles, you need to create separate flange features.

FIGURE 21.15

Establishing the limit of the flange angle

Flange Length

As mentioned earlier, if you have edited the Flange Profile sketch and a flange length dimension is applied in the sketch, then the flange length is taken from that sketch dimension. If this dimension has not been added to the profile sketch, then the options for this setting in the PropertyManager Flange Length panel are Blind and Up To Vertex. Using Up To Vertex is a nice way to link the lengths of several flanges.

Flange Position

The small icons for Flange Position should be fairly self-explanatory, with the dotted lines indicating the existing end of the material. The names for these options, in order from left to right, are

- Material Inside
- Material Outside
- Bend Outside
- Bend From Virtual Sharp (for use when an angle is involved)

Trim side bends

In situations where a new flange is created next to an existing flange, and a relief must be made in the existing flange to accommodate the new flange, you can select the Trim side bends option to trim back the existing flange. Leaving this option unselected simply creates a relief cut, as shown in Figure 21.16. This is functionality that requires some imagination from the user. A real sheet metal part manufactured like this would have an area at the corner where the deformation from the bends in different directions overlaps. This overlapping bend geometry is too complex for SolidWorks to create automatically, so it offers you a couple of options for how you would like to visually represent the corner. The Flat Pattern is correct, but the formed model requires some imagination.

Using the Trim side bends option

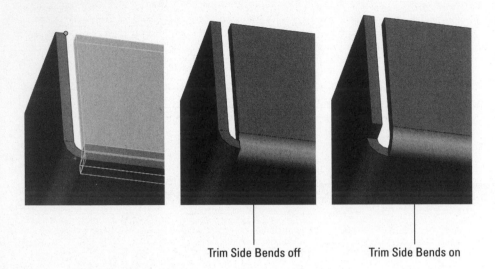

Trim Side Bends off   Trim Side Bends on

Curved edges

Edge Flanges can be created on curved edges, but the curved edge must be on a planar face. For example, if the part were the top of a mailbox, then an Edge Flange could not be put on the curve on the top of the mailbox. The flange would have to be made as a part of the flat end of the mailbox, instead.

Figure 21.17 shows Edge Flanges used on a part. Notice that reliefs are added to the ends of the bends, although they are not really needed.

Curved Edge Flanges on a part

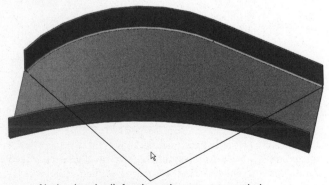

Notice bend reliefs where they are not needed

All the edges that you select to be used with a curved Edge Flange must be tangent. This means that in Figure 21.17, neither of the Edge Flanges could have been extended around the ends of the part. You would need to create separate Edge Flange features for those edges.

Because these Edge Flanges are made in such a way that they are developable surfaces, they can be (and are) flattened in such a way that they do not stretch the material of the flange when the flat is compared to the formed shape. Doubtless there is some deformation in between the two states in the actual forming of this flange, and so its manufacturing accuracy may not be completely reliable.

Using the Miter Flange feature

The Miter Flange feature can create picture frame–like miters around corners of parts, and correctly recognizes the difference between mitered inside corners and mitered outside corners. The PropertyManager and a sample Miter Flange are shown in Figure 21.18.

FIGURE 21.18

The Miter Flange PropertyManager and a sample part

A Miter Flange feature starts off with a sketch that is perpendicular to the starting edge of the Miter Flange feature.

Tip

A quick way to start a sketch for a Miter Flange that is on a plane perpendicular to a selected edge is to select the edge, and then click a sketch tool. This automatically creates a plane perpendicular to the edge at the nearest endpoint. ■

Miter Flange sketches can have single lines or multiple lines. They can even have arcs. Still, remember that just because you can make it in SolidWorks does not mean that the manufacturer can make it. It Is often a good idea to check with the manufacturer to ensure that the part can be made. Also, you usually learn something from the experience.

Tip

When selecting edges for the Miter Flange to go on, be sure to remain consistent in your selection. If you start by selecting an edge on the top of the part, then you should continue selecting edges on the top of the part. If you do not, then SolidWorks prompts you with a warning message in a tool tip that says that the edge is on the wrong face. ∎

Some of the controls in the Miter Flange PropertyManager should be familiar by now, such as Use default radius, Flange Position, Trim side bends, and Gap Distance. You have seen these controls before in the Edge Flange PropertyManager.

The Start/End Offset panel enables you to pull a Miter Flange back from an edge without using a cut. If you need an intermittent flange, then you may need to use cuts or multiple Miter Flange features, as shown in Figure 21.19.

FIGURE 21.19

The Start/End Offset settings for a Miter Flange

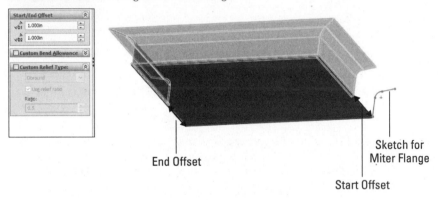

End Offset

Sketch for
Miter Flange

Start Offset

Using the Hem feature

 The Hem feature is used to roll over the edge of a sheet metal part. This feature is often used to smooth over a sharp edge or to add strength to the edge. You can also use it for other purposes, such as to capture a pin for a hinge. SolidWorks offers four different hem styles — Closed, Open, Tear Drop, and Rolled — which are shown as icons on the Hem PropertyManager. The PropertyManager for the Hem feature is shown in Figure 21.20.

One of the limitations to keep in mind with regard to hems is that SolidWorks cannot fold over a part so that the faces touch perfectly line on line. Doing this would cause the two sections of the part to merge into a larger piece, thus removing the coincident faces. SolidWorks, computers, and mathematics in general do not always handle the number zero very well. In reality, you can often see light through these hems, and so a perfectly flush hem may not be as accurate as it seems.

You can edit the profile of the Hem, like an Edge Flange, to control the length of the edge that is hemmed. To do this, click the Edit Hem Width button below the Edges selection box in the Hem PropertyManager, shown in Figure 21.20.

FIGURE 21.20

The Hem PropertyManager and a sample hem

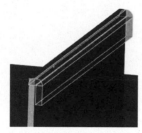

Using the Jog feature

The Jog feature puts a pair of opposing bends on a flange so that the end of the flange is parallel to, but offset from, the face where the jog started. The Jog PropertyManager and a sample jog are shown in Figure 21.21.

The Jog feature is created from a single sketch line on the face of a sheet metal part. The geometry to be jogged should not have any side bends; it should be a simple tab-like flange, as shown in Figure 21.21. The line to create the jog can be drawn at an angle, causing the jog to also be angled.

The three icons on the Jog Offset panel illustrate what dimension is being controlled by that setting.

Fixed Face

Like most sheet metal features, the Jog feature bends faces on the part, and when it does so, although it may be obvious to you as the user, it is not obvious to the software which face should remain stationary and which faces should be moved by the bend. The Fixed Face selection box enables you to select a face, or in this case, a part of a face, that you want to remain stationary as the rest of the faces move. The black dot on the face identifies it as stationary.

Tip

Problems can sometimes arise when you are using configurations that change sizes, because these markers for fixed faces can be pushed onto other faces. This can cause problems with assemblies and drawings, and in general makes visualization difficult. In cases like this, it may be advisable to select a larger face or one that has fewer changes, if possible, to be used as the fixed face. ■

FIGURE 21.21

The Jog PropertyManager and a sample jog

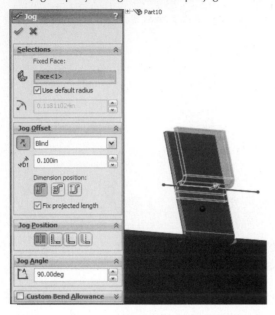

Jog Offset

You can control the direction of the jog by using the arrow button to the left of the end condition selection box. You can control the jog distance by selecting the end conditions Up To Surface, Up To Vertex, or Offset From Surface. The default setting is Blind, in which you simply enter a distance for the offset, in exactly the same way that end conditions are controlled for features such as extrudes.

Fix projected length

One setting that may not be obvious is the Fix projected length. This refers to the length of the flange that the jog is altering. In Figure 21.19, you can see that the height of the jogged feature is the same as the height of the original feature. The jog obviously requires more material than the original, but the Fix projected length option is selected, and so the height is maintained. If you deselected this option, then the finished height of the flange after the jog is added would be shorter, because the material is used by the jog and additional material would not be added. For comparison, the image to the right in Figure 21.19 shows this situation.

Jog Position

The Jog Position selection establishes the relationship between the sketched line and the first bend tangent line. The Jog Position icons have tool tips with the following names, from left to right: Bend Centerline, Material Inside, Material Outside, and Bend Outside.

Jog Angle

The Jog Angle enables you to change the angle of the short perpendicular section of the jog. You can angle it to smooth out the jog (angles of less than 90 degrees) or to curl back on itself (angles of more than 90 degrees). Again, be careful to check with your manufacturer's capabilities.

Using the Sketched Bend feature

 Sketched Bend works in some respects like half of a jog. It requires the sketch line and the Fixed Face selection. You define a bend position with the same set of icons that you used in the jog, and you assign a bend angle in the same way.

Tip

You can use the Sketched Bend feature to "dog ear" corners. You do this by drawing a line across the corner at an angle and setting the angle to 180 degrees and then overriding the default radius with a much smaller one, such as .001 inches. ∎

Unlike Jog, the Sketched Bend feature does not show you a preview. The Sketched Bend PropertyManager is shown in Figure 21.22.

FIGURE 21.22

The Sketched Bend PropertyManager

Using the Closed Corner feature

 The Closed Corner feature extends flanges on the sides to meet with other flanges. It is typically used when corners leave big open gaps in order to create a corner that is more easily welded shut. Figure 21.23 shows a part where angled flanges have been applied. This creates big gaps in the corners. Although a Miter Flange may have been better, these were created using regular Edge Flanges.

FIGURE 21.23

Applying the Closed Corner feature

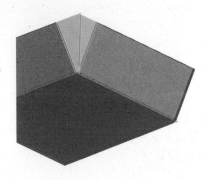

Faces to Extend

You must select the thickness face of one of the flanges in order to extend it. Selecting one face automatically selects the matching face from the other flange that you also want to extend. The Corner Type selection icons depict the selected face as red, and the three icons display tool tips: Butt, Overlap, and Underlap.

Faces to Match

The faces selected in the Faces to Match selection box act as an "up to" end condition for the faces to extend. Prior to SolidWorks 2010, the Closed Corner feature always automatically selected a matching face to extend for each face selected, when appropriate. SolidWorks 2010 enables you to manually select matching faces in the Faces to Match selection box for those times when the automatic selection does not work.

Note

If you deselect faces in either the Faces to Extend or Faces to Match selection boxes, the Auto Propagation option toggles off to enable you to make selections manually. ■

Gap

The Gap setting enables you to specify how close you want the closed corner to be. Keep in mind that you cannot use the number zero in this field. If you do, then SolidWorks reminds you to "Please enter a number greater than or equal to 0.00003937 and less than or equal to 0.86388126." It is good to know your limits.

Overlap/Underlap ratio

The Overlap/Underlap ratio setting controls how far across the overlapped face the overlapping flange reaches. Full overlap is a ratio of 1, and a Butt condition is (roughly) a ratio of zero. This ratio is only available when you have specified Overlap or Underlap for the corner type.

Open bend region

The Open bend region option affects how the finished corner looks in the bend area. If Open bend region is selected, then a small gap is created at the end of the bend. If the option is deselected, then SolidWorks fills this area with geometry. Figure 21.24 shows the finished model with this option selected and unselected, as well as the resulting Flat Patterns for each setting.

FIGURE 21.24

The Open bend region option, both selected and unselected, and the resulting Flat Patterns

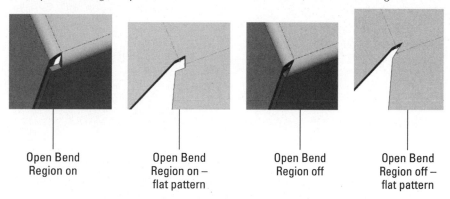

Open Bend
Region on

Open Bend
Region on –
flat pattern

Open Bend
Region off

Open Bend
Region off –
flat pattern

Coplanar faces

  When the Coplanar option is selected, any faces that are coplanar with any selected faces are also selected Corner Trim and Break Corner features. The Corner Trim feature is available only when the sheet metal part is in its flattened state. The Corner Trim PropertyManager also has the Break Corner Options interface built right into it. However, the Break Corner feature is only available when the sheet metal part is in its folded state. Figure 21.25 shows the combined interface. Both functions are included here, and SolidWorks treats them as if they are part of a single function.

When finished, the Corner Trim feature places itself after the Flat Pattern feature in the FeatureManager. It similarly follows the suppress/unsuppress state of the Flat Pattern feature. When the Break Corner feature is used on its own, it is placed before the Flat Pattern feature. With this in mind, it seems best to use Break Corner as a separate feature unless it is being used specifically to alter the Flat Pattern in a way that cannot be done from the folded state.

Break Corner on its own is primarily used to remove sharp corners using either a chamfer or a rounded corner. This tool is set up to filter edges on the thickness of sheet metal parts, which is useful, because these edges are otherwise difficult to select without a lot of zooming. Break Corner can also break interior corners.

One of the main functions of the Corner Trim feature is to apply bend relief geometry to the Flat Pattern. The three available options are Circular, Square, and Bend Waist. These options are shown in Figure 21.26.

FIGURE 21.25

The Corner Trim PropertyManager, including the Break Corner Options panel

FIGURE 21.26

Applying the Corner Trim Relief options

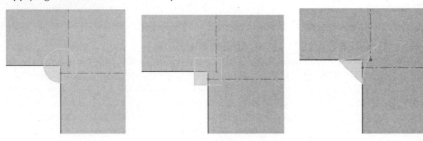

Mirroring and patterning in sheet metal

Most sheet metal features can be patterned or mirrored following the same logic as normal SolidWorks parts. Figure 21.27 shows a part with some features mirrored.

FIGURE 21.27

Mirroring some features on a sheet metal part

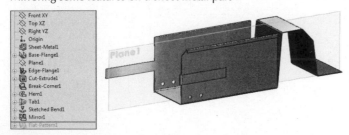

Mirroring sheet metal features

Notice that not all of the features are mirrored, though. In particular, the Corner Break and the Sketched Bend would not mirror. When you get into a situation where individual features don't mirror, you have two options, just like you would with mirroring a normal SolidWorks part: re-create the features on the other side manually or mirror the body rather than the features.

Figure 21.28 shows the same part from Figure 21.27 but modeled by mirroring the body instead of just the features, so all of the geometry is symmetrical. You can use this technique along with changing the feature order to make asymmetrical parts when the need arises.

FIGURE 21.28

Mirroring the entire sheet metal body

Patterning sheet metal features

Patterning also works for multiple sheet metal features. Figure 21.29 shows the patterned tabs with holes and hems. Controlling the bend placement of the first feature changes all of the patterned instances. This works nicely, especially because most patterns in sheet metal are going to be less demanding than general patterns.

FIGURE 21.29

Patterning multiple features in sheet metal

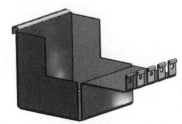

If you examine the part from the DVD (shown in Figure 21.29), it also contains a mirror feature that mirrors a Closed Corner feature. To me, this is very reasonable pattern/mirror functionality from SolidWorks.

Forming tool feature

 Forming tools in SolidWorks enable you to place features that are not formed on a brake press. These are features that are not straight-line bends but rather punched, drawn, formed, lanced, sheared, or otherwise deformed material.

One of the important things to understand about forming tools is that they do not stretch the material in the SolidWorks part in the same way that happens in a real-life forming operation. In real life, material is thinned when it is punched, stamped, or drawn. In SolidWorks, the thickness of a sheet metal part remains the same, regardless of what happens to it. For this reason, you need to be careful when using mass properties of sheet metal parts or doing stress analysis of parts that have formed features. You might consider taking your part weight from the Flat Pattern rather than from the formed sheet metal.

SolidWorks installs with a library of fairly simple forming tools that you can use as a starting point for your own personal customized library. You can also examine some of these tools to see how they create particular effects. You find this library in your Design Library in the Task pane. Some of the more interesting forming tools are the lances and louvers.

Creating forming tools

Forming tools are essentially a part that is used as a tool to form another part. One flat face of the forming tool part is designated as a Stopping Face, which is placed flush with the top face of the sheet metal part. You can move and rotate the tool with the Modify Sketch tool, and you can use dimensions or sketch relations to locate it.

Creating forming tools is far easier than it used to be. This section of the chapter gives you the information that you need to effectively create useful forming tools, addresses the limitations and unintended uses of forming tools, and provides a couple of hints for more complex forming tool creation.

To create a forming tool, click the Forming Tool button on the Sheet Metal toolbar. Figure 21.30 shows the PropertyManager interface for this tool.

FIGURE 21.30

The Form Tool PropertyManager and a sample tool with orientation sketch

The Stopping Face turns a special color, and so do any faces that are selected in the Faces to Remove selection box. Faces to Remove means that those faces will be cutouts in the sheet metal part.

Another aspect of the forming tool is the orientation sketch. Create the orientation sketch by using Convert Entities on the Stopping Face. If you have used this function in any of its previous versions, then you know that this latest iteration is far easier to create than before. However, to me, it looks like the orientation sketch has taken a step backward. The orientation sketch cannot be manually edited, and so for forming tools where *footprints* are symmetrical, but other features in the tool are not, you cannot tell from the sketch which direction the forming tool should face. Orientation could be managed more easily in earlier versions of forming tools because the placement sketch was just a manually created sketch.

When creating a forming tool, you must remember to build in generous draft and fillets, and not to build undercuts into the tool. Also keep in mind that when you have a concave fillet face on the tool, the radius becomes smaller by the thickness of the sheet metal; as a result, you must be careful about minimum radius values on forming tools. If there is a concave face on the tool that has a .060-inch radius and the tool is applied to a part with a .060-inch thickness, then the tool will cause an error because it forms a zero radius fillet, which is not allowed. Errors in applied forming tool features cannot be edited or repaired, except by changing forming tool dimensions.

Once the forming tool is created, special colors are used for every face on the part. For example, the Stopping Face is a light blue color, Faces to Remove are red, and all the other faces are yellow. Figure 21.31 shows the small addition that is made to the FeatureManager when you make a part into a forming tool. This feature did not exist in older versions of the tool.

FIGURE 21.31

The FeatureManager of a forming tool part

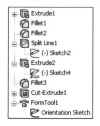

Forming Tool Library

The folder that the forming tools are placed into in the Design Library must be designated as a Forming Tool folder. To do this, right-click the folder that contains the forming tools and select Forming Tool Folder (a check mark appears next to this option).

Placing a forming tool

To place a forming tool on a sheet metal part (forming tools are only allowed to be used on parts with sheet metal features), you can drag the tool from the library and drop it on the face of the sheet metal part. Forming tools are limited to being used on flat faces.

From there, you can use the Modify Sketch tool or horizontal and vertical sketch relations to move and rotate the forming tool. It may be difficult to orient it properly without first placing it, seeing what orientation it ends up in, and then reorienting it if necessary because of the limitation mentioned earlier with not being able to edit the orientation sketch to give it some sort of direction identifier.

Configurations cannot be used with forming tools like they can with library features, although you can change dimensions by double-clicking the Forming Tool icon in the sheet metal part FeatureManager. Forming tools are suppressed when the part is flattened.

Special techniques with forming tools

One application of forming tools that is asked for frequently is the cross break to stiffen a large, flat sheet metal face. SolidWorks has a cosmetic cross break which I discuss next. Cross breaks are clearly not something that SolidWorks can do using straight bends, but a forming tool can do it.

You can create the forming tool by lofting a rectangle to a sketch point on a plane slightly offset from the plane of the rectangle. This creates a shallow pyramid shape. Open the part from the material on the DVD for Chapter 21 called Chapter 21 – Cross Break Sheet Metal.sldprt to examine how this part was made. Figure 21.32 shows the Cross Break forming tool applied to a sheet metal part.

FIGURE 21.32

The Cross Break forming tool applied to a part

Cross breaks

 Using a forming tool to create a cross break is overkill for most situations. You may need to do it if you need to actually show the indented geometry. The Cross Break feature is essentially a *cosmetic* cross break, and it enables you to specify the radius, angle, and direction used to create the cross break. It does not actually change the part geometry at all, but it does add two curve-like display entities.

When you place a Cross Break feature, you have the option to edit the sketch profile that creates the cross. This sketch has two intersecting lines. You cannot add more lines; the feature will fail if you have more than two lines in the sketch. (For example, if you wanted to put three breaks across a hexagonal face, the software will not allow this.) The lines do not have to end at a corner, but they do have to end at an edge. If the lines extend past or fall short of an edge, the feature will display a red X error icon, but it still creates the break lines where the sketch lines are.

Figure 21.33 shows the Cross Break PropertyManager and a part to which a cross break was applied. Notice that you can see the break lines through the solid, much like curves or cosmetic threads.

Creating a cross break

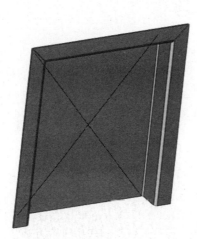

The Cross Break feature shows up in the FeatureManager just like any other feature, not like a cosmetic thread, which is the only other entity in the software that the cross break much resembles.

Form across bends

A second special technique is a gusset or a form that goes across bends. This can be adapted in many ways, but it is shown here going across two bends. I cannot confirm the practicality of actually manufacturing something like this, but I have seen it done.

The technique used here is to call the single long flat face of the forming tool the Stopping Face. The vertical faces on the ends and the fillet faces must be selected in the Faces to Remove selection box. The fillets of the outside of the forming tool also have to match the bends of the sheet metal part exactly. You may need to edit this part each time you use it, unless you apply it to parts with bends of the same size and separated by the same distance.

When you place the tool on the sheet metal part, you must place it accurately from side to side to get everything to work out properly. This part is in the same location as the Cross Break file and is called Chapter 21 – Form Across Bends Sheet Metal.sldprt. Figure 21.34 shows the tool and a part to which it has been applied.

FIGURE 21.34

Forming across bends

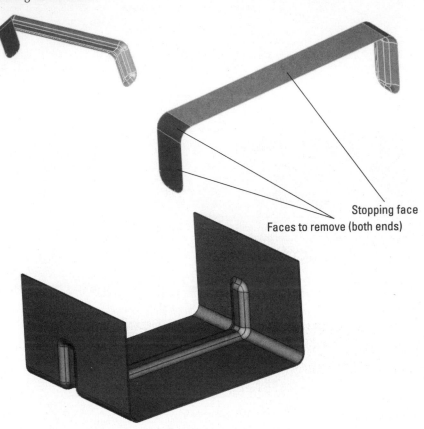

Stopping face
Faces to remove (both ends)

Using the Lofted Bends feature

The Lofted Bends feature enables you to create transitions between two profiles. The range of functionality available through the Loft feature is not available with Lofted Bends; it is limited to two profiles with no end conditions or guide curves. Both profiles also need to be open contours in order to allow the sheet metal to unfold.

Lofted Bends is not part of the Base Flange method, but it is part of the newer set of sheet metal tools available in SolidWorks. Figure 21.35 shows what is probably the most common application of this feature. The bend lines shown must be established in the PropertyManager when you create or edit the feature. Bend Lines are only an option if both profiles have the same number of straight lines. For example, if one of the profiles is a circle instead of a rectangle with very large fillets, then the Bend Lines options are not available in the PropertyManager.

FIGURE 21.35

The Lofted Bends PropertyManager, a sample, and a Flat Pattern with bend lines

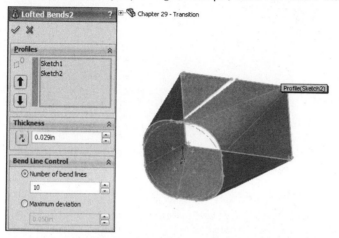

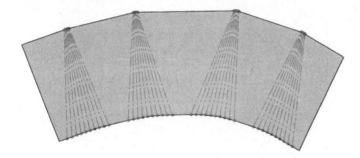

Like the forming tools, you can also use Lofted Bends in situations for which they were probably not intended. Figure 21.36 shows how lofting between 3D curves can also create shapes that can be flattened in SolidWorks. In this case, a couple of intermediate steps were required to get to the 3D curves, which involve surface features.

Note

This part is included on the DVD with the name `Chapter 21- wrap.sldprt`. ∎

Using 3D curves with Lofted Bends to create flatten complex shapes

Using the Unfold and Fold features

Unfold is a feature that unfolds selected bends temporarily. It is typically used in conjunction with a Fold feature to refold the bends. This combination is used to apply a feature that must be applied to the Flat Pattern; for example, a hole that spans across a bend.

Figure 21.37 shows the FeatureManager of a part where this combination has been applied, as well as the part itself, showing the bend across a hole, and the PropertyManager, which is the same for both features.

Applying the Unfold and Fold features

Both the Unfold and Fold features make it easy to select the bends without zooming in, even for small bends. A filter is placed on the cursor when the command is active, which allows only bends to be selected. The Collect All Bends option also becomes available. This feature also requires that you select a stationary face to hold still while the rest of the model moves during the unfolding and folding process.

Making Sheet Metal Parts from Generic Models

SolidWorks can also convert generic constant thickness models into sheet metal parts that flatten, and on which any of the dedicated sheet metal features can be used. You can make models from thin feature extrudes or regular extrudes with Shell features, and then use the Insert Bends feature to make them sheet metal parts. The structure of parts created with the Insert Bends feature is somewhat different. Figure 21.38 shows a comparison of the two methods' FeatureManagers for simple parts.

FIGURE 21.38

A comparison between default features for Base Flange and Insert Bends

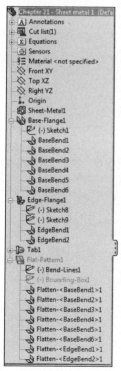

The most notable difference is that the Insert Bends part starts off with non–sheet metal features. The Rip feature also stands out, but the Rip feature is not exclusive to sheet metal. Although you can use Rip on any model, it is found only on the Sheet Metal toolbar.

The Sheet Metal feature is found in both the Base Flange and Insert Bends methods and has the same PropertyManager function in both methods.

The new features in the Insert Bends method are the Flatten Bends and Process Bends features. The way the Insert Bends method works is that the model that is built with the sharp-cornered non–sheet metal feature is flattened by the Flatten Bends feature. The model is then reconstructed with bends by the Process Bends feature.

The main rule that SolidWorks enforces on sheet metal models regardless of how they came to be sheet metal is that the parts should have a consistent wall thickness. When all the geometry is made from the beginning as a sheet metal part (using the Base Flange method), there is never a problem with this. However, when the part is modeled from thin features, cuts, shells, and so on, there is no telling what may happen to the model.

If you perform an Insert Bends operation on a model that does not have a consistent wall thickness, then the Flatten Bends and Process Bends features fail. If a thickness face is not perpendicular to the main face of the part, then the software simply forces the situation, making the face perpendicular to the main face.

Using the Normal cut feature

If a Cut feature is placed before the Sheet Metal feature, then as far as SolidWorks is concerned, the part is not a sheet metal part. However, if the cut feature is created after the Sheet Metal feature, then the model has to follow a different set of rules. The "normal shear" mentioned previously is one of those rules. In Figure 21.2, the sketch for a cut is on a plane that is not perpendicular to the face that the cut is going into. Under a normal modeling situation, the cut just goes through the part at an angle. However, in SolidWorks sheet metal, a new option is added to the PropertyManager for the cut. This is the Normal cut option, and it is selected by default. You could be modeling and never even notice this option, but it is important because it affects the geometrical results of the feature.

As shown in Figure 21.39, when the Normal cut option is selected, the thickness faces of the cut are turned perpendicular (or *normal*) to the face of the sheet metal. This is also important because if the angle between the angled face and the sketch changes, the geometry of the cutout can also change. This setting becomes more important as the material becomes thicker and as the angle between the sketch and the sheet metal face becomes shallower.

SolidWorks allows you to have angled faces on side edges and will maintain the angle when it flattens the part. In previous versions, angles on side faces cause the Flat Pattern feature to fail. Even a cut that does not use the Normal cut option and creates faces that are not perpendicular to the main face of the part will not cause the Flat Pattern to fail.

FIGURE 21.39

Using the Normal cut option

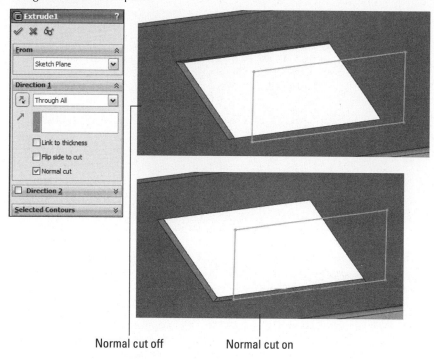

Normal cut off   Normal cut on

Using the Rip feature

When building a sheet metal part from a generic model, a common technique used to achieve consistent wall thicknesses is to build the outer shape as a solid and then shell the part. The only problem with this method is that it leaves corners joined in a way that cannot be flattened. You can solve this problem by using the Rip feature. Rip breaks out the corner in one or both directions in such a way that it can be unfolded. Bend reliefs are later added automatically by the Process Bends feature.

Figure 21.40 shows the Rip PropertyManager and the results of using this feature. The model was created to look like a Miter Flange part.

Notice also in Figure 21.3 that after the Rip, the edges of the material are still sheared at an angle. Because the top of the part was shelled, the thickness of the part is not normal to the main face of the sheet metal. You can fix this by using the Flatten Bends feature, which lays the entire part out flat, calculates the bend areas, and corrects any discrepancies at the edges of the part.

FIGURE 21.40

Using the Rip feature

Note

Rip functionality is included in the Insert Bends Sheet Metal PropertyManager when it is first initiated, although it is no longer there when you edit the part later. If you use it, the Rip data becomes a feature of its own and is placed before the Sheet Metal feature in the FeatureManager. Be aware that there are slight differences between using the Rip function as an independent feature and using it as a part of the Insert Bends feature. You may want to check this on a part you are working with to verify which method best suits your needs. ■

Using the Sheet Metal feature

 The Sheet Metal feature used in the Insert Bends method is very similar to the one used in the Base Flange method. However, two main differences exist: Insert Bends Sheet Metal requires the user to select a Fixed Face, and Base Flange Sheet Metal allows the use of Gauge Tables. Both features function as placeholders and otherwise contain the same information, use the same name and icon, and are inserted automatically when a different feature is created.

Using the Flatten Bends feature

 The Flatten Bends feature is added automatically by the Insert Bends tool. As mentioned earlier, it takes the model with sharp corners and lays it flat, adjusting the material in the bend area and normalizing the thickness faces around the Flat Pattern. The Merge Faces option is available in the Flat Pattern feature in the Insert Bends method; therefore, the Flat Pattern created by the Flatten Bends feature always has edges created by the tangent lines of the bends.

Notice in Figure 21.41 that the Flatten Bends feature has a sketch and several Sharp Bend features under it. The Sharp Sketch is simply an account of the bend lines, and you cannot edit it manually. The Sharp Bend features can be suppressed, in which case they are not re-formed in the Process Bends feature. You can also edit Sharp Bend features to change the default radius, bend allowance, and relief type.

FIGURE 21.41

Using the Flatten Bends feature

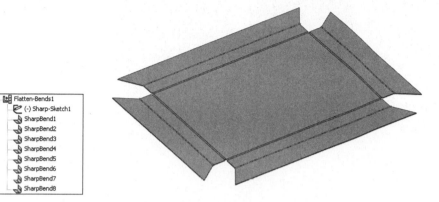

Using the Process Bends feature

 The Process Bends feature takes all the Flat Pattern information, the bend information, and entities in the Flat Sketch and rebuilds the model with the formed bends. The Flat Sketch under the Process Bends feature is the Insert Bends method version of a sketched bend. You can add sketch lines here to bend panels of the part. After you add lines to this sketch, exiting the sketch causes the part to be created with a default 90-degree bend corresponding to the line. Of course, all the Sketched Bend rules exist, such as that the line has to extend at least up to the edges of the part, the lines cannot extend across multiple faces, and construction lines are ignored.

For every bend created by a sketch line in the Process Bends Flat Sketch, a Flat Bend feature is added to the list under Process Bends. You can control the angle and radius of each of these Flat Bends by editing the Flat Bend feature. This is all illustrated in Figure 21.42.

Using the No Bends feature

You use the No Bends tool on the Sheet Metal toolbar to roll back the model before the Flatten Bends feature in the tree with a single button click. This is primarily to add new geometry that is turned into bends through the Flatten and Process Bends features.

Using the Flat Pattern feature

 The Insert Bends method uses the Flat Pattern feature as well as the Base Flange method. However, it was not part of the original scheme and was added at some point after the new tools had proved their value. This enables you to make use of the new features as well, as discussed later in this chapter in the section on mixing methods.

FIGURE 21.42

Using the Process Bends feature

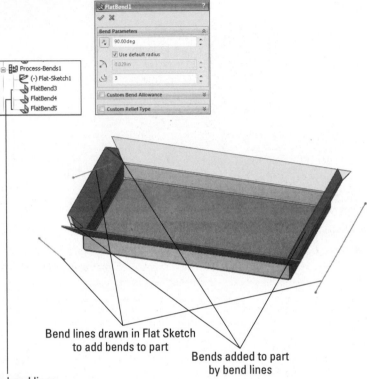

Bend lines drawn in Flat Sketch
to add bends to part

Bends added to part
by bend lines

Added by bend lines
added to the Flat Sketch

Using the Convert to Sheet Metal feature

 The Convert to Sheet Metal feature can use either SolidWorks native data or imported data. It can also use solids as well as surfaces. The model can be shelled or not shelled and have filleted edges or not. This feature enables you to identify which edges will become bends and automatically identifies the edges to rip. See Figure 21.43.

This tool is very useful for imported geometry and for parts with tricky shapes. Although the PropertyManager interface looks busy, it is fairly straightforward to use. Your first selection in the top Fixed Entity box should be a stable face, preferably an outer face on the bottom or the top. Inner faces generally do not work.

FIGURE 21.43

Using Convert to Sheet Metal

  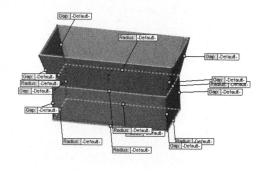

Note that you can reverse the thickness of the sheet metal, so that the solid that you start with can be treated as the volume inside the sheet metal enclosure, or the outer faces of the initial solid turn out to be the inner faces of the sheet metal part. Use the Reverse Thickness option to accomplish this.

Selecting Bend Edges is the next step, with the implication that any edge that is not a bend will be ripped. Also note that three bend edges cannot intersect at a point or one bend edge cannot intersect at the middle of another edge.

Setting default bend radius, thickness, and Auto Relief options are the same as in other sheet metal functions.

Using Other Methods

The sheet metal tools have been available in SolidWorks for quite some time and have had some time to mature and for users to become well acquainted with them and develop effective techniques using them.

Working with imported geometry

Working with imported geometry starts at the point where you use the Rip feature. While imported geometry can be geometrically manipulated to some extent in SolidWorks, this is beyond the scope of this chapter. The need for a model with walls of constant thickness still exists, even if the imported model has filleted edges showing bend geometry already in the model.

FeatureWorks may be used to recognize sheet metal features or to fully or partially deconstruct the model by removing bend faces as fillets. While FeatureWorks is not covered in this book, the technique may be useful when editing imported parts with overall prismatic geometry that is common to sheet metal parts.

When a sheet metal part is imported, whether it meets the requirements immediately or must be edited in one way or another to make a sheet metal part of it, you can simply use the Insert Bends feature or even the Convert to Sheet Metal feature.

Making rolled conical parts

One of the reasons for maintaining the legacy Insert Bends method is to have a way of creating rolled conical parts. You can create cylindrical sheet metal parts by drawing an arc that almost closes to an entire circle, and creating a Base Flange from it. However, no equivalent technique for creating tapered cones exists with the Base Flange method.

With the Insert Bends method, a revolved thin feature does the job nicely. You simply revolve a straight line at an angle to the centerline, so that the straight line does not touch or cross the centerline; the revolve cannot go around the full 360 degrees because there must be a gap. Sheet metal parts are not created by stretching the material (except for Forming Tools).

When creating a rolled sheet metal part, you cannot select a flat face to remain fixed when the part is flattened. Instead, you can use a straight edge along the revolve gap, as shown in Figure 21.44.

Note

When a conical sheet metal part is created, it does not receive the Flat Pattern feature at the end of the FeatureManager. This is because none of the new Base Flange method features are allowed on this type of part. ■

Mixing methods

If you use the Insert Bend tool on a part, you can still use the more advanced tools available through the Base Flange method, unless it is a cylindrical or conical part. A Flat Pattern feature is added to the bottom of most feature trees, and the presence of this feature is what signifies that the current part has now become a sheet metal part to the Base Flange features.

However, it is recommended that you avoid mixing the different techniques to flatten parts; for example, suppressing bends under Flatten and Process Bends, as well as using the Flat Pattern.

FIGURE 21.44

Selecting a straight edge for a conical part

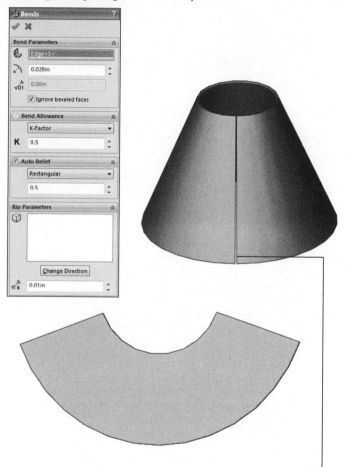

Select one of these edges in the
Fixed Face/edge selection box

Using Multi-Body Techniques with Sheet Metal

As of SolidWorks 2010, you can now use multi-body techniques with sheet metal models. For many of the same reasons you might want to make any other kind of model using multi-body techniques, you may also want to make sheet metal parts using similar techniques. The new rules have several implications for old limitations of sheet metal parts such as:

- You can now have multiple Base Flange features.
- With multiple Base Flange features you also get multiple Flat Pattern features.
- If you have multiple bent bodies, you can only show one body flattened at a time.
- Merging sheet metal bodies eliminates one Flat Pattern feature.
- You can use the Split feature to create multiple sheet metal bodies.
- The commands that can create new bodies in sheet metal parts are as follows:
  - Convert to Sheet Metal
  - Lofted Bend
  - Insert Bends
  - Base Flange
  - Insert Part
  - Split
- The commands that can merge bodies in sheet metal parts are as follows:
  - Edge Flange
  - Combine

The Mirror function enables you to mirror bodies, but the new bodies have to be merged manually with the existing body.

Using Insert Part

Using the Insert Part feature inserts an existing part as a new body inside a sheet metal part, but even if the inserted part was a sheet metal part initially, it does not show up as sheet metal after being inserted in the other part.

You can join the inserted part to the local sheet metal body by using the Combine feature, but not by using the merge option in an Edge Flange as you can to merge two bodies modeled within a single part. When the Combine feature is used, any sharp intersection between the parts is left sharp and will not flatten unless you use the Insert Bends feature to convert the sharp into a bend. This is an odd twist on combining the old (Insert Bends) method with the new (Base Flange) method.

Using multiple Base Flanges

Another method to get multiple bodies inside a sheet metal part is to start from disjoint Base Flange features. You can build flanges toward one another until flanges touch. Figure 21.45 illustrates a situation where a disjoint flange created by a Base Flange feature is connected to the main part using an Edge Flange feature with the Up To Edge And Merge flange length setting.

FIGURE 21.45

Using an Edge Flange to connect disjoint bodies in a sheet metal part

Tutorial: Working with the Insert Bends Method for Sheet Metal Parts

The Insert Bends method has been relegated to duty mainly for specialty functions. To gain an understanding of how this method works, follow these steps:

1. **Create a new blank part.**

2. **On the Top plane, open a sketch and sketch a rectangle centered on the Origin 12 inches in the Horizontal direction and 8 inches in the Vertical direction.**

3. **Extrude the rectangle 1 inch with 45 degrees of draft, Draft Outward, in Direction 1, and extrude 1 inch with no draft in Direction 2.** The two directions should be opposite from one another.

4. **Shell out the part to .050 inches, selecting the large face on the side where the draft has been applied.** The part should now look like Figure 21.46.

5. **Use the Rip feature to rip out the four corners.** Allow the Rip to rip all corners in both directions. The part should now look like Figure 21.47.

FIGURE 21.46

The part as of Step 4

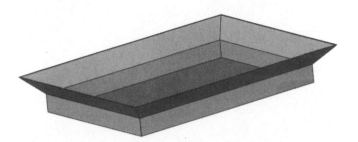

FIGURE 21.47

Ripping the corners

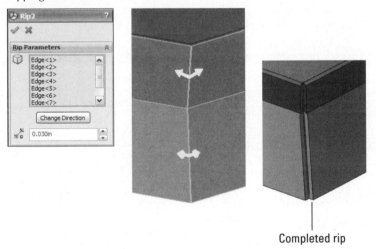

Completed rip

6. **Create an Insert Bends feature, accepting the default values, and picking the middle of the base of the part for the fixed face.**

7. **Draw a rectangle on one of the vertical faces of the part, as shown in Figure 21.48.**

8. **Use the sketch to create a Through All cut in one direction.** Notice that the Normal cut option is on by default. Examine the finished cut closely; notice that it is different from the default type of cut because it is not made in a direction normal to the sketch but rather in a direction normal to the face of the part. Details of this are shown in Figure 21.49.

FIGURE 21.48

Ripping the corners

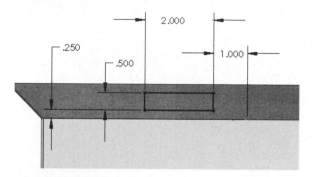

FIGURE 21.49

Using the Normal cut option

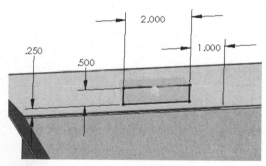

9. **Click the Flatten button on the Sheet Metal toolbar.** Notice that the Flat Pattern feature becomes unsuppressed and that the Bend Lines sketch under it is shown. This works just like it did in the Base Flange method. The finished part is shown in Figure 21.50.

FIGURE 21.50

The finished part with the Flat Pattern feature unsuppressed

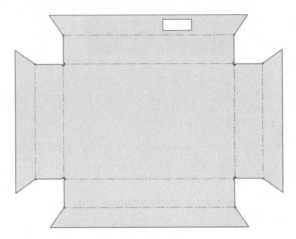

Tutorial: Using the Base Flange Sheet Metal Method

SolidWorks Base Flange method for sheet metal is fun and easy to use, as you will see in this tutorial:

1. **Open a new part using a special sheet metal template if one is available.**

2. **On the Top plane, draw a rectangle centered on the Origin, 14 inches in X by 12 inches in Y (or Z).**

3. **Initiate the Base Flange tool, set the thickness to .029 inches, and change the K-Factor to .43.** Notice that the default inside bend radius is not shown. This setting is made in the Sheet Metal feature that is placed before the Base Flange feature in the FeatureManager.

4. **After the Base Flange has been created, edit the Sheet Metal feature, and change the default bend radius to .050 inches.**

5. **Click one of the 14-inch edges and then select the Line tool from the Sketch toolbar.** This is a shortcut to creating a plane perpendicular to the end of the edge and opening a new sketch on the plane. This is useful in other situations in addition to working with sheet metal. Draw a sketch similar to that shown in Figure 21.51. The arc overrides the default inside bend radius setting and directly controls that particular bend.

6. **With the sketch still active, click the Miter Flange button on the Sheet Metal toolbar.** Use the settings shown in the image to the right in Figure 21.52. Select three edges as shown. Remember to select the edges on the same side of the Base Flange. In particular, notice the Start/End Offset settings. Click OK when you are satisfied with the settings.

FIGURE 21.51

The sketch to start a Miter Flange

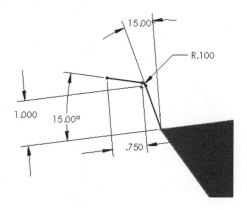

FIGURE 21.52

Specifying the Miter Flange settings

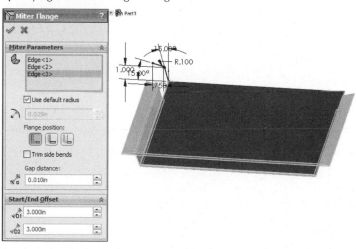

7. **Select the remaining edge that is not touched by the Miter Flange, and click the Edge Flange tool on the Sheet Metal toolbar.** Click the top point of one end of the Miter Flange to establish the flange length using the Up To Vertex end condition.

8. **Click the Edit Flange Profile button in the PropertyManager, and manually pull the sketch back from the ends of the flange.** Add dimensions to make the flange 3 inches from

the corner on the left side, and 5 inches from the corner on the right side, as shown in Figure 21.53; otherwise, use the default settings for the flange. Click OK to accept the feature when you are satisfied with the settings.

Creating an Edge Flange

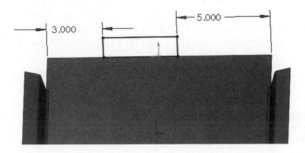

9. **Select the inside edge of the top of the Edge Flange that you have just created and initiate a Hem feature.** Use the settings Material Inside, Closed Hem, with a length of .25 inches, and make the material go toward the inside of the box. The settings and preview of the feature are shown in Figure 21.54.

Creating a hem

10. **Create a second Edge Flange the same height as the first, just to the right of the first flange, as seen from the point of view used in Figure 21.48.** Edit the flange profile and pull the new flange away from the existing flange. Add a dimension to make the new flange 2 inches wide. Click OK when you are satisfied with the settings.

11. **Open a sketch on the inside face of the new Edge Flange and draw a line across the flange .75 inches from the end.**

12. **Create a Jog feature with the settings shown in Figure 21.55.** Make sure to set a custom bend radius by deselecting the Use default radius option and entering **.025 inches**. If you do not set the custom radius, you may get a warning that the jog distance is less than a minimum jog value. Be careful when selecting the fixed face to select the side of the line with the largest area, or the face you want to remain where it is while the rest of the part bends and moves around it.

FIGURE 21.55

Creating a jog

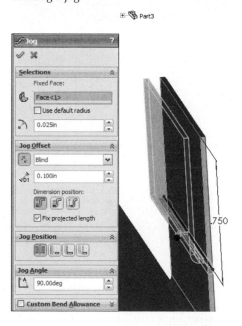

13. **From the DVD, in the folder for Chapter 21, find the part named** Chapter 21 – Cross Break.sldprt. Copy this file to a folder in the library that you have established outside of your SolidWorks installation folder, called Forming Tools.

14. **Make sure that this folder appears in the Design Library.** You may have to press F5 or click the Refresh button at the top of the Task pane. When the folder appears, right-click the folder and select the check mark next to Forming Tools Folder.

15. **When the file has been copied and the folder has been assigned as a Forming Tool folder, drag the Chapter 21 – Cross Break part from the folder and onto the big flat face of the sheet metal part.** You will be put into a sketch that looks like Figure 21.56.

FIGURE 21.56

Placing a forming tool

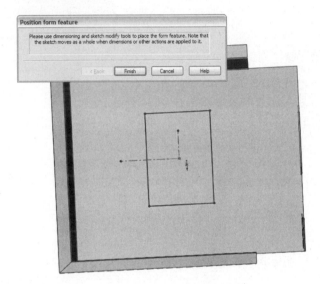

16. **Once you have dropped the feature into the sketch, drag the Origin of the sketch onto the Origin of the part, and then click Finish.** Notice that the cross break is in the middle of the part but is too small.

17. **Double-click the new feature in the FeatureManager; a set of dimensions appears on the screen.** Change the 4-inch dimension to 13.9 inches and the 6-inch dimension to 11.9 inches. The cross break should now look like Figure 21.57.

   Create a new configuration named Flat. In this configuration, suppress the forming tool that you just placed, and unsuppress the Flat Pattern feature at the bottom of the tree.

FIGURE 21.57

Resizing the cross break to 13.9

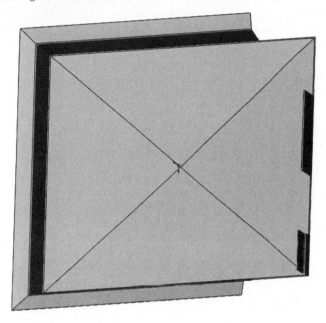

Summary

SolidWorks offers a broad range of sheet metal tools to tackle most of your modeling situations. Some of the tools still require a little imagination to visualize real-world results because the complex shapes created in the real world where bends intersect are problems for such highly automated software. The tools are able to deal with imported or generically modeled geometry as well as parts created using the dedicated sheet metal tools.

Creating Sheet Metal Drawings

After you have created your sheet metal models, you need to make drawings to get them manufactured. Fortunately, SolidWorks provides some nice tools to document, dimension, and annotate your parts in 2D.

Depending on whether your company does its own sheet metal manufacturing, you may or may not actually make flat pattern drawings. Many companies that use outside manufacturing for their sheet metal parts may just send them a drawing with views of a dimensioned part in the folded state. This is because it is the final formed dimensions that you want the shop to be responsible for, and if they use different flat dimensions to achieve that, it doesn't really matter.

Many users may think that providing a fully dimensioned flat pattern is a great value to the sheet metal shop. If your sheet metal shop is a professional outfit, they probably have their own software and their own way of doing things, in which case a flat pattern is redundant information and may cause more confusion than clarity.

On the other hand, if you are the sheet metal shop, or you specifically create drawings for the sheet metal shop, then creating the flat pattern is actually your business. This chapter will give you all the information you need to know to make sheet metal drawings, regardless of your role and without trying to tell you how to do your job.

IN THIS CHAPTER

Creating sheet metal drawings

Working with flat patterns

Making special sheet metal
drawing templates

Introducing Sheet Metal Drawings

Sheet metal drawings can take on various roles in your product development process — anything from general "make me a part that looks like this" to actually specifying how the work is to be done. Some drawings may need only the flat pattern, or only the formed part. Here I will assume that a sheet metal drawing will require both the formed and flat part, just to cover as much ground as possible.

If you need a drawing with both formed and flat geometry, you might consider making a two-page drawing — one page with the flat pattern and the other page with views of the 3D part. You might use one drawing sheet for the press operator and the other sheet for inspection. If you only need the flat pattern, you might consider using an isometric view of the part just for reference.

If your sheet metal parts are welded together with other sheet metal, structural, or plate parts, you might want to refer to the section later in this chapter on multi-body sheet metal drawings. You can accomplish the same things with an assembly (and in some cases the assembly will be the better option), but many people think that modeling in multi-bodies is easier. Sheet metal multi-body techniques are a little different, and in my opinion don't offer as many advantages as normal multi-body techniques. If you need to work in this mode, be careful to leave room on your drawing for exploded views and a weld list. Flat patterns require some extra thought if you have multiple sheet metal bodies in a single part.

You may also want to make a special drawing template for sheet metal drawings. The special template can contain custom blocks, title blocks, or table anchors.

Getting the Flat Pattern

When you need to make a drawing to build a sheet metal part from, getting the flat pattern is an essential part of the process. SolidWorks provides several ways to develop the flattened bend sections in the K-Factor, bend allowance, bend deduction, and bend calculation tables. Getting these values or equations correct is key in making the flat pattern the correct size to produce the finished part accurately. Chapter 21 covers how to use these methods, but you should obtain the actual values from your sheet metal shop.

You create the drawing of a sheet metal part in the same way that you would create one for any other type of part. You can use one of several methods, including the Create Drawing From Part command or dragging and dropping the part onto a drawing. Sheet metal drawings may serve different purposes. Usually a sheet metal drawing requires dimensioned orthogonal views of the finished part, and sometimes it also requires a flat pattern describing the blank the finished part is to be formed from.

To show a view of the flat pattern on a drawing where you already have a sheet metal part, select the view from the FeatureManager or the graphics window, and in the list of views below the Standard Views area of the Orientation panel of the PropertyManager, select Flat Pattern from the list. The Drawing View PropertyManager is shown in Figure 22.1.

FIGURE 22.1

Converting a view of a sheet metal part to a flat pattern

Understanding flat patterns and configurations

When a sheet metal part is put onto a drawing, SolidWorks automatically creates a derived configuration called SM-FLAT-PATTERN. The configuration doesn't exist until the part is put onto a drawing. For a part made with the Base Flange sheet metal method, this derived configuration in Figure 22.2 shows the default arrangement.

FIGURE 22.2

Automatically created derived configuration for the flat pattern

If your part already had multiple configurations, only the config that is showing on the drawing will get a derived flat pattern configuration. If you later show another configuration on the drawing, the derived flat pattern will not be automatically created until you show a flat pattern of that configuration.

Best Practice

You should be careful if you plan to make sheet metal parts with derived configurations for reasons other than the flat pattern. The automatic derived flat pattern configuration functionality may or may not be able to work with your manual or design table-driven derived configuration scheme. ■

Also be aware that there is a second way to get a flat pattern of a sheet metal part on the drawing. If you use the drop-down list in the Reference Configuration panel of the Drawing View PropertyManager, you can select the derived flat pattern configuration from there. The flat patterns that you get using these two methods may be oriented differently, and if you use the Flat Pattern selection from the More Views options, you will also get bend lines and annotations marking the direction, angle, and inside radius of the bend. The difference between the resulting views of these two methods is illustrated in Figure 22.3.

FIGURE 22.3

Comparing flat pattern views placed by using the More Views options, or by showing the derived flat pattern configuration

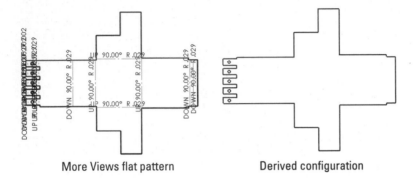

More Views flat pattern   Derived configuration

Showing bend lines and bend notes

If you show the derived configuration, the bend lines are not included in that view. To turn on the bend lines, you need to go to the FeatureManager for that view, scroll to the Flat Pattern feature, expand it, right-click the Bend Lines sketch, and select Show.

Figure 22.4 shows the drawing FeatureManager with the Bend Lines sketch highlighted.

To get the bend notes to show up, you need to use the Flat pattern view option shown in Figure 22.1. The bend notes are shown in Figure 22.5 and include which direction the bend is formed in, the angle of the bend, and the inside radius of the bend.

Other options for the display of bend notes are also available. Select Tools ➪ Options ➪ Document Properties ➪ Sheet Metal ➪ Bend Notes ➪ Style, and you can choose from the following options:

- Above bend line
- Below bend line
- With leader

When the notes are above or below the bend lines, they are aligned with the bend line, so the notes could be horizontal, vertical, or angled. If there is a succession of bends, interrupted in some way but close to one another, these notes can be on top of one another and difficult to read. This situation is shown in Figure 22.5.

FIGURE 22.4

Turning on the bend lines for a flat pattern view

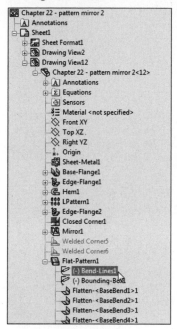

FIGURE 22.5

Showing the bend notes for a flat pattern

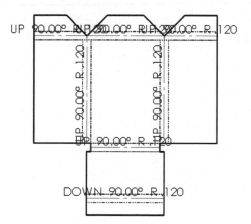

If you use the With leader option, all notes are horizontal with respect to the drawing sheet, and a leader points to the bend line.

Showing the bounding box for the flat pattern

SolidWorks automatically calculates a bounding box for your sheet metal flat pattern. This is the smallest rectangle that the flat pattern will fit into. This can be useful if your manufacturing process cuts the flat pattern from individual blanks rather than a bigger sheet with nested flat patterns. Generally, the bigger sheet allows you greater material efficiency, but it may also be difficult to manage if you don't have the equipment, and it may be unnecessary if you are making low volumes of certain parts.

The bounding box may not be aligned the way you might expect, but it represents the smallest rectangle that SolidWorks calculates will include your flat pattern. Many shops have separate nesting software which may allow for custom fits or some additional options. If you are not sure if your shop would benefit from a bounding box on the drawing, you may want to ask them directly.

You can have some control over the bounding box. If you specify a grain direction in the Flat Pattern PropertyManager, the bounding box aligns with the grain direction. You can use an edge, axis, or sketch to define the grain direction. The grain direction is the pattern of streaks on the face of the sheet metal that indicates the direction the sheets were processed in fabrication. Sheet metal properties can vary somewhat if measured with and against the grain. Sometimes the grain is specified in a certain orientation for aesthetic reasons.

The bounding box is stored in the sheet metal part as a sketch, which you can see right below the Bend Lines sketch shown in Figure 22.4. You can show this sketch, and the drawing will display it as a construction line. Figure 22.6 shows a flat pattern with a bounding box.

FIGURE 22.6

Showing a bounding box on a drawing

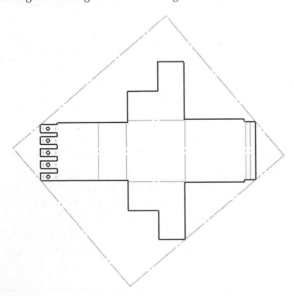

Showing bend areas on the part

If you want to show or hide the bend areas for all bends on the flattened part, open the part in its own window, and edit the Flat Pattern feature. You cannot edit the feature from the drawing; you have to do it from the part's own window. In the Flat-Pattern PropertyManager, make sure the Merge Faces option is turned off.

Figure 22.6 shows the bend lines (Merge Faces) turned off, and Figure 22.7 shows the bend lines (Merge Faces) turned on. Figure 22.7 also shows the setting which is available from the model. In Figure 22.7, the Tangent Edges are set to use a font. You can find this setting at View ➪ Display ➪ Tangent Edges With Font.

FIGURE 22.7

Showing the tangent bend lines on a flat pattern

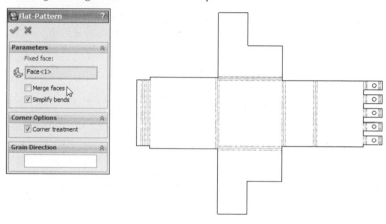

Making Drawings of Multi-Body Sheet Metal Parts

Multi-body sheet metal parts are still a bit of a curiosity in SolidWorks. You cannot flatten multiple sheet metal bodies simultaneously within a single sheet metal part. However, SolidWorks may be sending a confusing signal by adding more capabilities for drawings of multi-body parts. It is difficult to say what SolidWorks' intention was regarding multi-body sheet metal parts, but it is safe to say that you would do best to use them as a bridge to a single body, or when other parts such as small welded bits or PEM fasteners are pressed into a sheet metal part, creating an inseparable subassembly.

Figure 22.8 shows two different part scenarios that this chapter addresses. The part on the left is a simple sheet metal part with PEM standoffs from the SolidWorks Toolbox pressed into holes. The part on the right is a sheet metal part with multiple sheet metal parts and a simple plate, intended to be welded together. Both methods are valid uses of multi-body sheet metal parts.

FIGURE 22.8

Two multi-body sheet metal scenarios

Displaying bodies on the sheet metal drawing

SolidWorks allows you to hide bodies within a drawing view. To do this, click inside the view; at the top of the PropertyManager for the view in the Reference Configuration panel is a button labeled Select Bodies. Use this button to change the bodies that are visible in the drawing view. If you use the method of right-clicking a face of the body you want to hide, and choosing Show/Hide ⇨ Hide Body, you may get yourself into a situation where the body is hidden in multiple views, and you may have difficulty regaining control over which bodies are shown in which views again. The Select Bodies button and the body selection list are shown in Figure 22.9.

FIGURE 22.9

Selecting the bodies to show on the drawing

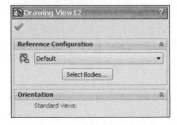
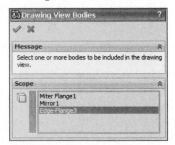

Caution

Use the Select Bodies button in the Reference Configurations panel of the View PropertyManager to hide bodies in views. If you use another method, you may not be able to control which bodies are shown in a particular view. Whether this is a bug or by design is unclear, but the functionality does not appear to be consistent. ∎

Another thing to be careful of is that in SolidWorks 2011 SP 1, the new functionality that allows you to use the part color on the drawing does not apply to bodies. If you use this setting, all of the bodies will use the part color. If your part uses an appearance, a color is always part of the appearance assignment, although the part may not display the color. For example, a steel appearance may still have a blue color assigned. You will see the texture-like appearance when the part is shaded, but you will see the associated color when the part is shown in wireframe mode.

Using a cut list in a sheet metal part

When you create a new sheet metal part, the FeatureManager automatically gets a new item called a cut list. The cut list is technically called a "weldment cut list," but it is used in sheet metal as well as in weldments to keep track of the parts modeled as bodies. The cut list is not very interesting until you have multiple pieces to list, and this only happens in a part file when you have multi-body parts. Beyond using multi-bodies as an interim condition where you're bridging between bodies, the cut list will be used when the final model is intended to have multiple bodies. The real use of the cut list is on the drawing for listing each of the individual pieces that go together to make the finished part. These pieces can be purchased hardware, other sheet metal parts, or welded plate parts, among others.

Cross-Reference

Weldments and Bills of Materials are covered in the SolidWorks 2011 Assemblies Bible (Wiley, 2011). ■

You can add several types of values to the cut list. It is essentially a Bill of Materials for welded assemblies. To access the interface for cut list properties, right-click a cut list item, and select Properties. Figure 22.10 shows a default cut list properties table.

FIGURE 22.10

Managing properties for a sheet metal cut list

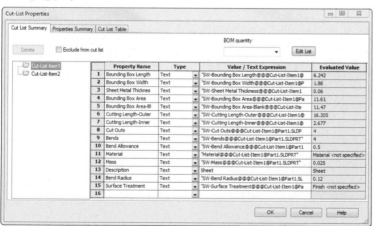

Managing cut list properties

To fill out the cut list properties, use the Cut List Summary the same way that you would use the Custom Properties data entry. Notice also that several properties already exist for the cut list. These include sheet metal–specific items like Bounding Box Length, Sheet Metal Thickness, the number of bends, material, or a special cut list–specific description. You can add additional custom properties as well.

Notice that on the left in Figure 22.10 is a list of all of the cut list items. This enables you to set the properties for each item. While most of the values use automated syntax, others, like the Description or any custom properties you might add, require manual data entry.

The next step after arranging all of your cut list properties is to create a drawing and add the cut list to a view. When you create a drawing of a multi-body sheet metal part, you can place the cut list on the drawing.

Placing the cut list on the drawing

Once you have created the multi-body sheet metal part, filled out the cut list properties, and created at least one drawing view of the part (flat or formed), you are ready to put a cut list on the drawing. I will assume you are placing a default cut list, and then need to create a customized one later. The next section will also go over how to create a cut list template once you have made one to suit your needs.

With the multi-body sheet metal drawing active, select Insert ⇨ Tables ⇨ Weldment Cut List. The Weldment Cut List PropertyManager is shown in Figure 22.11.

FIGURE 22.11

Configuring a Weldment Cut List for a multi-body sheet metal part

The first option in the Weldment Cut List PropertyManager is to select the template. By default, there is only the single sample table, which you will probably need to customize somewhat to suit your needs. You will do that shortly.

Once you have set the options to your satisfaction, place the cut list on the drawing by clicking where you want to place the table. Notice that as you drag the table around, it snaps to the drawing format border. You can place it at one of these snap locations or just place it in a blank area on the drawing.

The default cut list for a multi-body sheet metal part where the cut list properties have been filled out for each cut list item appears in Figure 22.12.

FIGURE 22.12

Placing the default cut list on the drawing

ITEM NO.	QTY.	DESCRIPTION	LENGTH
1	1	BOX	
2	1	LEFT LEG	
3	1	RIGHT LEG	
4	1	BASE PLATE	

When you select a column header (labeled with a letter), a Column PropertyManager appears, along with a text formatting bar (which appears to have a display bug affecting its top bar). This is all shown in Figure 22.13.

FIGURE 22.13

Customizing the cut list column

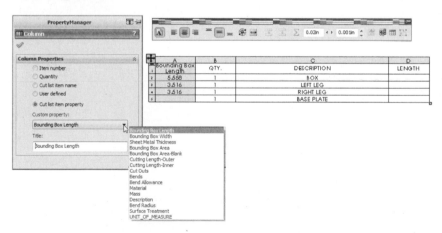

From here, you can change the information in the selected column. The first three column properties are built-in properties: Item Number, Quantity, and Description (cut list item name). The User Defined option lets you manually enter whatever text you want. The Cut List Item Property option allows you to select from a list of automated values, shown in Figure 22.13.

You can add additional columns by right-clicking a column and selecting Insert ➪ Column Right or Column Left. The additional columns can be formatted like the others.

Saving a cut list template

Once you have customized the cut list the way you like it — with the automated or manual entry fields set up to save you time the next time you need to use a similar table — you can save the table as a template. Right-click the table and choose the Save As option. The file type that is assigned is *.sld-wldtbt. This long file extension presumably stands for "weld table template." While a weld table and a cut list are not necessarily the same thing, they do use the same templates. You will learn more about weldments in the *SolidWorks 2011 Assemblies Bible* (Wiley, 2011).

Save the template file in the location established for your weldment table templates. You can find this location at Tools ⇨ Options ⇨ File Locations ⇨ Weldment Cut List Templates, which by default points to C:\Program Files\SolidWorks Corp\SolidWorks\lang\english, but you can (and should) keep all of your custom templates in a path that will not be overwritten by reinstalling or uninstalling the software, and that multiple users can share if necessary.

The next time you need to use this template, you can select it using the Table Template drop-down list in the Weldment Cut List PropertyManager.

Summary

SolidWorks has a lot of special drawing functionality built around sheet metal parts. You may want to create a special template or format for sheet metal drawings, or even use multi-page drawings for including both flat and formed views of the part.

Multi-body modeling in sheet metal opens up another whole range of possibilities in documenting inseparable subassemblies and small weldments using sheet metal parts. The use of a cut list is similar to the use of a Bill of Materials, and though originally intended for weldments, it is also useful for sheet metal parts.

Using Imported Geometry and Direct Editing Techniques

The direct editing set of tools in SolidWorks enables you to change a part without having access to the history of features that created the part. Direct editing works on both native and imported geometry either by simply moving faces or by editing the geometry directly rather than indirectly through feature definitions or sketches.

This chapter looks at recent direct editing developments in the CAD world and also describes the tools on the Direct Editing tab, which is shown in Figure 23.1.

The new tab has the following tools on it, listed from left to right from Figure 23.1:

- Move Face
- Move/Copy Bodies
- Fillet
- Chamfer
- Linear Pattern
- Delete Solid/Surface
- Delete Face
- Split
- Combine

Additional direct edit tools exist in SolidWorks that should possibly be added to the Direct Edit tab:

- Flex
- Deform
- Freeform

SolidWorks has a Direct Editing tab on the CommandManager.

Combining these tools with some of the new Instant 3D functionality gives direct editing tools in SolidWorks many of the advantages of the direct edit–only CAD software. Before a discussion of direct editing will make sense, you need to know a little bit about imported geometry.

Understanding the Basics of Imported Geometry

Geometry that is transferred between CAD packages is called imported geometry. The transfer usually happens through IGES (Integrated Geometry Exchange Standard; pronounced *eye-jess*), STEP (Standard for the Exchange of Product), Parasolid, or ACIS (named for the initials of three people and one company who created the standard: Alan, Charles, Ian, and Spatial) formats. SolidWorks also reads some native CAD data directly. For example, SolidWorks can read data directly from versions of Pro/ENGINEER, Unigraphics/SDRC (NX), Inventor, Solid Edge, CADKEY, and Rhino, as Figure 23.2 shows. In almost all cases, features are not transferred between CAD packages. The geometry that you wind up with is called "dumb" geometry because the smart parametrics and design intent (meaning the list of features) that the model had in its parent software is no longer there.

SolidWorks opens neutral format files as well as several native formats.

 You can bring in imported data in one of two ways. The most common way is to use the Open dialog box and switch the Files Of Type to an imported file format. The other way is to use the Imported Geometry feature by choosing Insert ➪ Features ➪ Imported Geometry from the menus. The Open dialog box creates a new part with the imported feature at the top of the FeatureManager, as shown in

Figure 23.3. Using the Imported Geometry feature enables you to insert imported geometry anywhere you like within the FeatureManager, even after other features have been added.

FIGURE 23.3

Imported geometry comes in without any feature history.

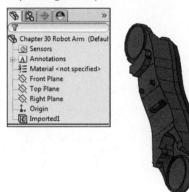

You can use the new Data Migration tab in the CommandManager to find tasks that support imported geometry. The tools on this tab are shown in Figure 23.4.

FIGURE 23.4

SolidWorks Data Migration tab on the CommandManager helps you find import tools.

The tools on the tab, listed in order from left to right, are

- Open
- Imported Geometry
- Import Diagnosis
- Check
- Draft Analysis
- Recognize Features (FeatureWorks)
- Heal Edges
- Knit Surface
- Move/Copy Bodies
- Move Face
- Delete Face

- Replace Face
- Split
- Combine
- Covert to Sheet Metal
- Insert Bends (sheet metal)

Many of these tools are not directly related to imports but may be frequently used with imports. FeatureWorks is a part of the SolidWorks Professional bundle, and as such is beyond the scope of this book; however, it is mentioned as part of one possible workflow for editing imported geometry toward the end of this chapter.

Gaining experience with imports

When SolidWorks imports data from another CAD program, the result is an Imported feature in the FeatureManager. The example shown in Figure 23.3 is the situation you are typically looking for: the result as a single solid body. Frequently, imports do not come in this clean. When imports start giving you trouble, you will see errors on a single body, or possibly multiple bodies, or even surface bodies. SolidWorks can address some types of errors automatically, and you can address some manually. From time to time and for various reasons, you might get a part that is such a mess that you just want to try a different method for importing it (for example, different import or export settings, or a different file type).

The best way to start to feel comfortable with imported data is to be exposed to a wide range of files, some that work and some that don't. This chapter is not intended to be a short course on import repair, but repair is certainly part of the reality of working with imported data. When imports fail, it is not often because of SolidWorks; it is often because the parent software fails. SolidWorks import tools are very good and have improved over time.

Understanding the results of imports

When you import geometrical data into SolidWorks, you can get a number of different types of results:

- Single solid body in a part file
- Assembly of multiple parts
- Multiple solid bodies in a part file
- Surface bodies in a part file
- Combination of solid and surface bodies in a part file

When you get an assembly of parts, SolidWorks uses the default template that you have designated in Tools ➪ Options ➪ Default Templates, creates new parts, and saves them to your hard drive automatically.

Some imports also create a report file with the extension *.rpt or *.err. This file includes statistics about the entities and precision of the data, filename, units, the originating system, and also some information about errors that occurred during the import.

Figure 23.5 shows the first section of a report written for the import of an IGES file.

FIGURE 23.5

Report files can help you understand the contents of the imported file.

```
****************************************************************
        SolidWorks Corporation - IGES Processor Status Report
****************************************************************
==============================================================
General Information
==============================================================
Sending System Product I.D. : cap for test cut.SLDPRT
Receiving System Product I.D.: cap for test cut.SLDPRT
File Name                    : E:\ARE\cap for test cut.IGS
Sending System               : SolidWorks 2004 by SolidWorks Corporation
Preprocessor Version         : version 5.3
File Creation Date           : 040430.111404
Model Creation Date          :
Units                        : IN
Model Space Scale            : 1
Author                       : matt lombard
organization                 :


==============================================================
Entity Processing Information
==============================================================
```

Demonstrating some data import

I am going to import a few parts that don't come in perfectly and ask you to follow along with the files on your DVD. This is not so much a click-by-click tutorial as a "watch over my shoulder" demonstration with commentary.

 Starting with a Parasolid import because these are the fastest and easiest, open the part called Chapter 23 Robot Arm.x_t from the material on the DVD for Chapter 23. You can open translated format files in a couple of different ways. Many people look for an Import or Translate option in the File menu, but it's not there. You can use the Open command, and select Parasolid from the Files Of Type drop-down list. That is one way to do it, but it is slow. I prefer to open a translated file using Windows Explorer, and drag-and-drop the file onto the SolidWorks window.

After you open the file, you will notice a couple of things. The first thing that stands out to me is that the model displays in Shaded mode, regardless of how you have the display set. For example, I like to use Shaded With Edges, but imports always set it back to Shaded.

 The next thing to notice is the Imported1 feature in the FeatureManager. In this case, the import was clean, so there are no warnings (yellow triangles) or errors (red circles). This is not always a good indication of the state of the part, though, because some errors that SolidWorks knows about are not displayed on the Imported feature icon. To investigate closer, right-click the Imported1 feature and select Import Diagnosis, or click Import Diagnosis from the Evaluate tab of the CommandManager.

In this case, the model really is clean. Running Import Diagnosis is the only way you can really know this. Figure 23.6 shows the FeatureManager, the Import Diagnosis, and the part itself.

Next, open the Parasolid file called bad face.x_t. This one also imports without an error or warning on the Import feature, but there is clearly a missing face. It is easier to visualize the separate faces of the part if you change the display mode to Shaded With Edges. If you examine the part closely, you can see that several faces are not lined up square with the rest of the part. Notice also that there are small sliver faces. This may be intentional, or it may be part of the problem. Triangular faces and sliver faces (with very sharp corners, usually long and narrow) are often the source of errors in translated parts.

FIGURE 23.6

Clean imports from Parasolid have the tendency to be fast and trouble-free.

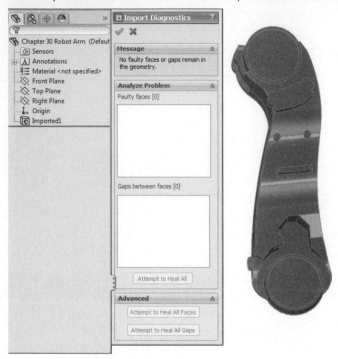

Right-click the Import feature and run the Import Diagnosis; you will see the faulty face listed. Click the Attempt to Heal All button to fix the faulty face. Figure 23.7 shows the part with the faulty face.

FIGURE 23.7

Three-sided and sliver faces are often the source of errors with imported parts.

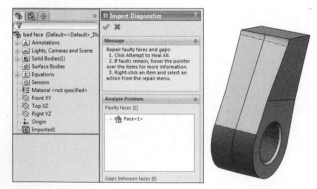

Now open the Pro/ENGINEER file called `bad face 2.prt.29`. Pro/ENGINEER files often end with version numbers as the extension of the file. You need to be careful if you see a file that looks like a Pro/ENGINEER file with no version extension. SolidWorks used the `*.prt` extension for the first couple of years and still opens this type of file as a native file. You may still find some of those parts in circulation.

Open the file using the Import Geometry Directly option, and switch the display to Shaded With Edges, and run an Import Diagnosis. The part has a bad face. If you click on the face in the Faulty Faces list, you can see that the face is next to a small, pointy triangular face, shown in Figure 23.8. The Attempt to Heal All option takes care of it.

FIGURE 23.8

Importing the same data in different ways can give you different results.

Import the same file, but this time choose the Analyze the Model Completely option. It should tell you that it recognizes 13 out of 13 features. Click the Features button and watch the part rebuild. Notice that this time the part comes up with a feature error. The error is on a fillet. It is not an accident that the previous error was on a face next to a fillet face.

Notice that the Parasolid parts came up almost immediately, but the Pro/ENGINEER parts take several seconds to process the data. As the imported files become larger and larger and branch into assemblies, this difference becomes more and more pronounced.

 Next is a sheet metal part. Open `sheet metal.x_t`. Change the display to Shaded With Edges. The part looks good, and Import Diagnosis says that it is okay. Because this is a sheet metal part, and it appears to have a consistent thickness, you will try to flatten it. Click the Sheet Metal CommandManager tab, and click the Insert Bends icon (on the far right side). Select the big flat face as the face to remain stationary (the top selection box), and click the green check mark button to accept the result.

The sheet metal features are added to the part, but notice in Figure 23.9 that they have failed. A close inspection of the part reveals that there is a small ledge between the big flat face and the inside bend on both ends. This was probably a modeling error rather than a translation error. You might be able to fix this to make it usable as a sheet metal part, but for imported geometry editing, you'll need to go to the end of this chapter. Here I cover the results of attempting to repair this model.

The last part I want to show in this "watch over the shoulder" demonstration is a part that I consider to be a complete loss. This is an IGES file that came from an Autodesk Mechanical product. In the DVD, open the file called `valve body.igs`. This part takes several seconds to import. When it does import, it has 11 surface bodies, 2 of those with errors, and some obvious problems with a couple of faces that somehow became out of control. This is one of the reasons so many users do not recommend using IGES files. This type of error is more prevalent with IGES files than other formats. Figure 23.10 shows the FeatureManager and the part on the screen. Again notice that the locations where the huge problem faces come off the model are pointy triangular faces.

FIGURE 23.9

Very small errors can cause special functionality in SolidWorks not to work, and repairing it is not always straightforward.

FIGURE 23.10

Some parts are simply beyond repair.

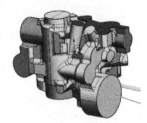

Note

If you get an error that says "There are no points that exist in this file" when importing an IGES file, it is probably because you have Scan To 3D selected in your add-ins list. IGES is one of the accepted file types for bringing in point cloud data, and Scan To 3D assumes you are trying to use the IGES for that. Scan To 3D is an add-in that comes with SolidWorks Premium, not with SolidWorks Standard, so it is beyond the scope of this book. To disable it, choose Tools ➪ Add-ins and deselect the check mark in the box next to Scan To 3D. ■

If you get a part that is this bad, your first move should be to try to get better data from the source. If that isn't available, you are going to have an uphill battle trying to make this part work. Automatic healing with the Import Diagnosis isn't going to touch this part. Repair is going to be an exercise in manual surface modeling. If you don't have the patience for that, you could try solid modeling from the reference faces on the part. If you look closely at the interaction of some of the fillets, it is no surprise that the translation failed so badly. Many of the fillets are badly hacked together. In addition, if this is a casting, someone is going to need to apply draft to the part, and with all the fillets on it, this part is not going to lend itself to that very well.

Using direct converters

SolidWorks contains some direct converters that either extract the kernel data (Parasolid information) or read the actual feature data and rebuild feature-based parts. The direct converter for Pro/ENGINEER data is probably the most widely used. Figure 23.11 shows the dialog box for the Pro/ENGINEER to SolidWorks Converter.

FIGURE 23.11

Converting Pro/ENGINEER files to SolidWorks gives you some options.

If you use the Import geometry directly option, you just get the dumb solid. Pro/ENGINEER uses its own "kernel," or underlying geometry engine, called Granite. SolidWorks shares its kernel with NX and Solid Edge (Parasolid). To read the geometry directly, SolidWorks has to read the Granite data stored inside the Pro/ENGINEER file and translate it to Parasolid geometry.

If you choose the Analyze Model Completely option, you get a dialog box similar to the one shown in Figure 23.12. In this case, the Pro/ENGINEER part had 42 features, and the SolidWorks converter can read them all. Here too, you are given the option to take the features or the body. It is not clear that the Body option is the same as the Import geometry directly option, but they both result in the import of the dumb solid.

You would want to click the Body option if the percentage of recognized features was low, or if you didn't really need the parametric features that much. Sometimes, even if it doesn't recognize all the features, you might still get all the sketches you need to re-create the part.

Note

When parts are re-created in this way, sketches are not made dependent on faces of the model; instead every sketch will lie on a reference plane. This is very similar to the skeleton approach discussed in Chapter 12. ∎

If you choose the Features option, SolidWorks rebuilds each sketch and feature to build a history-based model. This is not usually what people mean when they talk about imported geometry. Many CAD neophytes assume that features just automatically transfer from one CAD system to another, but this is by far the exception rather than the norm.

Figure 23.12 shows the Pro/ENGINEER to SolidWorks Converter dialog box and the finished imported model.

FIGURE 23.12

A Pro/ENGINEER part can be translated with a complete feature tree.

This translation depends on the version of the Pro/ENGINEER file. Check the SolidWorks documentation to see what versions of Pro/ENGINEER are supported.

Handling import errors

Import errors are usually caused by differences between the exporting and importing CAD software vendors. Some imports are more prone to errors than others. For example, the IGES format is interpreted different ways by different software vendors, and is, therefore, very prone to errors.

Another type of error is the error due to tolerance or accuracy issues. Catia is notorious for having very large tolerances on exported data. This is to enable Catia to work with large data sets more easily, but it means that when the geometry is read into SolidWorks, which typically requires more accurate data, you can see a lot of errors. The fact that the Catia to SolidWorks translation is one of the most problematic in the CAD industry seems odd because SolidWorks and Catia are both owned by Dassault Systemmes, but the difficulties have persisted for more than a decade, so it is not a technological difficulty, it is a business decision.

Repairing import errors automatically

SolidWorks has a tool called Import Diagnostics. Import Diagnostics can run automatically or manually to find the errors in imported data and to make repairs if possible. You can access Import Diagnostics by right-clicking an imported feature in the FeatureManager, as long as there are no native SolidWorks features that follow the imported feature. Figure 23.13 shows typical results from a faulty import.

FIGURE 23.13

Import Diagnostics helps you find and repair errors in imported data.

Sometimes the errors Import Diagnostics finds are things you can see, like missing faces, and sometimes they are things you can't see, like the edges of a face that don't intersect or inconsistent face normals. When errors can be found and repaired by Import Diagnostics, it is the best way to go. In fact, whenever I import a model, I always run Import Diagnostics on it to make sure everything is good.

Repairing import errors manually

Some errors are so big that the Import Diagnostics cannot fix them. An example of this type of error would be when a face is missing altogether from the imported data. When something like this happens, the only thing you can do is resort to surface modeling. If the import leaves you with surface bodies, and it cannot repair them automatically, you have to be able to remove the bad faces and replace them with new faces that you construct. This is all about using surface tools to create the new face, extending and possibly trimming the new face to fit into the gap caused by the bad face or faces, and then knitting everything together back into a solid. This may be an oversimplification of the workflow for manual import repair, but it is essentially the big-picture steps that you have to go through to get the task done.

There is such a thing as models that are so bad that you can't fix them, or that would not be worth your time to fix. If automatic repairs don't work, and simple manual repairs don't work, the next thing to do would be to go back to the source of the file and ask for better data.

Best Practice

Whenever you export data to another CAD system, it is considered best practice (and professional courtesy) to "round-trip" (save out, then read back in) the data to make sure that you can accurately read the data that you wrote out. You should not send someone else data that you cannot read back into the CAD system that created it. This may be of little comfort to you when you are the one receiving the bad data, but if you receive bad data, you have every right to go back to the creator and ask if he can round-trip his data. It might be that he can adjust tolerance or accuracy settings to give you better data, or possibly that his model had some problems that he didn't know about when he exported it out to you. ■

If you get bad data and you do not have access to the source, and automatic and manual errors prevent you from using the data, then the next best thing is to rebuild the part using the error-filled data as a reference. This is never a pretty thing, but if you really need the data to be clean, and there is no other way, this is what you need to do.

You can take measurements in one file and build a new part in another file, build one file in the context of an assembly directly over the problem file, or even rebuild it as a multi-body part.

Tricking data into working

Occasionally you can employ tricks to heal problem imports. Simply saving out of SolidWorks as Parasolid and reading back in repeatedly can sometimes heal troublesome imported geometry. I frequently use Rhino to import problem files, then export from Rhino as a Parasolid. Rhino is an inexpensive surfacing application. You can read more about it at www.rhino3d.com. You can download and install a trial version that allows you to save 25 times. Rhino works great as a translator because it reads and writes many file types that SolidWorks does not read. Sometimes when I get a very bad IGES file, I read it into Rhino, and save it out as Parasolid, then read the Parasolid into SolidWorks. Sometimes this will repair the data to the point that SolidWorks can deal with it more effectively.

This is not to say that Rhino is a better file translator than SolidWorks, because this workaround does not always improve things. It is sometimes effective, and because it is free, the only thing it will cost you to try it is time.

You can use the same trick with other CAD packages. For example, if you know that you have an IGES file from VX, and you are having difficulty reading it into SolidWorks, it might pay to download a trial version of VX (www.vx.com) and see if it can import the data and re-export. It is best to use the source program to read and re-export when possible.

Ensuring that you get good data

If you can't get a SolidWorks file from someone who needs to send you data, the type of translation file that you get has a huge influence on the likelihood that your translation will be successful. Ask for data in this order:

1. **Parasolid (including native formats that use Parasolid, such as NX, Unigraphics, and Solid Edge).** Parasolid can come in text format (`*.x_t`) or binary format (`*.x_b`). You may also see file extensions such as `.xmttxt` from older versions of Unigraphics. Of these, the binaries are smaller, but the text files have WordPad readable and editable headers that can be useful in various situations, such as correcting units or part scaling, as well as telling what the parent CAD program was.

2. **STEP (AP 214 or AP 203; Standard for the Exchange of Product model data).** The AP stands for application protocol. Most mechanical CAD programs use these two protocols, which were developed for automotive and configuration controlled design (read more at `www.steptools.com/library/standard/step_2.html`).

3. **ACIS (named for the initials of the three people and one company who created the standard: Alan, Charles, Ian, and Spatial).** ACIS creates `*.sat` files.

4. ***.VDAFS, *.VDA (Verband der Automobilindustrie ⇨ Flächenschnittstelle).** A German automotive geometry transfer format.

5. **IGES (Integrated Geometry Exchange Standard; pronounced *eye-jess*).** Because of the age and lack of clear definition in the IGES format, there is little that is truly standard about it any more, and many geometry creation software packages export data that SolidWorks cannot read correctly. While this format is an old standby for old-timers, it is one you probably want to avoid unless you are getting data from someone you know will give you something usable.

Another advantage of the Parasolid data is that SolidWorks reads it so quickly. A large IGES or STEP file can take minutes to read in, where SolidWorks can read equivalent Parasolid data in a couple of seconds. Once the data is read into SolidWorks, it should all be the same, with no difference between data from Parasolid and any other source, because it is all converted to Parasolid to be stored inside the SolidWorks file; but because it's now all Parasolid you save time on the initial read.

Whether or not the data you receive is of value to you depends in part on what you want to do with it. If your data only has to be a visual representation, and not a CAD-accurate NURBS (Non Uniform Rational B Spline) model, you may be able to accept a wider range of data types. If you are looking for manufacturing quality data, some formats are simply not worth your time to deal with. These file types are mesh data that SolidWorks can read and are useful for visual data, but useless for clean NURBS data:

- `*.stl`. Stereolithography, typically used for rapid prototypes
- `*.vrml`. Virtual reality markup language, typically used for games, an old format that allowed color to be transmitted with the mesh geometry
- `*.cgr`. Catia graphics

Converting point cloud data

One of the most common import questions is how to import data from file formats such as `*.obj` or `*.3ds`, among others. These file types are mesh files, which means they are simply point cloud data. SolidWorks and most other CAD programs create geometry that is based on NURBS data, where the surfaces are represented by very accurate mathematics. Mesh data is represented by points in space, which is much faster to work with because it is similar to the data used by graphics cards and drivers to display curvy shapes. Mesh data is used by Hollywood, video game developers, and computer graphics studios, and NURBS data is used in engineering and manufacturing. It is easy to convert NURBS to mesh, but more difficult to convert mesh to NURBS. The mesh to NURBS conversion can be done, but complex software and specialized expertise is needed for it to happen correctly.

Note

SolidWorks can make the mesh to NURBS conversion with the Scan To 3D software that is part of the Premium package. Because this is not included in the Standard package, it is beyond the scope of this book and will not be covered here. ■

Understanding the IFC file format

The *.ifc (Industry Foundation Classes) file format is from the AEC (Architecture, Engineering, and Construction) industry, which means it is for buildings. IFC is related to the BIM (Building Information Modeling) initiative that enables the transfer of more than just geometrical information about a building. Much of the AEC discussion is well beyond the scope of this book. If you want more information on IFC, BIM, and AEC modeling, a good place to start is at www.aecbytes.com/feature/2004/IFCmodel.html.

SolidWorks appears to be reaching into this market with a couple of enhancements in the 2011 release, including the large-scale design options with 3D sketches and weldments.

Understanding the Traditional Role of Direct Edit Tools

What I call "direct editing" is also known by other names. You may hear it referred to as direct modeling, explicit modeling, history-free modeling, or even synchronous technology. I call it direct editing because the way the geometry is created is all approximately the same and the difference is in the way edits are made. In fact, one of the claims to fame of direct editing software tools is that it is the only system that deals effectively with imported geometry, because "geometry is geometry," regardless of its source — native or imported. This is the reason why I cover imported geometry and direct edit tools together in this chapter.

Traditionally, direct editing CAD software has lived by the rule that how you create geometry should not affect how you edit the geometry. Therefore, direct edit CAD packages still use functions like extrude and revolve to build parts, but they would not return to those functions to edit the part; they would instead directly manipulate faces of the part by moving, offsetting, and rotating.

CAD software that depends on direct editing tools has existed for a long time: it has been around longer than history-based CAD software. In the last several years, some new direct edit CAD products (Sketchup and Spaceclaim) have appeared on the scene and have renewed an interest in direct edit techniques. Until this recent resurgence, the direct edit programs were seen as old-fashioned and inferior to parametric history-based programs.

Part of the charm of the direct edit scheme was that the software didn't add any information to the model. The model could be transferred between direct edit CAD packages without losing any information. This is clearly not the case with parametric history-based CAD software, where you basically lose the ability to edit the existing model when you transfer it from one parametric history-based program to another. You can add new features, but you can't change what originally appears.

Defining the role of direct edit tools

But direct edit CAD software has not taken over the market, even with all of the recent hype. History-based modelers are still popular with users who design things. There must be more to this story: the direct edit scheme does have some weaknesses. While making individual changes is easy and intuitive, making conceptual changes (changes to the design intent) can be just like starting over again with direct edit. There are also situations in which certain edits cannot be made, or reversing a set of edits does not result in the original configuration. People who are used to the control and power of history-based systems will be less likely to relinquish that control for simple ease of use.

It turns out that the simplified capabilities of direct edit tools are more suited to non-CAD specialists who still need to work with geometrical data either upstream or downstream from the main production modeling. This means that a non-specialist can do the equivalent of a 3D napkin sketch in Sketchup and hand it off to a specialist to create the detailed production model. It means that an FEA (Finite Element Analysis) analyst can make simple edits to a model given to her by a specialist. A machinist can add stock to a finished detail model without being highly CAD proficient. I don't see CAD power users or production modelers giving up history-based CAD software and changing over to direct edit-only tools any time soon.

As a part of the direct edit resurgence, CAD companies have figured out how to apply the concept of parametrics (driving dimensions and geometrical relationships) directly to the solid model, without using sketches or feature definitions as an intermediate step. Also, the history-based modelers are adding some direct-editing functionality. This cross-pollination helps bridge the gap that is now becoming mainly a discussion about how to combine direct edit and history-based modeling techniques. In this chapter, I do not cover the details of how each CAD program has implemented the direct editing scheme; I just want to help you understand where SolidWorks is today in the direct edit spectrum, and what you might have to look forward to as the comparison between the history-based and history-free worlds continues to take shape.

This background information is important as a part of the overall discussion of the place of these tools within the SolidWorks software. Adding direct edit tools to SolidWorks is not an earth-shattering change, but of secondary importance. Notice that the topic of direct edit does not dominate this book, just 1 chapter out of 24. SolidWorks includes the tools because they are useful, not because they are necessary.

Understanding the strengths and limitations of direct edit tools in SolidWorks

Some of the selling points for the direct edit CAD tools are that you don't have to worry about how a part was made (you just make the changes you want to make), and that feature trees with "history" always include feature rebuilds (which users tend to complain about taking a long time, especially for large parts and assemblies).

Without a doubt, grappling with feature order and feature rebuild times are problems that SolidWorks users face daily and often complain about.

Direct edit strengths include:

- Avoid feature order problems
- Avoid rebuild time
- Changes are more intuitive
- Concept of moving faces directly is very intuitive

Probably the most serious limitation of direct edit tools is that once a face has been eliminated from the model, you cannot bring it back using more direct edit tools. For example, take the part in Figure 23.14.

FIGURE 23.14

Editing limitations with direct editing

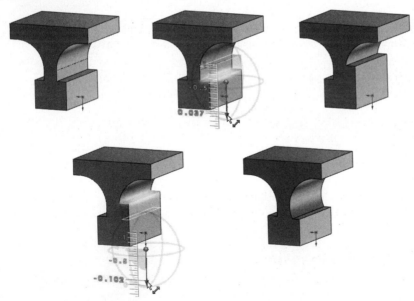

If you change the bottom square area such that the flat face between the bottom square and the arc disappears, you cannot get it back by just moving the face back to where it was; you would have to move the face and then make a cut to reinstate the flat face. This limitation is less serious when the direct edit tool is just another tool within a history-based modeler, because you can resort to the more powerful history-based tools to compensate, but with a dedicated direct edit–only tool you will be up against a more difficult task.

Other limitations of direct edit–only CAD software are going to center around features that themselves are some sort of process, such as fillets or shells. While fillets and shells are two of the most problematic features for history-based modeling, they are also two features that create the biggest limitations for direct edit software.

Using SolidWorks Direct Edit Tools

So how does SolidWorks, a history-based system, incorporate the advantages of direct editing techniques, which are *not* typically thought of as history-based? What does it look like when contradictory regimes collide and start sharing ideas? SolidWorks has taken ideas from a history-free scheme and incorporated them into a history-based scheme.

First, I will show you how this works in a simple example. Using the part from Figure 23.14, Figure 23.15 shows the FeatureManager and the original sketch. Notice that the original sketch has not changed, but the part itself has. Rolling back eliminates the Move Face features, and making changes to the original sketch changes the starting points for the Move Face features when they are unrolled.

FIGURE 23.15

Direct edits in a history-based part

You may be able to imagine that in a part with a much longer feature tree, where the relationships between the faces and the features are more complex, overriding that complexity by editing a face directly could have some appeal.

Combining direct edit with history

SolidWorks has several features that do not create new geometry, but edit existing geometry only, whether it is native or imported. These include the following:

- Move Face
- Delete Face

- Freeform
- Flex
- Deform
- Draft
- Scale

I'll show you a slightly more complex example. In traditional SolidWorks usage, if you wanted to move the face indicated in Figure 23.16, you would go back and edit the sketch or feature that was used to create it. That would be easy enough, and the fillets would update to match the new geometry.

The direct edit salesmen would say that first finding the feature you need to change is difficult, then waiting for the change to rebuild all the features, and last dealing with the downstream features like fillets that might fail due to the changes is frustrating, and he would be right. (You can find a feature in the tree by right-clicking geometry in the graphics window and selecting Go To Feature In Tree.) The problem is that the part, as shown in Figure 23.16, cannot be changed at all in the traditional direct edit scheme. In the direct edit scheme, the fillets are just faces; they are not intelligent features. If you move faces they are attached to, you have to also explicitly tell the fillet faces what to do.

FIGURE 23.16

Fillets greatly complicate direct editing schemes.

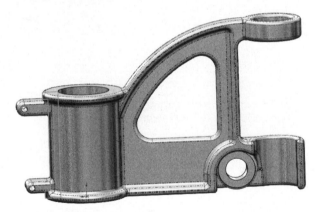

While the direct edit implementation in software such as Solid Edge ST3 is smart enough to make changes to models with fillets on them, the direct edit tools in SolidWorks are less sophisticated and cannot deal with the fillets at all.

Here's how to simplify the part by suppressing fillets and using the Move Face feature to change the part (see Figure 23.17). Here, I've moved the ring around the top of the barrel as well as the mounting boss.

FIGURE 23.17

Using Move Face to extend the length of the barrel of the cast part after the fillets have been removed

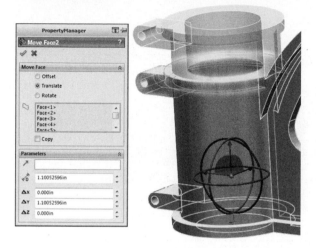

In order to make this move, I had to select seven faces:

1. Top of ring

2. Bottom of ring on left

3. Bottom of ring on right

4. Top of boss

5. Bottom of boss

6. Full round on end of boss

7. Hole in the mounting boss

Notice how the Web now extends up the side of the barrel. This is the type of edit that would be clumsy in SolidWorks if it were what you wanted to do. In direct edit, it is the kind of edit that would be clumsy if it were *not* what you wanted to do.

This is one of the limitations of direct edit techniques in general — not a limitation of SolidWorks, but a limitation of the concept as implemented in SolidWorks. Direct edit cannot make new faces without adding another feature and has problems with the intelligent type of face creation that you find in history-based systems. Direct edit programs are certainly not more powerful than SolidWorks or any other history-based CAD program. They have weaknesses in different areas, and the weaknesses are more limiting than SolidWorks history-based weaknesses.

Figure 23.18 shows where the weakness of using the direct edit tools within SolidWorks begins to show up. The first feature in the part is a revolve that uses a sketch. The last feature in the part is a Move Face feature that moves the faces created by the revolve. So if you want to change the geometry of the barrel, it is controlled by two different features. If you make the sketch a specific size, the Move Face feature will change it. Move Face can only change relative to a starting point; it cannot make something a specific dimension, so it will always either add or subtract a given amount from the geometry created by the original feature.

Move Face features put some geometry in double jeopardy — it can be changed from two different places.

Some SolidWorks power users consider this double-jeopardy condition sloppy design or bad practice. You can make a strong case that the direct edit tools should not be used on native SolidWorks parts, and that you should edit the feature the way it was created. There is certainly a place for that argument. But I know from my own modeling work that sometimes changing a feature way back in the tree can have unintended repercussions later in the tree, so using a Move Face feature late in the tree avoids fixing a lot of propagated errors. Is that a cheap, sleazy cheat? You will have to decide that for yourself.

Combining direct editing with imported geometry

Regardless of any argument against using direct edit tools on native SolidWorks data, there can be no such argument against using them on imported data. Direct edit tools may have their limitations, but when dealing with imported geometry in SolidWorks, your choices are limited, as you see from the following:

- Direct edit tools
- Cut and add modeling
- Manual surfacing tools
- FeatureWorks deconstruction

When faced with these options, direct edit tools look like the safe choice. The big problem will be that if the part is covered with fillets, you may not be able to change much. In cases like that, you might use a combination of tools, such as FeatureWorks to remove fillets, and then direct edit to make changes.

Handling imported data with FeatureWorks

 FeatureWorks is not part of the scope of this book because it is a part of SolidWorks Professional, and the book is limited to SolidWorks Standard. FeatureWorks is an add-in that rebuilds imported solid models as feature-based models. It can recognize and rebuild features automatically, or semi-automatically with you guiding it through the process.

FeatureWorks works by deconstructing, or "unbuilding," the part, removing faces of features that would be applied last. For example, first it will try to recognize fillets, and removes them from the model. Then it recognizes other types of features, including holes, and then finally it recognizes the base extrude or revolve feature.

You can use this as part of your process, but only deconstructing the part partially, leaving the portion of the part that is not assigned to a feature as an imported body. If you remove the fillets and the holes, you might be able to do the edits that remain using direct edit tools. This will leave you with a partially imported part with some parametric features and some direct edit features. Some folks might consider this a sloppy mess, but getting work done on schedule does count for something; if that is what it takes, then it removes the sting to some extent. The FeatureWorks PropertyManager is shown in Figure 23.19.

FIGURE 23.19

Use FeatureWorks to fully or partially deconstruct models to allow direct edit tools to work.

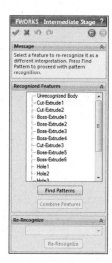

Evaluating Possible Future Improvements to a SolidWorks History-Based System

Recent developments in the CAD industry include a resurgence of direct editing CAD programs, and a direct edit type of functionality added to CAD programs that have been history-based for many years. Former SolidWorks CEO Jeff Ray has said that the future of SolidWorks will include more direct edit types of tools, and that the Instant3D functionality will play a role in that.

It is my strong belief that the marriage of direct edit and history modeling methods is far more beneficial to users than the either-or type of competition between the two that users have seen. Direct edit techniques do not have the power needed to tackle every type of task on their own, and history-based methods will certainly benefit from the additional flexibility that direct edit tools will bring. The details of this marriage as implemented in SolidWorks will remain to be seen for a couple of years.

The direct edit tools in SolidWorks 2011 are weak compared to those in Solid Edge ST3, but those tools are not widely used in SolidWorks. The industry as a whole, including CAD users, is becoming more aware of the potential benefits of direct editing, which does not require you to throw away your current history-based options, and this is a trend that can only grow. Modern direct edit CAD is also parametric; where it differs from SolidWorks is that it is not history-based.

One of the claims of direct edit marketing is that it unravels the tangled relationships created by history-based models. This is a double-edged sword, because most direct edit software cannot take advantage of the inherent benefits of performing operations in an order that you can control. Ironically, however, adding direct edit functionality to a history-based modeler in the way that SolidWorks has done actually compounds the tangled relationships. You need to establish some guidelines for how your company will implement these tools to get the greatest advantage while avoiding the potential pitfalls.

Tutorial: Importing and Repairing Solid Geometry

This tutorial walks you through the button-clicks to import CAD data from IGES and make some edits.

1. **From the DVD, open the file called** `cover.igs`. You can open this file by selecting it in the Open dialog box (File ⇨ Open) or dragging and dropping it from Windows Explorer.

2. **Right-click the Imported1 feature and run Import Diagnosis.** Notice that Import Diagnosis finds no errors on the part.

3. **Look at the inside of the part, in the area near the part origin. Notice on one end of the tab, all the fillets come to a point, as shown in Figure 23.20.** This is clearly not right, although Import Diagnosis did not identify it as a problem.

4. **Open a sketch on the flat face from which the tab protrudes.** Right-click any edge where the tab intersects the sketch face, and select Select Tangency. Then click the Convert Entities toolbar button, and click the green check mark icon to accept the result, and exit the sketch.

FIGURE 23.20

A corner where three fillets come together is not correct.

5. **Right-click one of the long faces of the tab and select Select Tangency.** This selects all but two faces of the tab. There are 16 faces altogether. Activate the Delete Face feature, and select the Delete and Patch option, select the two remaining faces of the tab, then accept the result. The model should remain a solid model, and the tab should be replaced by a smooth face.

6. **Select the sketch created in Step 4 and extrude it to blind depth of 0.050 inch.** Apply a fillet around the end face with a radius of 0.010 inch.

7. **Activate the Move Face feature, and select all the faces of the two side tabs and the snap feature on the end.** Use the Translate option, and the Right (YZ) plane as the direction, and use a distance of 0.25 inch. You should have no less than 21 faces selected. Faces that are parallel to the translate direction do not need to be selected, because they are automatically extended or trimmed to fit. If you are having trouble selecting the right faces, refer to Figure 23.21, and open the finished part on the DVD called `Tutorial1finished.sldprt`.

FIGURE 23.21

Moving tabs and snap in a single Move Face feature

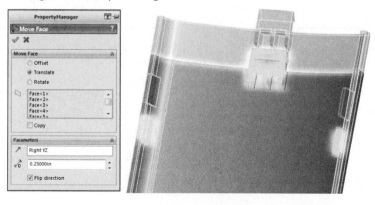

8. **Save the part under a different name and exit.**

Tutorial: Editing with Flex and Freeform Features

This tutorial steps you through importing and editing geometry using the Move Face, Flex, and Freeform features in SolidWorks.

1. **Open the Parasolid file from the DVD called** `ellipse.x_t`.

2. **Increase the size of the part by using the Move Face feature with the Offset option.** You can use the axis of the triad handle to drag the offset distance or key it in in the PropertyManager. Use an offset distance of about 0.08 inch. Make sure only the elliptical face of the model is selected.

3. **Activate the Flex feature, and use the settings shown in Figure 23.22:**

   - Select the body in the graphics window in the top selection box.
   - Select Bending option in the Flex Input section.
   - Select Hard edges in the Flex Input section.
   - Select 190deg for the angle.
   - In Trim Plane 1, set the distance to 1.9 inch.
   - In Trim Plane 2, set the distance to 4.5 inches.

   Accept the feature when you are done.

FIGURE 23.22

Using Flex Bending to bend an imported part

4. **Open a sketch on the Front (XY) plane, orient the view normal to it, and then sketch an ellipse with one end of the major axis at the origin and the rest dimensioned, as shown in Figure 23.23.**

FIGURE 23.23

Sketching an ellipse

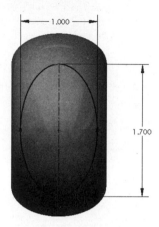

 5. **Initiate a Split Line (Insert ⇨ Curves ⇨ Split Line) and select the bent face of the part.** Accept the feature when you are done.

Note

The Split Line will split the outside and the inside of the curved face. If you select Shaded With Edges, you will be able to see the split on both sides. ■

6. **Initiate a Freeform feature, and select the elliptical split face on the outside of the bend created by the Flex feature.**

   Click the Direction 1 Symmetry option, and a gray plane should appear along the Right (YZ) plane.

7. **Click the Add Curves button, and then snap the cursor to the symmetry plane and click to add a curve.** The symmetry plane will highlight orange when it is selected. Add a second curve parallel to the first one about one-third of the way from the symmetry plane to the edge of the split.

8. **Click the Add Points button, and place a point approximately, as shown in Figure 23.24.**

   Place a point on the second curve in approximately the same location as the first point. Figure 23.24 shows one point on each curve.

   Click the Add Points button to deselect it when you are done.

9. **Change the Continuity flag pointing to the edge of the split from Contact to Curvature.**

10. **Click on the curve on the symmetry plane, then click on the point on that curve.** Drag the arrow handle to pull the point away from the part approximately, as shown in Figure 23.25.

FIGURE 23.24

Locating a point

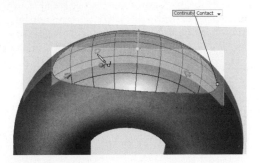

FIGURE 23.25

Pulling the point to create a freeform shape from the existing face

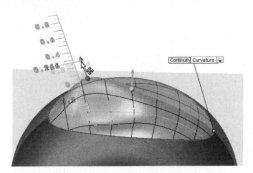

11. **Click on the second curve, and then click and move the second point in a way similar to the first point.** When you are done, the part should look similar to Figure 23.26.

FIGURE 23.26

The finished freeform surface

12. **Save the file as a different name.**

Summary

In recent years direct edit tools have received a lot of hyped press and marketing attention. However, CAD tools dedicated to working primarily as direct edit tools are not going to overtake the tools used by professionals who design and model for production. If anything, they will be used primarily by non-CAD specialists for simple editing and simple concept development, and possibly by downstream data consumers like FEA analysts or CNC (Computer Numerical Control) machinists.

The direct edit tools available within SolidWorks are powerful and are becoming more powerful with each release. While they might be best applied to imported data, they can also be applied to native SolidWorks data. This brings up questions of best practice and duplication of effort. Sometimes the changes involved in editing a feature that is near the top of a long feature tree can be time-consuming compared to simply moving a couple of faces.

Using Plastic Features

SolidWorks has several tools that are specific to modeling and evaluating plastic parts. These tools can help simplify and standardize some of the complex repetitive tasks involved with plastic part design. SolidWorks offers tools tailored to the needs of plastic part designers.

You can manually do all the work that these tools automate, which is useful when the automated tools do not provide the necessary options or flexibility. The more complex your models, the more comfortable you need to be with workaround techniques.

Because of the specific needs of plastic part modelers in some cases to prepare plastic parts for various molding methods, SolidWorks has a set of powerful evaluation tools that help you examine your models to check the amount of draft, thickness, and location of undercuts. Finding design-related manufacturability problems in manufacturing is expensive. Finding them in the design office is far less expensive and conserves time. A good grasp of the evaluation tools is an important component of good plastic part and mold modeling practice.

This chapter is written for the user who is already experienced in plastics practice and terminology, but needs to understand the SolidWorks tools used with the plastic and mold features. In this chapter, I assume that the reader already has a grasp of basic plastics and mold design.

IN THIS CHAPTER

Exploring plastic features

Learning about plastic evaluation tools

Using Plastic Features

The plastic features available in SolidWorks are the Mounting Boss, Snap Hook, Snap Groove, Vent, Lip/Groove, and Indent, as well as the more standard Draft and Shell. These features offer standardized but flexible geometry to help you make more consistent models more quickly, and with less tiresome repetition. You can find most of the features in this section on the Fastening Features toolbar, and the remaining features on the Features toolbar.

Some of these features have applications beyond just molded plastic parts. Many molding, casting, or "net shape" processes exist in plastic materials, as well as metals, ceramics, and composites.

Using the Mounting Boss

 The Mounting Boss feature enables you to place a boss with fins and either a hole or a pin on the end. It does not enable you to place a counterbored hole or a through hole to facilitate screw bosses. It is aimed primarily at press pins.

Figure 24.1 shows the Mounting Boss PropertyManager along with the preview of the boss in progress. The part used in this figure is on the DVD, with the filename `Chapter 24 – right frame.sldprt`.

The workflow for the Mounting Boss feature is as follows:

1. **Select a spot on the part that represents where the boss will attach to the part.** This can be either a flat or curved face. In the example in Figure 24.1, because I selected a curved face, it is necessary to also supply a direction of pull. If you select a flat face, the direction selection box in the next step is not available.

2. **Select a plane, planar face, edge, or axis to establish the axis of the boss.** This is usually the direction of draw. Notice in the part shown in Figure 24.1 that an axis established early in the part is named as the Direction of Draw. This step is optional. The default is the direction normal to the face selected in Step 1.

3. **Select an existing circular edge to align the boss.** The new boss will be concentric with the circular edge. This step is also optional. You can choose to use dimensions to locate the boss *after the feature is created*. If you use dimensions, you cannot locate the boss while the PropertyManager is active.

4. **The Boss panel of the Mounting Boss PropertyManager is used to establish the height and other dimensions of the central boss.** Diameter and draft dimensions are obvious. You can establish height by a dimension or by an "up to" face using the Select mating face option. There is no option for an "offset from face" end condition.

5. **The Fins panel of the Mounting Boss PropertyManager is used to control the alignment, draft, height, width, and patterning of the ribs around the boss.** The first box is for a direction vector such as a plane, edge, or axis to establish the rotational orientation of the ribs. You cannot use a sketch for this. The significance of the dimensional values is obvious. The fin pattern function is also obvious except for the Equally Spaced option, which is only available when the number selected is 2. Then you must select a vector to establish the orientation of the fins, which form a right angle for a corner.

6. **The Mounting Hole/Pin panel enables you to specify a pin or hole boss and the associated sizes.** It is interesting to me that it doesn't enable through holes or counterbore holes from the outside of the part, along with associated screw sizes for clearance.

7. **SolidWorks has renamed Favorites in the rest of the software to Styles, but in the Mounting Boss and the Lip/Groove, it is still called Favorites, and saves settings like other Favorites/Styles functionality.**

8. **After you have successfully accepted the creation of the boss, if you did not use a circular edge to locate the boss (Step 3), you can expand the Mounting Boss feature in the FeatureManager and edit the 3D sketch under the boss.** Inside this sketch is a point, which you can dimension to locate precisely. Remember that dimensions in 3D sketches follow some special rules. To get orthogonal dimensions parallel to X, Y, or Z axes, you will need to dimension from planes. Three-dimensional sketch dimensions do not snap to horizontal or vertical orientations like 2D sketches.

If you have selected a flat face for the initial position of the boss, you get a 2D sketch instead of a 3D sketch.

FIGURE 24.1

A Mounting Boss in progress

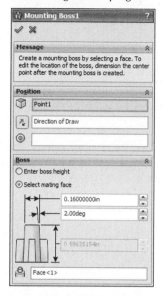

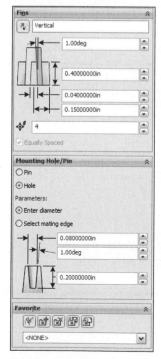

The features created by this tool are not manually editable. They are not made of extrudes and rib features that are accessible behind the Mounting Boss interface. You have to go through the Mounting Boss PropertyManager to edit the features and cannot edit sketches used to make the features.

SolidWorks designed this feature primarily as a way to create pin-and-hole press pin bosses. These are certainly needed, but also needed are screw bosses. You will have to size your own screw holes either for threaded inserts or for thread cutting screws. You will also need to manually create some of your own features if you want to make a counterbored clearance hole for a screw, as shown in the cross section in Figure 24.2.

FIGURE 24.2

Manually making a Mounting Boss into a typical screw boss

In this case, I created the screw boss by creating a Mounting Boss feature with a hole sized for the screw, then added an extrude around the base of the boss, and a cut from the outside to shell out the boss. The list of features is shown to the left in Figure 24.2. You might also consider using the Indent feature with a tool body the size of the hole you want to create.

An effective way to pattern a single Mounting Boss feature around a part is to use the Sketch Driven Pattern. This feature uses a sketch with a set of points where each point represents the center of a patterned instance. Refer to the model on the DVD and examine the sketch driven pattern at the bottom of the FeatureManager. Use the Chapter 24 - right frame.sldprt file, and change to the "nonmirror" configuration if it is not already there.

Using the Snap Hook and Snap Hook Groove

Snap Hook and Snap Hook Groove are two separate features. Lip/Groove combines both functions into a single PropertyManager to help you get results that work together more easily. Figure 24.3 shows the PropertyManager for the Snap Hook feature, along with a completed hook.

The workflow for the Snap Hook feature goes like this:

1. **Select a spot on the model that will correspond to the center of the undercut edge where the hook intersects the part.** It looks like you can select a face or an edge when you first create the feature, but the software always converts the selection to a 3D sketch point when the feature is accepted.

2. **Select a vector (face, edge, axis, not a sketch) to set the vertical orientation of the hook, or the "top."**

3. **Select another vector to define the "front" of the hook (the undercut side).**

4. **Choose to select a mating face or enter a number to define the height of the hook.**

FIGURE 24.3

The Snap Hook PropertyManager with a completed hook feature

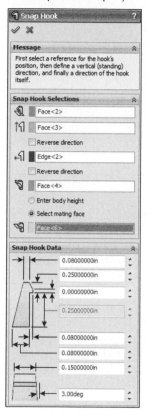

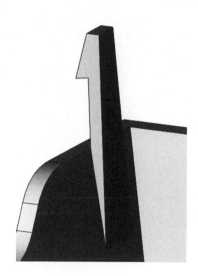

This feature uses a 3D sketch point where you made the selection in Step 1. You cannot dimension this point while setting up the feature, only by creating the feature and then going back and editing the 3D sketch absorbed under the feature. This is also the arrangement with the Lip/Groove. Remember that you cannot dimension 3D sketches the same way that you dimension 2D sketches. You may need to dimension to planes rather than edges or points to get the dimensions you really intend.

The Snap Groove PropertyManager interface is shown in Figure 24.4, along with a cross section of a finished Snap Hook and a Snap Hook Groove. To use the Snap Hook Groove feature, you must have already created a Snap Hook feature. The interface seems to imply that it requires the body the groove goes into to be in the same part as the body of the hook feature, but this is not the case. You can create this feature in-context between a part with a hook and the part to receive the groove, or in a multi-body part.

The Snap Hook Groove PropertyManager with a completed hook and groove

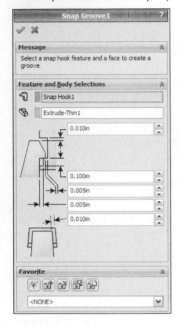

Note

Before designing extensive undercuts into a plastic part, it is advisable to talk to the mold builder if possible. They may have either limited or special capabilities that could impact on the practicality of one approach as opposed to another. I find it is frequently beneficial to work closely with a mold designer or builder on plastic part projects. ■

When I model plastic parts, rarely do situations call for a generic snap feature. Usually situations require more inventiveness due to space restrictions or curvature or material thickness considerations. The Snap Hook and Snap Hook Groove features are reasonably easy to use, but may not have the flexibility for application in all situations.

Using Lip/Groove

The Lip/Groove feature enables you to create a matching lip and groove in either a pair of parts in an assembly or a pair of bodies within a single part. Figure 24.5 shows the Lip/Groove PropertyManager creating a groove in a part. The same interface also creates the lip feature.

FIGURE 24.5

Using the Lip/Groove feature

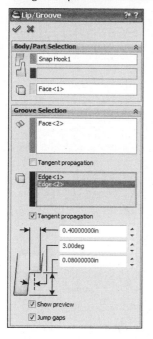
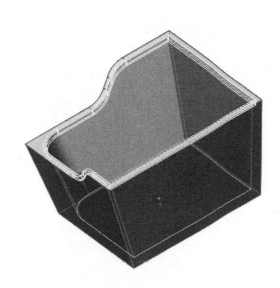

The workflow for this feature goes like this:

1. **Select the part or body to receive the groove.**
2. **Select the part or body to receive the lip. If you only want to create a groove, you can skip the lip steps.**
3. **Select a plane, planar face, straight edge, or axis to establish the direction of pull.**
4. **Select faces that represent the parting surface along the area to get the lip/groove.**
5. **Select edges that the lip/groove will affect.**
6. **Set dimensions for both lip and groove features.**

In some cases, the automated tools may not be able to create what you need to create. You can employ one of several manual workarounds to make lips and grooves. Several techniques exist:

- On a planar parting line, you can use sketches offset from the edges and then extrude either a boss or a cut.
- Using a thin feature extrude (boss or cut) can also be effective on planar parting lines.
- Using trimmed and thickened (again, boss or cut) surfaces can be effective but may also be more difficult.

- One of my favorite methods, especially for non-planar parting lines, is to combine a thin feature with an extrude up to an offset surface body.

- Using a sweep to cut or add material can be effective on either planar or non-planar parting lines.

Each of these is really a workaround technique and not a specific plastic modeling tool. I will not go into depth on these techniques here. On the DVD, you will find example parts that demonstrate each technique.

Using the Rib feature

The Rib feature is a flexible tool for creating ribs in a number of different situations. Ribs can be drawn in one of two different orientations, which the SolidWorks interface calls Parallel To Sketch and Normal To Sketch. The names appear only on tool tips when hovering over the icons. To be more precise, what they really mean is that the rib will be created either parallel or normal to the sketch *plane*. If the sketch is a single line, it can be very difficult to tell the difference between parallel and normal.

To me these names are not very descriptive. I call the two orientations *plan view* (view from the top, looking in the direction of draw, normal to the sketch plane) and *skyline* (looking from the side, perpendicular to the direction of draw, rib is parallel to the sketch plane). To me, these names are more intuitively descriptive, and better reflect the function of the rib.

Ribs can incorporate draft, extend, or trim the feature beyond the sketch automatically and break normal sketch rules (plan view ribs only).

Figure 24.6 shows a plan view rib that violates normal sketch rules. Also shown is the Rib PropertyManager. Several models on the DVD show examples of various rib techniques.

The Rib feature workflow should be self-explanatory:

1. **Draw the sketch, either the plan view or skyline.** The sketch represents the top of the Rib. Material can only be added between the sketch and the rest of the part. Remember that the sketch plane direction makes a difference.

2. **Initiate the feature, and set the type of rib and the direction.** Use the Flip Material Side toggle to change the direction of the gray arrow, which should point from the top of the rib toward the part.

3. **Set the thickness and draft amount and direction.**

Using draft in the Rib feature

When you create ribs, you almost always apply draft to them. You can apply draft as a separate feature, or you can apply draft as a part of the Rib feature. It is often easier to just do it as part of the Rib feature, but some people like to make all their drafts as separate Draft features to keep the part faces orthogonal for as long as possible, or they just like to organize all the Draft features into a folder at the end of the FeatureManager so that there is never any question about which feature controls the draft.

FIGURE 24.6

The Rib PropertyManager and a Rib feature

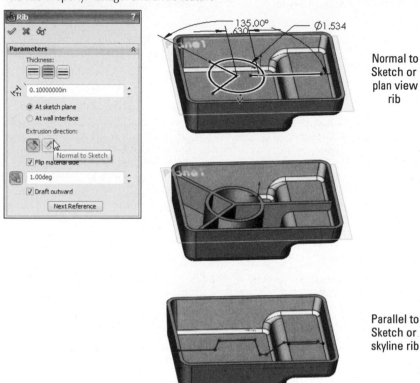

Normal to Sketch or plan view rib

Parallel to Sketch or skyline rib

By default, when you apply draft as a part of the Rib feature, the draft is applied from the sketch end of the rib. This can cause rib thickness problems if you have created a skyline rib where the rib may have various heights. In this case, the top of the rib will vary in thickness, and it may cause the base of the rib to be too thick. When you work this way, sometimes you have to experiment with the proper thickness at the top of the rib in order to get a thickness at the bottom of the rib that will not cause sink marks on the outside face of the part. A solution to this is to use the At Wall Interface option, which only appears once you enable draft in the PropertyManager. Then you can specify the thickness and draft so that the base of the rib maintains a specified thickness.

Best Practice

When modeling plastic parts, it is best practice to model the part at maximum material, and use draft to remove material. ∎

Understand the Rib feature and multi-bodies

The Rib feature is sensitive to changes in the number of solid bodies in the part. For example, if you build a part and put a Rib feature in it and it only has one body, then roll back before the rib and do something that makes two bodies when you unroll the FeatureManager, the Rib feature will fail. The way to fix this error is to edit the rib and use the Feature Scope at the bottom of the PropertyManager to select which body the rib is meant to intersect. The Feature Scope box does not appear unless the part has multiple bodies.

Caution

The Rib feature is very sensitive to changes in the number of solid bodies in a part. If the number of bodies that exist at the point in the FeatureManager where the Rib feature exists changes either by increasing or by decreasing, the Rib will fail with the message, "Please select a body on which you want to create a rib feature." You must edit the Rib feature to repair this condition. ■

Using Intersection Curves as reference

Ribs are features that typically go inside hollowed out parts. For that reason, they are often difficult to visualize, especially when they are on a plane that is deep down inside a part. You may find it useful to use some sort of a reference that shows where the current sketch plane intersects the wall of the part. For this I typically use Intersection Curves. This technique can be used in either Plan View or Skyline type ribs.

The Intersection Curve is on the Sketch toolbar. While in a 2D sketch, activate the tool and then select faces that intersect the current sketch plane. Deactivate the tool when you are done. You may want to select all the lines selected by the Intersection Curve tool and turn them into construction geometry. This provides a good reference for the rib sketch without interfering with the Rib feature.

Figure 24.7 shows an example of using an Intersection Curve as a reference for setting up a rib sketch. The construction lines at the ends and below the right end of the skyline rib sketch are Intersection Curves.

FIGURE 24.7

Using Intersection Curves as references

.133

At the ends of the shell, the intersection curves serve to give the sketch a reference point to be fully defined. Under the right end of the rib sketch, the intersection curve gives you a reference to dimension the height of the rib in the shallower section of the part. The part shown in Figure 24.7 is on the DVD, with the filename Chapter 24 – skyline.sldprt.

Terminating ribs

The Rib feature automatically extends and trims ribs based on your rib sketch. This is a great ease-of-use function, but it tends to lead to sloppy sketching for Rib features. If you sketch a rib, and the sketch does not lead all the way to the wall of the part, SolidWorks extends it. If your sketch line goes past the wall, SolidWorks trims the rib so that it only goes up to the wall of the part. Figure 24.8 shows how the two straight ribs are extended from the existing sketches on a pair of plan view ribs.

FIGURE 24.8

Extending ribs

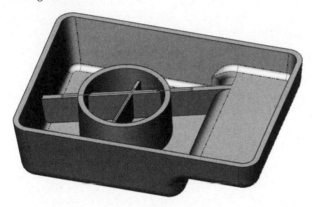

Sometimes you do not want a rib extended to the wall of the part. You may want to terminate a rib at a specific location in the middle of the part. The way to do this is to use a skyline rib and end the skyline sketch with a vertical (plus or minus draft) line that points to the base of the part. Figure 24.9 shows how to accomplish this. Notice that on the left end of the rib, it is extended straight down to the bottom of the part, and on the right side of the rib it is extended up to the next wall.

FIGURE 24.9

Terminating a skyline rib

A final termination situation I want to mention is one that can sometimes happen at curved edges. If the extension of the rib cannot be contained by the model, the rib will fail. This is not always as obvious a situation as you might think. When a non-horizontal rib intersects a curved edge, it usually forces you to fake something a little. Figure 24.10 shows an example of why this is.

FIGURE 24.10

The part wall does not terminate the rib.

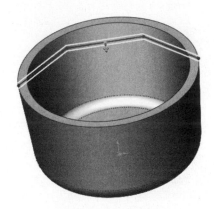

The reason for the error shown in Figure 24.10 is that even though the rib sketch intersects the edge of the part, the width of the top of the rib would go past the edge and not intersect anything. One way to deal with this is to make the sketch intersect the part a little closer to the center of the part from the edge. Another way would be to put a short vertical line at the end of the rib.

Using thin features

Thin feature extrusions are sometimes used in place of ribs. Thin features do not have all the specialized options available with the Rib feature, but they do offer simplicity as the main attraction. Thin features can substitute for Rib features when the rib is a stand-alone rib that doesn't touch the side walls of the part. They can be used to sketch and extrude from the bottom of the rib or from the top. When extruding a thin feature with draft, the end (thickness) faces get drafted as well, which might cause a problem if you are trying to attach the rib to a wall. Extruding a thin feature down from the top of the rib can replace a plan view rib, but it will not enable you to break sketch rules like the plan view rib.

I personally prefer to use Rib features, except for free-standing ribs where you do not want the sides extended up to the next wall.

Using Draft

SolidWorks Draft is surprisingly powerful for as simple as it is. All the aspects of working with Draft could take up an entire chapter all on its own. I will try to hit the most important points in this brief synopsis. The Draft feature creates three types of draft:

- **Neutral Plane draft.** Drafts faces from a plane or planar face where the intersection of the drafted face and the neutral plane is what the draft pivots about.
- **Parting Line draft.** Drafts faces pivot edge on selected edges.
- **Step draft.** Drafts faces from parting line edges and can create a step at the parting line. (similar to pivot draft in other software).

Figure 24.11 shows the PropertyManager of the draft feature, including the DraftXpert, which is mentioned later in this section.

FIGURE 24.11

Draft and DraftXpert PropertyManagers

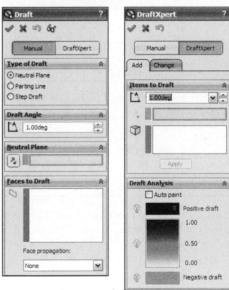

Neutral Plane draft

The workflow for Neutral Plane draft is as follows:

1. **Select Neutral Plane — plane or planar face at which the intersection of the drafted face does not move.** The direction of pull is always normal to the Neutral Plane.

2. **Set the draft angle — how many degrees from the direction of pull vector selected faces should be tilted.** This is *not* a cumulative angle, so applying 3 degrees of draft to a face that is already drafted 5 degrees results in 3 degrees rather than 8 degrees.

3. **Select the Direction — one side or the other side of the Neutral Plane.** The arrow points in the direction of decreasing material. If you are drafting a surface body, the "decreasing material" concept does not apply, so you just have to experiment to see which direction is the one you intend. The Draft feature does not have a preview option.

4. **Select faces to draft — use face propagation options.** Inner/Outer faces refer to inside or outside loops around the Neutral Plane face. All means all faces that have an edge on the Neutral Plane face.

Parting Line draft

The workflow for Parting Line draft is as follows:

1. **Select a direction of pull — this can be an edge, axis, sketch line, plane, or planar face.** You also have to set the direction to positive or negative along the selected direction.

2. **Select the parting lines — these are edges of the faces you want to draft.** The parting line edges remain stationary while the rest of the face tilts. Along with the parting line selection, you may also need to use the Other Face option. Every edge is adjacent to two different faces. The Draft feature automatically selects the face it thinks you want to draft, but it does not always get it right. Other Face enables you to intervene when the automatic selection is incorrect.

3. **Set the draft angle — remember that you can use the Allow Reduced Angle option if you need to.**

Step draft

The most complex of the types of draft that SolidWorks creates is the Step draft. Step draft is used on non-planar parting lines when Parting Line draft would cause the drafted faces to be split into multiple faces.

The word "step" can be said to refer to two different aspects of this feature. First, the parting line can said to be a "stepped" parting line because it is non-planar and at two different levels. Second, the draft actually steps out the drafted face at one level of the parting line. Step draft keeps the face intact and introduces an intentional mismatch ledge (step) at the parting line.

Figure 24.12 shows the difference between Parting Line draft and Step draft on a simplified part. The image on the left is the Parting Line draft. The middle image is Step draft, where a ledge is only created on one side of the parting line. The image to the right is essentially double Step draft, where the total step size is minimized by distributing it across both sides of the stepped parting line.

The draft in these images is slightly exaggerated to make it easier to see.

The workflow for Step draft is as follows:

1. **Start with a part that has a stepped split line, where the angled line makes angles of more than 90 degrees rather than less than 90 degrees.**

2. **Create a plane that defines the direction of pull and is located at the level of one of the split lines (for single Step draft) or at the midpoint of the angled line (for double Step draft).** The location of the plane will determine the "pivot" point for the drafted faces. Essentially the line of intersection between this plane and the drafted face will remain stationary and the rest of face will pivot around it.

3. **Initiate the Draft feature, and set the option to Step draft.** Consult your tooling people about whether to use tapered or perpendicular steps. Perpendicular are probably easiest to tool.

4. **Select the edges of the parting line.** Make sure that the yellow arrows indicate which faces you want to apply draft to.

FIGURE 24.12

Comparing Parting Line draft to Step draft

Parting line draft   Single step draft   Double step draft

Step draft can only draft faces on one side of the parting line at a time. To draft the faces on the other side of the parting line does not require another Step draft feature. You can use a Neutral Plane feature, using the plane created in Step 2 as the Neutral Plane. It will maintain the steps created by the Step draft feature.

Some draft limitations

One important limitation of draft in SolidWorks is that it cannot draft faces in both directions in the same feature. For example, if you have a parting line on a part, you must first draft the faces on one side of the parting line, then the faces on the other side of the parting line. This results in two separate draft features rather than one, and is simply an inconvenience.

Another inconvenience that affects many features in addition to draft is that you can only draft faces from a single body at a time — an understandable limitation, but annoying and inconvenient.

The biggest limitation is that you can't draft a face if it has a fillet on one of its edges that runs perpendicular to the direction of pull. To get around this, you usually have to tinker with the feature order. On imported parts you might have to use FeatureWorks to remove the fillet or Delete Face to reintroduce the sharp corner.

You may sometimes find that draft does not work if you do not draft all faces that are tangent to one another. This is the situation where the fillet is on an edge that is roughly parallel to the direction of pull.

What to do when draft fails

Part of the key to success with the Draft feature is that you have your expectations aligned with the actual capabilities of the software. If you recognize a situation where the draft can not work, you may be able to correct the situation by changing feature order, combining draft features into a single feature, breaking the draft into multiple features, or changing the geometry to be more "draft friendly."

Sometimes the Allow Reduced Angle option can be used for Parting Line draft. If you use this, follow it up with a draft analysis to make sure that you have sufficient draft in all areas of the model. This option enables the software to cheat somewhat in order to make the draft feature work. The SolidWorks Help documentation actually has a more detailed explanation of when to use this option. I tend to just select it if a draft fails, particularly if the parting line used becomes parallel or nearly parallel to the direction of pull.

Draft can fail for a number of reasons, including tangent faces, small sliver faces, complex adjacent faces that cannot be extended, or faces with geometry errors. When modeling, it is best to minimize the number of breaks between faces. This is especially true if the faces will be drafted later. Generally, the faces you apply draft to are either flat faces or faces with single direction curvature. You can't expect SolidWorks to draft anything you throw at it; you should try to give it good, clean geometry.

When draft does fail for a reason that doesn't seem obvious to you, you should use the Check utility under the Tools menu and also try a forced rebuild (Ctrl+Q) with Verification on Rebuild turned on. The Check utility checks the model for geometry errors. Verification on Rebuild checks more rigorously for features intersecting the model incorrectly. Some features may fail with the option on that would not fail with it off. When this happens, there is something wrong with that feature that the simplified default error checking did not catch.

DraftXpert

DraftXpert is a tool used to create multiple Neutral Plane draft features quickly. You can also use it to edit multiple drafted faces without regard for which features go to which faces.

Using Indent

Indent is a feature that uses a solid body as a tool, and indents a thin-walled area in the target part around the tool. For example, if you are building a plastic housing around a small electric motor, then the Indent feature shapes the housing and creates a gap between the housing and the motor. Figure 24.13 shows the PropertyManager interface for the Indent feature, as well as the geometry created by Indent.

In this case, the small motor is placed where it needs to be, but there is a wall in the way. Indent is used to create an indentation in the wall by using the same wall thickness and placing a gap of .010 inch around the motor. The motor is brought into the wall part using the Insert ⇨ Part command. This is a multi-body technique. (Multi-bodies are examined in detail in Chapter 19.)

The workflow for Indent is as follows:

1. **Open or create a thin-walled part (this can be plastic, sheet metal, machined, and so on) in which you want to create an indentation.**

2. **Create a new body that will be the positive shape of the negative indentation.** You can use Insert ⇨ Part to insert an external pre-existing part if you want.

3. **Start the Indent command by choosing Insert ⇨ Features ⇨ Indent.**

4. **Select the thin-walled part that you want to put the indentation into (as Target Body).**

5. **Click an area on the tool body and change the Keep or Remove option as necessary.**
Use Keep when you selected a location on the tool body where you want to create a thin-walled area, or Remove if you want the selected area to be free of material.

6. **Set the Thickness for the material thickness, and the Clearance for free space between the tool body and the new thin-walled material.**

FIGURE 24.13

Using the Indent feature

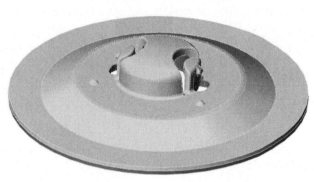

Indent is particularly effective if you have a part that is nearly finished with a lot of detail on it that might be lost by rolling back and making drastic changes to the feature history.

The "cut" option is good for non-thin features where you want an offset cut-with-body. It is just like the Combine (subtract) tool, only with the ability to add an offset.

Working with Shell

 The Shell feature is a powerful yet sometimes tricky feature to work with in SolidWorks. Many users just expect it to work regardless of the condition of the geometry, but it requires that some simple conditions be met. In general, to allow the Shell feature to work, you have to have a model where the minimum outside curvature (convex) is greater than the shell thickness. Shell works in 3D much like the offset sketch works in 2D. If the curvature is too small, you cannot offset an arc to the inside. The same applies to Shell; the thinner the shell, the more likely it is to work.

Also, generally speaking, if the body you are shelling doesn't have faces that are tangent to one another, you will have fewer problems, although faces that are nearly tangent or very pointy can sometimes cause problems.

You can use Shell to hollow out a solid, such as a bottle, as shown in Figure 24.14. You can also use Shell to "shell to outside," which adds material to the outside and removes the original solid.

The Shell feature can create multithickness shells.

Using Multithickness Shell

Figure 24.14 shows the PropertyManager set up for a multithickness shell. In this case, the bottom of the bottle is .150 inch thick, while the rest of the bottle is .050 inch. The top of the bottle is selected so that it is open. If you did not select a face to be open, the bottle would simply be hollow with no openings. The image on the right in Figure 24.14 shows half of the bottle in wireframe display to help you visualize the thickness differences. To get a better view of this model, you can find it on the DVD, with the filename `Chapter 24 - creased bottle.SLDPRT`.

An important part of using the multithickness settings is to remember that SolidWorks will not be able to assign different thicknesses to faces that are connected by tangency. All of the adjacent tangent faces must have the same thickness. Another way to say this is that adjacent faces that are to have different thicknesses must not be tangent to one another. The reason for this is that SolidWorks cannot transition between two thicknesses when the two faces are tangent.

Using Shell Outward

Shell Outward is another option, and is especially useful for bottles. You may be more interested in modeling the contents of a container than the actual container. To help you visualize this idea, think of modeling a liter of frozen water — not the bottle, just water frozen in the shape of the inside of the bottle. Now that you have the contents, you want to create the bottle. This is what the Shell Outward option is meant to do. Figure 24.15 shows the result, where the inside is the original modeled shape, and the bottle shown on the outside was "grown" by the Shell Outward option.

Figure 24.16 shows one of the trickier usages of the Shell feature. This figure shows a planter tray that is manufactured by thermoforming. It may be difficult to tell how to model a part like this, because it could be shelled from either side — the top or the bottom.

FIGURE 24.15

Creating a bottle from a shaped volume

FIGURE 24.16

Getting tricky with the Shell feature

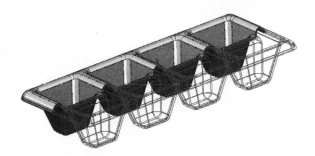

Open the file called Chapter 24 - potting tray.SLDPRT from the DVD. The final feature is used to allow you to better visualize the effects of the shell.

Understanding the Shell workflow

The workflow for using the Shell feature to produce the potting tray part goes like this:

1. **Create a solid part where one side of the solid represents the faces of the finished model.** The other side may be a simple block. Figure 24.17 shows the model before applying the Shell feature.

2. **Initiate the Shell command.** In the Faces To Remove selection box, select all the faces that should be removed or will become thickness faces. This should amount to the six faces of the block sitting on top of the tray.

3. **Use the Show Preview option if you are having difficulty visualizing the result.** Be aware that this option may slow down the operation of the software while the Shell PropertyManager is open, but it will help you see the result based on your current selection.

FIGURE 24.17

Preparing to shell the potting tray part

Using the Vent feature

The Vent feature is highly specialized and is intended for both sheet metal and plastic parts. Figure 24.18 shows examples of vents.

FIGURE 24.18

Examples of the Vent feature

The part used in Figure 24.18 can be found on the DVD in the file called Chapter 24 – Vents. SLDPRT.

A Vent feature has four main components:

1. Boundary
2. Ribs

3. Spars

4. Fill-In Boundary

Figure 24.19 shows the PropertyManager of the Vent feature. This is represented as a single column in the PropertyManager, but here it is split into two columns to fit the format of this book.

The Vent PropertyManager is used to specify the geometry of the feature.

The Vent feature also has several rules, most of which are not explained by the Help feature or the interface:

1. **All sketch elements must be in the same sketch.**

2. **The entire feature must exist on a single face.**

3. **No sketch elements can hang off of the face.**

4. **The Fill-in Boundary may not have a nested contour.**

5. **You must have one rib before you can create any spars.**

6. **Spars and Ribs can be interchangeable as long as at least one sketch element in the rib selection crosses the boundary.**

7. **If Ribs or Spars have sketch elements that are not tangent (lines meet at an angle), the intersections will have notches on the ends, as if each sketch line were extruded individually (see the circular and triangular examples in Figure 24.18).** As a workaround, you can remove the notches by using the Delete Face feature with the Delete and Patch option, selecting the two flat faces of the notch to be deleted.

The Boundary is the outline of the cutout. In Figure 24.20, the Boundary is the elements of the rectangle. The Ribs are the concentric circles, and the Spars are the radial lines.

FIGURE 24.20

Identifying components of a Vent feature

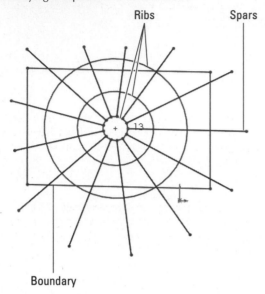

Ribs   Spars

Boundary

The workflow for a Vent feature is as follows:

1. **Create a sketch that contains the Boundary, Ribs, Spars, and Fill-in Boundary**. Rib and Spar sketch elements represent the mid-line of the feature.

2. **Select each element of each Boundary, Rib, Spar, and Fill-in Boundary in its respective selection box.**

3. **Set the widths and thicknesses of each item.**

4. **(Optional) Change the Radius For The Fillets option in the Geometry Properties panel to add fillets to all sharp corners of the feature**. If any of the fillets fail, it will not identify which corner failed; the whole feature will fail.

5. **Use the Flow Area panel to calculate the open space of the vent.**

6. **Use the Favorite panel of the Vent PropertyManager to store commonly used settings.** Favorites can be saved externally and shared with other users.

Using Plastic Evaluation Tools

The plastic evaluation tools in SolidWorks enable you to automatically check the model for manufacturability issues such as draft, undercuts, thickness, and curvature. The tools used to do this are the Draft Analysis, Thickness Analysis, Undercut Checker, and Curvature tools.

Using Draft Analysis

The SolidWorks Draft Analysis tool is a must when you are working with plastic parts. The part shown in Figure 24.21 has many of the situations that you are going to encounter in analyzing plastic parts. The Draft Analysis tool has four major modes of display:

- Basic
- Gradual Transition
- Face Classification
- Find Steep Faces

Draft Analysis is found in the View ⇨ Display menu and is either on or off, like the Section View tool. This is a benefit because it updates face colors dynamically as you model. It also has some drawbacks. The display method for the tool leaves the colors looking very flat, without highlights on curved faces, which makes parts — especially curved parts — very difficult to visualize.

Basic

The Basic draft analysis (with no options selected) simply colors faces red, green, or yellow. Colors may display transitioning if the draft shifts between two classifications. This transition type is shown in Figure 24.21 in the image to the right. For a clearer view of this method, look at the `Chapter 24 Draft Analysis.sldprt` part on the DVD.

FIGURE 24.21

Basic draft analysis results

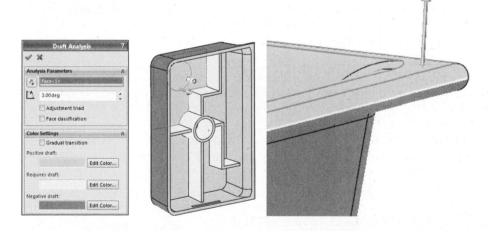

You can perform all types of draft analysis in SolidWorks by selecting a reference flat face or plane, and setting a minimum allowable angle. In Figure 24.21, all walls have at least a one-degree draft, except for the rounded edge shown in the image to the right and the dome. Both of these shapes transition from an angle less than one degree to an angle greater than one degree.

This basic analysis is good for visualizing changes in draft angle, but it also has some less desirable properties, which will become apparent as you study the other types of draft.

Gradual Transition

Although the Basic draft analysis is able to show a transitioning draft, the Gradual Transition draft analysis takes it a step further. With the Gradual Transition, you can specify the colors. It is also useful because it can distinguish drafts of different amounts by color. It may be difficult to tell in the gray-scale image in Figure 24.22, but the ribs, which were created at one degree, have a slightly different color than the floor of the part, and the walls also have a different color. Notice that cavity and core directions have different colors, as well (called Positive and Negative draft in the Draft Analysis). You may want to open this part in SolidWorks, re-create the settings, and run the analysis so that you can see the actual colors.

FIGURE 24.22

The Gradual Transition draft analysis

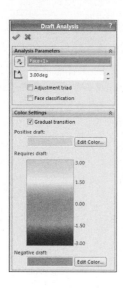
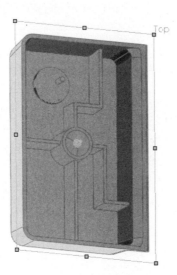

Some problems arise when you use this display mode, the first being the flat, non-OpenGL face shading that is used to achieve the transitioning colors. This often makes it difficult to distinguish curved faces, and faces that face different directions. The second problem is that you cannot tell that the boss on top of the dome has absolutely no draft. In fact, there is no way to distinguish between faces that lean slightly toward the cavity and faces that lean slightly toward the core. The third problem is the strange effect that appears on the filleted corners. The corners were filleted after you applied the draft and before the shell, and so the filleted corners should have exactly the same draft as the sides; however, from the color plot, it looks to be a few degrees more.

Caution

Software can sometimes interpret things differently from the way that a person does. As a result, any computer analysis must be interpreted with common sense.

Due to this and some of the other problems that I mentioned earlier, I recommend using the Gradual Transition draft analysis in conjunction with one of the other tests. Gradual Transition gives an interesting effect, but it is not a reliable tool for determining on its own whether or not a part can be manufactured. ∎

Face Classification

Face Classification draft analysis groups the faces into classifications using solid, non-transitioning colors. You will notice a big difference between the coloration of the Face Classification draft analysis faces and of the Basic or Gradual Transition faces. Face Classification uses OpenGL face shading, which is the same as that used by SolidWorks by default. This allows for better shading and differentiation between faces that face different directions. The Basic Analysis coloration looks like all the faces are painted the same flat hue, regardless of which direction they are facing, which makes shapes more difficult to identify. The non-OpenGL alternate shading method makes it possible to display a transition in color. SolidWorks OpenGL shading cannot do this.

Another advantage of using the OpenGL shading is that the face colors can remain on the part after you have closed the Draft Analysis PropertyManager.

Face Classification draft analysis also adds a classification that is not used by the Basic draft analysis. *Straddle faces* refer to faces that straddle the parting line, or faces that, due to their curvature, pull from both directions of the mold. These are faces that need to be split. On this part, a straddle face is shown in Figure 24.23.

FIGURE 24.23

Face Classification draft analysis and a straddle face

 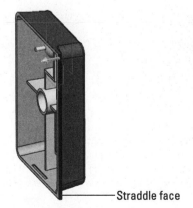

Straddle face

The light bulb icons to the left of the color swatches enable you to hide faces by classification. This is useful when you are trying to isolate certain faces, or visualize a group of faces in a certain way. This can be an extremely useful feature, especially when you have a very complex part with a large number of faces, some of which may be small and easily lost in the mix with other larger faces.

The face counts that appear in the color swatches are a very helpful feature that is absent from the Basic draft analysis.

Best Practice

I prefer Face Classification draft analysis because it is the clearest. If I need additional detail regarding other types of faces, then I may run a Steep Face draft analysis as a supplement. The best practice here is not that you follow my favorite type of draft analysis, but that you understand what you need to know and then use the appropriate tools to find this information. This may include running multiple analyses to collect all the necessary information. ■

Find steep faces

A *steep* face is defined as a face that transitions from less than the minimum angle to more than the minimum angle. Steep faces are different from straddle faces in that straddle faces are actually positive *and* negative, while steep faces are either entirely positive or entirely negative. On this part, the dome inside the part is classified as a steep face, as shown in Figure 24.24.

FIGURE 24.24

A steep face

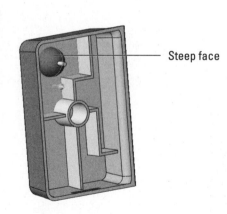

Steep face

Understanding the Draft Analysis workflow

The workflow for the Draft Analysis tool is as follows:

1. **Open a part for which you want to analyze the draft.**
2. **Select View ⇨ Display ⇨ Draft Analysis, or select it from the Evaluate tab of the CommandManager.**

3. **Select a plane or planar face for the direction of pull, and then set the options you want to use to visualize the draft on your part**. The draft colors display immediately after you select the direction of pull.

4. **If you want to keep the colors on while you work, click the green check icon.** The Draft Analysis icon on the toolbar and menu will display as selected. If you do not want to see the colors anymore, click the red X icon. If you click the green check icon and then later want to turn off the Draft Analysis display colors, you must deselect the Draft Analysis icon in the toolbar or menu.

Using Thickness Analysis

You can run Thickness Analysis in two modes: Show Thin Regions and Show Thick Regions. Of these, Show Thick Regions is the most versatile.

Using the Show Thin Regions option

The Show Thin Regions option, or the "Thinness" Analysis, requires you to input a minimum acceptable thickness. Every face with a thickness above this value is turned a neutral gray, and every face with a thickness below this value is displayed on a graduated scale.

Figure 24.25 shows the PropertyManager for this analysis and its result on the same part used for the draft work in the previous sections.

FIGURE 24.25

Results of the Thinness Analysis

One of the things to watch out for here is that some anomalies occur when you apply this analysis to filleted faces. The faces shown as colored were created by the Shell feature and should be exactly .100 inches thick. However, it does correctly represent the undercut on the end of the part and the thickness of the ribs. A nice addition to this tool would be the identification of minimum thickness faces. Perhaps you can submit an enhancement request.

Using the Show Thick Regions option

The Show Thick Regions option works a little differently from Show Thin Regions. You need to specify an upper thickness limit value, beyond which everything is identified as too thick. In these examples, the nominal wall thickness of the part is shown as .100 inches, and the thick region limit is set to .120 inches. For this type of analysis, the color gradient represents the thicknesses between .100 inches and .120 inches, while in the Thinness Analysis, the color gradient represents the values between .100 inches and 0 inches.

The analysis can produce some anomalous results, especially at the corners, and also in the middle. Again, this is a useful tool, if not completely accurate. You can use it to find problem areas that you may not have considered, but you should certainly examine the results critically.

The Treat Corners As Zero Thickness option should always be selected. I have never seen a situation where selecting it improved the results; in fact, I have found that deselecting it has always made corners and fillets behave worse.

This feature can generate a report, which to some extent answers questions about how or why it classifies faces in the way it does. To get a complete picture of the situation, it may be useful to look at the report when you are using the results to make design or manufacturing decisions. A sample of the report is shown in Figure 24.26.

FIGURE 24.26

A sample of a Thickness Analysis report

Summary

Total surface area analyzed	66.739in^2
Critical surface area(% of analyzed area)	1.533in^2 (2.30%)
Maximum deviation from target thickness	0.064in
Average weighted thickness on critical area	0.145in
Average weighted thickness on analyzed area	0.098in
Number of critical faces	6 Face(s)
Number of critical features	5
Minimum thickness on analyzed area	0.001in
Maximum thickness on analyzed area	0.182in

Analysis Details

Thickness range	Number of faces	Surface area	% of analyzed area
0.118in to 0.134in	4	0.57in^2	0.85%
0.134in to 0.15in	0	0.329in^2	0.49%
0.15in to 0.166in	0	0.359in^2	0.54%
0.166in to 0.182in	2	0.275in^2	0.41%

Understanding the Thickness Analysis workflow

The workflow for the Thickness Analysis tool is as follows:

1. **Open a thin-walled part with some variations in thickness.**
2. **Start the Thickness Analysis tool by selecting Tools ➪ Thickness Analysis or by clicking the icon on the Evaluate tab of the CommandManager.**
3. **Select the thin or thick regions option, depending on what you are most concerned about.**
4. **For a thin region analysis, enter in the lowest acceptable thickness.** For a thick region analysis, enter in the low and the high acceptable thickness values.
5. **(Optional) Select individual faces for local analysis in the Performance/Accuracy panel.** This also gives you the option to get a more accurate display. The default is the least accurate option. Accuracy comes at the cost of longer analysis time.
6. **Click Calculate.** This calculation may take a few seconds or longer, depending on the complexity of your part. It is not an instantaneous display.
7. **Observe the color gradient on the faces.** Blue indicates that the wall is too thin, and red indicates that it is too thick.

Undercut Detection

The Undercut Detection tool is in the View ➪ Display menu and on the Evaluate tab of the CommandManager. It is also an on or off display tool, which changes dynamically as you change the model. Undercut Detection is conceptually flawed in that it gives incorrect results every time. However, if you think of the labels as being changed slightly, the results become partially usable.

Even if you and your mold builder know that a part has absolutely *no* undercuts, the Undercut Detection tool will nonetheless always identify *all* the faces to be undercut. In fact, the only faces that this tool will identify as *not* undercut are faces that have no draft on them (even if they are in fact undercut). The only time it correctly identifies an undercut is when it classifies the undercut as Occluded Undercut. Faces that have no draft and are occluded undercut are improperly identified as simply No Undercut.

You may want to avoid this tool because too much interpretation of incorrect results is necessary; however, if you still want to use it, here is a translation guide that may help:

*   **Direction 1 Undercut.** Should read Pull from Direction 2
*   **Direction 2 Undercut.** Should read Pull from Direction 1
*   **Straddle Undercut.** Should read Straddle faces
*   **No Undercut.** Should read No draft in the primary draft direction, but may be occluded undercut faces
*   **Occluded Undercut.** Should read Occluded Undercut faces that have draft in the completely irrelevant primary draft directions; does not include occluded undercut faces that have no draft in the primary direction

Figure 24.27 shows the PropertyManager for this function and the results. If you would like to test it for yourself, the part is on the DVD with the filename Chapter 24 Draft Analysis.sldprt.

FIGURE 24.27

The results of the Undercut Detection tool

Understanding the Undercut Detection workflow

The workflow for the Undercut Detection tool is as follows:

1. **Open a plastic part model in which you want to find undercuts.**

2. **Open the Undercut Detection tool from View ⇨ Display or using the icon on the Evaluate tab of the CommandManager.**

3. **Select an axis, flat face, or plane to establish the direction of pull of the mold.**

4. **Interpret the results using the suggested labels listed earlier.**

5. **If you want to keep the colored display, click the green check icon.** If you want the model to display with the normal model colors, click the red X icon. If you chose the green check icon but want to turn off the color display, turn off the Undercut Detection tool by clicking on it again on the toolbar or in the menu.

Summary

SolidWorks provides a vast amount of plastics functionality. The more you use these features, the more power you will find in them. They will become second nature after you have used them for a while. The power and flexibility is amazing when you think of the incredible range of parts that you can make and evaluate with these features. Automated functions are not the answer to all problems, however. You need to be well versed in workaround techniques for more complex situations.

Part VI

Appendixes

Finding Help

SolidWorks software has been around for more than 15 years now. In that time, the resources available to users seeking help have increased dramatically. These resources take many forms, from personal Web sites with information from individual experience to commercial online magazines or forums with advanced interfaces. In this appendix, I have assembled some of the more worthy sources of quality information.

It is not the goal of this book to endorse any commercial sites or services, but some of the listed resources are commercial in nature, and may feature advertisements, logins, or paid subscriptions.

SolidWorks Help

The SolidWorks Help file contains some information you need to research how functions work. There are topics for which searchability is poor, or that do not appear under expected names, but this is the exception rather than the norm. It is more common to find that some features are poorly documented or not documented at all. For example, when you look up the significance of the Engage Belt option in the Belt/Chain sketch function described in Chapter 3, SolidWorks Help says, "Engage belt. Clear to disengage the belt mechanism," which may not be the help you are looking for.

However, some functions, such as sheet metal bend allowances and the referenced documents search routine, are extraordinarily well documented. Isolated topics are surprisingly thorough and extremely helpful.

SolidWorks Help is available in traditional Help files on the computer, as well as Web-based help. SolidWorks Web Help was created because it is easier for SolidWorks to keep it up to date. You can access the Web Help by turning on the Use SolidWorks Web Help option in the Help menu in SolidWorks or at `http://help.solidworks.com`.

SolidWorks Web Help

The SolidWorks Web Help was new in SolidWorks 2010. Web Help was introduced to help SolidWorks keep the Help files updated without having to send out help updates in the service packs. It also enables the use of other search tools and links to online data sources to make finding help that much easier.

You can access SolidWorks Web Help through the Help ⇨ SolidWorks Help menu selection as usual, but you need to make sure that the Use SolidWorks Web Help option also in the Help menu is activated. The following three sections only pertain to the traditional (non-Web) Help.

Contents

SolidWorks terminology has been a sticking point at times in the writing of this book because terms are either unclear or overlap. Still, it is difficult for two people to talk about the software if they are not using the same terminology. The Glossary, found at the bottom of the Help Contents list, is one of the most useful and yet most underused portions of the Help files. Often when a new user asks me a question, it can be impossible to discern what the user is talking about because he is not familiar with the SolidWorks terminology, is substituting AutoCAD or Inventor terminology, or is assuming all modeling terminology is universal. As dull as it may be, this Glossary should be required reading for all new users. Simply understanding the language being used by the training materials, Help files, and other users can give you a big head start when it comes to learning the software. Look through it. I promise you'll learn something useful.

Index

Starting in SolidWorks 2010, SolidWorks removed the Index from the regular Help, and of course, it does not exist in the Web Help either. An index is difficult to create, and this difficulty was the reason SolidWorks gave for not including it in the new version.

Search

The Search function is for when you are not exactly sure of what you are looking for. For example, you know there is a feature that has a funny name that uses stripes to analyze curvature across edges, but you cannot remember its name. Begin your search with the words *stripes* and *curvature*. If you use curvature, the Search function returns about 60 possibilities. The term you are looking for is Zebra Stripes, but you may not find it by scanning such a long list. If you search using the word stripe, Zebra Stripes appears at the top of the list. So a good search strategy might be to try multiple terms.

The biggest complaint you may have about the Search function in Help is that it will sometimes return too many options, and the connection between the word you searched on and the topic title shown in the list is not immediately clear. Still, too much information is better than not enough.

Many users overlook the three options at the bottom of the Search window: Search Previous Results, Match Similar Words, and Search Titles Only. All three are useful in narrowing your search. With the new Web Help, Search is improved, and includes a section that allows you to further narrow the search results that works like guided search. Guided search provides a list of results, but also provides an index-like set of topics (in the upper right-hand corner) that you can use to narrow the search further.

Additionally, most of the Help linked to from the search results has a link to search the Knowledge Base on a related phrase. This search of the Knowledge Base (KB) may or may not include any results. I have seen several links from the Help to the KB that were empty.

SolidWorks Web Site

Most of the valuable information on the SolidWorks Web site (`www.solidworks.com`) is behind the subscription login, but some free information is also available. It may be worthwhile to explore the SolidWorks site a bit, because it includes a large amount of information ranging from graphics cards evaluations to training files.

Graphics Cards Link

The link to this area of the SolidWorks Web site is `www.solidworks.com/sw/videocardtesting.html`, and appears on the SolidWorks Web site main page behind the Support ⇨ System Requirements link. SolidWorks has tested the range of most popular graphics cards and drivers for compatibility with various versions of SolidWorks and has rated them at various levels based on the following criteria:

> Passed all tests
>
> Passed with limitations
>
> Card has significant stability or repaint problems
>
> Uses the graphics card display settings for SolidWorks
>
> Multi-head hardware accelerated
>
> Supports RealView
>
> Provides 64-bit native support
>
> Supports 3D-Stereo effects

Customer Portal

The SolidWorks Customer Portal is full of useful information. It requires a login, and you can find it at `https://customercenter.solidworks.com`. Portions of the portal, such as the Forums, are available to anyone with or without subscription. Other areas, such as the service pack downloads, are only available to subscription customers.

SolidWorks Forums

The SolidWorks Forums have areas of wide interest for most users. These include about 40 different topic areas, each with a constant flow of information. SolidWorks employees sometimes answer questions, and knowledgeable users often give good answers and invaluable perspectives on not just modeling and CAD admin topics but also general mechanical engineering or materials sourcing.

You can read the forums without an account but need an account to post messages. Accounts can be granted to anyone even if you are not on maintenance. You can find the forums at `http://forum.solidworks.com`.

Make sure to read the Terms of Use available at the bottom of every Forum page. The moderators do not usually apply the rules strictly, but I have seen posts removed that should have been allowed and posts allowed that should have been removed. Generally if you ask, answer, or comment in good faith, you will not have any problems.

Knowledge Base

If you think you have used the Knowledge Base before and found it less than satisfying, you owe it to yourself to try it again. The KB is constantly updated with new information, which comes from several sources, including general technical support results and the Help documentation. Searches actually turn up a lot of useful information. Results may include tech support responses to customer issues, SPRs (software performance reports — also known as bug reports), white papers, articles, and so on. In addition, you can look up SPR numbers you have received from tech support to check the reports' statuses. I have consulted the Knowledge Base several times while writing this book. It has been built from vast amounts of internal SolidWorks corporate support documentation, as well as the support database. I give it very high usability marks!

Software downloads

Manually downloading and installing software and upgrades for SolidWorks is becoming outdated, although you can still do it. The SolidWorks Installation Manager works much like Microsoft Automatic Update. It downloads and even installs updates for you automatically. There is also a new Background Downloader that will download service packs while your internet connection is otherwise idle, to be available to you when you want to use it. You can also work with automated administrative image installations. I particularly like that it can download service packs before the links on the SolidWorks Web site are active. Of course, if you need or simply want to download them manually, this option is also available.

If you are still relying on DVDs to install software, you might consider using the SolidWorks Installation Manager (SWIM) to download not only service packs but also entire installation files for the software. You need adequate network bandwidth, as the downloads may take up several gigabytes. Still, this option is useful and convenient, and most importantly, it works much more reliably than it has in the past.

Release Notes

All the Release Notes for all the service packs of the current version are also available from the main Customer Portal window. This is essential information for CAD administrators. Technical Alerts, changes to the System Requirements (`www.solidworks.com/sw/support/System Requirements.html`), and new installation details are listed here.

Even if you think you do not need to know any of this information, it still makes for interesting (and at times alarming) reading. The Technical Alerts typically warn of severe bugs or other problems and how to work around or fix them.

What's New

What's New is a great document to refer to when you are learning a new version of SolidWorks. For the SolidWorks 2010 version, the What's New document comes in HTML and PDF formats. I find the PDF to be easier to access and read, but possibly less up to date than the HTML version. What's New is an important document to read before considering installing a new version, or if you have skipped versions. If you are looking for a What's New document from a version that you do not have installed, you can find all of the What's New documents on Ricky Jordan's blog (`www.rickyjordan.com/whats-new-guides`).

Installation and administration guides

Installation and administration guides are available for SolidWorks, eDrawings, and SolidWorks Simulation. They contain the basics about the topics and are not as detailed as other sources of information. For a complete installation and administration guide, please refer to the *SolidWorks Administration Bible* (Wiley, 2009).

PDMWorks Workgroup Vault Debug Guide

When the vault gives you an error code, you don't have to call tech support to find out what is going on. It is all listed in the PDMWorks Workgroup Vault Debug Guide. All the error codes appear with the name of the error. This is a must-have document for the PDMWorks administrator.

FLEXlm End Users Guide

The FLEXlm End Users Guide is required reading for a network license administrator. While the network license is easy to install, set up, and maintain, this guide explains many of the details and options that are available.

User Groups

The main SolidWorks site for user groups is `www.swugn.org`. There are too many individual user groups to keep track of or list here, but you can find a user group in your area on the SolidWorks User Group Network (SWUGN) site. You can also find user group information on the SolidWorks Forums.

Online Forums

There are many types of online forums for SolidWorks. I have already discussed the forum on the SolidWorks Web site. Other forums are not directly sponsored by SolidWorks Corporation, and they may vary in quality.

Blogs

Blogs for SolidWorks and related topics cover everything from opinion-based essays to speculation about future products, tips, and tricks or CAD industry news. Most are written by SolidWorks users rather than journalists, so you'll get specifics about a tool that you actually use.

I write a blog, which you can find at `http://dezignstuff.com/blog`. It covers advanced SolidWorks subjects such as surfacing, as well as consumer advocate type of articles, including information on enhancement request drives and subscription options. I also provide links to many other SolidWorks-related blogs, forums, and Web sites.

My blog has updates to books, notices of new books, lists of errors found in books, and a lot of other content. I deal with philosophical and ethical questions related to product design and CAD in general. I post advanced tips, and sometimes excerpts from books. I also post questions for readers and polls where readers can express their opinions; and I'm always looking for opinions as long as you can back up what you have to say.

Some SolidWorks blogs to check out include:

Matt Lombard at `www.dezignstuff.com/blog`

Ricky Jordan at `www.rickyjordan.com`

Rob Rodriguez – Rendering in SolidWorks at `www.robrodriguezblog.com`

Gabi Jack – Learning SolidWorks from the point of view of a student `http://gabijack.com/`

Jeff Cope – API at `http://extensiblecad.com/words/`

Lenny Kikstra – API at `http://designsmarter.typepad.com/lennyworks/`

Josh Mings at `www.solidsmack.com`

Matt Lorono at `www.fcsuper.com/swblog/`

Many other blogs exist, including very good general CAD or other non-SolidWorks topics, and you should be able to find most of them from the links on my blog and the others listed here. These blogs do not all fit the same mold. Some are highly optimistic; others focus on tech gadgets, social networking, tech tips, or CAD news; some simply parrot press releases; and so on. For the best list of other CAD, design, 3D, rendering, and engineering blogs, view the blog roll in the right column of my blog.

Forums

Some forums are commercial, which means they are likely to contain advertising. These forums include:

- `https://forums.solidworks.com`. This is SolidWorks' site with official forums. The forums are very active in a wide range of topics and lightly moderated. This requires a login but does not require current SolidWorks subscription.

- `www.productdesignhub.com`. This site is aimed at both industrial and product designers. It has an active forum for sharing ideas as well as a lot of great articles, videos, and other useful content.

- `www.core77.com`. This is probably the premier industrial design Web site available.

- `www.mcadforums.com`. This site has a lot of traffic and content, but also uses Flash advertisements.

- `www.eng-tips.com`. This forum receives plenty of traffic, has a sign-in popup, and is highly censored.

- `www.3dcadtips.com`. This site is run by the owners of the *Design World* magazine, and has a lot of information on general engineering topics as well as CAD.

Non-Commercial Web Sites

The sites listed here are run by individuals, lack advertising, and contain information created by the owner of the site. They are my favorite types of places to find information. Even though most of these folks are not professional HTML coders, the information is useful and presented well.

- **Rob Rodriguez** (www.robrodriguez.com) features rendering topics. Rob used to host the PhotoWorks rendering contest, but that has moved to http://rendercontest.com/.

- **Paul Salvador** (www.zxys.com) has some nice models and images.

- **Edgar Gidoni** (www.ragde3d.com) is a prolific creator of beautiful SolidWorks models, and he writes nice step-by-step tutorials, many of which are free.

- **Stefan Berlitz** (http://solidworks.cad.de) is the unofficial German SolidWorks site. If you read German, this site is loaded with great information. Although it does contain some advertisements, I still consider it a non-commercial site.

- **Scott Baugh** (www.scottjbaugh.com) has several sample models and a section on tips.

- **Mike Wilson** (www.mikejwilson.com) has some amazing things posted to his site that he has done with SolidWorks. They are great models from which to learn. The site has not been updated for some time, but the models and techniques shown are fascinating.

B

What's on the DVD

Extract the contents of the file to your hard drive in a location that is easy to access. The DVD contains example and tutorial parts, assemblies, and drawings, as well as templates, macros, and tables as appropriate for each chapter. The files are organized within folders for each chapter and are named for the chapter and the function they demonstrate. Some of the files are starting points for tutorials, and some are finished models meant to be examined.

If you make changes to files, I recommend that you use the Save As command (File ➪ Save As) to keep the original file intact. You also can retrieve originals from the DVD again if needed.

The DVD also includes several video tutorials. The videos are narrated, and offer another learning option to the print-only tutorials found in the book. The videos do not duplicate the print-only tutorials.

Caution

I do not recommend that you open files directly from the DVD or from the Zip file, because SolidWorks will respond with messages about read-only files. ■

System Requirements

Make sure that your computer meets the minimum system requirements listed in this section. If your computer doesn't match up to these requirements, you may have a problem using the contents of the DVD.

Windows versions

These requirements apply to Windows XP Professional, Windows Vista, and Windows 7:

- Intel and AMD processors, single, dual, or quad cores
- 1GB RAM minimum (2GB recommended)
- Virtual memory twice the amount of RAM (recommended)
- A certified OpenGL workstation graphics card and driver (Check the SolidWorks Web site for details: www.solidworks.com.)
- A mouse or other pointing device
- Microsoft Internet Explorer 6 minimum (IE 7 recommended)
- A CD drive minimum (DVD drive recommended)

For more details about the system requirements for SolidWorks 2011 and a list of certified graphics cards and drivers, visit www.solidworks.com.

Some older systems that run Windows XP Professional may not be compatible with Vista. Any hardware that runs Vista and most hardware that runs Windows XP should be able to work with Windows 7. For the latest information on system compatibility with Microsoft operating systems, visit www.microsoft.com. At this time, SolidWorks does not run on any non-Windows operating systems such as Mac OS X, Linux, or Google Chrome OS.

Realistically, you will never be satisfied with minimum requirements. If you are using PhotoWorks, PhotoView 360, or any simulation (Finite Element Analysis, or FEA) software, multiple processors or multiple cores are advantageous. Multi-body modeling makes use of multiple cores but also takes advantage of higher processor clock speeds. Maximum clock speeds are usually higher for a lower number of cores, so higher speeds take precedence over number of cores for general solid modeling. You may get better performance per dollar with dual-core processors than with quad-core processors for functionality other than rendering and FEA.

You can only take advantage of more RAM up to the limit needed by your data sets. You can check your Windows Task Manager to see how much memory your largest or most complex models consume. For example, if your largest models use 3GB of RAM, you should have at least 4GB of RAM but will probably not see a benefit from 16GB. You should use a 64-bit operating system if you intend to use more than 3GB of RAM.

All hardware produced in the last several years is 64-bit compatible, but in order to take advantage of it, you have to have a 64-bit operating system installed. XP, Vista, and Windows 7 all have 64-bit versions, but you need to have installed the 64-bit version to benefit from the huge memory advantages of a 64-bit operating system. A 32-bit operating system can handle a little over 3GB of RAM. To handle more than that, you need a 64-bit operating system.

Some software applications have 32- and 64-bit versions, and some do not. SolidWorks has both versions, and you need to make sure you have disks or downloaded data for the correct installation type. Data files are interchangeable between 32- and 64-bit versions, so the files on the DVD will work with either one.

SolidWorks versions

Files created in SolidWorks 2011 are not compatible with older versions of SolidWorks. So, if you have a version of SolidWorks older than 2011, you will have difficulty reading most of the files on the accompanying DVD. You may find some files that came from older versions on the DVD, but this only happens where the files have not been updated for new versions.

As a matter of policy, SolidWorks software does not open up future version files. So if you have SolidWorks 2009 installed, you cannot read files saved in SolidWorks 2011. If you have a question about this policy of the Dassault Corporation, you should contact your SolidWorks reseller. The author of this book does not have the ability to save 2011 files to previous versions.

This book was written using the SolidWorks 2011 version software, and while some of it may be applicable to previous versions, some of it may not due to annual changes that happen in the course of software development. Earlier versions of the book do exist (2010, 2009, and 2007) and are still available, which may benefit you if you have SolidWorks software in one of those versions.

Troubleshooting

If you have difficulty installing or using any of the material on the companion DVD, try the following solutions:

- **Turn off any antivirus software that you may have running.** Installers sometimes mimic virus activity and can make your computer incorrectly believe that it is being infected by a virus. (Be sure to turn the antivirus software back on later.)
- **Close all running programs.** The more programs you're running, the less memory is available to other programs. Installers also typically update files and programs; if you keep other programs running, installation may not work properly.
- **Contact the author.** For problems with the content of the DVD, visit my Web site (www. dezignstuff.com) or blog (www.dezignstuff.com/blog), or send me an e-mail (matt@dezignstuff.com).
- **See the ReadMe file.** Refer to the ReadMe file located at the root of the DVD for the latest product information at the time of publication.

Customer Care

If you have trouble with the DVD, please call the Wiley Product Technical Support telephone number at (877) 762-2974. Outside the United States, call 1 (317) 572-3993. You can also contact Wiley Product Technical Support at http://support.wiley.com. John Wiley & Sons will provide technical support only for installation and other general quality control items. For technical support on the applications themselves, consult the program's vendor or author.

To place orders or to request information about other Wiley products, you can call (877) 762-2974.

Index

Symbols and Numerics

Index

Index

Broken (Locked) category, 201
Broken View PropertyManager, 518
Broken-out Section View
    drawing closed loop, 515–516
    editing view, 517
    overview, 514–515
    selecting depth, 516–517
Broken-out Section View tool, Drawings toolbar, 531
*.btl file, 11
buttons, flyout, on toolbars, 45–46

C

calculator, sketching, 227–230
calloutformat.txt file, 11
Camera PropertyManager, 187
Camera View, 188
cameras, 186–189
Cameras DisplayManager, 186
Cap Ends option, 97, 142, 151
CapRad dimension, Revolve feature, 359
Cascade option, Window menu, 73
Cavity feature, 296
Center Creation option, Circle PropertyManager, 92
center marks, 550–551
centerline lofts, 249
centerlines, 95, 439, 550–551
Centerpoint Arc option, PropertyManager interface, 93
Centerpoint Straight Slot option, 152
Centroid option, Reference Point section, 330
*.cgr data, 739
chamfers
    dimensions of, 110
    edges of, 155
    in extruded feature, 153–155
    general discussion, 280–281
Change dimension direction option, Smart Dimension, 87
Change Sense button, Modify box, 88
Check Entity dialog box, 413
Check tool, 412–413, 427, 635
Check utility option, 770
Choose Option dialog box, 625
Circle option, 92
Circle PropertyManager, 92
circles, detail
    drawing in-line, 509
    pre-drawing, 508–509

Circular Pattern PropertyManager, 316
circular patterns
    creating, tutorial, 336–337
    overview, 325–326
Circular Sketch Pattern, 105, 315–316
Clear All option, SelectionManager, 249
Close loft option, SelectionManager, 250
Closed Corner feature
    Coplanar faces, 685–686
    Faces to Extend selection box, 684
    Faces to Match selection box, 684
    Gap setting, 684
    Open bend region option, 685
    Overlap/Underlap ratio setting, 684
    overview, 683–684
Closed loop cam profile sketch, 300
CNC (Computer Numerical Control), 620, 673
coincident sketch relations, 22
collapse tab, FeatureManager, 56
collapsing, automatically, 40–41
color
    applying automatically to features, 190
    assembly colors, using on drawings, 582
    changing, 81
    controlling, 223–226
    customizing, 64–66
    editing, 211
    of lines, 211, 225
    using with sketches, 211
Color button, Advanced Options panel, 394
Color Display Mode, 211, 212, 225, 491, 586
Colors dialog box, 81
Column PropertyManager, 725
columns, adding, 390, 391
Combine feature, 601–602, 626, 704
Combine PropertyManager, 601
Combine tool, 623, 771
combining macros with hotkeys, 82–83
CommandManager
    Auto Collapse option, 40–41
    basing tabs on document types, 41
    buttons of, 42
    changing appearance of, 41–43
    customizing, 40
    docking, 40
    limitations of, 43
    mixing with toolbars, 41

Index

Index

Index

Index

Index

Index

I

icons
    adding to flyout toolbar, 50
    large, setting, 43
    minimizing, 70
IFC file format, 740
IGES files, 730, 734
IIF function, 351–352
Import Diagnostics, 731, 733, 737, 748
imported geometry
    combining direct editing with, 746–747
    direct converters, 735–736
    IFC file format, 740
    imported and editing using Flex and Freeform, 750–753
    imports
        demonstrating data import, 731–735
        errors with, 736–739
        overview, 730
        results of, 730–731
    overview, 728
    point cloud data, converting, 740
    tutorial, 748–753
Imported Geometry feature, 728, 729
importing, options for, 505–506
Inch B Bible Template.drwdot drawing
        template, 528
Increment Value icon, Modify box, 88
indenting
    general discussion, 305–307
    using with multi-bodies, 599–601
    workflow for, 770–771
inferencing, 111–112
Infinite length line option, PropertyManager interface, 90
Inner/Outer faces, 768
Insert Bend, 696, 698, 699, 702, 706, 733
Insert Line PropertyManager interface, 91
Insert menu
    customizing, 80
    primary uses of, 54
    screenshot of, 53
Insert Part feature
    overview, 615–616
    PropertyManager for, 335
    starting point, 616
    using with sheet metal drawings, 704
    working with secondary operations, 616
Insert Part PropertyManager, 615
Insert Part technique, 133

inserted parts
    configurations of, 383
    controlling, 380–381
    overview, 28
inserting
    blank design table, 384
    blocks, 114, 545–547, 553
    model items, 555–557
    models, 496
    new branches, 542
Insertion Point panel, 123, 553
installing SolidWorks
    for first time, 3–5
    guide for, 791
Instances to Skip option, Linear Pattern feature, 324
Instant 3D
    creating extrudes with, 237–239
    editing geometry with, 239–240
    overview, 237–240
    purpose and capabilities of, 143–144
interface. *See also* customization
    2D Command Line Emulator, 63–64
    adding hotkeys, 81–82
    applying default settings to interface items, 76–77
    associativity, 27–28
    changing colors of, 81
    changing cursors, 55
    combining macros with hotkeys, 82–83
    CommandManager, 39–43
        Auto Collapse option, 40–41
        basing tabs on document types, 41
        changing appearance of, 41–43
        customizing, 40
        docking, 40
        limitations of, 43
        mixing with toolbars, 41
    controlling menus, 53–55
    copying existing settings, 76
    creating part templates, tutorial, 28–30
    customizing workflow, 51–52
    Design Intent
        editing, 26–27
        overview, 25
    history-based modeling, 18–21
    models, 55–58
        DisplayManager, overview of, 58
        working with in FeatureManager window, 55–57
        working with in PropertyManager window, 57–58

Index

Index

Index

O

Index

Index

Index

Index

Index

Wiley Publishing, Inc.
End-User License Agreement

READ THIS. You should carefully read these terms and conditions before opening the software packet(s) included with this book "Book". This is a license agreement "Agreement" between you and Wiley Publishing, Inc. "WPI". By opening the accompanying software packet(s), you acknowledge that you have read and accept the following terms and conditions. If you do not agree and do not want to be bound by such terms and conditions, promptly return the Book and the unopened software packet(s) to the place you obtained them for a full refund.

1. **License Grant.** WPI grants to you (either an individual or entity) a nonexclusive license to use one copy of the enclosed software program(s) (collectively, the "Software") solely for your own personal or business purposes on a single computer (whether a standard computer or a workstation component of a multi-user network). The Software is in use on a computer when it is loaded into temporary memory (RAM) or installed into permanent memory (hard disk, DVD, or other storage device). WPI reserves all rights not expressly granted herein.

2. **Ownership.** WPI is the owner of all right, title, and interest, including copyright, in and to the compilation of the Software recorded on the physical packet included with this Book "Software Media". Copyright to the individual programs recorded on the Software Media is owned by the author or other authorized copyright owner of each program. Ownership of the Software and all proprietary rights relating thereto remain with WPI and its licensers.

3. **Restrictions on Use and Transfer.**

    (a) You may only (i) make one copy of the Software for backup or archival purposes, or (ii) transfer the Software to a single hard disk, provided that you keep the original for backup or archival purposes. You may not (i) rent or lease the Software, (ii) copy or reproduce the Software through a LAN or other network system or through any computer subscriber system or bulletin-board system, or (iii) modify, adapt, or create derivative works based on the Software.

    (b) You may not reverse engineer, decompile, or disassemble the Software. You may transfer the Software and user documentation on a permanent basis, provided that the transferee agrees to accept the terms and conditions of this Agreement and you retain no copies. If the Software is an update or has been updated, any transfer must include the most recent update and all prior versions.

4. **Restrictions on Use of Individual Programs.** You must follow the individual requirements and restrictions detailed for each individual program in the "What's on the DVD" appendix of this Book or on the Software Media. These limitations are also contained in the individual license agreements recorded on the Software Media. These limitations may include a requirement that after using the program for a specified period of time, the user must pay a registration fee or discontinue use. By opening the Software packet(s), you agree to abide by the licenses and restrictions for these individual programs that are detailed in the "What's on the DVD" appendix and/or on the Software Media. None of the material on this Software Media or listed in this Book may ever be redistributed, in original or modified form, for commercial purposes.